Applied Financial Accounting

Implications for Analysts

by Alexander J. Sannella
Rutgers Business School

Hansen Publishing Group, LLC

Applied Financial Accounting: Implications for Analysts is published by Hansen Publishing Group, LLC,
302 Ryders Lane, East Brunswick, NJ 08816

16 15 14 13 12 11 10 1 2 3 4 5

International Standard Book Number: 978-1-60182-003-7

Book design and typography by Jon Hansen

Hansen Publishing Group, LLC
302 Ryders Lane
East Brunswick, NJ 08816

1-877-876-4716
http://hansenpublishing.com

Book web site
http://www.appliedfinancialaccounting.com

Dedicated to my family: Ann, Christopher, Eric, Anthony and Marissa

Contents

Applied Financial Accounting: Implication for Analysts

PREFACE
Applied Financial Accounting: Implications for Analysts

This work presents an analytical explanation as well as practical examples of Generally Accepted Accounting Principles (GAAP), written in a clear, lucid style for readers of all levels. Comprehensive coverage is provided for all accounting and reporting issues that are critical to the financial and credit analyst, with the exposition of GAAP made without the use of mechanical bookkeeping procedures. This is accomplished through an analysis of the financial accounting issue; the effects of GAAP on the balance sheet, income statement, and statement of cash flows; numerical illustrations; alternative treatments; and the impact of GAAP on financial ratios and analytical statistics.

The book offers a survey of basic financial statements, related footnote disclosures, and the general concepts underlying financial statements, as well as analyzes of specific statement items. The first three chapters discuss the conceptual foundation of the three basic financial statements, current assets, and noncurrent assets, and provide an analysis of liabilities and stockholders' equity. The study then turns to more complex accounting and reporting problems, including accounting for income taxes, computing earnings per share, and accounting for intercorporate investments, business combinations, pensions, employee options and leases. Professionals in the banking, investment, and accounting fields will find this work to be an effective resource, as will professors and students in business, accounting, and finance courses.

The book includes up to date references to the FASB Accounting Standards Codification. You will note that the references still use the FASB Statement numbers from the prior literature. This was done in order to simplify the transition into employing the codification in daily practice. The prior statement numbers are most familiar to the reader and using these numbers as the primary reference method will result in a better understanding by the experienced professional.

All mechanical debit and credit methodology is avoided through the use of Financial Modeling Worksheets in each illustration. The worksheets will permit all solutions and illustrations to "flow transactions through" the three basic financial statements and enhance the reader's understanding of the articulation among the balance sheet, income statement and the statement of cash flows. This snap shot can be reviewed and analyzed by the reader to ensure that he or she fully understands the financial statement impact of a particular accounting standard, rather than just concentrating on the debits and credits. The financial modeling worksheets will provide a direct link to statement analysis. This pedagogical device will also improve a reader's understanding cash flow and assist in the fundamentals of valuation. The use of the financial modeling worksheets in investment bank training programs have been well received by participants. Investment bank analysts and associates indicate that financial modeling worksheets provide a clear understanding of the impact of a particular transaction on an entity's financial position, earnings and cash flows. This is the type of critical understanding that participants in these training programs said they did not obtain by the traditional use of debits and credits and journal entries.

Chapter 1 | Introduction to GAAP and Implications for Analysis

INTRODUCTION

The implications of ***Generally Accepted Accounting Principles*** (GAAP) for users' understanding and the analysis of published financial statements are the central points of this book. This book incorporates the theory and assumptions underlying financial statements and uses detailed illustrations and sample disclosures to enhance the reader's understanding of fundamental accounting and reporting issues.

Throughout the book, the material is presented without utilizing a mechanical accounting framework (i.e., debit and credit bookkeeping procedures). Instead, the theoretical foundation underlying a particular accounting issue is presented along with detailed illustrations and, where appropriate, a financial modeling worksheet which provides the financial statement impact of the economic event or transaction. This approach provides an intuitive understanding of critical accounting and reporting issues facing the analyst.

This chapter begins by presenting the definition of GAAP to be used throughout the text. In addition, the issues of accounting risk and the quality of accounting numbers are related to this definition of GAAP. In the next section of this chapter, the primary sources of GAAP are identified. The following section provides an overview of the three basic financial statements, several financial metrics and the articulation among these statements. The conceptual foundation underlying the three basic financial statements is also discussed. In the final section of this chapter, the organization of the text is outlined.

Those readers familiar with the introductory accounting and reporting issues noted in the preceding paragraph should omit chapter 1.

GAAP DEFINED

As used throughout this book, ***Generally Accepted Accounting Principles*** are defined as broad reporting guidelines representing the "best" method or methods from many possible alternatives. Although only broad guidelines, the use of GAAP in financial reporting is essential in enhancing user confidence in published financial information. In addition, financial information based on GAAP assists in satisfying the primary objective of financial accounting: to provide information that enables users to make rational, economic decisions (e.g., credit and investment decisions). [1]

GAAP versus Tax Accounting

It should be noted that the terms ***financial accounting*** and ***financial information*** used above specifically highlight the fact that the primary focus of GAAP is financial accounting and reporting rather than tax accounting and reporting. As will be discussed in a later section of this book, there are different accounting methods for financial and tax accounting (i.e., the proverbial "two sets of books"). The use of different accounting methods should be expected, given the contrasting objectives of financial and tax accounting.

---

1. For a detailed discussion of this topic see *American Institute of Certified Public Accountants, Objectives of Financial Statements* (New York: AICPA, 1973) and *Financial Accounting Standards Board, Statement of Financial Accounting Concepts No. 1, Objectives of Financial Reporting* by Business Enterprises (Stamford, CT: FASB, 1978).

As indicated above, the primary objective of financial accounting is to provide information useful in making rational, economic decisions. Here are the objectives of tax accounting:

1. To raise revenues
2. To achieve stated economic objectives (for example, tax credits are granted to stimulate investment in research and development activities)
3. To achieve stated social objectives (for example, tax credits are granted for the rehabilitation of certain nonresidential, real property)

From the financial accounting standpoint, taxes are only considered to the extent that they impact published financial information. However, the manner in which the accountant reflects the impact of taxation is usually different from the information presented on the entity's income tax returns. Regardless of the accountant's treatment of income taxes, the analyst must be able to utilize the information provided in the annual report to assess the present and potential future cash flow consequences of the firm's tax information reported in the financial statements.

Reference to GAAP in the Annual Report

The fact that the financial statements are presented in accordance with GAAP is clearly stated in the independent registered public auditor's report. An independent registered public accounting firm's audit report for Park Ridge, Inc. is presented in Exhibit 1.1. In the third or opinion paragraph of the auditors' report, the accountant states that the financial statements were presented in conformity with U.S. GAAP. In addition, the independent registered auditors' report will indicate if GAAP has been applied consistently, period to period, or if there has been a change in accounting method. If there was a change in a GAAP accounting method, the next paragraph of the auditors' report would contain a statement similar to the one presented below.

As discussed in note 1 to the consolidated financial statements, the Company in 2011 and 2010 changed its method of accounting for variable interest entities.

The information provided in the explanatory paragraph of the auditors' report provides a signal to the analyst that certain financial information may no longer be comparable with prior years due to the change in GAAP method.

EXHIBIT 1.1: REPORT OF INDEPENDENT REGISTERED PUBLIC ACCOUNTING FIRM

The Board of Directors and Shareholders,
Park Ridge, Inc.

We have audited the accompanying consolidated balance sheets of Park Ridge, Inc. as of December 31, 2011 and 2010, and the related consolidated statements of income, shareholders' equity and cash flows for each of the three years in the period ended December 31, 2011. These financial statements are the responsibility of the Company's management. Our responsibility is to express an opinion on these financial statements based on our audits.

We conducted our audits in accordance with the standards of the Public Company Accounting Oversight Board (United States). Those standards require that we plan and perform the audit to obtain reasonable assurance about whether the financial statements are free of material misstatement. An audit includes examining, on a test basis, evidence supporting the amounts and disclosures in the financial statements. An audit also includes assessing the accounting principles used and significant estimates made by management, as well as evaluating the overall financial statement presentation. We believe that our audits provide a reasonable basis for our opinion.

In our opinion, the financial statements referred to above present fairly, in all material respects, the consolidated financial position of Park Ridge, Inc. at December 31, 2011 and 2010, and the consolidated results of its operations and its cash flows for each of the three years in the period ended December 31, 2011, in conformity with U.S. generally accepted accounting principles.

We also have audited, in accordance with the standards of the Public Company Accounting Oversight Board (United States), the effectiveness of Park Ridge, Inc.'s internal control over financial reporting as of December 31, 2011, based on criteria established in *Internal Control - Integrated Framework* issued by the Committee of Sponsoring Organizations of the Treadway Commission and our report dated February 18, 2012 expressed an unqualified opinion thereon.

Reagan & Vargas
Newark, New Jersey
February 18, 2012

The first footnote to the financial statements provides a summary of significant accounting policies (i.e., the GAAP) used by a firm. By reviewing the first footnote, the credit and financial analyst can identify the GAAP used by a firm; determine if these methods are consistent each period and if the GAAP methods are comparable with other firms in the same industry. Knowledge of the GAAP methods used is essential for understanding and interpreting the valuation of the economic resources and the measurement of profit or loss for the firm. The accounting policies footnote for Park Ridge, Inc. is presented in Exhibit 1.2. Note that in the partial footnote entitled "Summary of Significant Accounting Policies" the reader is informed as to the GAAP methods of accounting used for receivables, inventory, long-lived assets, etc.

EXHIBIT 1.2: PARTIAL FIRST FOOTNOTE: SUMMARY OF SIGNIFICANT ACCOUNTING POLICIES

Notes to Consolidated Financial Statements: Park Ridge, Inc.
Summary of Significant Accounting Policies

Receivables

Accounts receivable consist primarily of receivables from customers resulting from sales, of our major product lines.

Inventories

The Company values inventories at the lower of cost or market as determined primarily by using the last-in, first-out ("LIFO") method for substantially all merchandise inventories in the United States. Inventories of foreign operations are primarily valued by using the first-in, first-out ("FIFO") method. At December 31, 2011 and 2010, our inventories valued at LIFO approximate those inventories as if they were valued at FIFO.

Revenue Recognition

The Company recognizes sales revenue net of estimated sales returns at the time it sells merchandise to the customer.

Depreciation and Amortization

Depreciation and amortization for financial statement purposes are provided on the straight-line method over the estimated useful lives of the various assets. Depreciation expense, for fiscal years 2011, 2010 and 2009 was $5.7 billion, $5.1 billion and $4.6 billion, respectively. For income tax purposes, accelerated methods of depreciation are used with recognition of deferred income taxes for the resulting temporary differences. Estimated useful lives for financial statement purposes are as follows:

Buildings	15-20 years
Fixtures and fixtures	3-10 years
Transportation equipment	3–8 years

Estimates and Assumptions

The preparation of consolidated financial statements in conformity with generally accepted accounting principles requires Management to make estimates and assumptions. These estimates and assumptions affect the reported amounts of assets and liabilities, and the reported amounts of revenues and expenses during the reporting period. Actual results may differ from those estimates.

The analyst can use this footnote to determine if the company is implementing an income increasing or an income reducing financial reporting strategy.

An income increasing financial reporting strategy can be employed for several desired reasons:

1. Increase stock price
2. Improve credit ratings in the debt markets
3. Enhance management's stock-based compensation

An income reducing financial reporting strategy can be used for several desired reasons:

1. Justify price increases without invoking public criticism (e.g.,gasoline price increases)
2. Reduce the possibility of government interference (e.g., perceived monopoly positions through increased market share)
3. Minimize the possibility of tax modifications (e.g., excess profits tax triggered by earnings reported by oil and gas companies)

Financial reporting strategies can be firm specific or industry specific. Later in this text, we will discuss how choice of accounting methods can establish a firm's financial reporting strategy.

THE QUALITY OF ACCOUNTING INFORMATION AND ACCOUNTING RISK

In our definition of GAAP and in the review of the independent registered public auditors' report, several terms were couched in vague language such as "broad reporting guidelines," "best alternative method" and "presents fairly." The use of broad terminology indicates that accounting is not an exact science. In fact, accounting has often been criticized for the significant amount of flexibility, judgment and subjectivity afforded to management in three key areas:

1. The initial choice of a GAAP method
2. A change from one GAAP method to another
3. Discretion and judgment in the application of GAAP (e.g., the use of estimates)

The latitude afforded to management within these three areas implies that the analyst may have some difficulty in comparing the financial information reported for two firms in the same industry, if a different set of GAAP accounting methods or estimation techniques were used by the individual firms. In addition, the analyst may not be able to compare the same firm over time if that firm changes GAAP methods or modifies the estimation techniques used in the consistent application of a particular GAAP method.

Discretion in selection and application, and changes in GAAP, also provides management with an invaluable tool for smoothing or managing income by shifting reported income numbers among accounting periods. Depending on management's reporting objectives, an income-increasing or an income-reducing reporting strategy may be adopted.

These issues raise questions regarding the quality of the accounting numbers reported and subjects the analyst to "accounting risk," in addition to business and market risk, when making credit and investment decisions.

A major portion of this book addresses these issues and is devoted to providing the analyst with the background needed to better assess the quality of accounting numbers and to minimize the accounting risk associated with an investment choice or a credit-granting decision.

By presenting controversial GAAP accounting and reporting issues from the user's perspective, this book will provide the analyst with the tools needed to convert one GAAP method to another. Although it is not always possible to convert from one GAAP method to another on a quantitative basis, at a minimum the analyst should be able to understand the direction in which proforma adjustments should be made, in order to compare the financial statements of two firms in the same industry or for making comparisons of the financial information provided by the same firm over time.

SOURCES OF GAAP

In the analysis of published footnote information, there will be many references to the sources of GAAP used. For example, Park Ridge's *Share Based Compensation Plans* footnote indicates that:

> *On January 1, 2009, the Company adopted the expense recognition provisions of Statement of Financial Accounting Standards No. 123 ("SFAS 123"), restating results for prior periods. In December 2004, the Financial Accounting Standards Board issued a revision of SFAS 123 ("SFAS 123(R)"). The Company adopted the provisions of SFAS 123(R)at that time. The adoption of SFAS 123(R) did not have a material impact on our results of operations, financial position or cash flows. Currently, all share-based compensation is accounted at fair-value.*

The standards mentioned in the sample footnote are Statements of Financial Accounting Standards (SFAS) and are issued by the Financial Accounting Standards Board (FASB), which is the current standard setting body in the United States. In addition to the FASB, other sources of US GAAP include the pronouncements of the Accounting Principles Board (APB) and the Committee on Accounting Procedure (CAP) that are still in effect or have not been superseded by a subsequent FASB standard. These standard setting bodies and other sources of GAAP are briefly discussed in the next section.

The Financial Accounting Standards Board (FASB): (1973-Present)

The FASB is a full-time board that issues authoritative pronouncements called "Statements of Financial Accounting Standards" (SFAS), or simply "Statements" or "FASBs." To date, over 160 Statements have been issued. In addition, the FASB issues interpretations of its authoritative pronouncements.

The issuance of an FASB Statement is a public process implemented through a "due process" system consisting of ten steps:

1. A topic is placed on the FASB's agenda
2. A task force carefully defines the problems and accounting alternatives
3. Research and analysis of the issue is conducted by the FASB's technical staff
4. A Discussion Memorandum (DM) is released. The DM presents the issues, the rationale, and the advantages and disadvantages of alternative accounting and reporting solutions to the problem
5. A public hearing is held
6. The results of the public hearing are analyzed
7. An exposure draft of the Statement is issued
8. Public comment is requested for a 30-day period after the issuance of the exposure draft
9. The public comments are evaluated
10. The final Statement is issued[2]

This "due process" allows management, members of the financial and accounting community and academicians to lobby for those standards they support and to "vote" against those standards they oppose. It is interesting to note that the due process system does not end with the issuance of the final Statement. Several cases will be noted throughout this book which illustrate how various interest groups have lobbied the FASB, as well as the government, to suspend the effective dates or completely eliminate the requirements of a particular standard. In addition, if a standard is issued but is not used by the accounting profession, it is not "generally accepted." The lack of general acceptance, even without direct opposition and lobbying, could result in the suspension or elimination of a particular accounting standard. Therefore, GAAP consists of all standards issued by the FASB, or by the former authoritative bodies that have not been superseded by the FASB and have the general support of the members of the accounting profession.

The FASB also issues Consensus Decisions through its ***Emerging Issues Task Force (EITF).*** The EITF was formed in 1984, and its members include representatives of key associations of financial statement preparers. The Chief Accountant of the Securities and Exchange Commission and observers from the American Institute of Certified Public Accountants (AICPA) regularly attend EITF meetings.

---

2. Donald E. Kieso, Jerry J. Weygandt and Terry D. Warfield, *Intermediate Accounting* (Hoboken, New Jersey: John Wiley & Sons, Inc., 2007), 8-9.

The membership of the EITF is designed to include a diverse group that is aware of significant issues in financial reporting that need to be considered before the issues evolve into divergent practice.

If the group can reach a consensus on an issue, usually that consensus is accepted by the FASB as an indication that no Board action is needed. A consensus is reached when no more than one-third of the twelve voting members object to the decision. Consensus decisions reached by the EITF are considered part of GAAP.

The Accounting Principles Board (APB): (1959-1973)

The APB, a part-time board, issued pronouncements known as "Opinions." Over the period of its existence, the APB issued 31 Opinions, many of which have not been superseded by an FASB Statement, and therefore are still considered part of GAAP and have authoritative support.

The Committee on Accounting Procedure (CAP): (1939-1959)

The Committee on Accounting Procedure was primarily established to reduce the number of accounting alternatives in practice and to develop uniform standards of accounting, reporting, and disclosure. The CAP issued pronouncements known as "Accounting Research Bulletins" or simply"Bulletins." There were a total of 51 Bulletins, many of which remain in force today. Specific references to the Bulletins are rare because they became the basic foundation of GAAP.

Other Sources of GAAP

In addition to the semipublic (or semiprivate) bodies specifically designated by the accounting profession to promulgate accounting standards, there are other influential organizations that effect GAAP.

1. ***The Securities and Exchange Commission (SEC).*** The SEC's GAAP is found in Regulation S-X, Staff Accounting Bulletins (SABs), and Financial Reporting Releases (FRRs) (previously known as Accounting Series Releases [ASRs]). Filings with the SEC include Form 10-K (annual), Form 10-Q (quarterly) and Form 8-K, which must be filed within 15 days after the occurrence of a "material" event.

   Legally, the SEC has the authority to dictate accounting principles but historically has allowed the accounting profession to issue its own standards. Nonetheless, the SEC has used its power in limited cases and frequently exerts pressure on the FASB to issue or adopt certain standards of accounting, reporting, and disclosure.

2. ***The Internal Revenue Service (IRS).*** Accounting principles are based on a corresponding tax method in certain instances. The IRS can also force the use of certain tax accounting principles for financial reporting purposes. Inventory accounting is a current example of where the IRS requires conformity between the income tax and financial reporting if the LIFO method is used for tax purposes.

3. ***The American Institute of Certified Public Accountants (AICPA).*** Today, the AICPA is no longer directly involved in the standard setting process. However, the Accounting Standards Executive Committee (AcSec) of the AICPA continues to issue pronouncements called Statements of Position (SOPs) and Issue Papers which present accounting problems and issues and proposed accounting alternatives that are not currently being

addressed by the FASB. Although not initially part of GAAP on their own merit, SOPs and Issue Papers can be deemed GAAP by the SEC or the FASB, and can thereby have the same authoritative support as all other parts of GAAP.

The AICPA previously issued Statements on Auditing Standards (SASs), which provide the basis of the Generally Accepted Auditing Standards (GAAS) which today must be followed in order for the accountant to render an opinion on the financial statements, taken as a whole for privately held companies. In the auditor's opinion presented in Exhibit 1.1, there is a reference to the auditing standards of the Public Company Accounting Oversight Board (PCAOB). The auditing standards of the PCAOB must be following in the audits of publicly traded companies (i.e., companies reporting to the SEC).

The PCAOB is a private sector, non-profit corporation created by the Sarbanes-Oxley Act of 2002. It was established to oversee the audit of publicly traded companies to protect the public interest and the interests of financial statement users by ensuring the issuance of fair and independent reports. At this point in time, the PCAOB adopted the GAAS standards issued by the AICPA and has begun augmenting these rules with its own pronouncements or auditing standards.

As is the case in the use of GAAP, a clear statement that the accountant followed GAAS or the Auditing Standards of the PCAOB in the examination of financial statements provides the reader with certain assurances as to the quality of the audit work performed and the validity of the conclusions reached, as to the fair presentation of financial position, results of operations, and cash flows. Auditing is a specialized field of accounting and therefore auditing standards are not considered in this text.

4. ***The International Accounting Standards Board (IASB).*** Since 2001, the International Accounting Standards Board (IASB) assumed accounting standard-setting responsibilities from its predecessor body, the International Accounting Standards Committee. Standard setters in the United States have been working closely with the IASB to develop a common set of accounting standards, including a joint conceptual framework. In the interim, recently issued FASB standards have been based largely on the recommendations of and joint projects with the IASB and other international standard setters. International Financial Reporting Standards (IFRS) are expected to be adopted by US corporations and accepted by regulators and stock exchanges. A decision regarding the required full convergence of US GAAP with IFRS is expected in 2011.

The FASB recently created its ***codification database*** which arranges all sources of GAAP by topic.

THE THREE BASIC GENERAL PURPOSE FINANCIAL STATEMENTS AND THEIR RELATED CONCEPTS

The Three Basic General Purpose Financial Statements

In order to present financial statements in accordance with GAAP, published financial statements must include the three basic general purpose financial statements: the balance sheet or the statement of financial position; the income statement, the statement of profit and loss or the statement of operations; and the cash flow statement. In addition, a complete set of financial statements requires full disclosure in the form of footnotes. The statement of changes in shareholders' equity is presented in most cases and is the fourth basic financial statement in practice.

The three basic financial statements are said to be general purpose financial statements because they are designed to satisfy the needs of a wide spectrum of user groups, including investors, creditors, financial and credit analysts, insurance companies, labor unions, employees and government agencies.

Although considered general purpose, most financial information is provided to satisfy users with limited ability and authority to obtain additional information.[3] Usually, the primary users are identified as investors and creditors. However, from a practical standpoint, the investors are probably the primary user group addressed by the accounting profession in published annual reports. For the most part, the other user groups can demand and obtain additional information or request clarification of data included in the annual report. For example, if a firm wants to obtain additional financing, it would probably not hesitate to satisfy a potential creditor's demand for additional information.

The Balance Sheet or Statement of Financial Position

The balance sheet is a listing of the assets, liabilities and capital of the entity at a point in time. From an economic standpoint, the balance sheet presents the stock of wealth of the firm.

The assets of the firm have been defined as economic resources owned or controlled by the firm and having future service potential (economic benefit) to the firm. Notice that the assets of the firm do not have to be owned. As long as the economic resources are controlled and provide future economic benefit, they can be included among the assets of the entity. As will be discussed in a later chapter, under certain conditions leased equipment can be included among the assets of the firm (i.e., "capitalized"), even if not owned.

Liabilities are the debts owed to outsiders (i.e., creditors) by the firm. Liabilities are also known as "creditors' equity" or the creditors' claim against the assets of the firm.

The capital of the firm represents the owners' wealth which is a residual claim to the assets of the firm, or the owners' equity in the firm's assets. Because the creditors' claims must be satisfied first, the owners' equity has also been called net worth or net assets.

A balance sheet or statement of financial position for the Park Ridge, Inc. is presented in Exhibit 1.3.

3. American Institute of Certified Public Accountants, *Objectives of Financial Statements* (New York: AICPA, 1973), 17.

EXHIBIT 1.3: CONSOLIDATED BALANCE SHEET

Consolidated Balance Sheet: Park Ridge, Inc.

(Amounts in millions except per share data)

December 31,	**2006**	2005
Assets		
Current assets:		
Cash and cash equivalents	**$ 7,697**	$ 6,586
Receivables-Net	**3,194**	2,058
Inventories	**38,629**	35,714
Prepaid expenses	**3,068**	2,267
Total current assets	**52,588**	46,625
Property and equipment, at cost:		
Land	**19,972**	17,366
Buildings	**67,396**	55,889
Fixtures and equipment	**27,300**	25,753
Other equipment	**2,095**	1,836
Property and equipment, at cost	**116,763**	100,844
Less accumulated depreciation	**25,712**	22,364
Property and equipment, net	**91,051**	78,480
Property under capital lease:		
Property under capital lease	**6,694**	5,467
Less accumulated amortization	**2,596**	2,206
Property under capital lease, net	**4,098**	3,261
Goodwill and Other tangible assets	**14,626**	12,964
Other assets and deferred charges	**3,462**	2,855
Total assets	**$ 165,825**	$ 144,185
Liabilities and shareholders' equity		
Current liabilities:		
Commercial paper	**$ 4,505**	$ 4,574
Accounts payable	**30,448**	26,384
Accrued liabilities	**16,158**	14,544
Accrued income taxes	**1,608**	1,537
Long-term debt due within one year	**5,514**	4,511
Obligations under capital leases due within one year	**359**	268
Total current liabilities	**58,592**	51,818
Long-term debt	**31,715**	24,104
Long-term obligations under capital leases	**4,490**	3,805
Deferred income taxes and other	**5,462**	3,574
Commitments and contingencies		

Shareholders' equity:		
Preferred stock ($5 par value; 500 shares authorized, none issued)	—	—
Common stock ($0.25 par value; 20,000 shares authorized, 2,000 and 2,032 issued and outstanding at December 31, 2011 and December 31, 2010, respectively)	**500**	508
Capital in excess of par value	**3,115**	2,910
Accumulated other comprehensive income	**1,264**	3,233
Retained earnings	**58,926**	52,625
Shareholders' Equity	63,805	59,275
Noncontrolling Interest	1,760	1,608
Total shareholders' equity	**65,565**	60,884
Total liabilities and shareholders' equity	**$ 165,824**	$ 144,185

As noted in Exhibit 1.3, the balance sheet is based on the fundamental accounting or balance sheet equation:

Assets = Equities
Assets = Liabilities + Stockholders' Equity

Assets are usually thought of as uses of funds and liabilities and stockholders' equity are viewed as sources of funds.

In the asset section of the balance sheet, assets are listed in the "order of liquidity" (where liquidity is defined as the ability to convert an economic resource into cash with minimal risk of loss). It is common practice to report financial position through the use of a classified balance sheet.

In the classified balance sheet assets are classified as current if the economic resource is expected to be used or consumed in operations or converted into cash within one year from the balance sheet date or one operating cycle, whichever is longer.

The operating cycle is the "cash-to-cash cycle" or "cash conversion cycle" of the firm. The following diagram illustrates the operating cycle:

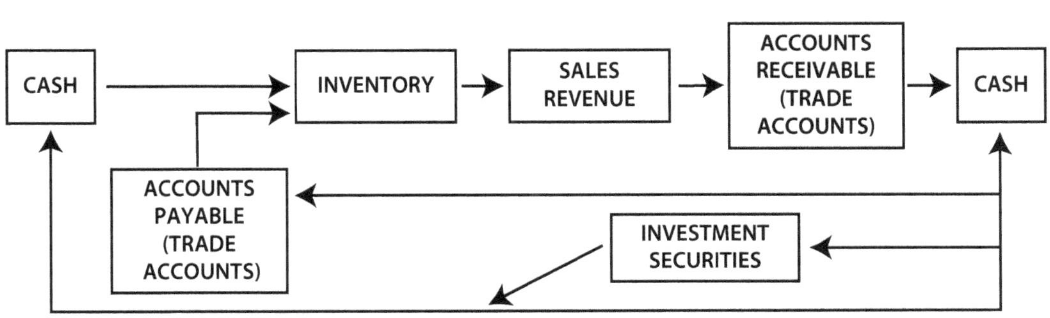

The operating cycle above assumes a manufacturing firm or retail operation. The cycle begins by investing cash and obtaining trade credit to acquire inventory. The inventory is sold on credit and ultimately cash is collected. When cash is collected, it is first applied to pay off trade accounts payable. Any excess cash is invested in securities in order to earn a return higher than if cash is held idle. Finally, the remaining cash is returned back to be used for next period's inventory purchases and the cycle begins again.

The operating cycle of a firm is a critical concept in financial statement analysis and can be measured through the application of basic financial ratios. The operating cycle and its implications for financial analysis will be presented in a subsequent chapter of this book.

For some operations, such as those requiring an aging process, a single operating cycle may extend beyond one year. In general, however, assets meeting the one-year criterion are classified as current. Conversely, if the asset is expected to provide economic benefit for a period longer than one year from the balance sheet date or it will take more than one year to convert into cash, it would be classified as a long-term or noncurrent asset.

On Exhibit 1.3, Park Ridge's current assets include: cash and cash equivalents, receivables, inventory, and prepaid expenses.

Cash equivalents are short term, highly liquid investments with maturities of three months or less when acquired. Cash equivalents include money market funds, commercial paper and treasury instruments. Receivables are amounts due to Park Ridge from the sale of products. Inventory represents Park Ridge's goods held for resale. Finally, prepaid expenses include rent paid in advance or advance payments on insurance policies. Prepaid expenses are assets not because they will be converted into cash, but are assets due to the fact that these prior expenditures will avoid cash outflows in the future.

The non-current or long-term assets for Park Ridge include: plant and equipment, property under capital lease, intangibles, such as goodwill, other assets and deferred charges. Property and equipment and property under capital lease are net of accumulated depreciation and accumulated amortization respectively. Depreciation and amortization represent the reduction of the asset's cost due to use in the operation of the business. Goodwill is an intangible asset representing the excess acquisition price over the fair value (appraisal value) of the assets and liabilities acquired in a business combination. Deferred charges are long-term prepaid expenses. An example of a deferred charge is an up front down payment on a long-term lease.

Liabilities are listed in the "order of maturity." It is common reporting practice to classify liabilities as current if due within one year of the balance sheet date, and noncurrent or long term if payable in a period greater than one year from the balance sheet date.

In theory, a current liability is defined as an obligation whose liquidation will require the use of economic resources properly classified as current assets or the creation of other current liabilities. Although the latter definition captures the operating cycle concept used in the discussion of current and noncurrent assets, the one-year criterion for the classification of liabilities is generally sufficient in practice.

Park Ridge's current liabilities include: commercial paper, accounts payable, accrued liabilities, accrued income taxes, long-term debt due within one year, and obligations under capital lease due within one year.

Commercial paper is used for short term financing and represents debt with maturities of usually less than six months and is issued on a discounted basis, (that is, with interest deducted on the date of issue). Commercial paper is only available to large corporations with high credit rating. Therefore, commercial paper usually carries a lower interest rate than comparable bank debt. Accounts payable are open trade accounts due to suppliers of inventory. Accrued expenses are expenses incurred but unpaid at the end of the accounting period. Examples, include wages, utilities, interest and taxes (accrued taxes) due but unpaid at the end of the accounting period. Finally, as long term debt comes due each year, that portion is classified as a current liability. Park Ridge has current portions of long term notes and long term lease obligations due within one year of the balance sheet date. The remaining portions of these long term obligations are classified as long term liabilities.

Park Ridge's long term liabilities also include deferred income taxes (taxes not due in the current period). The"noncontrolling interest" is now reported in stockholders' equity.

The commitments and contingencies line on the balance sheet is included for disclosure purposes only. It alerts the reader to read the commitments and contingencies footnote, which typically includes pending litigation, purchase commitments and off balance sheet arrangements (e.g., certain lease contracts not recorded on the balance sheet).

The current-noncurrent classification of assets and liabilities is useful for the analyst in "matching maturities" of these assets and liabilities. The excess of current assets over current liabilities, or working capital, is an important concept in the assessment of a firm's liquidity in the analysis of financial statements.

Finally, capital is known as stockholders' equity on a corporate balance sheet. The stockholders' equity section of the balance sheet consists of three major components:

1. Contributed or paid-in capital
2. Accumulated other comprehensive income
3. Retained earnings

Contributed or paid-in capital includes, but is not limited to, the capital stock (either common or preferred) issued by the entity at par or face value, and the amounts received above par value. The amounts received over par value are called additional paid-in capital, capital surplus or paid-in capital in excess of par. Preferred shares are senior equity securities with priority over common as to dividends and assets in liquidation. Preferred shares are typically not voting. Common shares are the basic ownership class and include the right to vote, to receive dividends, and the share in the earnings of the entity.

Accumulated Other Comprehensive Income, includes the cumulative record of unrealized gains and losses on investment securities; unrealized pension costs and unrealized foreign currency translation gains or losses. Unrealized gains and losses are what individuals call "paper" gains and losses. These unrealized items of profit and loss are not reported on the income statement due to a low probability of cash realization in the short run. These paper items were traditionally thought of as transitory components of income. However, disclosure of these unrealized events is important to the financial statement user due to the potential effects on a firm's earnings, financial position and cash flows. For example, future disposal of an investment can result in a significant realized gain or loss for the reporting entity.

The total comprehensive income is defined as the sum of net income from the income statement plus or minus other comprehensive income items. The other comprehensive income items are the "paper" gains and losses described above.

The change in other comprehensive income is usually reported in a Statement of Changes in Shareholders' Equity. A sample Statement of Changes of Shareholders' Equity for Park Ridge is presented in Exhibit 1.4. In the Park Ridge case we see that in fiscal 2011 the company reported $2,304 in unrealized losses on foreign currency translation adjustments. This amount represents a holding loss caused by a stronger US dollar relative to local currencies. If Park Ridge decided to liquidate its subsidiaries located in foreign countries and converted the local currencies into US dollars, a loss would result because fewer dollars would be obtained for each unit of the local currency. The company also reported unrealized gains on investments and pension asset and pension liability adjustments of $273.6 and $61.2 respectively.

Finally, retained earnings represent the historical record of earnings or losses that have not been paid out or distributed as dividends. The Statement of Changes in Shareholders' Equity for Park Ridge includes a retained earnings column which changes each year by adding net income and deducting dividends declared. There are also reductions for losses on the purchase of Park Ridge's own shares (i.e., treasury shares). Accounting for the acquisition of company shares or treasury shares will discussed in a subsequent chapter.

The noncontrolling interest represents the outside shareholders' claim against the net assets (i.e., assets - liabilities) of a subsidiary that Park Ridge does not wholly own. For example, if Park Ridge holds 90% of a subsidiary's voting shares, it controls 100% of that subsidiary's assets and liabilities. This creates an equity claim that is due to the outside 10% ownership: Park Ridge controls 100% of the net assets, but only owns 90%.

EXHIBIT 1.4 STATEMENT OF CHANGES IN STOCKHOLDERS' EQUITY

Park Ridge, Inc.

(Amounts in millions except per share data)	Number of Shares	Common Stock	Paid in Capital in Excess of Par Value	Accumulated Other Comprehensive Income	Retained Earnings	Total
Balance – December 31, 2008	5,274	$ 528	$ 2,345	$ (611)	$ 45,091	$ 47,353
Comprehensive income						
Net income from continuing operations					10,633	10,633
Net income from discontinued operation					231.6	231.6
Other comprehensive income:						
Foreign currency translation adjustment				2,022		2,022
Net unrealized loss on investments				(409)		(409)
Minimum pension liability				19.2		19.2
Total comprehensive income						12,497
Cash dividends					(1,883)	(1,883)
Purchase of Company stock	(110)	(11)	(218)		(5,826)	(5,826)
Stock options exercised and other	9.6		435.6			435.6
Balance – December 31, 2009	5,173	517.2	2,562	1021.2	48,247	52,348
Comprehensive income						
Net income from continuing operations					12,320	12,320
Other comprehensive income:						
Foreign currency translation adjustment				2,556		2,556
Net unrealized loss on investments				(233)		
Net pension adjustments				(112)		
Total comprehensive income						14,532
Cash dividends					(2,657)	(2,657)
Purchase of Company stock	(101)	(10)			(5,286)	(5,286)
Stock options exercised and other	4.8		511.2			511.2
Balance – December 31, 2010	**5,081**	**507.6**	**2,910**	**3,233**	**52,625**	**59,275**
Comprehensive income:						
Net income from continuing operations					**13,477**	**13,477**
Other comprehensive income:						
Foreign currency translation adjustment				**(2,304)**		
Net unrealized gain on investments				**273.6**		**273.6**
Net pension adjustment				**61.2**		**61.2**
Total comprehensive income						**11,508**
Cash dividends					**(3,013)**	**(3,013)**
Purchase of Company stock	**(89)**				**(4,163)**	**(4,163)**
Stock options exercised and other	**6**	**1.2**	**330**			**331.2**
Balance – December 31, 2011	**4,998**	**$ 500.4**	**$ 3,115**	**$ 1,264**	**$ 58,926**	**$ 63,805**

The Income Statement, (Statement of Profit and Loss or Statement of Operations).

The income statement is a flow statement listing revenues, expenses, and net income or net loss over a period of time. The income statement presents the change in owners' wealth or the flow of wealth for the accounting period (e.g., one month, one quarter or one year). The model of the income statement is simply:

Net Income (Loss) = Revenues - Expenses.

Revenues are defined as inflows of assets (not necessarily cash) or reduction of obligations resulting from providing goods and services. Expenses are defined as outflows of assets (not necessarily cash) or increases in obligations from providing goods and services. Gains and losses have the same effect on a company's assets and liabilities but gains and losses are a result of peripheral activities outside of typical operations. For example, if Toyota sells an automobile it is recorded as revenue, while if Dell Computer sells an automobile it can result in a gain or loss on disposal of an asset.

A sample income statement or statement of earnings for the Park Ridge, Inc. is presented in Exhibit 1.5.

EXHIBIT 1.5. PARK RIDGE, INC. STATEMENT OF EARNINGS

Consolidated Statements of Income
Park Ridge, Inc.

(Amounts in millions except per share data)

Fiscal Year Ended January 31,	2011	2010	2009
Revenues:			
Net sales	**$ 374,912**	$ 342,266	$ 307,595
Other income, net	**3,872**	3,492	2,822
	378,785	345,758	310,417
Costs and expenses:			
Cost of sales	**288,469**	263,752	238,496
Operating, selling, general and administrative expenses	**68,080**	61,498	53,891
Operating income	**22,236**	20,509	18,030
Interest:			
Debt	**1,405**	1120.8	874.8
Capital leases	**298.8**	303.6	320.4
Interest income	**(297.6)**	(241.2)	(196.8)
Interest, net	**1,406**	1183.2	998.4
Income from continuing operations before income taxes and minority interest	**20,830**	19,326	17,032
Provision for income taxes:			
Current	**7,118**	6,391	5,929
Deferred	**(154.8)**	315.6	212.4
	6,964	6,707	6,142
Income from continuing operations before minority interest	**13,866**	12,619	10,890
Minority interest	**(388.8)**	(298.8)	(256.8)
Income from continuing operations	**13,477**	12,320	10,633
Income from discontinued operation, net of tax			231.6
Net income	**$ 13,477**	$ 12,320	$ 10,865

Basic net income per common share:			
Income from continuing operations	**$ 3.216**	$ 2.892	$ 2.436
Income from discontinued operation			0.06
Basic net income per common share	**$ 3.216**	$ 2.892	$ 2.496
Diluted net income per common share:			
Income from continuing operations	**$ 3.216**	$ 2.892	$ 2.436
Income from discontinued operation			0.048
Diluted net income per common share	**$ 3.216**	$ 2.892	$ 2.484
Weighted-average number of common shares:			
Basic	**5,020**	5,111	5,236
Diluted	**5,026**	5,119	5,248
Dividends per common share	**$ 0.72**	$ 0.624	$ 0.432

Park Ridge's revenues consist of net sales (sales less any sales returns and allowances) and other income.

Costs and expenses include the cost of sales and operating, selling, general and administrative expenses. The cost of sales is the cost of merchandise purchased by Park Ridge for resale.

The difference between net sales and cost of sales is known as the gross profit. Gross profit is a critical measure because it indicates the amount of sales dollars remaining to cover operating expenses and contribute to overall profitability. Analysts will follow the trend in gross profit because any deterioration in this metric can indicate significant declines in bottom line net income.

Operating, selling, general and administrative expenses include sales salaries, sales commissions, administrative salaries and other corporate costs.

Operating income in this case is also equal to earnings before interest and taxes or EBIT. EBIT is a critical measure in financial analysis for three reasons:

1. EBIT represents the contribution of the core operations of the business to overall profitability. For example, Park Ridge's core operation is merchandising and not earning interest income on investments.
2. EBIT provides a measure of the ability to generate earnings, independent of the way in which the firm is financed: debt or equity financing. In this way an analyst can compare Park Ridge (with debt in it's capital structure or a levered firm) to another merchandiser (without debt in it's capital structure or an unlevered firm).
3. EBIT indicates the amount income available to cover distributions to all providers of capital and infrastructure: to stockholders in the form of dividends, to debt holders in the form of interest and to the government in the form of taxes.

Other income and expense includes revenues and expenses from peripheral activities such as investing, leasing and borrowing.

The provision for taxes is the sum of taxes currently due and payable and those taxes deferred to a future period.

The noncontrolling interest is the outside shareholders' claim to the net income of a subsidiary that Park Ridge does not wholly own. For example, if Park Ridge holds 90% of the voting stock of a subsidiary company the noncontrolling interest has the right to 10% of that subsidiary's income. This noncontrolling interests' share of income reduces the income available or allocated to the controlling common shareholders of Park Ridge.

Finally, bottom line net income is reported in aggregate and on a per share basis. Basic earnings per share is essentially unadjusted. Diluted earnings per share reflects assumptions regarding the effect of potential issuances of common stock. For example, earnings per share could be reduced if all investors holding Park Ridge stock options exercised those options resulting in diluted interest for the current Park Ridge shareholders.

Because the balance sheet is the stock of wealth at a point in time, it is a cumulative statement. On the other hand, the income statement is the flow of wealth or the change in capital resulting from the operations of the firm over a particular period of time. Therefore, the balance sheet is a permanent statement while the income statement is only a temporary statement. As a result, at the end of each accounting period, the change in owners' wealth from the income statement must be transferred to capital (specifically retained earnings) on the balance sheet. This transfer or "closing" process is illustrated in the following diagram.

Income Statement for the Year Ended 12/31/XX

← NET INCOME (LOSS) = REVENUES – EXPENSES

"Net Income or loss is closed out to capital"

BALANCE SHEET AT 12/31/XX

ASSETS = LIABILITIES ± STOCKHOLDERS' EQUITY

→ → → (B) Beginning Retained Earnings
(A) + NET Income or – LOSS
(S) – DIVIDENDS
(E) Ending Retained Earnings

Due to the fact that net income or loss is transferred or closed out to capital (i.e., retained earnings) at the end of each accounting period, all revenue and expense accounts begin each period with a zero balance. It is for this reason that income statement accounts are known as temporary accounts, and the income statement is said to reflect "completed accounting cycles." On the other hand, the balance sheet is said to consist of permanent accounts because their balances are cumulative and are carried forward period to period. Because of the cumulative nature of the balance sheet accounts, the balance sheet is said to reflect "incomplete accounting cycles." The balance sheet cycles will be completed when the economic resources of the firm generate revenues which are matched on the income statement with the expenses incurred to produce those revenues. Specifically, asset utilization will create revenue and expenses and sources and uses of cash. These changes in cash are reported in the statement of cash flows to be discussed in the next section.

The Statement of Cash Flows

Here are the primary objectives of the cash flow statement:

1. To provide information about the firm's cash receipts and cash payments from operating activities. In this case, cash receipts and payments relate to the current operating activities of the firm (i.e., the cash flows relating to current operating working capital accounts such as accounts receivable account payable and inventory). These are cash flows related to the income statement and operating working capital accounts.

2. To provide information about the firm's financing and investing activities over a period of time. The cash flows generated from these activities relate to long term and short term debt financing, equity financing and investments in plant and equipment and other noncurrent assets. Investments in long term and short term portfolios of securities are also included. These are cash flows primarily related to the noncurrent asset and debt and equity sections of the balance sheet.

In addition, an analysis of the cash flow statement, along with the income statement and footnote disclosures, enables the analyst to explain or reconcile the change in cash as well as other elements of the balance sheet. This interrelationship or "articulation" between the three general purpose financial statements is illustrated in the following financial reporting model.

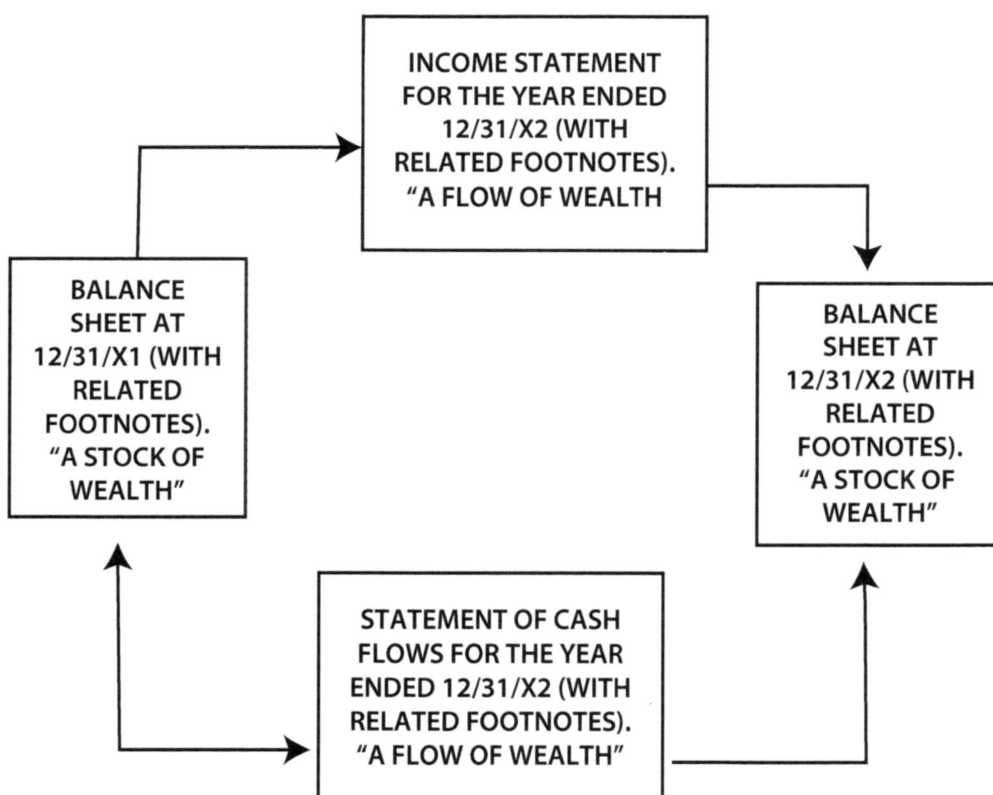

ASSETS	=	LIABILITIES + STOCKHOLDERS' EQUITY
(Use of Funds)	=	***(Source of Funds)***
Asset changes are inversely related to changes in cash flows	=	Liabilities and Stockholders' Equity changes are directly related to changes in cash flows

The cash flow statement should not include significant noncash financing and investing activities. These noncash transactions are either disclosed in the footnotes to the financial statements or below the statement of cash flows. Examples of significant noncash financing and investing activities include: acquisitions of fixed assets by issuing long term notes, bonds converted into common stock, dividends declared but unpaid, stock splits and stock dividends.

The statement of cash flows for the Park Ridge, Inc. is presented in Exhibit 1.6.

EXHIBIT 1.6: CONSOLIDATED STATEMENT OF CASH FLOWS

Consolidated Statements of Cash Flows
Park Ridge, Inc.

(Amounts in millions)

Fiscal Year Ended January 31,	**2011**	2010	2009
Cash flows from operating activities			
Income from continuing operations	**$ 13,477**	$ 12,320	$ 10,633
Adjustments to reconcile net income to net cash provided by operating activities:			
Depreciation and amortization	**5,660**	5,117	4,622
Deferred income taxes	**(154.8)**	315.6	212.4
Other operating activities	**744**	453.6	207.6
Changes in certain assets and liabilities, net of effects of acquisitions:			
Decrease (increase) in accounts receivable	**(547.2)**	(364.8)	447.6
Increase in inventories	**(2,080)**	(2,993)	(2,368)
Increase in accounts payable	**2,868**	2,033	3,104
Increase in accrued liabilities	**1191.6**	1171.2	2,275
Net cash provided by operating activities of continuing operations	**21,160**	18,053	19,135
Net cash provided by operating activities of discontinued operation			60
Net cash provided by operating activities	**21,160**	18,053	19,195
Cash flows from investing activities			
Payments for property and equipment	**(17,476)**	(15,472)	(12,370)
Investment in international operations, net of cash acquired	**(721.2)**	(378)	(45.6)
Proceeds from the disposal of fixed assets	**1,259**	1143.6	577.2
Proceeds from the sale of McLane			1,800
Other investing activities	**(81.6)**	(115.2)	93.6
Net cash used in investing activities of continuing operations	**(17,020)**	(14,821)	(9,944)
Net cash used in investing activities of discontinued operation			(30)
Net cash used in investing activities	**(17,020)**	(14,821)	(9,974)
Cash flows from financing activities			
Increase (decrease) in commercial paper	**(844.8)**	652.8	825.6

Proceeds from issuance of long-term debt	**9,229**	6,998	4,919
Purchase of Company stock	**(4,296)**	(5,459)	(6,055)
Dividends paid	**(3,013)**	(2,657)	(1,883)
Payment of long-term debt	**(3,269)**	(2,557)	(4,249)
Payment of capital lease obligations	**(294)**	(244.8)	(366)
Other financing activities	**(418.8)**	135.6	133.2
Net cash used in financing activities	**(2,906)**	(3,131)	(6,676)
Effect of exchange rate changes on cash	**(122.4)**	246	384
Net increase in cash and cash equivalents	**1111.2**	346.8	2,929
Cash and cash equivalents at beginning of year	**6,586**	6,239	3,310
Cash and cash equivalents at end of year	**$ 7,697**	$ 6,586	$ 6,239
Supplemental disclosure of cash flow information			
Income tax paid	**$ 7,154**	$ 6,712	$ 5,446
Interest paid	**1,668**	1,396	1,229
Capital lease obligations incurred	**343.2**	452.4	302.4

Operating cash flows are related to the income statement and begin with accrual basis net income, which is the bottom line on the income statement. These income flows are adjusted to remove the effects of items not using or providing cash, resulting in cash basis income or net cash flows from operating activities. Consider depreciation and amortization as an example of a non-cash expense. Depreciation and amortization is simply the reduction of the cost of productive and intangible assets respectively. This reduction does not use any cash (e.g., if the Blue Book value of your automobile declines, you do not have any cash outflows. In fact, the cash outflow occurred when you purchased the vehicle in the past). Depreciation reduces the value of the noncurrent asset in question and therefore reduces wealth and net income. However, since it does not use cash it is added back to net income.

Another example is the increase in accounts receivable. If accounts receivable increase, it represents net sales that were not collected and do not produce cash in the current period. Therefore, the increase in accounts receivable is deducted from net income to arrive at cash flow from operations. Finally, the increase in accounts payable is added back to net income because these are expenditures not yet paid. This is similar to charging your expenses on a credit card. You still have the expense, but you will pay for these charges in the next period, increasing your cash flow during the current period.

Investing activities include payments for plant assets, disposals of fixed assets and purchases and sales of investments, both short and long term investments.

Financing activities include short and long term borrowing, dividend payments to shareholders, and payments of short and long term debt.

The net change in cash is added to the beginning cash balance to reconcile to the ending cash balance on the balance sheet.

The financial reporting diagram presented earlier illustrates how the income statement and the statement of cash flows, with adequate footnote disclosure, can be used to explain or reconcile changes from one balance sheet to another. The ability to link or relate financial information contained on different financial statements is known as "articulation." Specifically, articulation refers to the interaction between assets, liabilities and equity elements with revenues and expenses. In other words, the elements of the three basic general purpose financial statements are intrinsically interrelated so that the elements of the balance sheet are dependent on the elements of the income statement and the elements of the income statement are dependent on the elements of the balance sheet. ***Financial Modeling Worksheets*** will be used to flow transactions through the financial statements and reinforce the concept of articulation. A sample financial modeling worksheet is presented below.

FINANCIAL MODELING WORKSHEET

INCOME STATEMENT (FIRST)	
REVENUES:	
EXPENSES:	
NET INCOME OR LOSS (a)	

STATEMENT OF CASH FLOWS (THIRD)	
OPERATING ACTIVITIES:	
NET INCOME OR LOSS (a)	
INVESTING ACTIVITIES:	
FINANCING ACTIVITIES:	
INCREASE (DECREASE) IN CASH (b)	
ADD: BEGINNING CASH BALANCE	
ENDING CASH BALANCE	

BALANCE SHEET (SECOND)			
ASSETS		***LIABILITIES***	
CURRENT ASSETS		***CURRENT LIABILITIES***	
CASH (b)			
		NONCURRENT LIABILITIES	
		STOCKHOLDERS'	
NONCURRENT ASSETS		***EQUITY***	
		CAPITAL STOCK	
		APIC	
		RETAINED	
		EARNINGS (a)	
		TOTAL	
		LIABILITIES &	
		STOCKHOLDERS'	
TOTAL ASSETS		***EQUITY***	

ILLUSTRATION OF ARTICULATION AMONG PARK RIDGE'S FINANCIAL STATEMENTS

An illustration of the concept of articulation for the Park Ridge financial statements is presented below. Be sure you can trace the numbers entered on the worksheet to the financial statements found in Exhibits 1.3 to 1.6.

FINANCIAL MODELING WORKSHEET: PARK RIDGE 2011

INCOME STATEMENT (FIRST)	
REVENUES:	
EXPENSES:	
NET INCOME OR LOSS (a)	*+13,477*

STATEMENT OF CASH FLOWS (THIRD)	
OPERATING ACTIVITIES:	
NET INCOME OR LOSS (a)	*+13,477*
INVESTING ACTIVITIES:	
FINANCING ACTIVITIES:	
INCREASE (DECREASE) IN CASH (b)	*+1111*
ADD: BEGINNING CASH BALANCE	*6,586*
ENDING CASH BALANCE (C)	*7,697*

BALANCE SHEET (SECOND)			
ASSETS		*LIABILITIES*	
CURRENT ASSETS		*CURRENT LIABILITIES*	
CASH (C)	*7,697*		
		NONCURRENT LIABILITIES	
		STOCKHOLDERS'	
NONCURRENT ASSETS		*EQUITY*	
		CAPITAL STOCK	
		APIC	
		RETAINED	
		EARNINGS (a)	*+13,477*
		TOTAL	
		LIABILITIES &	
		STOCKHOLDERS'	
TOTAL ASSETS		*EQUITY*	

Net income for the year ended December 31, 2011 is reported on the statements of income (Exhibit 1.5). Net income is then closed out to retained earnings on the balance sheet (see Exhibits 1.3 and 1.4). Finally, the opening line of the statement of cash flows (Exhibit 1.6) is net income, which comes directly from the statement of earnings. Accrual basis net income is converted to operating cash flows and when investing and financing cash flows are considered, the increase in cash is added to the beginning cash balance giving the ending cash balance on the balance sheet (Exhibit 1.3). The articulation described in the financial modeling worksheet can be further explained by a reconciliation of the change in retained earnings. The following illustration also employs the information contained in Exhibits 1.3 and 1.6 and will reconcile or explain the change in retained earnings on the Park Ridge balance sheets. As noted below, the retained earnings account increased by $6,301 during 2011. This change can be explained by net income less dividends declared and by the loss incurred on share repurchases.

Reconciliation of the Change in Retained Earnings

Exhibit 1.3: Consolidated Balance Sheet	2011	2010	Increase
Retained Earnings	$58,926	$52,625	$6,301

To Reconcile: All three statements must be used (Exhibits 1.3, 1.5, 1.6)

	2011
Net income (Exhibit 1.5)	$13,477
Less Dividends paid to Park Ridge shareholders (Exhibit 1.6; Statement of Cash Flows Financing Activities)	(3,013)
Less: Loss of purchase of company shares (Exhibit 1.4 Consolidated Statement of Shareholder's Equity)	(4,163)
Increase in retained earnings for 2011	$6,301

Therefore, all financial statements were used to reconcile or confirm the 2011 increase in Park Ridge's retained earnings.

THE CONCEPTUAL FOUNDATION FOR FINANCIAL STATEMENTS PREPARED IN ACCORDANCE WITH GENERALLY ACCEPTED ACCOUNTING PRINCIPLES

Concepts Related to the Balance Sheet

Although applicable to all financial information, the following concepts are generally identified with the balance sheet. These concepts include the historical cost concept, the going concern concept, conservatism, and the business entity concept.

The Historical Cost Concept. This principle states that assets are to be initially recorded at cost, and remain at cost until sold, consumed in operations or otherwise disposed of by the entity. Cost is the agreed upon acquisition price arrived at objectively through a bargained or "arms-length" transaction which involves a buyer and seller both attempting to maximize their own wealth.

Although unrelated to current market values and irrelevant in a period of inflation, accountants continue to use historical cost valuation because it is objectively determined and subject to independent verification.

For most assets and in most industries, this means that cost is the ceiling on asset valuation. Therefore, assets are generally not carried in the financial statements at market or appraisal values nor are they adjusted for inflation. However, if there are declines in market value that are deemed to be other than temporary, asset values can be written down (i.e., reduced due to conservatism). This is generally known as "asset impairment." We continue to use historical cost information for most assets and in most industries.

Fair value ("mark to market") accounting is currently permitted for investment securities held for trading or available for sale. Derivative securities are also carried at fair value on corporate balance sheets. In addition, companies have recently been permitted to employ a "fair value option" to report certain financial assets and liabilities on their balance sheets at fair value.

The Going Concern Concept. The going concern concept provides justification for the use of historical cost valuation. It states that, unless there is evidence to the contrary, accountants will record and report the results of transactions "as if" the entity will continue to operate for an indefinite period of time. That is, the entity will continue to operate for a period of time long enough to carry out contemplated operations, utilize existing productive capacity and liquidate outstanding obligations. This concept justifies accounting practices such as the long-term and short-term categories on a classified balance sheet, and the depreciation of plant assets for an extended period of time, such as thirty years.

As noted above, the going concern concept also justifies the use of the historical cost valuation. That justification states that if the business is going to exist for an indefinite period of time, productive assets are not for sale. If the firm's productive assets are not for sale, then current market values are not relevant. Therefore, if current market values are not relevant, only historical cost-based information is useful to the reader of financial statements. Of course, if there is evidence that the business will not continue to exist (e.g., bankruptcy), then liquidation values should be used as the basis of financial statement presentation.

Conservatism. In its basic form, conservatism means that if an accountant is faced with two alternative valuation bases or different accounting methods, he or she should select that basis or method that is least likely to overstate assets and income.

Conservatism supports historical cost in those cases where market values above original cost cannot be used. Conservatism also represents an exception to cost because as noted above, write-downs below cost are permitted under certain conditions. Thus, the accountant would rather understate assets and income than overstate assets and income.

Nonetheless, "over-conservatism" should be avoided. In many cases a firm may take excessive write-downs to smooth income or engage in "big bath accounting," and justify this action by the principle of conservatism. For example, if a firm expects a decrease in profits or a loss in the next accounting period, they could take write-downs today in order to make next year's decrease in profit or the loss appear less dramatic, or to keep earnings on a smooth trend. In addition, if a firm is going to report a loss in the current year, they may take excessive write-downs and increase the loss even further (i.e., take a "big bath"), so as to look better or make a significant improvement in the subsequent accounting period. The philosophy underlying big bath accounting is that a two million dollar loss is just as bad as a one million dollar loss. In any event, income smoothing and big bath accounting cannot be justified by conservatism because these techniques are essentially tools used to manipulate reported earnings or to shift accounting income numbers between reporting periods.

The Business Entity Concept. The business or accounting entity concept states that all transactions and events related to the reporting entity must be kept separate and distinct from the personal affairs of the owner(s), related businesses or other outside business interests of the owner(s) of the entity.

Although disclosures of related parties and financial information of affiliated businesses are provided in the financial statements, these entities may be kept "off-balance sheet" and make the resulting analysis of financial statements difficult. (e.g., related businesses, unconsolidated affiliates and research and development partnerships).

Concepts Related to the Income Statement

The concepts relating to the income statement are concerned with revenue and expense recognition and are fundamentally integrated with the accrual basis of accounting.

The Revenue Realization Concept. According to the revenue realization concept, revenue is recognized when

1. An exchange (delivery) has taken place and
2. The earning process is "essentially complete."

The earning process is considered to be essentially complete when there are no material uncertainties as to future costs to be incurred with respect to the transaction and as to collection.

An application of the revenue realization concept includes software sales. For example, software manufacturers defer and amortize a portion of revenues earned from the sales of their products using the theory that product support and rights to future upgrades are not delivered at the point of sale. As a result, the earnings process was not substantially complete at the point of sale. If the earnings process was not complete, then revenue could not be recognized in the year of the sale (the year of cash receipts). In this case, cash flow precedes revenue recognition and revenue will be recognized ratably over an estimated future period (sometimes called the creation of "Rainy Day Reserves"). It should be noted that a new standard governing revenue recognition is expected by 2011.

The Matching Principle. The matching principle states that expenses (costs) are to be recognized only in the period in which the related revenues (benefits) are received. For example, this principle would justify the deferral or "capitalization" of the cost of a productive asset (e.g., delivery van), and expense (i.e., depreciate) this cost only in the future when the deliveries are made and revenues are generated. In this way, the capitalized or deferred costs are allocated (matched) to future periods of expected benefit. However, if an economic resource is determined to have no future benefit, it should be expensed immediately in the period in which this determination is made.

The capitalization-expense alternative will be a critical issue to be discussed throughout this book. In practice, the matching principle could be used to justify the improper deferral (capitalization) of a cost as an asset in the current year and only expensed and matched against revenues in the future. This practice would overstate assets and book value over the asset's life. Income will be overstated in the current period and would be understated in all subsequent periods due to excess depreciation (unless the cost deferral can be implemented each year).

For example, internet providers capitalized part of the cost of mailing free "starter" disks as "deferred advertising" on the asset side of the balance sheet. The SEC criticized this practice and the firms were forced to take a one-time charge to write off the balance of its deferred advertising. Internet providers no longer follow this accounting policy.

The Cash versus the Accrual Basis of Accounting. Under GAAP, only the accrual basis of accounting is acceptable. However, the cash basis of accounting can be used under limited circumstances or when the financial statement effect of the transaction is not material.

Under the cash basis, revenues are recognized only when cash is received and expenses are recognized only when cash is paid. This approach to revenue and expense recognition is not acceptable because it only measures cash receipts and disbursements, and does not reflect economic activity. In addition, cash basis net income can be managed through the timing of cash flows. For example, if you wanted to employ an income reducing strategy on a cash basis, you could delay the receipt of cash to lower reported income or accelerate cash payments to increase expenses.

Under the accrual basis of accounting, revenues are recognized when earned in accordance with the revenue realization concept, and expenses are recognized when incurred in accordance with the matching principle, regardless of when the cash is received or paid. The accrual basis gives rise to accruals (i.e., the economic event is recognized before the cash event) and deferrals (i.e., the economic event is recognized after the cash event).

It should be noted that the statement of cash flows is not a violation of the accrual basis of accounting. Rather, this statement should be viewed as presenting the cash flows that result from the firm's economic activities properly recognized under the accrual basis of accounting.

ORGANIZATION OF THE TEXT

The next three chapters of this book provide a detailed analysis of corporate financial position. The corporate balance sheet is disaggregated and an in-depth discussion of assets, debt and stockholders' equity is provided.

In chapters 5 through 9, a discussion of critical issues in current corporate financial reporting is provided. In this discussion, complex areas such as accounting for income taxes, earnings per share, intercorporate investments business combinations, and accounting for leases are presented.

Issues relating to full disclosure are discussed in chapters 10 and 11. Areas such as revenue recognition, accounting changes and discontinued operations are analyzed in detail. The statement of cash flows is examined in the last chapter of this book.

Throughout the discussion of these areas, detailed illustrations are provided and a financial modeling worksheets used to reflect the impact of a particular event or transaction on the three basic purpose financial statements. In addition, modeling applications are provided within the discussion of key sections of the text. The modeling applications are designed to provide practical illustrations of the analytical issues addressed in the chapter.

CHAPTER 2 Corporate Assets: Special Accounting and Reporting Issues

INTRODUCTION

The classified balance sheet is the most common means of reporting corporate financial position. On the classified balance sheet, assets and liabilities are segregated into their current and noncurrent components. This classification assists the analyst in determining liquidity through matching the maturities of current assets with current liabilities.

The present chapter focuses on special accounting and reporting issues relating to corporate assets. In the analysis of corporate assets, a review of the basic principles of accounting for areas such as accounts receivable, investments, inventory and plant assets is provided. Readers familiar with the more basic accounting areas can omit these sections of the chapter. After the basic review, more complex issues such as the LIFO-FIFO analytical restatement and capitalization of interest will be discussed.

THE CURRENT ASSET SECTION OF THE BALANCE SHEET

As noted in Chapter 1, current assets are defined as assets that are reasonably expected to be converted into cash, sold or consumed within one year or operating cycle, whichever is longer. The operating cycle is the "cash-to-cash" cycle or cash conversion cycle of the firm. A typical operating cycle is illustrated in the following diagram.

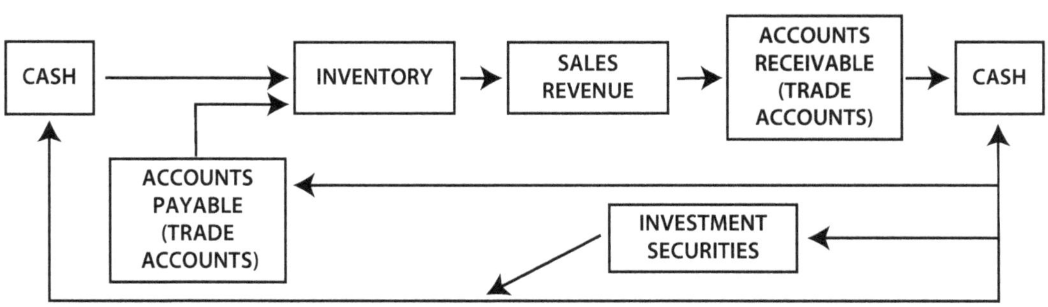

A firm will usually complete more than one operating cycle per year. However, in some industries such as tobacco, distilling or shipbuilding it may take longer than one year to complete a single operating cycle.

The operating cycle is a critical concept in the analysis of financial statements and can be measured through the application of some basic financial ratios. As will be discussed, converting the inventory turnover ratio into the number of days supply on hand or the "holding interval," and converting the accounts receivable turnover ratio into number of days sales in receivables or the "collection interval," provides the analyst with the variables needed to determine the length of the operating cycle. The holding interval measures the number of days from the acquisition or production of inventory to the point of sale. The collection interval measures the number of days required to convert the accounts receivable back into cash. The length of the operating cycle is the sum of the holding interval and the collection interval. The holding interval, the collection interval and the length of the operating cycle should be compared for the same firm over time, and it should also be assessed through comparison with industry standards.

As noted above, the operating cycle can be measured through the application of basic financial ratios.

Analysts use these operating cycle ratios for:

- Comparable company analysis
- Projections
- Debt capacity analysis

The operating cycle ratios are discussed in the following sections.

The Current (Working Capital) Ratio. The current or working capital ratio is simply the ratio of current assets to current liabilities:

$$\textbf{Current Ratio} = \frac{\textbf{Current Assets}}{\textbf{Current Liabilities}}$$

The numerator represents cash and the other current assets expected to be converted into cash within one year or operating cycle, whichever is longer. These resources are available to liquidate the short-term obligations due and payable during the same period.
A proper interpretation of the current ratio requires knowledge of trend and the industry in which the firm operates. The current ratio is a good starting point in the analysis of short-term liquidity and has been a reliable indicator of financial distress.
The following computations are based on the data provided for Nardo's Nuts and Bolts. The sample balance sheet and income statement are presented in Exhibit 2.1

EXHIBIT 2.1: NARDO'S NUTS AND BOLTS BALANCE SHEET AND INCOME STATEMENT

Nardo's Nuts and Bolts, Incorporated Balance Sheets at December 31, 2011 and 2010 Assets

	2011	***2010***
Cash	$250	$150
Accounts Receivable, net	$200	$100
Inventory	$350	$300
Total current assets	$800	$550
Noncurrent Assets		
Property, plant and equipment, net	$650	$500
Total Assets	$1,450	$1,050
Liabilities and Stockholders' Equity		
Liabilities		
Current Liabilities	***2009***	***2008***
Accounts payable	$400	$500
Noncurrent Liabilities		
Long term debt	$600	$400
Total liabilities	$1,000	$900
Stockholders' Equity		
Common stock	$ 90	$ 50
Retained earnings	$ 360	$ 100
Total stockholders' equity	$ 450	$ 150
Total liabilities and stockholders' equity	$ 1,450	$ 1,050

Nardo's Nuts and Bolts, Incorporated Income Statement For the year ended December 31, 2011	
Sales revenue	$3,000
Less: Cost of goods sold	$1,700
Gross profit	$1,300
Operating expenses:	
Salaries expense	$400
Utilities expense	$317
Depreciation expense	$100
Total operating expenses	$817
Operating income (EBIT)	$483
Less: Interest expense	$50
Income before tax	$433
Less: Income tax @ 40%	173
Net income	$260

The current ratio of Nardo's Nuts and Bolts is presented below:

Ratio	2011	2010
Current Ratio = Current Assets / Current Liabilities	$800 / 400 = 2 to 1	$550 / 500 = 1.1 to 1

In its purest form working capital is simply current assets minus current liabilities. Noncash or Operating working capital excludes cash and line items not considered part of operating working capital such as short-term bank debt, deferred taxes and pension (employee benefit) obligations. The change in noncash or operating working capital is used as a measure of the firm's investment in its short-term growth (this change is also called the investment in operating working capital). For Nardo's Nuts and Bolts we have the following:

DESCRIPTION	2011	2010
Working Capital = Current Assets - Current Liabilities	$800 - 400 = $400	$550 - 500 = $50
Noncash Working Capital = Current Assets - Cash - Current Liabilities	$550 - 400 = $150	$400 - 500 = ($100)

The change or investment in operating working capital is +$250 = $150 – (100).

Certain current assets, such as prepaid expenses, cannot be converted into cash quickly. As a result, many financial analysts will modify the current ratio by only including the most liquid current assets. The current ratio can be modified and computed as the Quick or Acid Test Ratio.

Quick or Acid Test Ratio. The quick or acid test ratio modifies the current ratio by only including those current assets expected to be converted into cash quickly. As a result, the numerator normally only includes cash, cash equivalents, marketable securities, and accounts receivable. A sample quick or acid test ratio is presented below.

$$\text{Quick or Acid Test Ratio} = \frac{\text{Cash and Cash Equivalents} + \text{Securities} + \text{Accounts Receivable}}{\text{Current Liabilities}}$$

However, depending on the type of company and industry, inventory may be more liquid than accounts receivable and replaces it in the denominator of the quick ratio.

The quick ratio of Nardo's Nuts and Bolts is presented below:

Ratio	2011	2010
Quick Ratio = Cash + Securities + Accounts Receivable / Current Liabilities	\$250 + 200 / 400 = 1.125 to 1	\$150 + 100 / 500 = .5 to 1

The ratios become more conservative when the Quick or Acid Test definition is used.

Accounts Receivable Turnover. The Accounts Receivable Turnover Ratio indicates on average how many times per year the firm goes from a full receivable balance to complete collection. This ratio is computed as follows:

$$\text{Accounts Receivable Turnover Ratio} = \frac{\text{Credit Sales}}{\text{Average Accounts Receivable}}$$

The denominator of each ratio uses the average balance, which is usually computed as the beginning balance plus ending balance divided by two. We use the average balance for two reasons. First, the numerator of the fraction is a flow variable, credit sales in this case, and the denominator is a static or stock variable, accounts receivable. Using the average accounts receivable balance for the period provides a flow characteristic for the denominator, giving an "apples to apples" measure. The second reason for using the average balance is to avoid any bias created by selecting either the beginning or ending balance of the account.

This ratio is also more useful when expressed in the expected number of days it takes to collect receivable balances. This ratio is sometimes called the Number of Days Sales in Accounts Receivable, the Collection Interval or Days Sales Outstanding (DSO). This ratio is computed by dividing 365 by the Accounts Receivable Turnover Ratio. That is:

$$\text{Collection Interval (DSO)} = \frac{365}{\text{Accounts Receivable Turnover Ratio}}$$

Inventory Turnover Ratio. The Inventory Turnover Ratio is designed to indicate on average how many times per year a company goes from full stock to stock out. This ratio is computed as follows:

$$\text{Inventory Turnover Ratio} = \frac{\text{Cost of Goods Sold}}{\text{Average Inventory}}$$

This ratio is more useful when expressed in the expected number of days it takes to sell inventory balances. This ratio is sometimes called the Number of Days Inventory Held (Stock on Hand) or the Holding Interval. This ratio is computed by dividing 365 by the Inventory Turnover Ratio as illustrated below:

$$\text{Holding Interval} = \frac{365}{\text{Inventory Turnover Ratio}}$$

Accounts Payable Turnover Ratio. The Accounts Payable Turnover Ratio indicates the number of times per year a company goes from full payable balances to full repayment. The ratio is computed as follows:

$$\text{Accounts Payable Turnover Ratio} = \frac{\text{Production or Purchases}}{\text{Average Accounts Payable}}$$

In many cases a company's beginning and ending inventory are approximately the same each year as a result, the cost of goods sold can be used as a proxy for purchases or production. This is reflected in the following cost of goods sold formula, using the assumption that beginning and ending inventories are equal.

ITEM	DOLLARS
Beginning Inventory	$ 2,000
Add: Cost of Goods Purchased or Produced	58,000
Goods Available for Sale	$ 60,000
Less: Ending Inventory	(2,000)
Cost of Goods Sold	$ 58,000

As a result, we usually compute the Accounts Payable Turnover Ratio using Cost of Goods sold as a proxy for purchases or production. This is illustrated below.

$$\text{Accounts Payable Turnover Ratio} = \frac{\text{Cost of Goods Sold}}{\text{Average Accounts Payable}}$$

This Accounts Payable Turnover Ratio is more useful when expressed in the expected number of days it takes to liquidate accounts payable balances. This ratio is sometimes called the Number of Days Accounts Payable Outstanding, the Payment Interval or the Credit Period. This ratio is computed by dividing 365 by the Accounts Payable Turnover Ratio:

$$\text{Payment Interval} = \frac{365}{\text{Accounts Payable Turnover Ratio}}$$

The length of the company's operating cycle can be measured as the sum of Collection Interval and Holding Interval. When the Payment Interval is netted against the Operating Cycle, the company's Cash Operating Cycle can be determined. The notation using parentheses, ( ), is designed to indicate a negative cash flow or "waiting for cash":

Cash Operating Cycle = (Collection Interval + Holding Interval) + Payment Interval

Cash Operating Cycle = (Operating Cycle) + Payment Interval

A cash operating cycle analysis for Nardo's Nuts and Bolts is presented below. The data for the computations are included in Exhibit 2.1.

2011 RATIO ANALYSIS FOR NARDO'S NUTS AND BOLTS

INVENTORY TURNOVER RATIO	=	COST OF GOODS SOLD / AVERAGE INVENTORY
	=	\$1,700 / [(\$350 + 300) / 2]
	=	5.2 TIMES
NUMBER OF DAYS SUPPLY ON HAND (HOLDING INTERVAL)	=	365 DAYS / INVENTORY TURNOVER RATIO
	=	365 DAYS / 5.2
	=	70 DAYS
ACCOUNTS RECEIVABLE TURNOVER RATIO	=	SALES REVENUES / AVERAGE RECEIVABLE
	=	\$3,000 / [(\$200 + 100) / 2]
	=	20 TIMES
NUMBER OF DAYS SALES IN RECEIVABLES (COLLECTION INTERVAL or DSO)	=	365 DAYS / ACCOUNTS RECEIVABLE TURNOVER RATIO
	=	365 DAYS /20
	=	18 DAYS.
ACCOUNTS PAYABLE TURNOVER RATIO	=	COGS (Proxy for Purchases) / AVERAGE ACCOUNTS PAYABLE
	=	\$1,700/ [(\$400 + 500)] /2
	=	3.8 TIMES
PAYMENT INTERVAL	=	365 / ACCOUNTS PAYABLE TURNOVER RATIO
	=	365 / 3.8
	=	96 DAYS

OPERATING CYCLE = HOLDING INTERVAL + COLLECTION INTERVAL
(88 DAYS) = (70 DAYS) + (18 DAYS)

CASH OPERATING CYCLE = OPERATING CYCLE + PAYMENT INTERVAL
8 Days = (88 DAYS) + 96 DAYS

No Need for Short term financing = Days before collection is received < Days until payment is due

There are several interesting points to note in the above results. First, Nardo is collecting its receivables in only 18 days, while the typical collection period is 30 days. A possible explanation is that Nardo offers its customers a discount for early cash payment. The discount is a cost to the seller, but it is outweighed by the benefits of having cash collections arrive earlier. The improved cash flows can avoid drawing on lines of credit and incurring interest charges or the excess cash can be invested on a short term basis or used to repay debt.

Second, Nardo's suppliers give them 96 days to pay off their accounts payable. Again, the average repayment terms provide for a 30 day repayment period. This extended credit period could be due to "seasonal dating of accounts receivable" by the suppliers. Seasonal dating is used in industries dependent on seasonal demand for their products. If the supplier did not use seasonal dating, the factory would be closed during slow periods and workers temporarily laid off. The lay offs increase drawing of unemployment benefits which increase the unemployment insurance premiums for the employer. When demand picks up during busy season, the factory is run overtime and salaries increase.

An alternative would be to run the factory at a level pace all year and stockpile inventory during slow seasons. However, this will increase inventory holding costs (e.g., handling costs, storage costs and insurance costs).

The optimal solution to the seasonal demand problem is to offer extended credit terms by "seasonal dating" the accounts receivable. In this case, Nardo's supplier allows an extended period (e.g., 3 months or more) to repay. These credit terms allow the supplier to run the factory at a constant level all year, avoid layoffs and overtime during seasonal fluctuations in demand. This policy also moves the inventory out of its warehouse and shifts it to Nardo's storage facility.

In this case, the combination of offering sales discounts and the seasonal dating offered by suppliers, allows Nardo to meet its short term obligations with an eight day float that avoids drawing on a line of credit, and may be invested in the interim.

KEY ISSUES IN THE ANALYSIS OF CURRENT ASSETS

These are two issues in the analysis of current assets. The first issue involves the use of operating cycle ratios to build projected financial statements in modeling applications. The second issue addresses how the use of alternative accounting methods can significantly bias several financial ratios.

Modeling Application. Holding all else constant, an analyst can use prior years' gross profit to determine the average (historical) gross profit and cost of sales percentages. Assume the five year average gross profit percentage for Nardo's Nuts and Bolts in Exhibit 2.1 is 43.3% ($1,300 / $2,000) and the cost of sales percentage is 56.7% (i.e., 100% - 43.3%). If an analyst estimates an 8% growth rate in Nardo's sales, then the 2012 sales forecast is $3,240, (i.e., 1.08 x $3,000). The cost of sales could be projected at $1,837 (i.e., 56.7% x $3,240 or 1.08 x $1,700). This information is used in building the proforma income statements.

If it is now assumed that Nardo's historical inventory turnover ratio is 5.2 times, then the ending inventory for 2012 could be estimated and used in building a proforma balance sheet as follows:

Inventory Turnover Ratio	=	Cost of Goods Sold / Average Inventory
5.2 Times	=	(Projected) $1,837 / X
Average Inventory	=	Cost of Goods Sold /Inventory Turnover Ration
x	=	(Projected) $1,837 / 5.2 Times
x	=	Average Inventory = $353
Average Inventory	=	[Actual Beg. Inv. + Projected End. Inv] / 2
$353	=	[$350 = Projected End. Inv.] / 2
Projected End. Inv.	=	$706 - 350 = $356

The Impact of GAAP alternatives on financial ratio measurement. The use of different GAAP methods can significantly bias these key financial statistics. For example, different methods of classification and accounting for assets such as accounts receivable and inventory can bias the interpretation of the liquidity and operating cycle of the firm.

Due to the importance of the operating cycle, the key topics discussed in the analysis of current assets are cash, accounts receivable and the bad debt expense, investments in marketable securities, and accounting for inventory.

CASH

Cash is typically the only asset without valuation problems. However, proper classification can be an issue. Cash is classified as current unless it is restricted from use in the current operating cycle. Restrictions on withdrawal, and therefore limitations on use, in the current operating cycle include foreign bank accounts, escrow account compensating balances and debt sinking funds.

When cash is restricted from use in the current operating cycle, it should be generally reclassified out of the regular cash line item on the balance sheet and disclosed in the footnotes. An account entitled "restricted funds" is used to indicate that there is some limitation on the use of cash. If the restriction extends beyond one year from the balance sheet date, the restricted funds account is classified as a noncurrent asset and is included in the Other Assets section of the balance sheet. If the restriction is for less than one year, the restricted funds account could still be classified as current, but segregated from the regular cash line item in the Current Assets section of the balance sheet.

Cash may be restricted from use due to compensating balance arrangements. Compensating balances are minimum cash balances that are "required" to be kept on deposit by debtors as support for existing credit agreements.

The key issue surrounding compensating balance requirements is also classification. According to the SEC, if the compensating balances are legally restricted, similar to an escrow account and held against short-term debt, the cash held as a compensating balance must be reclassified as another current asset. On the other hand, if the balance is held against long-term debt, the amount of cash held as a compensating balance must be reclassified as a noncurrent asset on the balance sheet. In either case, the legally restricted compensating balances cannot be combined with regular cash on the balance sheet.

If the compensating balances are not legally restricted, the amounts, terms and length of the arrangement must be disclosed in footnotes to the financial statements. However, a classification out of regular cash is not required.

Sample footnote disclosures for foreign cash balances and restrictive debt covenant provisions are presented in Exhibit 2.2 for Bruce Products, Inc. and the Newton Company.

EXHIBIT 2.2: RESTRICTED CASH DISCLOSURE FOR BRUCE PRODUCTS, INC. AND THE NEWTON COMPANY

BRUCE PRODUCTS, INC.
PARTIAL CONSOLIDATED BALANCE SHEETS
December 31,

(Dollar amounts in thousands)

	2011	2010
ASSETS		
CURRENT ASSETS		
Cash and cash equivalents	$ 236,957	$ 173,828
Accounts receivable, less allowance for doubtful accounts of $2,309 and $2,411 for 2011 and 2010, respectively	50,893	59,293
Inventories	73,397	77,881
Prepaid expenses and other current assets	8,935	9,252
Deferred taxes	5,069	5,585

NOTES TO CONSOLIDATED FINANCIAL STATEMENTS
December 31, 2011, 2010 and 2009
NOTE 1—SUMMARY OF SIGNIFICANT ACCOUNTING POLICIES

Cash Equivalents

For purposes of the statements of cash flows, the Company considers all highly liquid debt instruments purchased with an original maturity of three months or less to be cash equivalents. Included in cash and cash equivalents as of December 31, 2011 and 2010 is $18,947 and $7,850, respectively, held as compensating balances in foreign bank accounts.

Newton Company, Inc
Newton Company INC. FINANCIALS 2005
CONSOLIDATED BALANCE SHEETS

($ in millions except par value, shares in thousands)	January 28, 2006	January 29, 2005
Assets		
Current assets		
Cash and equivalents	$ 2,442	$ 2,694
Short-term investments	1142.4	980.4
Restricted cash	66	1,218
Merchandise inventory	2,035	2,177
Other current assets	601.2	495.6
Total current assets	6,287	7,565

Restricted Cash

Restricted cash consists of cash held as collateral and other cash that is restricted from withdrawal for use. Cash is held as collateral for other bank lines that backed our letter of credit agreements to finance our inventory purchases, and the remainder was primarily restricted for other obligations.

In those cases where compensating balances exist but the amount of cash is not legally restricted, the amount of available cash and liquidity may be overstated by use of conventional measures of liquidity. Although firms consider compensating balances as part of their minimum operating cash balances, these funds may not actually be available for use in the current operating cycle. That is, even if the compensating balances are not legally restricted from withdrawal, the firm may be reluctant to draw down a compensating balance because this action may result in technical default of the loan agreement or may seriously impair the firm's future credit standing.

In the case of the Bruce Products, Inc. in Exhibit 2.2, the extent of "restricted" cash can be estimated from the Cash and Cash Equivalent footnote. For example, $18,947 of the total 2011 cash balance reported as regular cash in the current asset section of the balance sheet at year end may not be available for use in the current operating cycle if the financial policies in the countries mentioned in the footnote restrict cash moving back to the company's domestic office. From a conservative standpoint, the foreign cash balances may not be considered by the analyst to be as "liquid" as the remainder of the cash balance. The analyst can also use this information to obtain a range of available cash balances in the assessment of liquidity (i.e., cash with and without the possible restrictions). In any event, the existence of restrictive debt covenants, including compensating balance restrictions, indicate some deterioration of the firm's credit rating.

As noted in Exhibit 2.2, the Newton Company, Inc. reports restricted cash in the current assets section of its balance sheet and in the footnotes to the financial statements. The restricted cash is classified as current because it is held against short term bank lines of credit.

Accounts Receivable and the Bad Debt Expense

In accounting for accounts receivable, or any asset with valuation issues, there are two major purposes or objectives:

1. The Balance Sheet Purpose is to properly value the asset at its Net Realizable Value (NRV), or the amount reasonably expected to be realized in cash. In addition, this objective includes the proper classification as either current or noncurrent, depending on the timing of expected cash realization.
2. Income Statement Purpose is to properly match costs and revenues.

As will be noted throughout the discussion of corporate assets, there is generally a trade-off between these two objectives. Specifically for accounts receivable, the valuation issue relates to the amount of cash ultimately expected to be collected. For all sales on credit, a firm must reasonably expect some uncollectible accounts. This is a cost or expense of doing business on credit. The loss from uncollectible accounts is known as the bad debt expense.

There are two methods to account for the bad debt expense:

- The direct write-off method (the tax method);
- The allowance method (the GAAP method).

The Direct Write-Off Method

Under the direct write-off, no provision is made for the expected losses from uncollectible accounts in the year of the sale. The bad debt expense is only recognized during the period in which the account is actually determined to be uncollectible. This could be several accounting periods after the sale was made.

The direct write-off method is primarily used for tax purposes. It can be used for financial reporting only if accounts receivable and the bad debt expense are immaterial to the financial position and operating results of the firm. However, in most cases the direct write-off method is not generally accepted.

The direct write-off method is not used for GAAP purposes because it is said to violate the two objectives of accounting for receivables noted above. In the year of the sale, the direct write-off method overstates assets by failing to provide a provision to reduce the balance of accounts receivable to its net realizable value, and overstates reported profit by not charging income for the expected loss from bad debts. For these reasons, the direct write-off method does not properly value the receivable and it does not match costs with revenues in the year of the sale. In addition, in the year of the write-off, income is reduced for a bad debt relating to sales revenue generated in a prior period. Again, there is a mismatch of costs and revenues. It is for these reasons that GAAP requires the use of the allowance method.

The Allowance Method

The allowance method is required under GAAP, and it is not acceptable for income tax purposes, with minor exceptions.

Under the allowance method, the bad debt expense is estimated and charged against income in the year of the sale in order to match costs with revenues. This is considered proper matching because the cost of selling on credit is matched with the additional revenue generated because the firm extends credit to its customers. That is, if the firm does not offer credit, overall sales will be reduced. The other side of the bad debt expense estimate is to create an allowance (i.e., a provision, a "cushion" or a "reserve") for the ultimate failure to collect the receivable. The allowance account is deducted from the gross accounts receivable balance to properly value accounts receivable at its net realizable value (i.e., the amount reasonably expected to be realized in cash).

The allowance account is considered a "contra asset account" and must be offset against accounts receivable on the balance sheet so that "accounts receivable-net" is reported in the financial statements.

The allowance account provides a cushion against future write-offs. In the year in which an account is actually determined to be uncollectible, the account is written off against the allowance. The write-off under the allowance method reduces the allowance account and the balance of accounts receivable (i.e., it has no effect on net realizable value). There is no income statement impact from the write-off under the allowance method because income was already reduced by the estimated bad debt expense in the year of the sale.

The differences between the direct write-off method and the allowance method are illustrated in Exhibit 2.3. Note that in both Exhibit 2.3 and in the financial modeling worksheet, there are no cash flow implications for accounting for uncollectible accounts.

EXHIBIT 2.3

Data:

In 2010 a firm has credit sales of $1,000. Assume there are no operating expenses during the year. The firm does not operate in 2011 (i.e., there are no sales or operating expenses). However, a customer with a $10 balance declares bankruptcy.

Partial Financial Statements Under The Direct Write-Off Method (Tax) And The Allowance Method (GAAP)

	TAX: THE DIRECT WRITE-OFF METHOD		GAAP: THE ALLOWANCE METHOD	
DESCRIPTION	2010	2011	2010	2011
INCOME STATEMENTS:				
CREDIT SALES	$1,000	$0	$1,000	$0
LESS: BAD DEBTS EXPENSE	0	*ACTUAL(10)	ESTIMATE(10)	0
NET INCOME (LOSS)	$1,000	($10)	$990	$0
BALANCE SHEETS:				
CURRENT ASSET SECTION				
ACCOUNTS RECEIVABLE	$1,000	*$ 990	$1,000	**$ 990
LESS: ALLOWANCE FOR BAD DEBTS	N/A	N/A	-10	**0
NET REALIZABLE VALUE (NRV)	$1,000	$990	$990	$990
STOCKHOLDERS' EQUITY SECTION				
RETAINED EARNINGS	$1,000	$990	$990	$990

NOTES:

*A write off of a bad debt under the Direct Write Off Method reduces income and accounts receivable.

**A write off of a bad debt under the Allowance Method reduces the allowance (provision) for bad debts and accounts receivable. That is, there is no effect on income when an account is written off under the Allowance Method. It is written off against a provision (reserve or cushion) that was created in the year of the sale. The expense was recognized in the year of the sale to match costs and revenue. Balance sheet totals are unchanged from 2010 to 2011 when there is a write off of an uncollectible account under the allowance method.

In Exhibit 2.3 it is assumed that $1,000 in credit sales are made in 2010 and there is no business activity in 2011. The bad debt expense is the firm's only operating expense. It is also assumed that a customer owing $10 declares bankruptcy in 2011. If we assume that the direct write-off method is used, the 2010 financial statements reflect $1,000 in income, assets and total equity. When the account actually becomes uncollectible in 2011, the firm reports a net loss of $10 under the direct write-off method, although there is no economic activity during this year. Not only are assets, total equity and income overstated in 2010, income is understated in 2011. Thus the use of the direct write-off method results in improper asset valuation and a mismatching of costs with revenues.

If the allowance method is used, a provision for estimated bad debts is made in 2010, the year of the sale, which reduces assets, total equity and reported income. The illustration assumes that bad debts are estimated with 100% accuracy. In 2011, when the account actually becomes uncollectible, the customer's account is written off against the provision created in 2010. The income statement correctly reflects no activity in 2011 and the balance sheet for the period is unchanged. This approach properly matches costs and revenues and carries the balance of accounts receivable at its net realizable value.

The financial statement effects of recording the bad debt estimate in 2010 and the bad debt write-off in 2011 under the allowance method are presented in the Financial Modeling Worksheets below. The worksheet illustrates the ***changes*** (not the balances) flowing through the three primary financial statements related to the above transaction.

The entry to record the estimated bad debt expense for 2010, reduces income and retained earnings, but there is no cash flow effect. The bad debt expense is a non-cash expense and is added back in the operating activities section of the Statement of Cash Flows.

FINANCIAL MODELING WORKSHEET (2010 ADJUSTMENT FOR THE ESTIMATED BAD DEBT EXPENSE: ALLOWANCE METHOD)

INCOME STATEMENT (FIRST)	
REVENUES:	
EXPENSES:	
Bad Debt Expense	*(10)*
NET INCOME OR LOSS (a)	*(10)*

STATEMENT OF CASH FLOWS (THIRD)	
OPERATING ACTIVITIES:	
NET INCOME OR LOSS (a)	*(10)*
Add back: Bad Debt Expense	*+10*
INVESTING ACTIVITIES:	
FINANCING ACTIVITIES:	
INCREASE (DECREASE) IN CASH (b)	*- 0 -*
ADD: BEGINNING CASH BALANCE	
ENDING CASH BALANCE	

BALANCE SHEET (SECOND)			
ASSETS		*LIABILITIES*	
CURRENT ASSETS		*CURRENT LIABILITIES*	
CASH (b)	*- 0 -*		
Accounts Receivable			
Less: Allowance	*(10)*		
		NONCURRENT LIABILITIES	
		STOCKHOLDERS' EQUITY	
NONCURRENT ASSETS			
		CAPITAL STOCK	
		APIC	
		RETAINED EARNINGS (a)	*(10)*
		TOTAL LIABILITIES & STOCKHOLDERS' EQUITY	
TOTAL ASSETS	*(10)*		*(10)*

When an account actually becomes uncollectible under the allowance method, the write-off only adjusts the accounts receivable and the allowance accounts, reducing both. The net realizable value of accounts receivable is not affected by the write off of the uncollectible account. There is no effect on any the statements. This is illustrated in the financial modeling work sheet below. Note when an allowance is reduced, accounts receivable net is increased.

FINANCIAL MODELING WORKSHEET (2011 ENTRY TO WRITE OFF THE ACCOUNT: ALLOWANCE METHOD)

INCOME STATEMENT (FIRST)	
REVENUES:	
EXPENSES:	
NET INCOME OR LOSS (a)	- 0 -

STATEMENT OF CASH FLOWS (THIRD)	
OPERATING ACTIVITIES:	
NET INCOME OR LOSS (a)	-0-
INVESTING ACTIVITIES:	
FINANCING ACTIVITIES:	
INCREASE (DECREASE) IN CASH (b)	- 0 -
ADD: BEGINNING CASH BALANCE	
ENDING CASH BALANCE	

BALANCE SHEET (SECOND)			
ASSETS		LIABILITIES	
CURRENT ASSETS		CURRENT LIABILITIES	
CASH (b)	- 0 -		
Accounts Receivable	-10		
Less: Allowance	+10		
		NONCURRENT LIABILITIES	
		STOCKHOLDERS'	
NONCURRENT ASSETS		EQUITY	
		CAPITAL STOCK	
		APIC	
		RETAINED	
		EARNINGS (a)	- 0 -
		TOTAL	
		LIABILITIES &	
		STOCKHOLDERS'	
TOTAL ASSETS	- 0 -	EQUITY	- 0 -

This illustration assumed that there were no estimation errors under the allowance method. However, estimation errors would not affect the basic principles of accounting for bad debts. If estimation errors occur, they would be corrected on a prospective basis where the future year's provision for bad debts would reflect both the current year's requirements as well as an adjustment for prior period estimation errors. Although prospective adjustments under the allowance method can create a matching problem, the allowance method is still considered superior to the direct write-off method.

As noted earlier, the allowance method is favored under GAAP because it better satisfies accounting and reporting objectives. However, the use of the allowance method results in several problems for analysts. First, there is a great deal of judgment and subjectivity in the bad debt estimate. This problem is compounded by the fact that there are no GAAP methods of estimation. In other words, GAAP is satisfied if the allowance method is used but the method used to estimate the bad debt expense is at the discretion of management. The prospective changes in estimate can also manipulate income.

Common estimation methods used in practice include a percentage of credit sales, a percentage of the accounts receivable balance, an analysis of an aging of accounts receivable, analysis of company and industry forecasts and a combination of these methods. The method used to estimate the bad debt expense can significantly affect reported net income and the net realizable value of accounts receivable on the balance sheet. However, no matter which method is used to account for the bad debt expense or to estimate the allowance for bad debts, there is no effect on cash flow when the expense is charged against income.

Second, there are usually inadequate disclosures regarding the techniques used to estimate the allowance for bad debts. A footnote disclosure would be required if the firm changes its estimation method and if that change results in a material effect on reported income. The lack of adequate disclosures coupled with the highly subjective nature of the estimation used increases the accounting risk and reduces the quality of reported earnings associated with the accounting for uncollectible accounts.

A SAMPLE FOOTNOTE DISCLOSURE

Allowance for Uncollectible Accounts

The company uses the percentage of credit sales, the aging of accounts receivable and specific reviews to establish the allowance for uncollectible accounts receivable.

Accounts receivable allowances were approximately $57 million, in 2012 and $63 million in 2011. Accounts receivable, net of allowances, were approximately $566 million, and $506 million, as of December 2012 and December 2011, respectively.

Other Issues in Accounting for Receivables

Pledging Assigning and Factoring Accounts Receivable. Pledging, assigning or factoring of accounts receivable can be used by a firm to convert their receivables into immediate cash.

When a firm "pledges" accounts receivable, the accounts receivable are pledged as collateral for a financing arrangement. The "assignment" of accounts receivable is also used directly in a borrowing arrangement, except that when accounts receivable are assigned, the receivables are still pledged as collateral for the loan but the receipts on collection of the receivables are directly used to pay down the debt. In either case, the accounts receivable are not removed from the current asset section of the balance sheet. Instead, footnotes to the financial statements indicate the contingent liability related to the transfer of the accounts receivable rights to others. Nevertheless, the analyst must consider the potential adverse effects on liquidity from a default on the debt relating to the receivables pledged or assigned to third parties.

In the case of a "factoring" of accounts receivable, the accounts receivable are sold at a discount to a third party called a factor. Here, customers instructed to remit payments directly to the factor. The accounting and reporting issues for factoring accounts receivable depend on whether the receivables are sold with recourse (with continuing involvement) or without recourse (without continuing involvement).

If the receivables are sold without recourse (without continuing involvement), the transaction is considered an outright sale and the accounts receivable are removed from the books and the related gain or loss on the transaction is recorded. The gain or loss is measured as the difference between the net proceeds on the sale and the face amount of the receivables factored.

If the receivables are factored with recourse (with continuing involvement), the risk of loss and collection remains with the seller. In that case, a sale is also recognized but an estimated recourse liability must be accrued. For factoring with or without recourse the primary issue is whether this is a sale or a secured borrowing arrangement? The answer to this question is provided by FASB Statement No. 140, "Accounting for Transfers and Servicing of Financial Assets and Extinguishments of Liabilities."[1]

Under SFAS 140, a transfer of accounts receivable either with or without recourse can be accounted for and reported as a sale with the gain or loss recognized, if all three of the following criteria are met:

(a) Transferor (i.e. the seller) surrenders control of the future economic benefits of the receivables

(b) Transferor's (i.e. the seller's) obligation under the recourse provisions can be reasonably estimated

(c) Transferee (i.e. the buyer) cannot require the transferor to repurchase the receivables

If all three conditions are met, a sale of accounts receivable is recorded along with an estimate of the recourse obligation if necessary. If these conditions are not met, the transfer is accounted for as a borrowing arrangement. If the seller does not meet all three criteria, the amount of the proceeds for the transfer of the receivables is recorded as a liability. A sale cannot be recorded and the amount of receivables transferred remains in the asset section of the balance sheet.

For the factoring of accounts receivable accounted for as a sale, the seller must provide the following disclosures:

- The proceeds received for each income statement presented
- If the information is available, the balance of the factored receivables that remains uncollected at the date of each balance sheet presented.

Although the provisions of SFAS 140 provide guidance as to the appropriate accounting and reporting of a transfer of receivables, there may still be some off-balance sheet financing. When a transfer is made with recourse and that transfer is recorded as a sale, the actual liability may not be reflected on the balance sheet. Even where the estimated recourse obligation is accrued in the financial statements, the seller's exposure to the risk on the transaction is no different from a primary debtor in a lending agreement. As a result, the analyst should carefully examine the footnotes to the financial statements in order to determine the extent of off-balance sheet financing resulting from factoring of accounts receivable with recourse. The disclosures for receivables should do the following:

(a) Segregate all different receivables, if material

(b) Insure that the allowance accounts are offset against the receivable accounts

1. FASB ASC 860 [Predecessor literature: "Accounting for Transfers and Servicing of Financial Assets and Extinguishments of Liabilities (a replacement of FASB Statement 125)," *Statement of Financial Accounting Standards No. 140* (Norwalk, Conn.: FASB, 2000)].

(c) Determine that receivables classified in the current asset section will be converted into cash within the year or the operating cycle, whichever is longer

(d) Disclose any loss contingencies related to receivables

(e) Disclose any receivables assigned or pledged as collateral

(f) Disclose all significant concentrations of credit risk (e.g., a single customer owes 30% of accounts receivable balances)

Imputed Interest on Sales Using Notes Receivable. According to APB Opinion No. 21, "Interest on Receivables and Payables"[2] when goods and services are exchanged for a note receivable, the interest rate is assumed to be fair unless:

- No interest rate is stated;
- The stated amount of interest is unreasonable;
- The face amount of the note receivable is materially different from the cash price of the goods or services provided or from the market value of the note.

When any of these conditions exist, it may be difficult to determine the separate amounts of the sales revenue and financing income earned on the transaction. Opinion No. 21 provides guidance as to the appropriate accounting for these types of notes receivable transactions.

If the current cash price of the goods or services provided is known, the sales revenue is set equal to the cash price. The difference between the face amount of the note receivable and the sales value is considered to be deferred interest income (i.e., discount on notes receivable) and is amortized to interest income over the life of the loan. At the end of each accounting period, the carrying value of the note receivable is reported as the face amount of the note less the unamortized balance of the deferred interest income. According to Opinion No. 21, the deferred interest income should be amortized by using the effective interest rate method of amortization. This method of amortization will be illustrated in the discussion of long-term debt.

If the goods or services have no established market so that a cash price cannot be determined, the sales value recorded is set equal to the present value of the note. If the note is publicly traded, then its fair value would be used. The present value of the note is determined by discounting the principal and interest (if any) at an imputed rate of interest. The imputed interest rate is a rate of interest that approximates that rate which would have resulted from an independent borrowing transaction under similar circumstances. Therefore, the imputation of a rate of interest requires consideration of factors such as the debtor's credit rating, the prime rate, and the rate on similar sources of financing by the debtor.

2. FASB ASC 835 [Predecessor literature: "Interest on Receivables and Payables," *Opinions of the Accounting Principles Board No. 21* (New York: AICPA 1971)].

Investments in Marketable Securities and the Fair Value Option

FASB Statement No. 115, "Accounting for Certain Investments in Debt and Equity Securities,"[3] sets forth the accounting requirements for investments in marketable securities. This standard is significant because it represents a major departure from the historical cost model by adopting a "mark-to-market" methodology for accounting for marketable securities. Recently, FASB Statement No. 159 "The Fair Value Option for Financial Assets and Liabilities"[4] allowing companies to apply the fair values option to most financial instruments, both debt and equity. Fair value is to be measured by applying the guidelines found in FASB Statement No. 157, "Fair Value Measurements."[5] All three standards are currently in effect and will be discussed in the following paragraphs.

FASB Statement 115

SFAS 115 applies to all debt and marketable equity securities with readily determinable fair values. Cost may be used when fair values are not readily determinable (e.g., the shares are not publicly traded). Equity securities include shares of common and preferred stock, warrants and options. SFAS 115 does not apply to long term investments accounted for under the equity method (to be discussed). The statement also does not apply to not-for-profit organizations and specialized industries that already account for their debt and equity securities at fair value.

Under SFAS 115, all debt and equity investments with determinable fair values must be classified into one of three portfolio classifications, based on management's intention.

a. Held-to-Maturity.
b. Trading.
c. Available-for-Sale.

A summary of the classifications and accounting used is presented in the following table.

3. FASB ASC 320 [Predecessor literature: "Accounting for Certain Investments in Debt and Equity Securities," *Statement of Financial Accounting Standards No. 115* (Norwalk, Conn.: FASB, 1993)].

4. FASB ASC 825 [Predecessor literature: "The Fair Value Option for Financial Assets and Financial Liabilities-Including an amendment of FASB Statement No. 115, "*Statement of Financial Accounting Standards No. 159* (Norwalk, Conn.: FASB, 2007)].

5. FASB ASC 820 [Predecessor literature: "Fair Value Measurements," *Statement of Financial Accounting Standards No. 157* (Norwalk, Conn.: FASB 2006)].

SFAS 115 CLASSIFICATIONS AND ACCOUNTING FOR DEBT AND EQUITY SECURITIES				
PORTFOLIO CLASSIFICATION	***TYPE OF SECURITY***	***MANAGEMENT'S INTENTION***	***BALANCE SHEET VALUATION***	***INCOME STATEMENT EFFECT***
a. Held-to-Maturity (A current asset if held as working capital)	***Debt***	***Positive intent and ability to hold to maturity. Holding for an "indefinite period of time" does not meet this criterion.***	***Amortized Cost***	***Interest is recognized as earned. Only realized gains or losses are recognized on sale.***
b. Trading (Always classified as a current asset)	***Debt and Equity***	***Acquired to sell in the short term.***	***Fair Value***	***Interest and dividends are recognized as earned. Premiums and discounts on debt securities are not amortized. The short-term nature of the investment results in immaterial amortization effects. Realized gains or losses are recognized on sale. Unrealized gains or losses are recognized as fair values fluctuate.***
c. Available-for-Sale (A current asset if held as working capital)	***Debt and Equity***	***Neither held to maturity or short term trading.***	***Fair Value As fair values fluctuate, unrealized gains or losses are recognized as adjustments to Stockholders' Equity. (In Comprehensive Income)***	***Interest and dividends are recognized as earned. Interest includes premium and discount amortization. Realized gains or losses are recognized on sale.***

The appropriateness of these categories should be reassessed each reporting period.

Balance Sheet Classification: All trading securities are classified as current assets. Securities classified as Held-to-Maturity and Available-for-Sale would be presented as current assets if the securities are considered working capital available for current operations. Otherwise, they would be classified as noncurrent assets.

Detailed Discussion of the Portfolio Classifications

Held-to-Maturity: If management demonstrates the intent and ability to hold a debt security to maturity, it should be classified as Held-to-Maturity. All debt securities in this category would be carried at amortized cost. That is, fair value accounting does not apply to this portfolio classification. As a result, only interest income and realized gains and losses on sale would be recorded on the income statement. Interest income is adjusted for premium and discount amortization.

Debt securities cannot be classified as Held-to-Maturity if the firm anticipates that a sale may be necessary due to these changes:

- Market interest rates and related prepayment risk of the security
- Liquidity needs availability and yield of alternative investments
- Funding sources and terms
- Foreign currency risk

Isolated, nonrecurring and unusual events that could not have been reasonably anticipated would not cause a sale or transfer out of this classification and would not be considered inconsistent with the initial classification as Held-to-Maturity. In addition, selling a security prior to maturity for the following reasons would not be inconsistent with classification in the Held-to-Maturity category:

- A significant increase in the credit risk of the security
- A change in tax law eliminating the tax exempt status of the interest on a security
- A major business combination or disposition that necessitates the sale or transfer of securities to maintain existing interest rate position or credit risk policy.
-

The sale of a security within three months of its maturity meets the requirement to hold to maturity since interest rate risk is substantially diminished at this point (i.e., interest rate risk is no longer an important pricing factor). Additionally, if a firm has already collected a substantial portion of the principal (at least 85%), the security is considered to have been held to maturity.

The classification on the balance sheet as current or noncurrent depends on whether the securities are considered working capital. All sales or transfers of securities in this category must disclose amortized cost, realized or unrealized gain or loss and circumstances leading to the decision to sell or transfer the security.

Trading Securities. If management intends to actively and frequently trade debt and equity securities they should be classified as Trading Securities. Trading Securities are carried on the balance sheet at fair value and classified as current assets. In addition to recognizing interest and dividend income and realized gains or losses on sales, unrealized gains or losses on the annual adjustment to fair value are reported on the income statement. These unrealized gains and losses are reported in the income statement because there is a high probability of short term cash realization as the securities are traded frequently. In addition active trading implies that these transactions are part of normal operations.

Available for Sale. Investments in debt and equity securities that are not classified as either Held-to-Maturity or Trading Securities are classified as Available for Sale. Available for Sale securities are also required to be carried on the balance sheet at fair value.

Interest and dividend income and realized gains and losses on the sale of Available for

Sale investments are included on the income statement. However, unlike trading securities, unrealized gains and losses on the annual adjustment to fair value are not included on the income statement. Instead, net unrealized gains or losses are reported as a separate component of stockholders' equity until realized on sale (i.e., the net gain or loss is deferred in other comprehensive income until the security is sold). The unrealized gain or loss is not reported in income due to the low probability of short term cash realization. The gain and loss is also not reported in income and is deferred in accumulated other comprehensive income because it is not part of normal operations and it avoids volatility in net income as gains and losses can offset as the market value of the securities fluctuate.

Deferred Tax Effects. The recognition of unrealized gains and losses for trading investments will not be recognized for tax purposes (until sold). Therefore, fair value accounting for financial statement purposes is likely to have deferred tax effects. Accounting for income taxes will be discussed in a subsequent section of this book.

Transfers Between Portfolio Classifications. All transfers between portfolios are to be accounted for at fair value. When transferred, any unrealized holding gains or losses are to be accounted as follows:

- All transfers to or from the trading portfolio must be made at fair value at the date of the transfer with any unrealized gain or loss recognized in income at the point of transfer
- Transfers only involving the available-for-sale and the held-to-maturity portfolios must be made at fair value with the unrealized gain or loss adjusted treated as follows:

    — if there is a transfer to the available-for-sale portfolio, the unrealized gain or loss is added to the balance of accumulated other comprehensive income in stockholders' equity

    — if there is a transfer to the held-to-maturity portfolio, the unrealized gain or loss in accumulated other comprehensive income in stockholders' equity is amortized against the allowance account on the balance sheet over the remaining life of the debt security

When it becomes probable that all contractual amounts due on Held-to-Maturity; Trading or Available for Sale securities will not be collected, the loss should be recognized immediately on the income statement. The FASB in EITF 03-1[6] that requires a "three step approach" be used to determine if there is an "other than temporary" impairment loss. The three step approach involves answering a series of questions:

6. FASB ASC 320 [Predecessor literature: *EITF Issue No. 03-1*, "The Meaning of Other-Than-Temporary Impairment and Its Application to Certain Investments," *Emerging Issues Task Force Abstracts* (September 30, 2004)].

1. *Is fair value less than cost?* That is, accountants must determine if the investment is impaired. This is typically determined by comparing fair value to carrying value and by consideration of several "impairment indicators":

- Deterioration of earnings
- Reduction of credit rating
- Adverse changes in the economy, the environment, technology, regulation, etc., that impacts the investee company

2. *Is it impossible to recover the loss during the expected holding period?* Here, an accountant needs to determine if there is adequate evidence to support the notion that the investor has the "ability and intent" to hold the investment over a period of time long enough to recover the lost investment value and bring it above cost. In this step, consideration must be given to the magnitude of the decline in value, the nature of the event causing the impairment, etc.

3. *If the first two steps are passed, the impairment loss is recorded.* The carrying value of the security after the write down to fair value becomes the new "cost" basis of the investment and this amount should *not be adjusted for subsequent recoveries in fair value.* That is, subsequent recoveries cannot be recognized in income. It should be noted that this treatment is justified because at the time of the write down and the recognition of the loss in income, the impairment was judged to be "other than temporary."

Similar to the bad debt expense adjustment, the impairment write off does not have any cash flow effects. The impairment loss will reduce assets, income and retained earnings, but that loss does not use cash.

To illustrate an impairment loss, assume that an investment held as a current asset is impaired by $50,000. The effect on the financial statements is presented in the Financial Modeling Worksheet below.

FINANCIAL MODELING WORKSHEET (IMPAIRMENT LOSS)

INCOME STATEMENT (FIRST)	
REVENUES:	
EXPENSES:	
Impairment Loss	(50,000)
NET INCOME OR LOSS (a)	(50,000)

STATEMENT OF CASH FLOWS (THIRD)	
OPERATING ACTIVITIES:	
NET INCOME OR LOSS (a)	(50,000)
Impairment Loss	+50,000
INVESTING ACTIVITIES:	
FINANCING ACTIVITIES:	
INCREASE (DECREASE) IN CASH (b)	- 0 -
ADD: BEGINNING CASH BALANCE	
ENDING CASH BALANCE	

BALANCE SHEET (SECOND)			
ASSETS		LIABILITIES	
CURRENT ASSETS		CURRENT LIABILITIES	
CASH (b)	- 0 -		
Investments	(50,000)		
		NONCURRENT LIABILITIES	
		STOCKHOLDERS'	
NONCURRENT ASSETS		EQUITY	
		CAPITAL STOCK	
		APIC	
		RETAINED	
		EARNINGS (a)	(50,000)
		TOTAL	
		LIABILITIES &	
		STOCKHOLDERS'	
TOTAL ASSETS	(50,000)	EQUITY	(50,000)

An illustration of "mark-to-market" accounting for an available-for-sale and trading portfolio is presented below. The data are provided for a company holding securities as investments on its balance sheet from 2008 to 2010.

MARKETABLE EQUITY SECURITIES (MES) ILLUSTRATION OF FAIR VALUE ACCOUNTING FOR TRADING AND AVAILABLE FOR SALE INVESTMENTS

PORTFOLIO OF MARKETABLE EQUITY SECURITIES								
SECURITY	* ORIGINAL COST AT 6/11/08	FAIR VALUE AT 12/31/08	2008 UNREALIZED GAIN OR (LOSS)	FAIR VALUE AT 12/31/09	2009 UNREALIZED GAIN OR (LOSS)	FAIR VALUE AT 12/31/10	2010 UNREALIZED GAIN OR (LOSS)
IBM	$ 5,000	$ 6,500	$1,500	$ 4,000	($2,500)	$ 5,000	$1,000
GM	8,000	7,000	(1,000)	6,000	(1,000)	8,000	2,000
GE	3,000	4,000	1,000	2,000	(2,000)	2,000	-
XEROX	10,000	5,500	(4,500)	13,000	7,500	15,000	2,000
TOTAL	$26,000	$23,000	($3,000)	$25,000	$2,000	$30,000	$5,000

****For an Available for Sale or Held to Maturity debt portfolio, this column would be the amortized cost of the security (i.e., original cost adjusted for premium or discount amortization). An Available for Sale debt portfolio carried at amortized cost would be adjusted to fair value at the end of the accounting period.*

Balance sheets and income statements for each year and for each portfolio type are presented in the following tables.

Assume that the Available for Sale Portfolio would be considered working capital and therefore classified as current. Trading securities are always current assets.

FINANCIAL STATEMENT: VALUATION AT FAIR VALUE			
CURRENT ASSET SECTION OF THE BALANCE SHEET FOR BOTH THE TRADING AND THE AVAILABLE FOR SALE PORTFOLIOS	***2008***	***2009***	***2010***
Investment in Marketable Securities: NOTE: A valuation allowance or contra asset (adjunct) account could be used and offset against (added to) original cost.	$23,000	$25,000	$30,000
PARENTHETICAL OR FOOTNOTE DISCLOSURE: At Historical Cost	$26,000	$26,000	$26,000

FINANCIAL STATEMENT: CLASSIFIED AS TRADING			
OTHER INCOME AND EXPENSE SECTION OF THE INCOME STATEMENT FOR THE TRADING PORTFOLIO	**2008**	**2009**	**2010**
OTHER INCOME AND EXPENSE (Closed to Retained Earnings to balance)	($ 3,000) **UNREALIZED LOSS**	$ 2,000 **UNREALIZED GAIN**	$ 5,000 **UNREALIZED GAIN**

FINANCIAL STATEMENT: CLASSIFIED AS AVAILABLE FOR SALE			
STOCKHOLDERS' EQUITY SECTION OF THE BALANCE SHEET FOR THE AVAILABLE FOR SALE PORTFOLIO: (Report in Comprehensive Income in Stockholders' Equity)	**2008**	**2009**	**2010**
CUMULATIVE VALUATION ADJUSTMENT: (NET UNREALIZED GAIN OR LOSS: NEGATIVE (CONTRA) OR ADJUNCT STOCKHOLDERS' EQUITY ACCOUNT).	($ 3,000) **NET UNREALIZED LOSS**	($ 1,000) **NET UNREALIZED LOSS**	$4,000 **NET UNREALIZED GAIN**

The 2008 financial statement effects of employing mark to market accounting for the trading and the available for sale portfolios are presented in the financial modeling worksheets below.

FINANCIAL MODELING WORKSHEET 2008 FOR THE TRADING PORTFOLIO

INCOME STATEMENT (FIRST)	
REVENUES:	
EXPENSES:	
Unrealized loss	*(3,000)*
NET INCOME OR LOSS (a)	*(3,000)*

STATEMENT OF CASH FLOWS (THIRD)	
OPERATING ACTIVITIES:	
NET INCOME OR LOSS (a)	*(3,000)*
Unrealized loss on trading portfolio	*+3,000*
INVESTING ACTIVITIES:	
FINANCING ACTIVITIES:	
INCREASE (DECREASE) IN CASH (b)	*- 0 -*
ADD: BEGINNING CASH BALANCE	
ENDING CASH BALANCE	

BALANCE SHEET (SECOND)			
ASSETS		*LIABILITIES*	
CURRENT ASSETS		*CURRENT LIABILITIES*	
CASH (b)	*- 0 -*		
Marketable Securities: Trading at Cost			
Allowance	*(3,000)*		
		NONCURRENT LIABILITIES	
		STOCKHOLDERS' EQUITY	
NONCURRENT ASSETS			
		CAPITAL STOCK	
		APIC	
		RETAINED EARNINGS (a)	*(3,000)*
		TOTAL LIABILITIES & STOCKHOLDERS' EQUITY	
TOTAL ASSETS	*(3,000)*		*(3,000)*

FINANCIAL MODELING WORKSHEET 2008 FOR THE AVAILABLE FOR SALE PORTFOLIO

INCOME STATEMENT (FIRST)	
REVENUES:	
EXPENSES:	
NET INCOME OR LOSS (a)	

STATEMENT OF CASH FLOWS (THIRD)	
OPERATING ACTIVITIES:	
NET INCOME OR LOSS (a)	
Unrealized loss on trading portfolio	
INVESTING ACTIVITIES:	
FINANCING ACTIVITIES:	
INCREASE (DECREASE) IN CASH (b)	*- 0 -*
ADD: BEGINNING CASH BALANCE	
ENDING CASH BALANCE	

BALANCE SHEET (SECOND)			
ASSETS		***LIABILITIES***	
CURRENT ASSETS		***CURRENT LIABILITIES***	
CASH (b)	*- 0 -*		
Marketable Securities: Available for Sale at Cost			
Allowance	*(3,000)*		
		NONCURRENT LIABILITIES	
NONCURRENT ASSETS		***STOCKHOLDERS' EQUITY***	
		CAPITAL STOCK	
		APIC	
		Accumulated Other Comprehensive Income	*(3,000)*
		RETAINED	
		EARNINGS (a)	
		TOTAL	
		LIABILITIES &	
		STOCKHOLDERS'	
TOTAL ASSETS	*(3,000)*	***EQUITY***	*(3,000)*

Realized Gains or Losses on Sale

Realized gains or losses are recognized on the sale of an individual security from *any* portfolio classification. For the Trading portfolio, the realized gain or loss on the sale is computed as the difference between the net selling price (i.e., selling price less any transactions costs) and the fair value (adjusted cost basis) on the balance sheet. The only difference for the Available for Sale portfolio is that the previously deferred net unrealized gain or loss recorded in stockholders' equity for the individual security sold must also be recognized in income.

To illustrate, assume that the Xerox shares are sold on January 2, 2011 for $20,000. **If the investment was carried in the Available for Sale portfolio,** a realized gain on sale of $10,000 would be recognized on the income statement in 2011. This would be determined as follows:

ASSUME: XEROX STOCK IS IN THE AVAILABLE FOR SALE PORTFOLIO	
Cumulative Net Unrealized Gain (Loss) for Xerox in Stockholders' Equity: 2008: ($4,500) 2009: 7,500 2010: 2,000 TOTAL:	$5,000
2011: Difference between Net Selling Price and the Fair Value reported on the Balance Sheet ($20,000 - 15,000).	5,000
TOTAL GAIN ON SALE IN 2011: Selling price – original cost = $20,000 – 10,000	$10,000

Removal of $5,000 of the net unrealized gain from the allowance account and from the balance of accumulated other comprehensive income, along with the recognition of this net gain on the income statement, results in a net balance of an unrealized loss of $1,000 in stockholders' equity and a balance of $1,000 in the allowance account (i.e., $4,000 - 5,000). This balance is the correct amount necessary to cover the difference between original cost and the fair value of the remaining securities in the Available for Sale portfolio. This is illustrated in the following table developed at December 31, 2010 (which is also the balance at the date of disposal, January 2, 2011).

SECURITY	**ORIGINAL COST AT 6/11/08**	**FAIR VALUE AT 12/31/10**	**2010 UNREALIZED GAIN OR (LOSS)**
IBM	$ 5,000	$ 5,000	-
GM	8,000	8,000	-
GE	3,000	2,000	($1,000)
TOTAL	$16,000	$15,000	($1,000)

The financial statement effects of selling the security out of the available for sale portfolio are presented in the following financial modeling worksheet.

FINANCIAL MODELING WORKSHEET SALE OF SECURITY FROM THE AVAILABLE FOR SALE PORTFOLIO

INCOME STATEMENT (FIRST)	
REVENUES:	
Gain on Sale of Investment	***+10,000***
EXPENSES:	
NET INCOME OR LOSS (a)	***+10,000***

STATEMENT OF CASH FLOWS (THIRD)	
OPERATING ACTIVITIES:	
NET INCOME OR LOSS (a)	***+10,000***
Less: Gain on sale of Investment	***(10,000)***
INVESTING ACTIVITIES:	
Sale of Available for Sale Securities	***+20,000***
FINANCING ACTIVITIES:	
INCREASE (DECREASE) IN CASH (b)	***+20,000***
ADD: BEGINNING CASH BALANCE	
ENDING CASH BALANCE	

BALANCE SHEET (SECOND)			
ASSETS		***LIABILITIES***	
CURRENT ASSETS		***CURRENT LIABILITIES***	
CASH (b)	***+20,000***		
Marketable Securities: Available for Sale at Cost	***(10,000)***		
Allowance	***(5,000)***		
		NONCURRENT LIABILITIES	
		STOCKHOLDERS' EQUITY	
NONCURRENT ASSETS			
		CAPITAL STOCK	
		APIC	
		Accumulated Other Comprehensive Income	***(5,000)***
		RETAINED EARNINGS (a)	***+10,000***
		TOTAL LIABILITIES & STOCKHOLDERS' EQUITY	
TOTAL ASSETS	***+5,000***		***+5,000***

Finally, it should be noted that the total gain recognized in the income statement **assuming that Xerox was included in the Trading portfolio** is also $10,000. The only difference is the period of recognition. The total gain recognized for the Trading portfolio consists of $5,000 of net unrealized gains recorded on the income statement from 2008 through 2011 and a realized gain on sale of $5,000 (i.e., $20,000 – 15,000) recognized in 2011. This is determined as follows:

ASSUME: XEROX STOCK IS IN THE TRADING PORTFOLIO	
Net Unrealized Gain (Loss) for Xerox Recognized in Income: 2008: ($4,500) 2009: 7,500 2010: 2,000 ***TOTAL INCOME RECOGNIZED IN PRIOR YEARS:***	$5,000
2011: Gain on Sale = Difference between Net Selling Price and the Fair Value reported on the Balance Sheet ($20,000 - 15,000)	5,000
TOTAL GAIN RECOGNIZED OVER THE LIFE OF THE INVESTMENT	$10,000

FINANCIAL MODELING WORKSHEET SALE OF SECURITY FROM THE TRADING PORTFOLIO

INCOME STATEMENT (FIRST)	
REVENUES:	
Gain on Sale of Investment	*+5,000*
EXPENSES:	
NET INCOME OR LOSS (a)	*+5,000*

STATEMENT OF CASH FLOWS (THIRD)	
OPERATING ACTIVITIES:	
NET INCOME OR LOSS (a)	*+5,000*
Less: Gain on sale of Investment	*(5,000)*
INVESTING ACTIVITIES:	
Sale of Available for Sale Securities	*+20,000*
FINANCING ACTIVITIES:	
INCREASE (DECREASE) IN CASH (b)	*+20,000*
ADD: BEGINNING CASH BALANCE	
ENDING CASH BALANCE	

BALANCE SHEET (SECOND)			
ASSETS		*LIABILITIES*	
CURRENT ASSETS		*CURRENT LIABILITIES*	
CASH (b)	*+20,000*		
Marketable Securities: Trading at Cost	*(10,000)*		
Allowance	*(5,000)*		
		NONCURRENT LIABILITIES	
		STOCKHOLDERS' EQUITY	
NONCURRENT ASSETS			
		CAPITAL STOCK	
		APIC	
		RETAINED EARNINGS (a)	*+5,000*
TOTAL ASSETS	*+5,000*	*TOTAL LIABILITIES & STOCKHOLDERS' EQUITY*	*+5,000*

The treatment of the gain on the cash flow statement reflects a reclassification out of operating activities into investing activities. The gain does not provide cash but the $20,000 proceeds provide positive cash flow from investing activities for both portfolios. As expected the cosmetic financial statement effects from the use of a GAAP standard does not affect cash flows.

Disclosures

For securities classified as Available for Sale and separately for securities classified as Held to Maturity, a company should disclose:

1. Aggregate fair value, gross unrealized holding gains, gross unrealized holding losses, amortized cost basis and security type (debt or equity).

2. Information about the contractual maturities of debt securities. Maturity information may be combined in appropriate groupings such as (a) within one year, (b) after one year through five years, (c) after five years through 10 years, and (d) after 10 years.

For each period for which an income statement is presented, a company must disclose:

1. The proceeds from sales of Available for Sale securities and the gross realized gains and gross realized losses on those sales.

2. The basis on which cost was determined in computing realized gain or loss. For example, specific identification, average cost, or FIFO. Note that on the sale of a security, the term "cost" includes original cost as well as the revised cost resulting from adjustments to fair value.

3. The change in net unrealized holding gain or loss on Available for Sale securities that has been included in the separate component in Stockholders' equity during the period.

4. The change in net unrealized holding gain or loss on trading securities that has been included in net income during the period.

Sample disclosures for investments in marketable securities are presented in Exhibit 2.4.

EXHIBIT 2.4 S. SATAF, INC. AND SUBSIDIARIES NOTES TO CONSOLIDATED FINANCIAL STATEMENTS

Investments—At December 31, 2011 and 2010, all short-term and long-term investments consist of debt securities (U.S. Treasury and other government securities, commercial paper and corporate notes) that are classified as available-for-sale and recorded at fair value. Fair value was determined based on quoted market prices.

Investments classified as long-term are restricted and held as collateral under certain letters of credit related to the Company's lease agreements.

Investments consist of the following at December 31:

	Cost			Gross Unrealized		Aggregate
	Due Under One Year	Due After One Year	Total	Gains	Losses	Fair Value
2011						
Available-for-sale securities:						
Investments — short-term:						
U.S. government obligations	$ 40,000	$ —	$ 40,000	$ —	$ (600)	$ 39,400
Corporate debt securities	11,000	342,000	353,000	1,000	(150)	353,850
	51,000	342,000	393,000	1,000	(750)	393,250
Investments — long-term:						
U.S. government obligations	600	—	600	—	—	600
Corporate debt securities	5,000	—	5,000	—	—	5,000
	5,600	—	5,600	—	—	5,600
Total	$ 56,600	$ 342,000	$ 398,600	$ 1,000	$ (750)	$ 398,850
2010						
Available-for-sale securities:						
Investments — short-term:						
Corporate debt securities	$ 3,000	$ 166,000	$ 169,000	$ 500	$ —	$ 169,500
Investments — long-term:						
U.S. government obligations	6,000	—	6,000	50	—	6,050
Total	$ 9,000	$ 166,000	$ 175,000	$ 550	$ —	$ 175,550

The Company also has investments in certain marketable equity securities with a fair value of approximately $1.5 million and $0.8 million as of December 31, 2011 and 2010, respectively, which are currently classified as available-for-sale securities and are recorded under the caption

"Other assets" in the consolidated balance sheets. The cost of such securities, net of write-downs for other-than-temporary impairment, was $1.0 million and $1.6 million as of March 31, 2006 and 2005, respectively.

FASB Statement No. 157: "Fair Value Measurements"

Introduction and Purpose of FASB Statement No. 157.

FASB Statement No. 157 does not require that any additional assets or liabilities to be measured at fair value. Rather, the statement has three primary objectives:

1. To provide a single definition of fair value that will be applied consistently to all existing standards and increase comparability in the fair value measurements employed.
2. To provide a framework to measure fair value.
3. To provide expanded disclosures for all assets and liabilities measured at fair value that will allow the financial statement user to assess the reliability of the fair values reported in the financial statements.

A summary comparison of prior GAAP with SFAS 157 is presented in the table below.

SUMMARY TABLE:

Issue	Prior GAAP	Current GAAP Under SFAS 157
Definition of fair value	Focus on Entry price. How much would be paid to acquire an asset or received to assume a liability?	Requires use of an EXIT price. How much would be received to sell the asset or paid to transfer the liability?
Assumptions	Entity specific measure	Market based measure
Measuring fair value	No consistent framework	Prescribes the use of one or more of three acceptable valuation techniques
Disclosures	Generic disclosure of fair valued assets with little transparency of approach / procedure	Detailed disclosures that allow the user to determine the reliability of the fair value measurements used.

THE DEFINITION OF FAIR VALUE

The definition of fair value is based on an exit price concept. The exit or exchange price is defined as the price that can be obtained on the disposal of an asset or the amount paid for the transfer of an obligation in an orderly transaction between market participants at the measurement date. This definition consists of several elements that require additional analysis:

- Exit or exchange price
- Orderly transaction
- Market participants in either the principal market or the most advantageous market

Exit or Exchange Price. The exit price is the price to be received on the sale of an asset or the amount paid to transfer a liability. This is not the price to be paid to purchase the asset or the amount received in incurring an obligation.

Orderly Transaction. This assumes that the hypothetical transaction used to measure fair value will be one in which the seller of an asset or the transferor of an obligation has the usual access to markets would not assume a forced sale as in the case of a liquidation or bankruptcy.

Market Participants. An interesting position taken in FASB Statement No. 157 is that the sale of the asset or transfer of the obligation must be taken from the standpoint of a typical market participant (using a principal or most advantageous market (to be discussed) and not from the entity's position. Market participants must possess four characteristics:

1. Be independent of the reporting entity and unrelated to the firm
2. Have the knowledge required to understand and execute the transaction
3. Have the financial and legal capacity to complete the transaction
4. Be able and willing to complete the transaction without being forced to do so

IMPLEMENTATION STEPS:

FASB 157 outlines six steps regarded to complete a fair value measurement. These steps are outlined below.

Step One:	Determine Unit of Account
Step Two:	Determine Potential Markets Based on the "Highest and Best Use"
Step Three:	Determine Markets for Basis of Valuation
Step Four:	Apply the Appropriate Valuation Technique(s)
Step Five:	Determine Fair Value
Step Six:	Determine Classification within the Fair Value Hierarchy

STEP ONE : UNIT OF ACCOUNT

This step determines what is being measured by considering level of disaggregation or aggregation used when applying other accounting pronouncements or based on guidance provided by other accounting standards.

For example:

- The unit of account for a derivative generally is the entire contract.
- The unit of account for the first step of a goodwill impairment analysis generally is the reporting unit.

STEP TWO: DETERMINE POTENTIAL MARKETS BASED ON HIGHEST AND BEST USE (VALUATION PREMISE)

Asset measurement at fair value assumes the ***"highest and best use"*** of the asset by market participants. The highest and best use refers to the use of an asset by market participants that would maximize the value of the asset or the group of assets within which the asset would be used.

The concept of the highest and best use of the asset will depend on if the asset is considered to be utilized in combination with other assets as a group or considered ***"in-use"*** or if the asset is to be valued on a standalone basis or considered ***"in-exchange."***

- *In-use.* The highest and best use of the asset is in-use if the asset would provide maximum value to market participants principally through its use in combination with other assets as a group (e.g., software and computer hardware).
- *In-exchange.* The highest and best use of the asset is in-exchange if the asset would provide maximum value to market participants principally on a standalone basis (e.g., financial assets or real estate investments).

The fair value of a liability represents what an entity would pay another entity to take over the liability. Fair value of a liability should reflect the entity's non performance risk (i.e. credit risk, delivery risk, etc.)

STEP THREE: DETERMINE MARKETS FOR BASIS OF VALUATION

Use either the principal market or the most advantageous market. FASB Statement No. 157 defines the ***principal market*** as the market with the greatest level of volume and level of activity where an asset can be sold or an obligation can be transferred. The principal market takes precedence in fair value measurements. However, if there is no principal market, then the most advantageous market must be used in measuring fair value.

The ***most advantageous market*** is the market where the reporting entity would maximize the net amount received to sell the asset or minimize the net amount paid to transfer the obligation.

For example, if a security can be sold for $500 in a domestic market (Market D) with a transaction cost of $120, (net amount received of $380) while the same security can be sold internationally (Market I) for $550 with a transaction cost of $200 (net amount received of $350), the most advantageous market is Market D. However, the fair value is measured at $500, without deducting the transaction costs. If neither market exists, a hypothetical market can be assumed.

STEP FOUR: APPLY THE APPROPRIATE VALUATION TECHNIQUE(S)

The primary objective of the valuation techniques required by FASB Statement No. 157 is to ***ensure that more reliance is placed on observable inputs than unobservable inputs***. The statement requires that the valuation techniques used to measure fair value be consistent with either: ***a market approach, an income approach or a cost approach***. A single or multiple approaches can be used in measuring fair value depending on the availability of data and the reliability of the inputs employed.

- ***Market approach.*** The market approach uses prices and other relevant information generated by market transactions involving identical or comparable assets or liabilities (including an entire business).

- *Income approach.* The income approach uses valuation techniques to convert future amounts such as cash flows or earnings, to a single present value amount (i.e., discounted cash flow applications such as the Black-Scholes-Merton formula).
- *Cost approach (a Replacement Cost Concept):* The cost approach is based on the amount that currently would be required to replace the service capacity of an asset (often referred to as current replacement cost adjusted for obsolescence and physical deterioration, etc).

Step Five: Determine Fair Value

The outcome of the market determination (Step Three) and the application of valuation technique(s) (Step Four) will be a fair value measurement.

To the extent that the valuation was applied to an asset that was valued in-use, the total calculated value must be allocated to each unit of account in the asset grouping based on the specific facts and circumstances.

To illustrate, assume that Company A has computer hardware asset (Division A) and a computer software asset (Division B). The assets of both divisions need to be measured at fair value. Unit of account is the software asset valued at $1 Billion and the hardware asset valued at $1 Billion. The unit of valuation is highest and best use of the combination of assets, valued at $2.5 Billion.

STEP SIX: DETERMINE CLASSIFICATION WITHIN THE FAIR VALUE HIERARCHY

The Fair Value Hierarchy

The fair value hierarchy was designed by the FASB in order to prioritize the inputs used in the valuation techniques. Note this hierarchy does not prioritize or rank the valuation techniques but simply ranks the level of reliability of the inputs used in the valuation process.

The key variable in the hierarchy is whether the inputs to the valuation process are observable or unobservable. The FASB emphasizes that we should maximize the use of observable inputs in determining fair value. The highest reliability ranking is given to quoted market prices in active markets for identical assets or liabilities (i.e., observable) and the lowest priority is given to the use of unobservable inputs created by utilization of the reporting entity's assumptions or projections.

The following table summarizes the FASB fair value hierarchy.

Fair Value Hierarchy for Inputs to the Valuation Techniques	
LEVEL	INPUTS
Level 1	Level 1 inputs are quoted prices (unadjusted) in active markets for identical assets or liabilities that the reporting entity has the ability to access at the measurement date. An active market for the asset or liability is a market in which transactions for the asset or liability occur with sufficient frequency and volume to provide pricing information on an ongoing basis. A quoted price in an active market provides the most reliable evidence of fair value and must be used to measure fair value whenever available. **EXAMPLE**: A NYSE quote for equity shares held by the entity.

Level 2	Level 2 inputs are inputs other than quoted prices included within Level 1 that are observable for the asset or liability, either directly or indirectly. If the asset or liability has a specified (contractual) term, a Level 2 input must be observable for substantially the full term of the asset or liability. Level 2 inputs include the following: a. Quoted prices for similar (comparable) assets or liabilities in active markets b. Quoted prices for identical or similar (comparable) assets or liabilities in markets that are *not* active, that is, markets in which there are few transactions for the asset or liability, the prices are not current, or price quotations vary substantially either over time or among market makers as found in some brokered markets, or in which little information is released publicly as in a principal-to principal market. c. Inputs other than quoted prices that are observable for the asset or liability. For example, interest rates and yield curves observable at commonly quoted intervals, volatilities, prepayment speeds, loss severities, credit risks, and default rates. d. Inputs that are derived principally from or corroborated by observable market data by correlation or other means (market-corroborated inputs). **EXAMPLES**: To estimate a valuation multiple such as the price per square foot for the building, we can use observable market data, such as multiples derived from prices in observed transactions involving comparable buildings in similar locations. Also, using a mid-point between bid and ask prices is derived from observable market data.
Level 3	Level 3 inputs are unobservable inputs for the asset or liability. Unobservable inputs will be used to measure fair value to the extent that observable inputs are not available, allowing for cases in which there is little, if any, market activity for the asset or liability at the measurement date. However, the fair value measurement objective remains the same, that is, an exit price from the perspective of a market participant that holds the asset or owes the liability. Therefore, unobservable inputs reflect the reporting entity's own assumptions about the assumptions that market participants would use in pricing the asset or liability, including assumptions about risk. Unobservable inputs are developed based on the best available information under the circumstances, which might include the reporting entity's own data. In developing unobservable inputs, the reporting entity need not undertake all possible efforts to obtain information about market participant assumptions. **EXAMPLE**: Projections of risk adjusted expected cash flows developed using the reporting entity's own data to value the initial recognition of an asset retirement obligation (ARO).

SAMPLE DISCLOSURES

The following sample footnote disclosures were adapted from FASB Statement No. 157.

ASSETS MEASURED AT FAIR VALUE ON A RECURRING BASIS

For assets and liabilities measured at fair value on a recurring basis during the period, quantitative disclosures about the fair value measurements must be provided separately for each major category of assets and liabilities For assets, that information might be presented as follows:

($ in 000s)		Fair Value Measurements at Reporting Date Using		
Description	12/31/X9	Quoted Prices in Active Markets for Identical Assets (Level 1)	Significant Other Observable Inputs (Level 2)	Significant Unobservable Inputs (Level 3)*
Trading securities	$138	$126	$12	
Available-for-sale securities	90	$ 90		
Derivatives	72	$ 30	$18	$24
Other investments	12			$12
Total	$312	$246	$30	$36

(Note: For liabilities, a similar table should be presented.)

** Level 3 inputs require additional disclosures in the form of a reconciliation of beginning and ending balances.*

ASSETS MEASURED AT FAIR VALUE ON A RECURRING BASIS USING SIGNIFICANT UNOBSERVABLE INPUTS (LEVEL 3)

For assets and liabilities measured at fair value on a recurring basis using significant unobservable inputs (Level 3) during the period, a reconciliation of the beginning and ending balances is required separately for each major category of assets and liabilities, except for derivative assets and liabilities, which may be presented on a net basis. For assets, the reconciliation might be presented as follows:

($ in 000s)	Fair Value Measurements Using Significant Unobservable Inputs (Level 3)		
	Derivatives	Other Investments	Total
Beginning balance	$ 17	$13	$30
Total gains or losses (realized/unrealized):			
Included in earnings (or changes in net assets)	13	(3)	10
Included in other comprehensive income	5		5
Purchases, issuances, and settlements	(8)	2	(6)
Transfers in and/or out of Level 3	(3)	0	(3)
Ending balance	$ 24	$ 12	$ 36
The amount of total gains or losses for the period included in earnings (or changes in net assets) attributable to the change in unrealized gains or losses relating to assets still held at the reporting date.	$ 8	$2	$11

(Note: For liabilities, a similar table should be presented.)

Gains and losses (realized and unrealized) included in earnings (or changes in net assets) for the period (above) are reported in trading revenues and in other revenues as follows:

	Trading Revenues	Other Revenues
Total gains or losses included in earnings (or changes in net assets) for the period (above)	$13	$(3)
Change in unrealized gains or losses relating to assets ***still held*** at reporting date	$ 8	$ 2

ASSETS MEASURED AT FAIR VALUE ON A NONRECURRING BASIS

For each major category of assets and liabilities measured at fair value on a nonrecurring basis during the period, disclosures about the fair value measurements are required. That information might be presented as follows:

($ in millions)		Fair Value Measurements Using			
Description	Year Ended 12/31/X9	Quoted Prices in Active Markets for Identical Assets (Level 1)	Significant Other Observable Inputs (Level 2)	Significant Unobservable Inputs (Level 3)	Total Gains (Losses)
Long-lived assets held and used	$90		$90		$ (30)
Goodwill	36			$36	(72)
Long-lived assets held for sale	31		31		(18)
					$ (120)

In accordance with the provisions of FASB Statement No. 144, long-lived assets held and used with a carrying amount of $120 million were written down to their fair value of $90 million, resulting in an impairment charge of $30 million, which was included in earnings for the period. In accordance with the provisions of FASB Statement No. 142, goodwill with a carrying amount of $108 million was written down to its implied fair value of $36 million, resulting in an impairment charge of $72 million, which was included in earnings for the period. In accordance with the provisions of FASB Statement No. 144, long-lived assets held for sale with a carrying amount of $42 million were written down to their fair value of $31 million, less cost to sell of $7 million (or $24 million), resulting in a loss of $18 million, which was included in earnings for the period.

FASB STATEMENT NO. 159: "THE FAIR VALUE OPTION FOR FINANCIAL ASSETS AND FINANCIAL LIABILITIES

Introduction

FASB Statement No. 159 permits entities to choose to measure eligible items at fair value (e.g., certain financial instruments, warranty contacts and insurance contracts). This is known as ***"the fair value option,"*** and this option applies to all reporting entities, including not-for-profit organizations.

Fair value is measured in accordance with FASB Statement No. 157. The unrealized gain or loss on the fair value measurement is to be reported in earnings. Any transaction costs (up front costs) and fees are to be recognized in earnings and are not to be recorded as a deferred charge on the asset side of the balance sheet. Once the fair value option is elected it is irrevocable with limited exceptions.

The purpose of allowing the fair value option is to improve financial reporting by providing entities with the opportunity to offset volatility in reported earnings caused by measuring related assets and liabilities differently without having to apply complex hedge accounting provisions.

The fair value option is to be applied on a "***contract by contract basis***" (also known as an "instrument by instrument basis"). This means that in general, the fair value option can be applied to one instrument but not to another, identical instrument, but there are exceptions.

Eligible Items for Applying the Fair Value Option

The fair value option can be elected for the following eligible items:

a. A recognized financial asset (including assets accounted for under the equity method) and financial liability, unless deemed ineligible as in Section (3) below.
b. A firm commitment that would otherwise not be recognized at inception and that involves only financial instruments (e.g., forward purchase contracts for loans that are not readily convertible into cash).
c. A written loan commitment.
d. The rights and obligations under an insurance contract that is not a financial instrument because it requires or permits the insurer to provide goods or services rather than a cash settlement but includes terms that permit the insurer to settle by paying a third party to provide those goods and services.
e. The rights and obligations under a warranty that is not a financial instrument because it requires or permits the warrantor to provide goods or services rather than a cash settlement but includes terms that permit the warrantor to settle by paying a third party to provide those goods or services.
f. A host financial instrument resulting from the separation of an embedded nonfinancial derivative instrument from a nonfinancial hybrid instrument.

RECOGNIZED FINANCIAL ASSETS AND FINANCIAL LIABILITIES THAT ARE NOT ELIGIBLE ITEMS

The fair value option may ***not*** be elected for the following financial assets and financial liabilities:

a. An investment in a subsidiary that the entity is required to consolidate
b. An interest in a variable interest entity that the entity is required to consolidate
c. Employers' and plans' obligations for pension benefits or assets representing net over funded positions, other postretirement benefits (including health care and life insurance benefits), post employment benefits, employee stock option and stock purchase plans, and other forms of deferred compensation arrangements.
d. Financial assets and financial liabilities recognized under lease. This exception does not apply to a guarantee of a third-party lease obligation or a contingent obligation arising from a cancelled lease.
e. Demand deposit liabilities of banks, savings and loan associations, credit unions, and other similar depository institutions
f. Financial instruments that are, in whole or in part, classified by the issuer as a component of permanent or temporary shareholder's equity. An example is a convertible debt security with a noncontingent beneficial conversion feature which is recorded in additional paid in capital.

Financial Statement Presentation of Items Measured at Fair Value

Balance Sheet: All assets and liabilities measured at fair value must be disclosed in a manner that separates these items from the carrying values of similar items not using the fair value option. These different measurement attributes can be disclosed either by separate line items (one for items measured at fair value and another for items not measured at fair value) or by parenthetical notation of the amount of the total line item that is measured at fair value.

A sample balance sheet for Christie Consultants, Inc. as of December 31, 2012, after the adoption of the fair value option is presented below.

Christie Consultants, Inc.
Statement of Financial Position
($ in 000s)

Description		At December 31, 2012
Assets		
Cash and Cash Equivalents		$600
Trading securities		300
Securities available-for-sale		20
Securities held-to-maturity		25
Loans and lease receivables ***($550 at fair value)***	$ 890	
Allowance for loan and lease losses	(200)	
Loans, net of allowance for loan and lease losses		790
Derivatives		100
Equity investments ***($120 at fair value)***		310
Property and Buildings-net		1,125
Other assets		50
Total assets		$3,500
Liabilities		
Accounts payable		$325
Short-term borrowings		1,400
Long-term debt ***($60 at fair value)***		1,225
Total liabilities		$1,950
Shareholders' equity		
Common stock (authorized 5,000,000 shares; issued 3,550,000 shares)		110
Capital surplus		700
Retained earnings		870
Accumulated other comprehensive income (loss)		(130)
Total shareholders' equity		$1,550
Total liabilities and shareholders' equity		$3,500

Adapted from the FASB illustration

Income Statement: All unrealized gains and losses from the application of the fair value option must be reported in the earnings of the current period. All transactions cost and fees must also be reported in current earnings.

The Statement of Cash Flows: The cash flows relating to items measured at fair value must be classified as operating, investing or financing activities based on the nature and purpose of holding the financial instrument, debt contract or other contract.

FASB ILLUSTRATION (ADAPTED): CUMULATIVE EFFECT ADJUSTMENT DISCLOSURES AT THE INITIAL ADOPTION OF FAIR VALUE OPTION (FVO):

An entity must provide information about the extent to which the fair value option is elected for existing eligible items at the time of initial adoption in a manner that reconciles to the cumulative-effect adjustment to retained earnings. That information might be presented as follows:

($ in 000s) Description	Balance Sheet 1/1/X9 prior to Adoption	Net Gain/(Loss) upon Adoption	Balance Sheet 1/1/X9 after Adoption of FVO
Loans net	$144	$(24)*	$120
Private equity investments	60	(12)	48
Long-term debt	(84)	5	(79)
Pretax cumulative effect of adoption of the fair value option		($31)	
Increase in deferred tax asset at 35%		11	
Cumulative effect of adoption of the fair value option (charge to retained earnings)		$(20)	

**The $24,000 net loss for loans recorded as part of the cumulative-effect adjustment to retained earnings upon initial adoption of this Statement includes $3,600, which was removed from the allowance for loan and lease losses.*

An entity can provide the following additional required disclosures in this same note: (a) management's reasons for electing the fair value option for each existing eligible item or group of similar eligible items and (b) if the fair value option is elected for some but not all eligible items within a group of similar eligible items, (1) a description of those similar items and the reasons for partial election and (2) information to enable users to understand how the group of similar items relates to individual line items on the statement of financial position.

FASB Illustration (Adopted): Fair Value Measurements and Changes in Fair Values Included in Current Period Earnings

The disclosure objective in this case is to provide information about (a) assets and liabilities measured at fair value on a recurring basis, (b) changes in fair values of assets and liabilities for which the fair value option has been elected in a manner that relates to the statement of financial position, and (c) fair value estimates and corresponding carrying amounts for major categories of assets and liabilities that include items measured at fair value on a recurring basis in accordance with the fair value disclosure requirements of FASB Statement No.107[7].

Table 1 below has been adapted from the FASB standards and reflects the fair value hierarchy, supplemented to (a) provide information about where in the income statement changes in fair values of assets and liabilities are included in earnings and (b) voluntarily integrate selected disclosures required annually by FASB Statement No. 107.

---

7. FASB ASC 825 [Predecessor literature: "Disclosures about Fair Value of Financial Instruments, "*Statement of Financial Accounting Standards No. 107* (Norwalk, Conn.: FASB 1991)].

Table 1 ($ in 000s)				Fair Value Measurements at December 31, 20X9, using			Changes in Fair Values for the 12-Month Period Ended December 31, 20X9, for Items Measured at Fair Value Pursuant to Election of the Fair Value Option				
Description	Total Carrying Amount in Statement of Financial Position 12/31/X9	Statement 107 Fair Value Estimate 12/31/X9	Assets/ Liabilities Measured at Fair Value 12/31/X9	Quoted Prices in Active Markets for Identical Assets (Level 1)	Significant Other Observable Inputs (Level 2)	Significant Unobservable Inputs (Level 3)	Trading Gains and Losses	Other Gains and Losses	Interest Income on Loans	Interest Expense on Long-Term Debt	Total Changes in Fair Values Included in Current-Period Earnings
Trading securities	$ 138	$ 138	$138	$126	$ 12		$12				$1
Available-for-sale securities	90	90	90	90							
Loans, net	480	494	180	0	120	$ 60		$ (4)	$12		8
Derivatives	72	72	72	35	18	24	6				6
Equity in-vestments	150	166	90	0	30	60		(22)			(22)
Long-term debt	(240)	(247)	(72)	(36)	(12)	(24)		16		$(5)	11

Loans are included in loans and lease receivables in the statement of financial position. As of December 31, 20X9, approximately $192,000 of lease receivables are included in loans and lease receivables in the statement of financial position and are not eligible for the fair value option.

An entity can provide the following additional required disclosures in this same note: (a) management's reasons for electing a fair value option for each eligible item or group of similar eligible items and (b) if the fair value option is elected for some but not all eligible items within a group of similar eligible items, (1) a description of those similar items and the reasons for partial election and (2) information to enable users to understand how the group of similar items relates to individual line items on the statement of financial position.

Table 2 is an alternative illustrative example that does not integrate disclosures required annually by FASB Statement No. 107 or the additional gain and loss amounts voluntarily displayed in Table 1. Table 2 represents the FASB Statement No. 157 fair value hierarchy table, supplemented to provide information about where in the income statement changes in fair values of assets and liabilities for which the fair value option has been elected are included in earnings.

Table 2 ($ in 000s)		Fair Value Measurements at December 31, 20X9, using			Changes in Fair Values for the 12-Month Period Ended December 31, 20X9, for Items Measured at Fair Value Pursuant to Election of the Fair Value Option			
Description	Fair Value Measurements 12/31/X9	Quoted Prices in Active Markets for Identical Assets (Level 1)	Significant Other Observable Inputs (Level 2)	Significant Unobservable Inputs (Level 3)	Other Gains and Losses	Interest Income on Loans	Interest Expense on Long-Term Debt	Total Changes in Fair Values Included in Current-Period Earnings
Trading securities	$138	$126	$ 12					
Available-for-sale securities	90	90						
Loans	180	0	120	$ 60	$ (4)	$12		$ 8
Derivatives	72	30	18	24				
Equity investments	90	0	30	60	(22)			(22)
Long-term debt	(72)	(36)	(12)	(24)	16		$(5)	11

Loans are included in loans and lease receivables in the statement of financial position. As of December 31, 20X9, approximately $192,000 of lease receivables are included in loans and lease receivables in the statement of financial position and are not eligible for the fair value option.

An entity can provide the following additional required disclosures in this same note: (a) management's reasons for electing a fair value option for each eligible item or group of similar eligible items and (b) if the fair value option is elected for some but not all eligible items within a group of similar eligible items, (1) a description of those similar items and the reasons for partial election and (2) information to enable users to understand how the group of similar items relates to individual line items on the statement of financial position.

INVENTORIES

In the analysis of inventory, the primary accounting and reporting issues focus on the components of the total inventory. Total inventory consists of these components:

- The units included in the ending inventory
- The composition of unit cost
- The allocation of unit cost to the units in ending inventory and to the units sold
- A change in the allocation method used
- The amount of obsolete or slow-moving items included in ending inventory

These issues will be discussed in the following sections of this chapter.

Units Included in Ending Inventory. The units included in ending inventory are ultimately determined by physical count. Either a perpetual or periodic inventory system can be used for the determination and control of the physical quantities in inventory throughout the accounting period.

Under a perpetual inventory system, inventory accounts are continually updated for acquisitions and sales of inventory, and the cost of goods sold is determined and charged against income after each sale. Regardless of how reliable the perpetual system is, a physical count of inventory must be taken at least once a year to verify the accuracy of the perpetual records.

If a periodic inventory system is used, the balance in inventory is only determined at the end of the accounting period by physical count and the cost of goods sold is determined by the formula to be discussed below. Obviously, a pure periodic system is not very effective in controlling inventory. Therefore, a hybrid system is usually employed whereby inventory is controlled internally by management through the use of a perpetual system, and a periodic system is used for financial reporting purposes.

Determination of Unit Cost. The unit cost of an item in inventory consists of the invoice price or manufacturing costs, plus all "reasonable and necessary" expenditures required to have the inventory item in its existing condition, location and ready for its intended use (i.e., sale or for use as input into the production process). Reasonable and necessary expenditures include transportation costs, packaging, etc. There is a great deal of discretion as to what constitutes a reasonable and necessary expenditure. If management considers a cost to be reasonable and necessary, it is capitalized as part of the unit cost of inventory. On the other hand, if the expenditure is not considered reasonable and necessary, it is charged to expense immediately. However in all cases, costs related to defective units, waste and excess spoilage should be expensed and cannot be capitalized.

When inventory costs are capitalized, current assets (i.e., inventory) increase and there will be no effect on reported profit until the item is sold. If the cost is expensed as incurred, income is reduced in the current period. As a result, identical firms taking different positions as to what is considered a reasonable and necessary expenditure will report different income and inventory amounts. A firm's capitalization policy may influence decision making because inventory could be the basis for collateral on a loan. In addition, the increased earnings resulting from capitalization could be used in the determination of a firm's ability to repay debt and to distribute dividends. Unfortunately for the analyst, there is generally little disclosure as to the composition of the unit cost of inventory. However, a footnote would be required if the firm changed its capitalization policy with respect to inventory costs, and that change had a material effect on inventory valuation, reported net income and earnings per share.

The Allocation of Unit Cost to the Items Included in Ending Inventory. The "allocation problem in inventory" is one of the most important issues in accounting for a retailer or manufacturer. The allocation problem consists of identification of the units remaining in ending inventory and the units sold, and the assignment or allocation of a unit cost to the units in ending inventory and to the units sold. The allocation problem is illustrated in Exhibit 2.5. Note that the input into the goods available for sale result in 16,000 units at a total cost of $60,000. The $60,000 must be assigned to the 5,500 units in inventory on the balance sheet and 10,500 units sold at the income statement.

EXHIBIT 2.5 ALLOCATION PROBLEM IN INVENTORY

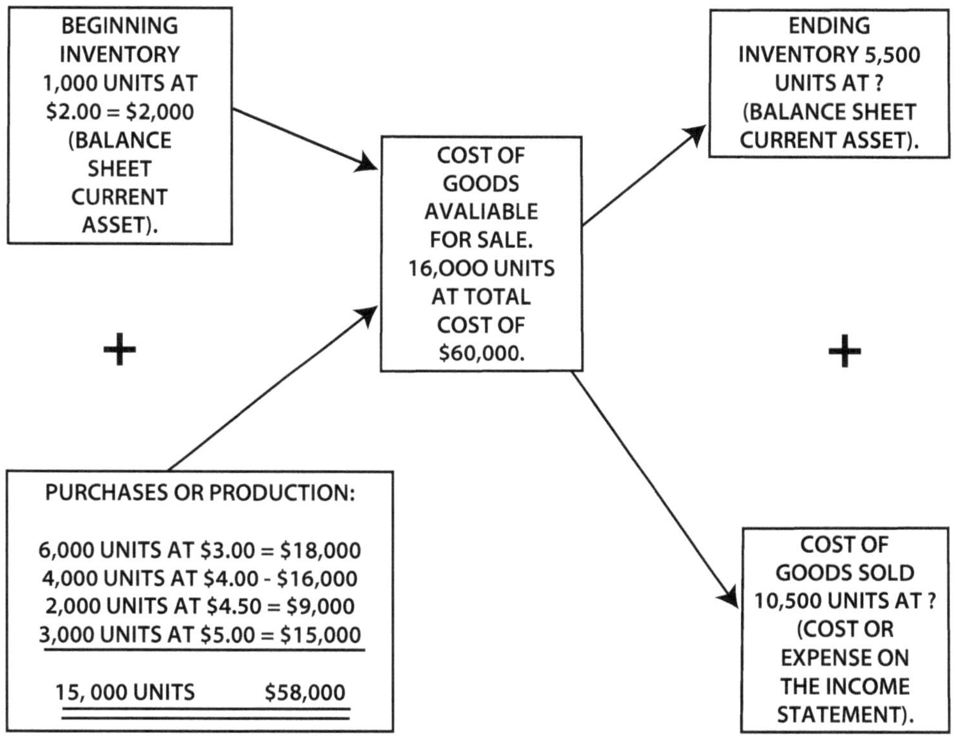

The allocation problem can also be illustrated by the cost of goods sold formula used in a periodic inventory system.

ITEM	UNITS	DOLLARS
Beginning Inventory	1,000	$ 2,000
Add: Cost of Goods Purchased	15,000	58,000
Goods Available for Sale	16,000	$60,000
Less: Ending Inventory	(5,500)	?
Cost of Goods Sold	10,500	?

The above formula points out the significance of the valuation assigned to ending inventory. Depending on management's reporting objectives, an allocation method can be used to overstate or understate inventory, which in turn will be directly related to reported net income and earnings per share.

If management selects an allocation method that increases ending inventory, assets will be increased, cost of goods sold will be reduced and reported income will increase. Conversely, an allocation method that reduces the valuation of ending inventory will reduce total assets, overstate cost of goods sold and understate net income. It should be noted that the ending inventory of the current year becomes the beginning inventory of the next year. Therefore, depending on the level of inventory and unit costs in the subsequent year, the income effects could reverse in the next accounting period. Management may also have quite different objectives in selecting an allocation method for tax purposes. The tax consequences relating to the choice of inventory valuation method have direct or real cash flow implications and will be discussed in a subsequent section of this chapter.

If unit prices were constant over time or if it were possible to specifically identify the exact cost of the units in inventory and units sold, there would be no allocation problem and the choice of inventory method would be irrelevant. However, unit prices of inventory are normally not stable and specific identification may not be possible. Even if specific identification is possible, management may wish to select another method of inventory valuation in order to satisfy some financial reporting or tax objective. In these situations, management is permitted to make certain cost flow assumptions.

There are three GAAP cost flow assumptions that can be used to allocate the total cost of goods available to ending inventory and cost of goods sold:

- The average cost method
- The first-in, first-out method (FIFO)
- The last-in, first-out method (LIFO)

Originally, sound accounting theory dictated that each cost flow assumption should be designed to match the cost flow to the unit flow of the items in inventory and the items sold. Thus, the average cost approach was originally designed for a firm selling a high volume of homogeneous goods. For example, the operations of a distributor of home heating oil may be well suited for the use of the average cost method.

The FIFO method was considered most useful for a firm selling a product subject to rapid obsolescence, style changes or perishability. Retail outlets would probably find that the FIFO cost flow assumption best matched their actual unit flow.

Finally, the LIFO approach was originally created for a firm with operations requiring a base stock. For example, a coal mining operation would maintain a base level in a pile of coal. All subsequent mining would be added to the top of the pile and all sales would be from the top of the pile. Sales would draw down the inventory level until the base stock level was reached. At this point, new inventory would be added to the top of the base stock. The base stock was rarely if ever sold or used in operations.

The theoretical objectives of matching unit flow and cost flow are no longer relevant. In today's accounting and reporting environment, the financial reporting objectives focus on balance sheet (i.e., inventory) valuation and income determination. As indicated in the discussion of accounts receivable and the bad debt expense, there is generally a trade-off between these two objectives. This trade-off of objectives will be more evident in the case of accounting for inventory. In addition, because of the IRS LIFO Conformity Rule, which requires that if a firm uses LIFO for tax purposes it must also be used for financial reporting, the inventory choice for financial reporting may be tied to the tax method selected and not related to the theoretical unit flow of inventory.

Exhibit 2.6 uses the same information provided in Exhibit 2.5 to illustrate the three GAAP cost flow assumptions.

EXHIBIT 2.6 ***ILLUSTRATION OF BASIC INVENTORY METHODS UNDER A PERIODIC INVENTORY SYSTEM:***

TRANSACTION	***UNITS***	***UNIT COST***	***TOTAL COST***
BEGINNING INVENTORY 1/1	1,000	$2.00	$2,000
PURCHASES			
30-Mar	6,000	3.00	18,000
16-Apr	4,000	4.00	16,000
13-Jun	2,000	4.50	9,000
5-Oct	3,000	5.00	15,000
TOTAL AVAILABLE FOR SALE	16,000		$60,000
ENDING INVENTORY PHYSICAL COUNT) 12/31	-5,500		
UNITS SOLD	10,500		

(1) Weighted Average Method (Periodic Method). (Original use: firms selling a high volume of a homogeneous product (e.g., oil and gas)).

WEIGHTED AVERAGE				
COST PER UNIT	=	TOTAL COST OF GOODS AVAILABLE	X	TOTAL NUMBER OF UNITS AVAILABLE
$60,000	=	16,000	X	$3.75/Unit
ENDING INVENTORY	=	5,500 x $3.75	X	$20,625
COST OF GOODS SOLD	=	GOODS AVAILABLE	—	ENDING INVENTORY
$39,375	=	$60,000	—	$20,625

(2) First-In, First-Out (FIFO) Method: Assigns The Most Recent Costs To Ending Inventory (EI) And The Oldest Cost To Cost Of Goods Sold (CGS). (Original use: Firms selling products subject to perishability, style changes, obsolescence or rapid technological changes.)

ITEM	UNITS	UNIT COST	TOTAL COST
MOST RECENT COST: OCTOBER 5th PURCHASE	3,000	$5.00	$15,000
NEXT MOST RECENT COST: JUNE 13th PURCHASE	2,000	4.50	9,000
NEXT MOST RECENT COST: APRIL 16th PURCHASE	500	4.00	2,000
FIFO ENDING INVENTORY	**5,500**		**$26,000**

COST OF GOODS SOLD = GOODS AVAILABLE - ENDING INVENTORY
$34,000 = 60,000 - 26,000

COST OF GOODS SOLD = [(1,000 x $2.00) + (6,000 x $3.00) + (3,500 x $4.00)]
= $34,000

(3) Last-In, First-Out (LIFO) Method: Assigns The Oldest Costs to Ending Inventory and the Most Recent Costs to Cost of Goods Sold. [Original use: Firms accumulating inventory, using from the most recent acquisitions and maintaining a base stock (e.g., mining)].

ITEM	UNITS	UNIT COST	TOTAL COST
OLDEST COST: BEGINNING INV. JAN. 1	1,000	$2.00	$ 2,000
NEXT OLDEST COST: MARCH 30 PURCHASE	4,500	3.00	13,500
LIFO ENDING INVENTORY	**5,500**		**$15,500**

COST OF GOODS SOLD = GOODS AVAILABLE - ENDING INVENTORY
$44,500 = $60,000 - 15,500

COST OF GOODS SOLD = [(3,000 x $5.00) + (2,000 x $4.50) + (4,000 x $4.00) + (1,500 x $3.00)]
= $44,500.

Note: Under the IRS LIFO Conformity Rule, if LIFO is used for tax purposes, then it must be used for financial reporting.

Summary of Inventory Valuation under the Three Accounting Alternatives

INVENTORY METHOD	***ENDING INVENTORY (BALANCE SHEET)***	***COST OF GOODS SOLD (INCOME STATEMENT)***
FIFO	$26,000	$34,000
WEIGHTED AVERAGE	$20,625	$39,375
LIFO	$15,500	$44,500

All of the calculations in Exhibit 2.6 assume:

- A periodic inventory system is used
- There is a period of rising inventory costs
- Inventory levels (i.e., units or quantities) are increasing

The average cost method is known as the weighted average method when applied in a periodic inventory system. The weighted average method applies a weighted average unit cost of $3.75 per unit to the number of units in ending inventory and the number of units sold. As noted in the summary of inventory valuation in Exhibit 2.6, the weighted average valuation will fall between the two extreme measures, FIFO and LIFO.

The FIFO method of inventory valuation assigns the most recent costs to ending inventory and the oldest costs to the cost of goods sold. FIFO results in an inventory valuation that approximates current cost. This provides the credit analyst with the most realistic valuation for assessing the collateral for an inventory-based loan, before considering the possibility of slow moving or obsolete inventory. In a period of rising prices, FIFO tends to provide the highest valuation of ending inventory. However, FIFO tends to mismatch costs with revenues in that it allocates the oldest low-unit cost to the cost of goods sold which are to be matched against inflated, current sales dollars. In a period of inflation this mismatch tends to overstate reported net income and earnings per share. The overstatement of FIFO income actually results in "phantom profits" because the additional reported income does not provide any incremental cash flows. Thus, in using the FIFO method, management trades-off proper balance sheet valuation for a mismatch of costs and revenues on the income statement.

The LIFO approach allocates the oldest cost to ending inventory and the most recent costs to the cost of goods sold. During a period of rising prices and with constant or increasing inventory levels, LIFO tends to significantly understate inventory valuation. However, the resulting cost of goods sold is considered to better match costs and revenues. Improved income statement matching results from the fact that current costs are matched with higher, current sales revenues.

Some believe that the use of LIFO actually adjusts the income statement for inflation. With the exception of the depreciation, depletion and amortization of old historical cost based assets, the use of LIFO in a period of inflation produces an income statement that matches current dollar revenues with current dollar operating expenses. Nonetheless, the LIFO method trades off balance sheet inventory valuation for proper matching on the income statement. In an inventory-based loan, the credit analyst must recognize the fact that before an actual appraisal is completed the use of LIFO will result in a highly conservative valuation for the inventory to be considered as collateral.

The summary of inventory valuation under the three GAAP alternatives in Exhibit 2.6 clearly illustrates the differences between the FIFO and LIFO methods. Specifically in comparing the three GAAP inventory methods, it is important to note that:

- Weighted average falls between the two extreme approaches, LIFO and FIFO.
- LIFO versus FIFO represents the classic trade-off in accounting between: (i) the balance sheet objective of proper inventory valuation (which is best satisfied by FIFO giving a valuation close to current cost); and (ii) the income statement objective of proper matching costs and revenues (which is best satisfied by LIFO by matching current sales dollars against current cost of goods sold).
- The use of the LIFO method will bias several key financial ratios. Specifically, LIFO will understate the current (working capital) ratio and will overstate the inventory turnover ratio.
- The relationships and rankings between the LIFO and FIFO hold only if there is a period of inflation and prices are rising for inventory acquisition or manufacturing costs, and inventory levels are constant or increasing.

Under the assumptions of this illustration, the FIFO method provides the highest inventory valuation and the lowest cost of goods sold, while the opposite is true for the LIFO method. The $10,500 difference between the inventory valuation under FIFO and LIFO is known as the LIFO reserve, (i.e., $26,000 – 15,500). The significance and uses of the LIFO reserve will be discussed in detail below.

It is critical to recognize the fact that the rankings in this illustration will only hold if there is a period of inflation and inventory levels are constant or increasing. If inventory levels decline, it is known as a LIFO liquidation. When a LIFO liquidation occurs, old low-cost base layers of LIFO inventory are assumed to be sold. If prices are rising, the matching of old low cost LIFO layers against high inflated sales dollars will increase LIFO profits, and can even result in a LIFO net income in excess of what would have been reported if the FIFO method was used.

In order to illustrate a LIFO liquidation, assume that the June 13th and October 5th purchases or production runs in Exhibit 2.6 were not made. In addition, assume that the same 10,500 units were sold so that the physical count of ending inventory resulted in 500 units on December 31st. Inventory levels decreased from 1,000 units at the beginning of the year to 500 units at year end.

Under these assumptions, the information presented in Exhibit 2.6 would be modified as follows:

LIFO Liquidation Scenario

TRANSACTION	*UNITS*	*UNIT COST*	*TOTAL COST*
BEGINNING INVENTORY 1/1	1,000	$2.00	$ 2,000
PURCHASES			
MARCH 30	6,000	3.00	18,000
APRIL 16	4,000	4.00	16,000
TOTAL AVAILABLE FOR SALE	11,000		$36,000
ENDING INVENTORY PHYSICAL COUNT) 12/31	(500)		
UNITS SOLD	10,500		

Given the FIFO method of inventory valuation, the 500 units in ending inventory would be valued at the most recent cost of $4.00 per unit or a total ending inventory value of $2,000. Cost of goods sold would be $34,000 (i.e., Goods available for sale – Ending inventory = $36,000 – 2,000), which is the same as the case of increasing inventory levels in Exhibit 2.6.

Therefore, with no change in the inflation assumption, declining inventory levels do not affect reported FIFO profits.

If the LIFO method is applied to the revised information, the ending inventory of 500 units would be valued at the oldest cost, or $2.00 per unit. In this case, it is said that management has "eaten into LIFO layers" or has "released LIFO layers." This results in a total ending inventory valuation of $1,000. However, the cost of goods sold would only be $35,000 (i.e., Goods available for sale – Ending inventory = $36,000 – 1,000). When compared to the original solution, cost of goods sold declines (and reported income before taxes increases) by $9,500 (i.e., $44,500 – 35,000). In addition, taxable income would increase by $9,500 as well.

The above comparison is not a valid representation of life liquidation profit because it includes the full effect of the two subsequent purchases or production runs. Accountants will generally compute liquidation profits only based on the hypothetical, subsequent purchase or production run that would have been required to cover the number of units liquidated (i.e., to avoid the LIFO liquidation).

In this illustration, the firm is considered to have liquidation profit of $1,000. Liquidation profit is computed as the difference between the actual cost of goods sold and the cost of goods sold that would have resulted if the firm had purchased or produced the same quantity of inventory as it sold, or if the firm had purchased or produced enough units to avoid the liquidation.

To avoid the liquidation, the firm would have been required to purchase or produce 10,500 additional units. The cost of the 10,500 units acquired and the liquidation profit are determined as follows:

Date	***Computation***	***Total Cost***
3/30	Actual purchase of 6,000 units at @$3.00	$18,000
4/16	Actual purchase of 4,000 units at @$4.00	16,000
	Hypothetical purchase to avoid the liquidation: 500 units at $4.00	2,000
	LIFO COST OF GOODS SOLD ***WITHOUT*** THE LIQUIDATION	$36,000
	LIFO COST OF GOOD SOLD ***WITH*** THE LIQUIDATION (ACTUAL)	(35,000)
	LIQUIDATION PROFIT	$ 1,000

An alternative method to compute the liquidation profit is to take the difference between the old LIFO cost and the most recent cost of inventory acquired during the year and multiply that difference by the number of units liquidated (i.e., the decrease in inventory):

Units Liquidated x (Most recent purchase cost – Liquidated cost) = Liquidation profit

500 units x ($4.00 - 2.00) = $1,000

LIFO and Taxes. The selection of the inventory method has increased significance when the tax implications of inventory valuation are considered. The consequences of selecting LIFO versus FIFO for income tax purposes is the only inventory issue that has cash flow implications for the firm. Without considering taxes, the LIFO-FIFO choice is purely a cosmetic financial reporting issue. However, with the IRS LIFO conformity rule, income tax and financial reporting issues become interrelated.

As noted earlier, the IRS LIFO conformity rule requires that if a firm uses LIFO for tax purposes, it must also use LIFO for financial reporting. In a period of rising prices and with constant or increasing inventory levels, LIFO could significantly increase cost of sales and result in large tax savings and increased cash flows for the firm, relative to the FIFO basis.

Before LIFO conformity, firms historically used FIFO or average cost for financial reporting and LIFO for tax reporting. As a result, when LIFO conformity was first enacted into law, many firms were required to switch to LIFO for financial reporting purposes. The switch to LIFO created a great deal of problems for credit and financial analysts in attempting to determine the value of inventory and to compare profitability over time and among firms in the same industry. In response to user needs, the accounting profession requires a significant amount of disclosure relating to the LIFO inventories presented on a firm's balance sheet.

The major disclosure requirements from the American Institute of Certified Public Accountants (AICPA's) LIFO Issues Paper are summarized in the following paragraphs.

The AICPA's LIFO Issues Paper. In 1984, the Accounting Standards Division of the AICPA (AcSec) issued a position paper on various LIFO topics[8]. The SEC subsequently declared that this paper should be viewed as part of GAAP as it addressed questions not covered in other authoritative pronouncements. Some of the disclosure requirements of the AICPA Issues Paper on LIFO topics include:

Disclosure of the LIFO reserve. The firm is required to disclose either the LIFO reserve (i.e., the difference between FIFO cost and the LIFO inventory value), or the replacement cost of inventory.

- ***Partial adoption of LIFO.*** The presumption is that if a company switches to LIFO it should do so for all of its inventories. The exception would be if a company has a valid reason for not adopting LIFO for a part of their inventory or a product line. For example, if a company can anticipate a reduction of certain lines of inventory or declining prices for a particular product, a non-LIFO inventory method can be used for that portion of the total inventory. In addition, LIFO is not permitted in many countries outside the United States and therefore, a company can report a significant amount on non-LIFO inventory on its balance sheet.
- ***Disclosure of the extent to which LIFO is used.*** Ideally the portion of cost of sales resulting from the use of LIFO should be provided. If this is not practical, the portion of the ending inventory valued under the LIFO method should be disclosed. The portion of inventory valued at LIFO can be disclosed as a percentage of the total inventory or as an absolute dollar amount. For example, a company with a significant international component may have a small percentage of its inventory on the LIFO basis, relative to other firms in the same industry.

LIFO liquidations. The effects on income from liquidating LIFO inventories should be disclosed, usually in the footnotes to the financial statements. A LIFO liquidation is not considered an unusual item. It should be noted that the effect of LIFO liquidation is not reported on the face of the income statement but is "buried" in the reduced cost of goods sold. Without careful review of the footnotes, a reader could misinterpret the reduced cost of goods sold from a LIFO liquidation as cost reduction or an improvement of operating efficiency.

Therefore, the disclosure of liquidation profits is important because it indicates to the analyst how much of reported net income was due to the firm's operating strength and what amount of income was simply caused by a decrease in the level of inventory on hand. In addition, the existence of liquidation profit has cash consequences because it results in a higher tax liability than would have been the case the absence of a liquidation.

8. FASB ASC 210-1—S99-3,6. [Predecessor literature: The AICPA Task Force on LIFO Inventory Problems, Issues Paper (New York, AICPA, November 30, 1984)]

Disallowance of replacement reserves. In the past, if LIFO inventories were involuntarily liquidated, firms would sometimes create replacement reserves on the balance sheet which anticipated replacement in the next accounting period of the units currently liquidated. In creating the reserve, a liability or an allowance for replacement would be reported on the balance sheet and cost of goods sold would be measured as if the liquidation did not occur. As a result, income would not be increased by the liquidation. The replacement reserve approach is not permitted in the annual financial statements. However, avoiding a LIFO liquidation by employing this technique is common in the quarterly reports.

Non-LIFO disclosures. Under the first LIFO conformity requirements, in order for LIFO to be accepted by the IRS companies were not allowed to report anything but LIFO values in their financial reports. However, this original conformity requirement was relaxed and a company may provide non-LIFO disclosures. Non-LIFO disclosures could include proforma inventory valuation and net income and earnings per share as if the FIFO method was used.

Non-LIFO disclosures enable the analyst to convert from the LIFO to the FIFO method of inventory valuation. The analytical restatement from LIFO to FIFO is important in comparing two firms in the same industry with materially different percentages of inventory on the LIFO basis or in conducting a pro-forma consolidation in a proposed merger or acquisition. In addition, the disclosures assist in restoring comparability over several accounting periods in the year in which a firm changes to the LIFO method for financial reporting purposes. An analytical restatement from LIFO to FIFO will be illustrated in the next section of this chapter.

It should be noted that the SEC cautioned companies that the supplemental LIFO disclosures must be considered carefully to avoid implying that FIFO earnings are the "real" earnings of a company using LIFO. The SEC believed that the risk of user misinterpretation is mitigated when such disclosures are made, if the companies that file their statements with the SEC also (a) state clearly that LIFO results in a better matching of costs and revenues; (b) indicate why the supplemental disclosures are being provided; and (c) present essential information about the supplemental income calculation to enable users to appreciate the quality of the information. In addition, the SEC believed that when companies made such disclosures, they should be made in the footnotes to the financial statements or in management's discussion and analysis. When non-LIFO disclosures are provided, the effects on net income and financial position should be reported net of tax.

Lower of cost or market (LCM). A company should report its inventory at the lower of cost or market. The LCM rules for inventory will be discussed in a later section of this chapter.

Analytical Restatement of Inventory from LIFO to FIFO. The LIFO disclosures are significant in that they represent a source of information that is available year after year, and which enables the analyst to restate both the inventory on the balance sheet and net income on the income statement from the LIFO basis to a pro-forma FIFO and/or average cost basis.

Specifically, when attempting to assess the fair values of a target company in a merger or acquisition, an analyst can use the LIFO reserve to adjust the target company's inventory from LIFO to a FIFO basis. The FIFO basis will provide an amount as close as possible to the current market value of the target company's inventory. Until an actual appraisal of the target company's assets is conducted, the adjusted inventory amount will provide a good first approximation of the inventory value for the target company.

The LIFO reserve can also be used to determine the extent of the bias in key financial ratios from the use of LIFO. This information is useful in comparable company analyses. The impact of using LIFO on financial ratios will be illustrated below.

Exhibits 2.7 and 2.8 provide an illustration of restating inventory and income from the LIFO to the FIFO method for Smokey Mountain Products, Inc.

EXHIBIT 2.7: 2011 FINANCIAL INFORMATION CONVERTED FROM LIFO TO FIFO. DATA ARE PRESENTED IN EXHIBIT 2.8

(a) Short cut determination of FIFO cost of goods sold using the change in the LIFO Reserve

Cost of Goods Sold (COGS)	
ITEM	**2011**
COGS-at LIFO as reported	$410,777
Deduct: Increase in the LIFO Reserve ($4,247 – 2,796)	-1,451
COGS-at FIFO as restated	$409,326

Alternative computation of FIFO Cost of Goods Sold:

First determine the cost of goods purchased or produced during the year as reported:

YEAR	*ITEM*	*As reported*
2011	Ending inventory	$106,294
	Add: Cost of goods sold	410,777
	Cost of goods available for sale	$517,070
	Less: Beginning inventory	-100,046
	Cost of goods purchased	$417,024

Next, we can compute the cost of goods sold as if FIFO was used during the current year:

YEAR	*ITEM*	*FIFO*
2011	***(See Note 10 for inventory amounts)***	
	Beginning inventory	$102,842
	Add: Cost of goods purchased (above)	417,024
	Cost of goods available for sale	$519,866
	Less: Ending inventory	-110,540
	Cost of goods sold-FIFO	$409,326

(b) Earnings Restatement

Operating Earnings Restated Under FIFO	
ITEM	**20**
LIFO operating earnings as reported	$183,215
Add: Increase in the LIFO Reserve	1,451
After tax earnings restated under FIFO	$184,666

(c) Comparative Financial Ratios

RATIO	FORMULA	LIFO AS REPORTED	FIFO AS RESTATED
Current Ratio	Current Assets / Current Liabilities	$391,570 = .901 to 1 / 434,531	($326,308 + 1,209)= .904 to 1 / 434,531
Inventory Turnover Ratio	Cost of Goods Sold / Average Inventory	$ 410,777 / [106,294 + 100,046/2] =3.98 Times	$409,326 / [($102,842 + 110,540)/2] =3.84 Times
Holding Interval	365 Days / Inventory Turnover	365 / 3.98= 91.7 days	365 / 3.84= 95 days

Although not significantly different from the FIFO basis in this case, the results presented in Part C of the exhibit illustration the general effects of using the LIFO basis of inventory valuation. LIFO tends to:

1. Understate liquidity (current ratio).

2. Overstate inventory turnover (reduces the estimated holding interval).

Note that this analysis ignores the tax effects (tax benefits) of using LIFO. Tax savings would increase cash (current assets) or reduce taxes payable (current liabilities) in the current ratio computation.

EXHIBIT 2.8: SMOKEY MOUNTAIN PRODUCTS, INC. PARTIAL CONSOLIDATED FINANCIAL STATEMENTS

Smokey Mountain Products, Inc.	**Dollars in thousands**	**31-December**		
		2011		2010
Assets				
Current Assets				
Cash and cash equivalents	**$**	**72,908**	$	107,281
Marketable securities		—		12,000
Accounts receivable		**189,930**		165,344
Inventories		**106,294**		100,046
Deferred income tax benefits		**6,644**		7,107
Prepaid and other Total		**15,794**		14,924
Current Assets	**$**	**391,570**	$	406,702
Product Development Assets		**78,769**		73,813
Property, Equipment and Technology		**122,548**		138,460
Intangible Assets		**362,861**		349,249
Goodwill		**238,099**		234,676
Deferred Income Tax Benefits		**4,571**		5,142
Other Assets		**32,794**		31,042
Total Assets	**$**	**1,231,211**	$	1,239,083
Liabilities and Shareholders' Equity				
Current Liabilities				
Accounts and royalties payable	**$**	**116,677**		85,150
Deferred subscription revenue		**172,708**		171,319
Accrued income taxes		**29,071**		43,651
Accrued pension liability		**7,289**		7,475
Other accrued liabilities		**108,786**		101,978
Total Current Liabilities	**$**	**434,531**		409,573

Partial Income Statement:

CONSOLIDATED STATEMENTS OF INCOME

Smokey Mountain Products, Inc.	For the years ended December 31		
Dollars in thousands except per share data	2011	2010	2009
Revenue	$1,253,022	$1,168,858	$1,107,554
Costs and Expenses			
Cost of sales	410,777	390,073	370,686
Operating and administrative expenses	642,833	596,071	569,882
Amortization of intangibles	16,198	13,056	11,731
Total Costs and Expenses	1,069,807	999,200	952,300
Operating Income	183,215	169,657	155,255

Note 10 - Inventories

Inventories at December 31 were as follows (in thousands):

	2011	2010
Finished Goods	**$95,267**	$87,517
Work-in-Process	**8,045**	8,092
Raw Materials	**7,229**	7,234
	110,540	102,842
LIFO Reserve	**-4,247**	-2,796
Total Inventories	**$106,294**	$100,046

LIFO inventories are restated to the FIFO basis by simply adding the LIFO reserve disclosed in the footnote to the LIFO inventory values reported on the balance sheet and in Note 10. Exhibit 2.7 also provides an estimation of the amount of purchases or production. This could be useful in a trend analysis. For example, if there is a decreasing trend in production and raw materials inventory, coupled with an increase in work in process and finished goods inventories, the analyst may conclude that management is expecting a slowdown in sales in the short run.

To determine the difference in pretax income, it is only necessary to compute the differences in cost of goods sold under LIFO and proforma FIFO.

The difference in cost of sales and therefore in pretax profit is $1,451, which means that pretax income is lower under LIFO. Part of the reason for this effect can be found in the analysis of the LIFO reserve. Note that Exhibit 2.7 presents a short-cut approach to determine the profit implications of the LIFO-FIFO switch. The difference in pretax profit is nothing more than the change in the LIFO reserve.

If the LIFO reserve increases, it implies that either prices are rising, inventory levels are constant or increasing, or there is a combination of both. The existence of inflation and constant or increasing inventory quantity levels cause the cumulative differences between LIFO and FIFO inventory values to increase, thereby resulting in a specific effect which increases the cost of sales and the resulting tax benefits under LIFO. That is, LIFO profit is less than FIFO profit. This is the case for Smokey Mountain in 2011.

When there is a decrease in the LIFO reserve, it implies that either prices are declining or inventory quantity levels are decreasing (i.e., there is a LIFO liquidation). Under these conditions, the cumulative difference between the LIFO and FIFO inventory valuation is reduced. In addition, the specific effect for the year results in a reduced cost of goods sold and a loss of tax benefits under LIFO. In this case, LIFO pretax profit could be greater than the FIFO pro-forma income before tax.

As noted above, Smokey Mountain experienced a decrease in its LIFO reserve in 2011. The specific pre-tax effect resulted in LIFO income lower than proforma FIFO income by $1,451 million. This specific effect could be due to increasing quantities or prices or both.

A decrease in the LIFO Reserve for the NJ MAX is presented below.

CONSOLIDATED BALANCE SHEETS (Partial)

(In thousands)	**December 31, *2011***	**December 31, *2010***
ASSETS		
CURRENT ASSETS		
Cash and cash equivalents	**$ 62,342**	$ 82,852
Accounts receivable Net	**382,235**	410,236
Inventories	**37,967**	42,077
Deferred income taxes	**94,484**	95,527
Other current assets	**94,840**	121,296
Total current assets	**671,868**	731,986

NOTE 3. INVENTORIES

Inventories are stated at the lower of cost or current market value. Inventory cost is generally based on the last-in, first-out ("LIFO") method for newsprint and magazine paper and the first-in, first-out ("FIFO") method for other inventories.

Inventories as shown in the accompanying Consolidated Balance Sheets were as follows:

(In thousands)	**December 31, 2011**	**December 31, 2010**
Finished Goods	**$34,130**	$36,767
Work-in-process and direct material	**3,836**	5,310
Total	**$37,967**	$42,077

Inventories are stated at the lower of cost or current market value. Cost was determined utilizing the LIFO method for 82% of inventory in 2011 and 86% of inventory in 2010. The replacement cost of inventory was approximately $40.6 million as of December 30, 2011 and $49.5 million as of December 31, 2010.

CONSOLIDATED STATEMENTS OF INCOME (Partial)

(In thousands, except per share data)	Year Ended December 31 2011
REVENUES	$3,619,150
COSTS AND EXPENSES	
Cost of Goods Sold	$1,635,437
Selling, general and administrative expenses	$1,534,436
Total	$3,169,873
OPERATING PROFIT	$ 449,277

In this case the LIFO reserve is determined as the difference between the FIFO (replacement) cost and LIFO carrying values. For NJ MAX case the LIFO reserve is computed as follows:

	2011	**2010**
Inventory at FIFO	$ 40.6	$49.5
Inventory at LIFO	38.0	**42.1**
LIFO Reserve	$ 2.6	$ 7.4

The LIFO reserve decreased by $4.8 million and operating profit under FIFO would be lower by that amount or restated to $444,477 (i.e., $449,277 – 4,800).

When there is a significant LIFO liquidation, the amount of liquidation profit is disclosed in the footnotes to the financial statements. The inventory footnote for Spin Move Corporation and Subsidiaries is presented below. You should also note the disclosure of the company's capitalization policy regarding inventory costs.

SPIN MOVE CORPORATION AND SUBSIDIARIES NOTES TO CONSOLIDATED FINANCIAL STATEMENTS (AMOUNTS IN THOUSANDS EXCEPT PER SHARE AMOUNTS)

Inventories. Inventories are stated at the lower of cost or market and include materials, labor and overhead. Cost for financial reporting purposes is determined by the last-in, first-out (LIFO) method. Inbound freight, purchasing and receiving costs, inspection costs, internal transfer costs and raw material warehousing costs are all ***capitalized*** into inventory and included in cost of goods sold as related inventory is sold. Finished goods warehousing costs and the cost of operating the Company's finished product distribution centers are included in Selling, General and Administrative ***expenses***. Inventories consist of the following at December 31, 2011 and December 31, 2010:

		December 31, 2011		December 31, 2010
Raw materials	**$**	**27,005**	$	26,876
Work-in-process		**7,344**		10,169
Finished goods		**14,603**		16,489
Inventory at FIFO		**48,952**		53,534
LIFO adjustment		**(3,559)**		(905)
Inventory at LIFO	**$**	**45,393**	$	52,629

During the years ended December 31, 2011 and December 31, 2010, inventory quantities were reduced. These reductions resulted in a liquidation of LIFO inventory quantities. The effect of the inventory reduction in 2011 decreased cost of goods sold by approximately $332, and increased net income by approximately $216 or $0.012 per share. The effect of the inventory reduction in 2010 was immaterial.

The footnote indicates that there was an increase in the LIFO reserve, but there was a decrease in the total LIFO inventory valuation. In this case, price increases may have more than offset a significant quantity decrease or the liquidation of inventory quantities under LIFO. However, liquidation profit resulted in the decrease in cost of goods sold. The liquidation provides evidence that the taxes actually paid increased. In other words, LIFO resulted in tax disadvantages for Spin Move in 2011. The extent of this tax disadvantage cannot be exactly determined by the information provided in the footnotes to the financial statements. However, the amount of the liquidation profit alone can provide some idea of the extent of the adverse tax consequences of using LIFO in 2011 relative to FIFO.

Using the footnote information, the difference between the pretax and after tax COGS effect is $116,000 or $116,000 of additional taxes (i.e., $332,000 – 216,000). This incorporates the effective tax rate and it may not be equal to the actual additional tax paid from the liquidation. Nonetheless, the disclosure of the liquidation profits provides useful information in approximating the cash effects of the liquidation and the impact on trend in gross profit and cost of goods sold.

Regarding this last point, it is important to note that the effect of the liquidation is not an unusual item and impacts the trend of cost of goods sold and gross profit. The gross profit trend for Spin Move is presented below with the adjustment for the LIFO liquidation profits recognized in fiscal 2011.

SPIN MOVE CORPORATION AND SUBSIDIARIES CONSOLIDATED STATEMENTS OF OPERATIONS (AMOUNTS IN THOUSANDS, EXCEPT PER SHARE AMOUNTS)

	Fiscal Year Ended		
	December 31, 2011	December 31, 2010	December 31, 2009
Net sales	**$ 269,621**	$ 346,974	$ 390,404
Cost of products sold	**234,917**	283,524	306,242
Gross profit	**34,704**	63,450	84,162
Gross profit margin	**12.9%**	18.3%	21.6%
Adjusted for the LIFO Liquidation: Cost of goods sold without the LIFO Liquidation: $34,704-332= $34,372 Gross Profit Margin without the Liquidation ($34,372 / $269,621) =	**12.7%**		

As noted in the above computation, the LIFO liquidation reduces cost of goods sold and overstates the gross profit margin. Although not significant in this case, the footnote information can assist in correcting the analyst's trend in gross profit.

The Lower of Cost or Market Rule for Inventory (LCM). The lower-of-cost-or-market rule for inventory is the accountant's test for obsolescence. At the end of each accounting period, auditing standards require that accountants compare the cost of the ending inventory, measured at LIFO, FIFO or average cost, with the market value of the inventory. If cost is greater than market, a write down of the inventory is required. Because LIFO tends to understate inventory cost in a period of inflation, an LCM problem is typically not expected if the firm uses the LIFO method.

Although similar in basic principle to the impairment rules for other assets, the LCM rules for inventory differ in several significant respects. First, the LCM rules for inventory can be applied to the aggregate inventory, product lines or individual items. The different levels of aggregation are permitted to allow for certain products in inventory that may be sold at a loss in order to stimulate sales of a related product. For example, a firm may sell a laser printer at a loss or very low profit margin in order to generate sales of toner cartridges at excessive markups. In this case, it would not be appropriate to write off the printers as obsolete because their cost is in excess of their market values. The printers are interrelated with the cartridges and therefore should be evaluated together, as a single unit. This would justify the application of the LCM rules to a particular product line or to the total inventory, rather than to the individual items in inventory.

Second, the market value for inventory is not obtained by simply referring to a published price list or quoted market prices as is the case with marketable securities. Conversely, the market value for inventory is not the current selling price of the item. Instead, market is the current replacement cost (CRC) subject to limitations or boundaries. These boundaries are known as the ceiling and floor, or the "NRV, (NRV-NP)" rules.

In the application of the LCM rules for inventory, CRC cannot exceed the ceiling which is defined as net realizable value (NRV). NRV is equal to the selling price of the item less any disposal costs such as commissions, packaging and freight. The NRV upper boundary or the ceiling on market is required in order to prevent overvaluation of inventory. That is, inventory should not be valued above an amount that is reasonably expected to be realized in cash from the disposal of the item.

In addition, CRC cannot fall below the floor. This lower boundary is defined as NRV less a normal profit (NP). The floor, or lower limit on the market value, is used to prevent undervaluation of inventory. Unnecessary or excessive write-offs of inventory (e.g., "big bath accounting") could result in smoothing income or reporting inflated profits in subsequent years when the undervalued inventory item is eventually sold at a normal selling price. The floor, or NRV-NP represents the most reasonable lower limit at which inventory can be carried.

The NRV-NP limit can be proven as follows:

Normal Profit = Selling Price - Cost of Inventory - Disposal Costs
Normal Profit = (Selling Price - Disposal Costs) - Cost of Inventory
Normal Profit = Net Realizable Value - Cost of Inventory
Cost of Inventory = Net Realizable Value - Normal Profit

That is, the minimum valuation for inventory cost is equal to NRV – NP.

An illustration of the LCM rules for inventory is presented in Exhibit 2.9.

EXHIBIT 2.9 ILLUSTRATION: LOWER OF COST OR MARKET RULE FOR INVENTORY

GROUP	*ITEM*	*CRC*	*SP*	*DISPOSAL*	*NP*	CEILING NRV	FLOOR NRV-NP	MARKET	COST	LCM
A	101	$14	$20	$5	$2	$15	$13	$14 CRC	$18	$14M
A	102	20	25	7	3	18	15	18 NRV	15	15C
B	110	50	80	20	8	60	52	52 NRV-NP	50	50C
B	112	70	95	20	10	75	65	70 CRC	72	70M
TOTAL								$154	$155	$149

Definitions:

CRC	= Current Replacement Cost.
SP	= Selling Price.
DISPOSAL	= Costs of Completion and Disposal.
NP	= Normal Profit.
NRV	= Net Realizable Value = SP - Disposal Costs

Application of LCM to:

(A) Total Inventory:

Cost - Market = $155-154 = ($1) Loss.

(B) Individual Items:

#101: Cost - Market = $18 - 14 = ($4) Loss

#112: Cost - Market = $72 - 70 = (2) Loss
Total ($6) Loss

(C) Group Basis:

A: Cost - Market = ($18 + 15) - ($14 + 18) = ($1) Loss

B: Cost - Market = ($50 + 72) - ($52 + 70) = 0

Total (Both Groups) ($1) Loss.

Assume that there are 1,000 units of each item and the individual items method is used A loss of $6,000, (i.e., $6 X 1,000 units), would be recorded.

As noted in Exhibit 2.9, Items #101 and #112 are carried at cost in excess of current market value as defined by the NRV NRV-NP rules.

The total or maximum write down of inventory using the individual items approach is $6 per unit. Assuming that there are 1,000 units of each item, the total write down is $6,000 (i.e., $4 x 1,000 + $2 x 1,000). The LCM inventory obsolescence write down would flow through the financial statements as follows:

FINANCIAL MODELING WORKSHEET

INCOME STATEMENT (FIRST)	
REVENUES:	
EXPENSES:	
Loss on inventory write down to market	(6,000)
NET INCOME OR LOSS (a)	(6,000)

STATEMENT OF CASH FLOWS (THIRD)	
OPERATING ACTIVITIES:	
NET INCOME OR LOSS (a)	(6,000)
ADD: Loss on inventory write down to market	+6,000
INVESTING ACTIVITIES:	
FINANCING ACTIVITIES:	
INCREASE (DECREASE) IN CASH (b)	- 0 -
ADD: BEGINNING CASH BALANCE	
ENDING CASH BALANCE	

BALANCE SHEET (SECOND)			
ASSETS		LIABILITIES	
CURRENT ASSETS		CURRENT LIABILITIES	
CASH (b)	- 0 -		
Inventory (direct write down or use of an allowance account)	(6,000)		
		NONCURRENT LIABILITIES	
		STOCKHOLDERS' EQUITY	
NONCURRENT ASSETS			
		CAPITAL STOCK	
		APIC	
		RETAINED EARNINGS (a)	(6,000)
		TOTAL LIABILITIES & STOCKHOLDERS' EQUITY	(6,000)
TOTAL ASSETS			

Note that the inventory obsolescence write down is not tax deductible and there are no cash flow implications until the inventory is actually sold at a loss.

NONCURRENT ASSETS

There are three major categories of noncurrent assets:

1. Tangible fixed assets or property, plant and equipment
2. Intangible assets
3. Natural resources or wasting assets

With the exception of land, goodwill and indefinite life intangible assets, all noncurrent assets have limited lives. The accountant must reflect this limited utility to the firm by systematic write-offs of the noncurrent asset's cost against income. This is considered a process of cost allocation rather than economic valuation. The cost of the noncurrent asset is allocated to the future periods of expected benefit in order to match costs with revenues.

TANGIBLE FIXED ASSETS

Characteristics of Tangible Fixed Assets. In order to be classified as a tangible fixed asset, the asset must possess three characteristics:

1. Tangible in nature
2. Long-lived
3. Used in the production and sale of other assets

The third characteristic is the most important in the analysis of financial statements because in order to conduct a proper analysis of fixed assets, this balance sheet category should only include active and productive assets, and therefore exclude idle plant and equipment. According to the SEC, if material in amount, idle plant assets should be disclosed in a footnote. In addition, if the plant asset is expected to be idle for an extended period of time, it should be segregated from plant assets and reclassified as "other assets" or "investments" in the noncurrent assets section of the balance sheet.

If idle plant assets are not properly identified, there could be a distortion of various profitability ratios and rates of return such as the ratio of pretax income to productive assets. The incorrect inclusion of idle plant assets in this computation would bias the ratio in a downward direction due to the fact that the idle plant in the denominator does not provide any contribution to production and income.

Plant Asset Accounting at Acquisition. At acquisition, plant assets must be recorded at cost, where cost includes invoice price (or production costs) plus all reasonable and necessary expenditures required to have the asset in its existing condition and location and ready for its intended use (e.g., production). Reasonable and necessary expenditures for plant assets include shipping, installation, special wiring and possibly interest charges for assets under construction. As was the case in the determination of the unit cost of inventory, what management considers to be reasonable and necessary depends on the firm's capitalization policy.

With respect to plant assets, capitalization policy can relate to either 1. the types of costs to capitalize, and 2. the magnitude of cost.

The Types of Costs to Capitalize and the Types of Costs to be Charged to Expense. Depending on management's judgment and capitalization policy, a reasonable and necessary cost could either be expensed or capitalized. For example, delivery charges can be expensed or capitalized depending on the theory followed by management. Expensing delivery costs can be justified under the theory that the cost of shipping the item does not add to the asset's productivity or efficiency and as a result does not have any future economic benefit to the firm. Conversely, delivery costs could be capitalized as part of the cost of the item under the theory that without the required delivery, the asset could not be put into place and would not contribute to production. Therefore, the choice is at the discretion of management and either expensing or capitalization can be justified. When a capitalization policy is selected by management, it should be followed consistently. Normally, the firm's capitalization policy is not disclosed in the footnotes to the financial statements, unless there has been a change in policy and the effect of the change on net income is material. It should be noted that the capitalization issue can also be a problem subsequent to acquisition with regard to repair and maintenance-type expenditures.

Section three the Magnitude of Costs to Capitalize. For example, some firms have a "materiality threshold" for capitalization. If an expenditure falls below a fixed dollar limit, it is expensed immediately rather than capitalized as part of the cost of an asset.

The capitalization issue is important for asset valuation and income determination. If a cost is inappropriately capitalized, both assets and income are overstated in the year of the expenditure. In subsequent accounting periods, the cost of the expenditure will be charged against income through higher depreciation charges. The effect is to understate future years' reported income. On the other hand, if an expenditure is inappropriately expensed as incurred, assets and income are understated in the year of acquisition. However, future income will be overstated through lower depreciation charges over subsequent accounting periods. Although cash flows and total income reported over the life of the asset will be the same, the profit reported each year will be misstated.

The capitalization-expense alternative could provide management with a valuable tool for shifting reported profit among accounting periods for purposes of smoothing income or avoiding technical default of a loan agreement. For example, improperly capitalizing costs could improve reported income in the current year so as to bring profitability ratios up to the levels required by restrictive covenants in debt agreements. Regardless of the accounting alternative selected, cash flows will be the same in total and for each year. There is only a single cash outflow in the year in which the expenditure is made. However, additional cash flow consequences could arise if certain expenditures are deducted for tax purposes rather than capitalized. These policies are governed by specific tax regulations.

Plant Asset Accounting Subsequent to Acquisition. Subsequent to acquisition, the two major accounting issues relating to fixed assets are repairs and maintenance, and depreciation. The repairs and maintenance issue involves the capitalization-expense alternative discussed above and will not be repeated again here. Depreciation is discussed in the following sections.

All plant assets, except land, are subject to depreciation. The accountant views depreciation as a process of allocation of the asset's cost to the expected future periods of benefit in order to properly match costs with revenues. Depreciation is not considered a process of economic valuation. This same view can be applied to the amortization of intangible assets and the depletion of natural resources.

The Nature of Depreciation. Depreciation is only an estimate and this estimation technique involves consideration of three factors:

1. The estimated useful or productive life;
2. The estimated scrap or residual value of the asset;
3. The estimated allocation method selected.

The estimated productive life of a plant asset can be estimated by consideration of factors such as past experience, IRS guidelines, industry practice, maintenance policy, the firm's usage versus normal usage, obsolescence and future inadequacy.

The estimated scrap, residual or salvage value is the amount expected to be realized upon disposal of the asset at the termination of its productive service to the firm. Scrap value can be based on past experience or industry practice. For example, most manufacturers leasing computers assume a zero scrap value in their depreciation computations.

The use of a scrap value was originally designed to avoid a gain or loss on disposal. The scrap value was set at an amount expected to be received on sale of the asset and the gain or loss would be minimal. The decision to use a scrap value in today's reporting environment is arbitrary.

The selection of an allocation method involves the choice of one of the four GAAP depreciation methods:

1. The straight-line method
2. The units-of-output (production) method
3. The sum-of-the-years digits method
4. The declining-balance method

The sum-of-the-years digits and the declining balance methods are also known as accelerated or decreasing charge methods.

The GAAP depreciation methods can also be used for most state and local taxes. However, the IRS requires the use of the Modified Accelerated Cost Recovery System (MACRS). MACRS depreciation is also accepted by state and local governments. The MACRS system will be considered in the chapter dealing with accounting for income taxes.

Originally, accounting theory prescribed that the depreciation method selected by management should reflect the operating and economic conditions facing the firm as well as the manner in which the asset was used. Therefore, the straight-line method should be used in those cases where there is relatively uniform periodic usage of the asset and a low obsolescence factor. The units of production or the activity method should be used when physical wear is the primary cause of depreciation and asset utilization varies year to year. Finally, the two accelerated methods should be used when the asset possesses greater usefulness in the earlier years of its life than in its later years. This is usually true for assets with a high obsolescence factor in earlier years and a high maintenance factor in later years. Due to the increased maintenance factor in later years, many believe that accelerated methods result in a relatively constant charge against income for each year of the asset's life. In earlier years, the charge against income would primarily consist of the higher accelerated depreciation expense and a lower maintenance factor. In later years of an asset's life, the total charge against income would consist of lower depreciation expense but increased maintenance costs. As a result, the cost of using the asset would be relatively constant year to year.

As was the case in selecting an inventory method, the choice of depreciation method in today's accounting and reporting environment will depend on management's reporting objectives: an income-increasing or income-reducing reporting strategy. Unlike the inventory valuation choice, there is no IRS conformity rule for depreciation. Therefore, the selection of depreciation method for financial reporting is typically independent from the method used for income tax purposes.

Regardless of the method selected, depreciation is usually recorded as an end of the period adjustment. Depreciation is charged against income on the income statement. On the balance sheet, the carrying value of the plant asset is reduced by increasing a contra-asset account called accumulated depreciation or the allowance for depreciation. The allowance for depreciation is netted or offset against the cost of the plant asset and the difference, the net book value (NBV), is reported in the noncurrent asset section of the balance sheet. This amount is also known as net fixed assets (NFA).

The use of the contra-asset account is necessary due to the fact that depreciation is only an estimate and may be revised. The only objectively determined information is the original historical cost of the asset. As a result, the accountant attempts to preserve the historical cost and records the estimated depreciation of the plant asset in the accumulated depreciation account. Nevertheless, the two accounts cannot be separated and must be viewed as a single unit, net book value. Regardless of the depreciation method used, the charge for depreciation is a noncash expense and the annual depreciation expense is an add-back in the reconciliation of accrual basis net income and cash generated from operations in the statement of cash flows.

Illustration of the GAAP Depreciation Methods. The four GAAP depreciation methods are illustrated in Exhibit 2.10. In addition, the exhibit presents an example of the optimal time to switch methods for income tax purposes.

EXHIBIT 2.10 ILLUSTRATION OF THE BASIC DEPRECIATION METHODS

Data:

Equipment Cost	**$125,000**
Useful Life	**5 Years or 100,000 Units of Output.**
Scrap (Salvage) Value	**$5,000**

(1) Straight line method (SL): Applies a constant rate of depreciation against a constant depreciable cost. Depreciable cost is equal to cost less estimated scrap value.

$$\text{DEPRECIATION EXPENSE} = \frac{\text{COST - SCRAP VALUE}}{\text{USEFUL LIFE}} = \frac{\$125{,}000 - 5{,}000}{\text{5 YEARS}} = \underline{\$24{,}000/\text{YEAR}}$$

or

= Straight line rate		x	Depreciable cost
= 1/ USEFUL LIFE x			(COST - SCRAP VALUE)
=	1/5	x	$125,000 - 5,000
=	20%	x	$120,000
=	<u>$24,000/YEAR.</u>		

STRAIGHT LINE DEPRECIATION SCHEDULE

YEAR	DEPRECIATION EXPENSE (INCOME STATEMENT)	COST (BALANCE SHEET)	ACCUMULATED DEPRECIATION AND RETAINED EARNINGS EFFECT (BALANCE SHEET)	NET BOOK VALUE (NBV) (BALANCE SHEET)
1	$24,000	$125,000	$24,000	$101,000
2	24,000	125,000	48,000	77,000
3	24,000	125,000	72,000	53,000
4	24,000	125,000	96,000	29,000
5	24,000	125,000	120,000	5,000
TOTAL	$120,000			

(2) Units of production method: Derives a rate of depreciation per unit produced.

$$\text{RATE OF DEPRECIATION EXPENSE PER UNIT} = \frac{\text{COST - SCRAP VALUE}}{\text{EST. UNITS OF OUTPUT}} = \frac{\$125{,}000 - 5{,}000}{100{,}000 \text{ UNITS}} = \underline{\$1.20/\text{UNIT}}$$

If in the first year of operation the firm manufactures 27,500 units, the depreciation expense for the year is computed as follows: $1.20 x 27,500 units = $33,000 depreciation expense.

(3) Sum-of-the-years-digits method (SYD or SOYD): Applies a declining rate of depreciation against a constant depreciable cost (defined as cost less salvage value).

$$\text{SYD DEPR RATE} = \frac{\text{\# OF YEARS REMAINING AS OF THE BEGINNING OF YEAR}}{\text{SUM OF THE YEARS}}$$

WHERE; SUM OF THE YEARS = n((n+1)/2) = 5((5+1)/2) = 15 = 5+4+3+2+1.

SYD Depreciation Schedule:

YEAR	DEPRECIABLE COST = (COST - SCRAP VALUE)	SYD FRACTION (DEPR. RATE)	DEPRECIATION EXPENSE (INCOME STATEMENT)	COST (BALANCE SHEET)	ACCUMULATED DEPRECIATION AND RETAINED EARNINGS EFFECT (BALANCE SHEET)	NET BOOK VALUE (BALANCE SHEET)
1	$120,000	15-May	$40,000	$125,000	$40,000	$85,000
2	120,000	15-Apr	32,000	125,000	72,000	53,000
3	120,000	15-Mar	24,000	125,000	96,000	29,000
4	120,000	15-Feb	16,000	125,000	112,000	13,000
5	120,000	15-Jan	8,000	125,000	120,000	5,000
TOTAL			$120,000			

(4) Double declining balance method (DDB): Applies a constant rate of depreciation against a declining net book value (defined as cost less accumulated depreciation). ***The DDB method ignores scrap value.***

DDB rate = "Twice the straight line rate"
Straight line rate = 1/useful life = 1/5 = 20%
DDB rate = 2 X 20% = 40%

DDB Depreciation Schedule: (c)

BEGINNING OF YEAR	COST (BALANCE SHEET)	ACCUMULATED DEPRECIATION AND RETAINED EARNINGS EFFECT (BALANCE SHEET)	BEGINNING NET BOOK VALUE (NBV) (BALANCE SHEET)	DDB %	DEPRECIATION EXPENSE (INCOME STATEMENT)
1	$125,000	$ 0	$125,000	40%	$50,000
2	$125,000	50,000	75,000	40%	30,000
3	$125,000	80,000	45,000	40%	18,000
4	$125,000	98,000	27,000	40%	10,800
5	$125,000	108,800	16,200	40%	6,480
(a) 6	$125,000	115,280	(b) 9,720		

Notes:

(a) This is the beginning of year 6 or the end of year 5.

(b) The ending net book value is greater than the planned scrap value of $5,000. There are three choices for financial reporting. First, the $9,720 can be treated as an imputed scrap value without further depreciation. Second, the $9,720 is depreciated over some estimated period of remaining life. Third, the depreciation in year 5 is increased to $11,200, (i.e., add $4,720 to depreciation expense in year 5). Thus, the NBV at the end of year 5 is exactly equal to the original estimated scrap value of $5,000.

(c) Declining balance methods are the only methods to ignore scrap value. As noted in (b) above, ignoring scrap value causes the additional analysis in the last year.

Optimal point to switch from DDB to Straight-line

(Assuming the firm uses DDB for tax purposes and switches to straight line in order to minimize the tax disadvantages of reversal)

END OF YEAR	BEGINNING OF YEAR	DDB REMAINING NBV	DDB DEPRECIATION EXPENSE	MODIFIED DDB OR MODIFIED STRAIGHT LINE CALCULATIONS (ASSUMING NO SCRAP VALUE)
0	1	$125,000	$50,000	$125,000/5 YRS = $25,000
1	2	75,000	30,000	75,000/4 YRS = 18,750
2	3	45,000	18,000	45,000/3 YRS = 15,000
3	**4	27,000	10,800	27,000/2 YRS = 13,500

*** OPTIMAL TIME TO SWITCH TO STRAIGHT LINE: MODIFIED S/L EXCEEDS DDB.*

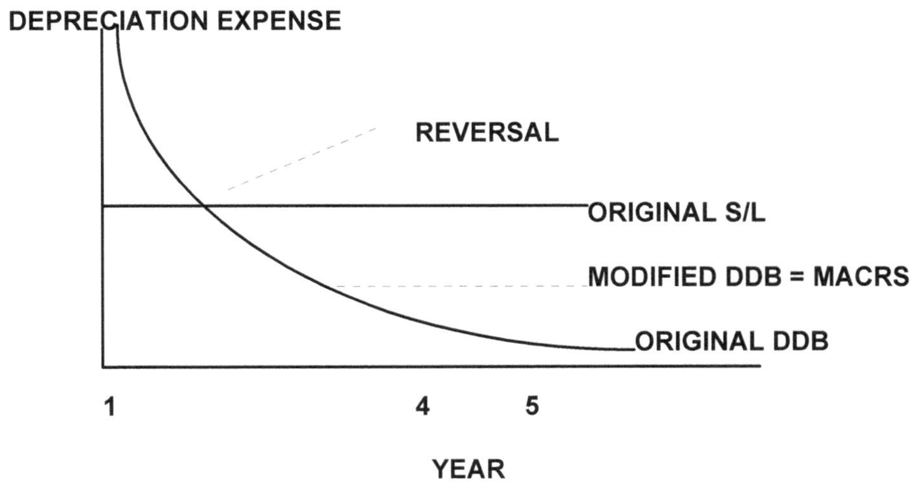

Note: The switch to SL does not prevent reversal but slows down the rate of reversal. The switch also enables the full write off of the asset for tax purposes.

Under the straight-line method, depreciable cost (i.e., cost less estimated scrap value) is divided by the estimated useful life of the asset. In this illustration, the depreciation expense of $24,000 would be charged against income in each of the five years of the asset's life. The end of the asset's life the total in the accumulated depreciation account is $120,000 (i.e., $24,000 x 5 years). Therefore, the net book value is equal to the estimated scrap value of $5,000.

The straight-line method can also be viewed as depreciating a constant depreciable cost at a constant rate. The straight-line rate is computed as one over the estimated useful life. In this case, the straight-line rate is 20% (i.e., 1/5 years). Thus, each year 20% of the $120,000 depreciable cost, or $24,000, is charged against income as depreciation expense.

The following financial modeling worksheet illustrates the effect of the depreciation expense adjustment. The straight-line method will be used for this illustration, but the effects of all other methods will be the same. Of course, the dollar amounts will differ for each method.

FINANCIAL MODELING WORKSHEET

INCOME STATEMENT (FIRST)	
REVENUES:	
EXPENSES:	
Depreciation Expense	(24,000)
NET INCOME OR LOSS (a)	(24,000)

STATEMENT OF CASH FLOWS (THIRD)	
OPERATING ACTIVITIES:	
NET INCOME OR LOSS (a)	(24,000)
Add back: Depreciation Expense	+24,000
INVESTING ACTIVITIES:	
FINANCING ACTIVITIES:	
INCREASE (DECREASE) IN CASH (b)	- 0 -
ADD: BEGINNING CASH BALANCE	
ENDING CASH BALANCE	

BALANCE SHEET (SECOND)			
ASSETS		LIABILITIES	
CURRENT ASSETS		CURRENT LIABILITIES	
CASH (b)	- 0 -		
		NONCURRENT LIABILITIES	
		STOCKHOLDERS'	
NONCURRENT ASSETS		EQUITY	
Plant Assets		CAPITAL STOCK	
Accumulated Depreciation	(24,000)	APIC	
Net book value		RETAINED	
		EARNINGS (a)	(24,000)
		TOTAL	
		LIABILITIES &	
		STOCKHOLDERS'	
TOTAL ASSETS	(24,000)	EQUITY	(24,000)

Under the units-of-production method, depreciable cost is divided by the estimated life in terms of productive output. The result is a rate of depreciation per unit of output. In Exhibit 2.10, the rate of depreciation is $1.20 per unit. For each unit produced, up to 100,000 units, $1.20 will be charged against income. After 100,000 units of production, the asset is fully depreciated and the accumulated depreciation account will equal $120,000. At this point, the net book value is equal to the estimated scrap value of $5,000. Note that under the units-of-output approach, the asset could be fully depreciated in a period greater than or less than the designated five year useful life. Again, useful life and the resulting cost allocation approach are based on units produced and not time.

The first accelerated method illustrated in Exhibit 2.10 is the sum-of-the-years digits method. The-sum-of-the-years digits method applies a declining rate of depreciation against a constant depreciable cost. The-sum-of-the-years digits rate for each year of the asset's life is determined as the ratio of the number of years of useful life remaining at the beginning of the year divided by the sum of the years. The acceleration of the depreciation charge is achieved through the declining sum of-the-years digits fraction. As with the straight-line and the units-of-output methods, the sum-of-the-years digits method depreciates the asset down to its estimated scrap value of $5,000.

The last accelerated depreciation method illustrated is the declining-balance method. Originally developed for income tax purposes, there are a series of declining balance methods based on multiples of the straight-line rate. For example, one and one-half declining balance (i.e., one and one-half times the straight-line rate), and double declining balance (i.e., twice the straight-line rate) are possible uses of the declining balance method. Double declining balance is the most common approach and is illustrated in Exhibit 2.10.

The double declining balance method applies a constant rate of depreciation against a declining net book value. The constant rate of depreciation is computed at twice the straight-line rate. In this case the straight-line rate is 20% so that the double declining-balance rate is 40%. The 40% is then applied against the net book value of the asset. Note that the net book value of the asset is equal to cost less accumulated depreciation. Acceleration is achieved due to the declining net book value over time. Even more significant is the fact that the double declining-balance method is the only depreciation method that does not consider the estimated scrap value.

As a result, at the end of the asset's useful life, the remaining net book value may be greater than or less than the estimated salvage value. In Exhibit 2.10, the remaining net book value is $9,720, which exceeds the planned scrap value of $5,000. When this occurs, the accountant has three alternatives for financial reporting purposes only (and not for tax).

First, the final net book value that results from the double declining-balance method can be maintained as the imputed scrap value. Second, the remaining net book value at the end of the asset's life can be depreciated over some estimated period of remaining life. Finally, the last year's depreciation expense can be "forced" so that the remaining net book value is exactly equal to the original estimated salvage value.

Optimal Point to Switch from Accelerated to Straight Line Depreciation. The last section of Exhibit 2.10 illustrates the determination of the optimal point to switch from accelerated to straight-line depreciation for income tax purposes. In order to determine the optimal switch point, the actual accelerated depreciation (double declining-balance in this case) is compared to a revised or modified straight line. The modified straight-line depreciation is determined by dividing the remaining net book value at the beginning of each year, determined under double declining balance, by the number of years of useful life remaining at the beginning of each year. It is assumed that the firm would not use a scrap value for income tax purposes because a scrap value reduces the amount of the available tax deductions for depreciation.

Based on the computations in Exhibit 2.10, the optimal time to switch is at the beginning of year four. This will result in a modified straight-line depreciation of $13,500 in years four and five. If the double declining-balance method was still employed, only $10,800 and $6,480 would be available for tax deductions in years four and five, respectively. Note that in the early years of the asset's life, there are tax advantages in using double declining balance over straight line. In the later years, reversal takes place causing the use of the accelerated method to be a tax disadvantage when compared to the straight-line method. The switch to straight line does not prevent reversal from taking place, but it slows down the rate of reversal. The switch to straight-line without a scrap value also allows a complete write off of the asset's cost without a residual value. In most cases, firms would elect to switch to straight line at the time it is optimal to do so. In fact, the IRS MACRS tables actually build in an automatic switch to straight line in the last few years of the asset's life.

Estimated Measures of Plant Age. Depreciation expense can result in a significant charge against income, but because depreciation is a noncash expense, it is added back to net income in the reconciliation of accrual basis net income and operating cash flows on the cash flow statement. However, depreciation should not be ignored by the analyst simply because it is a noncash expense. Eventually, equipment will have to be replaced in order to maintain current operating capacity. At the point replacement takes place, there could be a significant cash drain on the firm or it may require additional financing. This information is useful in the projection of future cash flows for input into discounted cash flow models that may be designed to predict the timing of additional financing requirements.

In order to estimate when mandatory replacement of plant and equipment will take place, measures of plant age can be developed. An illustration of estimated measures of plant age for the PAGE Incorporated is presented in Exhibit 2.11.

EXHIBIT 2.11 ANALYTICAL MEASURES OF PLANT AGE ILLUSTRATION

PAGE Incorporated 2012 Annual Report Footnote
(See footnote on subsequent pages):

$$\text{AVERAGE TOTAL LIFE SPAN} = \frac{\text{GROSS PP\&E***}}{\text{CURRENT DEPR. EXPENSE}} = \frac{\$1,572,700}{\$172,900} = \underline{\text{9.1 YRS}}$$

**** NOTE: Since land is not subject to depreciation, it could be excluded from Gross PP&E for purposes of this analysis, if material.*

DISAGGREGATION

$$\text{AVERAGE AGE} = \frac{\text{ACCUMULATED DEPRECIATION}}{\text{CURRENT DEPR. EXPENSE}} = \frac{\$680,533}{\$172,900} = \underline{\text{3.9 Years}}$$

$$\text{AVERAGE REMAINING LIFE} = \frac{\text{NET PP\&E}}{\text{CURRENT DEPR. EXPENSE}} = \frac{\$892,167}{\$172,900} = \underline{\text{5.2 Years}}$$

TOTAL LIFE SPAN AS ABOVE: 3.9 YRS + 5.2 YRS = 9.1 YRS.

At times, these measures are stated in percentage terms. For example, the Net Book Value (NBV) to Gross Book Value (GBV) ratio is presented below:

NBV / GBV = $686,283 / $1,209,770 = 56.7% of useful life remains on average.

When remaining useful life reaches 40% (i.e., 60% of the asset's productive life has expired) an analyst usually assumes that replacement is mandatory.

Applications

(1) Although depreciation is a noncash expense and is added back to income in the determination of cash flows, replacement of plant and equipment will require an actual cash disbursement. Capital investment reduces the projected free cash flows (i.e., free cash flows = cash flows from net income - capital expenditures - investment in working capital). The measure of average remaining life provides the analyst with an estimate of when the full replacement of existing capacity becomes mandatory.

(2) In the comparison of different firms, the capital intensive firm with older facilities (as determined by measures of average plant age) may report higher net income, profit margins and returns on total assets. This upward bias results from lower depreciation charges and lower net book values of property, plant and equipment.

PAGE Incorporated
NOTES TO CONSOLIDATED FINANCIAL STATEMENTS

Property, Plant and Equipment

	December 31,			
		2012		2011
		In thousands)		
Land	$	54,168	$	49,521
Buildings and improvements		382,442		365,106
Other equipment		452,670		368,281
Machinery and equipment		574,727		229,190
Furniture and office equipment		38,793		21,311
Assets Under Capital Leases		69,900		58,487
		1,572,700		1,091,896
Less accumulated depreciation and amortization		(680,533)		(531,081)
	$	892,167	$	560,815

Depreciation and amortization expense related to property, plant, and equipment for fiscal 2012, 2011, and 2009 was $172,900 million, $118,300 million and $144,700 million, respectively.

It should be noted that the measures of plant age utilized in Exhibit 2.11 assume that the straight-line method is used and there is no estimated salvage value. The footnotes to the financial statements should provide information regarding the firm's depreciation policy. If a method other than straight line is used and if a scrap value is included in the firm's computations, these estimated measures become less accurate.

The measure of average remaining life on Exhibit 2.11 provides the analyst with an estimate of when the full replacement of capacity becomes mandatory. In a comparison of different firms, a capital intensive firm with older facilities (as determined by the average age on Exhibit 2.11) may report higher income, profit margins and returns on total assets than a firm with more current acquisitions of plant and equipment. The upward bias for the older firm results from the lower depreciation charges and the reduced net book values of plant assets toward the end of their useful lives. By comparing the average age of plant and equipment of the two firms, the analyst is able to identify the potential bias in the comparison of the firm's financial ratios. Once identified, the analyst can control for that bias when drawing conclusions about the overall financial condition and operating strength of the two firms.

CAPITALIZATION OF INTEREST

A critical issue in accounting for certain acquisitions of plant assets is the determination of the proper treatment of the interest incurred on financing the plant asset acquisition or construction. Specifically, the accountant must determine if the interest on financing the acquisition is a cost of acquisition or construction or a pure finance charge. If the interest incurred is considered a cost of acquisition or construction it should be capitalized as part of the cost of the asset. On the other hand, if the interest incurred is considered a finance charge it should be expensed immediately on the current income statement.

FASB Statement No. 34, "Capitalization of Interest Cost" [9], requires the capitalization of "material" interest charges incurred in the acquisition or construction of certain assets. The interest capitalized is known as "avoidable interest." Avoidable interest is an opportunity cost concept because it represents the interest that could have been avoided if the plant asset had not been acquired or constructed.

The FASB concluded that capitalization of interest on certain assets was necessary in order to properly value the acquisition cost of the asset and to properly match costs with revenues by allocating the interest cost over the asset's productive life through higher depreciation charges. The provisions of SFAS 34 reinforce the balance sheet and income statement objectives of accounting for assets.

There are four major considerations in the application of the interest capitalization requirements:

1. The assets that qualify for interest capitalization
2. The expenditures on which interest should be computed
3. The rate of interest to be used in the computations
4. The period of capitalization

Qualifying Assets. According to SFAS 34 material, interest charges relating to the following projects should be capitalized:

- Assets constructed or otherwise produced for the firm's own use including assets constructed or produced for the enterprise by others for which deposits or progress payments have been made (e.g., a self-constructed power plant by a public utility). This category does not include the manufacture of inventory or other routine production.
- Assets intended for sale or lease that are constructed or otherwise produced as discrete projects (e.g., office buildings, land purchased for future development).
- Qualifying asset investments (equity, loans and advances) accounted for by the equity method while the investee has activities in progress necessary to commence its planned principal operations provided that the investee's activities include the use of funds to

9. FASB ASC 835 [Predecessor literature: "Capitalization of Interest Cost," *Statement of Financial Accounting Standards No. 34* (Norwalk, Conn.: FASB 1979)].

acquire qualifying assets for its operations.

Of course, interest accrued after the planned operations begin cannot be capitalized. In addition, interest cannot be capitalized on assets that are ready for intended use, even if held idle. It should be noted that the cost of equity or use of internal funds is not considered.

Expenditures on Which Interest Should be Computed. If the assets qualify for capitalization, interest should be computed on the "weighted average accumulated expenditures" for the year or the accounting period for which interest capitalization is required. The average accumulated expenditure is a measure of the amount of "outstanding debt" associated with the project, either directly or indirectly, for which the firm incurs finance charges. From the opportunity cost standpoint, debt could have been avoided or retired if the average expenditures for the period were not made.

The following example will illustrate the concept of the weighed average accumulated expenditure.

> ***EXAMPLE:*** Assume that a company borrows \$1,000,000 at 8% interest on October 1 of the current year. Interest is to be determined for the current year, but the debt is only outstanding for three months. Therefore, interest for the current year can be computed by weighting either the interest rate or the loan balance. If the interest rate is weighted, interest is computed as follows: 8% x 3/12 = 2% x \$1,000,000 = \$20,000. Alternatively, the loan balance can be weighted: \$1,000,000 x 3/12 = \$250,000 x 8% = \$20,000.

In interest capitalization, the expenditure for the year is weighted and serves as a proxy for the weighted average loan balance (this is the \$250,000 is the above example).

There are two approaches used to determine the average accumulated expenditure for interest capitalization. The following data will be used to illustrate these approaches.

> ***EXAMPLE:*** Assume a firm is constructing its own plant. During the first year of construction, the firm incurred expenditures equal to \$3,000,000. The \$3,000,000 was paid in four equal installments of \$750,000 at the end of each quarter. There are two ways to determine the weighted average accumulated expenditure:

(a) Weight each expenditure by the number of months "outstanding"

MARCH 31	**\$750,000 x 9/12**	**\$ 562,500**
JUNE 30	**\$750,000 x 6/12**	**375,000**
SEPT. 30	**\$750,000 x 3/12**	**187,500**
DEC. 31	**\$750,000 x 0/12**	**0**
TOTALS	**\$3,000,000 x 12/12**	**\$1,125,000**

(b) If expenditures are made of a uniform basis throughout the year, the weighted average accumulated expenditure can be estimated by a simple averaging process:

(Ending Balance in CIP - Beginning Balance in CIP) / 2

In this case we would have:

($3,000,000 - 0) / 2 = $1,500,000

In this case the average expenditure would be $1,500,000 (i.e., [$3,000,000 - 0] / 2), and avoidable interest would be determined on this amount.

The Rate of Interest. In determining the rate of interest to use for capitalization, a distinction is usually made between "direct debt" and "indirect debt." Direct debt is debt incurred specifically to finance the project (e.g., a state bond issue is passed to finance construction of a highway extension). If the weighted average accumulated expenditure for the accounting period is less than or equal to the face amount of the direct debt, then the actual effective rate of interest on the direct debt is multiplied against the weighted average accumulated expenditure for the period to determine the amount of interest to capitalize.

However, if the weighted average accumulated expenditure exceeds the outstanding balance of the direct debt, the accountant assumes that by undertaking the project, the firm foregoes the opportunity to liquidate all other outstanding debt. This other debt is the so-called indirect debt. Since this is only an assumption, since it may not be practical for the accountant to determine the order in which the indirect debt would have been liquidated. As a result, a weighted average interest rate for the all indirect debt is calculated and is applied against the excess of the weighted average accumulated expenditure over the amount of direct debt outstanding.

If the contractor only invoices one project, many firms have been using a single weighted average rate of interest determined by averaging the rates of interest on the direct debt and all of the indirect debt. This single average rate of interest is multiplied by the average accumulated expenditure for the period in order to determine the amount of interest to be capitalized.

Period of Interest Capitalization. According to SFAS 34, interest is to be capitalized from the time of the initial expenditure up to the time the asset is ready for its intended use. Therefore, if construction is completed but the asset is idle (e.g., protests blocking the operation of a nuclear power plant), interest incurred after the completion of the project must be charged to expense and cannot be capitalized.

Other Issues. Other requirements relating to interest capitalization include the following issues.

If direct debt is obtained but remains idle until construction begins, or during the construction period, the debt proceeds may be invested in interest earning assets on a temporary basis. According to FASB Technical Bulletin No. 81-5, any interest earned cannot be offset against the amount of interest capitalized and the amount of interest expensed. That is, the construction and financing decision must be accounted for separately from any subsequent investment decisions.

Due to the accountant's assumptions and the averaging procedures used in the SFAS 34 computations, it is possible that there could be an amount of interest to be capitalized in excess of the actual debt service for the period. This is not permitted. The maximum amount of interest to be capitalized to the actual interest incurred during the accounting period.

Capitalized interest is added to the cost of construction or production and is charged to a noncurrent asset account on the balance sheet, Construction in Progress. When construction is completed and the asset is ready for its intended use, it is reclassified out of construction in progress and into plant assets. The plant asset account is now subject to depreciation. The depreciation charges will increase by including a systematic write-down of previously capitalized interest. As a result, previously capitalized interest is ultimately charged against income via depreciation expense over the useful life of the asset.

When interest is capitalized as an asset on the balance sheet, the amount of interest expense charged against income on the income statement is not the total debt service for the period. However, SFAS 34, requires that the firm must disclose the amount of interest capitalized for the year, either in the financial statements or in the related footnotes. By adding the interest capitalized per the footnote to the interest expense charged on the income statement, the analyst can determine the total actual interest incurred for the year. This information is required in the computation of financial statistics such as the times-interest-earned ratio and other fixed charge coverage ratios. If the analyst only uses the interest expense reported on the income statement, these ratios and other statistics could be significantly misstated. In addition, capitalized interest overstates the investment in capital assets for the year. The actual amount of capital expenditures can be determined by deducting capitalized interest from the reported amount invested in plant assets.

The following example provides an illustration of many of the issues discussed above:

Illustration: Capitalization of Interest

Data: Assume a firm is constructing its own plant. The total expenditures of the first year amounted to $3,000,000. It is assumed that four equal payments are made to the contractor each quarter. Therefore, the average accumulated expenditure is equal to $1,500,000 ([$3,000,000 - 0] / 2).

The firm had the following debt structure:

10% Note	Directly related to the project	$1,000,000
12% Note	Not directly related to the project	200,000
9% Bonds	Not directly related to the project	1,000,000
	Totals	**$2,200,000**

(Assume that all debt is outstanding at the beginning of the year).

Required: Determine the amount of interest to be capitalized for the year.

Find the weighted average rate of interest on indirect debt: Because the average accumulated expenditure of $1,500,000 exceeds the direct debt of $1,000,000 by $500,000 (i.e., $1,500,000 – 1,000,000), we assume that the $500,000 excess expenditure is financed by indirect debt. Therefore, we must compute the weighted average interest rate on indirect debt.

The weighted average interest rate on indirect debt is computed in the following table:

PRINCIPAL	***RATE***	***INTEREST***	WEIGHTED AVERAGE RATE
$ 200,000	12%	(a) $24,000	
1,000,000	9%	(b) 90,000	
$1,200,000		$114,000	$114,000/$1,200,000 = **9 1/2%**

(b) Total capitalized interest:

DIRECT DEBT	**$1,000,000 X 10% =**	**(c) $100,000**
INDIRECT DEBT	**$500,000 X 9 1/2% =**	**47,500**
AVOIDABLE INTEREST TO BE CAPITALIZED		**$147,500**

Note: The maximum interest that can be capitalized is equal to the actual interest for the year [(a) + (b) + (c) = $214,000].

Although actual interest for the year is $214,000, interest expense reported on the income statement is only equal to $66,500:

INTEREST EXPENSE	**=**	**TOTAL INTEREST PAID-INTEREST CAPITALIZED**
$66,500	**=**	**$214,000 - 147,500**

A financial modeling worksheet for interest capitalization is presented below.

FINANCIAL MODELING WORKSHEET (CAPITALIZED INTEREST)

INCOME STATEMENT (FIRST)	
REVENUES:	
EXPENSES: Interest Expense	*(66.5)*
NET INCOME OR LOSS (a)	*(66.5)*

STATEMENT OF CASH FLOWS (THIRD)	
OPERATING ACTIVITIES:	
NET INCOME OR LOSS (a)	*(66.5)*
INVESTING ACTIVITIES:	
Increase in CIP (CAPEX)	*(147.5)*
FINANCING ACTIVITIES:	
INCREASE (DECREASE) IN CASH (b)	*(214)*
ADD: BEGINNING CASH BALANCE	
ENDING CASH BALANCE	

BALANCE SHEET (SECOND)			
ASSETS		*LIABILITIES*	
CURRENT ASSETS		*CURRENT LIABILITIES*	
CASH (b)	*(214)*		
		NONCURRENT LIABILITIES	
		STOCKHOLDERS' EQUITY	
NONCURRENT ASSETS			
CIP	*+147.5*	*CAPITAL STOCK*	
		APIC	
		RETAINED EARNINGS (a)	*(66.5)*
TOTAL ASSETS	*(66.5)*	*TOTAL LIABILITIES & STOCKHOLDERS' EQUITY*	*(66.5)*

***NOTE:* Capitalization of interest understates interest expense and overstates capital expenditures or CAPEX. Analytical restatements must be made to correct both interest expense and CAPEX to ensure comparability with other firms without debt in their capital structures.**

There are two key issues for financial analysis:

1. When computing the Interest Coverage (Times Interest Earned) Ratio, an analyst must be careful to examine all financial statement and footnote information to identify the interest capitalized for the period. Interest expense for the period is understated on the income statement whenever significant interest is capitalized.
2. When interest is capitalized, capital expenditure (CAPEX) on the cash flow statement is overstated and not comparable to a firm without debt in its capital structure. Here the capitalized interest must be added back to cash flows from investing activities (i.e., reduce the cash outflow for CAPEX).

An application using KeelyCom, Inc. (assuming In-process R&D is a recurring item), is presented below. The financial information needed for this application is presented in Exhibit 2.12.

EXHIBIT 2.12 SAMPLE FOOTNOTE DISCLOSURES FOR KEELYCOM, INC. AS REQUIRED BY FASB STATEMENT NO. 34

Note 8. Property, Plant and Equipment

At the end of 2012 and 2011, property, plant and equipment at cost and accumulated depreciation were:

(Dollars in Millions)

	2012	**2011**
Land and land improvements	$713	$566.4
Buildings and building equipment	6,263	5,237
Machinery and equipment	11,470	9,443
Construction in progress	2,017	1,931
	$20,462	$17,177
Less accumulated depreciation	8,647	6,725
	$11,815	$10,452

The company capitalizes interest expense as part of the cost of construction of facilities and equipment. Interest expense capitalized in 2012, 2011 and 2010 was $130 million, $118 million and $114 million, respectively.

Depreciation expense, including the amortization of capitalized interest in 2012, 2011 and 2009 was $1.7 billion, $1.6 billion and $1.3 billion, respectively.

Upon retirement or other disposal of fixed assets, the cost and related amount of accumulated depreciation or amortization are eliminated from the asset and accumulated depreciation accounts, respectively. The difference, if any, between the net asset value and the proceeds is adjusted to earnings.

Partial Consolidated Statements of Earnings – KeelyCom, Inc.

(Dollars in Millions Except Per Share Figures) (Note 1)

	2012	2011	2010
Sales to customers	$50,234	$43,558	$38,780
Cost of products sold	14,611	12,536	11,497
Gross profit	$35,623	$31,021	$27,283
Selling, marketing and administrative expenses	16,957	14,659	13,512
Research expense	5,621	4,748	4,309

Purchased in-process research and development (Note 17)	1101.6	226.8	126
Interest income	-212.4	-307.2	-547.2
Interest expense, net of portion capitalized (Note 3)	248.4	192	183.6
Other (income) expense, net	-462	352.8	222
	$23,254	$19,872	$17,806
Earnings before provision for taxes on income	$12,370	$11,149	$9,478

Partial Consolidated Statements of Cash Flows – KeelyCom, Inc.

(Dollars in Millions)

	2012	2011	2010
Cash flows from investing activities			
Additions to property, plant and equipment	(2,714)	(2,519)	(2,077)
Proceeds from the disposal of assets	402	187.2	195.6
Acquisition of businesses, net of cash acquired (Note 17)	(3,374)	(573.6)	(270)
Purchases of investments	(9,108)	(8,308)	(9,826)
Sales of investments	9,674	8,824	7,160
Other	(310.8)	(247.2)	(94.8)
Net cash used by investing activities	(5,431)	(2,636)	(4,912)
Supplemental cash flow data			
Cash paid during the year for:			
Interest	$247	169.2	222
Income taxes	3,775	2,407	2,508

The earnings before interest and taxes or EBIT for KeelyCom, Inc. are:

***EBIT* = $12,370 -212.4 + 248.4 – 462 = $11,944**

When computing the Interest Coverage (Times Interest Earned) Ratio, an analyst must be careful to examine all footnote information to identify the interest capitalized for the period. Interest expense for the period is understated on the income statement whenever significant interest is capitalized.

The Interest Coverage Ratio indicates the number of times EBIT exceeds interest expense and provides a measure of safety regarding the ability of a company to repay current debt service and the capacity to take on additional debt. This ratio is computed as follows:

$$\text{Times Interest Earned} = \frac{\text{EBIT}}{\text{Interest Expense}}$$

If an analyst simply computes this ratio from the income statement, the ratio would appear as follows:

$$\text{Times Interest Earned} = \frac{\$11{,}944}{\$248.4} = \underline{\textit{48.1 Times}}$$

However, even if the accountant only expenses \$248.4 on the income statement, the actual interest due and payable is \$378.4. That is, the \$130 capitalized interest from footnote 8, must be added to the \$248.4 interest expense deducted on the income statement in the denominator of the ratio. As a result, the correct times interest earned ratio for 2003 is:

$$\text{Times Interest Earned} = \frac{\$11{,}944}{\$378.4} = \underline{\textit{31.6 Times}}$$

Failure to take into account the total debt service can severely overstate the coverage ratio (approximately 34% in this case).

Capitalized interest is included the company's plant asset acquisitions (CAPEX) reported in investing activities on the accountant's cash flow statement. An analyst generally corrects this is his or her cash flow computations. For example, KeelyCom reported capital expenditures of \$2,714 on its 2012 cash flow statement. Included in capital expenditures was \$130 of capitalized interest reported in Footnote 8. From an analyst's perspective, its capital expenditures are \$2,584 (i.e., \$2,714 – 130).

Other Noncurrent Assets: Deferred Charges

Prepaid expenses are advance payments for goods and services to be received in the future (e.g., prepaid rent, prepaid insurance). Generally, prepaid expenses are capitalized as current assets on the balance sheet until expired. When expired, usually with the passage of time, they are charged to expense on the income statement. Analysts must consider the fact that prepaid expenses are not highly liquid assets because, even if classified as current, they are incapable of satisfying creditor claims or being converted into cash.

Deferred charges are essentially long-term prepaid expenses. Specifically, they are charges already incurred but are capitalized as assets. The charge against income is deferred to future periods when management expects to receive the benefits from these current period expenditures. This is justified by the matching principle. For example, if a firm pays for a significant amount of advance rentals at the end of an accounting period, management will defer the cost as a long-term prepaid asset and amortize it over the lease term so as to match the cost against the revenue generated from the use of the rented space.

As noted in the discussion of the capitalization-expense alternative for the cost of a plant asset, management has a great deal of discretion in determining which costs should be expensed and which costs should be capitalized. In addition, there is supporting theoretical justification for either alternative treatment. Therefore, care must be taken in the analysis of deferred expenses because many of these long-term "assets" may actually have no future economic value to the firm and may be nothing more than expenses erroneously capitalized as assets. Not only does this misclassification overstate asset value, none of which is available for collateral or for generating future income and cash flow, it also overstates income and earnings per common share.

An analyst must also consider the use of balance sheet reserves. Balance sheet reserves include:

1. Valuation Allowance Accounts used to reduce assets to net value:
   i. Receivables and loans (i.e., loan loss reserves)
   ii. Roncurrent assets (plant assets and intangibles)
   iii. Inventory obsolescence
   iv. Marketable securities and derivatives carried at fair value (mark to market accounting)
   v. Deferred tax assets
2. Deferred credit accounts, which include advance collections and other deferred revenues
3. Reserves for future expenditures (e.g., reserves for repairs and maintenance, major overhauls, etc.). Recent FASB standards limit the use of these types of reserves.

There are several analytical issues to consider when balance sheet reserves are analyzed:

- Are deferred credits, liabilities and other balance sheet reserves netted against "Other Assets" on the balance sheet? These credit balance accounts could include actual liabilities such as obligations for severance packages or legal settlements. These unpaid obligations have future cash flow implications, but may not be disclosed separately as liabilities on the balance sheet.
- Advance collections, including insurance premiums and subscriptions, are reported as deferred credits and are possibly netted against other assets (as above). However, in these cases cash is collected but future goods and services have to be provided. A problem arises if the cash is used before the goods and services are due to be delivered. This could erode the firm's ability to operate in the future without additional financing.
- Firms can increase contra accounts, such as the reserve for inventory obsolescence, to improve financial ratios (e.g., days inventory). In this case, the one time write off of inventory is discounted by the analyst, but the lower inventory balance improves turnover, liquidity and debt capacity implications. Here, an analyst must adjust for the bias in the financial ratios.

Accounting for Asset Impairments

According to FASB Statement No. 144, "Accounting for Impairment or Disposal of Long-Lived Assets,"[10] the process to determine an impairment loss includes three steps. Review events for possible impairment. These events include a significant decrease in the market value of the long-lived asset, a change in how the firm utilizes the asset or a change in the business climate that could affect the asset's value (e.g., a decrease in demand for the product like VHS tapes). If events suggest impairment, then determine if the sum of the undiscounted cash flows from the use and disposal of the asset is less than its carrying amount, (recoverability test) if so, then the loss is the amount by which the carrying amount of the asset is greater than the fair value of the asset (***fair market value test***). The fair market value of the long-lived asset is the amount at which the asset could be purchased or sold for in a current transaction between willing parties. The asset's fair market value can be determined in several ways. Quoted prices in active markets are the best evidence of fair value. Because

10. FASB ASC 360 [Predecessor literature: "Accounting for the Impairment or Disposal of Long-Lived Assets," *Statement of Financial Accounting Standards No. 144* (Norwalk, Conn.: FASB 2001)].

market prices are not always available, accountants should base fair-value estimates on the best information available or use valuation techniques such as ***market comparables, review of recent transactions and discounted cash flow valuation. This is consistent with applying the FASB 157 hierarchy.***

Cash flows should be determined based on the FASB's concepts of an ***Asset Group and a Disposal Group.***

Assets Held for Use must utilize the Asset Group Concept. The Asset Group Concept is defined as the lowest level of the firm where cash flows are substantially independent of the cash flows of other firm assets and liabilities. Here is some expamples of an ***asset group***:

- The entire company
- An operating segment as defined by FASB Statement No. 131
- A reporting unit as defined by FASB Statement No. 142
- A business
- A part of a business (e.g., a division)

In this case, the impairment write-down results in a reduced carrying value, an amount that is now considered the long-lived asset or asset group's new cost basis. No subsequent write-up is allowed for recoveries.

Assets Held for Sale use the concept of the Disposal Group. These are assets to be disposed of together, as a group, in a single transaction and includes the liabilities to be transferred in the transaction. If an impaired asset is expected to be disposed of, it should be recorded at the lower of cost or net realizable value, and it is not depreciated. When an impaired asset is held for disposal, it can be written up or down as long as the write-up is never greater than the carrying amount of asset at the time of the original impairment.

In either case, the loss on asset impairment is not an extraordinary item, but is classified as part of income from continuing operations before tax. The impairment loss has the same effect as the write down of obsolete inventory using the lower of cost of market rules.

The above are the ***General Impairment Standards.*** There are also ***Specific Industry Impairment Standards*** which would apply to oil and gas deposits and indefinite life intangibles such as goodwill, renewable broadcast rights, and other intangible assets with indefinite useful lives.

In the case of indefinite life intangibles, the ***recoverably test would not apply*** because this test would always result in no possible impairment with indefinite undiscounted future cash flows. Where the recoverability test does not apply, you would simply compare cost to fair value to determine if a write down is necessary.

The specific industry impairment standards will be discussed at appropriate points throughout the text.

INTANGIBLE ASSETS

Introduction

Intangible assets are defined as assets without physical substance but have economic value because of the rights they confer upon the holder. Intangible assets cannot be recorded unless acquired in an external transaction. According to the FASB's Statement of Financial

Accounting Standards No. 142, "Goodwill and Other Intangible Assets,"[11] there are two classes of intangible assets:

1. Intangible Assets Subject to Amortization. These intangibles are said to be specifically identifiable, separable from goodwill and have finite (or definite) and reasonably determinable useful lives. This class of intangible assets includes:

- Patents, copyrights, leaseholds and leasehold improvements, customer lists, covenants not to compete and franchises.

The useful life of intangible assets subject to amortization can be determined by factors such as: legal, regulatory or contractual provisions, the expected period of economic benefit of the asset, and the effects of obsolescence, demand or technological advances. The useful life may be known or estimated. The useful life is typically the shorter of the economic life or legal life, with a suggested maximum of 20 years. The 20 year maximum life can be avoided if future cash flows from use of the intangible are expected beyond 20 years. The method of amortization should be based on the pattern of expected revenue realization. If that pattern cannot be reasonably determined, the straight-line method of amortization should be used. A residual value may be employed in the amortization computation. Impairment losses should be recognized in accordance with SFAS No. 144: that is, employing the recoverability and fair value tests.

2. Intangible Assets Not Subject to Amortization. This class of intangible assets includes:

- Trademarks, trade names, and renewable broadcast licenses and goodwill.

These intangibles have ***indefinite (not infinite) useful lives***. Until a finite life is determinable, this class of intangible assets in ***not subject to amortization.*** These assets are subject to impairment using only the fair value test. The recoverability test would never be met as indefinite future cash flows will always exceed cost or carrying value of the intangible asset. Goodwill also has an indefinite life and employs a specific and more complex impairment test which will be discuss in the chapter covering merger and acquisition accounting.

Note also, that it is sometimes said that these intangibles are ***not specifically identifiable*** or their lives are tied to the existence of the entity or reporting unit to which they relate. The most significant intangible asset ***not subject to amortization*** is ***goodwill***. However, goodwill must be ***tested for impairment annually*** or whenever conditions indicate a decline in value. ***Goodwill*** is the excess cost over the fair value of the net assets acquired in merger and acquisition transactions. Goodwill has an indefinite life and is tied to the continued existence of the entity. As a result, goodwill cannot be recorded unless the entity is acquired in a business combination.

Goodwill Illustration. For example, assume an acquire (the Buy Company) pays $140,000 for a 100% ownership of a firm (the Sell Company) with net assets at book value (i.e., historical cost) of $80,000 (Total Assets = $100,000 and Total Liabilities = $20,000) and undervalued assets equal to $40,000. So, the fair value of the net assets acquired is equal to $120,000 (i.e., $80,000 at book value plus $40,000 upward adjustment to fair value). In this case, goodwill is computed as follows:

11. FASB ASC 350 [Predecessor literature: "Goodwill and Other Intangible Assets," *Statement of Financial Accounting Standards No. 142* (Norwalk, Conn.: FASB 2001)].

CALCULATION OF GOODWILL	
Purchase Price (Cost or Total Consideration Paid)	$ 140,000
Book Value (Historical Cost) of the Net Assets Acquired	(80,000)
Excess Cost Over Book.	$ 60,000
Excess Specifically Identified With Undervalued Assets (Write-up of Net Assets to Fair Market Value)	(40,000)
Unidentified Excess is Allocated to Goodwill (Excess Purchase Cost Over the Fair Market Value of Net Assets Acquired) ($140,000 – 120,000)	$ 20,000

Note that an entity could expend economic resources to develop, maintain and restore such intangible assets, (e.g., quality control, expenditures on training programs, research and development, etc.), but these expenditures are not recorded as assets. The economic value of the unrecorded asset can only be recognized if the entity is purchased in an objectively determined transaction (e.g., a merger or acquisition).

SPECIAL CASES: RESEARCH AND DEVELOPMENT COSTS AND COMPUTER SOFTWARE COSTS

Research and Development Costs (R&D). According to paragraph 12 of FASB Statement of Financial Accounting Standards No. 2, "Accounting for Research and Development Costs,"[12] "all R&D costs must be expensed as incurred," unless reimbursed under contract. If to be reimbursed, the R&D costs would be capitalized as a receivable. In addition, R&D equipment and patents purchased from outside research firms can be capitalized if they have alternative future use. SFAS 2, paragraph 13, also requires the disclosure of the level of R&D expenditures in the financial statements.

Prior to SFAS 2, R&D costs were capitalized as an intangible asset under the theory that these costs represented future economic benefit to the firm when a patented product was developed. For the most part, this theoretical justification is valid. However, accountants found it difficult to determine the asset value related to the R&D costs in practice. Specifically, it was difficult to estimate which R&D costs were going to result in successful products and which costs would become worthless. Due to the insurmountable problems involved in assessing potential marketability and value of these expenditures, accountants adopted a conservative position in that they decided to understate asset value and income (i.e., all R&D expenditures were assumed to be fully expired without any economic benefit) rather than overstate assets and income (i.e., by capitalizing R&D costs as an intangible asset). With expensing all R&D as incurred, the costs included in a patent account are now minimal (e.g., legal costs and registration fees). A patent can only include R&D costs if the reporting entity purchases the research leading to the patent from an outside research firm.

The fact that all R&D costs are expensed immediately is a result of a pragmatic solution by the FASB and does not literally imply that these expenditures have no future service potential. For certain industries, R&D is probably one of the most important investments made by the firm. This is precisely one of the reasons why SFAS 2 requires the disclosure of the firm's R&D activity. Sample disclosures of R&D activity are presented in Exhibit 2.13.

12. FASB ASC 730 [Predecessor literature: "Accounting for Research and Development Costs," *Statement of Financial Accounting Standards No. 2* (Norwalk, Conn.: FASB 1974)].

EXHIBIT 2.13: RESEARCH AND DEVELOPMENT DISCLOSURES FOR HIXON SYSTEMS, CO.

Sample Disclosures: Hixon Systems, Co. 2012 Annual Report

Research and Development:

Research and development expenses are expensed as incurred. Up front and milestone payments made to third parties in connection with research and development collaborations are expensed as incurred up to the point of regulatory approval. Payments made to third parties subsequent to regulatory approval are capitalized and amortized over the remaining useful life of the related product. Amounts capitalized for such payments are included in other intangibles, net of accumulated amortization.

Consolidated Statements of Earnings – Hixon Systems, Co. and Subsidiaries

(Dollars in Millions Except Per Share Figures)

	2012	2011	2010
Sales to customers	$50,234	$43,558	$38,780
Cost of products sold	14,611	12,536	11,497
Gross profit	35,623	31,021	27,283
Selling, marketing and administrative expenses	***16,957***	***14,659***	***13,512***
Research expense	***5,621***	***4,748***	***4,309***
Purchased in-process research and development	1101.6	226.8	126
Interest income	(212.4)	(307.2)	(547.2)
Interest expense, net of portion capitalized)	248.4	192	183.6
Other (income) expense, net	(462)	352.8	222
	23,254	19,872	17,806
Earnings before provision for taxes on income	12,370	11,149	9,478
Provision for taxes on income	$3,733	$3,233	$2,676
Net earnings	$8,636	$7,916	$6,802
Basic net earnings per share	$2.90	$2.64	$2.244
Diluted net earnings per share	$2.88	$2.592	$2.208

The disclosure of R&D activity can assist the analyst in estimating the value of the unrecorded asset related to a firm's research activity. This estimation cannot be made in the case of a firm's other significant unrecorded asset, goodwill. If an analyst believes that R&D is a significant investment for the firm, the disclosure of its R&D activity can be used to restate the financial statements on a proforma basis, under the assumption that the firm capitalizes R&D costs and amortizes these costs over the expected period of benefit.

After the issuance of SFAS 2, many firms attempted to circumvent the requirement to expense R&D as incurred by creating a limited partnership to conduct research for the parent or related company. Under the limited partnership treatment, the parent would treat the R&D as purchased and capitalize it as an asset, possibly in the patent account. The limited partnership would have its R&D reimbursed so that according to SFAS 2, it could be capitalized as a receivable from the parent. Under this scenario, neither party to the transaction would recognize the R&D expense as required by SFAS 2.

To resolve this problem, the FASB issued Statement No. 68, "Research and Development Arrangements,"[13] in 1982. According to SFAS 68 and the SEC, these arrangements are in substance lending agreements in which the parent has borrowed funds from the limited partnership and is using this financing to cover its R&D costs, which must be charged to expense. In general, the accountant must expense the R&D on the books of the entity that received the primary benefit from the research activity. Normally, the parent company would be required to charge income for the R&D expenditures and record the liability to the limited partnership. The limited partnership would record the receivable from the parent for reimbursement of the cash expended on its R&D activities.

Research Costs and Patents. As noted above, unless a firm purchases research from another entity in an objectively determined transaction, the amounts capitalized in the patent account on the balance sheet will be minimal. The patent account will normally only consist of registration fees and the legal costs involved with the successful defense of the patent.

Computer Software Costs. In recent years, questions have been raised regarding the nature of computer software costs incurred by firms that sell or lease software to outside entities. Specifically, it was uncertain if computer software costs were R&D, an intangible asset or a cost of inventory.

The nature of computer software costs was clearly defined by the FASB in Statement No. 86, "Accounting for the Costs of Computer Software to be Sold, Leased, or Otherwise Marketed."[14] According to SFAS 86, computer software costs for firms that develop software for external use are incurred in three distinct stages. At each stage, a different accounting treatment is required.

The three stages involved in the software development process are presented below:

1. Computer software costs expensed as research and development. According to SFAS 86, all costs incurred to establish the software's "technological feasibility" are classified as R&D and therefore must be expensed as incurred. These costs are considered necessary to determine the firm's ability to produce the software according to specification. This category of computer software costs would include the costs of planning, designing, coding and testing.

2. Computer software costs capitalized as an intangible asset. According to SFAS 86, after the technological feasibility of the software has been established, the remainder of the costs needed to generate product masters are to be capitalized as an intangible asset, "computer software production costs." The term product masters includes the completed versions of the software, documentation and training materials.

3. Computer software costs included in inventory. The costs incurred to duplicate and package the software, the documentation and the training materials are to be capitalized as part of the cost of inventory according to SFAS 86.

It should be noted that if computer software is purchased and it has alternative future uses, it may also be capitalized. Without alternative future use, the cost of purchased soft-

13. FASB ASC 730 [Predecessor literature: "Research and Development Arrangements," *Statement of Financial Accounting Standards No. 68* (Norwalk, Conn.: FASB 1982)].

14. FASB ASC 985 [Predecessor literature: "Accounting for the Costs of Computer Software to be Sold, Leased, or Otherwise Marketed," *Statement of Financial Accounting Standards No. 86* (Norwalk, Conn.: FASB 1985)].

ware must be expensed as incurred. The alternative future use test should also be applied to the acquisition of software that will be integrated with a product or process in which the R&D phase is not complete.

For those computer software costs capitalized as an intangible asset, SFAS 86, requires that a firm amortize these costs by using the greater of:

- The ratio of current gross revenues to the total current and expected future gross revenues (i.e., the percent of revenue approach), or
- The straight-line method over the remaining useful life of the asset.

SFAS 86 adopted a conservative approach in that all costs preceding the establishment of technological feasibility must be expensed as incurred. In addition, the Board expressed great concern over the valuation of the capitalized software costs presented in the balance sheet. As a result, SFAS 86, requires that the capitalized costs be carried at the lower of the net unamortized cost at year end or net realizable value. Although not specified in SFAS 86, net realizable value is usually defined as expected revenues less expected costs of disposal. If cost (i.e., the net unamortized cost of the intangible) exceeds net realizable value, the intangible asset must be written down to net realizable value without subsequent recovery. Of course, the costs included in inventory would be carried at either LIFO, FIFO or average cost, and would be subject to the LCM test for obsolescence discussed earlier in this text.

SFAS 86 requires a separate disclosure of a firm's software development activity. The disclosure should include the balance of the unamortized computer software costs included in each balance sheet presented, and the total amount charged to expense in each income statement presented for the amounts amortized and the amounts written down to net realizable value. The SFAS 2 disclosure requirements also apply to those computer software costs expensed as R&D.

Finally, SFAS 86 requires that the costs of improvement, maintenance and customer support should be charged to expense at the point at which the related revenue is recognized or when those costs are incurred, whichever comes first.

Internal Software Costs. In 1998, the AICPA issued a Statement of Position (SOP) dealing with internal software costs to provide consistent treatment for software development costs incurred on internally developed software. According to AICPA SOP 98-1, "Internal Software Costs,"[15] computer software costs incurred for internal use are capitalized after the "preliminary project stage" is reached. The costs of software (systems and programs) developed for internal use, and incurred prior to the "preliminary project stage" are expensed in the form of salary and supplies expense.

Sample disclosures of software costs and other intangible assets for Winter Corp. are presented in Exhibit 2.14.

15. FASB ASC 350 [Predecessor literature: "Accounting for the Costs of Computer Software Developed or Obtained for Internal Use," *Statement of Position 98-1* (New York: AICPA, 1998)].

EXHIBIT 2.14: CAPITALIZED SOFTWARE DEVELOPMENT COSTS

Sample Disclosures: Winter Corp. 2012 Annual Report

Other Assets (Partial Footnote)

a. Capitalized Software Development—In accordance with Statement of Financial Accounting Standards No. 86, "Accounting for the Costs of Computer Software to be Sold, Leased, or Otherwise Marketed," costs incurred in the research and development of new software products and enhancements to existing software products are expensed as incurred until technological feasibility has been established. After technological feasibility is established, any additional software development costs are capitalized and included in Other Assets. Software development costs are amortized using the straight-line method over the remaining estimated economic life of the product, not to exceed 5 years.

b. Internal Use Capitalized Computer Software Costs—We capitalize costs incurred to develop internal use computer software during the application development stage, in accordance with the AICPA Statement of Position 98-1, "Accounting for the Costs of Computer Software Developed or Obtained for Internal Use." Internal use computer software costs are amortized on a straight line basis over the remaining estimated economic life of the software, not to exceed 5 years. Costs become amortizable as functionality of the computer software is achieved.

c. Purchased Technology—We capitalize payments for purchased technology when it is considered probable that the technology will be brought to market in the near future and the profitability of the product is such that it can support recovery of the investment. Satisfaction of the above conditions requires that there be no significant uncertainty about attaining marketability and the remaining open issues necessary to have a saleable product are reasonably predictable. Purchased technology is amortized on a straight-line basis over the remaining estimated economic life of the technology.

5. Other Assets

Other Assets at December 31, 2012 and 2011 were comprised of the following:

	December 31, 2012	December 31, 2011
Capitalized software, net of accumulated amortization of $6,905 and $3,840	$19,600	$15,935
Intangible Assets	14,958	13,699
Goodwill	5,691	5,691
Purchased technology	2,800	--
Equity investments	2,621	2,176
Non-current deferred tax assets	979	--
Other non-current assets	2,187	1,743
	$48,836	$39,244

Amortization of capitalized software costs was $3.1 million in fiscal 2012, $1.3 million in fiscal 2011 and $1.2 million in fiscal 2010.

NATURAL RESOURCES

Introduction. Natural resources include oil and gas deposits, timberlands, and mineral deposits. Natural resources are recorded at cost and depleted over their economic lives. As in the case of depreciation and amortization, the cost of a natural resource is allocated to the expected future periods of benefit through systematic charges against income.

For financial reporting purposes, qualifying the natural resource is normally depleted by the units-of-production method. The depreciation of related costs (e.g., tunnels, shafts and offshore platforms) would be depreciated over the expected useful life of the natural resource if these assets were not movable or did not have alternative future uses. If the assets are movable and have an alternative future use, they would be depreciated over their own expected useful lives or the life of the natural resource, whichever is shorter.

For tax purposes, firms can deduct the greater of cost or percentage depletion. Percentage depletion can only be used under highly restrictive conditions. Under percentage or statutory depletion, the firm is allowed a depletion deduction based on a percentage of the gross revenue generated from the resource. The percentage allowed depends on the natural resource in question and size of the entity. Because percentage depletion is based on gross revenues rather than cost, depletion could be in excess of the total cost of the natural resource. Even if the firm uses a cost-based depletion method for tax purposes, it may not be the same as the deduction for financial reporting purposes due to other book-tax differences, such as the determination of the costs to be capitalized in the determination of the cost of the natural resource (i.e., the depletion base).

ACCOUNTING FOR NATURAL RESOURCES

Generally, accounting for natural resources is straightforward. However, there are several controversial accounting and reporting issues relating to oil and gas producing firms. The issues relating to proper accounting and reporting in the oil and gas industry is sometimes known as the "oil and gas controversy." As part of this controversy, the primary point of discussion centers around the proper treatment of the costs incurred in the exploration of nonproducing wells (i.e., dry holes). Once again, the argument is based on the capitalization-expense alternative facing management. That is, which costs incurred in the exploration activities of an oil and gas producing entity should be capitalized as part of the cost of the natural resource (i.e., the depletion base) and which costs should be expensed immediately. The nature of the costs associated with oil and gas producing activities and the alternative accounting methods are presented below.

***The Cost of a Natural Resource*: *The Depletion Base*.** The cost of a natural resource in the oil and gas industry consists of three elements:

1. ***Acquisition cost of the deposit*.** The acquisition cost is the price paid to obtain the property or the right to search and explore.
2. ***Development costs*.** The development costs include intangible development costs such as grading the land, construction of tunnels and shafts and the costs of constructing offshore drilling platforms. As noted earlier, some of these costs relate to individual assets that can be moved to be utilized in alternative future locations.
3. ***Exploration costs*.** These are the costs of staffing and drilling for oil and gas. The proper accounting treatment of exploration costs is the primary component of the oil and gas controversy.

Alternative Accounting Treatments of Exploration Costs. There are two methods of accounting for costs of exploration activities. These methods are known as full-costs and successful efforts.

Under the full-cost method, all costs associated with successful and producing wells, as well as unsuccessful or dry holes, are capitalized as part of the cost of the natural resource. The full-cost method's capitalization treatment of the cost of dry wells is justified by the theory that the costs of exploring and drilling dry wells are a "reasonable and necessary" expenditure required for the discovery of successful and producing wells from the same area (e.g., offshore tract of land). Of course, if the entire tract of land is found to be unproductive, all costs should be written off in the year in which the loss of value becomes evident.

The full-cost method is an income increasing alternative in the early years of the natural resource's useful life. By capitalizing the costs of dry wells, both assets and income are initially increased. However, in the later years, income will be reduced through recognition of higher depletion charges.

The full-cost method is normally used by the smaller, more aggressive oil and gas firms, "the independents," who are interested in initially reporting higher profits for purposes of raising capital by either debt or equity financing.

Under the successful-efforts method, only those costs associated with exploring successful and producing wells are capitalized as part of the depletion base. All costs associated with dry wells are expensed as incurred. By expensing all costs incurred in exploring the unsuccessful project, the successful-efforts method becomes the income reducing accounting alternative in the early years of the life of the natural resource. In the later years of the life of the natural resource, the depletion charges would be lower and reported profits would be higher relative to the full-cost method.

The use of the successful-efforts method is justified by the theory that dry wells produce no oil and gas and provide no future economic benefit. Therefore, the costs associated with the dry wells should be expensed at the point at which the particular deposit is determined to be nonproductive. As noted above, if all of the property is found to be unproductive, all costs associated with the project should be written off against income in the year in which the project is determined to be worthless.

The successful-efforts method is used by larger, established firms in an attempt to reduce reported profits. The large oil and gas firms tend to employ an overall income reducing reporting strategy in an attempt to reduce their "size" so as to minimize public criticism and possible government interference. Under either method after the wells go into production, all addition operating costs are expensed as incurred.

To illustrate the two alterative methods of accounting for oil and gas activities, assume that you are given the following data:

- Entry to record $4,000 total exploration cost, $6,000, as a natural resource for both productive and dry wells under the full cost method.
- Entry to record straight-line depletion under the full cost method, $6,000/10 years = $600.
- Entry to record exploration costs as a natural resource for successful wells, $2,000, and to expense the exploration costs associated with dry wells, $4,000, under the successful efforts method.
- Entry to record the depletion of the natural resource under the successful efforts method, $2,000/10 years = $200.

The effect of these transactions on the financial statement is presented in the financial modeling worksheets presented below:

FINANCIAL MODELING WORKSHEET: FULL COST METHOD

INCOME STATEMENT (FIRST)	
REVENUES:	
EXPENSES: Depletion Expense	(600)
NET INCOME OR LOSS (a)	(600)

STATEMENT OF CASH FLOWS (THIRD)	
OPERATING ACTIVITIES:	
NET INCOME OR LOSS (a)	(600)
Add back: Depletion Expense	+600
Cash Flow from Operating Activities	- 0 -
INVESTING ACTIVITIES:	
Purchase Oil and Gas Deposit	(6,000)
FINANCING ACTIVITIES:	
INCREASE (DECREASE) IN CASH (b)	(6,000)
ADD: BEGINNING CASH BALANCE	
ENDING CASH BALANCE	

BALANCE SHEET (SECOND)			
ASSETS		LIABILITIES	
CURRENT ASSETS		CURRENT LIABILITIES	
CASH (b)	(6,000)		
		NONCURRENT LIABILITIES	
		STOCKHOLDERS'	
NONCURRENT ASSETS		EQUITY	
		CAPITAL STOCK	
Oil and Gas Deposit	+6,000	APIC	
Less :Acc. Depletion	(600)	RETAINED	
Net Book Value	+5,400	EARNINGS (a)	(600)
		TOTAL	
		LIABILITIES &	
		STOCKHOLDERS'	
TOTAL ASSETS	(600)	EQUITY	(600)

FINANCIAL MODELING WORKSHEET SUCCESSFUL EFFORTS METHOD

INCOME STATEMENT (FIRST)	
REVENUES:	
EXPENSES: Exploration Expense	*(4,000)*
Depletion Expense	*(200)*
NET INCOME OR LOSS (a)	*(4,200)*

STATEMENT OF CASH FLOWS (THIRD)	
OPERATING ACTIVITIES:	
NET INCOME OR LOSS (a)	*(4,200)*
Add Back: Depletion Expense	*+200*
Cash Flow from Operating Activities	*(4,000)*
INVESTING ACTIVITIES:	
Purchase Oil and Gas Deposit	*(2,000)*
FINANCING ACTIVITIES:	
INCREASE (DECREASE) IN CASH (b)	*(6,000)*
ADD: BEGINNING CASH BALANCE	
ENDING CASH BALANCE	

BALANCE SHEET (SECOND)			
ASSETS		*LIABILITIES*	
CURRENT ASSETS		*CURRENT LIABILITIES*	
CASH (b)	*(6,000)*		
		NONCURRENT LIABILITIES	
		STOCKHOLDERS'	
NONCURRENT ASSETS		*EQUITY*	
		CAPITAL STOCK	
Oil and Gas Deposit	*+2,000*	*APIC*	
Less :Acc. Depletion	*(200)*	*RETAINED*	
Net Book Value	*+1,800*	*EARNINGS (a)*	*(4,200)*
		TOTAL	
		LIABILITIES &	
		STOCKHOLDERS'	
TOTAL ASSETS	*(4,200)*	*EQUITY*	*(4,200)*

Note that relative to the "successful efforts" company, the "full cost" company reports:

- Higher carrying values for its natural resources
- Higher net assets or book values
- Higher earnings (particularly when exploration costs are increasing)
- Higher cash flows from operations

The Oil and Gas Controversy. The oil and gas controversy began in 1977 with the FASB's issuance of Statement No. 19, "Financial Accounting and Reporting by Oil and Gas Producing Companies."[16] Under SFAS 19, only the successful-efforts method of accounting was permitted. The restriction of the use of the full-cost method raised significant protests and lobbying in Congress from the smaller oil and gas companies. Due to this pressure, along with the recent oil shortage the FASB issued Statement No. 25, "Suspension of Certain

16. FASB ASC 932 [Predecessor literature: "Financial Accounting and Reporting by Oil and Gas Producing Companies," *Statement of Financial Accounting Standards No. 19* (Norwalk, Conn.: FASB 1977)].

Accounting Requirements for Oil and Gas Producing Companies in 1979."[17] SFAS 25, suspended the effective date of SFAS 19. However, SFAS 25 has never been amended, so that both methods of accounting are currently accepted in practice.

Even with both the full-cost and successful-efforts methods in use by 1979, the SEC was not satisfied with the accounting and reporting standards for oil and gas producing activities. As a result, the SEC proposed the implementation of reserve recognition accounting (RRA). Under the RRA proposal, as soon as oil is discovered, the cost of the natural resource should be capitalized and set equal to the discounted value of the expected future net cash flows from proven oil and gas reserves. Income would also be recognized and measured by the amounts capitalized, net of the costs incurred in the acquisition, development and exploration of the natural resource. The RRA valuation would be reviewed each year. Revisions of the RRA valuation could be due to changes in interest rate assumptions, projected oil and gas prices, and proven oil and gas reserves. Changes in the discounted cash flow valuation would be reflected on the income statement as income if the RRA value increased from the prior year, and write-offs could result if the undepleted balance of the oil and gas deposit exceeded its discounted cash flow valuation.

Given the potential errors in geological surveys and interest rate assumptions, and the volatility of oil and gas prices, RRA could result in significant year-to-year fluctuations in reported profits. Therefore, the SEC abandoned its RRA proposal in 1982. As a compromise, the FASB expanded the disclosure requirements for oil and gas producing activities in 1982 with the issuance of Statement No. 69, "Disclosures about Oil and Gas Producing Activities."[18] SFAS 69, paragraphs 6 and 7, requires the disclosure of the following information about a firm's oil and gas producing activities.

1. Both publicly traded and privately held companies engaged in significant oil and gas producing activities must disclose:

- "the method of accounting for costs incurred" (i.e., full-cost or successful-efforts)
- "the manner of disposing of capitalized costs relating to those activities" (i.e., expensing immediately or capitalization and then depleting)

2. The following additional disclosures are required for publicly traded companies only:

- "Proved oil and gas reserve quantities" at the beginning and the end of the period
- "Capitalized costs relating to oil and gas producing activities" and the related accumulated depreciation, depletion, etc
- "Costs incurred for property acquisition, exploration and development activities"
- "Results of operations in the aggregate and for the separate geographical areas of activity"
- "A standardized measure of discounted future net cash flows relating to the proved oil and gas reserve quantities"

This last disclosure requirement is similar to the SEC's RRA proposal.

SFAS 69 disclosures can be extensive. Exhibit 2.15 presents the supplemental information on oil and gas exploration and production activities by Norton Oil Company.

---

17. FASB ASC 932 [Predecessor literature: "Suspension of Certain Accounting Requirements for Oil and Gas Producing Companies," *Statement of Financial Accounting Standards No. 25* (Norwalk, Conn.: FASB 1979)].

18. FASB ASC 932 [Predecessor literature: "Disclosures about Oil and Gas Producing Activities," *Statement of Financial Accounting Standards No. 69* (Norwalk, Conn.: FASB 1982)].

EXHIBIT 2.15: SAMPLE OIL AND GAS DISCLOSURES

Sample Oil and Gas Disclosures Required under FASB Statement No. 69
The Norton Oil Company 2003 Form 10-K:

THE NORTON OIL COMPANY
PARTIAL CONSOLIDATED BALANCE SHEETS
(in thousands, except share data)

	December 31, 2012	December 31, 2011
Assets:		
Cash and cash equivalents	$ 3,083	$ 21,637
Accounts receivable	105,539	104,056
Accounts receivable — Affiliate	8,080	3,727
Derivative financial instruments	4,150	—
Inventories	1,285	1,718
Deferred tax asset	23,573	14,702
Prepayments and other	6,982	2,635
Total current assets	152,690	148,476
Natural gas and oil properties, full cost method Unevaluated properties	161,389	115,430
Properties subject to amortization	2,788,813	2,193,792
Other property and equipment	15,140	12,839
	2,965,343	2,322,061
Less: Accumulated depreciation, depletion and amortization	1,319,988	1,095,164
	1,645,355	1,226,897
Other non-current assets	12,833	5,909
Total Assets	$ 1,810,878	$ 1,381,282

THE NORTON OIL COMPANY
CONSOLIDATED STATEMENTS OF OPERATIONS
(in thousands, except per share data)

	For the Years Ended December 31,		
	2012	2011	2010
Revenues:			
Natural gas and oil revenues	$540,584	$378,725	$425,872
Other	1,443	1,195	1,488
Total revenues	542,027	379,919	427,360
Operating expenses:			
Lease operating	51,779	37,374	27,820
Severance tax	17,554	10,436	12,139
Transportation expense	11,426	10,249	8,417
Asset retirement accretion expense	4,035	—	—
Depreciation, depletion and amortization	217,283	188,771	141,610
Write down in carrying value of natural gas and oil properties	—	—	6,787
General and administrative, net of amounts capitalized	21,496	14,385	18,821
Total operating expenses	323,573	261,214	215,593
Income from operations	218,455	118,705	211,767
Other (income) expense	(17320.6)	(9,977)	(130.9)
Interest expense, net of amounts capitalized	9,176	8,138	3,291
Income before income taxes	226,599	120,545	208,344
Provision for taxes	79,406	43,001	73,483

THE NORTON OIL COMPANY
NOTES TO CONSOLIDATED FINANCIAL STATEMENTS

Natural Gas and Oil Properties

Full Cost Accounting. We use the full cost method to account for our natural gas and oil properties. Under full cost accounting, all costs incurred in the acquisition, exploration and development of natural gas and oil reserves are capitalized into a "full cost pool." Capitalized costs include costs of all unproved properties, internal costs directly related to our natural gas and oil activities and capitalized interest. We amortize these costs using a unit-of-production method. We compute the provision for depreciation, depletion and amortization quarterly by multiplying production for the quarter by a depletion rate. The depletion rate is determined by dividing our total unamortized cost base by net equivalent proved reserves at the beginning of the quarter estimates for future development costs.

Costs associated amortization base until we have made a determination as the existence of proved reserves. We review our unevaluated properties at the end of each quarter to determine whether the costs incurred should be amortization. Sales of natural gas and oil properties are accounted for as adjustments to the full cost pool.

Under full cost accounting rules, total capitalized costs are limited to a ceiling equal to the present value of future net revenues, discounted at 10% per annum, plus the lower of cost or fair value of unproved properties less income tax effects (the "ceiling limitation"). We perform a quarterly ceiling test to evaluate whether the net book value of our full cost pool exceeds the ceiling limitation. If capitalized costs (net of accumulated depreciation, depletion and amortization) less related deferred taxes are greater than the discounted future net revenues or ceiling limitation, a write down or impairment of the full cost pool is required. A write down of the carrying value of the full cost pool is a non-cash charge that reduces earnings and impacts stockholders' equity in the period of occurrence and typically results in lower depreciation, depletion and amortization expense in future periods. Once incurred, a write down is not reversible at a later date.

The ceiling test is calculated using natural gas and oil prices in effect as of the balance sheet date and adjusted for "basis" or location differential, held constant over the life of the reserves. We use derivative financial instruments that qualify for cash flow hedge accounting under SFAS 133 to hedge against the volatility of natural gas prices, and in accordance with Securities and Exchange Commission guidelines, we include estimated future cash flows from our hedging program in our ceiling test calculation.

At December 31, 2012 and 2011, the carrying value of our full cost pool was less that the ceiling limitation by $528.8 million (after tax) for 2012 and by $335.3 million (after tax) for 2011. No write down was required.

At December 31, 2010, we reduced or "wrote down" the carrying value of our full cost pool and incurred a charge to earnings of $7.4 million ($4.8 million, after tax).

NOTE 18— Supplemental Information On Natural Gas and Oil Exploration, Development and Production Activities (Unaudited)

The following information concerning our natural gas and oil operations has been provided pursuant to Statement of Financial Accounting Standards No. 69, "Disclosures about Oil and Gas Producing Activities." Our natural gas and oil producing activities are conducted onshore within the continental United States and offshore in federal and state waters of the Gulf of Mexico. Our natural gas and oil reserves were estimated by independent reserve engineers.

Capitalized Costs of Natural Gas and Oil Properties

	As of December 31,		
	2012	2011	2010
		(in thousands)	
Unevaluated properties, not subject to amortization	$ 161,389	$ 115,430	$ 213,584
Properties subject to amortization	2,788,813	2,193,792	1,791,952
Capitalized costs	2,950,202	2,309,222	2,005,536
Accumulated depreciation, depletion and amortization	(1,310,488)	(1,087,307)	(882,308)
Net capitalized costs	$ 1,639,714	$ 1,221,915	$ 1,123,228

Capitalized Costs Incurred

Costs incurred for natural gas and oil exploration, development and acquisition are summarized below. Costs incurred during the years ended December 31, 2012, 2011 and 2010 include interest expense and general and administrative costs related to acquisition, exploration and development of natural gas and oil properties of $24.2 million, $25.3 million and $29.9 million, respectively.

	As of December 31,		
	2012	2011	2010
		(in thousands)	
Property acquisition and leasehold costs			
Unevaluated	$ 73,469	$ 17,520	$ 38,053
Proved	204,326	107,848	102,440
Exploration costs	79,511	31,876	86,467
Development costs	194,682	146,443	212,708
	551,988	303,687	439,668
Asset retirement obligation	37,982	–	–
Total costs incurred	$ 589,970	$ 303,687	$ 439,668

Standardized Measure of Discounted Future Net Cash Flows Relating to Proved Natural Gas and Oil Reserves (unaudited)

The following summarizes the policies we used in the preparation of the accompanying natural gas and oil reserve disclosures, standardized measures of discounted future net cash flows from proved natural gas and oil reserves and the reconciliations of standardized measures from year to year. The information disclosed, as prescribed by the Statement of Financial Accounting Standards No. 69 is an attempt to present the information in a manner comparable with industry peers.

The information is based on estimates of proved reserves attributable to our interest in natural gas and oil properties as of December 31 of the years presented. These estimates were prepared by independent petroleum consultants. Proved reserves are estimated quantities of natural gas and crude oil which geological and engineering data demonstrate with reasonable certainty to be recoverable in future years from known reservoirs under existing economic and operating conditions.

The standardized measure of discounted future net cash flows from production of proved reserves was developed as follows:

1. Estimates are made of quantities of proved reserves and future periods during which they are expected to be produced based on year-end economic conditions.
2. The estimated future cash flows are compiled by applying year-end prices of natural gas and oil relating to our proved reserves to the year-end quantities of those reserves.
3. The future cash flows are reduced by estimated production costs, costs to develop and produce the proved reserves and abandonment costs, all based on year-end economic conditions.
4. Future income tax expenses are based on year-end statutory tax rates giving effect to the remaining tax basis in the natural gas and oil properties, other deductions, credits and allowances relating to our proved natural gas and oil reserves.
5. Future net cash flows are discounted to present value by applying a discount rate of 10%.

The standardized measure of discounted future net cash flows does not purport, nor should it be interpreted, to present the fair value of our natural gas and oil reserves. An estimate of fair value would also take into account, among other things, the recovery of reserves not presently classified as proved, anticipated future changes in prices and costs and a discount factor more representative of the time value of money and the risks inherent in reserve estimates.

The standardized measure of discounted future net cash flows relating to proved natural gas and oil reserves is as follows and does not include cash flows associated with hedges outstanding at each of the respective reporting dates and is unaudited.

	As of December 31,		
	2012	2011	2010
		(in thousands)	
Future cash inflows	$ 5,202,803	$ 3,414,922	$ 1,765,868
Future production costs	(917,248)	(583,679)	(362,574)
Future development costs	(442,945)	(290,251)	(227,376)
Future income taxes	(1,020,317)	(651,338)	(253,429)
Future net cash flows	2,822,293	1,889,654	922,489
10% annual discount for estimated timing of cash flows	(1,017,006)	(619,976)	(260,659)
Standardized measure of discounted future net cash flows	$ 1,805,287	$ 1,269,678	$ 661,830

Of particular interest to the analyst is the comparison of the net carrying value of the natural resource with the discounted cash flow measure. In Exhibit 2.15, the net capitalized costs at December 31, 2012 and 2011 are equal to $1,639,714 and 1,221,915 respectively. The standardized measure of discounted future net cash flows relating to proved oil and gas reserve quantities are equal to $1,805,287 and 1,269,678 at December 31, 2012 and 2011, respectively. In this case, the net carrying value of the natural resource on Norton Oil Company's balance sheet is conservative and therefore possibly undervalued. Undervaluation of the carrying value of the natural resource would not be expected in Norton Oil's case due to its use of the full cost method. Overvaluation of the carrying value of the natural resource is expected under the full cost method. In fact, a write off was needed in fiscal 2010 amounting to $7,404. Net capitalized costs in that year were $1,123,228 while the net discounted cash flow measure was equal to $661,830. That means that the write down is much lower than the difference between the carrying amount and the standardized measure. This is due to the fact the discounted cash flow measure is only a tentative benchmark, due to the possible errors in estimating oil and gas reserve quantities and the assumptions used in projections such as future oil and gas prices, future operating costs and the appropriate discount rate to use in the computations. Write downs can also be avoided or limited if recoveries in oil and gas prices are expected in the mean term.

It is important to note that the SEC encouraged the FASB to require the current value disclosures in SFAS 69 due to the ceiling imposed by the SEC on the amounts to be capitalized under the full-cost method. Specifically, in 1986 the SEC sanctioned the use of full-cost accounting, but only with a ceiling on the total amount of costs to be capitalized in the carrying value of the natural resource. Costs can be capitalized, but only up to the present value of the company's reserves. All costs incurred in excess of the ceiling must be expensed as incurred. In Exhibit 2.15 the capitalized costs for 2012, 2011 and 2010 respectively, are $1,639,714, $1,221,915 and $1,123,228 and are less than the discounted cash flow measure each year except in 2010 (i.e., $1,805,287, $1,269,678 and $661,830). The write down for 2010 on the income statement was only $7,404, again, the amount of the loss can be reduced if short term recoveries are expected. In addition, if oil and gas prices or estimated reserves decrease, capitalized costs, net of accumulated depletion at the end of the year, could exceed the present value of the company's oil and gas reserves so that write-offs could be taken if these decreases are deemed to be permanent in nature.

As noted above, the full cost "ceiling" imposed on the carrying value of the natural resource, "oil and gas deposits," is equal to the present value of the future net cash flows from proven company reserves. If the capitalized cost or carrying value of the asset, (i.e., the historical cost, net of accumulated depletion), exceeds the present or discounted value, the excess must be written off against income. A write-off is likely when the accountant views a decline in estimated reserves and/or a decrease in oil and gas prices as "other than temporary." The ceiling was instituted by the SEC because the use of the full cost method could significantly overstate asset values by capitalizing the cost of dry wells. It should be noted that successful efforts companies must use a less stringent ceiling determined by "undiscounted" future cash flows from oil and gas activities. In practice, firms may switch from full cost to successful efforts, and make a retroactive accounting change to obtain the smaller impairment write down for those cases where the natural resource carrying value is greater than the "ceiling" (e.g., Pennzoil in 1988).

In sum, the maximum value to be carried on the balance sheet of full cost (successful efforts) company is the lower of the present value of the (undiscounted) future net cash flows from proven company reserves, or capitalized cost, net of accumulated depletion.

Thus given the SEC's imposed ceiling on the valuation of oil and gas deposits, if the discounted cash flow valuation was significantly less than the net carrying value at historical cost, it may imply that the natural resource on the balance sheet is overstated. If the fluctuation in the discounted cash flow valuation was other than temporary (e.g., a downward revision in the original estimate of proven oil and gas reserve quantities), a write-down of the cost of the natural resource may be considered appropriate. This is a very real possibility if one considers the potential overstatement of asset value under the full-cost method.

Due to the significance of the oil and gas activities of some firms and the different valuations that could result from the full-cost and the successful-efforts methods, it is important for the analyst to consider the possibility of overstatement of the natural resource and the potential write-off in subsequent accounting periods.

Utilization of the SFAS 69 supplemental disclosures of a firm's oil and gas producing activities, along with knowledge of industry trends and projections of oil and gas prices, can provide the analyst the sufficient data to assess the propriety of the valuation of the firm's natural resource base and the firm's ability to generate income and cash flows from its oil and gas producing activities. In addition, the analyst could use this information to project the need for future write-offs of the historical cost-based valuation of the carrying value of the firm's natural resources.

CHAPTER 3 | Analytical Issues in Accounting for Corporate Debt

ANALYSIS OF CORPORATE DEBT

INTRODUCTION

The most recent definition of liabilities by the Financial Accounting Standards Board is found in Statement of Financial Accounting Concepts (SFAC) No. 6 (SFAC 6)[1] defines a liability as a "probable future sacrifice of economic resources arising from the current obligations of an entity to transfer assets or to provide services to other entities in the future as a result of current or past transactions."

In this chapter, issues relating to reporting and accounting for current and long-term liabilities are discussed. For both classifications of liabilities, a basic review of accounting for corporate debt is provided. The discussion then moves on to special issues in measurement and classification of liabilities.

Classification of Corporate Debt

Liabilities are presented on the balance sheet in the order of maturity. Corporate debt is further classified as either current or long term.

Current Liabilities. Current liabilities are defined as obligations that will be liquidated through the use of economic resources properly classified as current assets or through the creation of other current liabilities. From a practical standpoint, current liabilities are usually due and payable within one year from the balance sheet date, or operating cycle, whichever is longer. Accounting and analytical issues related to the operating cycle were discussed in the chapter covering current assets.

Current liabilities include

- Trade accounts payable
- Income and other taxes payable
- Current portion of long-term debt (including capitalized lease obligations)
- Current deferred income taxes payable
- Short-term notes and loans payable
- Current obligations under pension plans
- Estimated liabilities for product warranties

Within the current liability classification, special analytical issues will arise with respect to the classification of short-term debt expected to be refinanced and long-term debt callable by the creditor.

Long-Term or Non-current Liabilities. Long-term liabilities are generally defined as those obligations that are due and payable in a period of time more than one year from the balance sheet date or operating cycle, whichever is longer. In addition, these obligations will not require the use of current assets or the creation of current liabilities in their liquidation. The long-term debt classification includes:

---

1. "Elements of Financial Statements," *Statement of Financial Accounting Concepts No. 6* (Stamford, Conn.: FASB, December 1985).

- Bonds payable
- Long-term notes payable
- Long-term obligations under pension plans
- Long-term obligations under capitalized leases
- Redeemable preferred stock

Special analytical issues relating to long-term corporate debt include early retirement or extinguishment of debt and troubled debt restructurings.

Accounting Limbo. Due to strong differences of opinion regarding the nature and proper classification of several items of corporate debt and stockholders' equity, accountants have created another section of the balance sheet located between liabilities and stockholders' equity. This grey area of the balance sheet is sometimes known as "accounting limbo." The items in this section are not specifically classified as debt or equity, but are left "unclassified" by the accountant. The ambiguous classification requires that analysts classify these items according to their own judgment and interpretation of the nature of the financial statement item. Commitments and contingences are typically found in the section of the balance sheet.

Contingent Liabilities. Contingent liabilities are defined as potential obligations that may become actual obligations of the entity depending on certain future events occurring or failing to occurring.

Examples include actual or threatened litigation, income tax investigations and guarantees of the debt of others.

Contingent liabilities are usually only disclosed in the footnotes to the financial statements, and are not formally recorded in the accounts. Some firms will include a line item entitled "commitments and contingencies" on the face of the balance sheet in the liabilities and stockholders' equity section, without including any dollar amounts in the financial statement totals. This disclosure will reference a footnote and makes the analyst aware of the potential obligations of the firm. Loss contingencies are discussed in detail in a subsequent chapter.

Many of the classification issues discussed above are included in the liabilities and stockholders' equity section of the JD Store's balance sheet presented in Exhibit 3.1.

EXHIBIT 3.1 CONSOLIDATED BALANCE SHEETS

JD Stores

(Amounts in millions except per share data)		
January 31,	2012	2011
Liabilities and shareholders' equity		
Current liabilities:		
Commercial paper	**$ 4,505**	$ 4,574
Accounts payable	**30,448**	26,384
Accrued liabilities	**16,158**	14,544
Accrued income taxes	**1,608**	1,537
Long-term debt due within one year	**5,514**	4,511
Obligations under capital leases due within one year	**358.8**	267.6
Total current liabilities	**58,591**	51,818
Long-term debt	**31,715**	24,104
Long-term obligations under capital leases	**4,490**	3,805
Deferred income taxes and other	**5,462**	3,574
Commitments and contingencies		

Shareholders' equity:		
Preferred stock ($0.10 par value; 100 shares authorized, none issued)	—	—
Common stock ($0.10 par value; 11,000 shares authorized, 4,165 and 4,234 issued and outstanding at January 31, 2006 and January 31, 2005, respectively)	**500.4**	507.6
Capital in excess of par value	**3,115**	2,910
Accumulated other comprehensive income	**1,264**	3,233
Retained earnings	58,926	52,625
Noncontrolling interset	1,760	1,608
Total shareholders' equity	65,565	60,883
Total liabilities and shareholders' equity	**$ 165,824**	$ 144,185

See accompanying notes.

SPECIAL ISSUES IN ACCOUNTING FOR CURRENT LIABILITIES

The analytical issues relating to current liabilities center on the proper classification of transactions involving refinancing short-term debt and the creditor's right to call long-term obligations. The professional standards relating to short-term debt expected to be refinanced and the classification of obligations that become callable by the creditor are discussed in the following sections.

Short-Term Debt Expected to be Refinanced. Short-term debt expected to be refinanced relates to an agreement or a transaction that will take place after the date of the balance sheet but before the financial statements are issued. The period between the balance sheet date and the date the financial statements are issued is known as the "post-balance sheet" or "subsequent events period."

Post-balance sheet or subsequent events result from the fact that there is usually a one-to-two-month lag between the fiscal year end, completion of the auditors' field work, and the release of the annual report. During this period of time, the auditor may become aware of events that could significantly influence the judgment of an informed user of the financial statements.

The key issue here is whether the accountant is required to account for events that take place during the post-balance sheet period and possibly modify the financial statements to be issued. That is, should the accountant reflect an event that occurs in 2008 in the financial statements for the year ended in 2007? The professional standards for accounting and auditing specify that the accountant is responsible for events that take place up to the last date of field work, which is also the date of the auditor's opinion.

With respect to post-balance sheet or subsequent events, profession pronouncements require the following procedures: 1. financial statement adjustment and disclosure or 2. footnote disclosure only. Here are two examples:

1. If the 2008 subsequent event was caused by other events and conditions which existed as of the date of the 2007 balance sheet and would have been accounted for in 2007 if brought to the attention of the accountant, the accountant must actually "go back" and adjust the 2007 financial statements for the subsequent event and make adequate footnote disclosures of the transaction. For example, if a major customer, with a significant outstanding receiv-

able balance, petitions for bankruptcy in January of 2008, the accountant must write-off this receivable in the 2007 financial statements and make adequate disclosure of the event because the conditions resulting in the customer's insolvency existed as of the balance sheet date.

2. Alternatively, if the 2008 subsequent event was caused by events and conditions that existed only during the post-balance sheet period, the accountant should only disclose the transaction in the footnotes to the 2007 financial statements, and would not make any adjustments to the 2007 financial statements. For example, the sale of additional stock or additional borrowing during the post-balance sheet period must be disclosed in a subsequent events footnote.

Short-term debt expected to be refinanced in the next accounting period may qualify as a post-balance sheet event, and if refinanced on a long-term basis, it may be reclassified as a non-current liability. FASB Statement No. 6, "*Classification of Short-term Obligations Expected to be Refinanced,*"[2] sets forth the conditions under which the short-term debt can be reclassified as long term.

Specifically, SFAS 6, covers situations where the short-term debt is expected to be (a) extended or replaced by additional short-term debt that will be due beyond one year from the balance sheet date, and (b) replaced or refinanced with either long-term debt or equity securities. In either case, the short-term obligation will no longer require the use of current assets or the creation of current liabilities in its liquidation. Therefore, the obligation no longer meets the definition of a current liability, and to the extent refinanced, would be reclassified as a noncurrent liability. In addition, adequate footnote disclosure providing the particulars of the terms of the refinancing is required.

It should be noted that the firm must first refinance (i.e., obtain the additional financing) and then liquidate the short-term obligation. If the sequence of events was reversed (i.e., the firm liquidates the short-term debt and then obtains new financing), the firm would be utilizing cash from current operations and the obligation would still meet the definition of a current liability and should not be reclassified as long term.

SFAS 6 set forth two criteria that must be met in order for the firm to exclude the short-term obligation from current liabilities and to reclassify the debt as long term. First, management must intend to refinance on a long-term basis. Second, management must demonstrate the ability to consummate the refinancing.

According to SFAS 6, the ability to refinance is demonstrated by either (a) actual refinancing during the post-balance sheet period, or (b) entering into a firm agreement which permits refinancing on a long-term basis and where the terms of the agreement are readily determinable. A commercial loan agreement containing a material adverse change clause would violate the second criterion of SFAS 6.

As noted earlier, only the portion of the short-term liability expected to be refinanced can be reclassified as a non-current obligation. The reclassification from short-term to long-term debt will improve the firm's liquidity statistics without changing total debt and without affecting cash flow. These results are due to the fact that the application of SFAS 6 causes a simple reclassification of the short-term debt into long-term debt. The details of the new financing agreement are only disclosed in a footnote to the financial statements, and the new debt obligation and the related cash inflow are not recorded until the contract is consummated in the next accounting period.

Classification of Obligations that are Callable by the Creditor. The case where long-term debt becomes callable by the creditor due to technical default is the converse of the case of

2. FASB ASC 470 [Predecessor literature: "Classification of Short-term Obligations Expected to be Refinanced," *Statement of Financial Accounting Standards No. 6* (Norwalk, Conn.: FASB, 1975)].

short-term debt expected to be refinanced. This second issue is concerned with obligations that, by their terms, are due on demand or will be due on demand within one year from the balance sheet date. The accounting and disclosure requirements for callable debt are set forth by FASB Statement No. 78, *"Classification of Obligations that are Callable by the Creditor."*

According to SFAS 78, this standard is applicable to obligations that are or will be callable by the creditor either because of the following circumstances:

- "The debtor's violation of a provision of the debt agreement at the balance sheet date makes the debt callable." For example, the debtor is in technical default due to violation of a restrictive covenant of a commercial loan agreement requiring maintenance of a certain level of working capital.
- If the violation is "not cured within a specified grace period," the obligation will become callable.

Under these circumstances the debt would be due and payable on demand and should be reclassified as a current liability. Nevertheless, the Board went on to specify that the callable obligation may continue to be classified as long term if one of the following conditions is met:

- The creditor either waives or loses the right to demand payment (e.g., the violation is cured)
- The obligation will not become callable because it is probable that the violation will be cured with the grace period

Although still classified as long-term debt, the conditions and circumstances justifying the noncurrent classification, given the technical default, should be disclosed in a footnote to the financial statements.

ANALYSIS OF SHORT-TERM DEBT

In a review of current liabilities, the analyst should note that large amounts of short-term bank debt may imply the inability of the firm to obtain financing on a long-term basis or that the firm has violated the terms of a long-term debt agreement, making the obligation callable. The application of SFAS 6 and SFAS 78 should provide adequate disclosures that assist the analyst in making informed judgments regarding the proper classification of the firm's debt.

However, some of the provisions of SFAS 6 and SFAS 78 are vague and may enable management to exercise some discretion in the classification of debt. For example, in applying the provisions of SFAS 6, management's "ability to refinance" and "demonstrating of the ability to refinance on a long-term basis" may be determined on a subjective basis. There can be a great deal of discretion on the part of management in determining if an agreement to refinance is "firm" and if the terms are "readily determinable." In this case, even if there is no actual refinancing during the post-balance sheet period, as long as there is an "agreement" to refinance there may be a reclassification of short-term to long-term debt. This improves the liquidity of the firm and may in fact prevent a technical default of another debt agreement containing a restrictive covenant based on working capital levels.

Similarly, a technical default of a long-term debt agreement would not result in reclassification to a current liability if management determines that under the provisions of SFAS 78, it is "probable" that the violation would be cured during the grace period. Although there should be disclosure of the rationale behind the decision not to reclassify the long-term obligation to short-term debt, the application of SFAS 78 still results in maintaining this debt as long-term, and prevents an adverse effect on the firm's liquidity position. Again, this could prevent violation of a liquidity based restrictive covenant in another debt agreement.

ACCOUNTING FOR LONG-TERM DEBT

Accounting for bonds payable will be discussed in this section of the chapter in order to illustrate the analytical issues surrounding long-term debt. After presenting the basic principles of accounting for bond discounts and premiums and the interest rate method of amortization, the discussion moves to more complex issues such as early extinguishment of debt and debt restructuring.

Basic Issues in Accounting for Bonds Payable. An individual bond is a promissory note with a par or face value of $1,000, a fixed maturity date and a stated rate of interest or the bond can be a zero coupon instrument. The bonds are sold in an issue through an underwriter or privately placed. For example, a $1,000,000 bond issue consists of 1,000, $1,000 par value bonds. Because there are multiple lenders, a contract between the corporation and the bondholders (represented by a trustee) must be drawn up to protect the bondholder/investor. The contract is called a bond indenture.

The bond indenture outlines the terms and provisions of the debt agreement. The terms and provisions of the debt agreement include dividend restrictions, debt compliance provisions or restrictive covenants (e.g., maintenance of a certain level of working capital or the establishment of compensating balances), manner of contract enforcement, the type of bonds, and the features associated with the bond. These features include whether the bonds are secured, mature in series, are registered, callable, redeemable or convertible.

Bonds can be issued at par, at a price above par (at a premium) or at a price below par (at a discount). In all cases, the bonds are priced to yield the market. That is, the issue price of the bonds will depend on the difference between the stated rate on the bonds (i.e., the nominal, cash, face or coupon rate) and the going market rate of interest. The nominal or face rate of interest is used in the determination of the coupon or cash interest. The semiannual cash interest is determined by multiplying the semiannual coupon rate of interest by the par value of the debt. The market rate is used to price the bonds. That is, the market rate is used to discount the future cash flows from the bond investment to determine the issue price of the bond.

The comparison of the coupon rate of interest with the market rate can result in three possible prices in relation to the par value of the bonds. In practice, bonds are priced instantaneously. However, in the discussion that follows, economic theory is used to illustrate the bond pricing.

- ***Par Value Case***: If the coupon rate is equal to the market rate, there is an equilibrium price which is equal to the par value of the bonds. The bonds can sell at their par value because, assuming that the rate of interest captures all pertinent factors such as risk, the investor is indifferent between the corporation's bond and any other bond investment in the market.

Example: An investor has the opportunity to acquire a $1,000, 10% bond without a maturity date (this is similar to a preferred stock). Coupon (cash) interest is $100 per year (10% x $1,000). If the market rate is 10%, the bonds will sell for par or $1,000.

Pricing Formula only if n = infinity:

$$\text{Price} = \frac{\text{Cash Interest}}{\text{Yield}} = \frac{\$100}{.1000} = \underline{\underline{\$1,000.}}$$

There is no discount or premium in this case.

This pricing formula reflects the bond price as the sum of the present values of the future cash flows. In this case, n = infinity. Therefore, as n goes to infinity, the present value factor for the principal, $[1 / (1+i)^{n})]$, goes to zero and the present value factor for the ordinary annuity (coupon interest), $\{[1 - 1 / (1+i)^{n}]/i\}$, goes to $1 / i = 1$ / Yield.

The following financial modeling worksheet presents the financial statement effects of bond issuance at par. The illustration assumes that there are no bond issue costs incurred at the date of sale.

FINANCIAL MODELING WORKSHEET BONDS ISSUED AT PAR

INCOME STATEMENT (FIRST)	
REVENUES:	
EXPENSES:	
NET INCOME OR LOSS (a)	

STATEMENT OF CASH FLOWS (THIRD)	
OPERATING ACTIVITIES:	
NET INCOME OR LOSS (a)	
INVESTING ACTIVITIES:	
FINANCING ACTIVITIES:	
Issued Bonds Payable	*+1,000*
INCREASE (DECREASE) IN CASH (b)	*+1,000*
ADD: BEGINNING CASH BALANCE	
ENDING CASH BALANCE	

BALANCE SHEET (SECOND)			
ASSETS		***LIABILITIES***	
CURRENT ASSETS		***CURRENT LIABILITIES***	
Cash (b)	*+1,000*		
		NONCURRENT LIABILITIES	
		Bonds Payable	*+1,000*
		STOCKHOLDERS' EQUITY	
NONCURRENT ASSETS			
		CAPITAL STOCK	
		APIC	
		RETAINED	
		EARNINGS (a)	
		TOTAL	
		LIABILITIES &	
		STOCKHOLDERS'	
TOTAL ASSETS	*+1,000*	***EQUITY***	*+1,000*

- ***Discount Case***: If the coupon rate is less than the market rate, the bonds will be issued at a price below par or at a discount. Since the investor can obtain a higher rate in the market, the supply of the corporation's bonds will exceed the demand and there will be downward price pressure. Prices fall until an equilibrium price is reached where the effective return for the investor and the effective cost of borrowing for the corporation is equal to the higher market rate.

Example: An investor has the opportunity to acquire a \$1,000, 10% bond without a maturity date (this is similar to a preferred stock). Coupon (cash) interest is \$100 per year (10% x \$1,000). If the market rate is 11.11%, the bonds will sell for \$900.

Pricing Formula only if n = infinity:

$$\text{Price} = \frac{\text{Cash Interest}}{\text{Yield}} = \frac{\$100}{.1111} = \underline{\$900.}$$

The discount in this case is $100 (i.e., $900 - 1,000)

The following financial modeling worksheet presents the financial statement effects of bond issuance at discount. The illustration assumes that there are no bond issue costs incurred at the date of sale.

FINANCIAL MODELING WORKSHEET BONDS ISSUED AT A DISCOUNT

INCOME STATEMENT (FIRST)	
REVENUES:	
EXPENSES:	
NET INCOME OR LOSS (a)	

STATEMENT OF CASH FLOWS (THIRD)	
OPERATING ACTIVITIES:	
NET INCOME OR LOSS (a)	
INVESTING ACTIVITIES:	
FINANCING ACTIVITIES:	
Issued Bonds Payable	***+900***
INCREASE (DECREASE) IN CASH (b)	***+900***
ADD: BEGINNING CASH BALANCE	
ENDING CASH BALANCE	

BALANCE SHEET (SECOND)			
ASSETS		***LIABILITIES***	
CURRENT ASSETS		***CURRENT LIABILITIES***	
Cash (b)	***+900***		
		NONCURRENT LIABILITIES	
		Bonds Payable-par	***1,000***
		Discount on Bonds	***(100)***
		Bonds Payable-net	***+900***
		STOCKHOLDERS' EQUITY	
NONCURRENT ASSETS			
		CAPITAL STOCK	
		APIC	
		RETAINED	
		EARNINGS (a)	
		TOTAL	
		LIABILITIES &	
		STOCKHOLDERS'	
TOTAL ASSETS	***+900***	***EQUITY***	***+900***

- ***Premium Case*:** Finally, if the coupon rate exceeds the market rate of interest, the bonds will sell at a price above par or at a premium. Since the investor obtains a greater interest rate than is available in the market, the demand for the corporation's bonds exceeds the supply and bids up the price. The upward price pressure continues until an equilibrium price is reached, where the effective return for the investor and the effective cost of borrowing for the corporation will equal the lower market rate.

Example: An investor has the opportunity to acquire a $1,000, 10% bond without a maturity date. Coupon (cash) interest is $100 per year (10% x $1,000). If the market rate is 8.33%, the bonds will sell for $1,200.

Pricing Formula only if n = infinity:

$$\text{Price} = \frac{\text{Cash Interest}}{\text{Yield}} = \frac{\$100}{.0833} = \underline{\$1{,}200}$$

In this case there is a $200 premium (i.e., $1,200 - 1,000).

The following financial modeling worksheet presents the financial statement effects of bond issuance at premium. The illustration assumes that there are no bond issue costs incurred at the date of sale.

FINANCIAL MODELING WORKSHEET BONDS ISSUED AT A PREMIUM

INCOME STATEMENT (FIRST)	
REVENUES:	
EXPENSES:	
NET INCOME OR LOSS (a)	

STATEMENT OF CASH FLOWS (THIRD)	
OPERATING ACTIVITIES:	
NET INCOME OR LOSS (a)	
INVESTING ACTIVITIES:	
FINANCING ACTIVITIES:	
Issued Bonds Payable	*+1,200*
INCREASE (DECREASE) IN CASH (b)	*+1,200*
ADD: BEGINNING CASH BALANCE	
ENDING CASH BALANCE	

BALANCE SHEET (SECOND)			
ASSETS		***LIABILITIES***	
CURRENT ASSETS		***CURRENT LIABILITIES***	
Cash (b)	*+1,200*		
		NONCURRENT LIABILITIES	
		Bonds Payable-par	*1,000*
		Premium on Bonds	*+200*
		Bonds Payable-gross	*+1,200*
		STOCKHOLDERS' EQUITY	
NONCURRENT ASSETS			
		CAPITAL STOCK	
		APIC	
		RETAINED EARNINGS (a)	
TOTAL ASSETS	*+1,200*	***TOTAL LIABILITIES & STOCKHOLDERS' EQUITY***	*+1,200*

It should be noted that the premium is an adjunct account to bonds payable, and bonds payable and the premium are usually reported in the aggregate. Conversely, the discount is a contra-liability account and is deducted from the par value of the debt. The bonds are usually reported net of the discount.

The discount and premium illustrations above clearly indicate that there is an inverse relationship between bond prices and market interest rates. It should also be noted that the differences between the coupon rate of interest and the market rate are due to the time lag between the dates the bond indenture is written, bonds are printed, etc., and the date the bonds are sold. Generally, with the exception of zero coupon bonds, the spread between the market rate and the coupon rate of interest is not as great as used in this chapter's illustrations.

After issuance, the bonds are reported on the balance sheet at their carrying or book value. At any point in time, the carrying value of the bonds should be equal to the present value of the future cash flows related to the bond issue, discounted at the historical market rate of interest. From an accounting standpoint, the carrying value of the bonds is equal to the par value plus the balance of the premium (i.e., the unamortized premium), or net of the balance of the discount (i.e., the unamortized discount).

In addition, bond issue costs include the costs of printing, accounting and legal fees, and underwriting costs. These costs are usually accounted for as a deferred charge "Unamortized Bond Issue Costs" and should be amortized over the life of the bond issue. The unamortized balance of the bond issue costs is also considered part of the bonds carrying value (APB Opinion No. 21). Bond issue costs are considered a "true deferred charge" and should be reported on the asset side of the balance sheet (probably included in "other assets"). The bond issue costs are considered assets because these costs are considered reasonable and necessary to raise the debt financing. Due to this future service potential, the bond issue costs are usually classified on the asset side of the balance sheet. Alternatively, bond issue costs are netted against the net book value of bonds payable on the liability side of the balance sheet.

Illustrations of accounting for bonds issued at a discount and at a premium will be presented in the following section. The illustrations assume that there are no bond issue costs.

ILLUSTRATION OF ACCOUNTING FOR BONDS SOLD AT A DISCOUNT

To illustrate accounting for bonds issued at a discount, assume that on January 1, 2008 the Auto-Stop Corporation issued $10,000 of its $1,000 par value 8%, three-year bonds. The bond issue consists of 10, $1,000 par value bonds. Interest is payable semiannually each January 1st and July 1st. If the market rate of interest is 10%, the issue price of the bonds is determined as follows:

Semiannual coupon or cash interest = $10,000 X 8% x 1/2 = $400

Total coupon interest = $400 x 6 = $2,400

To determine the issue price of the bonds, the future cash flows related to the bond are discounted at the semiannual market rate of interest so that the bonds will be priced to yield the market. In this case, the semiannual market rate of interest is 5% and should be discounted over six interest periods (i.e., 3 years with semi-annual interest payments).

Determination of Bond Price (equal to the sum of the present value of the future cash flows): All PV factors are at the semi-annual market rate because the bonds are priced to yield the market. Therefore, i = 5%, (10% / 2), and n = 6, (3 years x 2): Use the Present Value Tables found in the appendix at the end of this book.

CASH FLOWS:	***PV COMPUTATIONS***	AMOUNT
Par Value (An Amount of $1) (Appendix, Table 2)	$10,000 x .746 =	$ 7,460
Interest (An Ordinary Annuity) (Appendix, Table 4)	$400 x 5.076 =	+ 2,030
Selling Price		$ 9,490
Par Value		(10,000)
Discount on Bonds Payable		$ 510

In this case, the quoted bond price is 94.9 or 94.9% of par value.

Solving this problem on a **financial calculator** we have;

		END MODE
X = -$9,492.43	=	**PV**
10,000	=	**FV**
400	=	**PMT**
6	=	**n**
5	=	**i**

Nature of the Discount. Economically, the discount represents additional interest for the corporation. In other words, the corporation borrows, and has the right to use $9,490 today, but must repay the full $10,000 at the maturity date. The reporting issue for the accountant is to determine when this additional cost of borrowing should be recognized in the financial statements. Clearly, the discount is only paid at maturity. However, waiting until maturity and repayment to reflect the additional expense is cash basis accounting. GAAP requires the use of the accrual basis and therefore, the additional interest cost must be accrued over each period of expected benefit.

Specifically, the accountant gives recognition to this additional cost of borrowing by allocating or amortizing the discount over the life of the bond issue. There are two alternative methods of amortization: the straight-line method and the effective interest-rate method. The effective interest-rate method is required by APB Opinion No. 21, *"Interest on Receivables and Payables,"* unless the results obtained by using the straight-line method are not materially different from the effective interest rate method. Under either method, there are two primary effects of discount amortization:

- Discount amortization increases interest expense so that the corporation's effective cost of borrowing is brought up to the higher market rate of interest.
- Discount amortization reduces the balance of the discount, and therefore, increases the carrying value of the bonds so that at maturity date, the carrying value of the bonds is equal to the par value.

Discount amortization is nothing more than accrued by unpaid interest. The adjustment increases interest expense and increases the amount payable, as reflected in the increased balance of the debt.

The Straight-Line Method of Amortization. The straight-line method of amortization results in a constant amount of amortization each period. However, the results are incorrect from an economic standpoint because the effective cost of borrowing fluctuates from period to period. In addition, the resulting debt carrying value is no longer equal to the present value of the remaining cash flows, discounted at the historical market rate of interest.

In the Auto-Stop Corporation illustration, straight-line amortization is calculated as follows:

$$\text{S/L} = \frac{\$510}{\text{6 interest periods}} = \$85 \text{ / semi annual interest period.}$$

Interest expense and the amount of the debt both increase by $85 each year.

The results for the first year (i.e., the first two interest periods) are:

Period	*Computations*	*Cost of Borrowing = Interest Expense / Beginning Balance of the Debt*
1	($400 + 85) / $9,490 = $485 / 9,490 =	.0511
2	($400 + 85)/($9,490 + 85) = $485/$9,575 =	.0506

In each period, straight-line amortization results in a constant amount of interest expense charged against income, $485 (i.e., the coupon interest of $400 plus the $85 discount amortization). Although the straight-line method provides a constant amount of amortization each year, it results in a variable cost of borrowing. The effective cost of borrowing fluctuates each interest period with the cost of debt declining each year, a result that does not make economic sense given fixed rate debt. In addition, the balance of the debt after the first amortization period, $9,575, (the beginning balance plus the accrued interest = $9,490 +85), is not the present value of the remaining cash flows over the next five years. Therefore, the straight-line method of amortization is not considered theoretically correct by APB Opinion No. 21, *"Interest on Receivables and Payables."*

The Effective Interest Rate Method of Amortization. The effective interest-rate method of amortization is considered theoretically correct and is the method required by APB Opinion 21, unless the effects of using the straight-line method are not materially different.

The effective interest rate method is considered theoretically correct because the effective total interest is computed at a constant rate or constant cost of borrowing. This approach is also considered theoretically sound because at any point in time, the carrying value of the debt is equal to the present value of the remaining future cash flows discounted at the historical market rate of interest. The amount of discount amortized and allocated to each period is the difference between the effective total interest and the cash interest.

This constant cost of borrowing, called the effective total interest is determined by multiplying the historical semiannual market rate of interest (which was used to establish the issue price of the bonds) by the outstanding balance of the debt. The amount of the discount amortized or allocated to each accounting period is the difference between the effective total interest and the cash or coupon (nominal) interest.

Although the amount of discount amortization varies each period, the rate of interest applied against the outstanding balance of the debt is constant. This amount is determined as follows.

Effective Interest Expense = Semiannual market rate x Outstanding balance of the debt

Discount Amortization = Effective interest expense - Cash (coupon) interest

The results of applying the effective interest-rate method are illustrated on the discount amortization table presented in Exhibit 3.2.

As noted in Exhibit 3.2, the discount amortization table constructed under the effective interest rate method applies a constant rate of interest against the outstanding balance of the debt. Again, the difference between the effective total interest of 5% and the cash or coupon interest of 4% is the discount amortization for the period.

The effects of discount amortization are (a) to increase the effective cost of borrowing for the corporation to 5% semiannually (10% annually compounded on a semi-annual basis) or to a total of $2,910, which is the sum of the coupon interest ($2,400) plus the discount ($510); and (b) to reduce the amount of the discount and to increase the carrying value of the bonds up to $10,000, the amount due at maturity.

In each accounting period, the effective interest expense is charged against the income statement, but only the coupon interest is reported on the cash flow statement. These effects can be seen in the following financial modeling worksheet for the first semi-annual interest payment.

Note that discount amortization, as is the case for any interest accrual, is a non-cash expense and is added back to net income to obtain the cash interest paid. The non-cash component is also reflected by the increase in the bond liability (implemented through the reduction of the discount account).

EXHIBIT 3.2: DISCOUNT AMORTIZATION TABLE

AMORTIZATION TABLE UNDER THE INTEREST RATE METHOD:

PERIOD	4% CASH INTEREST	5% EFFECTIVE INTEREST	DISCOUNT AMORTIZATION	OUTSTANDING BALANCE OF DEBT
(1)	(2)	(3) = 5% x (5	(4) = (3)-(2)	(5)=PRIOR (5) + (4)
0	=	=	=	$9,490.00
1	$400	* $ 474.50	** $ 74.50	*** 9,564.50
2	$400	478.23	78.23	9,642.73
3	$400	482.14	82.14	9,724.87
4	$400	486.24	86.24	9,811.11
5	$400	490.56	90.56	9,901.67
6	$400	(r) 498.33	98.33	10,000.00
TOTALS	$2,400	(e) $2,910.00	$510.00	$0

NOTES:

* *= $9,490 x 5% = $474.50.*

** *= $474.50 - $400 = $74.50.*

*** *= $9,490 + 74.50 = $9,564.50.*

(r) *= ROUNDING ERROR = $3.25.*

(e) = EFFECTIVE COST OF BORROWING:

CASH OUTFLOW (PRINCIPAL + INTEREST = $10,000 + 2,400) = ($12,400)

CASH INFLOW (SELLING PRICE) = 9,490

EFFECTIVE COST OF BORROWING = ($ 2,910)

FINANCIAL MODELING WORKSHEET DISCOUNT AMORTIZATION FOR THE FIRST PERIOD

INCOME STATEMENT (FIRST)	
REVENUES:	
EXPENSES:	
Interest Expense	(474.50)
NET INCOME OR LOSS (a)	(474.50)

STATEMENT OF CASH FLOWS (THIRD)	
OPERATING ACTIVITIES:	
NET INCOME OR LOSS (a)	(474.50)
ADD: Bond Discount Amortization	+74.50
Operating Cash Flow	(400.00)
INVESTING ACTIVITIES:	
FINANCING ACTIVITIES:	
INCREASE (DECREASE) IN CASH (b)	(400.00)
ADD: BEGINNING CASH BALANCE	
ENDING CASH BALANCE	

BALANCE SHEET (SECOND)			
ASSETS		LIABILITIES	
CURRENT ASSETS		CURRENT LIABILITIES	
CASH (b)	(400.00)		
		NONCURRENT LIABILITIES	
		Bonds Payable	
		Discount on bonds	+74.50
		Bonds payable-net	+74.50
NONCURRENT ASSETS		STOCKHOLDERS' EQUITY	
		CAPITAL STOCK	
		APIC	
		RETAINED	
		EARNINGS (a)	(474.50)
		TOTAL	
		LIABILITIES &	
		STOCKHOLDERS'	
TOTAL ASSETS	(400.00)	EQUITY	(400.00)

ILLUSTRATION OF A BOND ISSUED AT A PREMIUM

In order to illustrate accounting for bonds issued at a premium, assume that on January 1, 2008, the Auto-Stop Corporation issued $10,000 of its $1,000 par value 8%, three-year bonds. The bond issue consists of 10, $1,000 par value bonds. Interest is payable semiannually each January 1st and July 1st. If the market rate of interest is 6%, the issue price of the bonds is determined as follows:

Semiannual coupon or cash interest = $10,000 x 8% x 1/2 = $400

Total coupon interest = $400 x 6 = $2,400.

To determine the issue price of the bonds, the future cash flows related to the bond are discounted at the semiannual market rate of interest so that the bonds will be priced to yield the market. In this case, the semiannual market rate of interest is 3% and should be discounted over six interest periods (i.e., 3 years with semi-annual interest payments).

Determination of Bond Price (equal to the sum of the present value of the future cash flows): All PV factors are at the semi-annual market rate because the bonds are priced to yield the market. Therefore, i = 3%, (6% / 2), and n = 6 (3 years x 2): Use the Present Value Tables found in appendix to this chapter:

Cash Flows:	***PV Computations***	***Amount***
Par Value (An Amount of $1): (Table 3A-2)	$10,000 x .838 =	$ 8,380
Interest (An Ordinary Annuity) (Table 3A-4)	$400 x 5.417 =	+2,167
Selling Price		$ 10,547
Par Value		(10,000)
Premium on Bonds Payable		$ 547

In this case, the quoted bond price is 105.47 or 105.47% of par value.

Using a **financial calculator** to determine the bond price we have:

END MODE

x = -$10,541.72 = PV

10,000 = FV

400 = PMT

3 = n

5 = i

The financial statement effects of this bond issue are presented below:

FINANCIAL MODELING WORKSHEET BONDS ISSUED AT A PREMIUM

INCOME STATEMENT (FIRST)	
REVENUES:	
EXPENSES:	
NET INCOME OR LOSS *(a)*	

STATEMENT OF CASH FLOWS (THIRD)	
OPERATING ACTIVITIES:	
NET INCOME OR LOSS *(a)*	
INVESTING ACTIVITIES:	
FINANCING ACTIVITIES:	
Issued Bonds Payable	***+10,547***
INCREASE (DECREASE) IN CASH *(b)*	***+10,547***
ADD: BEGINNING CASH BALANCE	
ENDING CASH BALANCE	

BALANCE SHEET (SECOND)			
ASSETS		***LIABILITIES***	
CURRENT ASSETS		***CURRENT LIABILITIES***	
Cash *(b)*	***+10,547***		
		NONCURRENT LIABILITIES	
		Bonds Payable-par	***10,000***
		Premium on Bonds	***+547***
		Bonds payable-gross	***+10,547***
NONCURRENT ASSETS		***STOCKHOLDERS' EQUITY***	
		CAPITAL STOCK	
		APIC	
		RETAINED	
		EARNINGS *(a)*	
		TOTAL	
		LIABILITIES &	
		STOCKHOLDERS'	
TOTAL ASSETS	***+10,547***	***EQUITY***	***+10,547***

Nature of the Premium. The premium represents "interest savings" for the corporation. That is, the corporation borrows and has the use of $10,547, but must only repay the creditor $10,000 at the maturity date. The interest savings from the premium are collected on the date of issue. We cannot recognize the interest savings at this point because we cannot use the cash basis. Rather, the interest savings are allocated over the expected period of benefit, or the bond term.

Similar to the discount case, the premium or interest savings must be allocated or amortized to each interest period over the life of the bond issue.

The effects of the premium amortization are two-fold:

- Reduce the interest expense so that the corporation's effective cost of borrowing is brought down to the lower market rate of interest
- Reduce the premium so that the carrying value of the bonds is brought down to the par value at the maturity date

As in the case of the bond discount, the premium could be amortized by the straight-line method or the effective interest-rate method of amortization. As noted earlier, according to APB Opinion 21, the effective interest-rate method is required, unless the effects of using the straight-line method are not materially different. The theoretical superiority of the effective interest rate method relative to the straight-line method was explained and illustrated in the discussion of accounting for bonds sold at a discount and will not be repeated here.

The Effective Interest Rate Method of Amortization. Under the effective interest-rate method of amortization, premium amortization is calculated in the same way as in the discount case. Specifically, the total effective interest for the period is determined by multiplying the semiannual market rate of interest by the outstanding balance of the debt. The amount of premium to amortize is the difference between the effective total interest and the cash or coupon interest for the period.

The premium amortization table under the effective interest rate method is presented in Exhibit 3.3.

EXHIBIT 3.3: PREMIUM AMORTIZATION TABLE

AMORTIZATION TABLE UNDER THE INTEREST RATE METHOD:

PERIOD	4% CASH INTEREST	3% EFFECTIVE INTEREST	PREMIUM AMORTIZATION	OUTSTANDING BALANCE OF DEBT
(1)	(2)	(3) = 3% x (5)	(4) = (3)-(2)	(5)=PRIOR (5) - (4)
0	-	-	-	$10,547.00
1	$400	* $ 316.41	** $ 83.59	***10,463.41
2	$400	**313.9**	86.1	10,377.31
3	$400	**311.32**	88.68	10,288.63
4	$400	308.66	91.34	10,197.29
5	$400	305.92	94.08	10,103.21
6	$400	(r) 296.79	103.21	10,000.00
TOTALS	$2,400	(e)$1,853.00	$547.00	$0

NOTES:

* = *$10,547 x 3% = $316.41.*

** = *$316.41 - $400 = $83.59.*

*** = *$10,547 - 83.59 = $10,463.41.*

(r) = *ROUNDING ERROR = $6.31.*

(e) = EFFECTIVE COST OF BORROWING:

CASH OUTFLOW (PRINCIPAL + INTEREST = $10,000 + 2,400)	*= ($12,400)*
CASH INFLOW (SELLING PRICE)	*= 10,547*
EFFECTIVE COST OF BORROWING	*= ($ 1,853)*

(s) *If the straight-line method was used, the premium would be amortized as follows:*

Straight Line Amortization = $547/6 Interest Periods = $91.17/Period

As noted in Exhibit 3.3, the premium amortization table constructed under the interest rate method applies a constant rate of interest against the outstanding balance of the debt. The difference between the effective total interest at 3% and the cash or coupon interest of 4% is the premium amortization for the period. The effects of premium amortization are (a) to decrease the effective cost of borrowing for the corporation to 3% semiannually or 6% annually, or to a total of $1,853, which is the difference between the coupon interest ($2,400) and the premium ($547); and (b) to reduce the amount of the premium and to reduce the carrying value of the bonds down to $10,000, the amount due at maturity.

In each accounting period, the effective interest expense is charged against the income statement, but the higher coupon interest is reported on the cash flow statement. These effects can be seen in the following financial modeling worksheet for the first semi-annual interest payment.

Note that the premium amortization is similar to a non-cash revenue (i.e., interest savings) and is deducted from net income to obtain the higher cash interest paid. The non-cash component is also reflected by the reduction in the bond liability (implemented through the reduction of the premium account).

Finally, the cash flows related to a particular bond issue are the same whether the bonds are issued at par, at a premium or at a discount. As noted in all the worksheets presented, the cash outflow for interest is always $400. The financial modeling worksheet for the premium case is presented below.

FINANCIAL MODELING WORKSHEET PREMIUM AMORTIZATION FOR THE FIRST PERIOD

INCOME STATEMENT (FIRST)	
REVENUES:	
EXPENSES:	
Interest Expense	***(316.41)***
NET INCOME OR LOSS (a)	***(316.41)***

STATEMENT OF CASH FLOWS (THIRD)	
OPERATING ACTIVITIES:	
NET INCOME OR LOSS (a)	***(316.41)***
LESS: Bond Premium Amortization	***(83.59)***
Operating Cash Flow	***(400.00)***
INVESTING ACTIVITIES:	
FINANCING ACTIVITIES:	
INCREASE (DECREASE) IN CASH (b)	***(400.00)***
ADD: BEGINNING CASH BALANCE	
ENDING CASH BALANCE	

BALANCE SHEET (SECOND)			
ASSETS		***LIABILITIES***	
CURRENT ASSETS		***CURRENT LIABILITIES***	
CASH (b)	***(400.00)***		
		NONCURRENT LIABILITIES	
		Bonds Payable	
		Premium on bonds	***(83.59)***
		Bonds payable-gross	***(83.59)***
NONCURRENT ASSETS		***STOCKHOLDERS' EQUITY***	
		CAPITAL STOCK	
		APIC	
		RETAINED EARNINGS (a)	***(316.41)***
		TOTAL LIABILITIES & STOCKHOLDERS' EQUITY	
TOTAL ASSETS	***(400.00)***		***(400.00)***

SPECIAL ISSUES RELATING TO CORPORATE DEBT

In accounting for corporate debt, several complex transactions can arise which either extinguish the debt or significantly modify the structure of the outstanding balance of the debt. Corporate debt can be retired by a call or an open market repurchase. The structure of the debt can be modified by an early settlement or a modification agreement. Some of these transactions pose formidable theoretical questions regarding proper accounting and reporting treatment.

In this section of the chapter, special issues related to accounting for corporate debt are examined. Specifically, this section presents the accounting and reporting standards for early extinguishment of debt and troubled debt restructurings.

EARLY EXTINGUISHMENT OF DEBT

If debt is retired before maturity at the option of the issuing corporation, the gain or loss is classified as a component of income from continuing operations on the income statement. Transactions qualifying as an early extinguishment of debt include: (i) calling in a bond issue, (ii) an open market repurchase and (iii) a refinancing of a bond issue.

FASB Statement No. 140, *"Accounting for Transfers and Servicing of Financial Assets and Extinguishments of Liabilities (a replacement of FASB Statement No. 125),"* requires that a liability be extinguished or derecognized if and only if either:

- The debtor pays the creditor and is relieved of its obligation for the liability or
- The debtor is legally released from being the primary obligor under the debt agreement either judicially or by the creditor.

For transactions that qualify as an early extinguishment of debt, the gain or loss is determined by taking the difference between the carrying value of the debt and the retirement price. If the corporation pays more than the carrying value of the debt, a loss is recorded. Conversely, if the corporation pays less than the carrying value of the debt, a gain on early retirement is recognized. For purposes of this calculation, the carrying value of the debt is reduced by the balance of any unamortized both issue cost. That is:

Gain or Loss Computation

Remaining Carrying Value of the Debt	**$ XXX**
Less: Retirement Price	**(XX)**
Gain (Loss) on Early Extinguishment	**$ XX**

To illustrate, assume the Auto-Stop Corporation decides to retire the debt originally issued at a discount at the end of period 4, (i.e., after two full years or 1 year to maturity). If the retirement price is $9,500, there would be an ordinary gain of $311.11. (i.e., $9,811.11 - 9,500). The carrying value of $9,811.11 was obtained from the discount amortization table found in Exhibit 3.2. As noted below the same amount could be obtained by using a financial calculator with a $2.95 rounding error.

		END MODE
x = -$9,814.06	=	PV
10,000	=	FV
400	=	PMT
2	=	n
5	=	i

Note that both the par value and the balance of the unamortized discount must be removed from the accounts when the bonds are retired. Any unauthorized bond issue costs would be removed as well. The remaining discount can obtained by adding the discount amounts for periods 5 and 6 from the amortization table presented in Exhibit 3.2 (i.e., $90.56 + 98.33 = $188.89)

Sample disclosures for an early extinguishment of debt found in the Sensor Corporation and Subsidiaries 2012 annual report are presented in Exhibit 3.4. The reported loss on debt repurchases was $4.8 million and $145.2 million in 2012 and 2011 respectively.

EXHIBIT 3.4: EARLY EXTINGUISHMENT OF DEBT

Partial Consolidated Statements of Income (In Millions, Except Per Share Amounts)

YEAR ENDED DECEMBER 31	**2012**	2011	2010
REVENUES			
Net Earned Premiums	$ **6,966.48**	$ 6,634.92	$ 5,882.16
Net Investment Income	**582.12**	557.52	562.08
Net Realized Investment Gains	**72.48**	240.96	84.12
Other	**0.24**	1.08	11.76
Total Revenues	**7,621.32**	7,434.48	6,540.12
EXPENSES			
Losses and Loss Adjustment Expenses	**4,362.00**	4,194.24	4,142.64
Amortization of Deferred Policy Acquisition Costs	**1167.72**	1109.52	1015.44
Other Underwriting and Operating Expenses	**794.4**	777.72	762.36
Interest Expense	**106.32**	129.84	152.52
Loss on Debt Repurchases	**4.8**	145.2	—
Restructuring Charges	**3.24**	6.48	11.04
Total Expenses	**6,438.48**	6,363.00	6,084.00
Income from Continuing Operations before Income Taxes	**1182.84**	1071.48	456.12
Provision for Income Taxes	**353.52**	327.24	113.52
Income from Continuing Operations	**829.32**	744.24	342.6

Note 10: Debt

In 2012, we repurchased $31.1 in principal amount of 8.1% long term notes for $35.8. Including transaction costs, we reported a loss on debt repurchase of $4.8 pretax ($3.1 after tax) in the Consolidated Statements of Income.

In 2011, we repurchased $568.1 in principal amount of our 9.7% bonds and $205.1 to $174 in principal amount of our 6.5% notes. Including transaction costs, we reported a loss on debt repurchases of $145.2 pretax ($94.4 after tax) in our Consolidated Statements of Income in 2011.

ACCOUNTING FOR A TROUBLED DEBT RESTRUCTURING

Accounting and reporting for troubled debt restructurings are set forth in FASB Statement No.118, "Accounting by Creditors for Impairments of a Loan-Income Recognition and Disclosures."[3] SFAS 118 amends FASB Statements Nos. 15 and 114. A troubled debt restructuring occurs when a creditor, for economic or legal reasons relating to the debtors financial difficulties, grants concessions to the debtor that it would not otherwise consider. Therefore, the standards do not apply to modifications of debt agreements that made in response to changes in general economic conditions (e.g., interest rate changes).

There are two primary accounting issues involved with troubled debt restructurings: loss recognition and loss measurement.

The resolution of the loss measurement issue utilizes criteria similar to the conditions needed under FASB No. 5, "Accounting for Contingencies,"[4] to accrue a loss contingency: the loss must be both probable and subject to reasonable estimation.

The loss measurement issue is more complex. Economically, one would expect that the creditor's loss on the restructuring should equal the debtor's gain. However, under the current accounting standards, an asymmetric model is employed. That is, the technique used to measure the creditor's loss is not the same as the method used to compute the debtor's gain. Specifically, we use a discounted cash flow approach for the creditor to maximize the creditor's loss but use an undiscounted cash flow methodology for the debtor to minimize the debtor's gain. Therefore, the purpose of the asymmetric model is to maximize the creditor's loss and minimize the debtor's gain. Maximizing the creditor's loss and minimizing the debtor's gain is a primary objective of the FASB in accounting for troubled debt. This can be illustrated by a simple restructuring case.

Assume that a company owes a financial institution $290 which is due today. The financial institution agreed to restructure the debt. Under the restructuring agreement, the debtor company must pay $100 per year for three years. Assume the company's cost of capital is 8%. The creditor uses a discounted cash flow approach to determine the present value of the restructured cash flows as $258. The creditor's loss is equal to $32 (i.e., $290 – 258). The debtor uses the sum of the undiscounted cash flows to determine the gain. In this case the gain recognized by the debtor is $10 (i.e., $300 – 290). The asymmetric model can be perfected by conservatism. Maximizing losses of financial institutions reflects the decline in values of the asset. It also seems prudent to minimize gain recognition caused by a debtor's financial difficulties.

There are two types of troubled debt restructurings: restructurings and impairments. Restructurings include both a full settlement of debt and a continuation of debt with a modification of terms. Therefore, a restructuring includes: transfers of noncash assets to settle the debt in full, granting an equity interest in full settlement of the debt, and continuation of the debt with a modification of terms. Terms that are modified on the restructured debt generally include these elements:

---

3. FASB ASC 310, ASC 470, ASC 310 [Predecessor literature: "Accounting by Creditors for Impairments of a Loan-Income Recognition and Disclosures," *Statement of Financial Accounting Standards No. 118* (Norwalk, Conn.: FASB, 1994)]; [Predecessor literature: "Accounting by Debtors and Creditors for Troubled Debt Restructurings," *Statement of Financial Accounting Standards No. 15* (Norwalk, Conn.: FASB, 1977)]; [Predecessor literature: "Accounting by Creditors for Impairment of a Loan, "*Statement of Financial Accounting Standards No. 114* (Norwalk, Conn.: FASB, 1993)].

4. FASB ASC 450 [Predecessor literature: "Accounting for Contingencies," *Statement of Financial Accounting Standards No. 5* (Norwalk, Conn.: FASB, 1975)].

- Reduction of the principal amount
- Extension of the maturity date
- Reduction of the face rate of interest
- Forgiving accrued interest

A troubled debt restructuring does not occur if the fair value of the assets transferred or the equity interest granted are at least equal to the face value of the debt (i.e., there is no creditor loss or debtor gain).

Impairment. The impairment loss is based on management's judgment and is not a transaction. An impaired loan exists when it is probable that the creditor will be unable to collect all amounts due (principal and interest) according to terms of the loan and the loss is subject to reasonable estimation. When a loan is impaired, the loan continues, but its carrying value is reduced (i.e. all or a portion is written off). This is similar to accounting for any bad debt. The differences between a loan impairment and recognition of an uncollectible account are the loss computation and the subsequent accounting for any deferred interest components.

The impairment loss is computed as the difference between the carrying value of the loan and the present value of the impaired or reduced future cash flows discounted at its original rate (i.e., the historical effective rate). Accounting for the creditor is similar to accounting for the bad debt expense. Also, as is the case in accounting for bad debts, the debtor makes no accounting entry for an impaired loan.

The use of the historical effective rate of interest is justified for the following reasons. First, an ongoing assessment of a loan should be made using historical amount. In addition, losses should only reflect deterioration in credit quality, which is reflected by changes in legally contracted terms and cash flows (i.e., interest payments, principal amount and loan term). This assessment should not reflect current market or economic conditions because the restructuring or impairment loss does not involve an external or market transaction. However, the fair value option under FASB 159 is available to mark the imared loan to market.

Recognition of interest income by the creditor after the impairment is questionable. If a loan is impaired, accrued interest may not be collected when due. However, if a creditor does not expect to collect accrued interest, then the loan may be without value and should be completely written off. Under this theory, a cash basis should be used to account for interest. Conversely, given that the loan is not totally written off, then some portion of the interest has value to the creditor and should be accrued. In this case, the accrual basis for a modified amount of interest income can be employed.

Restructuring. A restructuring is a transaction or an economic event and not simply an estimate, as is the case for a loan impairment. Accounting for a restructuring for the debtor and the creditor is summarized below.

ACCOUNTING FOR THE DEBTOR: FULL SETTLEMENT OF DEBT

One possible means of terminating a debt obligation is to transfer noncash assets to the creditor in full settlement of the debt. The debtor will recognize an ordinary gain on the settlement of debt. The gain on restructuring is equal to the excess carrying value of the debt over the fair value of the assets transferred.

The debtor will also recognize an ordinary gain or loss on the noncash asset transfer. The gain or loss on the asset transfer is equal to the difference between the fair value of the assets transferred and the net book value of the assets transferred.

As an alternative, the debtor can settle the debt in full by granting an equity interest to the creditor. In this case, the debtor will recognize an ordinary gain on the settlement of debt. The gain on restructuring is equal to the excess carrying value of the debt over the fair value of the equity interest granted. There is no gain or loss on the equity issuance. This is considered a capital transaction and is simply treated as any new stock issue or the sale of treasury stock.

In both types of full settlement of the debt, the gains recognized by the debtor are classified as income from continuing operations under FASB Statement No. 145 and qualify as an early extinguishment of debt.

ACCOUNTING FOR THE DEBTOR: MODIFICATION OF TERMS

The debtor's accounting for a troubled debt restructuring when there is a modification of terms depends on whether the total undiscounted future cash flows are greater or less than the carrying value of the debt.

Note that the debtor does not use discounted cash flows in determining the gain on a modification. This results in asymmetric accounting treatment between the debtor and the creditor when there are modifications of loan terms.

When the total undiscounted future cash flows are ***less than*** the carrying value of the debt, an ordinary gain on restructuring is recorded. The gain is the difference between the sum of the undiscounted future cash flows and the carrying value of the debt. In this case, the carrying value of the debt is restated to equal the sum of the undiscounted future cash flows. This means that the present value of the future cash flows is the same as the sum of the undiscounted cash flows. As a result, there is a zero effective interest rate so that all payments reduce the principal directly.

When the total undiscounted future cash flows ***exceed*** the carrying value of the debt, no gain is recognized (if the FASB's logic was followed a loss would be recorded!) However, this will result in a lower effective interest rate and in this way the "gain" on restructuring is spread over the remaining term of the debt.

ACCOUNTING FOR THE CREDITOR: FULL SETTLEMENT OF DEBT AT LESS THAN THE RECORDED AMOUNT

In this case, the creditor will accept a noncash asset or equity shares of the debtor in full settlement of the debt. The noncash assets or the equity securities received from the debtor are recorded at fair value. The excess carrying value of the receivable (i.e., the investment in the loan), over the fair value of the assets received is recorded as an ordinary loss. This ordinary loss is either recorded as a charge to the bad debt expense or the allowance for bad debts, if such a provision had been established for the loan, (e.g., a loan loss reserve).

ACCOUNTING FOR THE CREDITOR: CONTINUATION OF DEBT WITH A MODIFICATION OF TERMS

Unlike the debtor, the creditor must use a discounted cash flow methodology in accounting for a modification. According to FASB Statement No. 114, *"Accounting by Creditors for Impairment of a Loan,"* the loan is considered impaired when it is probable that the creditor will not be able to collect all amounts due under the terms of the loan.

The impairment is determined by first computing the present value of the modified future cash flows at the historical (original) effective interest rate.

The creditor's loss is equal to the difference between the present value of the modified future cash flows and the carrying value of the debt. This ordinary loss is either recorded as a charge to the bad debt expense or the allowance for bad debts, if such a provision had been established for the loan (e.g., a loan loss reserve).

ILLUSTRATIONS OF TROUBLED DEBT RESTRUCTURINGS ARE PRESENTED BELOW

Illustrations:

1. Full Settlement of Debt at Less Than the Recorded Amount.

Case A: Transfer of Noncash Assets.

Assume that the Proven Company owes $100,000 plus $20,000 of accrued interest to the Kimball County Bank. Due to Proven's financial problems, the bank agrees to accept a piece of equipment with a fair market value of $80,000. The asset has a net book value of $85,000 (Original cost $285,000 and accumulated depreciation up to the date of the settlement, $200,000).

Debtor Accounting:

Ordinary Gain on Restructuring	=	Carrying Value of the Debt	–	FMV of the Asset
$40,000	=	$120,000	–	$80,000
Ordinary Loss on Asset Transfer	=	Net Book Value	–	FMV of the Asset
($ 5,000)	=	$85,000	–	$80,000

A financial modeling worksheet for the above restructuring is presented below:

FINANCIAL MODELING WORKSHEET CASE 1A: TRANSFER OF NONCASH ASSETS IN FULL SETTLEMENT OF THE DEBT: DEBTOR

INCOME STATEMENT (FIRST)	
REVENUES:	
Gain on Restructure	***+40,000***
EXPENSES:	
Loss on Disposal	***(5,000)***
NET INCOME OR LOSS (a)	***+35,000***

STATEMENT OF CASH FLOWS (THIRD)	
OPERATING ACTIVITIES:	
NET INCOME OR LOSS (a)	***+35,000***
ADD: Loss on Disposal	***+5,000***
Less: Gain on Restructure	***(40,000)***
INVESTING ACTIVITIES:	
FINANCING ACTIVITIES:	
INCREASE (DECREASE) IN CASH (b)	***-0-***
ADD: BEGINNING CASH BALANCE	
ENDING CASH BALANCE	

BALANCE SHEET (SECOND)			
ASSETS		***LIABILITIES***	
CURRENT ASSETS		***CURRENT LIABILITIES***	
CASH (b)	***-0-***		
		NONCURRENT LIABILITIES	
		Notes Payable	***(120,000)***
		STOCKHOLDERS' EQUITY	
NONCURRENT ASSETS			
Equipment	***(285,000)***	***CAPITAL STOCK***	
Accumulated Depreciation	***+200,000***	***APIC***	
Net Book Value	***(85,000)***	***RETAINED***	
		EARNINGS (a)	***+35,000***
		TOTAL	
		LIABILITIES &	
		STOCKHOLDERS'	
TOTAL ASSETS	***(85,000)***	***EQUITY***	***(85,000)***

Creditor Accounting:

Ordinary Loss on Restructuring	=	Carrying Value of the Debt	–	FMV of the Asset
($40,000)	=	$120,000	–	$80,000

The creditor's accounting is presented in the following financial modeling worksheet.

FINANCIAL MODELING WORKSHEET CASE 1A: TRANSFER OF NONCASH ASSETS IN FULL SETTLEMENT OF THE DEBT: CREDITOR

INCOME STATEMENT (FIRST)	
REVENUES:	
EXPENSES:	
Bad Debt Expense	(40,000)
NET INCOME OR LOSS (a)	(40,000)

STATEMENT OF CASH FLOWS (THIRD)	
OPERATING ACTIVITIES:	
NET INCOME OR LOSS (a)	40,000
Less: Bad Debt Expense	(40,000)
INVESTING ACTIVITIES:	
FINANCING ACTIVITIES:	
INCREASE (DECREASE) IN CASH (b)	-0-
ADD: BEGINNING CASH BALANCE	
ENDING CASH BALANCE	

BALANCE SHEET (SECOND)			
ASSETS		LIABILITIES	
CURRENT ASSETS		CURRENT LIABILITIES	
CASH (b)	-0-		
		NONCURRENT LIABILITIES	
		STOCKHOLDERS' EQUITY	
NONCURRENT ASSETS			
Note Receivable	(120,000)	CAPITAL STOCK	
Equipment	+80,000	APIC	
		RETAINED EARNINGS (a)	(40,000)
TOTAL ASSETS	(40,000)	TOTAL LIABILITIES & STOCKHOLDERS' EQUITY	(40,000)

Case B: Transfer of an Equity Interest.

Assume that the Proven Company owes $100,000 plus $20,000 of accrued interest to the Kimball County Bank. Due to Proven's financial problems, the bank agrees to accept Proven Company no-par common shares with a fair market value of $80,000.

Debtor Accounting:

Ordinary Gain on Restructuring	=	Carrying Value of the Debt	–	FMV of the Asset
<u>$40,000</u>	=	$120,000	–	80,000

FINANCIAL MODELING WORKSHEET CASE 1B: TRANSFER OF AN EQUITY INTEREST IN FULL SETTLEMENT OF THE DEBT: DEBTOR

INCOME STATEMENT (FIRST)	
REVENUES:	
Gain on Restructure	+40,000
EXPENSES:	
NET INCOME OR LOSS (a)	+40,000

STATEMENT OF CASH FLOWS (THIRD)	
OPERATING ACTIVITIES:	
NET INCOME OR LOSS (a)	+40,000
Less: Gain on Restructure	(40,000)
INVESTING ACTIVITIES:	
FINANCING ACTIVITIES:	
INCREASE (DECREASE) IN CASH (b)	- 0 -
ADD: BEGINNING CASH BALANCE	
ENDING CASH BALANCE	

BALANCE SHEET (SECOND)			
ASSETS		LIABILITIES	
CURRENT ASSETS		CURRENT LIABILITIES	
CASH (b)	- 0 -		
		NONCURRENT LIABILITIES	
		Notes Payable	(120,000)
		STOCKHOLDERS' EQUITY	
NONCURRENT ASSETS			
		CAPITAL STOCK	+80,000
		APIC	
		RETAINED	
		EARNINGS (a)	+40,000
		TOTAL LIABILITIES & STOCKHOLDERS' EQUITY	
TOTAL ASSETS	- 0 -		- 0 -

Creditor Accounting:

Ordinary Loss on Restructuring	=	Carrying Value of the Debt	–	FMV of the Asset
($40,000)	=	$120,000	–	80,000

FINANCIAL MODELING WORKSHEET CASE 1B: TRANSFER OF AN EQUITY INTEREST IN FULL SETTLEMENT OF THE DEBT: CREDITOR

INCOME STATEMENT (FIRST)	
REVENUES:	
EXPENSES:	
Bad Debt Expense	(40,000)
NET INCOME OR LOSS (a)	(40,000)

STATEMENT OF CASH FLOWS (THIRD)	
OPERATING ACTIVITIES:	
NET INCOME OR LOSS (a)	+40,000
Less: Gain on Restructure	(40,000)
INVESTING ACTIVITIES:	
FINANCING ACTIVITIES:	
INCREASE (DECREASE) IN CASH (b)	- 0 -
ADD: BEGINNING CASH BALANCE	
ENDING CASH BALANCE	

BALANCE SHEET (SECOND)			
ASSETS		LIABILITIES	
CURRENT ASSETS		CURRENT LIABILITIES	
CASH (b)	- 0 -		
		NONCURRENT LIABILITIES	
		STOCKHOLDERS' EQUITY	
NONCURRENT ASSETS			
Notes Receivable	(120,000)	CAPITAL STOCK	
Investments	+80,000	APIC	
		RETAINED EARNINGS (a)	(40,000)
		TOTAL LIABILITIES & STOCKHOLDERS' EQUITY	
TOTAL ASSETS	(40,000)		(40,000)

Continuation of Debt with a Modification of Terms.

Case A: Debtor Gain Case

DeMarco Industries has an outstanding debt amounting to $2,950,000. The notes carried a face rate of 8% and were issued at par. The debt is due today and is payable to the First Liquidity Bank.

DeMarco is experiencing financial difficulties and requested a debt restructuring. First Liquidity Bank agreed to the following terms:

- Extend the maturity date of the debt for three years.
- Reduce the face rate of interest to 6%.
- Reduce the balance of the debt to $2,000,000 (the new principal) and write-off $950,000.

Debtor Accounting:

To determine if a gain can be recorded, the debtor must compare the total undiscounted future cash flows with the carrying amount of the debt. If the total undiscounted future cash flows under the modified terms are less than the pre-restructuring carrying value of the debt, an ordinary gain can be recorded.

The debt is reduced by the difference between the total undiscounted future cash flows and the carrying amount of the debt. In other words, the debt is now carried at the total undiscounted future cash flows. This results in the same present and nominal values of the future cash flows, providing a zero effective interest rate. Therefore, all interest payments are used to reduce the principal.

In this case, DeMarco would make the following computations:

Modified Principal	$2,000,000
Interest (6% x $2,000,000 x 3 years)	360,000
Total Undiscounted Future Cash Flows	$2,360,000

The pre-restructuring carrying amount of the debt is $2,950,000 so that the ordinary gain on restructure is $590,000. The debtor reduces the note payable and records the ordinary gain on debt restructuring for $590,000. The modified carrying value of the debt is also equal to $2,360,000 and the effective interest rate is zero.

Each year, the debtor pays interest of $120,000 and this is recorded as a reduction of the note payable. After three years (at maturity), the debt is reduced to $2,000,000. The financial modeling worksheet for the debtor is presented below.

FINANCIAL MODELING WORKSHEET CASE 2A: CONTINUATION OF DEBT WITH MODIFIED TERMS: DEBTOR

INCOME STATEMENT (FIRST)	
REVENUES:	
Gain on Restructure	*+590,000*
EXPENSES:	
NET INCOME OR LOSS (a)	*+590,000*

STATEMENT OF CASH FLOWS (THIRD)	
OPERATING ACTIVITIES:	
NET INCOME OR LOSS (a)	*+590,000*
Less: Gain on Restructure	*(590,000)*
INVESTING ACTIVITIES:	
FINANCING ACTIVITIES:	
INCREASE (DECREASE) IN CASH (b)	*-0-*
ADD: BEGINNING CASH BALANCE	
ENDING CASH BALANCE	

BALANCE SHEET (SECOND)			
ASSETS		*LIABILITIES*	
CURRENT ASSETS		*CURRENT LIABILITIES*	
CASH (b)	*-0-*		
		NONCURRENT LIABILITIES	
		Notes Payable	*(590,000)*
		STOCKHOLDERS' EQUITY	
NONCURRENT ASSETS			
		CAPITAL STOCK	
		APIC	
		RETAINED EARNINGS (a)	*+590,000*
TOTAL ASSETS	*-0-*	*TOTAL LIABILITIES & STOCKHOLDERS' EQUITY*	*-0-*

The debtor's revised amortization schedule indicates that all payments will be applied against the principal amount of the debt and there is a zero effective interest rate for the remaining debt term.

SCHEDULE FOR INTEREST AND PRINCIPAL AMORTIZATION—
EFFECTIVE INTEREST METHOD
$2,360,000 NOTE MODIFIED TO YIELD 0%

Date	6% Cash Interest	0% Effective Interest	Principal Amortized	Carrying Amount
1/01/X0				$2,360,000
12/31/X1	$120,000	$0	$120,000	2,240,000
12/31/X2	120,000	0	120,000	2,120,000
12/31/X3	120,000	0	120,000	2,000,000
Total	$360,000	$0	$360,000	

Creditor Accounting:

The creditor must use a discounted cash flow methodology. The loss on restructuring is equal to the difference between the present value of the modified cash flows and the carrying value of the debt.

The present value of the modified cash flows can be determined using the present value tables in the appendix:

CASH FLOWS:		PV COMPUTATIONS	AMOUNT
Modified Principal =	$2,000,000 (Table 3A-2)	X.79383 =	$1,587,660
Interest =	120,000 (Table 3A-4)	X 2.57710 =	309,252
Present Value			$1,869,912

Financial calculator keystrokes to determine the present value of the modified cash flows are presented below:

$2,000,000	=	**FV**
3	=	**n**
8	=	**i**
$120,000	=	**PMT**
X	=	**PV**

PV = $1,896,916.

The ordinary loss recorded by the First Liquidity Bank is determined as follows:

PV of the Restructured Cash Flows	$1,896,916
Carrying Amount of the Debt	(2,950,000)
Ordinary loss on Debt Restructure	($1,053,084)

The loss is recorded as a charge to the bad debt expense (or an allowance for bad debts) and a reduction of notes receivable. The receivable is now carried at its present value using modified terms (i.e., $1,896,916) and is amortized at the historical effective rate of 8%. A standard amortization table would be used. This is the true economic loss to the creditor and economic gain to the debtor, but it is not recognized by the debtor. In meeting the FASB's objectives, the debtor's gain is minimized at $590,000 and the creditor's loss is maximized at $1,053,084.

It should be noted that by discounting at the historical effective rate, the loss only reflects the change in cash flows due to the modification. It does not reflect any current market factors. The financial modeling worksheet for the creditor is presented below.

FINANCIAL MODELING WORKSHEET CASE 2A: CONTINUATION OF DEBT WITH MODIFIED TERMS: CREDITOR

INCOME STATEMENT (FIRST)	
REVENUES:	
EXPENSES:	
Bad Debt Expense	(1,053,000)
NET INCOME OR LOSS (a)	(1,053,000)

STATEMENT OF CASH FLOWS (THIRD)	
OPERATING ACTIVITIES:	
NET INCOME OR LOSS (a)	(1,053,000)
ADD: Bad Debt Expense	+1,053,000
INVESTING ACTIVITIES:	
FINANCING ACTIVITIES:	
INCREASE (DECREASE) IN CASH (b)	- 0 -
ADD: BEGINNING CASH BALANCE	
ENDING CASH BALANCE	

BALANCE SHEET (SECOND)			
ASSETS		LIABILITIES	
CURRENT ASSETS		CURRENT LIABILITIES	
CASH (b)	- 0 -		
		NONCURRENT LIABILITIES	
NONCURRENT ASSETS		STOCKHOLDERS' EQUITY	
Notes Receivable	(1,053,000)	CAPITAL STOCK	
		APIC	
		RETAINED EARNINGS (a)	(1,053,000)
		TOTAL LIABILITIES & STOCKHOLDERS' EQUITY	
TOTAL ASSETS	(1,053,000)		(1,053,000)

Case B: Debtor No Gain Case

DeMarco Industries has an outstanding debt amounting to $2,950,000. The notes carried a face rate of 8% and were issued at par. The debt is due today and is payable to the First Liquidity Bank.

DeMarco is experiencing financial difficulties and requested a debt restructuring. First Liquidity Bank agreed to the following terms:

- Extend the maturity date of the debt for eight years
- Reduce the face rate of interest to 6%
- Reduce the balance of the debt to $2,000,000 (the new principal)

Debtor Accounting:

To determine if a gain can be recorded, the debtor must compare the total undiscounted future cash flows with the carrying amount of the debt. If the total undiscounted future cash flows under the modified terms ***exceed*** the pre-restructuring carrying value of the debt, an ordinary gain ***cannot*** be recorded. No entry is made on the books of the debtor and a new (lower) effective interest rate is determined. ***Economically, the lower effective cost of borrowing spreads the gain over the modified term of the loan.***

In this case, DeMarco would make the following computations:

Modified Principal	$2,000,000
Interest (6% x $2,000,000 x 8 years)	960,000
Total Undiscounted Future Cash Flows	$2,960,000

The pre-restructuring carrying amount of the debt is only $2,950,000 so that the ordinary gain cannot be recorded. No journal entry is made on the date of the restructure. The debtor continues to carry the note payable at $2,950,000 and the new effective interest rate is determined as follows:

$2,000,000	=	**FV**
8	=	**n**
-$2,950,000	=	**PV**
$120,000	=	**PMT**
X	=	**i**

i = .0493%

Each year, the debtor pays $120,000 and this is allocated between interest expense and a reduction of the note payable. After eight years (at maturity), the debt is reduced to $2,000,000 on the amortization table.

Note that with the effective interest rate now lower than the coupon rate on the debt, the amortization table presented below functions as a premium amortization.

**SCHEDULE FOR INTEREST AND DISCOUNT AMORTIZATION—
EFFECTIVE INTEREST METHOD
$2,950,000 NOTE MODIFIED TO YIELD .0493%**

Date	6% Cash Interest	.0493% Effective Interest	Discount Amortized	Carrying Amount
1/1/X1				$ 2,950,000
12/31/X1	$120,000	$1,454	$118,546	2,831,458
12/31/X2	120,000	1,396	118,604	2,712,853
12/31/X3	120,000	1,337	118,663	2,594,191
12/31/X4	120,000	1,279	118,721	2,475,470
12/31/X5	120,000	1,220	118,780	2,356,690
12/31/X6	120,000	1,162	118,838	2,237,852
12/31/X7	120,000	1,103	118,897	2,118,955
12/31/X8	120,000	1,044	118,955	2,000,000
Total	$960,000	$9,995	$950,000	

Creditor Accounting:

The creditor must use a discounted cash flow methodology. The loss on restructuring is equal to the difference between the present value of the modified cash flows and the carrying value of the debt.

The present value of the modified cash flows can be determined using the present value tables in the appendix:

CASH FLOWS:	*PV COMPUTATIONS*	AMOUNT
Modified Principal = $2,000,000 (Table 3A-2)	X .54027 =	$1,080,540
Interest = 120,000 (Table 3A-4)	X 5.74664 =	689,597
Present Value		$1,770,137

Financial calculator keystrokes to determine the present value of the modified cash flows are presented below:

$2,000,000	=	**FV**
8	=	**n**
8	=	**i**
$120,000	=	**PMT**
X	=	**PV**

PV = $1,770,134.

The ordinary loss recorded by the First Liquidity Bank is determined as follows:

PV of the Restructured Cash Flows	$1,770,134
Carrying Amount of the Debt	(2,950,000)
Ordinary loss on Debt Restructure	($1,179,866)

The loss is recorded as a charge to the bad debt expense (or an allowance for bad debts) and a reduction of notes receivable. The receivable is now carried at its present value using modified terms or at $1,770,134 and is amortized at the historical effective rate of 8%. A standard amortization table is used (not shown). Note that this is the true economic loss to the creditor and economic gain to the debtor, but it is not recognized by the debtor. In meeting the FASB's objectives, the debtor's gain is minimized at zero, and the creditor's loss is maximized at $1,179,866.

Note that by discounting at the historical effective rate, the loss only reflects the change in cash flows due to the modification. It does not reflect any current market factors. This transaction has the same impact on the financial statements as Case A.

ANALYSIS OF PENSION OBLIGATIONS

This section of the chapter will provide a detailed overview of accounting for pension plans. The accounting and reporting requirements for other post-retirement benefits are parallel to the pension standards and will not be discussed here.

Employers can adopt two types of pension plans; defined contribution plans and defined benefit plans. Under a defined contribution plan, the employer's only responsibility is to make the periodic contributions to the pension plan as defined by a contribution formula. An example of a defined contribution plan is a 401(k) plan. Because the employer's contributions are fixed (i.e., defined), the risk of loss from the assets accumulated by the fund are borne by the employee. In accounting for the defined contribution plan, the accountant simply charges the income statement for the amount of the defined contribution. If the contribution is less than the defined amount, a liability is recorded. Conversely, if the employer contributes more to the fund than required by the plan's contribution formula, a prepaid pension asset is recorded. In the case of a defined contribution plan, the footnote disclosures required include a description of the plan, the employee group covered, the formula for determining the defined contribution and the nature and impact of significant events affecting financial statement comparability from period to period.

Under the defined benefit plan, the benefits to be received by the employee are determined by a formula which usually provides for pension benefits based on a particular percentage of a salary level (e.g., the average of an employee's last three years of employment) and the number of years of service provided. Because the future benefits are defined, the risk of loss on the plan assets are borne by the employer. In addition, the employer must determine the magnitude of current funding requirements (i.e., contributions to the plan) in order to meet the mandatory pension benefit payments over the employee's retirement years. Because the employer's pension cost and obligation are dependent on future variables, the accounting and disclosure requirements for a defined benefit pension plan are more complex than for a defined contribution plan.

Defined benefits can be expressed in equation form as indicated below:

Defined Benefit = % X Salary Level X Credits for Years of Service

It should be noted that either a defined benefit or defined contribution plan can be "qualified" by the IRS for preferential tax treatment. Under a qualified plan, contributions made by the employer are tax deductible. In addition, plan earnings are not taxed at the employer level. The employees are only taxed upon receipt of the pension benefits for the portion contributed by the employer, plus any earned income on invested plan assets.

The accountant determines the pension liability or prepaid pension asset by implementation of FASB Statement No. 87, *"Employers' Accounting for Pensions"*[5] and its amendment, FASB Statement No. 158, *"Employers' Accounting for Defined Benefit Pension Plans and Other Postretirement Benefit Plans."*[6] There are extensive footnote disclosures required by the FASB reporting standards.

SFAS 87 requires the use of actuarial information provided by the pension plan but without adjustment, the accountant's pension asset or obligation will not always equal the funded status of the plan (i.e., the difference between the person assets and obligations). The pension plan is a separate legal and accounting entity. As a result, the pension plan may have its own management and a separate set of financial statements audited by a different, independent registered CPA firm. In fact, accounting for the pension plan itself is covered by FASB Statement No. 35, *"Accounting and Reporting by Defined Benefit Pension Plans."*[7] Due to the separation of the two entities (i.e., the employer and the defined benefit pension plan), SFAS 158 requires that the funded status of the pension plan (either an over-funded or under-funded plan), as determined by the actuary, be reported on the corporation's balance sheet. The adjustments to the bring accounting determined pension asset or liability to the funded status of the plan will flow through accumulated other comprehensive income in the stockholders' equity section of the balance sheet.

The purpose of this section of the chapter is to provide a discussion of the determination of the actuary's funded status, and compare it to the accountant's computation of the pension asset or obligation and the annual pension expense under a defined benefit plan. In addition, this section will illustrate the required adjustments that bring the accountant's pension asset or obligation to the actuarially determined funded status of the plan reported on the balance sheet.

The Actuarial Present Value of the Pension Obligation. The actuary determines the pension obligation by taking the present value of the future pension benefits to be distributed under the terms of the pension plan. The computation requires several assumptions as to employee base, salary levels, life expectancy, expected rates of return on plan assets and the expected discount rate at which the liability will ultimately be settled, appropriately called the ***"settlement rate."*** The settlement rate is the return necessary to settle the pension obligation by purchasing an annuity contract. The rate of return on this quality corporate debt has also been used as the settlement rate.

The actuarial present value of the benefit obligation is measured in three ways, based on the assumptions as to salary levels and whether or not the benefits are vested. In all three cases, the pension obligation is equal to the present value of the future defined benefits. The difference among each of these measures is how we compute the defined benefit. The key variables are the salary levels used and the employee base included in the computation.

5. FASB ASC 715 [Predecessor literature: "Employers' Accounting for Pensions," *Statement of Financial Accounting Standards No. 87* (Norwalk, Conn.: FASB, 1985)].

6. FASB ASC 715 [Predecessor literature: "Employers' Accounting for Defined Benefit Pension and Other Postretirement Plans-an amendment of FASB Statements No. 87, 88, 106, and 132R," *Statement of Financial Accounting Standards No. 158* (Norwalk, Conn.: FASB, 2006)]

7. FASB ASC 960 [Predecessor literature: "Accounting and Reporting by Defined Benefit Pension Plans," *Statement of Financial Accounting Standards No. 35* (Norwalk, Conn.: FASB, 1980)].

The salary level assumed will impact the future obligation because the defined pension benefits to be paid are usually determined by a formula that is based on salary levels and years of service. Typically, there is a minimum service requirement that must be met before an employee can vest in the pension plan. Vested benefits represent the pension benefits an employee is entitled to receive that are not contingent on further employment.

The different measures of the pension liability are discussed in the next section.

Different Measures of the Actuarial Pension Obligation. The three different measures of the pension obligation are the vested benefit obligation, the accumulated benefit obligation, and the projected benefit obligation.

The first measure of the pension obligation is the ***vested benefit obligation.*** The vested benefit obligation is determined by taking the present value of the future cash flows for the expected years of service by ***vested employees only***, using ***current salary levels*** in the benefit formula. This measure excludes all non-vested employees. The vested benefit obligation is the "most restrictive" pension liability for the corporation because these benefits are not dependent on additional years of service by the employee and are legally protected. The vested benefit obligation is protected by the Employee Retirement Income Security Act (ERISA) of 1974.

The general purpose of the ERISA legislation is to protect an employee's rights under pension plans. Specifically, ERISA requirements result in minimum funding amounts, guaranty of equal employee participation in the plan and protection of vested pension benefits. The Pension Benefit Guaranty Corporation (PBGC) was established by ERISA for the purpose of administering terminated plans. Upon termination of a plan, the PBGC can impose a lien against an employer's assets for the excess of vested benefit obligations over the fair value of the plan's assets. Although limited to 30% of the employer's net worth, the lien imposed by the PBGC takes priority over most creditors' claims and has the status of a tax lien. After settling the vested benefit obligation, any remaining plan assets may revert back to the corporation, subject to PBGC approval. Under ERISA requirements the corporation cannot obtain excess pension assets unless the original provisions of the plan specifically permit asset reversion. In addition, there could be excise tax penalties on plan termination.

The excise tax on reversions of surplus pension plan assets is generally imposed on asset reversions but is minimized if a portion of the reverted assets are transferred to a replacement plan. Reversions in which the transferred assets are used to fund employee medical plans are exempt from the excise tax. In addition to the excise tax, the value of the reverted assets is subject to tax at ordinary income rates.

Due to the restrictive provisions of the ERISA legislation with respect to vested benefits, the excess of the vested benefit obligation over the fair value of the plan's assets is generally considered part of a firm's off-balance sheet debt in the analysis of financial statements. It should be noted that this off-balance sheet debt only arises in the event of plan termination and is not to be considered part of an employer's obligation as a going concern. The unfunded vested benefit obligation is considered a termination basis liability. Unfortunately, the vested benefit obligation is no longer included in the accountant's pension disclosures.

The next measure of the pension obligation is known as the ***accumulated benefit obligation***. The accumulated benefit obligation is determined by taking the present value of the future pension benefits to be paid to all employees, vested and nonvested, computed by using the current salary levels in the benefit formula. Because it includes ***all employees*** (both vested and non-vested), the accumulated benefit obligation will be larger than the vested benefit obligation, and the difference between the two represents the obligation for unvested benefits. In addition, since it is based on ***current salary levels*** and does not account for expected increases in salaries, the accumulated benefit obligation is considered by many to be an understatement of the pension obligation of the firm and is therefore the least conservative going concern approach. The unfunded accumulated benefit obligation is commonly viewed as the minimum liability for the employer. The accumulated benefit obligation maybe disclosed in the footnotes to the financial statements.

The final measure of the pension liability is called the ***projected benefit obligation***. The projected benefit obligation is typically the largest pension obligation because it is determined by taking the present value of benefits to be paid to ***all employees***, both vested and unvested, and by using ***expected future salary levels*** in the benefit formula. The projected benefit obligation is favored by the FASB for the accountant's computation of the pension expense and the resulting pension asset or obligation because it considers the most realistic situation facing the corporation: a commitment to make pension payments based on a benefit formula using expected salary levels over current and future years of service, rather than simply applying the current salary level to all future years of service. The projected benefit method usually results in the largest and therefore the most conservative pension obligation.

The excess of the projected benefit obligation over the fair value of the plan's assets represents the employer's pension obligation on an ongoing (i.e., a going-concern) basis. It assumes a continuing plan with no changes in actuarial assumptions.

As will be illustrated below, pension accounting and the footnotes to the financial statements will provide the analyst with information that is sufficient to determine the composition of the funded status of the plan on an ongoing basis (i.e., the difference between the projected benefit obligation and the fair value of the plan's assets), as reported on the balance sheet as noted earlier the accumulated benefit can be included in the footnotes to the financial statements. Information regarding the vested benefit obligation is no longer disclosed in the financial statements must be obtained directly from the pension plan.

Other Actuarial Considerations. The actuarial present value of the pension obligation, determined under any method, considers all prior service costs, the actual gains and losses on pension assets and any gains or losses from changes in assumptions due to experience and additional information.

Prior or past service costs represent the cost of retroactive benefits for past service relating to an amendment or an initial adoption of a pension plan.

The actuarial gains or losses include the actual gains or losses on pension fund investments and adjustments to the pension obligation resulting from changes in actuarial assumptions. The actuary can revise assumptions such as those relating to life expectancy, rates of return on plan assets, employee turnover, expected salary levels and the settlement rate.

Accounting for Pension Obligations. The accountant's measurement of pension expense and the resulting pension asset or obligation is based on the provisions of SFAS 87 as amended by SFAS 158. SFAS 158 did not change the computation of pension expense as required by the original standard.

According to SFAS 87, the annual pension expense consists of six elements. These are the service or normal cost, interest on the beginning projected benefit obligation, the expected return on beginning plan assets, amortization of prior service costs, amortization of the transition element, and the recognition of actuarial gains and losses. The elements of pension expense are discussed in the following sections of this chapter.

Service or normal cost. The service cost component of the total pension expense is the actuarial present value of the formula benefits for services rendered by employees during the current period. Service cost is simply the change in the projected benefit obligation due to the change in the defined pension benefit component resulting from one additional year of employee service.

The total change in the projected benefit obligation would include increases for interest on the opening balance and decreases for benefit payments made during the year, in addition to the change in the defined pension benefit. It should be noted that the service cost component is provided in the actuary's report.

Interest on the projected benefit obligation. Interest on the projected benefit obligation represents the change in the pension liability "due to the passage of time." It is computed by multiplying the settlement rate by the beginning balance of the projected benefit obligation. This is similar to any interest accrual under the effective interest rate method of amortization.

The expected return on plan assets. The actual return on the plan assets is also provided in the actuary's report. However, SFAS 87, requires the use of the expected return rather than the actual return on plan assets. This is the first difference between the accounting and the actuarial computations. The difference between the actual and the expected return, the "unexpected return," is included as an adjustment in the actuarial gain or loss recognition for the year. The gain or loss recognized is a separate component of the total pension expense. The expected return is computed by multiplying the expected rate of return on plan assets by the fair market value of the plan assets at the beginning of the year. For example, if the plan holds an equity portfolio and the average return for such a portfolio is 12%, accountants simply multiply the five-year moving average value of the portfolio at the beginning of the year by 12%. The five-year moving average portfolio value is called the "market related asset value."

The use of the expected return and the market related asset value are part of the SFAS 87 "income smoothing objective." A primary objective of SFAS 87 was to determine a measure of pension expense that would not cause wide fluctuations in reported net income and earnings per share whenever there were significant changes in actuarial assumptions or material gains and losses on plan assets.

Amortization of prior service costs. Unlike the actuary, the accountant does not recognize the full amount of the cost of retroactive benefits for past service in the year of an amendment or at the initial adoption of a plan. Instead, the total prior service is amortized over the future service lives of the employees expected to receive benefits from the plan. The prior service cost is usually amortized by an accelerated method, similar to the sum of the year's digits method, under the assumption that the employer is more likely to realize greater productivity from the labor force in the earlier years than in the later years of an employee's service life.

Amortization of the transition amount. The transition amount resulted from adopting SFAS 87 and switching out of the old pension requirements of APB Opinion No. 8, *"Accounting for the Cost of Pension Plans."* The transition amount is the funded status of the plan at the date the firm adopts SFAS 87, where the funded status of the plan is the difference between the projected benefit obligation and the fair market value of the plan assets. The transition element also includes any existing asset or liability reported on the balance sheet on the date SFAS 87 was first adopted.

The transition amount could be a net asset (unrecognized transition gain) or liability (unrecognized transition loss) at the date of the change to SFAS 87. The amortization of the transition amount is usually done on a straight-line basis over the average remaining service lives of the employee base. The transition amortization could either increase or decrease the pension expense for the year, depending on the funded status of the plan at the date of the change in method. Regardless of the direction of the amortization, it is usually combined with the amortization of the prior service cost. SFAS 87 has been in effect since 1987 and as a result, the amount of the transition asset or liability is typically not expected to be significant today.

Actuarial gain or loss recognition. This component includes the adjustment to bring the actual return on plan assets up or down to the expected return (i.e., "the unexpected return"). In addition, the accountant recognizes a portion of the actuarial experience gain or loss and is included in this component of pension expense. Gain or loss recognition is subject to a materiality test (i.e., the corridor test).

As noted earlier, the objective of SFAS 87 with respect to experience gains or losses is to minimize or smooth the amount of gain or loss recognized in any one year. This was done in order to avoid wide fluctuations in the amount of pension expense charged against income which were caused by modifications in actuarial assumptions and estimates.

In order to accomplish this smoothing objective, SFAS 87, requires the use of the "corridor approach." The "corridor" is a materiality threshold for gain or loss recognition. The corridor is defined as 10% of the greater of the beginning projected benefit obligation or the fair value of plan assets at the beginning of the year. If the beginning balance of the cumulative unrecognized net gain or loss (including the cumulative unexpected return as of the beginning of the period) exceeds the corridor, the excess is amortized over the average remaining service life of the employees, but only for the current year. This is known as the "minimum amortization." According to SFAS 87, another "systematic method of amortization" can be used. However, the method must be "applied consistently, applied similarly to both gains and losses and must be disclosed." In addition, the minimum amortization must be used in any year in which the "minimum amortization is greater (reduces the net balance more)" than the other systematic approach.

In each subsequent year, another corridor test must be performed and if the balance of the unrecognized net gain or loss is less than the corridor, the amortization is suspended and no part of the net gain or loss is recognized in that period. An illustration of the corridor approach is presented below.

Illustration of the Corridor Approach: Assume that Clarke Company provides the following information regarding the balances of unrecognized gains and losses, plan assets and the projected benefit obligation (PBO) at the end of 2005.

2005: Unrecognized (Gain) Loss:	***Amount***
Beginning balance	$ -0-
Actuarial loss during the year	600,000
Amortization	-0-
Ending balance	$600,000
Average remaining service life	10 years
Ending PBO	$4,100,000
Ending plan assets (market related value)	$4,000,000

With a zero beginning balance in the unrecognized (gain) loss schedule, ***no corridor test is required in 2005.*** However, the 2005 ending balance of the unrecognized (gain) loss schedule is the beginning balance of 2006, requiring the corridor test below.

2006 Corridor Test:	***Amounts***
Corridor: 10% of the larger of the beginning PBO or beginning plan assets at market related value: PBO is larger: (10% x $4,100,000)	$410,000
Excess unrecognized loss over corridor: ($600,000 – 410,000)	$190,000
Minimum amortization: Add to pension expense for 2006: ($190,000 / 10 years)	$19,000

In this case, the accountant will increase pension expense by $19,000 for fiscal 2006. At this point, the balances of unrecognized gains and losses, plan assets and the projected benefit obligation (PBO) at the end of 2006 are presented in the following table:

2006: Unrecognized (Gain) Loss:	***Amount***
Beginning balance	$600,000
Actuarial loss during the year (assumed)	- 0 -
Amortization (See table above)	(19,000)
Ending balance	$581,000
Average remaining service life	10 years
Ending PBO (Assumed)	$6,000,000
Ending plan assets (market related value) (Assumed)	$6,200,000

The 2006 ending balances are used to test for the corridor minimum amortization at the beginning of 2007.

2007 Corridor Test:	***Amounts***
Corridor: 10% of the larger of the beginning PBO or beginning plan assets at market related value: Plan Assets are larger (10% x $6,200,000)	$620,000
There is ***no excess unrecognized loss over corridor:*** ($581,000 – 620,000)	$ - 0 -
Minimum amortization: NONE: There is no amortization for 2007.	$ - 0 -

Because the cumulative unrecognized loss at the beginning of 2007 falls below the corridor, there is no minimum amortization for the year.

Pension Expense and the Funded Status of the Plan. The accountant's pension expense charged against current income is equal to the net result of combining these six components. The combined amount is expensed on the income statement. In addition, pension footnote disclosures report the individual components of pension expense.

The amount of the accounting pension asset or liability is based on the pension contribution or funding made during the period. The funding decision by the employer is dependent on current and future cash flow requirements as well as on the ERISA minimum funding requirements and the maximum tax deduction permitted by the IRS code.

Over time, if the cumulative amount of pension contributions are equal the cumulative pension expense, there is no accounting pension asset or liability. If the cumulative contributions exceed the cumulative pension expense, there is an accounting prepaid pension asset and if the cumulative contributions are less than the cumulative pension expense, an accounting pension obligation results. Nonetheless, the accounting asset or liability is not usually equal to the funded status of the plan due to unrecognized gains and losses and unrecognized prior service cost. Therefore, after the determination of the pension expense and the resulting accounting pension asset or liability, SFAS 158 requires that the unrecognized components of the actuary's pension cost be included on the corporate balance sheet to reflect the funded status of the plan. Any adjustments made to the accounting prepaid pension asset or obligation will flow through accumulated other comprehensive income in the stockholders' equity section of the balance sheet.

Comprehensive Pension Illustration. The data for the illustration are contained in Exhibit 3.5. The information provided in Exhibit 3.5 includes balances at December 31, 2008 through December 31, 2010 and all assumptions required to implement SFAS 158.

The illustration will take a step-by-step approach which first builds the six components of the pension expense defined by SFAS 87 and then determines the accounting pension asset or liability. Finally, the funded status of the plan is computed and the accountant's pension asset or obligation is adjusted to correct this amount and report the funded status of the plan on the balance sheet. Deferred tax effects are not considered in the illustrations that follow.

EXHIBIT 3.5 PENSION ILLUSTRATION

Footos Candy Company offers a defined benefit pension plan to its salaried employees. The following information summarizes events related to the Footos pension plan for 2008 through 2010.

Description	2008	2009	2010
Plan assets at the beginning of the year (at fair value = market related asset value)	$540,000	***Solve***	***Solve***
Projected benefit obligation (PBO) at the beginning of the year	540,000	***Solve***	***Solve***
Service cost for the year	32,400	33,600	34,800
Settlement rate	9%	9%	9%
Expected return on plan assets	7%	7%	7%
Actual return on plan assets	37,800	50,000	33,600
Contributions for the year	38,400	54,800	88,400
Benefit payments for the year	20,400	28,800	24,000
Accumulated benefit obligation (ABO) at the end of the year	510,000	683,732	810,500
Vested benefit obligation (VBO) at the end of year	450,450	603,293	765,700
Accrued/prepaid pension cost at the beginning of the year	- 0 -	***Solve***	***Solve***
Prior service costs granted on 1/1/2009 (at present value)	- 0 -	50,400	- 0 -
Amortization of prior service costs	- 0 -	21,000	25,200
Increase in the ending projected benefit obligation due to changes in actuarial assumptions (i.e., actuarial loss)	- 0 -	90,000	- 0 -
Average remaining service life of employee base (ARSL)	10 years	10 years	10 years

Using the data presented in Exhibit 3.5 for 2008, the accounting measure of the accrued pension liability is the same as the actuarially determined funded status of the plan. Note that the vested benefit obligation and the accumulated benefit obligation amounts are presented each year for comparative purposes. The vested benefit obligation is provided in the actuarial report but is not included in the GAAP pension computations and disclosures.

The computation of pension expense is based on the information provided by the actuary. Since the 2008 expected return is equal to the 2008 actual return on plan assets and there are no plan amendments or actuarial gains and losses, the accounting data and the actuarial information are the same in this case. This is illustrated in the pension expense computation below.

Computation of Pension Expense for the year: 2008

Component of Pension Expense	Amount
+ Service cost	$ 32,400
+ Interest on beginning PBO (9% x $540,000)	48,600
- Expected return on beginning plan assets at market related value (7% x $540,000)	(37,800)
+ Amortization of prior service costs	- 0 -
+/- Amortization of cumulative unrecognized (gain) or loss (Corridor Method)	- 0 -
+/- Amortization of transition element: obligation (asset)	- 0 -
Pension expense for the year	$43,200

Given the pension expense of $43,200 and the fact that the actual contributions into the plan only amount $38,400, there is an accrued pension liability of $4,800.

The reconciliations of the beginning and ending projected benefit obligation (PBO) and plan assets at fair value as computed by the actuary are presented in the following tables. The use of parenthesis indicates a liability or a credit balance. The individual components used to build the projected benefit obligation and the plan assets at fair value will also be included in the pension footnote disclosures in the financial statements.

Actuarial Computation of the PBO	Amount
Beginning balance of the PBO	($540,000)
+ Adjustment for prior service cost granted at the beginning of the year	- 0 -
Adjusted beginning balance of the PBO	($540,000)
+ Service cost	(32,400)
+ Interest on adjusted beginning PBO	(48,600)
- Benefits paid during the year	20,400
+/- Actuarial loss (from changes in actuarial assumptions) at year end	- 0 -
Ending balance of the PBO	($600,600)

Actuarial Computation of Plan Assets at Fair Value	Amount
Beginning balance of plan assets	$540,000
+/- Actual return	37,800
+ Contributions made during the year	38,400
- Benefits paid during the year	(20,400)
Ending balance of plan assets	$595,800

Determination of the Balance Sheet Pension Asset or Obligation and Related Adjustments: 2008

Description	Amount
Projected benefit obligation (PBO): (Credit)	($600,600)
Less: Plan assets at fair value: Debit	595,800
Funded status: Plan assets in excess of (or less than) PBO reported by the plan	($4,800)
(Accrued)/prepaid pension cost computed by the accountant:	($ 4,800)
Credits: Increase the Obligation or Reduce the Asset	
Unamortized prior service cost: (Credit)	- 0 -
Cumulative unrecognized net loss: (Credit)	- 0 -
Unrecognized net obligation at transition: (Credit)	- 0 -
Debits: Reduce the Obligation or Increase the Asset	
Cumulative unrecognized net gain: Debit	- 0 -
Unrecognized net asset at transition: Debit	- 0 -
Total Cumulative Adjustments in Comprehensive Income (Credit Balance)	($ - 0 -)
Funded Status of the Plan Reported on the Balance Sheet (Obligation)	($ 4,800)

Because the accounting measure of the pension liability is the same as the funded status of the plan there are no adjustments needed to the accounting measure of the accrued pension liability. Note that the pension asset or liability is typically classified as noncurrent because the pension assets are restricted and cannot be used in current operations. Any liability liquidated from noncurrent assets must be classified as a noncurrent liability.

The financial modeling worksheet for the 2008 pension accrual is presented below.

FINANCIAL MODELING WORKSHEET 2008 PENSION ACCRUAL

INCOME STATEMENT (FIRST)	
REVENUES:	
EXPENSES:	
PENSION EXPENSE	(43,200)
NET INCOME OR LOSS (a)	(43,200)

STATEMENT OF CASH FLOWS (THIRD)	
OPERATING ACTIVITIES:	
NET INCOME OR LOSS (a)	(43,200)
Increase in the pension liability	+4,800
INVESTING ACTIVITIES:	
FINANCING ACTIVITIES:	
INCREASE (DECREASE) IN CASH (b)	(38,400)
ADD: BEGINNING CASH BALANCE	
ENDING CASH BALANCE	

BALANCE SHEET (SECOND)			
ASSETS		LIABILITIES	
CURRENT ASSETS		CURRENT LIABILITIES	
CASH (b)	(38,400)		
		NONCURRENT LIABILITIES	
		PENSION LIABILITY	+4,800
NONCURRENT ASSETS		STOCKHOLDERS' EQUITY	
		CAPITAL STOCK	
		APIC	
		ACCUMULATED OTHER COMPREHENSIVE INCOME	
		RETAINED	
		EARNINGS (a)	(43,200)
		TOTAL	
		LIABILITIES &	
		STOCKHOLDERS'	
TOTAL ASSETS	(38,400)	EQUITY	(38,400)

Again, there is no adjustment to comprehensive income on the 2008 balance sheet However, this adjustment is required for 2009 as illustrated below. Pension expense for 2009 is determined as follows:

COMPUTATION OF PENSION EXPENSE FOR THE YEAR: 2009

Component of Pension Expense	Amount
+ Service cost	$ 33,600
+ Interest on beginning PBO (9% x ($600,600 + 50,400 PSC))	58,590
- Expected return on beginning plan assets at market related value (7% x $595,800)	(41,706)
+ Amortization of prior service costs (Given)	21,000
+/- Amortization of cumulative unrecognized (gain) or loss (Corridor Method)	- 0 -
+/- Amortization of transition element: obligation (asset)	- 0 -
Pension expense for the year	$ 71,484

Note carefully how the retroactive benefits provided within the past service cost component (i.e., PSC), increases the beginning balance of the projected benefit obligation and impacts the interest component.

The cash contribution into the plan for 2009 is $54,800 and with the expense of $71,484, the accountant's accrued pension liability increases by $16,684. The beginning balance of the liability is $4,800 and with the 2009 increase of $16,684, the ending balance of the accrued liability is $21,484.

The reconciliations of the beginning and ending projected benefit obligation (PBO) and plan assets at fair value as computed by the actuary are presented in the following tables. This information will also be included in the pension footnote disclosures in the financial statements.

Actuarial Computation of the PBO	Amount
Beginning balance of the PBO	($600,600)
+ Adjustment for prior service cost granted at the beginning of the year	(50,400)
Adjusted beginning balance of the PBO	($651,000)
+ Service cost	(33,600)
+ Interest on adjusted beginning PBO	(58,590)
- Benefits paid during the year	28,800
+/- Actuarial loss (from changes in actuarial assumptions) at year end	(90,000)
Ending balance of the PBO	($804,390)

Actuarial Computation of Plan Assets at Fair Value	Amount
Beginning balance of plan assets	$595,800
+/- Actual return	50,000
+ Contributions made during the year	54,800
- Benefits paid during the year	(28,800)
Ending balance of plan assets	$671,800

Computation of Unamortized Prior Service Cost (PSC)	Amount
Beginning balance of unamortized PSC	$50,400
Amortization for the year	(21,000)
Ending balance of unamortized PSC	$29,400

The corridor test is not needed this year because there is no beginning balance of the unrecognized gain or loss. This is verified in the following computation.

Computation of Cumulative Unrecognized (Gain) or Loss	Amount
Beginning balance of unrecognized (gain) or loss	$ -0-
Unrecognized (gain) or loss for the year from changes in actuarial assumptions	90,000
Unexpected return: (Expected Return - Actual Return) = $41,706 - 50,000 =	(8,294)
Amortization for the year (based on Corridor Test)	-0-
Ending balance of unrecognized (gain) or loss	$81,706

The funded status of the plan is presented in the following table. Note that the unrecognized prior service cost ($29,400) and the unrecognized loss ($81,706) cause the $111,106 difference between the actuary's funded status, which is an obligation of $132,590, and accounting accrued liability of $21,484. The $111,106 difference will be charged to the accumulated other comprehensive income account in the stockholders' equity section of the balance sheet.

DETERMINATION OF THE BALANCE SHEET PENSION ASSET OR OBLIGATION AND RELATED ADJUSTMENTS: 2009

Description	Amount
Projected benefit obligation (PBO): (Credit)	($804,390)
Less: Plan assets at fair value: Debit	671,800
Funded status: Plan assets in excess of (or less than) PBO reported by the plan	($132,590)
(Accrued)/prepaid pension cost computed by the accountant:	($ 21,484)
Credits: Increase the Obligation or Reduce the Asset	
Unamortized prior service cost: (Credit)	(29,400)
Cumulative unrecognized net loss: (Credit)	(81,706)
Unrecognized net obligation at transition: (Credit)	-0-
Debits: Reduce the Obligation or Increase the Asset	
Cumulative unrecognized net gain: Debit	-0-
Unrecognized net asset at transition: Debit	-0-
Total Cumulative Adjustments in Comprehensive Income (Credit Balance)	($111,106)
Funded Status of the Plan Reported on the Balance Sheet (Obligation)	($132,590)

As noted earlier, the total adjustments will be charged to the accumulated other comprehensive income account in the stockholders' equity section of the balance sheet. The accounting pension accrual and the adjustment to bring the liability to the funded status of the plan are illustrated in the financial modeling worksheet presented below.

Note that the net changes are computed by using the shaded boxes. The beginning and ending balances are presented for reference purposes only.

FINANCIAL MODELING WORKSHEET 2009 ACCOUNTANT'S PENSION ACCRUAL AND ADJUSTMENT TO BRING THE ACCOUNTING ACCRUED PENSION LIABILITY TO THE ACTUARY'S FUNDED STATUS

INCOME STATEMENT (FIRST)	
REVENUES:	
EXPENSES:	
PENSION EXPENSE	*(71,484)*
NET INCOME OR LOSS (a)	*(71,484)*

STATEMENT OF CASH FLOWS (THIRD)	
OPERATING ACTIVITIES:	
NET INCOME OR LOSS (a)	*(71,484)*
Increase in the pension liability	*+16,684*
INVESTING ACTIVITIES:	
FINANCING ACTIVITIES:	
INCREASE (DECREASE) IN CASH (b)	*(54,800)*
ADD: BEGINNING CASH BALANCE	
ENDING CASH BALANCE	

BALANCE SHEET (SECOND)			
ASSETS		*LIABILITIES*	
CURRENT ASSETS		*CURRENT LIABILITIES*	
CASH (b)	*(54,800)*		
		NONCURRENT LIABILITIES	
		Pension Liability	
		Beginning Balance:	*4,800*
		2009 Accrual	*+16,684*
		2009 Adjustment	*+111,106*
		Ending Balance: Funded Status	*132,590*
		STOCKHOLDERS' EQUITY	
NONCURRENT ASSETS			
		CAPITAL STOCK	
		APIC	
		*AOCI** Beginning Balance*	*-0-*
		2009 Adjustment	*(111,106)*
		Ending Balance	*(111,106)*
		RETAINED	
		EARNINGS (a)	*(71,484)*
		TOTAL LIABILITIES & STOCKHOLDERS'	
TOTAL ASSETS	*(54,800)*	*EQUITY*	*(54,800)*

*** AOCI = Accumulated Other Comprehensive Income*

The accounting determined liability before adjustment is $21,484, consisting of the $4,800 beginning balance and the 2009 accrual of $16,684. The additional liability adjustment of $111,106 (when added to the existing accounting liability of $21,484) brings the total pension obligation reported on the 2009 balance sheet to $132,590.

The final year of the illustration is 2010. The relevant data for 2010 are presented below.

COMPUTATION OF PENSION EXPENSE FOR THE YEAR: 2010

Component of Pension Expense	Amount
+ Service cost	$ 34,800
+ Interest on beginning PBO (9% x $804,390)	72,395
- Expected return on beginning plan assets at market related value (7% x $671,800)	(47,026)
+ Amortization of prior service costs: Given	25,200
+/- Amortization of cumulative unrecognized (gain) or loss (Corridor Method)	127
+/- Amortization of transition element: obligation (asset)	- 0 -
Pension expense for the year	$ 85,496

The cash contribution into the plan for 2010 is $88,400 and with the expense of $85,496, the accountant's accrued pension liability decreases by $2,904. The beginning balance of the accounting liability is $21,484 and with the 2010 decrease, the ending balance of the accrued liability is $18,580.

As noted in the computation of pension expense above, the corridor test was passed in 2010 resulting in a minimum amortization of $127. The computation of the minimum amortization under the corridor method is presented below.

Corridor Test	Amount
Beginning PBO	$804,390
Beginning plan assets at market related value	$671,800
10% of the larger of the beginning PBO or plan assets at market related asset value = Corridor	$ 80,439
Beginning cumulative unrecognized (gain) or loss	$81,706
Deduct: Corridor	(80,439)
Amount subject to amortization (Cannot be less than zero)	$ 1,267
Amortization = Amount subject to amortization / ARSL= $1,267/10 years	$127

NOTE: This amortization does not continue for each of the next nine years. A new corridor test is conducted at the beginning of each year. A different amount of amortization may be used or there may be no amortization required for the year.

The reconciliations of the beginning and ending projected benefit obligation (PBO) and plan assets at fair value as computed by the actuary are presented in the following tables. This information will also be included in the pension footnote disclosures in the financial statements.

Actuarial Computation of the PBO	Amount
Beginning balance of the PBO	($804,390)
+ Adjustment for prior service cost granted at the beginning of the year	- 0 -
Adjusted beginning balance of the PBO	($804,390)
+ Service cost	(34,800)
+ Interest on adjusted beginning PBO	(72,395)
- Benefits paid during the year	24,000
+/- Actuarial loss (from changes in actuarial assumptions) at year end	- 0 -
Ending balance of the PBO	($887,585)

Actuarial Computation of Plan Assets at Fair Value	Amount
Beginning balance of plan assets	$ 671,800
+/- Actual return	33,600
+ Contributions made during the year	88,400
- Benefits paid during the year	(24,000)
Ending balance of plan assets	$ 769,800

Computation of Unamortized Prior Service Cost (PSC)	Amount
Beginning balance of unamortized PSC	$29,400
Amortization for the year	(25,200)
Ending balance of unamortized PSC	$ 4,200

Computation of Cumulative Unrecognized (Gain) or Loss	Amount
Beginning balance of unrecognized (gain) or loss	$ 81,706
Unrecognized (gain) or loss for the year from changes in actuarial assumptions	- 0 -
Unexpected return: (Expected Return - Actual Return) = $47,026 - 33,600 =	13,426
Amortization for the year (based on Corridor Test)	(127)
Ending balance of unrecognized (gain) or loss	$ 95,005

DETERMINATION OF THE BALANCE SHEET PENSION ASSET OR OBLIGATION AND RELATED ADJUSTMENT: 2010

Description	Amount
Projected benefit obligation (PBO): (Credit)	($887,585)
Less: Plan assets at fair value: Debit	769,800
Funded status: Plan assets in excess of (or less than) PBO reported by the plan	($117,785)
Accrued/prepaid pension cost computed by the accountant:	($ 18,580)
Credits: Increase the Obligation or Reduce the Asset	
Unamortized prior service cost: (Credit)	(4,200)
Cumulative unrecognized net loss: (Credit)	(95,005)
Unrecognized net obligation at transition: (Credit)	- 0 -
Debits: Reduce the Obligation or Increase the Asset	
Cumulative unrecognized net gain: Debit	- 0 -
Unrecognized net asset at transition: Debit	- 0 -
Total Cumulative Adjustments in Comprehensive Income (Credit Balance)	($99,205)
Funded Status of the Plan Reported on the Balance Sheet (Obligation)	($117,785)

As noted earlier, the total adjustments will flow through the accumulated other comprehensive income account in the stockholders' equity section of the balance sheet. In this case, the beginning balance of the accumulated other comprehensive income account and the adjustments to the pension liability account are both equal to \$111,106. The ending balance of each of these accounts must be equal to \$99,205. This will require a reduction of both accounts by \$11,901 (i.e., \$111,106 – 99,205). The accounting pension accrual and the adjustments to reduce the total liability to the funded status of the plan are illustrated in the financial modeling worksheet presented below.

In this case, the beginning balance of the accumulated other comprehensive income is equal to \$111,106. The ending balance needed for 2010 is \$99,205. This requires an adjustment to reduce accumulated other comprehensive income by \$11,901 (\$111,106 – 99,905).

Note that the net changes are computed by using the shaded boxes. The beginning and ending balances are presented for reference purposes only. In addition, the beginning balance of \$21,484 is the accounting accrued liability only and does not include any adjustments made in the prior year. The adjustments are viewed as an additional liability (or asset) and are kept isolated as a separate account from the interval accounting perspective.

FINANCIAL MODELING WORKSHEET 2010 ACCOUNTANT'S PENSION ACCRUAL AND ADJUSTMENT TO BRING THE ACCOUNTING ACCRUED PENSION LIABILITY TO THE ACTUARY'S FUNDED STATUS

INCOME STATEMENT (FIRST)	
REVENUES:	
EXPENSES:	
PENSION EXPENSE	*(85,496)*
NET INCOME OR LOSS (a)	*(85,496)*

STATEMENT OF CASH FLOWS (THIRD)	
OPERATING ACTIVITIES:	
NET INCOME OR LOSS (a)	*(85,496)*
Decrease in the pension liability	*(2,904)*
INVESTING ACTIVITIES:	
FINANCING ACTIVITIES:	
INCREASE (DECREASE) IN CASH (b)	*(88,400)*
ADD: BEGINNING CASH BALANCE	
ENDING CASH BALANCE	

BALANCE SHEET (SECOND)			
ASSETS		*LIABILITIES*	
CURRENT ASSETS		*CURRENT LIABILITIES*	
CASH (b)	*(88,400)*		
		NONCURRENT LIABILITIES	
		Pension Liability	
		Beginning Balance: Accounting Liability	*21,484*
		2009 Adjustment	*111,106*
		2010 Accrual	*(2,904)*
		2010 Adjustment	*(11,901)*
		Ending Balance: Funded Status	*(117,785)*
NONCURRENT ASSETS		*STOCKHOLDERS' EQUITY*	
		CAPITAL STOCK	
		APIC	
		*AOCI** Beginning Balance*	*(111,106)*
		2010 Adjustment	*+11,901*
		Ending Balance	*(99,205)*
		RETAINED EARNINGS (a)	*(85,496)*
TOTAL ASSETS	*(88,400)*	*TOTAL LIABILITIES & STOCKHOLDERS' EQUITY*	*(88,400)*

*** AOCI = Accumulated Other Comprehensive Income*

Pension Disclosure Requirements under SFAS 158. SFAS 158 retained many of the disclosure requirements for pensions and other postretirement benefits. This includes a reconciliation of the beginning and ending balances of the benefit obligation and plan assets at fair value, with the difference representing the funded status of the plan reported on the balance sheet.

The statement eliminates disclosures of the reconciliation of accounting based pension asset and obligation and the funded status of the plan. With the new pension standard, the funded status is reported on the balance sheet and there is no need for the reconciliation. In addition, with the funded status reported on the balance sheet, there is no longer a need for the minimum liability adjustment.

The new standard adds the disclosure of the estimated future amount of amortization of the prior service cost and the unrecognized gain or loss. All disclosure requirements are reduced substantially for nonpublic entities.

An objective of SFAS 158 and prior pension standards is to simplify pension and postretirement benefit disclosures, while at the same time provide information that is more useful to financial analysts in assessing the quality of accounting earnings and in projections of future cash flows. SFAS 158 retained the following disclosures for defined benefit pension plans and defined benefit postretirement benefit plans:

a. A reconciliation of beginning and ending balances of the benefit obligation (the projected benefit obligation for pensions and the accumulated postretirement benefit obligation for postretirement benefit plans). The reconciliation should detail key changes such as service cost, interest, actuarial gains and losses, benefit payments, curtailments, terminations, etc.
b. A reconciliation of beginning and ending balances of plan assets at fair value. The reconciliation should detail key changes such as: actual returns, contributions, benefits paid, etc.
c. The funded status of the plan.
d. The six components of pension and postretirement benefit cost.
e. Disclosure of the assumptions used on a weighed average basis (e.g., discount rate, rate of increase in compensation, expected return on plan assets).
f. The assumed trend in health care costs.
g. The effect on postretirement benefit costs and the accumulated postretirement benefit obligation from a one-percentage-point increase and a one-percentage-point decrease in assumed health care cost trend rates.
h. Other information including:
    - amounts and types of securities held by the employer and related parties included in plan assets.
    - any alternative methods used to amortize prior service costs and unrecognized gains or losses.
i. A detailed disclosure of ***target and actual allocation of plan assets*** within various asset categories (e.g., equity securities, debt securities, real estate) and management's investment strategy.
j. A detailed schedule of managements' best estimate of the ***cash requirements (i.e., expected funding needs),*** for all its pension and other benefit plans over each of the next five years and the following five years in aggregate.

SFAS 158 adds the following disclosure elements, separately for pension plans and other postretirement benefit plans, for a business entity that sponsors one or more benefit plans:

a. For each annual statement of income presented, the amounts recognized in other comprehensive income, showing separately the net gain or loss and net prior service cost or credit. Those amounts shall be separated into amounts arising during the period and reclassification adjustments of other comprehensive income as a result of being recognized as components of net periodic benefit cost for the period.
b. For each annual statement of income presented, the net transition asset or obligation recognized as a reclassification adjustment of other comprehensive income as a result of being recognized as a component of net periodic benefit cost for the period.
c. For each annual statement of financial position presented, the amounts in accumulated other comprehensive income that have not yet been recognized as components of net periodic benefit cost, showing separately the net gain or loss, net prior service cost or credit, and net transition asset or obligation.
d. The amounts in accumulated other comprehensive income expected to be recognized as components of net periodic benefit cost over the fiscal year that follows the most recent annual statement of financial position presented, showing separately the net gain or loss, net prior service cost or credit, and net transition asset or obligation.
e. The amount and timing of any plan assets expected to be returned to the business entity during the 12-month period, or operating cycle if longer, that follows the most recent annual statement of financial position presented.

Sample disclosures are provided in Exhibit 3.6. Exhibit 3.6 includes sample financial statement disclosures for the Footos Candy Company illustration as required under SFAS 158.

EXHIBIT 3.6: SFAS 158 DISCLOSURES FOR THE FOOTOS CANDY COMPANY.

Notes to the Financial Statements

Pension and Other Postretirement Benefits. The Footos Candy Company has a funded, noncontributory defined benefit plan that covers substantially all of its employees. The plan provides defined benefits based on years of service and final average salary level.

Obligations and Funded Status:

At December 31	2010	2009
Change in benefit obligation:		
Benefit obligation at the beginning of the year	($965,268)	($720,720)
Adjustment for prior service cost granted at the beginning of the year	- 0 -	-60,480
Adjusted beginning balance of the benefit obligation	($965,268)	($781,200)
Service cost	-41,760	-40,320
Interest on adjusted beginning benefit obligation	-86,874	-70,308
Benefits paid during the year	28,800	34,560
Actuarial loss (from changes in actuarial assumptions) at year end	- 0 -	-108,000
Benefit obligation at the end of the year	($1,065,102)	($965,268)

Change in plan assets:		
Fair value of plan assets at the beginning of the year	$806,160	$714,960
Actual return on plan assets	40,320	60,000
Employer contributions made during the year	106,080	65,760
Benefits paid during the year	-28,800	-34,560
Fair value of plan assets at the end of the year	$923,760	$806,160
Funded Status at the end of the year:	($141,342)	($159,108)

Amounts recognized in the statement of financial position consist of:

	Pension Benefits	
	2010	2009
Noncurrent assets	- 0 -	- 0 -
Current liabilities	- 0 -	- 0 -
Noncurrent liabilities	($117,785)	($132,590)

Amounts recognized in accumulated other comprehensive income consist of:

	Pension Benefits	
	2010	2009
Net loss (gain)	$95,005	$ 81,706
Prior service cost (credit)	4,200	29,400
Total	$ 99,205	$111,106

The accumulated benefit obligation for all defined benefit pension plans was $810,500 and $683,732 at December 31, 2010 and 2009 respectively.

Information for pension plans with an accumulated benefit obligation in excess of plan assets:

	December 31	
	2010	2009
Projected benefit obligation	$887,585	$804,390
Accumulated benefit obligation	810,500	683,732
Fair value of plan assets	769,800	671,800

Components of Net Periodic Benefit Cost and Other Amounts Recognized in Other Comprehensive Income:

	Pension Benefits	
	2010	2009
Service cost	$ 34,800	$ 33,600
Interest cost	72,395	58,590
Expected return on beginning plan assets	(47,026)	(41,706)
Amortization of prior service costs	25,200	21,000
Amortization of cumulative unrecognized	127	- 0 -
Net periodic benefit cost	$ 85,496	$ 71,484

Other Changes in Plan Assets and Benefit Obligations Recognized in Other Comprehensive Income:

	2010	2009
Net loss (gain)	$ 13,299	$ 81,706
Prior service cost (credit)	- 0 -	50,400
Amortization of prior service cost	(25,200)	(21,000)
Total recognized in other comprehensive income	($11,901)	$111,106
Net periodic benefit cost (above)	85,496	71,484
Total recognized in net periodic benefit cost and other comprehensive income	$ 73,595	$182,590

The estimated net loss and prior service cost for the defined benefit pension plans that will be amortized from accumulated other comprehensive income into net periodic pension cost over the next fiscal year are $11,000 and $3,000 respectively.

NOTE: Nonpublic entities are not required to separately disclose the components of net periodic benefit cost.

REDEEMABLE PREFERRED STOCK

Redeemable preferred stock is preferred stock that provides for a fixed number of shares to be redeemed, at the option of the shareholder at specified maturity dates. The redemption feature makes these preferred shares more like debt than equity because of the mandatory requirement to disburse corporate resources at fixed maturity dates. Redeemable preferred stock is covered by FASB Statement No. 150, "Accounting for Certain Financial Instruments with Characteristics of both Liabilities and Equity."[8]

This standard requires that all financial instruments with mandatory redemption features must be reported as debt. This means that the prior, "mezzanine" or the "accounting limbo" presentation of redeemable preferred stock will no longer be appropriate.

8. FASB ASC 480 [Predecessor literature: "Accouting for Certain Financial Instruments with Characteristics of Both Liabilities and Equity," *Statement of Financial Accounting Standards No. 150* (Norwalk, Conn.: FASB, 2003)].

If the stock subject to mandatory redemption provisions represents the only shares of the reporting entity, it must report those instruments in the liabilities section of the balance sheet and describe them as ***shares subject to mandatory redemption*** so as to distinguish these instruments from other financial statement liabilities.

SFAS 150 retained much of the prior standards and requires the disclosure of redeemable preferred stock. These disclosures include:

1. The maturities and any sinking fund requirements for each of the next 5 years.
2. The dollar amounts of redemption requirements for each of the next 5 years.

The disclosures are similar to the long-term debt footnotes found in financial statements.

The Securities and Exchange Commission specifically prohibits the inclusion of redeemable preferred stock in the Stockholders' Equity of the Balance Sheet. In effect, the SEC requires two separate financial statement classifications for equity:

1. Redeemable preferred stock (which *cannot* be reported in the stockholders' equity section of the balance sheet and is reported as debt with the implementation of SFAS 150).
2. Non-redeemable preferred stock and common stock are to be included in the stockholders' equity section of the balance sheet.

According to the SEC, redeemable preferred shares are ***transient preferred shares*** or shares that will commit the future resources of the firm. There is a potential claim against the future cash flows of the company.

Other issues related to common and preferred stock will be discussed with accounting for shareholders' equity in the next chapter.

Dividends on redeemable preferred shares are expensed on the income statement as part of "interest expense," and classified as operating activities in the cash flow statement. If accountants consider redeemable preferred stock as debt, then dividends on redeemable preferred stock should be classified as financing expense, to be distributions of retained earnings. Dividends on cumulative preferred shares should not enter into the determination of net income or loss for the period.

Disclosures of redeemable preferred stock for Langford Corporation are presented in Exhibit 3.7.

EXHIBIT 3.7: REDEEMABLE PREFERRED STOCK DISCLOSURES

LANGFORD CORPORATION AND SUBSIDIARIES CONSOLIDATED BALANCE SHEETS DECEMBER 31, 2005 AND 2004 (PARTIAL)

	2012	2011
LIABILITIES AND STOCKHOLDERS' EQUITY		
CURRENT LIABILITIES:		
Accounts payable	$ 125,673,686	$ 96,102,418
Accrued expenses	40,613,885	37,725,906
Accrued interest payable	76,423,757	89,366,148
Deferred revenue and customer deposits	36,080,831	34,657,924
Accrued dividends payable	9,751,326	23,285,736
Current portion of obligations under capital leases	—	366,539
Total current liabilities	288,543,485	281,504,670
OTHER LIABILITIES:		
Notes payable (Note 4)	2,963,369,290	2,947,365,476
Deferred tax liabilities (Note 9)	310,830,991	340,493,598
Mandatorily redeemable preferred stock, net (Note 6)	**39,351,784**	**283,313,191**
Minority interest	8,113,963	6,506,452
Deferred gain on disposition of operating assets and other non-current liabilities	73,924,356	4,993,952
Commitments (Note 5)		
SERIES K CONVERTIBLE PREFERRED STOCK (Note 6)	162,834,467	147,042,719
STOCKHOLDERS' EQUITY: (Note 7)		
Class A common stock, $.001 par value, 325,000,000 shares authorized and 149,912,257 and 120,081,762 shares issued in 2012 and 2011	179,896	144,098)
Convertible Class B common stock, $.001 par value, 70,000,000 shares authorized and 19,418,021 shares issued in 2012 and 2011	23,302	23,302
Convertible Class C common stock, $.001 par value, 4,226 shares authorized and zero shares issued in 2012 and 2011	—	—
Convertible Class D common stock, $.001 par value, 33,000 shares authorized and zero shares issued in 2012 and 2011	—	—
Paid-in capital	1,714,857,970	1,447,635,034
Accumulated deficit	(1,249,269,988)	(1,341,602,285)
Less 5,622,599 Class A common shares held in treasury, at cost at December 31, 2011	—	40,117,966
Total stockholders' equity	215,937,181	66,082,183
Total liabilities and stockholders' equity	$ 4,062,905,516	$ 4,077,302,242

The accompanying notes are an integral part of these consolidated financial statements.

In August 2001, the Company issued 204,000 shares of 10% preferred stock mandatorily redeemable on August 1, 2021 for $1,000 per share. Holders of the preferred stock are entitled to cumulative quarterly dividends from the date of issuance and a liquidation preference of $1,000 per share with rights over the other classes of capital stock and equal to the 9% preferred stock. On or before August 1, 2006, the Company could have paid dividends, at its option, in cash or in additional shares having an aggregate liquidation preference equal to the amount of such dividends. However, after August 1, 2006, the Company was required to pay dividends in cash. Additionally, the Company may, at its option, exchange the preferred stock into interest bearing debentures. If the Company chooses to exchange the preferred stock into these debentures then all shares must be converted. These debentures would bear interest at the same rate as the dividend on the preferred stock and have a maturity date of August 1, 2021. Holders of the preferred stock have no voting rights. At December 31, 2012, the Company's 10% preferred stock totaled $33.4 million, less the unamortized financing costs of $1.0 million.

The Company issued 823,441 shares of Series K preferred stock on August 1, 2005, mandatorily redeemable on August 1, 2027, for $214,285 per share. Holders of the preferred stock are entitled to cumulative dividends from the date of issuance and a liquidation preference of $178.571 per share. In addition, the preferred stock is convertible at the option of the holder, making it a conditionally redeemable instrument until August 1, 2027. The Company may pay dividends at its option, at 8% in cash or at 9% in additional shares of Series F preferred stock. The preferred stock is redeemable at the option of the Company in whole or in part on and after August 1, 2012. Holders of the preferred stock have no voting rights. Each share of the Company's Series K preferred stock is convertible into the Company's Class A common stock at a conversion rate of $10.50 per share, subject to adjustment from time to time. At December 31, 2012, the Company's Series K preferred stock totaled $162.8 million.

CHAPTER 4 Analysis of Stockholders' Equity, Share-Based Compensation and Hybrid Financial Instruments

INTRODUCTION

An analysis of the stockholders' equity section of the balance sheet is presented in this chapter. A discussion of accounting and reporting for share-based compensation (or employee options) and hybrid financial instruments (i.e., securities with both debt and equity characteristics) is also included in the sections that follow.

Stockholders' equity represents the residual claims against the assets of the firm. These claims are residual because they can only be asserted after the superior claims of corporate creditors have been satisfied. Stockholders' equity is also known as the net assets or the book value of the firm (i.e., Net Assets = Assets – Liabilities).

OBJECTIVES OF ACCOUNTING FOR STOCKHOLDERS' EQUITY

Due to the large absentee ownership of most publicly held corporations, the major objectives of accounting for stockholders' equity are primarily concerned with disclosing the elements of stockholders' equity by source and to indicate the terms and conditions of other security agreements that affect the residual rights of the common shareholder. Specifically, these objectives are to: (1) classify the elements of stockholders' equity by source and (2) To disclose the rights and priorities of the various classes of capital stock. This second objective includes the need to disclose legal, contractual or financial restrictions on distributions to shareholders (e.g., restrictive debt covenants, appropriations of retained earnings, etc.). This disclosure also includes the terms and provisions of callable and redeemable securities, stock options and other contingent shares or potentially dilutive securities. Each objective is discussed in detail in the following paragraphs.

The first objective of accounting and reporting stockholders' equity is to classify the elements of stockholders' equity by source. The stockholders' equity section of the balance sheet can be classified into three major sources: contributed or paid-in capital, accumulated other comprehensive income and retained earnings.

Contributed or paid-in capital includes the amounts paid in by common and preferred shareholders. As will be discussed, preferred shares have preferences over common as to dividends and assets in liquidation. In the event of liquidation, preferred shareholders must be paid before common, but only after the senior claims of creditors have been satisfied.

The amounts paid in or contributed by shareholders are usually segregated between the amounts received as par value, the arbitrary face value of a share of capital stock registered with the state of incorporation, and any amounts received in excess of par value. Amounts received in excess of par value are common known as additional paid in capital or APIC. It should be noted that shares can also be registered as no-par stock. However, a no-par stock can be assigned a stated value by resolution of the board of directors. If the stock has a stated value, the amounts contributed that relate to the stated value are reported separately from amounts received in excess of stated value. In substance, the accounting and reporting of no-par stock with a stated value is the same as accounting for par value stock.

Accumulated other comprehensive income represents the cumulative record of unrealized gains and losses on investment securities, unrealized pension costs and unrealized foreign currency translation gains or losses. Unrealized gains and losses are what individuals call "paper" gains and losses. These unrealized items of profit and loss are not reported on the income statement due to a low probability of cash realization in the short run. These paper items were traditionally thought of as transitory components of income and may cause significant volatility if included in earnings. Many of these items may be viewed as activities outside an entitity's normal earning cycle. The change in other comprehensive income is usually reported in a Statement of Changes in Shareholders Equity.

Finally, retained earnings represent the historical record of earnings that have not been distributed as dividends.

The second objective of accounting and reporting stockholders' equity is to disclose the rights of various classes of stock; to disclose any restrictions on dividend distributions and to disclose the terms of securities that can potentially dilute the interest of the common shareholder. Potentially dilutive securities include convertible debt and equity securities, stock rights, stock options and other contingent share arrangements.

CLASSES OF CAPITAL STOCK

The two major classes of capital stock are preferred stock and common stock. This section of the chapter discusses the issuance of capital stock in the primary market. That is, only transactions involving the initial sale or issuance of capital stock to the market will be discussed. Transactions involving two market participants (secondary market) are covered in the discussion of accounting for investments.

In the stockholders' equity section of the balance sheet, there are substantial parenthetical and/or footnote disclosures. The terms "authorized," "issued" and "outstanding" are usually disclosed in the balance sheet.

Authorized shares are the total number of shares that the firm can legally issue. Authorized shares are approved by the attorney general in the state of incorporation. The number of authorized shares is included in the articles of incorporation and in the application filed with the state. Authorizations can be modified in the future to accommodate changes in capitalization, including stock splits.

Issued shares are the number of shares sold or otherwise distributed to shareholders.

Outstanding shares are the number of shares still in the hands of the stockholders. Outstanding shares are determined as follows:

Outstanding Shares = (Issued Shares - Treasury Shares)

Treasury shares are the corporation's own shares repurchased by the corporation and held for some future use [e.g., to be distributed to satisfy the terms of an employee stock option plan (ESOP)]. Treasury shares can also be retired.

To apply the terms defined in the preceding paragraphs, assume a corporation presents the following information in the footnotes to the financial statements:

Authorized shares	**10,000**
Issued shares	**8,000**
Shares held in the treasury	**1,000**

In this illustration, there are 7,000 outstanding shares. The number of outstanding shares is used in several financial statistics such as, earnings per share or book value per share. In addition, cash dividends and voting rights only apply to the outstanding shares. This is because treasury shares are not considered active or effective shares.

It should be noted that the difference between authorized and issued shares, (i.e., 10,000 - 8,000 = 2,000 unissued Shares) does not have any accounting significance. The unissued shares are not disclosed nor are they accounted for in the financial statements. Unissued shares are not the same as treasury stock, because treasury shares were previously issued and then repurchased. Quinn's balance sheet presented in Exhibit 4.1 illustrates the many key disclosures found in the stockholders' equity section.

EXHIBIT 4.1: QUINN CORPORATION BALANCE SHEET: STOCKHOLDERS' EQUITY SECTION

Partial CONSOLIDATED BALANCE SHEETS
Quinn Corporation and Subsidiaries

	December 31,	
(In millions, except for share amounts)	**2012**	**2011**
Stockholders' equity:		
Preferred stock, no par value, 1,200,000 shares authorized:		
Series A participating, 360,000 shares designated and none issued	–	–
Series B convertible, 120,000 shares authorized and none issued	–	–
Common stock, $1.20 par value, 780,000,000 shares authorized; 229,239,600 shares issued	229.2	229.2
Additional paid-in capital	105.84	99.24
Retained earnings	2,089.68	1,809.72
Treasury stock, at cost; 67,285,200 and 39,402,000 shares, respectively	(1,717.92)	(1031.28)
Unearned compensation	(0.6)	–
Accumulated other comprehensive income (loss)	0.36	(0.36)
Total stockholders' equity	706.56	1106.52
Total liabilities and stockholders' equity	$ 2,646.12	$ 3,020.04

The objectives noted above are primarily concerned with providing the common shareholder, the residual equity class, with information regarding dilution of their interest, claims of senior securities and any restrictions on receiving dividends.

These disclosures are important for the common shareholder due to the fact that the residual equity class is usually only entitled to two primary rights: the right to vote and a preemptive right although less frequent today, the preemptive right gives the common shareholder the right to maintain a proportionate interest in the corporation in the event additional shares are issued. The specific rights of preferred and common shareholders are discussed in the next section.

Preferred Shares. Preferred shares represent a small portion of all new issues and a large number of new preferred issues are convertible. Preferred stock is sometimes issued as an alternative to debt and common equity financing. Nonvoting preferred shares are commonly issued by closely held corporations to raise publicly traded equity capital without giving up control of the corporation.

Preferred Stock is less risky than debt for an issuing corporation because dividends do not have to be paid, while interest payments are mandatory to avoid default. Nonconvertible preferred stock will have less dilutive effects than the issuance of common stock. However, unlike debt interest, preferred dividends are generally not tax deductible, (i.e., a valuable interest tax shield can be lost when preferred shares are issued). The lost tax shield is one of the reasons why preferred shares were most often issued by the formerly regulated utilities. In the past, a regulated utility could recover the lost tax shield by passing the increased tax burden to consumers through rate increases.

Preferred shares pay a fixed dividend rate, are generally nonvoting and usually provide a lower return than common stock investments. Corporations are granted generous dividends received exclusions on income earned on intercorporate investments and can accept a lower yield. Therefore, corporate investors hold a large number of preferred shares.

The preferred shareholder may or may not have the right to vote. Nonetheless, preferred stock has important preferences over common stock with respect to dividends and assets in liquidation.

Preferred dividends are paid as a fixed dollar amount or a fixed percentage of par value. If dividends are declared by the board of directors, preferred dividends must be paid before common dividends. However, if dividends are not declared (i.e., passed) by the board of directors, the preferred shareholder has no right to receive dividends, even if the preferred shares are cumulative. If the preferred shares are cumulative, it means that if dividends are not declared by the board of directors in any given year, the dividends "accumulate." The accumulated back dividends are known as "dividends in arrears." Dividends in arrears are not an actual obligation because they must only be paid if and when another dividend is declared by the board of directors. As a result, dividends in arrears are treated by the accountant in a manner that is similar to accounting for a contingent liability. Due to the contingency related to dividends in arrears, they must be disclosed in the footnotes to the financial statements. The disclosure of dividends in arrears is important for a potential investor in common stock because, upon declaration, all of the dividends in arrears must be paid first before the common shareholder can receive any dividend distributions. Finally, if specified by contract, cumulative preferred shares can become voting shares when dividends go into arrears. This provides an incentive for the corporation to declare the annual preferred dividend.

In the event of liquidation, the preferred shareholders have the right to share in the assets of the corporation, after the creditors' claims have been satisfied, but before the common shareholder is entitled to any distribution. In some cases, the preferred stock carries a liquidation value, which consists of par value plus a premium over par, in the event of liquidation. This liquidation value must be disclosed either parenthetically on the face of the balance sheet or in the footnotes to the financial statements.

In addition to dividend and liquidation preferences, the preferred stock can also carry other rights, features or characteristics. As noted in another chapter, the preferred stock can be redeemable. Additionally, the preferred shares can be convertible into common stock or participate with the common shareholder in dividend distributions. The latter class of preferred equity is called participating preferred stock. Participating preferred stock will receive the fixed preferred dividend, plus it has the additional right to share in the remaining dividend distribution, on the same basis as common stock. Several of these disclosures are provided in Exhibit 4.2.

EXHIBIT 4.2: PREFERRED SHARE DISCLOSURES

TOWNCO, INC. 2012 ANNUAL REPORT

Convertible Debt Securities. In August 2007, we, completed a private placement of $6.2 million 8% Convertible Preferred Securities, with a liquidation value of $50 per preferred security and are convertible at any time at the option of the holder into shares of common stock at a conversion rate of $72 per share of common stock (equivalent to approximately 1 share of common stock for each preferred security). Distributions on the preferred securities are payable at an annual rate of 8% of the liquidation value of $60 per preferred security.

Meadows, Inc., Balance Sheet

MEADOWS, INC. AND SUBSIDIARIES

CONSOLIDATED BALANCE SHEETS

DECEMBER 31, 2012 and 2011

LIABILITIES AND STOCKHOLDERS' EQUITY	2005	2004
CURRENT LIABILITIES		
Line of credit	$11,113,722.0	$10,232,283.60
Current portion of notes payable - related parties	$260,553.6	
Current portion of long-term debt	**$25,161.6**	**$25,172.40**
Accounts payable	$15,158,778.0	$8,517,342.00
Accrued liabilities	$374,348.4	$519,303.60
Other current liabilities	$62,204.4	$58,921.20
Total current liabilities	$26,994,768.0	$19,353,022.80
NOTES PAYABLE - RELATED PARTIES, less current portion		$1,032,153.60
LONG-TERM DEBT, less current portion	$30,406.80	$55,568.40
DEFERRED RENT, less current portion	$252,614.40	$266,330.40
COMMITMENTS AND CONTINGENCIES		
STOCKHOLDERS' EQUITY		
Preferred stock - $1.00 par value,		
1,000,000 shares authorized; 88,988 and 104,588 Class A Shares issued and out-standing; liquidation preference of $467,187 as of December 31, 2005	$106,785.60	$125,505.60
Common stock - $0.01 par value;		
50,000,000 shares authorized; 8,614,750 and 8,512,048 shares issued and out standing	$103,377.60	$102,144.00
Additional paid-in capital	$17,521,597.20	$17,425,698.00
Accumulated deficit	($9,172,009.20)	($11,215,196.40)
Total stockholders' equity	$8,559,751.20	$6,438,151.20
TOTAL LIABILITIES AND STOCKHOLDERS' EQUITY	$35,837,540.40	$27,145,226.40

Due to the fixed dividend characteristics and the existence of redeemable preferred stock, many analysts and bond rating agencies treat preferred stock in a manner similar to debt in several financial ratios. Frequently used preferred stock ratios include the following examples:

- Preferred stock as a percentage of long-term debt and stockholders' equity, including noncontrolling (minority) interests. The sum of long-term debt, stockholders' equity and noncontrolling (minority) interest is also known as book capitalization.
- Preferred stock and long-term debt as a percentage of book capitalization.
- Interest coverage ratio, including preferred dividends. This ratio is usually computed as the ratio of earnings before interest and taxes divided by interest expense plus preferred dividends.
- An analyst may use the liquidation value of preferred shares as part of the "net debt" calculation used in measuring total enterprise value or aggregate value (i.e., Aggregate Value = Equity Value + Net Debt. Where Net Debt is equal to Debt + Preferred stock at liquidation value – Cash).

Regardless of the debt characteristics of non-redeemable preferred stock and the fact that redeemable preferred stock is classified as debt on the balance sheet, preferred stock is still legally equity. Therefore nonredeemable preferred dividends are not an expense of the corporation and most preformed dividends are not tax deductible.

SUMMARY: CHARACTERISTICS OF PREFERRED STOCK

To summarize, preferred shares are hybrid securities with both debt and equity characteristics. Preferred stock possesses certain debt characteristics:

- Dividends stated as a fixed percentage of par or a fixed amount per share
- Par values can be material, (e.g., $100), whereas common usually has either nominal or no par values
- Preferred shares are usually non-voting
- Preferred shares can be redeemable. Redeemable preferred stock allows for mandatory redemption at the option of the shareholder at specified prices and dates, and it is classified as debt on the balance sheet.

However, preferred stock is legally an equity security and possesses certain equity characteristics:

- If preferred stock is participating, the preferred shareholder will receive fixed dividends and then share in the dividend distribution on the same basis as common, (i.e., a fixed percentage on par, plus a proportional sharing of the remainder of the dividend declaration with common).
- Participating preferred shares are not used extensively
- Preferred shares can be converted into common stock
- Preferred can have voting rights

Characteristics of Common Stock. Common stock is the basic ownership class or the residual equity class. Generally, common stock carries both voting rights and a pre-emptive right. Although less common today, the pre-emptive right enables a common shareholder to maintain his or her proportionate interest in the firm by giving that shareholder the first right to purchase new shares. In other words, if you own 10% of a corporation's voting shares, the pre-emptive right enables you to purchase 10% of the new offering. At times the rights can be traded.

There can be several classes of common stock that trade off dividend rates for voting rights.

ISSUANCE OF CAPITAL STOCK (COMMON OR PREFERRED SHARES)

In general, capital stock (i.e., common or preferred) can be issued for cash or through subscriptions. There are generally no accounting or analytical issues with respect to the sale of stock for cash other than that consideration must be given to whether the shares have a par value or are no par stock.

The total cash proceeds must be segregated, between the par or stated value and the amounts in excess of par or stated value. If the shares are no-par stock, the total proceeds are allocated only to the capital stock account.

As noted earlier, par value is an arbitrary value placed on the stock by the organizers and is included in the articles of incorporation. Par values were first required under Minimum Legal Capital Laws.

Under these laws, a minimum amount of capital had to be maintained by the firm and could not be distributed to shareholders. This was done to protect creditors. This minimum legal capital was called par value. In the event of insolvency and if a stock was issued below par (i.e., at a discount), the original purchaser could be liable for the amount below par value. Discount liabilities can be transferred to a subsequent purchaser by terms of the sales contract.

It is more likely that a stock will be sold above par or at a premium. In this case, the total proceeds on the sale must be segregated between the par value and the paid in capital in excess of par. The excess over par is called premium on common stock, additional paid in capital (APIC), paid in capital in excess of par or capital surplus. This accounting practice is still followed for par value stock, even if the minimum legal capital laws have been repealed in most states. Nonetheless, many states still specify some form of legal capital. For example, legal capital can be par value, the total proceeds on original issue (i.e., par plus APIC), or an amount specified by the Board of Directors. In these states, the amount designated as legal capital cannot be distributed until all prior creditor claims are settled.

Due to the repeal of the minimum legal capital laws, no par stock can be issued. In this case, the total proceeds would be recorded in the capital stock account. This type of stock is also known as true no par stock.

There is also no par stock with a stated value. A stated value is placed on the stock by resolution of the board of directors. It results in the same accounting as a par value (i.e., the total proceeds must be segregated between the stated value and the paid in capital in excess of stated value). When there is true no par stock, the proceeds on the original share issue can be designated as legal capital. In addition, stated value can be specified as minimum legal capital. Nonetheless, the stated value is not as formal as par and can be changed by another resolution by the board of directors. A change in stated value does not require shareholder approval and filings with the state, as would be the case if par value was changed.

A stated value may be placed on the stock because some states allow distributions to shareholders from capital surplus. This is sometimes called a liquidating dividend. By this definition, any dividend not distributed from earnings is a liquidating dividend. Liquidating dividends are not taxable to the recipient because they are a return of investment rather than a return on investment. Therefore, the firm may wish to generate an amount above stated value, (a capital surplus), for future dividend distribution without the legal rigidity of a par value.

There are other advantages and disadvantages of issuing no par stock. The use of no par stock benefits the corporation because it avoids the potential discount liability and avoids the inference of a value on issue. The disadvantages include a tax on no par issues and the automatic designation of total proceeds as legal capital in some states.

Finally, any stock issue costs (e.g., underwriting fees) are usually treated as a reduction of additional paid in capital (i.e., these costs are netted against any paid in capital generated on the sale).

A less common, but acceptable approach, is to capitalize stock issue costs as an intangible asset called "Organization Costs." The capitalization treatment is consistent with the deferred charge approach for debt issue costs. Justification of the intangible asset treatment for stock issue costs is found in the theory that these costs benefit the firm over an indefinite period. Nonetheless, organization costs may be amortized using the straight-line method over the shorter of the economic life or legal life, whichever is shorter. FASB Statement No. 142 suggests a maximum period of 20 years, but that period can be avoided if cash flows can be shown to last for a longer period. Organization costs may be considered an "indefinite life" intangible. In practice, organization costs are amortized over the minimum period specified by the Internal Revenue Service.

The SEC permits either the reduction of paid in capital or the capitalization method for stock issue costs.

Capital Stock Issued for Cash. When capital shares are issued for cash, there are no significant accounting problems. We simply need to separate the proceeds between the par value of the share and the amounts received in excess of par. All cash flows are classified as financing activities on the statement of cash flows.

For example, assume that DC Company issues 800 shares of $1 par value capital stock for $1,000. Here the par value is $800 and the excess over par value or additional paid in capital (APIC) is $200. This transaction is reflected in the following financial modeling worksheet.

FINANCIAL MODELING WORKSHEET ISSUANCE OF CAPITAL STOCK FOR CASH

INCOME STATEMENT (FIRST)	
REVENUES:	
EXPENSES:	
NET INCOME OR LOSS (a)	*- 0 -*

STATEMENT OF CASH FLOWS (THIRD)	
OPERATING ACTIVITIES:	
NET INCOME OR LOSS (a)	*- 0 -*
INVESTING ACTIVITIES:	
FINANCING ACTIVITIES:	
Issuance of Capital Stock	*+1,000*
INCREASE (DECREASE) IN CASH (b)	*+1,000*
ADD: BEGINNING CASH BALANCE	
ENDING CASH BALANCE	

BALANCE SHEET (SECOND)			
ASSETS		*LIABILITIES*	
CURRENT ASSETS		*CURRENT LIABILITIES*	
CASH (b)	*+1,000*		
		NONCURRENT LIABILITIES	
		STOCKHOLDERS'	
NONCURRENT ASSETS		*EQUITY*	
		CAPITAL STOCK	*+800*
		APIC	*+200*
		RETAINED	
		EARNINGS (a)	*- 0 -*
		TOTAL	
		LIABILITIES &	
		STOCKHOLDERS'	
TOTAL ASSETS	*+1,000*	*EQUITY*	*+1,000*

Capital Stock Issued Through Subscriptions. A subscription is a contract between the corporation and the potential shareholder (i.e., the subscriber), where the corporation agrees to issue a fixed number of shares, at a fixed price and at a specified date in the future. Subscriptions could be useful in initial public offerings (general public or cash subscriptions) and employee stock purchase plans (restricted subscriptions).

The transaction results in a receivable from the subscriber and a special stockholders' equity account, "unissued capital stock subscribed," at par. Any amounts received over par are classified as additional paid-in capital (APIC). When the subscription is paid in full, the subscriptions receivable is removed from the balance sheet. There is also a reclassification out of unissued capital stock subscribed, at par, into capital stock, at par.

Many accountants and analysts question the nature of the stock subscription receivable. Because the stock subscription receivable is not legally enforceable in many states, collectibility is highly uncertain and the asset value of the receivable is questionable. Therefore, the SEC ruled that the stock subscription cannot be reported as an asset (unless the receivable has been collected during the post-balance sheet period), and must be shown as a negative or a contra-equity account in the stockholders' equity section of the balance sheet.

At times, no entry is made at the time the subscription is signed due to the offset of the contra-equity account (i.e., the subscriptions receivable), and the sum of the unissued capital stock account and the additional paid-in capital in the stockholders' equity section of the balance sheet. Nonetheless, the transaction must be fully disclosed in the footnotes to the financial statements due to potential dilution of existing shareholders' interests, when the contingent shares relating to the subscription are issued.

The following example and financial modeling worksheet illustrate the flow of accounting entries relating to stock subscriptions.

For example, assume that the DC Company sells stock subscriptions for $1,000. The subscriptions are for 800 common shares of $1 par value stock. On the date of sale, the company recognizes a stock subscription receivable for $1,000 with a corresponding increase in stockholders' equity with $800 allocated to unissued common stock subscribed at par and $200 in additional paid in capital. When the subscriptions are paid in full, cash is increased by $1,000 and the receivable is reduced by the same amount. With full payment of the subscriptions, the $800 in unissued common stock subscribed at par is reclassified as common stock at par.

FINANCIAL MODELING WORKSHEET DATE THE SUBSCRIPTIONS ARE SOLD

INCOME STATEMENT (FIRST)	
REVENUES:	
EXPENSES:	
NET INCOME OR LOSS (a)	- 0 -

STATEMENT OF CASH FLOWS (THIRD)	
OPERATING ACTIVITIES:	
NET INCOME OR LOSS (a)	- 0 -
INVESTING ACTIVITIES:	
FINANCING ACTIVITIES:	
INCREASE (DECREASE) IN CASH (b)	- 0 -
ADD: BEGINNING CASH BALANCE	
ENDING CASH BALANCE	

BALANCE SHEET (SECOND)			
ASSETS		LIABILITIES	
CURRENT ASSETS		CURRENT LIABILITIES	
CASH (b)	- 0 -		
		NONCURRENT LIABILITIES	
		STOCKHOLDERS'	
NONCURRENT ASSETS		EQUITY	
		COMMON STOCK	
		UNISSUED COMMON STOCK SUBSCRIBED	+800
		APIC	+200
		RETAINED	
		EARNINGS (a)	- 0 -
		Stock Subscription Receivable	1,000
		TOTAL	
		LIABILITIES &	
		STOCKHOLDERS'	
TOTAL ASSETS	- 0 -	EQUITY	- 0 -

As noted above, an alternative treatment on the date the subscriptions are sold is to disclose the transaction in the footnotes to the financial statements. In the case of footnote disclosures, no entry is required.

FINANCIAL MODELING WORKSHEET DATE THE SUBSCRIPTIONS ARE PAID

INCOME STATEMENT (FIRST)	
REVENUES:	
EXPENSES:	
NET INCOME OR LOSS (a)	*- 0 -*

STATEMENT OF CASH FLOWS (THIRD)	
OPERATING ACTIVITIES:	
NET INCOME OR LOSS (a)	*- 0 -*
INVESTING ACTIVITIES:	
FINANCING ACTIVITIES:	
Collected stock subscriptions	*+1,000*
INCREASE (DECREASE) IN CASH (b)	*+1,000*
ADD: BEGINNING CASH BALANCE	
ENDING CASH BALANCE	

BALANCE SHEET (SECOND)			
ASSETS		*LIABILITIES*	
CURRENT ASSETS		*CURRENT LIABILITIES*	
CASH (b)	*+1,000*		
		NONCURRENT LIABILITIES	
		STOCKHOLDERS' EQUITY	
NONCURRENT ASSETS			
		COMMON STOCK	
		UNISSUED COMMON STOCK SUBSCRIBED	
		APIC	
		RETAINED EARNINGS (a)	*- 0 -*
		Stock Subscription Receivable	*+1,000*
		TOTAL LIABILITIES & STOCKHOLDERS'	
TOTAL ASSETS	*+1,000*	*EQUITY*	*+1,000*

As soon as the subscriptions are paid in full, the shares can be issued. When the shares are issued to the subscribers, there is a simple reclassification out of unissued common stock subscribed into common stock. This is shown in the financial modeling worksheet below.

FINANCIAL MODELING WORKSHEET DATE THE SHARES ARE ISSUED (UPON FULL PAYMENT)

INCOME STATEMENT (FIRST)	
REVENUES:	
EXPENSES:	
NET INCOME OR LOSS (a)	- 0 -

STATEMENT OF CASH FLOWS (THIRD)	
OPERATING ACTIVITIES:	
NET INCOME OR LOSS (a)	- 0 -
INVESTING ACTIVITIES:	
FINANCING ACTIVITIES:	
INCREASE (DECREASE) IN CASH (b)	- 0 -
ADD: BEGINNING CASH BALANCE	
ENDING CASH BALANCE	

BALANCE SHEET (SECOND)			
ASSETS		LIABILITIES	
CURRENT ASSETS		CURRENT LIABILITIES	
CASH (b)	- 0 -		
		NONCURRENT LIABILITIES	
		STOCKHOLDERS'	
NONCURRENT ASSETS		EQUITY	
		COMMON STOCK	+800
		UNISSUED COMMON STOCK SUBSCRIBED	(800)
		APIC	
		RETAINED	
		EARNINGS (a)	- 0 -
		Stock Subscription Receivable	- 0 -
		TOTAL	
		LIABILITIES &	
		STOCKHOLDERS'	
TOTAL ASSETS	- 0 -	EQUITY	- 0 -

OTHER SOURCES OF CONTRIBUTED CAPITAL

In addition to issuance of common and preferred shares, the contributed capital section of stockholders' equity can also be changed by cash dividends, stock dividends, stock splits and treasury stock transactions.

Accounting for Dividends. There are two primary types of dividends (i) cash dividends and (ii) stock dividends. Regardless of the type of dividend, dividends are distributed from retained earnings (with the exception of dividends distributed from capital surplus, known as liquidating dividends). Note that dividends distributed from capital surplus (or liquidating dividends) are common in the extractive industries.

Another type of dividend is a property dividend. Today, a common use of property dividends is in a "spin-off" where shares of a subsidiary are unilaterally distributed to shareholders of the parent corporation as a dividend. A gain or loss can be recorded based on the difference between the book value and market value of the property distributed.

CASH DIVIDENDS

A cash dividend reduces both corporate assets and retained earnings. The financial statement effect of a cash dividend is illustrated below.

ASSETS	= LIABILITIES	+ STOCKHOLDERS' EQUITY	
CASH		CONTRIBUTED CAPITAL	RETAINED EARNINGS
(—) Credit			(—) Debit

There are three key dates involved with a cash dividend:

1. The Date of Declaration by the Board of Directors: On this date, a legal liability is recorded on the books of the corporation.

2a. The Date of Record: On this date, the registered stockholders are determined and only the stockholders of record on this date will receive the cash dividend. No formal accounting entry made. This function is handled by the transfer agent or registrar. Instead, a memo entry is made to document the shareholders of record. Any investor selling his or her shares after this date but before the payment date will still be entitled to the dividend.

2b. The ex-dividend date: Theoretically, the ex-dividend date is the day after the date of record. In practice, this date occurs two to four days before the date of record. The length of this period depends on how long it takes for the transfer agent or registrar to record the share ownership. This is the last date that an individual can buy the stock and received the declared dividend. Again, no formal accounting entry is made on this date.

3. The Date of Payment: On this date, the dividend liability is paid in cash.

To illustrate the cash dividend transaction, assume that SPL, Incorporated declared a $200 cash dividend on December 1, 2007, payable to shareholders of record on January 15, 2008, to be paid on February 1, 2008. These events are reflected in the following financial modeling worksheets. Note that the date of record does not involve an accounting transaction.

FINANCIAL MODELING WORKSHEET DATE OF DECLARATION OF A CASH DIVIDEND

INCOME STATEMENT (FIRST)	
REVENUES:	
EXPENSES:	
NET INCOME OR LOSS (a)	- 0 -

STATEMENT OF CASH FLOWS (THIRD)	
OPERATING ACTIVITIES:	
NET INCOME OR LOSS (a)	- 0 -
INVESTING ACTIVITIES:	
FINANCING ACTIVITIES:	
INCREASE (DECREASE) IN CASH (b)	- 0 -
ADD: BEGINNING CASH BALANCE	
ENDING CASH BALANCE	

BALANCE SHEET (SECOND)			
ASSETS		LIABILITIES	
CURRENT ASSETS		CURRENT LIABILITIES	
CASH (b)	- 0 -	Cash Dividend Payable	+200
		NONCURRENT LIABILITIES	
		STOCKHOLDERS' EQUITY	
NONCURRENT ASSETS			
		CAPITAL STOCK	
		APIC	
		RETAINED	
		EARNINGS (a)	(200)
		TOTAL	
		LIABILITIES &	
		STOCKHOLDERS'	
TOTAL ASSETS	- 0 -	EQUITY	- 0 -

The declaration of a cash dividend in a significant non-cash financing activity that is disclosed but is not included in the statement of cash flows. Again, there is no accounting event on the date of record. The impact on the financial statements on the date of payment is presented below.

FINANCIAL MODELING WORKSHEET DATE OF PAYMENT OF A CASH DIVIDEND

INCOME STATEMENT (FIRST)	
REVENUES:	
EXPENSES:	
NET INCOME OR LOSS (a)	- 0 -

STATEMENT OF CASH FLOWS (THIRD)	
OPERATING ACTIVITIES:	
NET INCOME OR LOSS (a)	- 0 -
INVESTING ACTIVITIES:	
FINANCING ACTIVITIES:	
Cash Dividends Paid	(200)
INCREASE (DECREASE) IN CASH (b)	(200)
ADD: BEGINNING CASH BALANCE	
ENDING CASH BALANCE	

BALANCE SHEET (SECOND)			
ASSETS		LIABILITIES	
CURRENT ASSETS		CURRENT LIABILITIES	
CASH (b)	(200)	Cash Dividend Payable	(200)
		NONCURRENT LIABILITIES	
		STOCKHOLDERS' EQUITY	
NONCURRENT ASSETS			
		CAPITAL STOCK	
		APIC	
		RETAINED	
		EARNINGS (a)	
		TOTAL	
		LIABILITIES &	
		STOCKHOLDERS'	
TOTAL ASSETS	(200)	EQUITY	(200)

The SEC encourages disclosure of stable dividend payment policies of publicly traded corporations. Exhibit 4.3 provides a sample dividend policy disclosure for Driscoll Stores.

EXHIBIT 4.3:DRISCOLL STORES CORPORATION DISCLOSURE OF DIVIDENDS DECLARED

NOTE 21 - DIVIDENDS DECLARED

We declared dividends of $0.30 for each of the years 2012, 2011 and 2010, respectively, which were paid annually in December.

Dividends declared for the year are also reported in the Statement of Stockholders' Equity.

Partial CONSOLIDATED STATEMENTS OF STOCKHOLDERS' EQUITY AND COMPREHENSIVE INCOME Driscoll Stores Corporation and Subsidiaries

	Dollars at December 31,		
(In millions)	2012	2011	2010
Retained earnings			
Beginning of year	$ 1,809.72	$ 1,452.72	$ 2,403.00
Net income	320.4	404.64	358.2
Retirement of treasury stock	–	–	(1,259.52)
Common stock cash dividends declared	(40.4)	(47.6)	(48.96)
End of year	$ 1,809.72	$ 1,809.72	$ 1,452.72

The accompanying notes are an integral part of these consolidated financial statements.

STOCK DIVIDENDS

A stock dividend may be declared to avoid passing a dividend but at the same time preserving corporate assets. Stock dividends can also be used to supplement a cash dividend without a permanent dividend increase. The stock dividend also "permanently capitalizes" retained earnings by allowing the company to plow earnings back on a permanent basis. That is, the reduction of retained earnings caused by the stock dividend may limit the company's ability to distribute cash dividends and permit the use of cash for expansion, etc.

A stock dividend has no effect on total assets and total stockholder's equity. There is no legal liability to distribute a stock dividend, even if declared, because there is no effect on total assets and total stockholders' equity. There is also no obligation to distribute corporate assets. In addition, no liability is created because the Board of Directors can reverse the declaration of the stock dividend. Stock dividends are common in practice.

A stock dividend results in a simple reclassification from retained earnings into contributed capital (capital stock at par and paid in capital in excess of par). A stock dividend is sometimes called an "intra-equity transaction" or a "capitalization of retained earnings." The intra-equity nature of the stock dividend is illustrated below.

ASSETS	= LIABILITIES	+ STOCKHOLDERS' EQUITY	
CASH		CONTRIBUTED CAPITAL	RETAINED EARNINGS
		(+) Credit ?	(—) Debit ?
			ACCOUNTING VALUATION ISSUE

Without a signaling effect in the market, a stock dividend does not change total market value but only reduces market value per share. Therefore, as the above diagram indicates that the primary issue in accounting for stock dividends is accounting valuation. The total book value of the company does not change, but there is a proportional decrease in book value per share.

On the surface, the stock dividend does not seem to pose any significant analytical or accounting questions. However, the primary issue facing the accountant is the valuation of the stock dividend. The accountant must determine the "value" distributed to the shareholder or what amount of retained earnings should be capitalized. That is, "what accounting value has the corporation distributed to the shareholder or how much retained earnings should be capitalized in contributed capital?" The answer to these questions depends on the size of the stock dividend. A stock dividend can be classified as either: (i) a small stock dividend or (ii) a large stock dividend. The rules represent materiality thresholds affecting the book or accounting valuation of the stock dividend.

(i) Small (Ordinary) Stock Dividend (Valued at market)

A stock dividend is considered a small stock dividend if the number of shares issued does not exceed approximately 25% of the previously outstanding shares. Unless there is evidence to the contrary, the accountant assumes that a dividend of this size would not have a materially negative effect on the market price of the stock when the additional shares are distributed. We know stock prices will decline proportionately but 25% is not considered material. Therefore, the dividend should be valued (i.e., retained earnings capitalized) at the market price at the date of declaration. This is the approximate accounting value that the shareholder can receive if the shares are sold and converted into cash.

(ii) Large Stock Dividend (Valued at par or accounted for as a stock split)

A stock dividend is considered a large stock dividend if the number of shares issued is over 25% of the previously outstanding shares. Unless there is evidence to the contrary, the accountant assumes that a dividend of this size would materially reduce the market price of the stock when the additional shares are distributed. Therefore, the value given to the shareholder is not known, but the dividend cannot be valued below minimum legal capital. As a result, the dividend is valued at (i.e., retained earnings capitalized at) the par value of the stock.

It should be noted that a large stock dividend is sometimes accounted for as a stock split. In fact, a large stock dividend is sometimes called "a stock split effected in the form of a stock dividend." For example, a 50% stock dividend has the same effect as a 3-for-2 stock split. The stock split treatment is convenient when the stock does not have a par or stated value.

The split treatment for no par stock simply increases the number of outstanding shares disclosed in the stockholders' equity section of the balance sheet. There is no change in any of the line item totals in the stockholders' equity section of the balance sheet.

If the stock has a par value, split treatment will transfer the appropriate amount of par value from additional paid in capital into the capital stock account. The key point to note is that the stock split treatment for a large stock dividend does not affect retained earnings.

Some states permit stock dividends to be distributed to shares held as treasury stock.

ILLUSTRATION: ACCOUNTING FOR STOCK DIVIDENDS

Data for the Illustration. The JT Company reports the following Stockholders' Equity Section in its most recent Balance Sheet:

STOCKHOLDERS' EQUITY	*BALANCE*
Common Stock ($10 par, 200,000 shares authorized, 110,000 shares issued)	$1,100,000
Contributed Capital in Excess of Par	480,000
Total Contributed Capital	$1,580,000
Retained Earnings	2,000,000
Total	$3,580,000
Less: Cost of Treasury Stock (10,000 shares)	(400,000)
Total Stockholders' Equity	$3,180,000

Assume that a stock dividend was declared on a date when the firm's common stock was selling for $30/share (the market price of the stock on the date of declaration). Also assume that the shares issued to satisfy the stock dividend are newly issued shares, not treasury shares, and treasury shares are not entitled to the stock dividend. The accounting problem is to determine the valuation of the stock dividend for two independent cases: Case 1: The stock dividend was equal to 23,000 shares and Case 2: The stock dividend was equal to 26,500 shares.

Solution: Case 1

Outstanding Shares = (Issued — Treasury Shares)
100,000 = (110,000 — 10,000)

Type Of Stock Dividend: 23,000/100,000 = 23% or a Small Stock Dividend.

Retained Earnings Capitalized at FMV = 23,000 X $30 = $690,000.

$230,000 is classified as common stock par ($10 per share), and the difference, $460,000, is classified as contributed capital in excess of par. The stockholder's equity section after the declaration of the small stock dividend is presented below.

STOCKHOLDERS' EQUITY	*BALANCE*	*CHANGE*
Common Stock ($10 par, 200,000 shares authorized, 133,000 shares issued)	$1,330,000	+$230,000
Contributed Capital in Excess of Par	940,000	+ 460,000
Total Contributed Capital	$2,270,000	+$690,000
Retained Earnings	1,310,000	- 690,000
Total	3,580,000	$0
Less: Cost of Treasury Stock (10,000 shares)	(400,000)	0
Total Stockholders' Equity	$3,180,000	$0

Solution: Case 2

Type Of Stock Dividend: 26,500/100,000 = 26.5% or a Large Stock Dividend.

Retained Earnings Capitalized At Par = 26,500 X $10 = $265,000.

The stockholders' equity section after the declaration of the large stock dividend is presented below:

STOCKHOLDERS' EQUITY	*BALANCE*	*CHANGE*
Common Stock ($10 par, 200,000 shares authorized, 136,500 shares issued)	$1,365,000	+$265,000
Contributed Capital in Excess of Par	480,000	0
Total Contributed Capital	$1,845,000	+$265,000
Retained Earnings	1,735,000	- $265,000
Total	$3,580,000	$ 0
Less: Cost of Treasury Stock (10,000 shares)	(400,000)	0
Total Stockholders' Equity	$3,180,000	$ 0

Alternative Treatment of a Large Stock Dividend. For a large stock dividend with no par stock, we can treat the large stock dividend as a stock split by increasing the number of outstanding shares disclosed on the balance sheet. There is no change in any balance sheet total but the parenthetical notation must be modified accordingly.

If the stock has a par value, the appropriate amount of additional paid in capital is transferred into the common stock account. Sample disclosures for Cohen Corporation and Howard Corporation are presented in Exhibit 4.4.

EXHIBIT 4.4: COHEN CORP. AND HOWARD CORP. STOCK SPLIT FOOTNOTE DISCLOSURE

Cohen Corporation 2012 Annual Report NOTE 5 - STOCK SPLIT

On June 1, 2012, the Company's Board of Directors declared a two-for-one split of Cohen common stock for stockholders of record at the close of business on June 30, 2012, payable on August 1, 2012. This resulted in the issuance of 63.2 million shares of common stock along with a corresponding decrease of $63.2 million in additional paid-in capital. Treasury shares were not split; however, an adjustment was made to the Company's stockholders' equity section of the balance sheet to split the cost of treasury stock (in effect a cancellation of treasury shares). All references to the number of shares of common stock issued or outstanding, per share prices, and income per common share amounts in the consolidated financial statements and the accompanying notes have been adjusted to reflect the split on a retroactive basis. Previously awarded stock options, restricted stock awards, and all other agreements payable in the Company's common stock have been adjusted or amended to reflect the split. Additionally, cash dividends which were $0.24 per share per quarter prior to the two-for-one split have been adjusted to $0.12 per share per quarter to reflect the two-for-one split.

Howard Corporation Annual Report

Stock Split. On October 1, 2012, we announced our Board of Directors had approved a two-for-one split of the common stock. The stock split was affected by issuing an additional share of common stock for each outstanding share of that common stock. The additional shares were distributed December 1, 2012 to shareholders of record at the close of business on October 31, 2012. Accordingly we have restated our earnings (loss) per share calculations, as well as reclassified amounts between common stock and additional-paid-in-capital to reflect the impact of the stock split of the outstanding common stock for all periods presented. In accounting for the stock split, 19.6 million shares of treasury stock were deemed reissued and an additional 11.5 million shares were issued. As the treasury shares that were reissued as part of the stock split had been purchased by us during fiscal year 2012 and previous fiscal years, treasury stock has only been reclassified to show the effect of the stock split as of December 31,2012.

For a true stock split, there would be a proportionate increase in the number of shares and a proportionate decrease in the par value, if any. This would only affect the disclosures for stockholders' equity and would have no impact on any balance sheet account. For example, assume a corporation has 10,000 shares of $10 par value stock authorized, issued and outstanding. If the corporation implements a 2 for 1 stock split, it would increase the number of outstanding shares to 20,000 and reduce the par value to $5 per share. There would be no change in the total book value or the total market value of the firm. However, the book value per share and market value (price) per share are reduced proportionately.

Before: 10,000 shares at $10 par = $100,000 Total par value
After: 20,000 shares at $ 5 par = $100,000 Total par value

Finally, it should be noted that all shares split, even those held in the treasury.

ACCOUNTING FOR TREASURY STOCK TRANSACTIONS

Treasury stock is a corporation's own stock that was authorized, issued and previously outstanding. Treasury shares are reacquired by the corporation with the intention to reissue these shares for some specific purpose. Generally, the shares are not to be retired.

Treasury shares can be acquired to satisfy several objectives. For example, treasury shares can be purchased:

- To be used in stock option plans, stock bonus plans, ESOP's, etc.
- To be used in exchange for another firm's voting shares in a merger or acquisition.
- To support the market price of the stock.
- To prevent takeover attempts.
- To distribute cash to shareholders without formally increasing the dividend per share.

In some cases, the treasury shares are retired. Additionally, the SEC encourages publicly traded companies to disclose their stock repurchase plans. Share repurchase plans are not commitments and do not have to be fulfilled. Sample disclosures for Levy Associates are presented in Exhibit 4.5.

EXHIBIT 4.5: LEVY ASSOCIATE STOCK REPURCHASE FOOTNOTE DISCLOSURES

NOTE 6 - STOCK REPURCHASE PROGRAM

On February 25, 2012, our Board of Directors approved a share repurchase program with no expiration date authorizing management to repurchase up to $300 million in open market purchases. We repurchased 5.6 million shares of our common stock for $150.1 million for the year ended December 31, 2012, under our approved repurchase programs (but excluding the OSR). The funding required for these repurchases came from cash generated from net sales and operating revenues and cash and cash equivalents. We also repurchase shares in the open market to offset the sales of shares to our employee benefit plans. As of March 3, 2013, there was $209.9 million available under the $300 million share repurchase program. Management suspended purchases under the $300 million share repurchase program, while the financial institution completed the overnight share repurchase program ("OSR") described below.

As of March 3, 2013 management has not resumed share repurchases under the $300 million program. On August 5, 2012, we entered into an agreement with a financial institution to purchase 24 million shares of our common stock from the financial institution under the OSR. The share price upon completion of the transaction was $28.98. We funded this payment from available cash on hand and short-term borrowings in the commercial paper market.

NOTE 11 - TREASURY STOCK RETIREMENT

In December 2009, our Board of Directors approved the retirement of 54 million shares of our common stock held as treasury stock. These shares returned to the status of authorized and unissued. Additional details of the transaction can be found in our 2009 Consolidated Statement of Stockholders' Equity.

The treasury stock acquisition is not an investment asset. Under the cost method, treasury stock is treated a negative equity or a contra-stockholders' equity account. It is reported as a reduction of total stockholders' equity on the balance sheet. As noted earlier, the treasury shares reduce the number of shares outstanding. In addition, treasury stock is not active or effective stock. That is, treasury shares are no longer outstanding and do not have voting rights and cannot receive cash dividends. However, treasury shares do split and can receive stock dividends in some states. Note that the cost method is used by approximately 60 to 70% of companies in the United States.

Treasury Stock Transactions under the Cost Method. On the date of acquisition the cost (not the par value) of the shares is the basis for recording. It reduces cash and total stockholders' equity.

To illustrate, assume that in 2008 the Locke Corporation purchases treasury shares for $100.

FINANCIAL MODELING WORKSHEET TREASURY STOCK AT ACQUISITION

INCOME STATEMENT (FIRST)	
REVENUES:	
EXPENSES:	
NET INCOME OR LOSS (a)	*-0-*

STATEMENT OF CASH FLOWS (THIRD)	
OPERATING ACTIVITIES:	
NET INCOME OR LOSS (a)	*-0-*
INVESTING ACTIVITIES:	
FINANCING ACTIVITIES:	
Purchase Treasury Shares	*(100)*
INCREASE (DECREASE) IN CASH (b)	*(100)*
ADD: BEGINNING CASH BALANCE	
ENDING CASH BALANCE	

BALANCE SHEET (SECOND)			
ASSETS		*LIABILITIES*	
CURRENT ASSETS		*CURRENT LIABILITIES*	
CASH (b)	*(100)*		
		NONCURRENT LIABILITIES	
		STOCKHOLDERS' EQUITY	
NONCURRENT ASSETS			
		CAPITAL STOCK	
		APIC	
		RETAINED EARNINGS (a)	*-0-*
		TREASURY STOCK	*(100)*
TOTAL ASSETS	*(100)*	*TOTAL LIABILITIES & STOCKHOLDERS' EQUITY*	*(100)*

The treasury shares can now be reissued at a price either above or below cost. If the treasury shares are sold at a price above cost, the excess over cost ("gain") is classified as additional paid in capital from treasury stock transactions. This "gain" is not reported on the income statement because this event is considered to be a capital transaction. In addition, the "gain" cannot create retained earnings.

To illustrate, assume that in 2009 the Locke Corporation sells the treasury shares it acquired at $100 for a net selling price of $110. By collecting an additional $10, the shareholder contributes an extra amount for the same shares purchased.

	2008 Purchase Treasury Stock	*2009 Reissue Treasury Stock*	*Net Gain (Loss)*
Corporation	($100)	+$110	+$10
Stockholder	+100	($110)	($10)

FINANCIAL MODELING WORKSHEET REISSUE TREASURY SHARES AT AN AMOUNT ABOVE COST

INCOME STATEMENT (FIRST)	
REVENUES:	
EXPENSES:	
NET INCOME OR LOSS (a)	*-0-*

STATEMENT OF CASH FLOWS (THIRD)	
OPERATING ACTIVITIES:	
NET INCOME OR LOSS (a)	*-0-*
INVESTING ACTIVITIES:	
FINANCING ACTIVITIES:	
Disposal of Treasury Shares	*+110*
INCREASE (DECREASE) IN CASH (b)	*+110*
ADD: BEGINNING CASH BALANCE	
ENDING CASH BALANCE	

BALANCE SHEET (SECOND)			
ASSETS		***LIABILITIES***	
CURRENT ASSETS		***CURRENT LIABILITIES***	
CASH (b)	*+110*		
		NONCURRENT LIABILITIES	
		STOCKHOLDERS' EQUITY	
NONCURRENT ASSETS			
		CAPITAL STOCK	
		APIC ("Gain")	*+10*
		RETAINED EARNINGS (a)	
		TREASURY STOCK	*+100*
		TOTAL LIABILITIES & STOCKHOLDERS' EQUITY	
TOTAL ASSETS	*+110*		*+110*

Finally, if the treasury shares are sold at price below cost, the amount below cost ("loss") is first used to reduce additional paid in capital from prior treasury stock transactions, if any. If this account is reduced to zero, the remainder is used to reduce retained earnings (i.e., a dividend effect). Some states permit the entire loss to be deducted from additional paid in capital from all sources. This "loss" is not reported on the income statement because this is considered a capital transaction.

To illustrate, assume that in 2009 the Locke Corporation sells the treasury shares it acquired at $100 for a net selling price of $80. In this case, the shareholder receives a distribution from the corporation and continues to hold the same number of shares.

	2008 Purchase Treasury Stock	*2009 Reissue Treasury Stock*	*Net Gain (Loss)*
Corporation	($100)	+$ 80	($20)
Stockholder	+100	($80)	+$20

Again, note that some states permit the reduction of additional paid in capital (APIC) from regular share issuances. If this APIC is reduced to zero, then APIC from treasury stock transactions and retained earnings will be reduced in that order. In general, contributed capital accounts cannot be reduced below zero (i.e., have a negative balance), but a negative balance can exist in retained earnings. A negative balance in retained earnings is known as a "deficit."

The reduction of retained earnings reflects the "in-substance dividend distribution" interpretation of the "loss." To understand this last point, assume that the purchase and the reissuance of the treasury shares were both cash transactions, and if the shares are reissued below cost, the stockholders hold the same number of shares but now have a cash distribution from the corporation. This interpretation justifies, the reduction of retained earnings or the dividend treatment of the loss as noted above. In fact, many states restrict dividend distributions to the extent of the cost of treasury shares held by the corporation.

The "gain" or "loss" on treasury stock transactions have no tax consequences. These "gains" or "losses" are considered to be the result of capital (equity) transactions and are not an element of corporate taxable income. Therefore, capital transactions have no effect on income (neither financial accounting nor taxable income).

Paid in capital from treasury stock transactions is usually a separate category of contributed capital and must be kept separate from regular paid in capital from the issuance of stock or other sources. This treatment satisfies one of the objectives of accounting for stockholders' equity: to maintain each source of capital separately. The separate contributed capital accounts are typically found in the footnotes to the financial statements if material.

The financial modeling worksheet for the "loss" treasury stock transaction is presented below. Here we assume the loss can be deducted from additional paid in capital.

FINANCIAL MODELING WORKSHEET REISSUE TREASURY SHARES AT AN AMOUNT BELOW COST

INCOME STATEMENT (FIRST)	
REVENUES:	
EXPENSES:	
NET INCOME OR LOSS (a)	- 0 -

STATEMENT OF CASH FLOWS (THIRD)	
OPERATING ACTIVITIES:	
NET INCOME OR LOSS (a)	- 0 -
INVESTING ACTIVITIES:	
FINANCING ACTIVITIES:	
Disposal of Treasury Shares	+80
INCREASE (DECREASE) IN CASH (b)	+80
ADD: BEGINNING CASH BALANCE	
ENDING CASH BALANCE	

BALANCE SHEET (SECOND)			
ASSETS		LIABILITIES	
CURRENT ASSETS		CURRENT LIABILITIES	
CASH (b)	+80		
		NONCURRENT LIABILITIES	
		STOCKHOLDERS' EQUITY	
NONCURRENT ASSETS			
		CAPITAL STOCK	
		APIC ("Loss")	(20)
		RETAINED EARNINGS (a)	
		TREASURY STOCK	+100
		TOTAL LIABILITIES & STOCKHOLDERS' EQUITY	
TOTAL ASSETS	+80		+80

Disclosure of "gains" on treasury stock disposals is presented in Exhibit 4.6 and is classified as "other capital."

EXHIBIT 4.7: BAVER TECHNOLOGIES SHARE OWNERS' EQUITY FOOTNOTE

Notes to Consolidated Financial Statements
Note 24: Shareowner's Equity (Partial)

(In millions)	2012	2011	2010
OTHER CAPITAL			
Balance at January 1	$ 20,996	$ 20,746	$ 20,032
Gains on treasury stock dispositions and other(a)	5,538	250.8	714
Issuance of subsidiary shares		–	–
Balance at December 31	$ 29,118	$ 20,996	$ 20,746
RETAINED EARNINGS			
Balance at January 1	$ 99,823	$ 90,851	$ 82,570
Net earnings	20,183	18,283	17,000
Dividends	(10,313)	(9,311)	(8,719)
Balance at December 31	$ 109,693	$ 99,823	$ 90,851
COMMON STOCK HELD IN TREASURY			
Balance at January 1	$ 29,516	$ 31,952	$ 32,299
Purchases	2,270	1,412	3,421
Dispositions	(16,472)	(3,848)	(3,768)
Balance at December 31	$ 15,314	$ 29,516	$ 31,952

SHARES OF BAVER COMMON STOCK

December 31 (In thousands)	2012	2011	2010
Issued	**13,374,254**	**13,374,254**	**13,374,254**
In treasury	**(670,625)**	**(1,298,510)**	**(1,410,382)**
Outstanding	**12,703,630**	**12,075,744**	**11,963,873**

THE RETAINED EARNINGS SECTION

In addition to the net income or loss for the period and dividend declarations, retained earnings will be affected by prior period adjustments and appropriations of retained earnings.

Prior Period Adjustments. According to FASB Statement Nos. 16, "Prior Period Adjustments," corrections of errors made in financial statements of prior periods are reported as adjustments to opening retained earnings, net of tax. If the entity prepares comparative financial statements, the correction should be applied retroactively with the prior period adjustment reflected in the retained earnings section of the first balance sheet presented.

For example, assume that a $4,000 sale was not recorded in 2002 and therefore, sales and accounts receivable were understated. This error was discovered in 2009 and the accounts receivable was never collected. Assuming a tax rate of 40%, the firm's stockholders' equity section at December 31, 2009 would appear as follows:

Stockholders' Equity	
Contributed Capital:	
Capital Stock, At par	$12,000
Paid in Capital in Excess of Par	5,000
	$17,000
Retained Earnings:	
Retained Earnings 1/1/2009 As Previously Reported	$ 14,000
Add or Deduct: Prior Period Adjustment, net of tax	2,400
Retained Earnings 1/1/2009 As Adjusted	$ 16,400
Add: Net Income for the Year ended 12/31/2009	3,000
Less: Dividends	(1,000)
Retained Earnings 12/31/2009	$ 18,400
Stockholders' Equity	$35,400

In addition to the $2,400 adjustment to opening retained earnings, accounts receivable is increased by $4,000 and a $1,600 tax liability is reported (i.e., $4,000 x 40%).

Appropriations of Retained Earnings. An appropriation of retained earnings is a disclosure device which indicates the reasons why dividends are not paid or were less than expected. Simply stated, the appropriation is a disclosure of dividend restrictions.

There are three types of appropriations: voluntary, legal and contractual.

- ***Voluntary or discretionary.*** These appropriations are at the discretion of the board of directors and include appropriations for plant expansion or self-insurance.
- ***Legal or statutory.*** As indicated earlier, certain states require a restriction on dividend distributions equal to the cost of treasury stock held by the corporation.
- ***Contractual.*** Restrictive covenants in debt agreements may place limitations on dividend distributions.

There are two accounting alternatives for an appropriation of retained earnings. The first, and most common, is a footnote disclosure. The second type of disclosure requires a reclassification of retained earnings into two categories: free and unappropriated retained earnings and retained earnings-appropriated. This does not change the total of retained earnings but simply makes the disclosure of the appropriation on the face of the balance sheet.

Regardless of the accounting approach used, it should never be assumed by the reader of the financial statements that there is a fund of cash or other economic resources available to satisfy the purpose for which the appropriation is established. The appropriation is simply a disclosure of a restriction or limitation on dividend distributions.

Reporting Comprehensive Income. FASB Statement No. 130, "Reporting Comprehensive Income" [1] is designed to report a measure of changes in the equity of an enterprise that result from recognized transactions and all economic events of the period other than transactions with owners in their capacity as owners. This measure is comprehensive income.

It is believed that the information provided by reporting comprehensive income should assist investors, creditors and others in assessing an enterprise's activities and the timing and magnitude of an enterprise's future cash flows. Here, information about the components of comprehensive income is more important than the total.

Comprehensive income is best defined as all changes in equity during a period from all sources except those resulting from investments by owners and distributions to owners. This concept can be formulated as follows:

Comprehensive		**Net**		**Other Comprehensive**
Income	=	**Income**	+/-	**Income**
(CI)		**(NI)**		**(OCI)**

The elements of net income (NI) are revenues, expenses, gains and losses. There are also components of income from continuing operations and income or loss from discontinued operations and extraordinary items.

The elements of other comprehensive income (OCI) currently consist of the following:

- Unrealized gains and losses from the available for sale portfolio of investment securities and derivatives classified as cash flow hedges
- Foreign currency translation gains and losses
- Unrealized gain and loss adjustments to the balance sheet need to reflect the funded status of defined contribution pension plans

All elements are not reported on the income statement because they have a very low probability of cash flow realization in the short term and could result in significant earnings volatility. If the probability of short-term cash flow realization is high, a transaction is reported on the income statement.

SFAS No. 130 does not require a specific format but does require that all components of comprehensive income be reported in a financial statement that is displayed with the same prominence as other financial statements and an amount representing total comprehensive income for that period be displayed in that financial statement. Most firms have elected to report the other comprehensive income items (net of tax), in a Statement of Changes in Stockholders' Equity (See Exhibit 4.3).

The enterprise is also required to report the accumulated balance of other comprehensive income separately from retained earnings and additional paid in capital in the stockholders' equity section of the balance sheet. The term used for this account is "Other Accumulated Comprehensive Income."

Earnings per share on comprehensive income is not required. However, net income must be displayed as a component of comprehensive income.

1. FASB ASC 220 [Predecessor literature: "Reporting Comprehensive Income," *Statement of Financial Accounting Standards No. 130* (Norwalk, Conn.: FASB, 1997)].

ACCOUNTING FOR STOCK-BASED COMPENSATION AND HYBRID FINANCIAL INSTRUMENTS

Accounting for Stock-Based Compensation: Introduction

Employee stock options are financial instruments that give an employee the right to purchase shares of a company's stock, directly from the company, at fixed price and for a specific period of time. The fixed price is called the "exercise" or "strike" price.

These compensation arrangements are known as "incentive option plans" because the assumption is that the employee will be more productive as he or she wants the market price of the company's stock to increase substantially above the exercise price. In this way the employee purchases the shares from the company at a fixed exercise price that is lower than the market price at the time of exercise. The employee can then sell the shares in the market at a significant gain.

When the market price is above the exercise price of the company's stock, the options are "in the money."

Types of Employee Stock Option Plans

There are two types of employee stock option plans:

- Nonqualified or Nonstatutory Stock Option Plans
- Incentive Stock Option or Qualified Plans

Nonqualified or nonstatutory stock option plans provide a significant tax advantage for the employer corporation. In a nonqualified stock option plan, the corporation receives a tax deduction equal to the difference between the market price and the exercise price on the date the employee purchases the stock (i.e., on the date the options are exercised).

However, this results in a taxable event for the employee. An employee who receives a nonqualified stock option must pay taxes, at ordinary income rates, on the difference between the market price and the exercise price on the date the stock is purchased (i.e., on the date of exercise). This represents a burden for the employee who now has to pay cash for the shares, as well as the tax at ordinary income rates.

Incentive or qualified stock option plans provide a significant tax advantage for the employee. In these types of plans, an employee pays no tax on the difference between the market price of the stock and the option price when the stock is purchased (i.e., when the options are exercised). The only taxable event arises when the employee sells his or her shares and here, the tax is paid at favorable capital gains rates. Effectively, all tax consequences are deferred until the shares are sold in the market.

Conversely, an incentive or qualified plan provides no tax benefit for the employer. No tax deduction is permitted for an incentive or qualified plan.

Tax law requires that the market price and the exercise price be equal on the date of the grant in order to have the plan classified as a qualified or incentive stock option plan. This means that there is no intrinsic value on the date of the grant of the option.

The equality of the market price and exercise price is not required in nonqualified plans. In this case, there can be a positive intrinsic value on the date of the grant.

To illustrate, assume that Costline.com grants options to purchase 200,000 shares at an option price of $200 per share on a date when the market price of the stock is also $200 per share. The options are exercised on a date when the shares are also selling for $400 per share and are sold at $400 a year later. Tax rates are assumed to be 36% for individuals on ordinary income and 28% on capital gains and the corporate tax rate is assumed to be 34%.

A comparison of both types of plans are presented below.

Effects on Employee and Employer Corporation	Assuming Incentive Stock Options	Assuming Nonqualified Stock Options
Employee (36% tax rate):		
Profit on exercise (200,000 X [$400 – 200])	$40,000,000	$40,000,000
Tax on exercise ($40,000,000 X 36%)	- 0 -	$14,400,000
Tax on sale ($40,000,000 x 28%)	$11,200,000	- 0 -
After tax benefit	$28,800,000	$25,600,000
Employer Corporation (34% tax rate):	No tax deduction resulting in no tax benefit.	$40,000,000 tax deduction resulting in a $13,600,000 tax benefit.

COMPENSATION EXPENSE IN THE FINANCIAL STATEMENTS

The key issue in accounting for employee stock options is whether or not to record compensation expense in the financial statements. This issue was first addressed by the accounting profession in APB Opinion 25, "Accounting for Stock Issued to Employees,"[2] replaced by FASB Statement No. 123, "Accounting for Stock Based Compensation,"[3] and more revised in FASB Statement No. 123R, "Accounting for Stock Based Compensation (Revised)."[4] SFAS 123R requires that all employee stock based compensation plans are to be expensed (at fair value) on the income statement over the expected period of benefit.

Unlike prior accounting, where no compensation expense was recognized if there was no intrinsic value at the date of the grant, all employee options must be expensed, even if there is no intrinsic value.

Intrinsic value is defined as the difference between the exercise price and the market price on the date of the grant to the employee. When the exercise price and the market price are the same, there is no intrinsic value. However, an employee would not accept the options as compensation for services if they had no value. Therefore, even if there is no intrinsic value, there is an economic or fair value that must be recognized and exercised.

By expensing stock based compensation plans, the FASB is using an accounting method consistent with all other forms of nonmonetary exchanges. For example, if a consultant is paid is shares of stock, there is an expense charged for the consultant's services and this expense is measured at the fair value of the consideration given (i.e., the fair value of the stock) or the fair value of the consideration received, whichever is more clearly evident. This is the theoretical foundation supporting SFAS 123R.

The following section of this module presents the accounting for employee stock options.

Accounting for Employee Stock Options under SFAS 123R. As implied in the introductory paragraphs, the two primary accounting issues for employee stock based compensation are: the measurement of compensation expense and the allocation of compensation expense to the expected period of benefit

2. "Accounting for Stock Issued to Employees," *Opinions of the Accounting Principles Board No. 25* (New York: AICPA 1972).

3. FASB ASC 718 [Predecessor literature: "Accounting for Stock-Based Compensation," *Statement of Financial Accounting Standards No. 123* (Norwalk, Conn.: FASB, 1995)]

4. FASB ASC 718 [Predecessor literature: "Accounting for Stock-Based Compensation," *Statement of Financial Accounting Standards No. 123R* (Norwalk, Conn.: FASB, 2004)].

Determination of Compensation Expense. SFAS 123R requires that we measure stock based compensation expense at fair value. Fair value is based on the number of options expected to vest. When vesting occurs, an employee's right to receive the stock based compensation (or any employee fringe benefit), is no longer dependent on continued employment with the corporation.

The fair value of the stock based compensation can be measured by either:

i. The Black-Scholes Option Pricing Model (most commonly used in practice)
ii. A Binominal or Lattice Model (preferred but not required by the FASB)

A key point to note is that under the fair value method equity classified awards compensation expense is not adjusted for changes in the market price of the stock. Even if the options are not "in the money" (i.e., the market price falls below the exercise price) at the end of the accounting period, there is no adjustment made in the compensation expense. However, compensation expense is adjusted as the probability of vesting changes (i.e., accountants must adjust stock-based compensation expense for estimated forfeitures before vesting).

Options can be classified as liabilities (i.e., liability classified awards). Unlike equity classified awards (the focus of this presentation), liability classified awards are adjusted each year changes in fair value of the options with the expense adjustment flowing through income and an adjustment is made to the liability (e.g., Stock appreciation rights).

Options could be classified (credited) as liabilities if the option is for the acquisition of securities classified as liabilities, such as redeemable preferred stock (considered debt under FASB 150) or if the shares acquired can be sold back to the employer corporation at the exercise price within a "reasonable period of time"(e.g., six months). Here the employee does not absorb any risk if the award is indexed to a factor, such as a commodity price.

CONVERTIBLE BONDS WITH BENEFICIAL CONVERSION OPTIONS

Since convertible debt is a hybrid (compound) financial instrument (possessing both debt and equity features), accountants have argued that the debt and equity components should be separated at issuance and reported as part debt and part equity on the balance sheet. The EITF provides guidance regarding the separate recognition of the conversion option. The EITF's[5] guidance is presented in the following illustration.

Illustration. Assume that a company issues a 5 year, 5% convertible bond at par, $1,000. The yield on the bond is therefore, 5%. Each $1,000 bond converts into 50 shares of common stock at the option of the bondholder beginning two years after the date of issue. There were no bond issue costs. The market price of the common stock on the purchase commitment date was equal to $25 per share.

In order to determine if the debt and equity features of this financial instrument can be separated, we must first test to see if there is a beneficial conversion option. A beneficial conversion option exists if the implied purchase (exercise or strike) price of the stock is less that the market price of the shares on the purchase commitment date (i.e., the conversion option is "in the money" or it is said to have positive intrinsic value).

The implied strike price is $20 per share: $1,000/50 shares and the intrinsic value of the option is $5 per share: $25 – 20. This means that the value of the beneficial conversion option is $250 ($5 intrinsic value x 50 shares) and the bonds are value at $750.

The financial modeling worksheet to record the bond issue with a beneficial conversion option is presented below.

5. FASB ASC 470 [Predecessor literature: *EITF Issue No. 98-5*, "Accounting for Securities with Beneficial Conversion Features or Contingently Adjustable Conversion Ratios," *Emerging Issues Task Force Abstracts* (June 12, 2008)].

FINANCIAL MODELING WORKSHEET CONVERTIBLE BONDS ISSUED WITH BENEFICIAL A CONVERSION OPTION

INCOME STATEMENT (FIRST)	
REVENUES:	
EXPENSES:	
NET INCOME OR LOSS (a)	*- 0 -*

STATEMENT OF CASH FLOWS (THIRD)	
OPERATING ACTIVITIES:	
NET INCOME OR LOSS (a)	*- 0 -*
INVESTING ACTIVITIES:	
FINANCING ACTIVITIES:	
Proceeds from Convertible Bond issue	*+1,000*
INCREASE (DECREASE) IN CASH (b)	*+1,000*
ADD: BEGINNING CASH BALANCE	
ENDING CASH BALANCE	

BALANCE SHEET (SECOND)			
ASSETS		*LIABILITIES*	
CURRENT ASSETS		*CURRENT LIABILITIES*	
CASH (b)	*+ 1,000*		
		NONCURRENT LIABILITIES	
		Bonds Payable – par	*+1,000*
		Discount on Bonds	*(250)*
		STOCKHOLDERS'	
NONCURRENT ASSETS		*EQUITY*	
		CAPITAL STOCK	
		APIC	
		APIC –Beneficial Conversion Option	*+250*
		ACCUMULATED OTHER COMPRE-HENSIVE INCOME	
		RETAINED EARNINGS (a)	
TOTAL ASSETS	*+1,000*	*TOTAL LIABILITIES & STOCKHOLDERS' EQUITY*	*+1,000*

The discount would be expensed immediately if the bonds were immediately exercisable. If exercisable only with the passage of time, the discount account is used.

With the discount recorded, a new effective interest rate (yield or discount) rate must be computed in order to amortize the discount. Using a **financial calculator,** the new effective rate is 11.92%

		END MODE
- 750	=	**PV**
1,000	=	**FV**
50 ($1,000 x 5%)	=	**PMT**
5	=	**n**
X = 11.92%	=	**i**

Allocation of Compensation Expense. Compensation expense is allocated over the vesting period. This is the period from the date of the grant to the date the employee is able to exercise the option. The theory underlying this allocation period is that during this period, employees will increase their productivity in order to increase the market price of the stock. As a result, the compensation expense should be matched against the income generated from increased employee motivation (incentive) and productivity.

Therefore, compensation expense is allocated to the income statement by using a straight line amortization method over the vesting period.

ILLUSTRATION: EMPLOYEE STOCK OPTION ALTERNATIVES UNDER SFAS 123R

The following information is available for employee stock options granted on January 2, 2008 (which is also the measurement date). The measurement is the first date on which the number of shares and the exercise price are both known:

- Options to acquire 50,000 shares of $1 par value common stock
- Market price on January 2, 2008 = $4 per share
- Exercise (option, strike) price = $4 per share
- Estimated service period = 2 years
- The options can only be exercised at this time, (i.e., after the end of a two year vesting period)
- The options expire after a 5-year period
- Estimated fair value of the options using the Black-Scholes Option Pricing Model: $8 per share or a total of $400,000 (i.e., 50,000 shares x $8 per share)

Note that the intrinsic value is equal to zero on the grant date. Where:

Intrinsic Value = Market Price - Exercise Price = ($4 - 4) = $ - 0 -

Accounting Under SFAS 123R. Compensation expense is measured at fair value of the options at the grant date. Adequate footnote disclosure is also required.

Optional Entry on the date of the grant. Note that because the net effect on Stockholders' Equity is zero, this entry is not required and is only a form of disclosure. This is similar to stock subscriptions. The entry for the date of the grant is presented in the financial modeling worksheet below.

FINANCIAL MODELING WORKSHEET: DATE OF THE GRANT

INCOME STATEMENT (FIRST)	
REVENUES:	
EXPENSES:	
NET INCOME OR LOSS (a)	

STATEMENT OF CASH FLOWS (THIRD)	
OPERATING ACTIVITIES:	
NET INCOME OR LOSS (a)	
INVESTING ACTIVITIES:	
FINANCING ACTIVITIES:	
INCREASE (DECREASE) IN CASH (b)	
ADD: BEGINNING CASH BALANCE	
ENDING CASH BALANCE	

BALANCE SHEET (SECOND)			
ASSETS		LIABILITIES	
CURRENT ASSETS		CURRENT LIABILITIES	
CASH (b)			
		NONCURRENT LIABILITIES	
		STOCKHOLDERS' EQUITY	
NONCURRENT ASSETS			
		CAPITAL STOCK	
		APIC	
		APIC-OPTIONS	+400
		RETAINED EARNINGS (a)	
		DEFERRED COMPENSATION	(400)
		TOTAL LIABILITIES & STOCKHOLDERS' EQUITY	
TOTAL ASSETS	-0-		-0-

Deferred (unearned) compensation is a negative stockholders' equity accounting and will be amortized to compensation expense on the income statement over the employees' service period (See Exhibit 4.1).

Subsequent entries assuming a two-year amortization (service) period: matching compensation expense against increased employee productivity.

FINANCIAL MODELING WORKSHEET: AMORTIZATION EACH YEAR OVER THE SERVICE PERIOD

INCOME STATEMENT (FIRST)	
REVENUES:	
EXPENSES: COMPENSATION EXPENSE	*(200)*
NET INCOME OR LOSS (a)	*(200)*

STATEMENT OF CASH FLOWS (THIRD)	
OPERATING ACTIVITIES:	
NET INCOME OR LOSS (a)	*(200)*
ADD BACK: STOCK BASED COMPENSATION EXPENSE	*+200*
CASH FLOW FROM OPERATING ACTIVITIES	*-0-*
INVESTING ACTIVITIES:	
FINANCING ACTIVITIES:	
INCREASE (DECREASE) IN CASH (b)	*-0-*
ADD: BEGINNING CASH BALANCE	
ENDING CASH BALANCE	

BALANCE SHEET (SECOND)			
ASSETS		*LIABILITIES*	
CURRENT ASSETS		*CURRENT LIABILITIES*	
CASH (b)	*-0-*		
		NONCURRENT LIABILITIES	
NONCURRENT ASSETS		*STOCKHOLDERS' EQUITY*	
		CAPITAL STOCK	
		APIC	
		APIC - OPTIONS	
		RETAINED EARNINGS (a)	*(200)*
		DEFERRED COMPENSATION	*+200*
		TOTAL LIABILITIES & STOCKHOLDERS' EQUITY	
TOTAL ASSETS	*-0-*		*-0-*

Next, assume all options are exercised on January 2, 2007. This assumes that the options are "in the money" or the market price exceeds the exercise price (e.g., assume the market price is now $17 per share). Again, the current market price of the shares is not reflected in the financial statements.

Note that the corporation issues new shares with a total value of $600,000 received in exchange: $400,000 in services rendered plus $200,000 in cash. The shares have a $50,000 par value with the $550,000 excess over par reported as additional paid in capital (APIC).

FINANCIAL MODELING WORKSHEET: DATE OF EXERCISE

INCOME STATEMENT (FIRST)	
REVENUES:	
EXPENSES:	
NET INCOME OR LOSS (a)	- 0 -

STATEMENT OF CASH FLOWS (THIRD)	
OPERATING ACTIVITIES:	
NET INCOME OR LOSS (a)	- 0 -
INVESTING ACTIVITIES:	
FINANCING ACTIVITIES:	
ISSUED COMMON STOCK	+200
INCREASE (DECREASE) IN CASH (b)	+200
ADD: BEGINNING CASH BALANCE	
ENDING CASH BALANCE	

BALANCE SHEET (SECOND)			
ASSETS		LIABILITIES	
CURRENT ASSETS		CURRENT LIABILITIES	
CASH (b)	+200		
		NONCURRENT LIABILITIES	
		STOCKHOLDERS' EQUITY	
NONCURRENT ASSETS			
		CAPITAL STOCK	+50
		APIC	+550
		APIC - OPTIONS	(400)
		RETAINED EARNINGS (a)	- 0 -
		DEFERRED COMPENSATION	
		TOTAL LIABILITIES & STOCKHOLDERS' EQUITY	
TOTAL ASSETS	+200		+200

If the options expire and are not exercised, there is a simple reclassification of the $400,000 option value out of Additional Paid in Capital – Stock Options and into Additional Paid in Capital – Expired Options. This occurs if the options are not in the money or the market price is less than the exercise price (e.g., assume the market price is now $2 per share, but this is not reflected in the accounting process for options).

FINANCIAL MODELING WORKSHEET: EXPIRED OPTIONS

INCOME STATEMENT (FIRST)	
REVENUES:	
EXPENSES:	
NET INCOME OR LOSS (a)	- 0 -

STATEMENT OF CASH FLOWS (THIRD)	
OPERATING ACTIVITIES:	
NET INCOME OR LOSS (a)	- 0 -
INVESTING ACTIVITIES:	
FINANCING ACTIVITIES:	
INCREASE (DECREASE) IN CASH (b)	- 0 -
ADD: BEGINNING CASH BALANCE	
ENDING CASH BALANCE	

BALANCE SHEET (SECOND)			
ASSETS		LIABILITIES	
CURRENT ASSETS		CURRENT LIABILITIES	
CASH (b)	- 0 -		
		NONCURRENT LIABILITIES	
		STOCKHOLDERS'	
NONCURRENT ASSETS		EQUITY	
		CAPITAL STOCK	
		APIC	
		APIC - OPTIONS	(400)
		APIC – EXPIRED OPTIONS	+400
		RETAINED	
		EARNINGS (a)	
		DEFERRED COMPENSATION	
		TOTAL	
		LIABILITIES &	
		STOCKHOLDERS'	
TOTAL ASSETS	- 0 -	EQUITY	- 0 -

For deferred tax accounting, qualified options give rise to permanent book/tax differences as the stock-based compensation is expensed for books, but never tax deductible. This increases the firm's effective tax rate. Nonqualified options give rise to a deferred tax asset because the compensation expense is recognized for book purposes over the vesting period, while this expense is only tax deductible on actual exercise.

Change in Vesting Assumptions. As noted earlier, SFAS 132R did not require any accounting adjustments for changes in the market value of the shares. However, the amount of compensation expense must be adjusted for changes in vesting assumptions. An illustration of the effects of a change in vesting assumptions is presented in the following table.

Description	*12/31/2008*	*12/31/2009*
Total compensation expense at fair value	$400,000	$400,000
Vesting probability	X 100%	X 40%
Expected compensation expense	$400,000	$160,000
Cumulative rate of amortization	X 1/2	X 2/2
Cumulative compensation expense	$200,000	$160,000
Less: Expense recognized in prior years	(- 0 -)	(200,000)
Compensation expense (income): Current Year	$200,000	($ 40,000)

The change in the vesting probability indicates that deferred compensation and APIC-Options are both overstated by $240,000 (i.e., $400,000 – 160,000). In addition, $40,000 of "compensation income" is recognized for the year ended December 31, 2009. This $40,000 income adjustment was necessitated by the excess compensation expense recognized in 2008 that must be corrected and reversed out in 2009. Note that changes in vesting probabilities are considered changes in estimate and are prospective in nature (prior periods are not restated).

Below are the financial statement adjustments required for the change in vesting probability.

FINANCIAL MODELING WORKSHEET: ADJUSTMENTS FOR CHANGES IN VESTING ASSUMPTIONS-CORRECTION OF DEFERRED COMPENSATION AND APIC-OPTION ACCOUNTS

INCOME STATEMENT (FIRST)	
REVENUES:	
EXPENSES:	
NET INCOME OR LOSS (a)	*- 0 -*

STATEMENT OF CASH FLOWS (THIRD)	
OPERATING ACTIVITIES:	
NET INCOME OR LOSS (a)	*- 0 -*
INVESTING ACTIVITIES:	
FINANCING ACTIVITIES:	
INCREASE (DECREASE) IN CASH (b)	*- 0 -*
ADD: BEGINNING CASH BALANCE	
ENDING CASH BALANCE	

BALANCE SHEET (SECOND)			
ASSETS		*LIABILITIES*	
CURRENT ASSETS		*CURRENT LIABILITIES*	
CASH (b)	*- 0 -*		
		NONCURRENT LIABILITIES	
		STOCKHOLDERS' EQUITY	
NONCURRENT ASSETS			
		CAPITAL STOCK	
		APIC	
		APIC - OPTIONS	*(240)*
		RETAINED EARNINGS (a)	
		DEFERRED COMPENSATION	*+240*
		TOTAL LIABILITIES & STOCKHOLDERS' EQUITY	
TOTAL ASSETS	*- 0 -*		*- 0 -*

After this adjustment, the APIC-Options account is reduced from $400,000 to $160,000, which is equal to the cumulative compensation expense at December 31, 2009 (or the proper value of employee services received). This account in now correctly stated.

The deferred compensation account began with a $400,000 and was reduced by amortization of $200,000 in 2008. The 2009 amortization of $240,000 resulted in a negative or "credit" balance of $40,000 in the deferred (unearned) compensation account. This negative balance is removed by recognizing $40,000 of "compensation revenue" in 2009. The financial modeling worksheet below reflects the adjustment to the deferred compensation account.

FINANCIAL MODELING WORKSHEET: ADJUSTMENTS FOR CHANGES IN VESTING ASSUMPTIONS

INCOME STATEMENT (FIRST)	
REVENUES:	
EXPENSES:	
Compensation Adjustment	+40
NET INCOME OR LOSS (a)	+40

STATEMENT OF CASH FLOWS (THIRD)	
OPERATING ACTIVITIES:	
NET INCOME OR LOSS (a)	+40
Compensation Adjustment	(40)
INVESTING ACTIVITIES:	
FINANCING ACTIVITIES:	
INCREASE (DECREASE) IN CASH (b)	- 0 -
ADD: BEGINNING CASH BALANCE	
ENDING CASH BALANCE	

BALANCE SHEET (SECOND)			
ASSETS		LIABILITIES	
CURRENT ASSETS		CURRENT LIABILITIES	
CASH (b)	- 0 -		
		NONCURRENT LIABILITIES	
		STOCKHOLDERS'	
NONCURRENT ASSETS		EQUITY	
		CAPITAL STOCK	
		APIC	
		APIC - OPTIONS	
		RETAINED	
		EARNINGS (a)	+40
		DEFERRED COMPENSATION	(40)
		TOTAL	
		LIABILITIES &	
		STOCKHOLDERS'	
TOTAL ASSETS	- 0 -	EQUITY	- 0 -

The final financial modeling worksheet reflects the exercise of the options and assumes the vesting probability does not change. This exercise would provide for the issuance of 20,000 shares at the strike price of $4 per share (i.e., $80,000 in cash is paid into the corporation). When the amount of the APIC-Options or $160,000 is added to the cash received the total value received by the corporation is $240,000. This represents the total value received in exchange for the shares issued ($160,000 in employee service plus $80,000 in cash). The shares have a $1 par value or a total par of $20,000. The balance or $220,000 is reported as APIC.

FINANCIAL MODELING WORKSHEET EXERCISE OF OPTIONS ASSUMING NO CHANGE IN VESTING PROBABILITY

INCOME STATEMENT (FIRST)	
REVENUES:	
EXPENSES:	
NET INCOME OR LOSS (a)	*- 0 -*

STATEMENT OF CASH FLOWS (THIRD)	
OPERATING ACTIVITIES:	
NET INCOME OR LOSS (a)	*- 0 -*
INVESTING ACTIVITIES:	
FINANCING ACTIVITIES:	
Exercise of Stock Options	*+80*
INCREASE (DECREASE) IN CASH (b)	*+80*
ADD: BEGINNING CASH BALANCE	
ENDING CASH BALANCE	

BALANCE SHEET (SECOND)			
ASSETS		*LIABILITIES*	
CURRENT ASSETS		*CURRENT LIABILITIES*	
CASH (b)	*+80*		
		NONCURRENT LIABILITIES	
		STOCKHOLDERS' EQUITY	
NONCURRENT ASSETS			
		CAPITAL STOCK	*+20*
		APIC	*+220*
		APIC - OPTIONS	*(160)*
		RETAINED EARNINGS (a)	*- 0 -*
		DEFERRED COMPENSATION	
TOTAL ASSETS	*+80*	*TOTAL LIABILITIES & STOCKHOLDERS' EQUITY*	*+80*

Stock option disclosures for King Corporation are presented in Exhibit 4.7.

EXHIBIT 4.7: KING CORPORATION. STOCK BASED COMPENSATION DISCLOSURES UNDER FASB STATEMENT NO. 123R

Stock Based Compensation. Prior to fiscal year 2006, we accounted for our stock incentive plans under the recognition and measurement principles of Accounting Principles Board Opinion No. 25, "Accounting for Stock Issued to Employees" (APB No. 25) and related interpretations, Financial Accounting Standards Board (FASB) Statement No. 123, "Accounting for Stock-Based Compensation," (SFAS No. 123), and complied with the disclosure provisions of FASB Statement No. 148, "Accounting for Stock-Based Compensation Transition and Disclosure, and Amendment of FASB Statement No. 123."

Effective August 1, 2005, we adopted Statement of Financial Accounting Standards No. 123 (revised), "Share-Based Payment" ["SFAS No. 123(R)], which requires the use of the fair value method of accounting for all stock-based compensation, including stock options. SFAS No. 123(R) was adopted using the modified prospective method. Under this method, in addition to reflecting compensation expense for new share-based awards, expense is also recognized for those awards vesting in the current period based on the value that had been included in pro forma disclosures in prior periods. Results from prior periods have not been restated.

Prior to the adoption of SFAS No. 123(R), we presented all benefits of tax deductions resulting from the exercise of share-based compensation as operating cash flows in the Statements of Cash Flows. SFAS No. 123(R) requires the benefits of tax deductions in excess of the compensation cost recognized for those options (excess tax benefits) to be classified as financing cash flows. We have elected to calculate the SFAS No. 123(R) APIC pool under FSP123R-(3) ("simplified method").

ACCOUNTING FOR HYBRID FINANCIAL INSTRUMENTS

Hybrid financial instruments include all securities with both debt and equity characteristics. Examples of hybrid securities include convertible preferred shares and convertible debt.

The most problematic issues involved with accounting and reporting these hybrid securities is proper classification of the debt and equity components. Under current GAAP standards, we generally do not separate the debt and equity elements of the security. Therefore, the accounting before the conversion is usually identical to accounting for straight debt and equity securities. Separate accounting for the debt and equity components is only made when there is a "beneficial conversion option" embedded in the hybrid security.

Convertible Preferred Shares: Definition and Rationale for Use. As noted earlier, preferred shares represent a small portion of all new issues and many new preferred issues are convertible. Preferred stock is sometimes issued as an alternative to debt and common equity financing.

Convertible preferred stock is a financial instrument the enables a holder to convert into a fixed number of shares of common stock (based on a fixed exchange ratio). Convertible preferred shares are sometimes used in merger and acquisitions and reorganizations.

Accounting for convertible preferred stock without a beneficial conversion option at the time of issuance and at each dividend date is the same as accounting for straight preferred stock. On conversion, the book value method is the only approach permitted in accounting for convertible preferred stock. This results from the fact that gains and losses are never permitted in transactions involving equity of the corporation (i.e., a capital transaction). The market value approach is prohibited because it results in gain or loss recognition.

The key issue in accounting for the conversion of the preferred shares is the relationship between the par value of the common stock and the book value of the preferred shares:

- When the book value of the preferred stock exceeds the par value of the common stock, the excess is recorded in the additional paid in capital of the common shares.
- When the book value of the preferred stock is less than the par value of the common stock, then there is a charge to retained earnings for the difference. In some states, the charge reduces additional paid in capital.

ILLUSTRATION OF THE BOOK VALUE METHOD OF ACCOUNTING FOR CONVERTIBLE PREFERRED SHARES

Case 1: The Book Value of the Preferred Stock is greater than the Par Value of the Common Stock. Assume that the Danny Steel Company issues 2,000 shares of $1 par value common stock on the conversion of 300 shares of $10 par value convertible preferred stock. When the preferred shares were issued there was a premium of $500 (i.e., additional paid in capital-preferred stock). The financial modeling worksheet in this case is presented below: Note that the book value of the preferred shares is transferred into the common-equity accounts. Disclosure of this noncash financing activity is made in the notes to the financial statements.

FINANCIAL MODELING WORKSHEET THE BOOK VALUE OF THE CONVERTIBLE PREFERRED STOCK IS GREATER THAN THE PAR VALUE OF THE COMMON STOCK

INCOME STATEMENT (FIRST)	
REVENUES:	
EXPENSES:	
NET INCOME OR LOSS (a)	*- 0 -*

STATEMENT OF CASH FLOWS (THIRD)	
OPERATING ACTIVITIES:	
NET INCOME OR LOSS (a)	*- 0 -*
INVESTING ACTIVITIES:	
FINANCING ACTIVITIES:	
INCREASE (DECREASE) IN CASH (b)	*- 0 -*
ADD: BEGINNING CASH BALANCE	
ENDING CASH BALANCE	

BALANCE SHEET (SECOND)			
ASSETS		*LIABILITIES*	
CURRENT ASSETS		*CURRENT LIABILITIES*	
CASH (b)	*- 0 -*		
		NONCURRENT LIABILITIES	
		STOCKHOLDERS'	
NONCURRENT ASSETS		*EQUITY*	
		COMMON STOCK	*+2,000*
		APIC-COMMON	*+1,500*
		PREFERRED STOCK	*(3,000)*
		APIC-PREFERRED	*(500)*
		RETAINED	
		EARNINGS (a)	
		TOTAL	
		LIABILITIES &	
		STOCKHOLDERS'	
TOTAL ASSETS	*- 0 -*	*EQUITY*	*- 0 -*

Case 2: The Book Value of the Preferred Stock is less than the Par Value of the Common Stock. Conversely, if the 300 shares of preferred only had a par value of $3 per share, with the same issue premium of $500, the following financial modeling worksheet would apply.

FINANCIAL MODELING WORKSHEET THE BOOK VALUE OF THE CONVERTIBLE PREFERRED STOCK IS LESS THAN THE PAR VALUE OF THE COMMON STOCK

INCOME STATEMENT (FIRST)	
REVENUES:	
EXPENSES:	
NET INCOME OR LOSS (a)	*-0-*

STATEMENT OF CASH FLOWS (THIRD)	
OPERATING ACTIVITIES:	
NET INCOME OR LOSS (a)	*-0-*
INVESTING ACTIVITIES:	
FINANCING ACTIVITIES:	
INCREASE (DECREASE) IN CASH (b)	*-0-*
ADD: BEGINNING CASH BALANCE	
ENDING CASH BALANCE	

BALANCE SHEET (SECOND)			
ASSETS		*LIABILITIES*	
CURRENT ASSETS		*CURRENT LIABILITIES*	
CASH (b)	*-0-*		
		NONCURRENT LIABILITIES	
		STOCKHOLDERS' EQUITY	
NONCURRENT ASSETS			
		COMMON STOCK	*+2,000*
		APIC-COMMON	
		PREFERRED STOCK	*(900)*
		APIC-PREFERRED	*(500)*
		RETAINED EARNINGS (a)	*(600)*
		TOTAL LIABILITIES & STOCKHOLDERS' EQUITY	
TOTAL ASSETS	*-0-*		*-0-*

The charge to retained earnings is sometimes justified by capital transactions theory. That is, one may think of the above treatment as analogous to accounting for treasury shares: all gains are recorded in additional paid in capital and all losses are recorded as a reduction of retained earnings. Again, the transaction simply reclassifies the book value of the prefined stock as common equity with disclosure of this noncash event.

MEZZANINE FINANCING

Definition. The term mezzanine financing is typically associated with the second or third stage financing of a company. It is typically used in leveraged buyouts (LBOs) and this debt is generally not secured and is not is given priorities or seniority over first stage debt, (e.g., higher coupon rates, but subordinated). Mezzanine financing includes debt with detachable warrants, redeemable preferred shares and other quasi-debt or hybrid financial instruments. Nonetheless, preferred shares are senior equity securities.

Long-term debt is sometimes issued with warrants (longer term options) and may be considered somewhere between long-term debt and preferred stock in a firm's capitalization.

In general, stock warrants can be issued:

- As an "equity kicker" to make debt or preferred shares more attractive.
- To satisfy preemptive rights on common shares.
- As a part of employee stock options.

When stock warrants are issued with other securities (e.g., debt issued as mezzanine financing), the warrants can either be nondetachable or detachable. Assuming no beneficial conversion option at issuance:

- If the warrants are nondetachable, then the total debt proceeds received are fully assigned to the debt issue and there is no allocation between debt and equity.
- If the warrants are detachable and can be traded separately, there is an allocation of the total proceeds received on the financing between the debt and equity components. There are two methods of allocating the debt proceeds when issued with detachable warrants:

1. The Proportional Method (based on relative fair market values of the debt and equity securities).
2. The Incremental Method (part of the proceeds are allocated to the fair market value of one security and the balance of the proceeds are allocated to the other security).

CONVERTIBLE BONDS WITH BENEFICIAL CONVERSION OPTIONS

Since convertible debt is a hybrid (compound) financial instrument (possessing both debt and equity features), accountants have argued that the debt and equity components should be separated at issuance and reported as part debt and part equity on the balance sheet. The EITF provides guidance regarding the separate recognition of the conversion option. The EITF's guidance is presented in the following illustration.

Illustration: Assume that a company issues a 5 year, 5% convertible bond at par, $1,000. The yield on the bond is therefore, 5%. Each $1,000 bond converts into 50 shares of common stock at the option of the bondholder beginning two years after the date of issue. There were no bond issue costs. The market price of the common stock on the purchase commitment date was equal to $25 per share.

In order to determine if the debt and equity features of this financial instrument can be separated, we must first test to see if there is a beneficial conversion option. A beneficial conversion option exists if the implied purchase (exercise or strike) price of the stock is less that the market price of the shares on the purchase commitment date (i.e., the conversion option is "in the money" or it is said to have positive intrinsic value).

The implied strike price is $20 per share: $1,000/50 shares and the intrinsic value of the option is $5 per share: $25 – 20. This means that the value of the beneficial conversion option is $250 ($5 intrinsic value x 50 shares) and the bonds are value at $750.

The financial modeling worksheet to record the bond issue with a beneficial conversion option is presented below.

FINANCIAL MODELING WORKSHEET CONVERTIBLE BONDS ISSUED WITH BENEFICIAL A CONVERSION OPTION

INCOME STATEMENT (FIRST)	
REVENUES:	
EXPENSES:	
NET INCOME OR LOSS (a)	- 0 -

STATEMENT OF CASH FLOWS (THIRD)	
OPERATING ACTIVITIES:	
NET INCOME OR LOSS (a)	- 0 -
INVESTING ACTIVITIES:	
FINANCING ACTIVITIES:	
Proceeds from Convertible Bond issue	+1,000
INCREASE (DECREASE) IN CASH (b)	+1,000
ADD: BEGINNING CASH BALANCE	
ENDING CASH BALANCE	

BALANCE SHEET (SECOND)			
ASSETS		LIABILITIES	
CURRENT ASSETS		CURRENT LIABILITIES	
CASH (b)	+ 1,000		
		NONCURRENT LIABILITIES	
		Bonds Payable – par	+1,000
		Discount on Bonds	(250)
		STOCKHOLDERS'	
NONCURRENT ASSETS		EQUITY	
		CAPITAL STOCK	
		APIC	
		APIC –Beneficial Conversion Option	+250
		ACCUMULATED OTHER COMPREHENSIVE INCOME	
		RETAINED EARNINGS (a)	
TOTAL ASSETS	+1,000	TOTAL LIABILITIES & STOCKHOLDERS' EQUITY	+1,000

The discount would be expensed immediately if the bonds were immediately exercisable. If exercisable only with the passage of time, the discount account is used.

With the discount recorded, a new effective interest rate (yield or discount) rate must be computed in order to amortize the discount. Using a **financial calculator,** the new effective rate is 11.92%

		END MODE
- 750	=	PV
1,000	=	FV
50 ($1,000 x 5%)	=	PMT
5	=	n
X = 11.92%	=	i

ILLUSTRATIONS OF ACCOUNTING FOR STOCK WARRANTS

Case 1: The Warrants Are Not Detachable

Assume that the Grey City Company issued 1,000 of its $1,000 par value bonds for $1,200. The bonds are sold with 20,000 warrants to acquire 20,000 shares of the company's common stock.

Grey City has existing bonds outstanding that currently trade without warrants at $1,020. There are other Grey City warrants outstanding that trade for $20 each. The financial modeling worksheet that reflects the issuance of the 1,000 bonds is presented below. Note that the cash flow from financing activities will be the same in all cases. In this first case, if the warrants are not detachable the issue is recorded as straight debt.

FINANCIAL MODELING WORKSHEET ISSUANCE OF BONDS WITH WARRANTS, CASE 1: THE WARRANTS ARE NOT DETACHABLE AND CANNOT BE TRADED SEPARATELY

INCOME STATEMENT (FIRST)	
REVENUES:	
EXPENSES:	
NET INCOME OR LOSS (a)	- 0 -

STATEMENT OF CASH FLOWS (THIRD)	
OPERATING ACTIVITIES:	
NET INCOME OR LOSS (a)	- 0 -
INVESTING ACTIVITIES:	
FINANCING ACTIVITIES:	
Issuance of Bonds Payable	+1,200
INCREASE (DECREASE) IN CASH (b)	+1,200
ADD: BEGINNING CASH BALANCE	
ENDING CASH BALANCE	

BALANCE SHEET (SECOND)			
ASSETS		LIABILITIES	
CURRENT ASSETS		CURRENT LIABILITIES	
CASH (b)	+1,200		
		NONCURRENT LIABILITIES	
		Bonds Payable - Par	+1,000
		Premium on Bonds	+200
		STOCKHOLDERS' EQUITY	
NONCURRENT ASSETS			
		CAPITAL STOCK	
		APIC	
		RETAINED EARNINGS (a)	
		TOTAL LIABILITIES & STOCKHOLDERS' EQUITY	
TOTAL ASSETS	+1,200		+1,200

Case 2: The Warrants are Detachable and Can be Traded Separately.

Using the same data as in case 1 except that we now assume that the warrants are detachable and trade separately.

a. The Proportional Method:

Number of Units	Market Value of Existing Units	Total Market Value	Proportion for Allocation
1,000	$1,020	$1,020,000	72%
20,000	$20	400,000	28%
		$1,420,000	100%

Issue Price: $1,200,000

Allocation to Bonds: $1,200,000 X 72% = $864,000. (The implied discount on bonds is equal to $136,000 (i.e., $1,000,000 – 864,000)

Allocation to Warrants: $1,200,000 X 28% = $336,000.

FINANCIAL MODELING WORKSHEET ISSUANCE OF BONDS WITH WARRANTS: CASE 2: THE WARRANTS ARE DETACHABLE AND CAN BE TRADED SEPARATELY, THE PROPORTIONAL METHOD

INCOME STATEMENT (FIRST)	
REVENUES:	
EXPENSES:	
NET INCOME OR LOSS (a)	*- 0 -*

STATEMENT OF CASH FLOWS (THIRD)	
OPERATING ACTIVITIES:	
NET INCOME OR LOSS (a)	*- 0 -*
INVESTING ACTIVITIES:	
FINANCING ACTIVITIES:	
Issuance of Bonds Payable	*+1,200*
INCREASE (DECREASE) IN CASH (b)	*+1,200*
ADD: BEGINNING CASH BALANCE	
ENDING CASH BALANCE	

BALANCE SHEET (SECOND)			
ASSETS		*LIABILITIES*	
CURRENT ASSETS		*CURRENT LIABILITIES*	
CASH (b)	*+1,200*		
		NONCURRENT LIABILITIES	
		Bonds Payable - Par	*+1,000*
		Discount on Bonds	*(136)*
		STOCKHOLDERS' EQUITY	
NONCURRENT ASSETS			
		CAPITAL STOCK	
		APIC	
		APIC-STOCK WARRANTS	*+336*
		RETAINED EARNINGS (a)	
		TOTAL LIABILITIES & STOCKHOLDERS' EQUITY	
TOTAL ASSETS	*+1,200*		*+1,200*

b. Incremental Method:

Assuming the market value of the bonds is more reasonably determined, the incremental method will be applied as follows:

Allocation to Bonds (1,000 X $1,020)	=	$1,020,000 (The implied premium on bonds is $20,000, the amount above par)
Allocation to Warrants ($1,200,000 - 1,020,000):	=	$180,000.

FINANCIAL MODELING WORKSHEET ISSUANCE OF BONDS WITH WARRANTS: CASE 2: THE WARRANTS ARE DETACHABLE AND CAN BE TRADED SEPARATELY; INCREMENTAL METHOD

INCOME STATEMENT (FIRST)	
REVENUES:	
EXPENSES:	
NET INCOME OR LOSS (a)	*- 0 -*

STATEMENT OF CASH FLOWS (THIRD)	
OPERATING ACTIVITIES:	
NET INCOME OR LOSS (a)	*- 0 -*
INVESTING ACTIVITIES:	
FINANCING ACTIVITIES:	
Issuance of Bonds Payable	*+1,200*
INCREASE (DECREASE) IN CASH (b)	*+1,200*
ADD: BEGINNING CASH BALANCE	
ENDING CASH BALANCE	

BALANCE SHEET (SECOND)			
ASSETS		*LIABILITIES*	
CURRENT ASSETS		*CURRENT LIABILITIES*	
CASH (b)	*+1,200*		
		NONCURRENT LIABILITIES	
		Bonds Payable - Par	*+1,000*
		Premium on Bonds	*+20*
		STOCKHOLDERS' EQUITY	
NONCURRENT ASSETS			
		CAPITAL STOCK	
		APIC	
		APIC-STOCK WARRANTS	*+180*
		RETAINED EARNINGS (a)	
		TOTAL LIABILITIES & STOCKHOLDERS' EQUITY	
TOTAL ASSETS	*+1,200*		*+1,200*

On exercise, the warrants are accounted for in the same way as the exercise of stock options (see previous illustrations).

Convertible Bonds: Definition and Rationale for Use. Convertible bonds are financial instruments that enable the holder to convert a debt (fixed income) security into a specified number of shares of common stock (based on the "exchange ratio" included in the bond indenture).

Convertible bonds are issued by corporations as a vehicle to ultimately raise equity capital. This is sometimes known as "back door equity financing." These situations arise when equity prices are temporarily depressed and the firm needs to raise a requisite amount of capital.

For example, assume a company needs to raise $18,000,000 in new financing. If the current market price of the company's equity is $5 per share, the company would have to issue an additional 3,600,000 shares of stock (i.e., $18,000,000 / $5 per share = 3,600,000 shares). This equity issue would have significant dilutive effects on the company's share price and earnings per share.

As an alternative, the company could issue 18,000, $1,000 par value convertible bonds. Each bond is convertible into 30 shares of the company's common stock. If the company expects share price to increase, there is an incentive for conversion and only 540,000 new shares would be issued (i.e., 18,000 bonds x 30 shares per bond = 540,000 shares). In addition, the coupon rate on the convertible debt is less generally than on straight debt.

The company usually has a call option attached to convertible debt. Here the company can call in the debt to "force conversion." The call price can be at a premium (above par). This is generally known as the "call premium."

For example, if the market price of the stock increases to $40 per share assuming the price already factors in the dilutive efforts of conversion and bondholders do not convert in anticipation of further market appreciation, the company can call in the debt at a call price of $1,010 per bond (i.e., there is a $10 call premium per bond). There is usually a grace period where bondholders can decide to convert the bonds or allow the call to take place. If bondholders allow the call to take place, the total value of the call is $18,180,000 (i.e., 18,000 bonds x $1,010 call price). Conversely, if bondholders convert, the market value of the equity securities received is equal to $21,600,000 (i.e., 18,000 bonds x 30 shares per bond x $40 market price per share). Clearly, the bondholder will convert before the call takes effect. Therefore, the corporation used its call option to force conversion.

ACCOUNTING ALTERNATIVES FOR CONVERTIBLE DEBT ASSUME NO BENEFICIAL CONVERSION AT ISSUANCE

Assuming no beneficial conversion option, accounting for convertible debt at issuance and at each interest period is the same as accounting for straight debt. When the bonds are converted into shares of the company's common stock, (i.e., bonds retired prior to maturity at the option of the bondholder), either the book value or market value approach is used to value the common stock issued on the debt conversion. That is, either the carrying (book) value of the bonds or the market value of the bonds or common shares (whichever is more clearly evident) is recorded as the carrying amount of the common stock issued. The debt is removed from the corporation's books.

No gain or loss is recognized on the conversion of debt into equity securities using the book value approach. The book value approach is preferred and is justified under the theory that this is a capital transaction and no gain or loss should result. The same theory is used when accounting for "gains" or "losses" on treasury stock transactions.

When the market value approach is used, a gain or loss can be recognized. The gain or loss is computed as the difference between the market value of the bonds or common stock and the carrying value of the bonds. The gain or loss on bond conversion is classified as ordinary income. This approach is justified under the theory that the conversion is a constructive early retirement of debt.

ILLUSTRATION OF THE BOOK VALUE AND MARKET VALUE METHODS

Assume that a company has convertible debt with a book value of $9,811. The bonds have a total par of $10,000 and an unamortized discount of $189. Each $1,000 bond is convertible into 600 shares of $1 par value common stock. For this bond issue there are 10 bonds ($10,000 / $1,000 par), and a total of 6,000 shares of common stock would be issued (i.e., 600 shares per bond x 10 bonds).

All bondholders convert into common stock on a date when the market price of the company's stock is $1.5833 per share. The total market value of the company's stock issued on conversion is $9,500 (i.e., 6,000 x $1.5833). It is assumed the market price of the debt is also equal to $9,500 at that time. If recognized, the gain on conversion would amount to $311 (i.e., $9,811 – 9,500).

The financial modeling worksheets under the both the Book Value and Market Value Methods are presented below.

The Book Value Method (the preferred approach): Under the Book Value Method, the carrying value of the convertible debt is simply transferred into the equity accounts (par plus APIC), without any gain or loss recognition. The event would be disclosed as a significant noncash financing activity either in a footnote as a separate schedule for the cash flow statement.

FINANCIAL MODELING WORKSHEET BOND CONVERSION UNDER THE BOOK VALUE APPROACH: NO GAIN OR LOSS RECOGNIZED ON CONVERSION

INCOME STATEMENT (FIRST)	
REVENUES:	
EXPENSES:	
NET INCOME OR LOSS (a)	*- 0 -*

STATEMENT OF CASH FLOWS (THIRD)	
OPERATING ACTIVITIES:	
NET INCOME OR LOSS (a)	*- 0 -*
INVESTING ACTIVITIES:	
FINANCING ACTIVITIES:	
INCREASE (DECREASE) IN CASH (b)	*- 0 -*
ADD: BEGINNING CASH BALANCE	
ENDING CASH BALANCE	

BALANCE SHEET (SECOND)			
ASSETS		*LIABILITIES*	
CURRENT ASSETS		*CURRENT LIABILITIES*	
CASH (b)	*- 0 -*		
		NONCURRENT LIABILITIES	
		Bonds Payable - Par	*(10,000)*
		Discount on Bonds	*+189*
		STOCKHOLDERS' EQUITY	
NONCURRENT ASSETS			
		CAPITAL STOCK	*+6,000*
		APIC	*+3,811*
		RETAINED EARNINGS (a)	
		TOTAL LIABILITIES & STOCKHOLDERS' EQUITY	
TOTAL ASSETS	*- 0 -*		*- 0 -*

The Market Value Method: Under the Market Value Method, either the market value of the stock or the market value of the bonds, whichever is more clearly evident, is transferred into the equity accounts. In this case the market value of both the common shares and the convertible debt is assumed to be equal to $9,500. Actually, the market value of the common stock issued is preferred because it is what the company had to give up to retire its debt. The difference between the market value used and book (carrying value) of the debt is recorded as an ordinary gain or loss on conversion. This transaction is similar to a constrictive early retirement of debt. It is as if the entity issued new shares for $9,500 in cash and then retired debt with a carrying value of $9811.

FINANCIAL MODELING WORKSHEET BOND CONVERSION UNDER THE MARKET VALUE APPROACH: GAIN OR LOSS IS RECOGNIZED ON CONVERSION

INCOME STATEMENT (FIRST)	
REVENUES:	
GAIN ON BOND CONVERSION	+311
EXPENSES:	
NET INCOME OR LOSS (a)	+311

STATEMENT OF CASH FLOWS (THIRD)	
OPERATING ACTIVITIES:	
NET INCOME OR LOSS (a)	+311
LESS: GAIN ON BOND CONVERSION	(311)
INVESTING ACTIVITIES:	
FINANCING ACTIVITIES:	
INCREASE (DECREASE) IN CASH (b)	-0-
ADD: BEGINNING CASH BALANCE	
ENDING CASH BALANCE	

BALANCE SHEET (SECOND)			
ASSETS		LIABILITIES	
CURRENT ASSETS		CURRENT LIABILITIES	
CASH (b)	-0-		
		NONCURRENT LIABILITIES	
		Bonds Payable – Par	(10,000)
		Discount on Bonds	+189
		STOCKHOLDERS'	
NONCURRENT ASSETS		EQUITY	
		CAPITAL STOCK	+6,000
		APIC	+3,500
		RETAINED	
		EARNINGS (a)	+311
		TOTAL	
		LIABILITIES &	
		STOCKHOLDERS'	
TOTAL ASSETS	-0-	EQUITY	-0-

Note that under the market value approach, the gain is separately identified and reported on the income statement. Under the book value method, the gain or loss was buried in the additional paid in capital account in the stockholders' equity section of the balance sheet. Again, this significant noncash financing activity is disclosed and not included in the cash flow statement.

CHAPTER 5 | Accounting For Income Taxes

INTRODUCTION

Accounting for income taxes involves reporting the tax consequences of a firm's transactions on its financial statements, accounted for under the accrual basis and prepared in accordance with GAAP. The traditional purpose of accounting for income taxes was to properly match costs with revenues. That is, the accountant was to determine and report an amount of income tax expense that was matched with accounting income. Accounting income was assumed to be based on the accountant's principles of revenue and expense recognition, and therefore may not be directly related to accounting techniques used on the firm's federal, state and local income tax returns.

In this chapter, accounting for income taxes will focus on reporting the impact of taxation on accrual basis financial statements. The discussion will provide an analysis of the traditional purpose of accounting for income taxes: to properly match the tax expense with revenues earned. Again, the matching of tax expense with revenues earned is based on the accountant's principles of revenue and expense recognition and not based on the firm's federal, state and local and foreign income tax returns.

With the issuance of FASB Statement No. 109, "Accounting for Income Taxes (amended)"[1], accountants have become more concerned with the proper measurement and classification of the tax liability or tax asset to be paid or received currently and in the future resulting from current economic events and transactions reflected on the firm's financial statements. Nonetheless, with the firm's financial statements tied to the accrual basis of accounting and prepared in accordance with GAAP, the determination of income tax expense is still based on accounting income and not the taxable income found on the firm's tax returns. The current approach to accounting for income tax is a balance sheet methodology and is known as the Asset-Liability Method or simply the Liability Method.

The traditional and the SFAS 109 Asset-Liability approaches to income tax accounting will be integrated throughout in this chapter.

INTERPERIOD TAX ALLOCATION: THE TRADITIONAL APPROACH

The use of the matching principle results in interperiod tax allocation specifically under the matching principle, income tax expense must be recognized in the period in which the related accounting earnings are reported. That is, the accountant's income tax expense must be allocated to the periods in which the related accounting income is reported, regardless of the amounts actually due to the applicable taxing jurisdictions. The amounts due to each taxing jurisdiction are based on applicable tax laws.

In short, the application of interperiod tax allocation results in the recognition of income tax expense on the income statement based on "book" or pre-tax accounting income and the recognition of income taxes payable on the balance sheet, (the ultimate cash outflow for taxes), based on taxable income on the tax returns. Income tax expense and income taxes payable are rarely equal due to different accounting methods used in the financial statements and tax returns. The difference between income tax expense (on the income statement) and the income taxes payable (from the tax return and reported on the balance sheet) is known as the deferred income tax (asset or liability).

---

1. FASB ASC 740 [Predecessor literature: "Accounting for Income Taxes," *Statement of Financial Accounting Standards No. 109* (Norwalk, Conn.: FASB, 1992)].

The different methods of accounting used for tax and GAAP purposes are justified due to the different reporting objectives for each. The primary objective of financial reporting is to provide information useful in making rational economic decisions. On the other hand, the primary objective of tax accounting is to raise revenues However, the primary revenue raising objective can be traded off to achieve both economic and social objectives. Economic objectives include granting tax credits for investment in research and development activities. Social objectives include tax credits for rehabilitation of certain real property intended for commercial use. Due to these different objectives, there will be different accounting methods for GAAP and tax accounting.

The financial statement effects of interperiod tax allocation are illustrated below. For example, assume that Florentine Company reports $100,000 in taxable income using an accelerated method of depreciation. Florentine's GAAP or book income before tax using a straight-line depreciation is $120,000. The company's tax rate is assumed to be 40%. Based on this information, Florentine's tax provision can be determined as follows:

Tax Expense on GAAP Income Statement	($120,000 X 40%) = $48,000
Tax Payable on GAAP Balance Sheet (From the tax return)	($100,000 X 40%) = 40,000
Deferred Tax Liability on GAAP Balance Sheet	($ 20,000 X 40%)= $ 8,000

Income tax expense (provision) cannot always be computed by multiplying book income by the federal tax rate. Rather, there is a sequence or order used in the computation of the income tax provision. The computation of income tax expense is the sum of the current provision (the change in the income tax payable) plus the deferred provision (the change in the deferred tax account).

The above illustration is reorganized in the typical order of preparation in the table below. This computation can be followed in a clockwise fashion.

THIRD: INCOME STATEMENT (BOOK) BASED ON GAAP	**FIRST:** TAX RETURN (TAX) BASED ON TAX CODES
Pre-tax Accounting Income	Taxable Income $100,000
LESS; Income Tax Expense (Reported by the accountant on the Income Statement) **$48,000**	X Income Tax Rate X 40%
Net Income or Loss	Income Taxes Payable (Reported by the accountant on the Balance Sheet) **$40,000**

SECOND: DIFFERENCE BETWEEN TAX EXPENSE AND TAXES PAYABLE =

DEFERRED INCOME TAXES = TEMPORARY BOOK TAX DIFFERENCE X TAX RATE
$8,000 = $20,000 X 40%
(Taxes deferred to a future period when the event becomes taxable or can be used as a tax deduction).

Note that income tax expense on the income statement is equal to the sum of current income taxes payable and deferred income taxes. That is:

Income tax expense = Income tax payable ± Deferred income tax expense
$48,000 = $40,000 + 8,000
Income tax provision = Current Provision ± Deferred provision.
$48,000 = $40,000 + 8,000

As noted in the introduction, the difference between the tax paid to the government and the tax expense reported on the income statement is called the deferred tax. The deferred tax account can result in either a deferred tax asset or a deferred tax liability. In the case of the deferred tax liability, less tax is paid to the government today but will be paid at some point in the future. In effect, this is an additional "accrued tax". For the deferred tax asset, more tax is paid to the government today but there will be tax savings at some point in the future. In effect, this is a "prepaid tax".

The discussion will first focus on the deferred tax liability. The presentation of the deferred tax asset will be included in the section covering the net operating loss carryforward.

To illustrate a deferred tax liability using the typical sequence of preparing the tax provision, we will consider a personal transaction. Assume that you earn $50,000 during 2007. You decide to open an Individual Retirement Account (IRA) and make a deposit of $2,000 for the 2007 tax year. If you were in a 35% tax bracket, your tax return would be completed as follows:

2007 Income Tax Return	
Wages	$50,000
IRA deduction	(2,000)
Taxable income	$48,000
Tax rate	X 35%
Tax due (Income tax payable)	$16,800

By making a deposit into your IRA account you saved $700 (i.e., $2,000 x 35%) on your 2007 tax. However, this is not a permanent tax savings or a tax exemption. Rather, you have a deferred tax (i.e., a deferred tax liability) because the book/tax difference is only temporary. When you withdraw the $2,000 from the IRA account you will pay back the $700 in taxes, assuming your tax rate does not change. Of course, the $700 is worth more to you today than it will in the future. However, accountants do not consider the time value of money in computing deferred taxes. Note that your financial reported income is still $50,000 even though your taxable income is only $48,000. If you are interested in matching tax expense with your financial income, your personal financial statements would include the following information. Note that without permanent differences (to be discussed), tax expense can be computed by either of two approaches: (1) book income multiplied by the tax rate or (2) the sum of the current and the deferred tax provisions.

2007 Statement of Earnings	
Wages	$ 50,000
Less: Income tax expense (35% x $50,000)	(17,500)
Net income after tax	$ 32,500

Your personal financial statements reflect a tax expense that matches with your total wages for the year. The tax expense includes the amount you will pay the government this year plus the additional tax expected on the future withdrawal of the IRA deposit (i.e., the deferred income tax). In other words, using the proper sequence for the computation the income tax expense ($17,500) is equal to the current tax payable ($16,800) plus the additional deferred tax provision ($700, accrued but unpaid in the current period).

The effects of this transaction are reflected on the financial modeling worksheet presented below. Note that the worksheets reflect financial statement changes and not cumulative balances. There is no cash outflow for taxes in 2007 because it is assumed that neither the current provision nor the deferred tax provision is paid this year. Although not illustrated, the payment of the current tax provision would be a use of cash in operating activities on the statement of cash flows.

FINANCIAL MODELING WORKSHEET FOR 2007

INCOME STATEMENT (FIRST)	
REVENUES:	
EXPENSES:	
Income Tax Expense	(17,500)
NET INCOME OR LOSS (a)	(17,500)

STATEMENT OF CASH FLOWS (THIRD)	
OPERATING ACTIVITIES:	
NET INCOME OR LOSS (a)	(17,500)
Increase in Deferred Tax Liability Increase in Income Tax Payable	+700 +16,800
Cash Flow from Operating Activities	-0-
INVESTING ACTIVITIES:	
FINANCING ACTIVITIES:	
INCREASE (DECREASE) IN CASH (b)	-0-
ADD: BEGINNING CASH BALANCE	
ENDING CASH BALANCE	

BALANCE SHEET (SECOND)			
ASSETS		LIABILITIES	
CURRENT ASSETS		CURRENT LIABILITIES	
CASH (b)	-0-	Income Tax Payable	+16,800
		NONCURRENT LIABILITIES	
		Deferred Tax Liability	+700
		STOCKHOLDERS'	
NONCURRENT ASSETS		EQUITY	
		CAPITAL STOCK	
		APIC	
		RETAINED	
		EARNINGS (a)	(17,500)
		TOTAL	
		LIABILITIES &	
		STOCKHOLDERS'	
TOTAL ASSETS	-0-	EQUITY	-0-

If you retire in 2010 and decide to withdraw half of your pension in each of the next two years, (2010 and 2011), you will be responsible for paying $350 of the deferred tax liability each year assuming a constant tax rate. The financial modeling worksheet for each year there is a repayment of the deferred tax liability is presented below.

FINANCIAL MODELING WORKSHEET FOR 2010 AND 2011

INCOME STATEMENT (FIRST)	
REVENUES:	
EXPENSES:	
NET INCOME OR LOSS (a)	- 0 -

STATEMENT OF CASH FLOWS (THIRD)	
OPERATING ACTIVITIES:	
NET INCOME OR LOSS (a)	
Decrease in Deferred Tax Liability	(350)
INVESTING ACTIVITIES:	
FINANCING ACTIVITIES:	
INCREASE (DECREASE) IN CASH (b)	(350)
ADD: BEGINNING CASH BALANCE	
ENDING CASH BALANCE	

BALANCE SHEET (SECOND)			
ASSETS		LIABILITIES	
CURRENT ASSETS		CURRENT LIABILITIES	
CASH (b)	(350)		
		NONCURRENT LIABILITIES	
		Deferred Tax Liability	(350)
		STOCKHOLDERS' EQUITY	
NONCURRENT ASSETS			
		CAPITAL STOCK	
		APIC	
		RETAINED	
		EARNINGS (a)	- 0 -
		TOTAL	
		LIABILITIES &	
		STOCKHOLDERS'	
TOTAL ASSETS	(350)	EQUITY	(350)

BOOKTAX DIFFERENCES AND ACCOUNTING FOR DEFERRED INCOME TAXES

There are two types of book/tax differences:

a. Temporary Differences
b. Permanent Differences

Temporary (Timing) Differences

The personal pension illustration above is an example of temporary book/tax differences. Temporary differences represent items of revenue and expense that are recognized for financial reporting in a different period(s) from when these same economic events are recognized on the income tax return. These differences will reverse because the revenue and expense will ultimately be reported for both book and tax purposes. That is, at the end of the life of the transaction, the differences caused by the timing of recognition will fully offset (reverse) and additional taxes will be due or a reduction of taxes will be realized.

Examples of Temporary (Timing) Differences

Common examples of temporary differences include the following:

1. ***Installment sales***. In general, installment sales are accounted for under the accrual basis for financial reporting and accounted for under the cash basis (installment method) for tax purposes. Under these circumstances, the entire amount of the sale would be accrued and recognized as revenue for financial reporting, but only an amount of the gross profit in proportion to the cash collected would be recognized as income on the tax return. Therefore, GAAP income tax expense is based on the full amount of the sale, while the tax liability is based on income recognized in proportion to the amount of cash received. Because the tax expense exceeds the income taxes payable, (less tax is paid today), a deferred tax liability would be recorded. The deferred liability would be due and payable to the government as taxable income is reported in proportion to the balance of the cash collected (i.e., reversal takes place as cash is collected).
2. ***Excess Tax Depreciation***. In practice, the straight-line method is generally used for financial reporting while an accelerated method is used on the firm's income tax return (e.g., the Federal Modified Accelerated Cost Recovery System, MACRS). Because tax depreciation is higher in the earlier years of the asset's useful life, tax deductions are accelerated and less tax is paid today. However, the tax expense per book is based on a lower depreciation charge so that the income tax expense on the GAAP income statement is greater than the income taxes payable on the balance sheet. The difference is reported as a deferred income tax liability on the current balance sheet. The deferred liability is due and payable in the later years of the asset's useful life when the depreciation differences reverse and the higher tax deductions are lost.
3. ***Advance collections for subscriptions***. If a publisher collects subscriptions in advance, the cash receipt is not recognized as income for financial reporting until the books, magazines, etc., are delivered to the subscriber. The advance collections are considered unearned revenues for GAAP purposes and as such, are recorded as liabilities on the balance sheet. However, if the firm uses the cash basis for tax purposes, the entire amount of the cash received would be included in taxable income in the year of the advance collection. As a result, more taxes are paid today than the income tax expense reported on the income statement by the accountant. The excess of income taxes paid over the income tax expense on the income statement is always reported as a deferred tax asset on the balance sheet, subject to an impairment test. The impairment test will be discussed. The deferred tax asset represents a "prepaid tax" in the current period, the benefit from which will be realized in the future when reversal takes place. In this case, when the books, magazines, etc., are actually delivered to the subscriber, accounting income is recognized but there is no taxable income during the periods of delivery because taxable income was already recognized in the year of the advance collection. This is the point of reversal, and the benefits of the prepaid taxes are realized in the form of lower income taxes payable than the income tax expense reported for financial reporting purposes.
4. ***Estimated Warranty Expense Accruals***. Estimated warranty costs are expensed for book purposes in the year the product is sold but are not tax deductible until the actual repairs take place. In the year of the sale, the estimated warranty expense is recorded on the GAAP income statement, reducing both book income and tax

expense. However, because the estimated warranty cost is not tax deductible, more tax is paid to the government today. The excess tax payment to the government over the amount of GAAP tax expense is recognized as a deferred tax asset, subject to an impairment test. When the actual repairs take place, that amount is tax deductible lowering the tax due and payable to the government. This is the period when the deferred tax asset benefits are realized.

Temporary differences related to depreciation will be illustrated below.

Illustration

Assume a plant asset is acquired at a cost of $120,000 at the beginning of the year. The asset is assumed to have an estimated useful life of five years with no residual value. The firm uses an accelerated method for tax purposes (e.g., sum of the year's digits or SYD) and the straight-line method (SL) for book or financial reporting purposes. The depreciation and deferred tax schedules are presented below. Note that the parentheses indicate a tax advantage or the accrual of the deferred tax liability. This is not standard notation and can vary in practice. In addition, you should clearly differentiate between the income statement (flow effects) from the balance sheet (cumulative effects) of deferred tax accounting.

	DEPRECIATION		***( ) = TAX ADVANTAGE***	***INCOME STATEMENT***	***BALANCE SHEET***
YEAR	***SYD (TAX)***	***SL (BOOKS)***	***TEMPORARY BOOK / TAX DIFFERENCE***	***DEFERRED TAX PROVISION AT 40%***	***CUMULATIVE DEFERRED TAX LIABILITY***
1	$ 40,000	$24,000	($16,000)	($6,400)	($ 6,400)
2	32,000	24,000	(8,000)	($3,200)	(9.600)
3	24,000	24,000	- 0 -	- 0 -	(9,600)
4	16,000	24,000	8,000	3,200	(6,400)
5	8,000	24,000	16,000	6,400	- 0 -
TOTAL	$120,000	$120,000	$ - 0 -	$ - 0 -	

Government Tax Returns

Assume that the annual tax payable is based on $100,000 taxable income before depreciation is deducted. The tax returns are presented below. Income tax payable is also reported on the balance sheet as a current liability. Note that in this illustration the amount of tax payable each year increases as the company foregoes valuable tax deductions from depreciation.

DESCRIPTION	***YEAR 1***	***YEAR 2***	***YEAR 3***	***YEAR 4***	***YEAR 5***
Income before depreciation	$100,000	$100,000	$100,000	$100,000	$100,000
Less: Depreciation	(40,000)	(32,000)	(24,000)	(16,000)	(8,000)
Taxable income	$60,000	$68,000	$76,000	$84,000	$92,000
Tax rate 40%	x 40%	x 40%	x 40%	x 40%	x 40%
Income tax payable	$ 24,000	$ 27,200	$ 30,400	$ 33,600	$ 36,800

GAAP Income Statements

The determination of GAAP income tax expense deducted on the income statement is equal to the sum of the current and the deferred tax provisions. That is the income tax expense is equal to the change in the current tax liability plus the change in the deferred tax liability.

Computation of Income Tax Expense: ( ) = Expense

DESCRIPTION	YEAR 1	YEAR 2	YEAR 3	YEAR 4	YEAR 5
Income tax payable	($ 24,000)	($ 27,200)	($ 30,400)	($ 33,600)	($ 36,800)
Deferred Tax provision	(6,400)	(3,200)	- 0 -	3,200	6,400
Income tax expense	($30,400)	($30,400)	($30,400)	($30,400)	($30,400)

Based on the assumptions in this illustration, income before tax and depreciation is constant each year, there is no change in the straight-line depreciation deduction and therefore, GAAP income before tax is the same each year. Logically, with a stable 40% income tax rate, tax expense should be constant. The implementation of SFAS 109 ensures that we have a normalized or constant income tax expense. This approach also matches accounting income tax expense with pretax GAAP income. Therefore, given no change in any economic variables, GAAP net income is equal to $45,600 each year after deducting a constant tax expense of $30,400.

Income before tax and depreciation	**$100,000**
Less: Depreciation expense	**(24,000)**
Income before tax	**$ 76,000**
Less: Income tax expense	**(30,400)**
Net income	**$ 45,600**

The effective (or actual) tax rate is defined below:

$$\text{Effective (Actual) Tax Rate} = \frac{\text{GAAP Income Tax Expense}}{\text{Pretax GAAP Accounting Income}}$$

The effective (actual) tax rate is also constant or normalized at 40%. That is:

$$\text{Effective (Actual) Tax Rate} = \frac{\text{GAAP Income Tax Expense}}{\text{Pretax GAAP Accounting Income}} = \frac{\$30,400}{\$76,000}$$

$$\text{Effective (Actual) Tax Rate} = \underline{40\%}$$

If deferred taxes are not accrued and we use tax payable as tax expense, the effective (actual) tax rate becomes volatile and increases each year as the increased tax payable is divided by the constant pretax GAAP or accounting income of $76,000. This process would result in mismatching tax expense with income on the GAAP income statement and is not acceptable. Note that the first direction the deferred tax account takes (either liability or asset) is called "originating" or an "originating difference". When the account changes direction it is known as "reversing" or a "reversing difference".

The financial modeling worksheets for years 1 and 4 are presented below:

FINANCIAL MODELING WORKSHEET FOR YEAR 1: ORIGINATING DIFFERENCE

INCOME STATEMENT (FIRST)	
REVENUES:	
EXPENSES:	
Income Tax Expense	*(30,400)*
NET INCOME OR LOSS (a)	*(30,400)*

STATEMENT OF CASH FLOWS (THIRD)	
OPERATING ACTIVITIES:	
NET INCOME OR LOSS (a)	*(30,400)*
Increase in Deferred Tax Liability *Increase in Income Tax Payable*	*+6,400* *+24,000*
Cash Flow from Operating Activities	*- 0 -*
INVESTING ACTIVITIES:	
FINANCING ACTIVITIES:	
INCREASE (DECREASE) IN CASH (b)	*- 0 -*
ADD: BEGINNING CASH BALANCE	
ENDING CASH BALANCE	

BALANCE SHEET (SECOND)			
ASSETS		*LIABILITIES*	
CURRENT ASSETS		*CURRENT LIABILITIES*	
CASH (b)	*- 0 -*	*Income Tax Payable*	*+24,000*
		NONCURRENT LIABILITIES	
		Deferred Tax Liability	*+6,400*
NONCURRENT ASSETS		*STOCKHOLDERS' EQUITY*	
		CAPITAL STOCK	
		APIC	
		RETAINED EARNINGS (a)	*(30,400)*
TOTAL ASSETS	*- 0 -*	*TOTAL LIABILITIES & STOCKHOLDERS' EQUITY*	*- 0 -*

There is no cash flow effect because it is assumed that there are no taxes paid in Year 1.

FINANCIAL MODELING WORKSHEET FOR YEAR 4 REVERSING DIFFERENCE

INCOME STATEMENT (FIRST)	
REVENUES:	
EXPENSES:	
Income Tax Expense	(30,400)
NET INCOME OR LOSS (a)	(30,400)

STATEMENT OF CASH FLOWS (THIRD)	
OPERATING ACTIVITIES:	
NET INCOME OR LOSS (a)	(30,400)
Decrease in Deferred Tax Liability Increase in Income Tax Payable	(3,200) +33,600
Cash Flow from Operating Activities	-0-
INVESTING ACTIVITIES:	
FINANCING ACTIVITIES:	
INCREASE (DECREASE) IN CASH (b)	-0-
ADD: BEGINNING CASH BALANCE	
ENDING CASH BALANCE	

BALANCE SHEET (SECOND)			
ASSETS		LIABILITIES	
CURRENT ASSETS		CURRENT LIABILITIES	
CASH (b)	-0-	Income Tax Payable	+33,600
		NONCURRENT LIABILITIES	
		Deferred Tax Liability	(3,200)
NONCURRENT ASSETS		STOCKHOLDERS' EQUITY	
		CAPITAL STOCK	
		APIC	
		RETAINED EARNINGS (a)	(30,400)
TOTAL ASSETS	-0-	TOTAL LIABILITIES & STOCKHOLDERS' EQUITY	-0-

When the higher tax payable of $33,600 is paid, the payment will cover the tax for current economic activity (i.e., tax expense of $30,400) plus the previously deferred liability of $3,200.

PERMANENT DIFFERENCES

The second type of book/tax difference is known as a permanent difference. A permanent difference represents an item of revenue and expense that will be reported on the firm's tax return, but never on its financial statements or it is reported on the firm's financial statements, but never on its tax returns. Therefore, permanent differences represent differences between book and taxable income that never "reverse." The difference between book and taxable income is permanent, (i.e., the item neither becomes taxable nor can it be used as a tax deduction) and cannot be deferred.

Examples of Permanent Differences

Common examples of permanent differences include the following:

1. Interest Received on Tax Free Securities. Interest received on tax exempt investments is reported on the GAAP income statement as an item of revenue. Although this interest is considered income for financial reporting purposes, it is never taxable.
2. Insurance Expense for Officers' Life Insurance. Payments made to an insurance carrier for a policy covering the life of a key company executive is an expense for financial reporting, but is never tax deductible.

In both cases, the differences between GAAP and taxable income will never reverse and are not deferred. If there are no deferred tax implications, we then need to establish the role of permanent differences in GAAP accounting and reporting.

THE ROLE OF PERMANENT DIFFERENCES

As noted above, permanent differences never reverse and as a result are not deferred. If there are only permanent differences, the accountant simply sets the income tax expense on the income statement equal to the change in income tax liability that was obtained from the tax return and reported on the balance sheet as an increase in a current liability.

Although permanent differences do not affect accounting for deferred taxes, these differences will impact the effective (actual) tax rate. A reconciliation between the effective (actual) and the statutory tax rate is required as part of the income tax disclosures. The reconciliation can be presented in either dollars, percentages or both. Permanent differences are common reconciling items in the footnote.

To illustrate the role of permanent differences, assume the firm reports no temporary differences and the only book/tax difference is permanent (i.e., tax exempt interest). Under these assumptions, the firm's income tax return would be determined to follows:

Income Tax Return	***Amount***
Income Before Taxes (before adjustments for tax exempt income based on GAAP)	$10,000
Less: Tax Exempt Income	- 2,000
Taxable Income (IRS)	$ 8,000
Income Tax Rate	x 40%
Income Taxes Payable (Tax Liability)	$ 3,200

Income tax expense is still equal to the sum of the current plus the deferred provision, however without temporary differences there is no deferred provision so we have: Income Tax Expense = Income Taxes Payable + Deferred Tax (Expense) Provision = $3,200 + 0 = $3,200. In this case, the firm's effective (actual) tax rate is 32% (i.e., $3,200 / $10,000).

The required footnote reconciliation would be presented as follows:

FOOTNOTE RECONCILIATION	DOLLARS	%
Tax at the statutory rate: (40% x $10,000)	$ 4,000	40%
Tax exempt interest: (Tax savings = 40% x $2,000 = $800 **or** $800/$10,000 = 8%)	(800)	(8%)
Tax at the effective (actual) rate ($3,200/$10,000)	$ 3,200	32%

Note in this case that we cannot determine tax expense by multiplying a federal tax rate by GAAP pre-tax accounting income. Using that procedure would result in a tax expense of $4,000 which incorrect. The sum of the current plus the deferred provision approach is required to compute tax expense whenever there are permanent differences.

A sample footnote reconciliation for Allen Devices is presented in Exhibit 5.1

EXHIBIT 5.1: ALLEN DEVICES: TAX RATE RECONCILIATION

Notes to Consolidated Financial Statements

A reconciliation of the (provision for) and benefit from income taxes to income tax expense computed by applying the statutory federal income tax rate to pre-tax income (loss) for the fiscal years ended December 31, is as follows (dollars in thousands):

	2012		2011		2010	
Year Ended December 31,	**Amount**	**Percentage**	**Amount**	**Percentage**	**Amount**	**Percentage**
Income tax benefit (expense) at statutory federal rate	**$ (8,489)**	**35.00%**	$ 27,496	35.00%	$ (12,682)	35.00%
Decrease (increase) resulting from:						
State tax, net of federal benefit	**2,441**	**(10.06)**	5,989	7.62	1,472	(4.06)
Research and development credits	**2,562**	**(10.56)**	7,784	9.91	3,720	(10.27)
Foreign sales corporation benefit	**2,972**	**(12.25)**	9,464	12.05	1,739	(4.80)
Foreign tax rate difference	**458.4**	**(1.89)**	(1,228)	(1.56)	550.8	(1.52)
Change in reserve for deferred tax assets	**(4,968)**	**20.49**	(47,958)	(61.05)	4,154	(11.47)
In-process research and development	—	—	(2,604)	(3.32)	—	—
Other	**366**	**(1.53)**	358.8	0.46	463.2	(1.27)
	$ (4,657)	**19.20%**	$ (697.2)	(0.89)%	$ (582)	1.61%

As noted in Exhibit 5.1 Allen Devices discloses both dollars and percentages in its effective tax rate reconciliation. The reconciliation only applies to the federal tax rate and as a result, state and foreign taxes are part of the reconciling items. In Allen Devices' case, effective tax rates are reduced by state and foreign tax benefits. The research and development (R&D) tax credit is an example of a permanent difference. These are credits granted for tax purposes, but are not revenues per GAAP or book reporting. This credit reduces the company's effective tax rate. The reserve or allowance for reduction impairment of the deferred tax asset will be discussed in the section of this chapter covering the net operating loss.

THE BASIS PERSPECTIVE UNDER THE LIABILITY (ASSET-LIABILITY) METHOD

Under the SFAS 109 liability (asset-liability) method, deferred taxes are also analyzed by comparing the book and tax bases (i.e., the net carrying values or net book values, NBV) of the asset or liability underlying the transaction. In the depreciation illustration, the underlying asset is the plant asset.

To illustrate, assume the following for an asset with an original cost of $450,000 and a 5-year useful life.

	DEPRECIATION	
YEAR	***SL (BOOKS)***	***SYD (TAX)***
1	$90,000	$150,000
2	90,000	120,000
3	90,000	90,000
4	90,000	60,000
5	90,000	30,000
TOTAL	$450,000	$450,000

As noted in the table above, the company uses straight line depreciation for GAAP and employs an accelerated method for tax purposes. If we use the traditional approach to deferred tax accounting, we would focus on the depreciation expense differences to determine the change in the deferred tax provision (the income statement effect) To determine the cumulative balance sheet effect, we must add that change to the existing balance of the deferred tax account.

However, under the Liability (Asset-Liability) Method, we focus on the basis or carrying value differences and compute the cumulative balance of the deferred tax account on the balance sheet. Then, the change in the cumulative balance of the deferred tax account would represent the income statement effect or the deferred tax provision.

The following tables employ the Liability Method for the first two years of the asset's useful life.

Year 1:

Description	***Book (GAAP)***	***Tax***	***Cumulative Book Tax Difference***
Cost	$450,000	$450,000	$ - 0 -
Less: Accumulated Depreciation (end of year one)	(90,000)	(150,000)	(60,000)
Net Book Value	$360,000		
Tax Basis		$300,000	
Book / Tax Basis Difference			(60,000)
Tax Rate			X 40%
Cumulative Balance of the Deferred Tax Liability			($24,000)

The deferred tax expense in year one is also $24,000 (charge in the cumulative deferred tax liability (i.e., $24,000 - 0).

Year 2:

Description	***Book (GAAP)***	***Tax***	***Cumulative Book Tax Difference***
Cost	$450,000	$450,000	$ - 0 -
Less: Accumulated Depreciation (end of year two)	(180,000)	(270,000)	(90,000)
Net Book Value	$270,000		
Tax Basis		$180,000	
Book / Tax Basis Difference			(90,000)
Tax Rate			X 40%
Cumulative Balance of the Deferred Tax Liability			($36,000)

The deferred tax expense in year two is the difference between the cumulative balances of the deferred tax liability on the balance sheet or $12,000 (i.e., $36,000 – 24,000).

The basis approach could be rationalized by assuming that the asset is sold at the end of year two for $290,000. The gain for book purposes would be $20,000 while the gain for tax purposes would amount to $110,000. The book/tax difference on the gain is $90,000, resulting in an additional $36,000 tax liability on the sale, (given a 40% tax rate). The date of sale is the reversal point.

Although the results are the same in this case for both the traditional and the liability methods, an important application of the liability method is on the date of a merger and acquisition transaction. For example, if there is a tax free merger transaction for tax purposes, the carryover or historical bases of net assets would be used. Conversely, for GAAP purposes, the acquisition method must be used and this method results in a basis step up or writes up the historical bases to fair value. The difference between the carryover tax bases and the fair value used for GAAP reporting creates a deferred tax account on the date of acquisition that must be included in the net assets acquired on the date of the deal. This new account will change the net assets acquired and therefore, impact the valuation of any goodwill computed.

A summary review of accounting for deferred income taxes is presented in Exhibit 5.2.

EXHIBIT 5.2: SUMMARY OF DEFERRED TAX ACCOUNTING

Summary Table for Temporary Differences

	REVENUE	**EXPENSE**
BOOK > TAX	Deferred tax liability (e.g., installment sales)	Deferred tax asset (e.g., warranty costs)
BOOK < TAX	Deferred tax asset (e.g., advance collections)	Deferred tax liability (e.g., accelerated depreciation)

Summary Table for Computation of Income Tax Expense

As illustrated earlier, the accountant does not calculate income tax expense by multiplying income before tax on the income statement by the tax rate. The income tax expense must be calculated as follows:

Increase in Income Taxes Payable
(From the tax return and included in the
balance of income tax payable
on the balance sheet).......................................$XXX

<u>The Deferred Tax Expense or</u>
<u>The Deferred Tax Provision:</u>
ADD: Originating deferred tax liabilities
Reversing deferred tax assets....................+ XX
or
LESS: Originating deferred tax assets
Reversing deferred tax liabilities................<u>- XX</u>

Income Tax Expense (On the
income statement)...<u>$XXX</u>

Income Tax Expense (Plug)	=	Income Tax Payable	+/-	Deferred Tax Provision	+ Increase in the DTL + Decrease in the DTA - Decrease in the DTL - Increase in the DTA

SUMMARY TABLE FOR TEMPORARY VERSUS PERMANENT DIFFERENCES

Book / Tax Difference	Impact Deferred Tax Accounts	Impact Effective Tax Rate
Temporary	*YES*	*NO*
Permanent	*NO*	*YES*

Exhibit 5.2 can be used as a summary and as a tool to understand the basics of deferred tax accounting. The summary table provides a matrix that can be used to determine whether a transaction results in a deferred tax asset or a deferred tax liability, depending on the magnitude of book versus taxable revenues and expenses. The computation of income tax expense provides two vehicles to build the income tax provision as the sum of the current provision plus the deferred tax provision.

A comprehensive illustration including both temporary and permanent differences is presented below.

COMPREHENSIVE DEFERRED TAX LIABILITY ILLUSTRATION

To illustrate accounting for the deferred tax liability, we will consider a firm that uses straight-line depreciation for financial reporting and the MACRS for Federal (IRS) tax reporting. This is the firm's only temporary difference. The receipt of tax-exempt interest represents the only permanent difference. Depreciation information and an analysis of the temporary book/tax difference are presented below.

Depreciation Information:

Machinery Cost = $40,000
Depreciation Methods:
Book: 5 Year Property Using The Straight Line Method.
Tax: 5 Year Property Using Federal MACRS.

For both book and tax there is a 1/2-year depreciation in the first and the last years.

Book Depreciation:
S/L Rate = 1 / 5 Years = 20%
$40,000 / 5 Years = $8,000 Per Year

TAX DEPRECIATION: MACRS TABLE ASSUMING 5 YEAR PROPERTY

As noted in the chapter discussing non-current assets, MACRS depreciation is based on double declining balance, with a switch to straight line at the optimal point. For a five year asset, we determined that the optimal point begins in year four. MACRS also builds in partial year depreciation directly in its tables. In the case of five year property, it is assumed that there will be a half year taken in the first and last years, regardless of the actual date of asset acquisition. The development of the relevant MACRS percentages is illustrated the following table.

Year	***DDB %***	***½ Year***	***Adjusted %***	***% of Net Book Value (NBV) Remaining at the Beginning of the year***	***MACRS % = (Adjusted % x % of NBV Remaining)***
1	40%	1/2	20%	100%	20.00%
2	40%		40%	80%	32.00%
3	40%		40%	48%	19.20%
Total Depreciation to date in Percentage Terms					71.2%
4	Switch to Straight Line = Remaining NBV in % terms / 2.5 years = (100% - 71.2 %) / 2.5 years = 28.8% / 2.5 years = 11.52% per year				
Year	***SL %***	***½ Year***	***Adjusted %***	***% of Net Book Value (NBV) Remaining at the Beginning of the year***	***MACRS %***
4	11.52%		11.52%	NA	11.52%
5	11.52%		11.52%	NA	11.52%
6	11.52%	1/2	5.76%	NA	5.76%

Application of the MACRS depreciation percentages to this illustration we have:

Year	*MACRS %*	*Depreciation Computations*
1	20.00%	20.00% X $40,000 = $8,000
2	32.00%	32.00% X $40,000 = 12,800
3	19.20%	19.20% X $40,000 = 7,680
4	11.52%	11.52% X $40,000 = 4,608
5	11.52%	11.52% X $40,000 = 4,608
6	5.76%	5.76% X $40,000 = 2,304

An analysis of the book/tax differences caused by the depreciation of the plant asset and a summary of income and taxes are presented in the next schedule. The income before tax and depreciation and the tax exempt interest amounts are assumed. The income before tax and depreciation includes the tax exempt interest for each year.

Analysis of Temporary Book/Tax Differences

	DEPRECIATION EXPENSE			*DEFERRED TAX EXPENSE OR PROVISION (BOOK/TAX DIFFERENCE @ 40%*	*CUMULATIVE BALANCE IN THE DEFERRED TAX ACCOUNT*
YEAR	*BOOK*	*TAX*	*BOOK / TAX DIFF.*	*REPORTED ON THE INCOME STATEMENT AS PART OF DETERMINATION OF INCOME TAX EXPENSE*	*REPORTED ON THE BALANCE SHEET*
2007	$4,000	$8,000	($4,000)	($1,600)	($1,600)
2008	8,000	12,800	($4,800)	($1,920)	(3,520)
2009	8,000	7,680	320	128	(3,392)
2010	8,000	4,608	3,392	1,357	(2,035)
2011	8,000	4,608	3,392	1,357	(678)
2012	4,000	2,304	1,696	678	- 0 -
TOTAL	$40,000	$40,000	$ - 0 -	$ - 0 -	

Schedule of Income and Taxes:

	2007		2008		2009		2010		2011		2012	
ITEM	BOOK	TAX	BOOK	TAX	BOOK	TAX	BOOK	TAX	BOOK	TAX	BOOK	TAX
INCOME BEFORE TAX & DEPR.	$40000	$40000	$65000	$65000	$50000	$50000	$60000	$60000	$80000	$80000	$60000	$60000
LESS: DEPR.	-4000	-8000	-8000	-12800	-8000	-7680	-8000	-4608	-8000	-4608	-4000	-2304
LESS: TAX EXEMPT INTEREST.	0	-5000	0	-7000	0	-10000	0	-11000	0	-15000	0	-10000
INCOME BEFORE TAX	$36000	$27000	$57000	$45200	$42000	$32320	$52000	$44392	$72000	$60392	$56000	$47696
	2007 TAX PROVISION		2008 TAX PROVISION		2009 TAX PROVISION		2010 TAX PROVISION		2011 TAX PROVISION		2012 TAX PROVISION	
TAXES PAYABLE @40% (REPORTED ON THE BALANCE SHEET).	($10,800)		($18,080)		($12,928)		($17,757)		($24,157)		($19,078)	
ADD: DEFERRED TAX EXPENSE (PROVISION).	(1600)		(1,920)		128		1,357		1,357		678	
INCOME TAX EXPENSE (REPORTED ON THE INCOME STATEMENT).	($12,400)		($20,000)		($12,800)		($16,400)		($22,800)		($18,400)	
DEFERRED TAXES PAYABLE (CUMULATIVE) (REPORTED ON THE BALANCE SHEET).	($1,600)		($3,520)		($3,392)		($2,035)		($ 678)		$ - 0 -	

The tax provisions for each year are computed in a similar fashion. Using 2007 as an illustration we have:

Account	Computation	Amount
Income tax payable (current provision)	Tax rate x Taxable income before tax = 40% x $27,000 =	$10,800
Deferred Provision	Taken directly from the analysis of book/tax differences	1,600
Income tax expense (provision)	The sum of the current plus the deferred provision	$12,400

An alternate approach to computing the income tax expense is to deduct the permanent differences from pretax accounting or book income and multiply that result by the tax rate. For example:

Pretax accounting income	**$36,000**
Tax exempt interest	**(5,000)**
Net amount	**$31,000**
Tax rate	**X 40%**
Income tax expense (provision)	**$12,400**

This method is not favored by accountants because the "net amount" does not exist for financial reporting purposes and cannot be traced through the statements.

Footnote Reconciliation with both Temporary and Permanent Book/Tax Differences: 2007

FOOTNOTE RECONCILIATION	*DOLLARS*	%
Tax at the statutory rate: (40% x $36,000)	$14,400	40.0%
Tax exempt interest: (Tax savings = 40% x $5,000 = $2,000 OR $2,000/$36,000 = 5.6%)	(2,000)	(5.6%)
Tax at the effective (actual) rate: ($12,400 / $36,000)	$12,400	34.4%

Financial modeling worksheets for 2007 and 2009 are presented below.

FINANCIAL MODELING WORKSHEET FOR 2007 ORIGINATING DIFFERENCE

INCOME STATEMENT (FIRST)	
REVENUES:	
EXPENSES:	
Income Tax Expense	(12,400)
NET INCOME OR LOSS (a)	(12,400)

STATEMENT OF CASH FLOWS (THIRD)	
OPERATING ACTIVITIES:	
NET INCOME OR LOSS (a)	(12,400)
Increase in Deferred Tax Liability Increase in Income Tax Payable	+1,600 +10,800
Cash Flow from Operating Activities	- 0 -
INVESTING ACTIVITIES:	
FINANCING ACTIVITIES:	
INCREASE (DECREASE) IN CASH (b)	- 0 -
ADD: BEGINNING CASH BALANCE	
ENDING CASH BALANCE	

BALANCE SHEET (SECOND)			
ASSETS		LIABILITIES	
CURRENT ASSETS		CURRENT LIABILITIES	
CASH (b)	- 0 -	Income Tax Payable	+10,800
		NONCURRENT LIABILITIES	
		Deferred Tax Liability	+1,600
NONCURRENT ASSETS		STOCKHOLDERS' EQUITY	
		CAPITAL STOCK	
		APIC	
		RETAINED EARNINGS (a)	(12,400)
TOTAL ASSETS	- 0 -	TOTAL LIABILITIES & STOCKHOLDERS' EQUITY	- 0 -

Once again, it is assumed that no taxes are paid during the current year and as a result, the tax provision has no effect on the company's cash flows.

FINANCIAL MODELING WORKSHEET FOR 2009 REVERSING DIFFERENCE

INCOME STATEMENT (FIRST)	
REVENUES:	
EXPENSES:	
Income Tax Expense	(12,800)
NET INCOME OR LOSS (a)	(12,800)

STATEMENT OF CASH FLOWS (THIRD)	
OPERATING ACTIVITIES:	
NET INCOME OR LOSS (a)	(12,800)
Decrease in Deferred Tax Liability	(128)
Increase in Income Tax Payable	+12,928
Cash Flow from Operating Activities	- 0 -
INVESTING ACTIVITIES:	
FINANCING ACTIVITIES:	
INCREASE (DECREASE) IN CASH (b)	- 0 -
ADD: BEGINNING CASH BALANCE	
ENDING CASH BALANCE	

BALANCE SHEET (SECOND)			
ASSETS		LIABILITIES	
CURRENT ASSETS		CURRENT LIABILITIES	
CASH (b)	- 0 -	Income Tax Payable	+12,928
		NONCURRENT LIABILITIES	
		Deferred Tax Liability	(128)
		STOCKHOLDERS' EQUITY	
NONCURRENT ASSETS			
		CAPITAL STOCK	
		APIC	
		RETAINED EARNINGS (a)	(12,800)
		TOTAL LIABILITIES & STOCKHOLDERS' EQUITY	
TOTAL ASSETS	- 0 -		- 0 -

There is a reversal in 2009 that results in more taxes paid to the government (i.e., $12,928) than the amount of tax expensed on the income statement (i.e., $12,800). The amount to be paid ($12,928) covers the amount due for current economic activity (tax expense of $12,800) plus payment of a previously deferred liability ($128).

KEY ISSUES IN THE APPLICATION OF THE SFAS 109 BALANCE SHEET APPROACH

In applying SFAS 109, there are three key issues to consider. These issues are: The Liability (Asset-Liability) Method; Balance Sheet Classification Rules and Accounting for the Deferred Tax Asset. Each issue is discussed in the following sections.

1. ***The Liability (Asset-Liability) Method.*** To properly value the deferred tax asset and deferred tax liability, FASB 109 requires that deferred tax accounts are measured at the tax rate expected to be in effect at the future reversal date. A future tax rate can only be used if enacted into law. In addition, if a tax rate change is enacted into law, the cumulative balance

of a deferred tax account must be revalued to reflect the change in tax rate. The revaluation is recorded in the year the tax rate change is enacted into law. Accounting for tax rate changes and implementation of the asset-liability method results in increased volatility of a firm's effective tax rate, tax expense, net income and earnings per share.

2. Balance Sheet Classification Rules. The deferred tax account is classified as current or noncurrent depending on the classification of the underlying asset or liability causing reversal. For example, if the balance of the deferred tax liability is caused by depreciation differences, the deferred tax liability is classified as long term because the underlying plant asset is a noncurrent (long term) asset. That is, as the net book value of the plant asset is reduced through depreciation, reversal takes place and the deferred liability is paid. However, if reversal is not related to an underlying asset or liability, (e.g., net operating loss carryforward benefits), the deferred tax account is classified based on expected reversal date (i.e., current if reversing within one year from the balance sheet date and noncurrent if reversing more than one year from the balance sheet date).

3. Accounting for Deferred Tax Assets. When based on future events, asset recognition may not be supported by accounting theory. Specifically, because the realization of the tax benefit is dependent on future income it violates conservatism. Under SFAS 109, asset recognition is always permitted but is subject to an impairment test. Specifically, all available evidence regarding the realization of future taxable income, (both positive and negative evidence), must be considered to determine whether it is "more likely than not", (slightly more than a 50% chance), that the asset's value will be realized. A valuation allowance (i.e., a reserve or contra asset account) is created to reduce the asset's value, if available evidence indicates that all or a portion of the asset may not be realized.

It should be noted that both the use of the valuation allowance and the liability method for tax rate changes may cause significant volatility in a firm's effective tax rate, tax expense, net income and earnings per share.

Each of these issues is discussed in the following sections of this chapter.

The Liability Method (or Asset-Liability Method): Detailed Discussion

SFAS 109 requires that the liability method (or the asset-liability method) be used in accounting for the deferred tax account. Along with the use of the valuation allowance for the deferred tax asset, the liability method is consistent with the FASB's objective of proper deferred tax asset and deferred tax liability valuation and classification. This approach will focus on proper balance sheet valuation and classification and trades off income statement matching. The liability method consists of two major provisions:

(1) The use of future tax rates.
(2) The adjustment of the cumulative balance of the deferred tax account whenever tax rate changes are been enacted into law.

Future Tax Rates

Under the liability method, deferred income taxes should be recorded at the amounts at which they will be recovered or settled when the underlying temporary differences reverse. That would require valuation at the future tax rates in effect at reversal.

SFAS 109 requires that a tax rate other than the current rate may be used only when the future tax rates have been enacted into law. Even if it is probable that tax law will change, if it has not yet been enacted into law, the current rate must be used.

Revision of Future Tax Rates

When a change in the tax rate is enacted into law, its effect on the cumulative balances of the deferred tax accounts and the related tax expense should be recorded immediately. That is, in the year of the tax rate change, all cumulative deferred tax account balances must be increased or decreased to reflect the new tax rates. The tax rate change adjustment is prospective in nature so that prior year's financial statements are not adjusted or restated. The effect of a tax rate change is illustrated below.

Tax Rate Change Illustration. Using the data from the Comprehensive Deferred Tax Liability Illustration, assume that tax rates increase from 40% to 41% effective at the beginning of 2009 or year three.

GAAP and Tax Information for 2009. Assume that pretax GAAP income is $42,000 and taxable income is $32,320. Taxable income excludes $10,000 of tax exempt interest. The revised analysis is presented below:

	DEPRECIATION EXPENSE			*DEFERRED TAX EXPENSE OR PROVISION (BOOK/TAX DIFFERENCE x Tax Rate)*	*CUMULATIVE BALANCE IN THE DEFERRED TAX ACCOUNT*
YEAR	**BOOK**	**TAX**	**BOOK / TAX DIFF.**	**REPORTED ON THE INCOME STATEMENT AS PART OF DETERMINATION OF INCOME TAX EXPENSE**	**REPORTED ON THE BALANCE SHEET**
2007	$4,000	$8,000	($4,000)	($4,000) x 40% =($1,600)	($1,600)
2008	8,000	12,800	($4,800)	($4,800) x 40% =($1,920)	(3,520)
2009***				**Adjustment:** **($8,800) x 1% = (88)**	(3,608)
	8,000	7,680	320	320 x 41% = 131	(3,477)
2010	8,000	4,608	3,392	3,392 x 41% = 1,391	(2,086)
2011	8,000	4,608	3,392	3,392 x 41% = 1,391	(695)
2012	4,000	2,304	1,696	1,696 x 41% = 695	- 0 -
TOTAL	$40,000	$40,000	$ - 0 -	$ - 0 -	

****Year of tax rate change*

Given the increased tax rate the proper amount of the cumulative deferred tax liability should be $3,608 at the end of 2008. This is the amount that is due and payable at reversal using the new 41% tax rate. Specifically, the cumulative book/tax difference is $8,800 at the end of 2008 (i.e., $4,000 in 2007 and $4,800 in 2008). If the tax rate was always equal to 41%, the deferred tax liability should be equal to $3,608 (i.e., 41% x $8,800). However, the balance at the point is only $3,520. The adjustment needed to bring the deferred tax liability to its correct valuation of $3,608 is $88 (i.e., $3,608 – 3,520). This adjustment is also determined by multiplying the 1% tax rate increase by the cumulative book/tax difference of $8,800.

Regardless of the method of computation, the adjustment is applied prospectively: in the year of the tax rate change and in all future periods. There are no retroactive adjustments made to prior years. With the cumulative balance of the deferred tax liability valued at 41%

and all reversals made at 41%, the deferred tax account clears to a zero balance at the end of the asset's useful life.

The following tables are based on the data provided in the comprehensive illustration presented earlier. The key difference is the implementation of the new 41% tax rate beginning in 2009.

Tax Returns:

DESCRIPTION	2007	2008	2009***	2010	2011	2012
Taxable income	$27,000	$45,200	$32,320	$44,392	$60,392	$47,696
Tax rate 40%	x 40%	x 40%	x 41%	X 41%	x 41%	41%
Income tax payable	$10,800	$18,080	$13,251	$18,201	$24,761	$19,555

****Year of tax rate change*

Income Statements

Computation of Income Tax Expense: ( ) = Expense

DESCRIPTION	2007	2008	2009***	2010	2011	2012
Income tax payable	($10,800)	($18,080)	($13,251)	($18,201)	($24,761)	($19,555)
Tax rate change adjustment Deferred Tax provision	(1,600)	(1,920)	(88) 131	1,391	1,391	695
Income tax expense	($12,400)	($20,000)	($13,208)	($16,810)	($23,370)	($18,860)
Effective (Actual) Tax Rate	34.4%	35.1%	31.4%	32.3%	32.5%	33.7%

****NOTE: there is net reversal in 2009 of $43 ($131-88)*

Income Statement each year:

DESCRIPTION	2007	2008	2009***	2010	2011	2012
Income before tax	$36,000	$57,000	$42,000	$52,000	$72,000	$56,000
Less: Income tax expense	(12,400)	(20,000)	(13,208)	(16,810)	(23,370)	(18,860)
Net income	$23,600	$37,000	$28,792	$35,190	$48,360	$37,140

****Year of tax rate change*

Footnote Reconciliation with both Temporary and Permanent Book/Tax Differences and a Tax Rate Change enacted into Law in 2009:

FOOTNOTE RECONCILIATION	DOLLARS	%
Tax at the statutory rate: ($42,000 x 41%)	$17,220	41.0%
Tax exempt interest: (Tax savings = $10,000 x 41% = $4,100 or $4,100 / $42,000 = 9.8%)	(4,100)	(9.8%)
Tax rate change adjustment ($88 / $42,000)	88	.2%
Tax at the effective (actual) rate: ($13,208 / $42,000)	$13,208	31.4%

The tax rate change adjustment increases the deferred tax liability and tax expense for GAAP or book purposes, but this is not tax deductible. As a result of the lack of tax deductibility, the company's effective tax rate increases.

Financial modeling worksheet for 2009 (the year of the tax rate change) is presented below.

FINANCIAL MODELING WORKSHEET FOR 2009 YEAR OF THE TAX RATE CHANGE

INCOME STATEMENT (FIRST)	
REVENUES:	
EXPENSES:	
Income Tax Expense	*(13,208)*
NET INCOME OR LOSS (a)	*(13,208)*

STATEMENT OF CASH FLOWS (THIRD)	
OPERATING ACTIVITIES:	
NET INCOME OR LOSS (a)	*(13,208)*
Decrease in Deferred Tax Liability	*(43)*
Increase in Income Tax Payable	*+13,251*
Cash Flow from Operating Activities	*-0-*
INVESTING ACTIVITIES:	
FINANCING ACTIVITIES:	
INCREASE (DECREASE) IN CASH (b)	*-0-*
ADD: BEGINNING CASH BALANCE	
ENDING CASH BALANCE	

BALANCE SHEET (SECOND)			
ASSETS		***LIABILITIES***	
CURRENT ASSETS		***CURRENT LIABILITIES***	
CASH (b)	*-0-*	*Income Tax Payable*	*+13,251*
		NONCURRENT LIABILITIES	
		Deferred Tax Liability (131-88)	*(43)*
		STOCKHOLDERS' EQUITY	
NONCURRENT ASSETS			
		CAPITAL STOCK	
		APIC	
		RETAINED EARNINGS (a)	*(13,208)*
TOTAL ASSETS	*-0-*	***TOTAL LIABILITIES & STOCKHOLDERS' EQUITY***	*-0-*

Balance Sheet Classification of Deferred Income Taxes

The deferred tax liability and the deferred tax asset can be classified as either current or long-term. The deferred tax account is the result of many book/tax differences. Some of these differences will give rise to deferred tax liabilities and others will result in deferred tax assets. Similarly, some within each group will be current and others will be noncurrent.

At the end of each accounting period, the accountant must analyze the composition of the deferred tax account and classify each reversal of a book/tax difference as either current or long term. The accountant will then determine the net liability and the net asset. Technically, netting is permitted as long as the right to offset exists (i.e., the amounts are payable and receivable from the same taxing jurisdiction). However, some entities may reflect net balances on the financial statements with the gross amounts disclosed in the footnotes. The result will be a net current liability or asset and a net noncurrent liability or asset.

Classification Rules

An individual deferred tax asset or liability is classified as current or noncurrent based on the classification of the related asset or liability for financial reporting.

A relationship exists if the reduction of the underlying asset or liability causes the temporary book/tax difference to reverse. For example, if the firm uses straight-line depreciation for financial reporting and the MACRS system for tax purposes, the depreciation of the plant asset and the reduction of its net book value in subsequent periods will cause the reversal of the deferred tax liability. The plant asset is classified as a fixed or noncurrent asset. Therefore, the deferred tax liability related to this plant asset is also classified as noncurrent.

A deferred tax asset or liability that is not related to an asset or liability for financial reporting is classified as current or noncurrent based on expected reversal date.

Therefore, if the expected reversal is within one year from the balance sheet date, the deferred tax account is classified as current. If the expected reversal date is more than one year from the balance sheet date, the deferred tax account is classified as noncurrent. For example, a net operating loss carryforward benefit giving rise to a deferred tax asset can be realized at any time over a 20-year period. In this case to be discussed, if there is no short term reversal expected, the deferred tax asset would probably be classified as noncurrent. Otherwise, a position would be current (realization expected within one year) and the remainder long term.

Financial Statement Presentation

After deferred tax assets and liabilities are classified as current and noncurrent, the net current asset or liability and the net noncurrent asset or liability should be determined and reported on the balance sheet. It should be noted that even if netting is reflected on the balance sheet, the gross deferred tax asset, the gross deferred tax liability and the valuation allowance, if any, should be disclosed in the footnotes to the financial statements. The classification rules and the related accounting processes are illustrated below.

TEMPORARY DIFFERENCE	DEFERRED TAX		RELATED BALANCE SHEET ACCOUNT	BALANCE SHEET CLASSIFICATION	
	ASSET	(LIABILITY)		RELATED ACCOUNT	DEFERRED TAX ACCOUNT
ADVANCE COLLECTION OF A ONE YEAR SUBSCRIPTION (ACCRUAL BASIS FOR BOOKS AND CASH BASIS FOR TAX)	$20,000		UNEARNED REVENUE	CURRENT LIABILITY	CURRENT ASSET
STRAIGHT LINE DEPRECIATION FOR BOOKS AND MACRS FOR TAX		($100,000)	PLANT ASSETS	LONG TERM ASSET	LONG TERM LIABILITY
ESTIMATED WARRANTY LIABILITY FOR A ONE YEAR BASIC PRODUCT WARRANTY (ACCRUAL BASIS FOR BOOKS AND CASH BASIS FOR TAX)	$4,000		ESTIMATED WARRANTY LIABILITY	CURRENT LIABILITY	CURRENT ASSET
INSTALLMENT SALES RECOGNIZED ON THE ACCRUAL BASIS FOR BOOKS AND THE INSTALLMENT (CASH) BASIS FOR TAX		(15,000)	INSTALLMENT SALES RECEIVABLE	CURRENT ASSET	CURRENT LIABILITY

This analysis results in the classification of $9,000 of the deferred taxes as a net current deferred tax asset (i.e., $20,000 + 4,000 - 15,000). The $100,000 is classified as a noncurrent deferred tax liability.

ACCOUNTING FOR DEFERRED TAX ASSETS (DTA)

Deferred tax assets result from expected tax reductions to be realized in the future resulting from the reversal of current, temporary book-tax differences, (i.e., future deductible amounts or future tax deductions). As noted earlier, deferred tax assets arise from several book tax differences including advance collections, estimated warranty accruals, net operating loss carryforwards or NOLs. The net operating loss carryforward is the most complex of the deferred tax assets. As a result, deferred tax assets will be illustrated by using the net operating loss in the following section of this chapter.

Accounting for the Net Operating Loss (NOL)

A Net Operating Loss (NOL) is simply a net loss for tax purposes. That is, an NOL occurs when tax-deductible expenses exceed taxable revenues. As in the case of deferred tax accounting, the NOL is treated differently for tax purposes than for financial accounting (GAAP) purposes.

(a) Tax Law

According to tax law, a firm (within limitations to be discussed) can elect one of two options. Once an option is elected it is irrevocable. The NOL provisions of the IRS code are designed as an income smoothing or income averaging mechanism.

(1) NOL Carryback/Carryforward Option

Companies can carryback the NOL for two years and claim a refund for taxes previously paid in those years, but it must be carried back to the earliest year first. Any remaining NOL can be carried forward up to 20 years to offset future taxable income. Any unused carryforward expires.

(2) NOL Carryforward Option

A company can elect to carryforward the NOL for a period of 20 years to offset future taxable income. This is the carryforward only option. Any unused carryforward expires. The carryforward only option may make sense if there is no taxable income available in the two prior years. In addition, the entity may expect higher taxable income or tax rates in the future or the firm may not wish to open up previous tax years.

Limitation on the NOL Carryforward Benefit

After a change in ownership of more than 50% (over a three year period) of the value of the stock in a loss corporation, however effected, (e.g., merger, acquisition, etc.), the future taxable income available for offset each year by the pre-acquisition NOL's is limited to the following amount.

Annual Income Limit on NOL Benefit Realization	=	Long Term Exempt Rate	X	The Value of NOL Corporation's Equity

Where:

- The Long Term Tax Exempt Rate to be used is the highest published Applicable Federal Rate, (AFR), over the three months immediately before the acquisition. The AFR is close to the T-Bond rate.
- The Value of the NOL Corporation's Equity is measured by the fair market value (i.e., the purchase price) of the equity interests before the ownership change. This value will be modified to reflect the IRS upward adjustments to asset bases, etc.

For example, if the long-term tax-exempt rate is 8% and the purchase price of the loss subsidiary is $1,000,000, then the annual income limitation on the use of NOL carryforward benefits is $80,000. This is the maximum amount of income available for offset each year.

Annual Income Limit on NOL Benefit Realization	=	Long Term Tax Exempt Rate	X	The Value of NOL Corporation's Equity
$80,000	=	8%	X	$1,000,000

This annual limitation is known as the Section 382 Limitation. In addition, NOL carryforwards are disallowed unless the loss corporation satisfies the continuity-of-business enterprise rule that applies to tax-free reorganizations for the two-year period following the ownership change. Note that there are other elements related to Section 382 and many more complex restrictions on the NOL that are beyond the scope of this text.

The next illustration provides an overview of the NOL carryback/carryforward rules and moves into the accounting requirements for the NOL.

Illustration

The following diagram will illustrate the NOL provisions of the IRS code. The data assume that there are no book/tax differences so that taxable income is the same as pre-tax accounting (book) income. We also assume that there is no Section 382 limitation and that the NOL carryback/carryforward option will be elected.

Assume that a company began operations in 2005 and reported income during its first two years. The company incurred a loss in 2007 followed by two profitable years. The tax rates used in the following computations were assumed to be in effect for the years presented.

ITEM	***2005***	***2006***	***NOL 2007***	***2008***	***2009***
TAXABLE INCOME OR (NOL)	$100,000	$59,000	($184,000)	$10,000	$25,000
TAX RATE	X 35%	X 25%			
TAXES PAID	*(a) 35,000*	*(a) 14,750*			
CARRYBACK	***FIRST*** (100,000)	***SECOND*** (59,000)	← $159,000		
BALANCE			$(25,000)		
CARRYFORWARD			→ $ 25,000	***FIRST*** ***(b)*** (10,000)	***SECOND*** ***(c)*** (15,000)
BALANCE			$-0-		
Valuation of the Deferred Tax Asset at 15% (b)			***$25,000 x 15% $ 3,750***	***($10,000) x 15% ($1,500)***	***($15,000) x 15% ($2,250)***

NOTES:

(a) Refund applied for in 2007 (i.e., the year of the loss) is $49,750 (i.e., 35,000 + 14,750).

(b) There are no taxes due in 2008 because the available NOL carryforward fully offsets taxable income. Assuming a 15% tax bracket for the short term, the value of the NOL carryforward benefit (i.e., valuation of the deferred tax asset) is $3,750 (15% x $25,000). Of this amount, $1,500 (i.e., 15% x $10,000), is realized in 2008.

(c) There will be $1,500 of taxes due in 2009. The tax liability is calculated as follows:

Taxable Income	$25,000
Less: NOL Carryforward Taxable Income after the application of available	(15,000)
NOL Carryforwards	$10,000
Tax Rate	x15%
Tax liability	$ 1,500

This calculation is part of the corporate income tax return. Note that the remaining $2,250 (i.e., 15% x $15,000) of the carryforward benefit is realized in 2009.

(b) Accounting for the NOL

The primary accounting issue for the NOL is to determine when to recognize the related tax benefits: in the year of the loss, in the year in which the future income is earned or in some combination of the year of the loss and future years.

(1) NOL Carryback

In the case of an NOL carryback, the NOL gives rise to a refund that is both measurable and currently realizable. As a result, accountants are fairly certain as to the refund and recognize the NOL carryback benefits in the year of the loss. The recognition results in recording a receivable (i.e., a current asset) for the tax refund and increasing ordinary income (or reducing the loss) on the income statement. The income tax benefit flows through the income tax provision (expense) line on the income statement. This is treated as negative tax expense.

In the previous illustration, accounting for the NOL carryback in 2007 (the year of the loss) will result in a $49,750 refund receivable in the current asset section of the balance sheet and an item of income for $49,750 on the income statement. This income item, benefit due to NOL carryback, is a reduction of income tax expense (i.e., negative tax expense).

The financial modeling worksheet for the NOL carryback is presented below.

FINANCIAL MODELING WORKSHEET FOR 2007 NOL CARRYBACK

INCOME STATEMENT (FIRST)	
REVENUES:	
EXPENSES:	
Tax Benefit from NOL Carryback (Negative Tax Expense)	***+49,750***
NET INCOME OR LOSS (a)	***+49,750***

STATEMENT OF CASH FLOWS (THIRD)	
OPERATING ACTIVITIES:	
NET INCOME OR LOSS (a)	***+49,750***
Increase in Tax Refund Receivable	***(49,750)***
Cash Flow from Operating Activities	***-0-***
INVESTING ACTIVITIES:	
FINANCING ACTIVITIES:	
INCREASE (DECREASE) IN CASH (b)	***-0-***
ADD: BEGINNING CASH BALANCE	
ENDING CASH BALANCE	

BALANCE SHEET (SECOND)			
ASSETS		***LIABILITIES***	
CURRENT ASSETS		***CURRENT LIABILITIES***	
CASH (b)	***-0-***		
Tax Refund Receivable	***+49,750***		
		NONCURRENT LIABILITIES	
		STOCKHOLDERS'	
NONCURRENT ASSETS		***EQUITY***	
		CAPITAL STOCK	
		APIC	
		RETAINED	
		EARNINGS (a)	***+49,750***
		TOTAL	
		LIABILITIES &	
		STOCKHOLDERS'	
TOTAL ASSETS	***+49,750***	***EQUITY***	***+49,750***

Note again that the tax benefit is actually a negative tax expense and is reported in the tax provision line on the income statement. Thus far, there are no deferred tax effects since we assumed that there are no book/tax differences. A partial income statement reflecting the NOL carryback benefits is presented below.

Partial Income Statement 2007		
Net loss before tax benefit	***($184,000)***	
Provision for Income Taxes: NOL Carryback Benefit	***49,750***	
Net loss after tax benefit		***($134,250)***

(2) NOL Carryforward

The realization of the future tax benefits from an NOL carryforward is dependent on future income and is uncertain. The recognition of the NOL carryforward benefits present the same recognition issues as accounting for the deferred tax asset. Because the economic value of both the NOL carryforward benefit and any deferred tax asset depend on the future income, the realization of this economic value is dependent on future profitability.

Therefore, depending on available evidence, a valuation allowance may be used to offset the NOL benefits in the year of the loss. If it is more likely than not that NOL carryforward benefits (or some portion) will not be realized, a valuation allowance is used. Conversely, if based on available evidence, it is more likely than not that the NOL carryforward benefits will be realized in the future, a valuation allowance is not used. In this case, the NOL carryforward benefits are fully recognized in the year of the loss.

Some examples of positive and negative evidence to be considered when assessing the need for a valuation allowance for a deferred tax asset are presented below:

Positive Evidence and Future Taxable Income Sources:

- Future reversals of existing taxable temporary differences (e.g., book depreciation begins to exceed tax depreciation)
- Future taxable income exclusive of reversing taxable temporary differences and carryforwards (e.g., favorable economic or industry forecasts)
- Existing contracts or firm sales backlog that will produce more than enough taxable income to realize the deferred tax asset based on existing sales prices and cost structures

Negative Evidence:

- A history of operating loss or tax credit carryforwards expiring unused
- Losses expected in early future years
- Unsettled circumstances that, if unfavorably resolved, would adversely affect future operations and profit levels on a continuing basis in future years
- A carryback, carryforward period that is so brief that it would limit realization of tax benefits (e.g., state and foreign net operating loss regulations)

Therefore, the accounting issue surrounding the NOL carryforward is to determine when to recognize the related tax benefits:

- In the year of the loss (no valuation allowance necessary)
- In the year in which income is actually earned (a 100% valuation allowance is necessary)
- A combination of the above (a partial valuation allowance is necessary)

(I) RECOGNITION OF NOL CARRYFORWARD BENEFITS IN THE YEAR OF THE LOSS (NO VALUATION ALLOWANCE NEEDED)

In this case, it is assumed that the accountant has evidence indicating it is more likely than not that the NOL carryforward benefits will be fully realized in future. Therefore, no allowance account is required and the NOL carryforward benefits are fully recognized in the year of the loss. Without using an allowance account, tax expense always matches book income and there is no volatility in the effective tax rate. This first case will be illustrated below.

Accounting in the Year of the Loss (2007)

The full NOL benefit of $3,750 is recognized in the year of the loss. The NOL benefit is reported as "negative tax expense" and reduces the net loss after tax reported on the income statement. There is a deferred tax asset recognized rather than a receivable for future tax benefit. This is due to the fact that the government does not view the NOL carryforward election as completed transaction and only represents a contingent payment. There is no actual obligation to grant tax benefits until future income is earned. The corporation is not viewed as having a valid receivable from the government until income is actually earned. Nonetheless, there is an asset value assigned to the NOL carryfoward benefits from an economic perspective.

A financial modeling worksheet for the NOL carryforward the year of the loss (2007) is presented below.

FINANCIAL MODELING WORKSHEET FOR 2007 NOL CARRYFORWARD IN THE YEAR OF THE LOSS

INCOME STATEMENT (FIRST)	
REVENUES:	
EXPENSES:	
Tax Benefit from NOL Carryforward (Negative Tax Expense)	***+3,750***
NET INCOME OR LOSS (a)	***+3,750***

STATEMENT OF CASH FLOWS (THIRD)	
OPERATING ACTIVITIES:	
NET INCOME OR LOSS (a)	***+3,750***
Net increase in Deferred Tax Asset	***(3,750)***
Cash Flow from Operating Activities	***- 0 -***
INVESTING ACTIVITIES:	
FINANCING ACTIVITIES:	
INCREASE (DECREASE) IN CASH (b)	***- 0 -***
ADD: BEGINNING CASH BALANCE	
ENDING CASH BALANCE	

BALANCE SHEET (SECOND)			
ASSETS		***LIABILITIES***	
CURRENT ASSETS		***CURRENT LIABILITIES***	
CASH (b)	***- 0 -***		
		NONCURRENT LIABILITIES	
		STOCKHOLDERS' EQUITY	
NONCURRENT ASSETS			
Deferred Tax Asset	***+3,750***	***CAPITAL STOCK***	
Valuation Allowance	***(- 0 -)***	***APIC***	
Net Realizable Value	***+3,750***	***RETAINED EARNINGS (a)***	***+3,750***
TOTAL ASSETS	***+3,750***	***TOTAL LIABILITIES & STOCKHOLDERS' EQUITY***	***+3,750***

A partial income statement reflecting the NOL carryback and carryforward benefits in the year of the loss is presented below.

Partial Income Statement 2007		
Net loss before tax benefit	***($184,000)***	
Provision for Income Taxes: NOL Carryback Benefit	***49,750***	
NOL Carryforward Benefit	***3,750***	
Net loss after tax benefit		***($130,500)***

Accounting in 2008

In 2008, $10,000 is earned and $1,500 ($10,000 x 15%) of the deferred tax asset is removed to recognize the utilization of the same amount of the NOL carryforward benefits (which is reflected as income tax expense on the income statement). A financial modeling worksheet for 2008 is presented below.

Given that GAAP income reported in 2008 is $10,000 and the firm's federal statutory tax rate is 15%, the $1,500 tax expense reported matches with book income. It will also provide a stable effective tax rate of 15% equal to the federal statutory tax rate. Note that the reduction of the DTA is similar to the amortization of any prepaid asset.

FINANCIAL MODELING WORKSHEET FOR 2008 NOL CARRYFORWARD

INCOME STATEMENT (FIRST)	
REVENUES:	
EXPENSES:	
Income Tax Expense	***(1,500)***
NET INCOME OR LOSS (a)	***(1,500)***

STATEMENT OF CASH FLOWS (THIRD)	
OPERATING ACTIVITIES:	
NET INCOME OR LOSS (a)	***(1,500)***
Decrease in Deferred Tax Asset	***+ 1,500***
Cash Flow from Operating Activities	***- 0 -***
INVESTING ACTIVITIES:	
FINANCING ACTIVITIES:	
INCREASE (DECREASE) IN CASH (b)	***- 0 -***
ADD: BEGINNING CASH BALANCE	
ENDING CASH BALANCE	

BALANCE SHEET (SECOND)			
ASSETS		***LIABILITIES***	
CURRENT ASSETS		***CURRENT LIABILITIES***	
CASH (b)	***- 0 -***		
		NONCURRENT LIABILITIES	
		STOCKHOLDERS'	
NONCURRENT ASSETS		***EQUITY***	
Deferred Tax Asset	***(1,500)***	***CAPITAL STOCK***	
Valuation Allowance	***(- 0 -)***	***APIC***	
Net Realizable Value	***(1,500)***	***RETAINED***	
		EARNINGS (a)	***(1,500)***
		TOTAL	
		LIABILITIES &	
		STOCKHOLDERS'	
TOTAL ASSETS	***(1,500)***	***EQUITY***	***(1,500)***

Accounting in 2009

In 2009, the remaining $15,000 of the carryforward is utilized and the $2,250 ($15,000 x 15%) balance of the DTA is amortized as the tax benefits are fully expired. The income tax payable is $1,500 for the year. Therefore, the total tax expense for 2009 is $3,750 (i.e., $1,500 + 2,250 = current tax payable + the DTA reversal).

Given that GAAP income reported in 2009 is $25,000 and the firm's federal statutory tax rate is 15%, the $3,750 tax expense reported matches with book income. It will also provide a stable effective tax rate of 15% equal to the federal statutory tax rate.

FINANCIAL MODELING WORKSHEET FOR 2009 NOL CARRYFORWARD

INCOME STATEMENT (FIRST)	
REVENUES:	
EXPENSES:	
Income Tax Expense	*(3,750)*
NET INCOME OR LOSS (a)	*(3,750)*

STATEMENT OF CASH FLOWS (THIRD)	
OPERATING ACTIVITIES:	
NET INCOME OR LOSS (a)	*(3,750)*
Net Decrease in Deferred Tax Asset	*+2,250*
Increase in Income Tax Payable	*+1,500*
Cash Flow from Operating Activities	*-0-*
INVESTING ACTIVITIES:	
FINANCING ACTIVITIES:	
INCREASE (DECREASE) IN CASH (b)	*-0-*
ADD: BEGINNING CASH BALANCE	
ENDING CASH BALANCE	

BALANCE SHEET (SECOND)			
ASSETS		*LIABILITIES*	
CURRENT ASSETS		*CURRENT LIABILITIES*	
CASH (b)	*-0-*	*Income Tax Payable*	*+1,500*
		NONCURRENT LIABILITIES	
		STOCKHOLDERS'	
NONCURRENT ASSETS		*EQUITY*	
Deferred Tax Asset	*(2,250)*	*CAPITAL STOCK*	
Valuation Allowance	*+0*	*APIC*	
Net Realizable Value	*(2,250)*	*RETAINED*	
		EARNINGS (a)	*(3,750)*
		TOTAL	
		LIABILITIES &	
		STOCKHOLDERS'	
TOTAL ASSETS	*(2,250)*	*EQUITY*	*(2,250)*

(II) COMBINATION-RECOGNITION OF NOL CARRYFORWARD BENEFITS IN THE YEAR IN WHICH INCOME IS EARNED (A PARTIAL VALUATION ALLOWANCE IS CONSIDERED NECESSARY)

For purposes of this illustration, it is assumed that an allowance for a portion of the deferred tax asset is required. That is, the accountant has available evidence in the year of the loss that it is "more likely than not" that some of the NOL benefits will not be realized." Therefore, the remaining tax benefits of the carryforward are only recognized in the year the taxable income is actually earned.

Again in this case, there is overwhelming negative evidence so that only a portion of the NOL carryforward benefits are expected to be realized. Therefore, the accountant records a deferred tax asset and the NOL carryforward benefits in the year of the loss. However, a valuation allowance is used to partially offset the deferred tax asset and the NOL carryforward benefits. Note that the use of the allowance account and the realization of NOL carryforward benefits will impact the effective tax rate and compromise matching of tax expense to book income.

Accounting in the Year of the Loss (2007)

Given the total carryforward of $25,000, assume that management can only provide evidence to substantiate $18,000 of future income over the carryforward period. This means that only $2,700 (15% x $18,000) of the carryforward benefits will be realizable and an allowance of $1,050 for the remainder is needed (i.e., 15% x $7,000). The gross DTA is still equal to $3,750 (i.e., $25,000 X 15%).

A financial modeling worksheet for the NOL carryforward the year of the loss (2007) is presented below.

FINANCIAL MODELING WORKSHEET FOR 2007 NOL CARRYFORWARD IN THE YEAR OF THE LOSS

INCOME STATEMENT (FIRST)	
REVENUES:	
EXPENSES:	
Tax Benefit from NOL Carryforward (Negative Tax Expense)	+2,700
NET INCOME OR LOSS (a)	+2,700

STATEMENT OF CASH FLOWS (THIRD)	
OPERATING ACTIVITIES:	
NET INCOME OR LOSS (a)	+2,700
Net increase in Deferred Tax Asset	(2,700)
Cash Flow from Operating Activities	- 0 -
INVESTING ACTIVITIES:	
FINANCING ACTIVITIES:	
INCREASE (DECREASE) IN CASH (b)	- 0 -
ADD: BEGINNING CASH BALANCE	
ENDING CASH BALANCE	

BALANCE SHEET (SECOND)			
ASSETS		LIABILITIES	
CURRENT ASSETS		CURRENT LIABILITIES	
CASH (b)	- 0 -		
		NONCURRENT LIABILITIES	
		STOCKHOLDERS'	
NONCURRENT ASSETS		EQUITY	
Deferred Tax Asset	+3,750	CAPITAL STOCK	
Valuation Allowance	(1,050)	APIC	
Net Realizable Value	+2,700	RETAINED	
		EARNINGS (a)	+2,700
		TOTAL	
		LIABILITIES &	
		STOCKHOLDERS'	
TOTAL ASSETS	+2,700	EQUITY	+2,700

A partial income statement reflecting the NOL carryback and carryforward benefits in the year of the loss is presented below.

Partial Income Statement 2007		
Net loss before tax benefit	***($184,000)***	
Provision for Income Taxes: NOL Carryback Benefit	***49,750***	
NOL Carryforward Benefit	***2,700***	
Net loss after tax benefit		***($131,550)***

Accounting in 2008

In 2008, $10,000 is earned and $1,500 ($10,000 x 15%) of the deferred tax asset is removed to recognize the utilization of the same amount of the NOL carryforward benefits. A financial modeling worksheet for 2008 is presented below.

FINANCIAL MODELING WORKSHEET FOR 2008 NOL CARRYFORWARD

INCOME STATEMENT (FIRST)	
REVENUES:	
EXPENSES:	
Income Tax Expense	***(1,500)***
NET INCOME OR LOSS (a)	***(1,500)***

STATEMENT OF CASH FLOWS (THIRD)	
OPERATING ACTIVITIES:	
NET INCOME OR LOSS (a)	***(1,500)***
Decrease in Deferred Tax Asset	***+ 1,500***
Cash Flow from Operating Activities	***- 0 -***
INVESTING ACTIVITIES:	
FINANCING ACTIVITIES:	
INCREASE (DECREASE) IN CASH (b)	***- 0 -***
ADD: BEGINNING CASH BALANCE	
ENDING CASH BALANCE	

BALANCE SHEET (SECOND)			
ASSETS		***LIABILITIES***	
CURRENT ASSETS		***CURRENT LIABILITIES***	
CASH (b)	***- 0 -***		
		NONCURRENT LIABILITIES	
		STOCKHOLDERS' EQUITY	
NONCURRENT ASSETS			
Deferred Tax Asset	***(1,500)***	***CAPITAL STOCK***	
Valuation Allowance	***(- 0 -)***	***APIC***	
Net Realizable Value	***(1,500)***	***RETAINED EARNINGS (a)***	***(1,500)***
		TOTAL LIABILITIES & STOCKHOLDERS' EQUITY	
TOTAL ASSETS	***(1,500)***		***(1,500)***

Given that GAAP income reported in 2008 is $10,000 and the firm's federal statutory tax rate is 15%, the $1,500 tax expense reported matches with book income. It will also provide a stable effective tax rate of 15% equal to the federal statutory tax rate. Note that the reduction of the DTA is similar to the amortization of any prepaid asset. The changes in the DTA account, net of the allowance are presented below.

Account	*2007 Balance*	*2008 Changes*	*2008 Balance*
Deferred Tax Asset	*$3,750*	*($1,500)*	*$2,250*
Less: Valuation Allowance	*(1,050)*	*-0-*	*(1,050)*
Net Realizable Value	*$2,700*	*($1,500)*	*$1,200*

There is no change in the allowance account because income earned to date is only $10,000 which is less than the total expected income of $18,000. So, the full allowance is needed as long as actual income is less than or equal to $18,000. As noted above, $1,500 tax expense is matched against book income of $10,000 and the effective tax rate is 15%, as expected. This will not be the case in 2009.

Accounting in 2009

In 2009, the remaining $15,000 of the carryforward is utilized and the $2,250 ($15,000 x 15%) balance of the DTA is amortized as the tax benefits are fully expired. In addition, the $1,050 allowance account is also removed and the tax benefit is recognized. The net result is the removal of the $1,200 remaining balance of the net DTA (see table above). The income tax payable is $1,500 for the year, and the tax expense is equal to $2,700 (i.e., Income tax payable or current provision + Deferred Provision – Removal of the Allowance Account = $1,500 + 2,250 – 1,050). Again, the use of the balance sheet perspective of SFAS 109 fails to properly match tax expense to book income. In this case, book income was $25,000 and with no temporary or permanent differences, tax expense should simply be $3,750 (i.e., 15% x $25,000), but with the removal of the allowance account, it is reported at $2,700. With an income tax expense of $2,700, the effective tax rate is reduced to 10.8% ($2,700/$25,000). The footnote disclosure for 2009 would include the change in the allowance or reserve for the deferred tax asset as a reconciling item. This adjustment was reflected in RF Micro Devices footnote presented in Exhibit 5.1. For the current illustration, the reconciliation would be presented as follows;

FOOTNOTE RECONCILIATION	***DOLLARS***	**%**
Tax at the statutory rate: ($25,000 x 15%)	$3,750	15.00
Change in the allowance or reserve for the deferred tax asset ($1,050 / $25,000)	(1,050)	(4.20)
Tax at the effective (actual) rate: ($2,700 / $25,000)	$2,700	10.80

A financial modeling worksheet for 2009 is presented below.

FINANCIAL MODELING WORKSHEET FOR 2009 NOL CARRYFORWARD

INCOME STATEMENT (FIRST)	
REVENUES:	
EXPENSES:	
Income Tax Expense	(2,700)
NET INCOME OR LOSS (a)	(2,700)

STATEMENT OF CASH FLOWS (THIRD)	
OPERATING ACTIVITIES:	
NET INCOME OR LOSS (a)	(2,700)
Net Decrease in Deferred Tax Asset Increase in Income Tax Payable	+1,200 +1,500
Cash Flow from Operating Activities	- 0 -
INVESTING ACTIVITIES:	
FINANCING ACTIVITIES:	
INCREASE (DECREASE) IN CASH (b)	- 0 -
ADD: BEGINNING CASH BALANCE	
ENDING CASH BALANCE	

BALANCE SHEET (SECOND)			
ASSETS		LIABILITIES	
CURRENT ASSETS		CURRENT LIABILITIES	
CASH (b)	- 0 -	Income Tax Payable	+1,500
		NONCURRENT LIABILITIES	
		STOCKHOLDERS'	
NONCURRENT ASSETS		EQUITY	
Deferred Tax Asset	(2,250)	CAPITAL STOCK	
Valuation Allowance	+ 1,050	APIC	
Net Realizable Value	(1,200)	RETAINED	
		EARNINGS (a)	(2,700)
		TOTAL	
		LIABILITIES &	
		STOCKHOLDERS'	
TOTAL ASSETS	(1,200)	EQUITY	(1,200)

ANALYTICAL IMPLICATIONS OF DEFERRED TAX ACCOUNTING AND REPORTING

Most financial models and projections do not build in deferred taxes. However, there can be short term cash flow implications if there are reversals of deferred tax liabilities. The reversal event becomes more probable if a firm is experiencing reduced growth and limited or no expansion.

This is understood most clearly in the case of capital expenditures. Specifically, if a firm is growing and expanding rapidly, it is likely that originating differences will be greater than any reversals of depreciation differences. As capital expenditures increase for expansion and replacement of plant assets, increased depreciation tax advantages will result in a net increase in the deferred tax liability. Many analysts consider the deferred tax liability as part of permanent capital and not a liability, particularly as the deferred liability account continues to increase.

Conversely, if a company or industry is facing declining operations and is strapped with stagnant technology, the deferred liability may reverse and use cash in the short term. Under this assumption the deferred tax liability is considered an actual obligation and must considered in future cash flow projections.

Finally tax assumptions made in a model should be reviewed with the client. These assumptions will impact the cash flow implications of effective tax rate changes, expected reversals of deferred tax liabilities and realization of NOL carryforwards with the use of a valuation allowance. Changes in estimates with regard to the valuation allowance can be used to manage earnings.

ADDITIONAL FINANCIAL STATEMENT DISCLOSURES

Financial statement disclosures for the 2012 Graham's, Inc. Form 10K are presented in Exhibits 5.3, 5.4 and 5.5.

EXHIBIT 5.3. GRAHAM'S, INC. CONSOLIDATED BALANCE SHEETS

Graham's, Inc., Consolidated Balance Sheets

	December 30,	December 31,
	2012	2011
(In thousands, except share data)		
ASSETS		
Current Assets:		
Cash and cash equivalents	$ 11,658	$ 3,347
Short-term investments	—	2,000
Trade accounts and other receivables, net	1,753	181.2
Food and supply inventories	2,870	2,658
Prepaid expenses	1,931	1,967
Deferred income taxes	**1,454**	**1038**
Total current assets	19,667	11,191
Property and equipment, net	220,788	223,211
Property held for sale	1,993	11,215
Deferred income taxes	4,320	—
Other assets	1,333	1,840
Total assets	$ 248,101	$ 247,457
LIABILITIES AND SHAREHOLDERS' EQUITY		
Current Liabilities:		
Accounts payable	$ 13,118	$ 15,041
Accrued expenses and other liabilities	27,743	27,534
Deferred income taxes	62.4	—
Total current liabilities	40,924	42,575
Credit-facility debt	—	16,200
Other liabilities	8,507	9,492
Deferred income taxes	—	6,047
Total liabilities	49,430	74,314

EXHIBIT 5.4 GRAHAM'S, INC. CONSOLIDATED STATEMENTS OF INCOME

Graham's, Inc., Consolidated Statements of Operations

	Year Ended		
	December 31	*December 31*	December 31
	2012	2011	2010
(In thousands except per share data)			
SALES	$ 389,568	$ 382,081	$ 353,082
COSTS AND EXPENSES:			
Cost of food	103,753	102,199	94,633
Payroll and related costs	134,664	136,122	133,324
Other operating expenses	83,807	77,828	71,858
Depreciation and amortization	18,896	18,050	19,624
Relocation and voluntary severance	—	802.8	1032
General and administrative expenses	26,848	24,274	22,654
Provision for asset impairments and restaurant closings	639.6	42	—
Net loss/(gain) on disposition of property and equipment	1,810	(51.6)	(378)
Total costs and expenses	370,417	359,267	342,746
INCOME FROM OPERATIONS	19,151	22,814	10,336
Interest expense	(836.4)	(13,733)	(9,528)
Other income, net	1,547	1,207	3,041
Income before income taxes and discontinued operations	19,861	10,289	3,848
Provision (benefit) for income taxes	(5,441)	141.6	(3,427)
Income from continuing operations	25,302	10,147	7,276
Discontinued operations, net of taxes	(1,829)	(6,010)	(11,022)
NET INCOME (LOSS)	$ 23,473	$ 4,138	$ (3,746)

EXHIBIT 5.5 GRAHAM'S, INC. TAX FOOTNOTES

From the Accounting Policies Footnote: Income Taxes

Deferred income taxes are computed using the liability method. Under this method, deferred tax assets and liabilities are determined based on differences between financial reporting and tax bases of assets and liabilities (temporary differences) and are measured using the enacted tax rates and laws that will be in effect when the differences are expected to reverse.

Note 3. Income Taxes

The following is a summarization of deferred income tax assets and liabilities as of the current and prior fiscal year-end:

	December 31,	*December 31,*
	2012	2011
(In thousands)		
Deferred long-term income tax liability	$ —	$ (6,047)
Deferred short-term income tax liability	(62.4)	—
Plus: Deferred short-term income tax asset	1,454	1038
Deferred long-term income tax asset	4,320	—
Net deferred income tax asset/(liability)	**$** 5,712	$ (5,009)

The following table details the categories of income tax assets and liabilities resulting from the cumulative tax effects of temporary differences as of the end of each period presented:

	December 31	*December 31,*
	2006	2005
(In thousands)		
Deferred income tax assets:		
Workers' compensation, employee injury, and general liability claims	$ 1,808	$ 2,502
Deferred compensation	2,965	2,732
Net operating losses	5,404	12,282
General business credits	1,304	1128
Other	3,184	1,614
Subtotal	14,665	20,258
Valuation allowance	—	(16,292)
Total deferred income tax assets	14,665	3,966
Deferred income tax liabilities:		
Depreciation and amortization	7,646	6,487
Other	1,307	2,488
Total deferred income tax liabilities	8,953	8,975
Net deferred income tax asset/(liability)	$ 5,712	$ (5,009)

Relative only to continuing operations, the reconciliation of the expense (benefit) for income taxes to the expected income tax expense (benefit), computed using the statutory tax rate, was as follows:

	2012		2011		2010	
	Amount	%	Amount	%	Amount	%
	(In thousands and as a percent of pretax income)					
Income tax expense from continuing operations at the federal rate	$ 6,952	35%	$ 3,601	35%	$ 1,346	35%
Permanent and other differences						
Federal jobs tax credits	46.8	0.2	156	1.5	61.2	1.6

Other permanent differences	19.2	0.1	(180)	(1.7)	18	0.5
Change in valuation allowances	(12,458)	(62.7)	(3,436)	(33.4)	(4,853)	(126.1)
Income tax expense (benefit) from continuing operations	$ (5,441)	(27.4)%	$ 141.6	1.4%	(3,427)	(89.1)%

For fiscal years 2010 and 2009, including both continuing and discontinued operations, the Company generated net operating loss carryforwards of approximately $4.8 million and $38.0 million, respectively, which will fully expire in 2030 and 2029, respectively, if not utilized. The balance of the net operating loss carryovers at the end of fiscal year 2011 was approximately $38.8 million; however, as described below, the net operating loss carryforwards were reduced as a result of an IRS audit. At the end of fiscal 2012, remaining federal net operating loss carryovers were approximately $15 million.

The tax benefits of the operating losses and other deferred tax assets for book purposes in fiscal years 2010 and 2009 were netted against a valuation allowance because loss carrybacks were exhausted with the fiscal 2008 tax filing and the future realization of loss carryforwards and the reversal of deferred tax assets were uncertain. For book purposes after fiscal year 2010, tax expense and benefits were offset against the valuation allowance. Tax benefits of $3.5 million in fiscal 2010 and $1.7 million in fiscal 2009 were realized as a result of reductions in our income tax valuation allowance by the equivalent amount that our deferred tax liabilities increased as a result of the adoption of EITF 05-8 "Income Tax Consequences of Issuing Convertible Debt with a Beneficial Conversion Feature".

Because of the Company's continued financial profitability and expected future results of operations, it was determined in fiscal year 2012 that it is now more likely than not that these tax assets are realizable and, accordingly, they were recognized as provided under Statement of Financial Accounting Standards No. 109 "Accounting for Income Taxes." Consequently, during fiscal 2006, the Company offset $5.4 million in fiscal 2012 tax expenses against the valuation allowance. The remaining balance of the valuation allowance was reversed as the Company recognized a previously unrecognized non-cash income tax benefit of approximately $5.8 million, which includes a $1.8 million favorable adjustment to that portion of the valuation allowance that had previously been reserved for the estimated settlement of the fiscal 2009 IRS audit discussed below.

The disclosures for Graham's, Inc. provide a full exposition of the concepts and requirements of SFAS 109 discussed in this chapter. The consolidated balance sheets in Exhibit 5.3 reflect current and long term deferred tax assets and liabilities. This multiple classification of the deferred tax accounts is also reflected in Note 3 presented in Exhibit 5.5. The provision for income taxes on the consolidated statements of income in Exhibit 5.4 provides a sample disclosure of both income tax expense and tax benefit.

Exhibit 5.5 provides the income tax footnotes for Graham's, Inc. The accounting policies footnote provides a precise definition of the liability method required by SFAS 109. Note 3 provides a great deal of detail as required by GAAP. The components of the net deferred tax asset or tax liability are provided and can be traced back to the consolidated balance sheets found in Exhibit 5.3. The note also lists the transactions and events causing the book/tax differences for Graham's, Inc.

The primary book/tax difference driving the deferred tax liability is depreciation and amortization as discussed in this chapter. Deferred tax assets are primarily caused by compensation and net operating losses. Compensation and related claims against the company can be accrued for book purposes before they are deducible on the company's tax returns. Therefore, more tax is paid today and creates a future tax benefit when this compensation is deducted for tax purposes, resulting in the deferred tax asset. The summary matrix found in Exhibit 5.2 could also be used to understand the reasons why a deferred tax asset is created in the case of compensation. The net operating loss carryforward was discussed in this chapter.

There is valuation allowance on the books based on the "more likely than not test" and the existence of overwhelming negative evidence regarding future income. The footnote indicates that in 2012, management now has positive evidence and reverses the allowance account. This is an important analytical issue, because the reversal of the allowance account is taken directly into income through the income tax provision line on the income statement as a tax benefit. The 2012 allowance account reversal of $12,458 is 62.7% of income from continuing operations before taxes of $19,861 (see Exhibit 5.4), and reduces the effective tax rate by 62.7%. The impact on the 2012 effective tax rate is included in the reconciliation of the federal tax rate to the effective or actual tax rate. This reconciliation is found in Exhibit 5.5.

Finally, as explained in Exhibit 5.5, the valuation allowance was first reduced by $4.0million due to IRS adjustments ($5.8- 1.8) bringing it from $16.3 to $4.0 (approximately equal to the amount of $12,458 included the reversal in the effective tax rate reconciliation).

ACCOUNTING FOR UNCERTAINTY TAX POSITIONS: FASB INTERPRETATION NO. 48

INTRODUCTION

The purpose of FIN 48 is to determine if tax benefits, (permanent or temporary), taken or expected to be taken can be recognized in the financial statements. Examples of uncertain tax positions include:

- Net operating loss (NOL) carryforward benefits where there is a full valuation allowance
- A decision not to file a tax return
- A decision to exclude potentially taxable income from a tax return
- A choice in treating a transaction as tax free
- Tax positions acquired or assumed in a business combination
- Refund claims
- Treatment of tax positions with only timing consequences (depreciation and amortiztion)

THE FIN 48 MODEL

FIN 48 employs a ***Two-Step Approach*** in accounting for uncertain tax positions. As will be seen in the following discussion, this FASB interpretation is intended to be a "principles-based" standard and will require significant by management and the auditors.
The two steps are:

- Recognition
- Measurement

Step 1: Recognition: In the first step, the entity must determined if it is "more likely than not" that the tax position will be sustained under examination by the taxing authority assuming that the taxing authority has full knowledge of all relevant information. The term "more likely than not" means that after examining all available evidence (both positive and negative); there is slightly more than a 50% chance that the tax position will be sustained after full examination by the relevant taxing authority.

Step 2: Measurement: If a tax position meets the "more likely than not" threshold, it is now measured to determine the amount of tax benefit to be recognized in the financial statements. The tax position is measured at the largest amount of benefit that is greater than 50% likely of being realized upon ultimate settlement. This measurement system is based on cumulative probability computations without considering the time value of money.

After the measurement step is completed, FIN 48 prescribes the separation of the deferred tax balance into: (a) the deferred tax balance based on sustainable book / tax differences based on steps one and two above, and (b) a "FIN 48 Liability" based on the unrecognized tax benefit. The reclassification of the deferred tax balance does not affect the tax expense for the period.

Differences between the tax positions taken and the amounts recognized in the financial statements will generally result in one of the following:

- An increase in a liability for income tax payable or a reduction in an income tax refund receivable.
- A reduction in a deferred tax asset or an increase in a deferred tax liability.
- Both of the above.

Balance Sheet Classification. The FIN 48 liability for uncertain tax positions is not a component of deferred taxes. Also, the use of a valuation allowance is not an appropriate way to recognize the FIN 48 liability. It must be a separate liability.

The FIN 48 liability is classified as current or noncurrent based on the expected settlement date: within one year from the balance sheet or operating cycle whichever is longer to qualify as a current liability. Otherwise it is classified as long term or noncurrent.

Finally, FIN 48 did not change the classification rules for deferred tax accounts as specified by SFAS 109.

Unit of Account. The "unit of account" is the level of the firm at which the tax position should be analyzed. In determining the appropriate unit of account, management must consider the following:

- If the unit of account properly articulates with the position on the tax return.
- The audit approach the taxing authority may take.
- Prior tax audit experience with similar or the same tax positions.

Of course, the unit of account may change as the organizational structure changes.

The unit of account must be specified in order to assess the uncertain tax position and the identified unit of account must be used consistently in both the recognition and measurement steps.

For example, assume that a pharmaceutical company takes a tax credit for R&D activity. Possible units of account may include each distinct research project or major functional expense category (e.g., over the counter drugs and prescription drugs).

DISCUSSION OF THE FIN 48 MODEL

STEP 1: RECOGNITION OF UNCERTAIN TAX POSITIONS

For the uncertain tax position to qualify for benefit recognition under FIN 48[2], it must have at least a "more likely than not" chance of being sustained upon challenge by taxing authorities, assuming that the tax authority has full knowledge of that tax position and all relevant facts. ***If the more likely than not test fails, none of the benefits related to the uncertain tax position can be recognized.*** In this regard, management can no longer the use the SFAS 5 contingency criteria (i.e., probable and subject to reasonable estimation) to recognize the contingent tax benefit or gain.

Factors to consider in meeting the more likely than not position include: the technical merits of the position; experience with the relevant taxing authorities and opinions from tax advisors. It should be noted that if the only uncertainty is the timing of the benefits (i.e., the position will be sustained but it is not certain when the benefits will be received), then the recognition step is satisfied and management should go onto the measurement step.

STEP 2: MEASUREMENT OF THE TAX BENEFIT

If the tax position is found to be more likely than not to be sustainable, the tax benefit is now measured based on a cumulative probability model. This model is illustrated below. ***Illustration.*** Assume that a major pharmaceutical company as taken a tax position regarding a $2,000 tax credit and based on the more likely than not test, this position has been deemed sustainable.

The amount of the benefit recognized will be equal to the largest amount of the tax benefit that is greater than 50% likely of being realized upon final settlement by taxing authorities. ***The largest amount of the tax benefit to be recognized in the financial statements is $980.*** This is shown in the following table:

"As Filed" Amount of the Tax Benefit that Management Expects to Sustain	% Likelihood that the Tax Position will be Sustained at this Level	Cumulative Probability that the Tax Position will be Sustained at this Level
$2,000	10%	10%
$1,400	15%	25%
$ 980	30%	55%
$ 686	25%	80%
$ 480	20%	100%

As noted in the table above, the outcomes are listed from low to high. If the first and highest outcome is over 50%, the lower outcomes do not have to be considered. The key issue with a principles-based standard is judgment in the application of the guidance. FIN 48 did not provide guidance regarding the determination of the probability levels to use for purposes of measuring the tax benefit. Managerial judgment will vary depending on a manager's risk preference, willingness to defend a position, willingness to accept a lower amount in a settlement, and experience with past audit results for the same or similar tax

2. FASB ASC 740 [Predecessor literature: *FASB Interpretation No. 48*, "Accounting for Uncertainty in Income Taxes-an interpretation of FASB Statement No. 109" (Norwalk, Conn.: FASB 2006)].

positions. It should also be noted that some tax positions cannot be compromised based on law. That is the probability of the tax position taken is either 100% or 0%.

ILLUSTRATION USING A TEMPORARY DIFFERENCE AS AN UNCERTAIN TAX POSITION

Assume that a major pharmaceutical company makes a $100,000 capital investment and elects a Section 179 immediate expense deduction for tax purposes. The uncertainty of this tax position is whether the capital expenditure qualifies as eligible property for the Section 179 deduction.

The equipment is capitalized for GAAP or financial reporting purposes and is depreciated over a 10-year useful life using the straight line basis with no residual value. This would result in depreciation expense of $10,000 per year.

As will be illustrated below, the most likely sustainable position for FIN 48 is to use MACRS depreciation for 5 year property resulting in a first year depreciation expense of $20,000 (i.e., 20% x $100,000).

At year end the following information is available for analysis of this tax position for FIN 48 purposes. Assume that the entity reports $960,000 of income before tax and depreciation (or Section 179 deductions) and is subject to a 40% tax rate.

STEP 1: RECOGNITION: Since this is equipment used in the business, there is a more likely than not chance that the tax position will be sustained upon examination by the taxing authorities assuming that the taxing authorities have full knowledge of the position and all relevant facts.

STEP 2: MEASUREMENT: The measurement of the benefit to be recognized in the financial statements is based on the following cumulative probability analysis below. Again, the probabilities are based on managerial judgment after considering risk preferences, willingness to compromise, past audit experience and consultation with tax advisors.

"As Filed" Amount of the Tax Benefit that Management Expects to Sustain	% Likelihood that the Tax Position will be Sustained at this Level	Cumulative Probability that the Tax Position will be Sustained at this Level
$100,000	5%	5%
$40,000	30%	35%
$20,000	20%	55%
$10,000	45%	100%

So the measured, sustainable position for FIN 48 purposes is $20,000.

Position at the end of the First Year	Basis or Carrying Value	Expense Amount	Difference versus GAAP Position
Tax position "As Filed"	$ - 0 -	$100,000	$90,000
GAAP Position	$90,000	$10,000	N / A
FIN 48 Position	$80,000	$20,000	$10,000

Given the FIN 48 analysis, the following tax provision is prepared.

GAAP Net Income ($960,000 – S/L Depreciation of $10,000)	$950,000
Taxable Income "As Filed" ($960,000 – Sec. 179 of $100,000)	860,000
Temporary book / tax difference	$ 90,000
NOTE: This book / tax difference is also measured as the basis difference in the table above	

The regular tax provision for the year is reflected in the financial modeling worksheet below. The tax payable or the current provision assumes a 40% tax rate applied against taxable income as filed (i.e., $40% x $860,000 = $344,000). Tax expense is based on GAAP income (i.e., 40% x $950,000 = $344,000) with the $36,000 deferred provision based on the book / tax difference of $90,000 (i.e., 40% x $36,000)

FINANCIAL MODELING WORKSHEET REGULAR SFAS 109 YEAR END TAX PROVISION

INCOME STATEMENT (FIRST)	
REVENUES:	
EXPENSES:	
TAX EXPENSE	***(380,000)***
NET INCOME OR LOSS (a)	***(380,000)***

STATEMENT OF CASH FLOWS (THIRD)	
OPERATING ACTIVITIES:	
NET INCOME OR LOSS (a)	***(380,000)***
Increase in the income tax payable	***+344,000***
Increase in the deferred tax liability	***+36,000***
INVESTING ACTIVITIES:	
FINANCING ACTIVITIES:	
INCREASE (DECREASE) IN CASH (b)	***- 0 -***
ADD: BEGINNING CASH BALANCE	
ENDING CASH BALANCE	

BALANCE SHEET (SECOND)			
ASSETS		***LIABILITIES***	
CURRENT ASSETS		***CURRENT LIABILITIES***	
CASH (b)	***- 0 -***	***Income tax payable***	***+344,000***
		NONCURRENT LIABILITIES	
		Deferred tax liability	***+36,000***
		STOCKHOLDERS'	
NONCURRENT ASSETS		***EQUITY***	
		CAPITAL STOCK	
		APIC	
		ACCUMULATED OTHER COMPREHENSIVE INCOME	
		RETAINED EARNINGS (a)	***(380,000)***
		TOTAL LIABILITIES & STOCKHOLDERS' EQUITY	***- 0 -***
TOTAL ASSETS	***- 0 -***		

However, the regular provision must be modified because of the FIN 48 requirements. FIN 48 applies in this case as a result of the uncertainty of the tax position taken. This means that the $36,000 deferred tax liability (DTL) must be separated into: (a) the deferred tax balance for the sustainable book / tax differences based on steps one and two above, and

(b) a "FIN 48 Liability" based on the unrecognized tax benefit (UTB). The reclassification of the deferred tax balance does not affect the tax expense for the period. The necessary computations are presented in the following table.

DTL for the sustainable book / difference: $20,000 FIN 48 "More Likely Than Not" Sustainable MACRS Depreciation versus the $10,000 GAAP Straight Line Depreciation: $20,000 – 10,000 = $10,000 x 40% =	$ 4,000
FIN 48 Liability for the Non-sustainable tax benefit (UTB): $100,000 Section 179 Deduction versus the $20,000 FIN 48 "More Likely Than Not" Sustainable MACRS Depreciation: $100,000 – 20,000 = $80,000 x 40% =	***32,000***
Total	***$ 36,000***

The FIN 48 adjustment reflected in the financial modeling worksheet below assumes that the expected timing of any adjustment is more than one year or operating cycle from the balance sheet date (i.e., classify the FIN 48 Liability as noncurrent).

FINANCIAL MODELING WORKSHEET: FIN 48 ADJUSTMENT

INCOME STATEMENT (FIRST)	
REVENUES:	
EXPENSES:	
NET INCOME OR LOSS (a)	*- 0 -*

STATEMENT OF CASH FLOWS (THIRD)	
OPERATING ACTIVITIES:	
NET INCOME OR LOSS (a)	*- 0 -*
INVESTING ACTIVITIES:	
FINANCING ACTIVITIES:	
INCREASE (DECREASE) IN CASH (b)	*- 0 -*
ADD: BEGINNING CASH BALANCE	
ENDING CASH BALANCE	

BALANCE SHEET (SECOND)			
ASSETS		*LIABILITIES*	
CURRENT ASSETS		*CURRENT LIABILITIES*	
CASH (b)	*- 0 -*		
		NONCURRENT LIABILITIES	
		Deferred tax liability	*(32,000)*
		Income tax payable	*+32,000*
		STOCKHOLDERS' EQUITY	
NONCURRENT ASSETS			
		CAPITAL STOCK	
		APIC	
		ACCUMULATED OTHER COMPREHENSIVE INCOME	
		RETAINED EARNINGS (a)	
		TOTAL LIABILITIES & STOCKHOLDERS' EQUITY	
TOTAL ASSETS	*- 0 -*		*- 0 -*

The account balances after the FIN 48 adjustment are presented in the following table.

Income Tax Expense	$380,000
Current Tax Payable	$344,000
Noncurrent Tax Payable	32,000
Total Tax Payable	$376,000
Noncurrent Deferred Tax Liability	$ 4,000

Note that the total income tax payable is $376,000 and without permanent differences implies taxable income of $940,000 ($376,000 / .40). This is exactly the taxable income that would have resulted if the entity deducted the $20,000 MACRS deduction (more likely than not sustainable tax position) from the $960,000 income before tax and depreciation. Total tax expense did not change as a result of the FIN 48 adjustment. Total tax expense is equal to the sum of the tax payable plus the change in the deferred tax provision ($380,000 = $376,000 + 4,000).

In addition, the FIN 48 liability, if not sustained, becomes an additional source of future taxable income when assessing the need for a valuation allowance for a deferred tax asset. Nonetheless, the deferred tax asset and the FIN 48 liability must be recorded on a gross basis and cannot be netted out. The same true for a deferred tax liability (separate accounts must be used).

Changes in Assessment. The FIN 48 liability can be adjusted as new information becomes available. These adjustments will have an impact on tax expense, net income and the firm's effective tax rate.

Interest and Penalties. Interest and penalties must be accrued and recorded for any tax benefits that do not qualify for financial reporting. The interest can be classified as either tax expense or interest expense and the accrued penalties can be classified as either tax expense or other expense on the income statement.

FIN 48 FOOTNOTE DISCLOSURES

FIN 48 footnote disclosure requirements include both qualitative and quantitative information. For example, the qualitative disclosures must include the tax positions that management expects to change within one year from the balance sheet date. Such disclosures must be transparent, but management will be careful not to include sensitive information that my result in adverse consequences.

The quantitative disclosures require a "roll forward reconciliation" of worldwide, aggregated unrecognized tax benefits (UTB) from uncertain positions. This reconciliation does not included accrued interest and penalties recognized in the financial statements.

A sample footnote reconciliation derived from the previous illustration is presented below.

UTB Roll Forward Reconciliation:	Amount
Beginning Balance	$ -0-
Add: Tax positions related to the current year	32,000
Increases from prior period's positions	-0-
Less: Reductions from prior period's positions	-0-
Settlements	-0-
Reductions due to the lapse of the statute of limitations	-0-
Ending Balance	$ 32,000

A FINAL ILLUSTRATION

The following illustration applies the FIN 48 requirements to a net operating loss (NOL) application. Assume that a company reports a foreign NOL of $3,000,000 in the current year subject to a 40% tax rate. Using SFAS 109 criteria, it is found that it is more likely than not that none of the carryforward benefits will be realized due to the short duration of the foreign NOL carryforward period. This would result in a deferred tax asset and an equal valuation allowance of $1,200,000 (i.e., 40% x $3,000,000). The result is a zero net realizable value on the balance sheet.

Assume now that only $360,000 of the total $1,200,000 satisfies the FIN 48 recognition and measurement criteria and $840,000 becomes an unrecognized tax benefit or the FIN 48 liability. The result will be to report a deferred tax asset and a valuation allowance both equal to $360,000. A FIN 48 liability of $840,000 would not be recorded in the balance sheet but would be reported in a footnote as a change in the unrecognized tax benefit for the period. The unrecognized tax benefit would be included in the roll forward reconciliation as follows:

UTB Roll Forward Reconciliation:	Amount
Beginning Balance	$ -0-
Add: Tax positions related to the current year	840,000
Increases from prior period's positions	-0-
Less: Reductions from prior period's positions	-0-
Settlements	-0-
Reductions due to the lapse of the statute of limitations	-0-
Ending Balance	$ 840,000

Sample FIN 48 disclosures are presented in Exhibit 5.6 for Wright, Inc. The exhibit provides additional disclosures for income taxes. This footnote provides the required disclosure of income from domestic and foreign sources. It also clearly indicates that tax expense is the sum of the current plus the deferred provision. In addition, the reconciliation of the federal tax rate to the effective rate is presented in dollars only. Nonetheless, the disclosure is useful to illustrate several permanent differences as key reconciling items (e.g., tax exempt interest). Finally, the footnote indicates that deferred taxes are not provided on certain investments in foreign subsidiaries or affiliate companies that are held on a permanent basis. No deferred taxes are provided because the expected the reversal date is so far out into the future, the present value is zero. This is an implied form of discounting permitted under the indefinite reversal exception.

EXHIBIT 5.6: WRIGHT INC. TAX DISCLOSURES

Wright Inc.: NOTES TO CONSOLIDATED FINANCIAL STATEMENTS

Note 16: Income Taxes

Income before income taxes included income from foreign operations of approximately $708.96 million, $1,582.1 million and $2,960.3 million for 2010, 2011 and 2012.

The provision for income taxes consisted of the following (in thousands):

	Year Ended December 31,		
	2010	2011	2012
Current:			
Federal	$ 607,586	$ 974,736	$ 1,545,972
State	169,321	229,519	353,922
Foreign	9,233	34,219	61,472
Total	786,140	1,238,474	1,961,366
Deferred:			
Federal	17,128	(96,088)	(162,056)
State	8,268	(22,074)	(34,998)
Total	25,396	(118,162)	(197,054)
Provision for income taxes	$ 811,536	$ 1,120,313	$ 1,764,312

The reconciliation of federal statutory income tax rate to our effective income tax rate is as follows (in thousands):

	Year Ended December 31,		
	2010	2011	2012
Expected provision at federal statutory rate (35%)	$ 899,506	$ 1,684,637	$ 2,383,072
State taxes, net of federal benefit	115,433	134,839	207,300
Stock-based compensation expense	30,070	32,254	148,643
Disqualifying dispositions of incentive stock options	(55,310)	(7,354)	—
Foreign rate differential	(161,022)	(606,875)	(846,480)
Federal research credit	(14,744)	(93,431)	(97,763)
Tax exempt interest	(24,212)	(37,900)	(60,794)
Other permanent differences	21,817	14,142	30,335
Provision for income taxes	$ 811,536	$ 1,120,313	$ 1,764,312

We provide U.S. income taxes on the earnings of foreign subsidiaries unless the subsidiaries' earnings are considered permanently reinvested outside the U.S. To the extent that the foreign earnings previously treated as permanently reinvested are repatriated, the related U.S. tax liability may be reduced by any foreign income taxes paid on these earnings. As of December 31, 2012, the cumulative amount of earnings upon which U.S. income taxes have not been provided is approximately $4,680.7 million. Determination of the amount of unrecognized deferred tax liability related to these earnings is not practicable.

Deferred Tax Assets

Deferred income taxes reflect the net effects of temporary differences between the carrying amounts of assets and liabilities for financing reporting purposes and the amounts used for income tax purposes. Significant components of our deferred tax assets and liabilities are as follows (in thousands):

	As of December 31,	
	2011	2012
Deferred tax assets:		
Stock-based compensation	$ 48,926	$ 141,956
State taxes	—	103,507
Depreciation	31,211	64,680
Vacation accruals	13,507	22,642
Deferred Rent	11,478	20,998
Accruals and reserves not currently deductible	8,240	11,789
Unrealized losses on investments and other	2,395	—
Other	5,090	17,609
Total deferred tax assets	120,848	383,180
Deferred tax liabilities:		
Identified intangibles	(129,337)	(153,240)
Undistributed earnings of foreign subsidiaries	—	(66,395)
Unrealized gains on investments and other	—	(36,224)
Other	(4,361)	(5,213)
Total deferred tax liabilities	(133,698)	(261,072)
Net deferred tax assets (liabilities)	$ -12,850	$ 122,108

As of December 31, 2012, our federal net operating loss carryforwards for income tax purposes were approximately $26.5 million. If not utilized, the federal net operating loss carryforwards will begin to expire in 2032. The net operating loss carryforwards are subject to various limitations under Section 382 of the Internal Revenue Code.

Uncertain Tax Positions

Effective January 1, 2012, we adopted the provisions of FIN 48. This interpretation clarifies the accounting for uncertainty in income taxes recognized in an enterprise's financial statements in accordance with SFAS No. 109 and prescribes a recognition threshold of more-likely-than-not to be sustained upon examination. Upon adoption of FIN 48, our policy to include interest and penalties related to gross unrecognized tax benefits within our provision for income taxes did not change. The adjustment to retained earnings upon adoption to FIN 48 on January 1, 2012 was $2.8 million.

The following table summarizes the activity related to our gross unrecognized tax benefits from January 1, 2012 to December 31, 2012 (in thousands):

Balance as of January 1, 2012	$	292,306
Increases related to prior year tax positions		35,825
Decreases related to prior year tax positions		(22,796)
Increases related to current year tax positions		159,290
Decreases related to settlements with taxing authorities		—
Decreases related to lapsing of statute of limitations		—
Balance as of December 31, 2012	$	464,624

Our total unrecognized tax benefits that, if recognized, would affect our effective tax rate were $234.8 million and $340.2 million as of January 1, 2012 and December 31, 2012.

As of December 31, 2012, we had accrued $14 million for payment of interest. Interest included in our provision for income taxes was not material in all the periods presented. We have not accrued any penalties related to our uncertain tax positions as we believe that it is more likely than not that there will not be any assessment of penalties.

CHAPTER 6 Long Term Investments In Equity Securities

INTRODUCTION

In accounting for intercorporate investments in equity securities, the accounting method used depends on the percentage of voting stock held by the investor company and its implied control over the investee company. Implied or economic control is inferred from the percentage ownership of voting stock, as well as from other information regarding the relationship between the investor and investee companies.

The following table summarizes the general percentage rules regarding the implied levels of control over the investee company and the related method to use in accounting for investments in equity securities. The fair value option under FASB 159 was discussed in Chapter Two. The fair value option can be elected for the following investments. Under this option, the investments are carried at fair value, with unrealized gains and losses recorded in earnings.

GENERAL GUIDELINES			
PERCENT OF VOTING STOCK HELD	***IMPLIED CONTROL***	***ACCOUNTING METHOD***	***PURPOSE OF INVESTMENT SIGNALLED BY ACCOUNTING METHOD USED***
1 — 19%	***NO ECONOMIC (EFFECTIVE) CONTROL***	***COST OR FAIR VALUE*** *(SFAS STATEMENT NOS. 107, 115 AND 159).*[1]	***PASSIVE***
20 — 50%	***ECONOMIC (EFFECTIVE) CONTROL***	***EQUITY METHOD*** *(APB OPINION NO. 18*[2] *or FASB STATEMENT NO. 159).*	***INFLUENCE***
51 — 100%	***LEGAL CONTROL***	***CONSOLIDATION ACCOUNTING*** *(SFAS STATEMENTS NO. 94, 141 (R) and 142).*[3] ***NOTE: The Equity Method is also used to report investments where there is both effective or legal control and separate company financial statements are issued.***	***CONTROL***

1. FASB ASC 825, ASC 320, ASC 825 [Predecessor literature: "Disclosures about Fair Value of Financial Instruments," *Statement of Financial Accounting Standards No. 107* (Norwalk, Conn.: FASB, 1991)]; [Predecessor literature: "Accounting for Certain Investments in Debt and Equity Securities," *Statement of Financial Accounting Standards No. 115* (Norwalk, Conn.: FASB, 1993)]; ["The Fair Value Option for Financial Assets and Financial Liabilities-Including an amendment of FASB Statement No. 115," *Statement of Financial Accounting Standards No. 159* (Norwalk, Conn.: FASB, 2007)].

2. FASB ASC 323 [Predecessor literature: "The Equity Method of Accounting for Investments in Common Stock," Opinions of the *Accounting Principles Board No. 18* (New York: AICPA 1971)].

3. FASB ASC 810, ASC 805, ASC 350 [Predecessor literature: "Consolidation of All Majority-Owned Subsidiaries," *Statement of Financial Accounting Standards No. 94* (Norwalk, Conn.: FASB, 1987)]; [Predecessor literature: "Business Combinations," *Statement of Financial Accounting Standards No. 141* (R) (Norwalk, Conn.: FASB, 2007)]; [Predecessor literature: "Goodwill and Other Intangible Assets," *Statement of Financial Accounting Standards No. 142* (Norwalk, Conn.: FASB, 2001)]

It should be emphasized that these are only general guidelines. With the exception of a majority owned subsidiary, all information must be considered when determining the extent of economic control exercised by the investee company. In FASB Interpretation No. 35, "Criteria for Applying the Equity Method of Accounting for Investments in Common Stock," and APB Opinion No. 18, "The Equity Method of Accounting for Investments in Common Stock"[4], several illustrations are provided which indicate the areas in which judgment is required in determining the appropriate accounting method to use. For example, if an investor corporation holds 25% of the voting stock of the investee corporation, but was rejected membership on the investee's board of directors, it may indicate that the investor does not exercise considerable economic control over the investee company. In this case, the equity method of accounting may not be appropriate. Fair value or "mark to market" accounting would be used. Mark to market accounting was covered in the discussion of current assets.

Conversely, if the investor corporation only holds 15% of the voting stock of the investee company, but has controlling membership on the investee's board of directors, is a major supplier or customer of the investee company, or exchanges management or technology with the investee, it may provide evidence that the investor has the ability to exercise economic control over the investee company and that the equity method should be used, regardless of the percentage of voting stock held. Thus, the use of the equity method is based on the ability of the investor to "control" the investee company. With less than a majority ownership, control must be determined by considering all factors and not by simply utilizing the general guidelines based on the percent of voting stock held. The details of applying the equity method of accounting are discussed in the following section.

THE EQUITY METHOD OF ACCOUNTING FOR INTERCORPORATE INVESTMENTS

When economic (effective) control is indicated by the percentage of voting stock held and all other available information, accountants conclude that the investor corporation has the ability to exercise "significant influence and control" over the financing, operating and investing activities of the investee corporation. Due to this influence and control, the investment is accounted for as an "unconsolidated subsidiary." In this case, the investor's ("the parent's") long-term investment account is carried on the balance sheet at its percentage ownership of investee voting stock multiplied by the book value (i.e., the net assets) of the investee's ("the sub's") equity. This is sometimes known as a "one-line consolidation". Therefore, whatever events affect the book value of the investee's stockholders' equity must be reflected in the carrying value of the investor's equity investment account and financial statements. This last point is reflected in the equation for the equity investment account.

Investor's Investment Account on the Balance Sheet @ Equity (Carrying Value)	=	**% of Voting Stock Held by the Investor**	X	**Investee's Net Assets (A-L) or Book Value (Stockholders' Equity)**

If the investor ("parent") pays more than book value for the subsidiary's net assets, "goodwill" can be recorded in a separate account entitled "the excess cost over the book value of net assets acquired." Using the excess cost over the book value of the subsidiary's net assets is not the same as recording goodwill and other asset revaluations in a true business

4. FASB ASC 323 [Predecessor literature: *FASB Interpretation No. 35*, "Criteria for Applying the Equity Method of Accounting for Investments in Common Stock (APB Op. No. 18)" (Norwalk, Conn.: FASB 1981)].

combination or under the complex equity method. It should be noted that either the cost or the partial equity method is sometimes used internally when the investor has legal control and separate company financial statements are not expected to be prepared in addition to consolidated statements (which is commonly the case).

Under the partial equity method, the parent records its share of subsidiary net income or loss but does not charge the additional amortization and depreciation from asset write-ups. The excess cost over book value of the net assets acquired is called goodwill.

In general, goodwill is an intangible asset, not subject to amortization but subject to an annual review for impairment (SFAS No.142). However, there is no impairment test for goodwill created on an equity method investment. This type of investment is subject to write-downs whenever declines in value are considered other than temporary.

The following spreadsheet is presented to illustrate the "one-line consolidation" concept. Assume Company A owns 100% of Company B. In addition to consolidated financial statements, Company A and B present separate company financial statements because Company B has publicly traded debt. When moving from separate company statements (i.e., "de-consolidation"), to full consolidation, the elimination of intercompany accounts is required. In this case, the only intercompany elimination involves the reciprocal accounts: the investor's investment account and the investee's stockholders' equity accounts. After the elimination of the reciprocal accounts, the investment account (i.e., the one-line consolidation) is effectively replaced by the individual assets and liabilities of the investee company. This elimination converts the one-line consolidation into a full or multi-line consolidation. Finally, only the investor's (parent's) stockholders' equity accounts are reported in the consolidated financial statements. The investee's (subsidiary's) equity accounts are no longer held by any party outside the consolidated entity.

Description	***Company A***	***Company B***	***Elimina-tions***	***Consoli-dated***
Assets	5,000	3,000		8,000
Investment in Company B (100%)	1,000	- 0 -	(1,000)	- 0 -
Total Assets	6,000	3,000	(1,000)	8,000
Liabilities	100	2,000		2,100
Stockholders' Equity	5,900	1,000	(1,000)	5,900
Total Equities	6,000	3,000	(1,000)	8,000

Due to the judgment that can be involved in determining the appropriate accounting treatment for a long-term investment in common stock, it is interesting to compare the financial statement effects of using the cost or mark-to-market methods and the equity method. When the equity method is not appropriate the cost method is only used if the investee company's shares are not publicly traded. If the shares are publicly traded (i.e., the shares have a readily determinable fair value), then fair value or mark to market accounting must be used.

The following table summarizes the main points of the previous discussion by listing the differences in accounting for an intercorporate investment under the cost, fair value and equity methods.

COST AND FAIR VALUE VERSUS EQUITY METHOD OF ACCOUNTING FOR INTERCORPORATE INVESTMENTS	
COST AND FAIR VALUE METHOD	***EQUITY METHOD***
1. The investment is originally recorded at cost and is carried at cost or fair value, until sold or permanently written down to market (i.e., the decline is other than temporary).	1. The investment is originally recorded at cost but is adjusted to reflect changes in the net assets of the investee company (see 2 and 3 below).
2. Cash dividends are recorded as dividend income or a return on investment.	2. Cash dividends are recorded as a return of investment and a reduction of the investment account.
3. Investor proportionate share of investee net income or loss is not recognized.	3. The carrying value of the investment account is increased (decreased) by the investor's proportionate share of investee net income (loss).
4. The carrying value of the investment is adjusted to fair value by use of an allowance account. As noted earlier, unrealized gains or losses on adjustments to fair value are recorded on the income statement for a trading portfolio and recorded as an element of stockholders' equity for an available for sale portfolio (included in other comprehensive income) The FASB 159 fair value option can also be elected.	4. Fluctuations in market value are not recognized, unless the FASB 159 fair market option is elected.
5. Goodwill is not recorded.	5. Goodwill is recorded and is measured as either the excess cost over the book value of net assets acquired (if partial equity is employed) or the excess cost over the fair value of net assets acquired (if the full or complex equity method is used).
6. Realized gains and losses are recorded on disposal as the difference between the net selling price minus the carrying value of the investment.	6. Same as under the cost method.
7. Stock dividends: No entry -- only a memo of the increased number of shares and the reduction in cost per share. For example: ***Before stock dividend:*** 1,000 shares at $10 per share = $10,000 total cost. ***After a 10% stock dividend:*** 1,100 shares but total cost is still $10,000 and cost per share is now $10,000 / 1,100 = $9.09	7. Same as under the cost method.

It should be noted that in determining the percentage ownership for evaluation of economic (effective) control, both voting common and voting preferred, if any, are included. Generally, for the investor's recognition of its share of investee net income or loss, only the percentage of voting common stock is used. However, EITF standards change the approach used for loss recognition when the investor holds securities of the investee, other than common stock (to be discussed).

In the case of a decline in an investment's value that is "other than temporary" there must be a write-down to market. This write-down is required for both cost, fair value and equity methods and is accounted for as a realized loss on the income statement. Finally, the valuation under the equity method is based on the book value of the investee company and therefore, should not be equal to the current market value of the investee's common stock.

The following example illustrates the financial statement effects of the cost and equity methods. It is assumed that the shares are not publicly traded without a readily determinable fair value. It is also assumed that the fair value option is not elected. As a result, mark to market accounting is not appropriate. For simplicity, it is assumed that there is no goodwill on the acquisition and that there are no income tax provisions made for the equity income. The tax considerations under the equity method will be discussed in a subsequent section of this chapter.

ILLUSTRATION: BASIC EQUITY METHOD VERSUS COST METHOD TRANSACTIONS

In this illustration, assume that an investor company acquires 20% of the voting shares of the investee corporation. The following transactions are determined under both the cost and equity methods. The relevant transactions are listed below and will be reported in financial modeling worksheets.

(a) Entry to record the initial investment of $1,000 under either the equity or the cost method. The investee shares are acquired at book value. This implies that the book value or stockholders' equity of the investee is $5,000 and with the 20% ownership at book value, the investment cost is $1,000. ***It is assumed that the investee shares are not publicly traded and that cost is always equal to fair value. As a result, an allowance account is not required.***

(b) Entry to record the receipt of a $50 cash dividend under the equity method.
Assume a 20% ownership and a $250 dividend declared by the investee company.

(c) Entry to record the receipt of a $50 cash dividend under the cost method. ***Assume a 20% ownership and a $250 dividend declared by the investee company.***

(d) Entry to record the investor's share of investee net income under the equity method. No entry is required under the cost method. ***Assume a 20% ownership and a $2,000 net income reported by the investee company for the first half of the year (or recognize $400 in income).***

(e) Entry to record the investor's share of investee net loss under the equity method. No entry is required under the cost method. ***Assume a 20% ownership and a $1,000 net loss reported by the investee company for the last six months of the year (or recognize a $200 loss).***

Under the equity method, the investor company will report $200 in net equity income for the year (i.e. $400 income for the first six months and a $200 lost for the last half of the year). An acquisition at book value enables us to tie the investment account directly to the investee's stockholders' equity as illustrated in the following table.

Description	***Investee Stockholders' Equity***	***Percentage Ownership***	***Investor Investment Account***
Beginning Balance	$ 5,000	20%	$1,000
Add: Net Income (Loss)			
1st Half of the Year	2,000	20%	400
2nd Half of the Year	(1,000)	20%	(200)
Subtract: Dividends	(250)	20%	(50)
Ending Balance	$5,750	20%	$1,150

Financial modeling worksheets will be presented for the individual transactions above.

FINANCIAL MODELING WORKSHEET ENTRY (A) FOR BOTH THE COST AND EQUITY METHODS

Entry to record the initial investment of $1,000 under either the equity or the cost method. It is assumed that cost is always equal to fair value so that an allowance account is not required.

INCOME STATEMENT (FIRST)	
REVENUES:	
EXPENSES:	
NET INCOME OR LOSS (a)	-0-

STATEMENT OF CASH FLOWS (THIRD)	
OPERATING ACTIVITIES:	
NET INCOME OR LOSS (a)	
INVESTING ACTIVITIES:	
Purchase of Investment Securities	(1,000)
FINANCING ACTIVITIES:	
INCREASE (DECREASE) IN CASH (b)	(1,000)
ADD: BEGINNING CASH BALANCE	
ENDING CASH BALANCE	

BALANCE SHEET (SECOND)			
ASSETS		LIABILITIES	
CURRENT ASSETS		CURRENT LIABILITIES	
CASH (b)	(1,000)		
		NONCURRENT LIABILITIES	
		STOCKHOLDERS' EQUITY	
NONCURRENT ASSETS			
Investment in Equity Securities	+1,000	CAPITAL STOCK	
		APIC	
		RETAINED EARNINGS (a)	
		TOTAL LIABILITIES & STOCKHOLDERS' EQUITY	
TOTAL ASSETS	-0-		-0-

Note that the transaction changes the composition of the assets but not the total. The cash outflow is reported as an investing activity on the cash flow statement.

FINANCIAL MODELING WORKSHEET ENTRY (B) DIVIDENDS RECEIVED UNDER THE EQUITY METHOD

Entry to record the receipt of a $50 cash dividend under the equity method. Assume a 20% ownership and a $250 dividend declared by the investee company.

INCOME STATEMENT (FIRST)	
REVENUES:	
EXPENSES:	
NET INCOME OR LOSS (a)	- 0 -

STATEMENT OF CASH FLOWS (THIRD)	
OPERATING ACTIVITIES:	
NET INCOME OR LOSS (a)	- 0 -
Dividends received in excess of equity income	+50
Cash flow from Operating Activities	+50
INVESTING ACTIVITIES:	
FINANCING ACTIVITIES:	
INCREASE (DECREASE) IN CASH (b)	+50
ADD: BEGINNING CASH BALANCE	
ENDING CASH BALANCE	

BALANCE SHEET (SECOND)			
ASSETS		LIABILITIES	
CURRENT ASSETS		CURRENT LIABILITIES	
CASH (b)	+50		
		NONCURRENT LIABILITIES	
		STOCKHOLDERS' EQUITY	
NONCURRENT ASSETS			
Investment in Equity Securities	(50)	CAPITAL STOCK	
		APIC	
		RETAINED	
		EARNINGS (a)	- 0 -
		TOTAL	
		LIABILITIES &	
		STOCKHOLDERS'	
TOTAL ASSETS	- 0 -	EQUITY	- 0 -

Cash dividends received under the equity method are not reported as income but are a return of capital (i.e., return of investment). The receipt of cash dividends will therefore reduce the investment account, similar to collection of a claim against the investee's net assets. Although, not reported as income, the dividends received provide cash and requires an add back in the operating activities section of the cash flow statement.

FINANCIAL MODELING WORKSHEET ENTRY (C) DIVIDENDS RECEIVED UNDER THE COST METHOD

Entry to record the receipt of a $50 cash dividend under the cost method. Assume a 20% ownership and a $250 dividend declared by the investee company.

INCOME STATEMENT (FIRST)	
REVENUES:	
Dividend Income	***+50***
EXPENSES:	
NET INCOME OR LOSS (a)	***+50***

STATEMENT OF CASH FLOWS (THIRD)	
OPERATING ACTIVITIES:	
NET INCOME OR LOSS (a)	***+50***
INVESTING ACTIVITIES:	
FINANCING ACTIVITIES:	
INCREASE (DECREASE) IN CASH (b)	***+50***
ADD: BEGINNING CASH BALANCE	
ENDING CASH BALANCE	

BALANCE SHEET (SECOND)			
ASSETS		***LIABILITIES***	
CURRENT ASSETS		***CURRENT LIABILITIES***	
CASH (b)	***+50***		
		NONCURRENT LIABILITIES	
		STOCKHOLDERS'	
NONCURRENT ASSETS		***EQUITY***	
		CAPITAL STOCK	
		APIC	
		RETAINED	
		EARNINGS (a)	***+50***
		TOTAL	
		LIABILITIES &	
		STOCKHOLDERS'	
TOTAL ASSETS	***+50***	***EQUITY***	***+50***

Cash dividends received under the cost method are reported as income or a return on investment. The accounting for cash dividends increase both net income and retained earnings with a corresponding increase in cash. The cash flow from dividend income is classified as part of operating activities on the statement of cash flows. The same is true for investments carried at fair market value.

FINANCIAL MODELING WORKSHEET ENTRY (D) EQUITY INCOME FOR THE FIRST SIX MONTHS

Entry to record the investor's share of investee net income under the equity method. No entry is required under the cost method. Assume a 20% ownership and a $2,000 net income reported by the investee company for the first half of the year.

INCOME STATEMENT (FIRST)	
REVENUES:	
Equity Income	+400
EXPENSES:	
NET INCOME OR LOSS (a)	+400

STATEMENT OF CASH FLOWS (THIRD)	
OPERATING ACTIVITIES:	
NET INCOME OR LOSS (a)	+400
Undistributed Equity Income	(400)
Cash flow from Operating Activities	- 0 -
INVESTING ACTIVITIES:	
FINANCING ACTIVITIES:	
INCREASE (DECREASE) IN CASH (b)	- 0 -
ADD: BEGINNING CASH BALANCE	
ENDING CASH BALANCE	

BALANCE SHEET (SECOND)			
ASSETS		LIABILITIES	
CURRENT ASSETS		CURRENT LIABILITIES	
CASH (b)	- 0 -		
		NONCURRENT LIABILITIES	
		STOCKHOLDERS' EQUITY	
NONCURRENT ASSETS			
Investment at Equity	+400	CAPITAL STOCK	
		APIC	
		RETAINED	
		EARNINGS (a)	+400
		TOTAL	
		LIABILITIES &	
		STOCKHOLDERS'	
TOTAL ASSETS	+400	EQUITY	+400

The recognition of equity income increases the investment account, net income and retained earnings. The investment account increases as investee company net income increases the investor's claim against the investee's net assets. However, this income does not generate any cash and requires a deduction in the operating activities section of the cash flow statement.

FINANCIAL MODELING WORKSHEET ENTRY (E) EQUITY LOSS FOR THE LAST SIX MONTHS

Entry to record the investor's share of investee net loss under the equity method. No entry is required under the cost method. Assume a 20% ownership and a $1,000 net loss reported by the investee company for the last six months of the year.

INCOME STATEMENT (FIRST)	
REVENUES:	
EXPENSES:	
Equity Loss	*(200)*
NET INCOME OR LOSS (a)	*(200)*

STATEMENT OF CASH FLOWS (THIRD)	
OPERATING ACTIVITIES:	
NET INCOME OR LOSS (a)	*(200)*
Add: Equity Loss	*+ 200*
Cash flow from Operating Activities	*- 0 -*
INVESTING ACTIVITIES:	
FINANCING ACTIVITIES:	
INCREASE (DECREASE) IN CASH (b)	*- 0 -*
ADD: BEGINNING CASH BALANCE	
ENDING CASH BALANCE	

BALANCE SHEET (SECOND)			
ASSETS		*LIABILITIES*	
CURRENT ASSETS		*CURRENT LIABILITIES*	
CASH (b)	*- 0 -*		
		NONCURRENT LIABILITIES	
		STOCKHOLDERS' EQUITY	
NONCURRENT ASSETS			
Investment at Equity	*(200)*	*CAPITAL STOCK*	
		APIC	
		RETAINED EARNINGS (a)	*(200)*
		TOTAL LIABILITIES & STOCKHOLDERS' EQUITY	
TOTAL ASSETS	*(200)*		*(200)*

The recognition of an equity loss decreases the investment account, net income and retained earnings. The investment account decreases as an investee company net loss reduces the investor's claim against the investee's net assets. However, this loss does not use cash and requires an add back in the operating activities section of the cash flow statement.

The financial modeling worksheets illustrate an important difference between the cost and equity methods. Under the cost method, there is a positive correlation between the recognition of income from the investment and the underlying cash flows. When cash dividends are received (or accrued), income is recognized on the investor's income statement with limited exceptions.

Conversely, when cash dividends are received on an equity investment, the carrying value of the investment is reduced and there is no recognition of income. When the proportionate equity income or loss is recognized on the investor's income statement, there is no cash flow. Therefore, the accountant will make adjustments to accrual basis net income for undistributed equity earnings on the statement of cash flows for an entity using the equity method.

Even with adjustments on the cash flow statement, an analyst should realize that, regardless of the accounting method used, the cash flows from the investment are identical for each accounting period and over the life of the investment. These points will be illustrated in the extension of the transactions analyzed in the previous financial modeling worksheets.

Finally, in reviewing this illustration and its extension below, the reader should compare the effects on reported income and earnings per share with the cash flow consequences of each transaction. In addition, note that over the life of the investment cash flows are identical under both methods for each accounting period; cash flows are identical for both methods over the life of the investment; and the total accrual basis income from the investment measured under both methods will be identical over the life of the investment. Therefore, only the timing of accrual-based income recognition will vary from period to period when comparing the cost and equity methods of accounting.

To illustrate this last point, assume the investment is sold at the beginning of the following year for $1,700. The gain or loss on the disposal of the investment is computed below:

CARRYING VALUE OF THE INVESTMENT ON THE BALANCE SHEET	***AT EQUITY***	***AT COST***
Purchase price	$1,000	$1,000
Equity income (for the first half of the year)	400	- 0 -
Equity loss (for the second half of the year)	(200)	- 0 -
Dividend	(50)	- 0 -
Ending balance of the investment	$1,150	$1,000
Selling price of the investment	1,700	1,700
Gain on disposal of the investment	$ 550	$ 700

The gain on disposal will result in an equality of income over the life of the investment. The following summary provides proof of the equality of total income over the life of the investment.

INCOME OVER THE LIFE OF THE INVESTMENTS	***AT EQUITY***	***AT COST OR FAIR VALUE***
INVESTEE INCOME: FIRST HALF OF THE YEAR (Equity Income)	$400	$ - 0 -
INVESTEE LOSS: SECOND HALF OF THE YEAR (Equity Loss)	(200)	- 0 -
DIVIDEND INCOME DURING THE YEAR		50
GAIN ON SALE OF INVESTMENT IN THE NEXT YEAR	**550**	**700**
TOTAL INCOME FROM INVESTMENT	***$750***	= ***$750***
NOTE: Cash flows are the same each year for both methods. Income differs year to year, but is the same over the life of the investment.		

Again, this example illustrates that over the life of the investment, the total income and cash generated from the investment are the same. Only the timing of income recognition will vary from period to period under the equity method.

An analyst must be aware of a common adjustment needed in building a cash flow statement when the client holds an equity investment. As noted above, the cash flows must be the same under either method of accounting.

The only cash flows in the year of acquisition are the purchase of $1,000 and the cash dividend received of $50. However, there is $200 of net equity income reported under the equity method. To bring this amount to the $50 cash dividend received, accountants make an adjustment called "undistributed equity income" or "income retained by the investee". This adjustment is always equal to the growth in the equity investment, which is equal to $150 in this case. The cash flow statements under the two accounting alternatives are presented below.

Statements of Cash Flow for the year first year of the Investment	***AT EQUITY***	***AT COST***
Operating Activities:		
Net Income:		
Net Equity Income ($400 – 200)	$200	$ - 0 -
Dividend Income	- 0 -	50
Adjustments to reconcile net income to operating cash flow:		
Undistributed Equity Income ($200 – 50)	(150)	- 0 -
Cash Flow from Operating Activities	***$ 50***	= ***$ 50***
Investing Activities		
Purchased Investment	(1,000)	(1,000)
Net cash flows relating to the first year of the investment	***($950)***	= ***($950)***

There will be an add back in the operating activities section of the cash flow statement in the case of the net equity loss or dividends received in excess of equity income.

A major implication here is that an analyst needs to assess the ability of the parent company to access the undistributed equity income. The analytical question focuses on whether the income from the investee company is the equity earnings recognized or the cash dividends received. Several related questions must be asked regarding the inclusion of equity earnings in an income or cash flow projection. Are the equity earnings sustainable? What is the company's legal ability to obtain cash (i.e., can the investor collect the undistributed equity earnings)? Foreign governments or state insurance commissions can restrict or limit the cash distributed to the investor company. The probabilty of cash collection from equity income will help an analyst determine if such earnings should be included in EBITDA and other cash flow projections.

DISCLOSURES UNDER THE EQUITY METHOD

Investments accounted for under the equity method should include the following disclosures:

1. The name of the investment and the percentage of voting stock held.

2. The investor's accounting policies used in implementing the reporting requirements for the equity investment (e.g., if the investee's financial reporting period does not coincide with the investor's, the investor should use the most recent available financial statements of the investee, and the time lag should be consistent from period to period). Significant intercompany transactions must be disclosed.

3. The difference between the carrying value of the investment and the underlying net assets of the investee company (i.e., goodwill). Material goodwill impairment write-downs must be disclosed along with reasons for the write-down.

4. If significant, the investor must disclose the assets, liabilities and the results of operations of an equity investment in a footnote or in a separate statement. This disclosure typically takes the form of condensed financial statements of the investee company or aggregate financial statements for all investee company investments carried under the equity method.

5. If significant, the impact on the investor of any convertible securities of the investee company.

6. An explanation is required if the equity method is not used for an investment of 20% or more, or if the equity method is used for an investment of less than 20%. The name of the investee companies for these situations must also be disclosed.

Financial statement presentation of the investment account on the balance sheet, equity earnings on the income statement, statements of cash flows and the footnote disclosures for the equity investments of Barry Company and Subsidiaries presented in Exhibit 6.1 through 6.4.

The Barry Consolidated Statements of Income presented in Exhibit 6.1 reflects a significant of net equity income ranging from 8% to 11% of operating income each year. There are also gains from the issuance of shares by equity investees. The nature of these gains will be discussed in a subsequent section of this chapter.

EXHIBIT 6.1 BARRY COMPANY AND SUBSIDIARIES CONSOLIDATED STATEMENTS OF INCOME

THE BARRY COMPANY AND SUBSIDIARIES
CONSOLIDATED STATEMENTS OF INCOME

Year Ended December 31,	**2005**	2004	2003
(In millions except per share data)			
NET OPERATING REVENUES	**$27,724.8**	$26,090.4	$25,028.4
Cost of goods sold	**9,834**	9,209	9,331
GROSS PROFIT	**$17,891**	$16,882	$15,697
Selling, general and administrative expenses	**10,487**	9,468	8,744
Other operating charges	102	576	687.6
OPERATING INCOME	**$7,302**	$6,838	$6,265
Interest income	**282**	188.4	211.2
Interest expense	**288**	235.2	213.6
Equity income — net	**816**	745.2	487.2
Other loss — net	**(111.6)**	(98.4)	(165.6)
Gains on issuances of stock by equity investees	**27.6**	28.8	9.6
INCOME BEFORE INCOME TAXES	**$8,028**	$7,466	$6,594

Barry's Consolidated Balance Sheets are presented in Exhibit 6.2. Investments are classified as both equity investments and cost method investments. The total investments for Barry represent 20% or more of the company's total assets.

EXHIBIT 6.2. BARRY COMPANY AND SUBSIDIARIES CONSOLIDATED BALANCE SHEETS

December 31, (In millions except par value)	**2012**	2011
ASSETS		
CURRENT ASSETS		
Cash and cash equivalents	**$5,641.2**	$8,048.4
Marketable securities	**79.2**	73.2
Trade accounts receivable, net	**2,737**	2,693
Inventories	**1,709**	1,704
Prepaid expenses and other assets	**2,134**	2,219
TOTAL CURRENT ASSETS	**$12,300**	$14,737
INVESTMENTS		
Equity method investments:		
Barry Enterprises Europe	**$2,077**	$1,883
Barry China	**1,247**	1,280
Barry South America	**1178.4**	950.4
Barry UK	**897.6**	883.2
Other	**2,474**	2,080
Cost method investments	**432**	426
TOTAL INVESTMENTS	**$8,306**	$7,502
OTHER ASSETS	**3,178**	3,577
PROPERTY, PLANT AND EQUIPMENT — net	**6,943**	7,309
TRADEMARKS WITH INDEFINITE LIVES	**2,335**	2,444
GOODWILL	**1,256**	1,316
OTHER INTANGIBLE ASSETS	**993.6**	842.4
TOTAL ASSETS	**$ 35,312**	$ 37,727

Exhibit 6.3 reflects the cash flow effects of investments in equity securities. The cash paid for the investments is reported in investing activities as "acquisitions and investments, principally trademarks and bottling companies." The deduction of undistributed equity income is reported in the operating activities section of the statement of cash flows. Note also that the gains on issuances of stock by equity investees are non-cash gains and are subtracted in operating activities. Undistributed equity income is computed as equity income less dividends received. As illustrated in the examples discussed in this chapter, the adjustment for undistributed equity income in the cash flow statement converts net equity income into cash received from investee company dividends. In Barry's case we can compute the cash dividends received from equity investees as follows:

Description	***2012***	***2011***	***2010***
Equity income-net (Exhibit 6.1)	$816	$745.2	$487.2
Undistributed equity income (Exhibit 6.3)	(535.2)	(571.2)	(352.8)
Cash dividends received from equity investees	$280.8	$174	$134.4

The amount of cash dividends received from equity investees can be verified in Exhibit 6.4 under the caption "Net Receivables and Dividends from Equity Method Investees."

EXHIBIT 6.3: BARRY COMPANY AND SUBSIDIARIES CONSOLIDATED STATEMENTS OF CASH FLOWS

Year Ended December 31,	**2012**	2011	2010
(In millions)			
OPERATING ACTIVITIES			
Net income	**$ 5,846.4**	$ 5,816.4	$ 5216.4
Depreciation and amortization	**118.4**	1017.6	1020
Stock-based compensation expense	**388.8**	414	506.4
Deferred income taxes	**(105.6)**	194.4	(225.6)
Equity income or loss, net of dividends	**(535.2)**	(571.2)	(352.8)
Foreign currency adjustments	**56.4**	(70.8)	(94.8)
Gains on issuances of stock by equity investees	**(27.6)**	(28.8)	(9.6)
Gains on sales of assets, including bottling interests	**(108)**	(24)	(6)
Other operating charges	**102**	576	396
Other items	**358.8**	524.4	298.8
Net change in operating assets and liabilities	**516**	(740.4)	(201.6)
Net cash provided by operating activities	**$7,708**	$7,162	$6,547
INVESTING ACTIVITIES			
Acquisitions and investments, principally trademarks and bottling companies	**$(764.4)**	$(320.4)	$(430.8)
Purchases of investments and other assets	**(63.6)**	(55.2)	(212.4)
Proceeds from disposals of investments and other assets	**39.6**	193.2	176.4
Purchases of property, plant and equipment	**(1078.8)**	(906)	(974.4)
Proceeds from disposals of property, plant and equipment	**105.6**	409.2	104.4
Other investing activities	**(33.6)**	75.6	213.6
Net cash used in investing activities	**$(1,795.2)**	$(603.6)	$(1,122)

Exhibit 6.4 provides the disclosures required under the equity method. These disclosures are particularly extensive for Barry due to this company's significant investment in equity investees.

EXHIBIT 6.4: BARRY EQUITY INVESTMENTS FOOTNOTE

NOTE 2: Equity Investments
Barry Enterprises Europe (BEE).

BEE, producer and distributor of our products, operating in eight countries. On December 31, 2012, our Company owned approximately 30.68% of the outstanding common stock of BEE. We account for our investment by the equity method of accounting and, therefore, our operating results include our proportionate share of income resulting from our investment in BEE. As of December 31, 2012, our proportionate share of the net assets of BEE exceeded our investment by approximately $337.2 million. This difference is not amortized.

A summary of financial information for BEE is as follows (in millions):

December 31,	**2012**	2011
Current assets	**$ 4,074**	$ 4,045.2
Noncurrent assets	**26,354**	27,708
Total assets	**$ 30,428.4**	$ 31,753.2
Current liabilities	**$ 4,615.2**	$ 4,141.2
Noncurrent liabilities	**19,042**	21,158
Total liabilities	**$ 23,656.8**	$ 25,299.6
Shareowners' equity	**$ 6,771.6**	$ 6,453.6
Company equity investment	**$ 2,077.2**	$ 1,882.8

Year Ended December 31,	**2012**	2011	2010
Net operating revenues	**$ 22447.2**	$ 21,789.6	$ 20,796
Cost of goods sold	**13,422**	12,925	12,198
Gross profit	**$ 9,025.2**	$ 8,864.4	$ 8,598
Operating income	**$ 1,717.2**	$ 1,755.6	$ 1,892.4
Net income	**$ 616.8**	$ 715.2	$ 811.2
Net income available to common shareowners	**$ 616.8**	$ 715.2	$ 808.8

A summary of our significant transactions with BEE is as follows (in millions):

Year Ended December 31,	**2012**	2011	2010
Primary Product sales to BEE	**6150**	6243.6	6100.8
Primary product purchases from BEE	**513.6**	513.6	483.6
Other Purchases	**330**	370.8	373.2
Payments made by us directly to BEE	**578.4**	730.8	1056
Payments made to third parties on behalf of BEE	**163.2**	124.8	138
Marketing program reimbursements from BEE	**294**	295.2	265.2
Payments made to BEE for repair services	**84**	75.6	74.4

Other Equity Method Investments

Our other equity method investments include our ownership interests in Barry China, Barry South America and Barry UK for which we own 28.8 percent, 48 percent and 48.4 percent of their common shares, respectively.

Operating results include our proportionate share of income (loss) from our equity method investments. A summary of financial information for our equity method investments in the aggregate, other than BEE, is as follows (in millions):

December 31,	**2012**	2011
Current assets	**$ 7,803**	$ 6,723
Noncurrent assets	**20,698**	19,107
Total assets	**$ 28,501**	$ 25,830
Current liabilities	**$ 7,705**	$ 5,507
Noncurrent liabilities	**8,395**	8,924
Total liabilities	**$ 16,100**	$ 14,431
Shareowners' equity	**$ 12,401**	$ 11,399
Company equity investment	**$ 4,831**	$ 4,328

Year Ended December 31,	**2012**	2011	2010
Net operating revenues	**$ 29,266.8**	$ 25,442.4	$ 23,756.4
Cost of goods sold	**16,969**	14,558	13,993
Gross profit	**$ 12,297.6**	$ 10,884	$ 9,763.2
Operating income	**$ 3,202.8**	$ 2,887.2	$ 1,999.2
Net income (loss)	**$ 1,801.2**	$ 1,666.8	$ 696
Net income (loss) available to common shareowners	**$ 1,772.4**	$ 1,636.8	$ 696

Net sales to equity method investees other than BEE, which are located outside the United States, were approximately $8.9 billion in 2012, $6.2 billion in 2011 and $4.8 billion in 2010. Total support payments, primarily marketing, made to equity method investees other than BEE were approximately $570 million, $530 million and $613.2 million in 2012, 2011 and 2010, respectively.

If valued at the December 31, 2013 quoted closing prices of shares actively traded on stock markets, the value of our equity method investments in publicly traded bottlers other than BEE would have exceeded our carrying value by approximately $2.9 billion.

Net Receivables and Dividends from Equity Method Investees

The total amount of net receivables due from equity method investees, including BEE, was approximately $772.8 million and $687.6 million as of December 31, 2012 and 2011, respectively. The total amount of dividends received from equity method investees, including BEE, was approximately $280.8 million, $174 million and $134.4 million for the years ended December 31, 2012, 2011 and 2010, respectively.

ADDITIONAL CONSIDERATIONS UNDER THE EQUITY METHOD

Tax Implications

Tax on income generated on intercorporate investments is based only on the cost method. Cash dividends received and the gain on sale are the only taxable events under either method. In the basic illustration, the $50 cash dividend would be taxable, net of the corporate dividends received exclusion. Under current tax law, a corporation may exclude all or a portion of intercorporate dividends. The amount of the exclusion depends on the percentage ownership of the voting stock of the investee company. The corporate dividend received exclusion rules are summarized below.

PERCENT OWNERSHIP	***PERCENT EXCLUDED***
1 - 19%	70%
20 - 79%	80%
80 - 100%	100%

The 70% dividend received exclusion is automatic and it goes to 80% if 20% of the voting stock of the investee company is held. Note also that 80% ownership is required for tax consolidation. That is, a company can file consolidated tax returns with 80% ownership of a subsidiary, but it is not required to do so.

Applying the dividend received exclusion rules to the basic illustration with a 20% ownership and assuming a 40% tax rate, the company would pay tax of $4 (i.e., $50 x (1 - .80) x 40%) on the $50 cash dividend received. This would be the case for both the cost, fair value and equity methods.

The tax (and cash flow) implications for the $700 gain on sale will be the same under either method. There is no exclusion on the gain and the tax at 40% would be $280 for both methods (i.e., 40% x $700). This illustration assumes that there are no existing capital loss carryovers.

The Effect of Deferred Taxes on the Equity Method

An investor using the equity method reports equity income or loss in the current period. However, as indicated above, for income tax purposes the investor only reports dividends received and gains or losses on the disposal of the investment. Thus, temporary book tax differences are created and according to SFAS 109, the investor must provide deferred taxes on the undistributed equity earnings in most cases (exceptions will be discussed). The amount of deferred taxes to provide will depend on the investor's assumptions regarding the ultimate realization of the undistributed equity earnings; through future dividend distributions or by gain or loss on the disposal of the investment.

Illustration

Assume that on January 2, 2008, FuzziLou Enterprises acquires a 30% share of the Drifter Too Company for $700,000. This amount is also equal to the book value of the investee net assets acquired (i.e., there is no goodwill). Drifter Too reported $300,000 in net income and distributed dividends of $50,000 in 2008. FuzziLou's tax rate is 35% (for both ordinary income and capital gains, as there is no preferential treatment for corporate capital gains under the current tax law).

CASE A

In the computation of FuzziLou's tax provision for 2008, management assumes that undistributed equity earnings will be realized as future dividends. Undistributed equity earnings are determined below:

Equity income: $300,000 x 30%	**$90,000**
Dividends received: $50,000 x 30%	**(15,000)**
Undistributed equity income (increase in the investment account)	**$75,000**

Given FuzziLou's 30% ownership, it qualifies for the 80% dividends received exclusion (i.e., only 20% is taxable). Therefore, FuzziLou's 2008 tax provision is computed as follows:

Undistributed equity income (above)	**$75,000**
Taxable percentage	**x 20%**
Taxable future dividends	**$15,000**
Tax rate	**x 35%**
Deferred income tax liability	**$ 5,250**
Current taxes payable: ($15,000 x 20% x 35%)	**$ 1,050**
Income tax expense: ($5,250 + 1,050)	**$ 6,300**

A financial modeling worksheet for CASE A is presented below:

FINANCIAL MODELING WORKSHEET (CASE A)

INCOME STATEMENT (FIRST)	
REVENUES:	
EXPENSES:	
Income Tax Expense	*(6,300)*
NET INCOME OR LOSS (a)	*(6,300)*

STATEMENT OF CASH FLOWS (THIRD)	
OPERATING ACTIVITIES:	
NET INCOME OR LOSS (a)	*(6,300)*
Increase in the Deferred Tax Liability	*+5,250*
Increase in Income Tax Payable	*+1,050*
Cash Flow from Operating Activities	*- 0 -*
INVESTING ACTIVITIES:	
FINANCING ACTIVITIES:	
INCREASE (DECREASE) IN CASH (b)	*- 0 -*
ADD: BEGINNING CASH BALANCE	
ENDING CASH BALANCE	

BALANCE SHEET (SECOND)			
ASSETS		***LIABILITIES***	
CURRENT ASSETS		***CURRENT LIABILITIES***	
CASH (b)	*- 0 -*	*Income tax payable*	*+1,050*
		NONCURRENT LIABILITIES	
		Deferred Tax Liability	*+5,250*
		STOCKHOLDERS' EQUITY	
NONCURRENT ASSETS			
		CAPITAL STOCK	
		APIC	
		RETAINED EARNINGS (a)	*(6,300)*
		TOTAL LIABILITIES & STOCKHOLDERS' EQUITY	
TOTAL ASSETS	*- 0 -*		*- 0 -*

Assuming that the $90,000 of GAAP income reported in 2008, FuzziLou's effective (actual) tax rate is only 7% (i.e., $6,300/$90,000 = 7%). The reconciliation of the federal statutory tax rate and the effective (actual) tax rate is:

Federal statutory income tax rate	**35.00%**
Dividend received exclusion: **$90,000 X 80% x 35% = $25,200: ($25,200/$90,000) =**	**(28.00%)**
Effective (actual) tax rate	**7.00 %**

CASE B

Assume now that FuzziLou's management believes that the undistributed equity earnings will be realized on a future disposal of the investment. Under this assumption, FuzziLou's

2008 income tax provision is determined as follows:

Undistributed equity income (above)	**$75,000**
Tax rate	**x 35%**
Deferred income tax liability	**$ 26,250**
Current taxes payable: ($15,000 x 20% x 35%)	**$ 1,050**
Income tax expense: ($26,250 + 1,050)	**$ 27,300**

A financial modeling worksheet for CASE B is presented below:

FINANCIAL MODELING WORKSHEET (CASE B)

INCOME STATEMENT (FIRST)	
REVENUES:	
EXPENSES:	
Income Tax Expense	*(27,300)*
NET INCOME OR LOSS (a)	*(27,300)*

STATEMENT OF CASH FLOWS (THIRD)	
OPERATING ACTIVITIES:	
NET INCOME OR LOSS (a)	*(27,300)*
Increase in the Deferred Tax Liability	*+26,250*
Increase in Income Tax Payable	*+1,050*
Cash Flow from Operating Activities	*- 0 -*
INVESTING ACTIVITIES:	
FINANCING ACTIVITIES:	
INCREASE (DECREASE) IN CASH (b)	*- 0 -*
ADD: BEGINNING CASH BALANCE	
ENDING CASH BALANCE	

BALANCE SHEET (SECOND)			
ASSETS		*LIABILITIES*	
CURRENT ASSETS		*CURRENT LIABILITIES*	
CASH (b)	*- 0 -*	*Income tax payable*	*+1,050*
		NONCURRENT LIABILITIES	
		Deferred Tax Liability	*+26,250*
		STOCKHOLDERS' EQUITY	
NONCURRENT ASSETS			
		CAPITAL STOCK	
		APIC	
		RETAINED EARNINGS (a)	*(27,300)*
		TOTAL LIABILITIES & STOCKHOLDERS' EQUITY	
TOTAL ASSETS	*- 0 -*		*- 0 -*

Assuming that the $90,000 of GAAP income reported in 2008, FuzziLou's 2008 effective (actual) tax rate is now 30.33% (i.e., $27,300/$90,000 = 30.33%). The reconciliation of the federal statutory tax rate and the effective (actual) tax rate is:

Federal statutory income tax rate	**35.00%**
Dividend received exclusion: **$15,000 x 80% x 35% = $4,200: ($4,200/$90,000) =**	**(4.67)**
Effective (actual) tax rate	**30.33%**

The Use of the Liability Method under SFAS 109

Under SFAS 109, adjustments to the deferred income tax account can result if tax rates change or if the estimated valuation allowance for a deferred tax asset is revised. In addition, the deferred tax account must be adjusted if the undistributed equity earnings are realized in a manner other than anticipated.

For example, assume that in CASE A FuzziLou sells the investment prior to any additional investee earnings or dividends. The net selling price is $810,000. The $5,250 of deferred taxes provided in CASE A are reversed on the disposal. The tax implications are presented in the table below:

Description	***Tax (Cost)***	***Book (Equity)***
Selling price	$810,000	$810,000
Cost ($700,000) and equity (700,000 + 90,000 - 15,000) carrying value	(700,000)	(775,000)
Gain on sale	$110,000	$35,000
Tax rate	35%	
Tax liability	$38,500	

Assuming that the only income earned is from the sale of the investment. The book income reported is $35,000 and the taxable income is $110,000. Income tax expense is $33,250 and is determined as follows:

Current taxes payable	**$38,500**
Deferred income tax liability reversal	**(5,250)**
Income tax expense: ($38,500 - 5,250)	**$33,250**

The income tax expense on this transaction can be further analyzed by component:

Tax on book income ($35,000 x 35%)	**$12,250**
Undistributed equity income multiplied by the difference between the full tax rate on capital gains and the tax rate applicable to dividends: **$75,000 x [35% - (35% x 20%)]** **$75,000 x [35% - 7%]** **$75,000 x 28% = $21,000**	**21,000**
Income tax expense	**$33,250**

The 28% represents the lost tax benefits from converting the future dividends into a gain on sale, taxed at the marginal tax rate of 35%. The effective tax rate resulting from this reversal adjustment is 95%! (i.e., $33,250 / $35,000 = 35%). This is due to the fact that with the reversal adjustment, more tax is paid or payable in the current year than the income tax expense reported on the income statement. A financial modeling worksheet for Case A with a reversal is presented below:

FINANCIAL MODELING WORKSHEET (CASE A: REVERSAL)

INCOME STATEMENT (FIRST)	
REVENUES:	
EXPENSES:	
Income Tax Expense	(33,250)
NET INCOME OR LOSS (a)	(33,250)

STATEMENT OF CASH FLOWS (THIRD)	
OPERATING ACTIVITIES:	
NET INCOME OR LOSS (a)	(33,250)
Decrease in the Deferred Tax Liability	(5,250)
Increase in Income Tax Payable	+38,500
Cash Flow from Operating Activities	- 0 -
INVESTING ACTIVITIES:	
FINANCING ACTIVITIES:	
INCREASE (DECREASE) IN CASH (b)	- 0 -
ADD: BEGINNING CASH BALANCE	
ENDING CASH BALANCE	

BALANCE SHEET (SECOND)			
ASSETS		LIABILITIES	
CURRENT ASSETS		CURRENT LIABILITIES	
CASH (b)	- 0 -	Income Tax Payable	+38,500
		NONCURRENT LIABILITIES	
		Deferred Tax Liability	(5,250)
		STOCKHOLDERS'	
NONCURRENT ASSETS		EQUITY	
		CAPITAL STOCK	
		APIC	
		RETAINED	
		EARNINGS (a)	(33,250)
		TOTAL	
		LIABILITIES &	
		STOCKHOLDERS'	
TOTAL ASSETS	- 0 -	EQUITY	- 0 -

If FuzziLou sells the investment and previously provided for deferred taxes assuming that the undistributed equity earnings would be realized from sale (i.e., this is the CASE B: Reversal assumption, then the following entry would be made on a financial modeling worksheet. The tax expense reported on the income statement is $12,250 computed below:

Current taxes payable	**$38,500**
Deferred income tax liability reversal	**(26,250)**
Income tax expense: ($38,500 - 5,250)	**$12,250**

Note that the effective tax rate is equal to the federal tax rate of 35% (i.e., $12,250 / $35,000 = 35%). The effective tax rate is correct in this case because the future earnings were realized from the sale of the investment as originally anticipated by management in developing the deferred tax provision.

FINANCIAL MODELING WORKSHEET (CASE B: REVERSAL)

INCOME STATEMENT (FIRST)	
REVENUES:	
EXPENSES:	
Income Tax Expense	*(12,250)*
NET INCOME OR LOSS (a)	*(12,250)*

STATEMENT OF CASH FLOWS (THIRD)	
OPERATING ACTIVITIES:	
NET INCOME OR LOSS (a)	*(12,250)*
Decrease in the Deferred Tax Liability	*(26,250)*
Increase in Income Tax Payable	*+38,500*
Cash Flow from Operating Activities	*- 0 -*
INVESTING ACTIVITIES:	
FINANCING ACTIVITIES:	
INCREASE (DECREASE) IN CASH (b)	*- 0 -*
ADD: BEGINNING CASH BALANCE	
ENDING CASH BALANCE	

BALANCE SHEET (SECOND)			
ASSETS		*LIABILITIES*	
CURRENT ASSETS		*CURRENT LIABILITIES*	
CASH (b)	*- 0 -*	*Income Tax Payable*	*+38,500*
		NONCURRENT LIABILITIES	
		Deferred Tax Liability	*(26,250)*
		STOCKHOLDERS' EQUITY	
NONCURRENT ASSETS			
		CAPITAL STOCK	
		APIC	
		RETAINED	
		EARNINGS (a)	*(12,250)*
		TOTAL	
		LIABILITIES &	
		STOCKHOLDERS'	
TOTAL ASSETS	*- 0 -*	*EQUITY*	*- 0 -*

The "Indefinite Reversal" Exception

The "indefinite reversal" exception refers to situations where deferred taxes are not provided on undistributed equity earnings. The FASB the IASB decided to retain SFAS 109's exception to recognizing deferred taxes on investments in foreign subsidiaries.

The exception to recognizing deferred taxes on investments in foreign subsidiaries reduces the amounts of deferred tax liabilities and deferred tax expense that must be recognized. That is, companies do not recognize a deferred tax liability on undistributed equity income from an investment in a foreign subsidiary or foreign corporate joint venture that is considered permanent in nature. However, the deferred tax liability will be recognized when it becomes evident that the differences will reverse in the near future.

The Effect of Investee Capital Transactions

Investee capital transactions include investee company acquisitions and disposals of treasury stock and the issuance of additional shares. When the investee engages in a capital transaction that alters the investor's percentage share, a "gain or loss" can arise.

The amount of the "gain or loss" depends on whether the price paid for treasury shares acquired or the price received for new or treasury shares issued is greater or less than the investor's per share carrying value of its investment in the investee company. As is the case for any capital transaction for GAAP accounting and reporting (a transaction involving a firm's own shares), no "gain or loss" is reported in the income statement. Rather, there will be an adjustment in additional paid in capital or retained earnings. However, the SEC permits income recognition based on the theory that the investor is disposing a portion of its investment in the investee as a result of the investee's capital transaction.

For example, if the investee company issues new shares at a price above the investor company's carrying value and the investor does not participate proportionately, the investor can record a gain, (See Coca Cola Company Income Statement in Exhibit 6.1 and disclosures at the end of Exhibit 6.4).

Illustrations of the effects of investee capital transactions are presented below.

Illustration Using the GAAP Approach

Assume an investor acquires 30,000 shares of an investee's 100,000 shares for $150,000 (i.e., a 30% interest obtained at a cost of $5 per share). The investee's net assets were equal to $500,000 on the date of acquisition. So the investor paid book value (i.e., 30% x $500,000). At the end of the first year after the acquisition, the investee acquires 15,000 treasury shares at a cost of $8 per share or $120,000. It is assumed that the investor does not sell back any shares to the investee company. To isolate the effect of the capital transaction, it is assumed that the investee reports no income and there are no dividends for the year. There are two important effects of this capital transaction:

1. Reduction of the investee net assets to $380,000 (i.e., $500,000 - 120,000).

2. The investor's percentage share of voting stock is increased while the carrying value of the investment account is decreased:

30,000 shares / (100,000 - 15,000) shares = <u>35.29%</u>

The carrying value of the investment is reduced to $134,102 (i.e., $380,000 x 35.29%).

There is a $15,898 "loss" in the carrying value of the equity investment (i.e., $150,000 - 134,102). For ***GAAP purposes***, this "loss" is recorded as reduction of the investor's additional paid in capital (APIC) from prior investee capital transactions, if any. If there is no APIC from prior investee capital transactions or if this account is reduced to zero, the investor's retained earnings are reduced. Any "gains" on investee capital transactions can only be recorded as increases in investor APIC. Retained earnings can never be created or increased by capital transactions. The SEC permits income recognition as a result of investee capital transactions. A financial modeling worksheet for this transaction is presented below. In this case it is assumed that there is no APIC from prior investee capital transactions. Therefore, the entire loss is charged against retained earnings. This is a significant non-cash investing activity requiring footnote disclosure or a separate schedule.

FINANCIAL MODELING WORKSHEET INVESTEE CAPITAL TRANSACTION: GAAP TREATMENT

INCOME STATEMENT (FIRST)	
REVENUES:	
EXPENSES:	
NET INCOME OR LOSS (a)	- 0 -

STATEMENT OF CASH FLOWS (THIRD)	
OPERATING ACTIVITIES:	
NET INCOME OR LOSS (a)	- 0 -
INVESTING ACTIVITIES:	
FINANCING ACTIVITIES:	
INCREASE (DECREASE) IN CASH (b)	- 0 -
ADD: BEGINNING CASH BALANCE	
ENDING CASH BALANCE	

BALANCE SHEET (SECOND)			
ASSETS		LIABILITIES	
CURRENT ASSETS		CURRENT LIABILITIES	
CASH (b)	- 0 -		
		NONCURRENT LIABILITIES	
		STOCKHOLDERS'	
NONCURRENT ASSETS		EQUITY	
Investment at Equity	(15,898)	CAPITAL STOCK	
		APIC	
		RETAINED	
		EARNINGS (a)	(15,898)
		TOTAL	
		LIABILITIES &	
		STOCKHOLDERS'	
TOTAL ASSETS	(15,898)	EQUITY	(15,898)

Illustration Using the SEC Approach. Assume an investor acquires 30,000 shares of an investee's 100,000 shares for $150,000 (i.e., a 30% interest obtained at a cost of $5 per share). The investee's net assets were equal to $500,000 on the date of acquisition. So the investor paid book value (i.e., 30% x $500,000). Immediately after the acquisition, the investee issues 10,000 shares of voting common stock at $7 per share or $70,000. The investor does not participate in this new issue. To isolate the effect of the capital transaction, it is assumed that the investee reports no income and there are no dividends for the year.

Using the SEC rules, the gain or loss and the value of the investor company's investment account after the investee issuance of shares are presented below.

With the new issue of common equity, the investee net assets increase to $570,000 (i.e., $500,000 + 70,000). As a result of the new stock issue, the investor's percentage share of voting stock is decreased while the carrying value of the investment account is increased. The percentage ownership falls from 30% to 27.27% (i.e., [30,000 shares / (100,000 + 10,000) shares = 27.27%]) and the carrying value of the investment is increased to $155,440 (i.e., $570,000 x 27.27%). This transaction results in a $5,440 "gain" in the carrying value of the equity investment (i.e., $155,440 - 150,000). The financial modeling worksheet using the SEC's approach is presented below where the $5,440 gain is reported in income.

FINANCIAL MODELING WORKSHEET INVESTEE CAPITAL TRANSACTION: SEC TREATMENT

INCOME STATEMENT (FIRST)	
REVENUES:	
Gains on issuances of stock by equity investee	+5,440
EXPENSES:	
NET INCOME OR LOSS (a)	+5,440

STATEMENT OF CASH FLOWS (THIRD)	
OPERATING ACTIVITIES:	
NET INCOME OR LOSS (a)	+5,440
Less: Gains on issuances of stock by equity investee	(5,440)
INVESTING ACTIVITIES:	
FINANCING ACTIVITIES:	
INCREASE (DECREASE) IN CASH (b)	-0-
ADD: BEGINNING CASH BALANCE	
ENDING CASH BALANCE	

BALANCE SHEET (SECOND)			
ASSETS		LIABILITIES	
CURRENT ASSETS		CURRENT LIABILITIES	
CASH (b)	-0-		
		NONCURRENT LIABILITIES	
		STOCKHOLDERS' EQUITY	
NONCURRENT ASSETS			
Investment at Equity	+5,400	CAPITAL STOCK	
		APIC	
		RETAINED EARNINGS (a)	+5,440
		TOTAL LIABILITIES & STOCKHOLDERS' EQUITY	
TOTAL ASSETS	-0-		-0-

The gain is a noncash revenue and is deducted in the operating activities section of the statement of cash flows (See Exhibits 6.1 and 6.3 for similar results for Coca-Cola). The transaction is a significant noncash investing activity requiring footnote disclosure or a separate schedule.

INVESTEE LOSSES IN EXCESS OF EQUITY CARRYING VALUE

A question arises when the investee incurs significant losses and the investor's share of these losses result in a negative equity investment account. According to the provisions of APB Opinion No. 18, the investor should not provide for additional losses and must suspend the use of the equity method unless:

- profitable investee operations are expected in the near future, or
- investor losses are not limited to the original investment.

With regard to this last point it should be noted that investor losses are typically limited to the amount of the equity investment. However, the investor can guaranty investee obligations or pledge other means of financial support. In this case, the negative balance in the equity investment is permitted because it is representative of the investor's obligation (commitment) to the investee.

The EITF also requires that if the investor holds other securities of the investee company, then losses must continue to be recognized and are allocated in the reverse order of liquidation priority:

1. to reduce the equity investment, but not below zero.
2. to reduce all other investments (unless classified as trading) in reverse order of liquidation priority (i.e., investments in preferred would be first, investments in debt would be second).

When future income occurs, the investment balances could be restored in reverse order (i.e. in the order of liquidation priority): all other securities first (debt first, preferred second, etc.), then the equity investment account.

COMPLEX OR FULL EQUITY ACCOUNTING

Goodwill Computations and Net Asset Revaluations Under the Complex or Full Equity Method

According to APB Opinion No. 18, in applying the equity method, the difference between the book and fair market values of the net assets acquired should be identified and allocated to asset revaluations and goodwill. However, depending on the cost and availability of fair value information, goodwill may be simply computed as the excess cost over the book value of the net assets acquired. This is a form of the partial equity method. In the following illustration, it is assumed that fair value information is readily available to the investor and the complex or full equity method will be used. The complex or full equity method produces the same results as using proportional consolidation techniques.

To illustrate the complex or full equity method, assume that FuzziLou Enterprises has significant influence over an investee company and a long-term plan to acquire a controlling interest in the investee. Therefore, it is economically feasible to obtain enough information to revalue the subsidiary's net assets (e.g., a detailed appraisal can be made). On January 2, 2008, FuzziLou acquires a 30% interest in the Drifter Too Company, paying $1,000,000 to acquire this share. The book and fair market values of Drifter Too's net assets are presented in the following table.

Account	Book Value	FMV	Difference	30% x Difference
Cash	$ 600,000	$ 600,000	$ - 0 -	$ - 0 -
Accounts receivable - net	100,000	100,000	- 0 -	- 0 -
Inventory (at FIFO)	433,334	533,334	100,000	30,000
Land	700,000	900,000	200,000	60,000
Plant and equipment - net	1,500,000	2,000,000	500,000	150,000
Total Assets	$3,333,334	$4,133,334	$800,000	$240,000
Liabilities	(1,000,000)	(1,000,000)	(- 0 -)	(- 0 -)
Net assets (Stockholders' Equity)	$2,333,334	$3,133,334	$800,000	$240,000

With the fair values of the investee net assets identified, the excess cost over book can be allocated. This allocation results in a $240,000 revaluation of the investee's net assets and recognition of a $60,000 as goodwill. The computation is proved below:

Purchase cost	**$1,000,000**
Book value of net assets acquired ($2,333,334 x 30%)	**(700,000)**
Excess cost over book	**$ 300,000**
Revaluation of net assets (above)	**(240,000)**
Goodwill (unallocated excess)	**$ 60,000**

The financial modeling worksheet used to reflect the acquisition indicates how the $1,000,000 investment will be reflected in the balance sheet and the statement of cash flows.

FINANCIAL MODELING WORKSHEET

INCOME STATEMENT (FIRST)	
REVENUES:	
EXPENSES:	
NET INCOME OR LOSS (a)	- 0 -

STATEMENT OF CASH FLOWS (THIRD)	
OPERATING ACTIVITIES:	
NET INCOME OR LOSS (a)	- 0 -
INVESTING ACTIVITIES:	
Purchase of DTC shares	(1,000,000)
FINANCING ACTIVITIES:	
INCREASE (DECREASE) IN CASH (b)	(1,000,000)
ADD: BEGINNING CASH BALANCE	
ENDING CASH BALANCE	

BALANCE SHEET (SECOND)			
ASSETS		LIABILITIES	
CURRENT ASSETS		CURRENT LIABILITIES	
CASH (b)	(1,000,000)		
		NONCURRENT LIABILITIES	
		STOCKHOLDERS' EQUITY	
NONCURRENT ASSETS			
Investment at Equity	+940,000	CAPITAL STOCK	
Goodwill*	+60,000	APIC	
		RETAINED EARNINGS (a)	
		TOTAL LIABILITIES & STOCKHOLDERS' EQUITY	
TOTAL ASSETS	- 0 -		- 0 -

* Not reported separately. Goodwill is part of the investment account. It is isolated here only for the purpose of this illustration.

The investment account can be established by the investor at $1,000,000, without separate recognition of the asset revaluations and goodwill. However, the excess cost over book value will result in additional depreciation and amortization charges, which reduce the equity earnings recognized by the investor. This is known as the "earnings drag effect" of using acquisition accounting. These charges not only reduce equity income, but they will also reduce the carrying value of the investment. Note that under FASB 142, goodwill is no longer subject to amortization but is subject to an impairment test each year. Again, goodwill generated on an equity investment is not subject to the annual test for impairment. Rather, these investments are written down whenever declines in value are found to be other than temporary. The goodwill impairment loss adds to the earnings drag effect of net asset revaluations.

To illustrate the earnings drag effect that results in this case, assume that Drifter Too (DTC) reports net income of $300,000 at December 31, 2008 (the first year of operations following the acquisition) and declares and pays a cash dividend of $50,000 on the same date. Assuming that all the investee's beginning inventory is sold (i.e., a FIFO assumption), goodwill is impaired by $2,000 and plant assets are depreciated over a 5 year useful life, the equity income and the additional charges on recognized on the investor's income statement are:

Account	***30% x Difference at FMV***	***Useful life or method***	***2008 Additional Expense***
Inventory (at FIFO)	$ 30,000	FIFO-sold	$ 30,000
Land	60,000	N/A	- 0 -
Plant and equipment – net	150,000	5 years	30,000
Goodwill	60,000	Impairment	2,000
Excess cost over book	$300,000		
Additional charges against equity income			$62,000

Equity income (30% x $300,000 Sub NI))	**$90,000**
Additional charges (above)	**(62,000)**
Net equity income recognized	**$28,000**

Investment Account Balance at 12/31/08

Cost	$1,000,000
Equity income (30% x $300,000)	90,000
Additional charges against income	(62,000)
Dividends (30% x $50,000)	(15,000)
Balance at 12/31/08	$1,013,000

The $13,000 growth in the investment account represents the undistributed equity earnings. The undistributed equity earnings are reconciled as follows:

Equity income: $300,000 x 30%	**$90,000**
Additional charges against income	**(62,000)**
Dividends received: $50,000 x 30%	**(15,000)**
Undistributed equity income (increase in the investment account)	**$13,000**

The effects of reporting equity income can be analyzed by reviewing the following financial modeling worksheet. Note that equity income could be reported on a net basis or $28,000, without separate disclosure of the additional operating expenses. Barry Company reports net equity income in Exhibit 6.1. The dividends received increase cash flows by $15,000 and are included as part of operating activities after the adjustment of undistributed equity income.

FINANCIAL MODELING WORKSHEET

INCOME STATEMENT (FIRST)	
REVENUES:	
Equity Income - NET (90,000 - 62,000)	+28,000
EXPENSES:	
NET INCOME OR LOSS (a)	+28,000

STATEMENT OF CASH FLOWS (THIRD)	
OPERATING ACTIVITIES:	
NET INCOME OR LOSS (a)	+28,000
Undistributed Equity Income	(13,000)
Cash Flow from Operating Activities	+15,000
INVESTING ACTIVITIES:	
FINANCING ACTIVITIES:	
INCREASE (DECREASE) IN CASH (b)	+15,000
ADD: BEGINNING CASH BALANCE	
ENDING CASH BALANCE	

BALANCE SHEET (SECOND)			
ASSETS		LIABILITIES	
CURRENT ASSETS		CURRENT LIABILITIES	
CASH (b)	+15,000		
		NONCURRENT LIABILITIES	
		STOCKHOLDERS' EQUITY	
NONCURRENT ASSETS			
Investment in DTC	+28,000	CAPITAL STOCK	
	(15,000)	APIC	
		RETAINED EARNINGS (a)	+28,000
		TOTAL LIABILITIES & STOCKHOLDERS' EQUITY	
TOTAL ASSETS	+28,000		+28,000

Additional Illustration

On January 1, 2008, Pendant Publishing, PLC acquired 4,000 shares of voting common stock of the J. Peterman Company, Incorporated. J. Peterman Company is a privately held company. Pendant paid $120,000 and the shares acquired represent a 20% interest in J. Peterman Company. The stockholders' equity of J. Peterman Company on the date of acquisition was equal to $550,000. Any asset write-ups are depreciated over a 5 year period and any goodwill on the acquisition is not subject to amortization.

During 2008 J. Peterman Company reported net income of $80,000 and declared and paid cash dividends of $24,000. Ignore taxes and deferred tax effects of the transaction for purposes of this illustration.

Goodwill results in the case because the investor pays more than the fair value of the net assets acquired. Assume that J. Peterman Company's plant assets were undervalued by $6,000 on the date of acquisition.

CALCULATION OF GOODWILL	
Purchase Price (Cost or Total Consideration Paid)	$ 120,000
Book Value (Historical Cost) of the Net Assets Acquired ($550,000 x 20%)	(110,000)
Excess Cost Over Book	$ 10,000
Excess Specifically Identified With Undervalued Assets (Write-up of Net Assets to Fair Market Value)	(6,000)
Unidentified Excess is Allocated to Goodwill (Excess Purchase Cost Over the Fair Market Value of Net Assets Acquired)	$ 4,000

Income Recognized under the Equity Method:	
Share of investee net income ($80,000 x 20%)	$16,000
Depreciation of asset write ups	—
$6,000 / 5 years................................	(1,200)
Income recognized................................	$14,800
Cash dividends received ($24,000 x 20%).....	$ 4,800
Undistributed Equity Income................	$ 10,000

The effects of these transactions (i.e., reporting equity income, asset revaluations and dividends) are shown on the following financial modeling worksheet. It is assumed that the additional operating expenses from the net asset write ups are not reported as a separate line item on the income statement.

FINANCIAL MODELING WORKSHEET

INCOME STATEMENT (FIRST)	
REVENUES:	
Equity Income - NET (16,000 - 1,200)	+14,800
EXPENSES:	
NET INCOME OR LOSS (a)	+14,800

STATEMENT OF CASH FLOWS (THIRD)	
OPERATING ACTIVITIES:	
NET INCOME OR LOSS (a)	+14,800
Undistributed Equity income	(10,000)
Cash Flow from Operating Activities	+ 4,800
INVESTING ACTIVITIES:	
FINANCING ACTIVITIES:	
INCREASE (DECREASE) IN CASH (b)	+ 4,800
ADD: BEGINNING CASH BALANCE	
ENDING CASH BALANCE	

BALANCE SHEET (SECOND)			
ASSETS		LIABILITIES	
CURRENT ASSETS		CURRENT LIABILITIES	
CASH (b)	+4,800		
		NONCURRENT LIABILITIES	
		STOCKHOLDERS'	
NONCURRENT ASSETS		EQUITY	
Investment at Equity	+14,800	CAPITAL STOCK	
	(4,800)	APIC	
		RETAINED EARNINGS (a)	+14,800
		TOTAL LIABILITIES & STOCKHOLDERS' EQUITY	
TOTAL ASSETS	+14,800		+14,800

Changing Methods of Accounting for Investments in Equity Securities

As the investor's level of ownership and the ability to exercise significant influence over the investee changes, it may be necessary to switch from cost to equity or from equity to cost.

Change from Equity to Cost

When the level of ownership falls below 20% and the investor's ability to exercise significant influence over the investee ceases to exist, the investor must terminate the use of the equity method and adopt the cost or fair value approach. Under these circumstances:

- the equity carrying value on the date of the change becomes the new "cost" basis of the investment account.
- the additional charges for depreciation, cost of sales and intangible asset amortization are suspended.

• there is no retroactive adjustment for previously recognized investee income.

However, adjustments are made on a prospective basis. Specifically, for all subsequent years after the switch from equity to cost, the investment account must be reduced for the cumulative difference between excess dividends received over what would have been the investor's share of investee net income.

This test is used to determine if the dividends received in subsequent years are income or a return of investment to the investor. Therefore, if from the date of the change, cumulative dividends are less than what would have been the investor's cumulative share of income, it implies that the investment value has been maintained, and is perhaps even undervalued. In this case, the entire amount of the dividend is recorded as income.

Conversely, if the cumulative dividends exceed what would have been the investor's cumulative share of investee net income, the underlying carrying value of the investment has not been maintained. Here, the excess dividend received reduces the carrying value of the investment. The dividends are coming out of previously recognized equity earnings. When previously recognized equity earnings are reduced to zero, the excess is charged against investor retained earnings. The portion of the dividend that does not exceed the cumulative equity earnings can be recorded as income.

It should be noted that although not frequently experienced in practice, the same methodology must be applied to all cost investments. The cumulative excess dividends over cumulative investee earnings are a form of liquidating dividend. To illustrate these concepts for the equity method, assume that FuzziLou had to suspend the use of the equity method early in 2009 as another investor gained control of Drifter Too. FuzziLou's 30% share of Drifter Too's income and dividends for the next four years is presented below.

Year	*Share of Dividends*	*Cumulative Dividend*	*Share of Net Income*	*Cumulative Net Income*	*Dividend Income*	*Reduction of Investment Account*
2009	$5,000	$ 5,000	$7,000	$ 7,000	$5,000	$ - 0 -
2010	6,000	11,000	8,000	15,000	6,000	- 0 -
2011	7,000	18,000	4,000	19,000	7,000	- 0 -
2012	7,000	25,000	4,000	23,000	5,000	2,000

The 2012 dividend of $7,000 is partially a liquidating dividend or a return of FuzziLou's investment because it fails to maintain the equity carrying value of the investment. The 2012 dividends would be reflected on the financial modeling worksheet as a $7,000 cash inflow that is allocated to reduce the investment account by $2,000 on the balance sheet and the remaining $5,000 is reported on the income statement as dividend income.

FINANCIAL MODELING WORKSHEET

INCOME STATEMENT (FIRST)	
REVENUES:	
Dividend Income	*+5,000*
EXPENSES:	
NET INCOME OR LOSS (a)	*+5,000*

STATEMENT OF CASH FLOWS (THIRD)	
OPERATING ACTIVITIES:	
NET INCOME OR LOSS (a)	*+5,000*
Cash received in excess of dividends	*+2,000*
INVESTING ACTIVITIES:	
FINANCING ACTIVITIES:	
INCREASE (DECREASE) IN CASH (b)	*+7,000*
ADD: BEGINNING CASH BALANCE	
ENDING CASH BALANCE	

BALANCE SHEET (SECOND)			
ASSETS		*LIABILITIES*	
CURRENT ASSETS		*CURRENT LIABILITIES*	
CASH (b)	*+7,000*		
		NONCURRENT LIABILITIES	
		STOCKHOLDERS'	
NONCURRENT ASSETS		*EQUITY*	
Investment in Equity	*(2,000)*	*CAPITAL STOCK*	
		APIC	
		RETAINED EARNINGS (a)	*+5,000*
		TOTAL LIABILITIES & STOCKHOLDERS' EQUITY	
TOTAL ASSETS	*+5,000*		*+5,000*

Note that if the investment was in a public company or if the fair value option is elected, the adjustments for fair value or "mark-to-market" accounting would be required each time financial statements are provided.

CHANGE FROM COST (FAIR VALUE) TO EQUITY

If the level of ownership increases over 20% or there is an increase in the ability of the investor to exercise significant influence over the investee, the investor must switch from the cost to the equity method. This situation is quite common in piecemeal corporate acquisitions. As of the date the investment qualifies for use of the equity method the investor:

- adopts the equity method, and
- adjusts the carrying value of the investment, net income and beginning retained earnings in a "step-by-step acquisition" approach, as if the equity method had always been used.

This requires a prior period adjustment to opening retained earnings, net of tax. The prior period adjustment is classified as a correction of an error. The adjustment also increases the investment account for the undistributed equity earnings for the years prior to the change in investor status. If comparative financial statements are presented, income statements are retroactively adjusted with the prior period adjustment reflected in the first balance sheet provided.

To illustrate, assume that FuzziLou's original 30% interest was not adequate for use of the equity method (e.g., another corporation held 35% of Drifter Too voting common stock). However, on January 2, 2009, FuzziLou acquires an additional 10% of Drifter Too stock for $150,000 and now switches from the cost to the equity method. The following adjustments are required on the date of the change to the equity method (assuming asset revaluations and goodwill are recognized and that undistributed earnings will be realized through future dividends):

Equity earnings in Drifter Too (30% x $300,000)	**$ 90,000**
Dividends received (30% x $50,000)	**(15,000)**
Additional charges for asset revaluations and goodwill impairment	**(62,000)**
Pre tax prior period adjustment (undistributed earnings)	**$ 13,000**
Taxable percentage (35% ownership; 80% exclusion)	**x 20%**
Taxable portion	**$ 2,600**
Tax rate	**x 35%**
Deferred income tax provision	**$ 910**
Prior period adjustment - net of tax: ($13,000 - 910)	**$12,090**

The prior period adjustment, (correction of an error), is reported as an adjustment to opening retained earnings. The deferred tax provision is increased by $910. Finally, the carrying value of FuzziLou's investment is increased by $13,000 and with the purchase of an additional $150,000 of voting stock, is now equal to $1,163,000:

Investment account at cost (30% share)	**$1,000,000**
Retroactive adjustment for change to the equity method	**13,000**
Cost of the additional 10% share of Drifter Too	**150,000**
Investment account at equity (40% share)	**$1,163,000**

If the investment was in a publicly traded company or if the fair value option was elected, fair value or mark-to-market accounting would have been used by the investor company. It is likely that the investment would have been classified as available for sale. In changing to the equity method the allowance account and any balance in accumulated other comprehensive income must be reversed out along with the revaluation to the equity method. The financial modeling worksheet reflecting the change to the equity method is presented below.

FINANCIAL MODELING WORKSHEET

INCOME STATEMENT (FIRST)	
REVENUES:	
EXPENSES:	
NET INCOME OR LOSS (a)	- 0 -

STATEMENT OF CASH FLOWS (THIRD)	
OPERATING ACTIVITIES:	
NET INCOME OR LOSS (a)	- 0 -
INVESTING ACTIVITIES:	
Purchase of Equity Investment	(150,000)
FINANCING ACTIVITIES:	
INCREASE (DECREASE) IN CASH (b)	(150,000)
ADD: BEGINNING CASH BALANCE	
ENDING CASH BALANCE	

BALANCE SHEET (SECOND)			
ASSETS		LIABILITIES	
CURRENT ASSETS		CURRENT LIABILITIES	
CASH (b)	(150,000)		
		NONCURRENT LIABILITIES	
		Deferred Tax Liability	+910
		STOCKHOLDERS'	
NONCURRENT ASSETS		EQUITY	
Investment in DTC	+150,000	CAPITAL STOCK	
	+13,000	APIC	
		RETAINED	
		EARNINGS (a)	+12,090
		TOTAL	
		LIABILITIES &	
		STOCKHOLDERS'	
TOTAL ASSETS	+13,000	EQUITY	+13,000

INTERCOMPANY TRANSACTIONS UNDER THE EQUITY METHOD

As noted earlier, the complex or full equity method produces results identical to the use of proportional consolidation. Therefore, this accounting will require adjustments to eliminate the effects of intercompany transactions. A common intercompany transaction is the purchase and sale of merchandise inventory.

When assets are transferred between investor and investee companies at historical cost (or book values), no adjustments are required. However, when there is a profit component on the transfer, the intercompany profit must be eliminated. To illustrate, assume that FuzziLou Enterprises purchases inventory from Drifter Too Company. The inventory was marked up by $600 over cost and FuzziLou sold none of the inventory. The following adjustment is required on the investor's books. Again, it is assumed that FuzziLou is a 30% investor and both the investor and investee are subject to a 35% tax rate. The adjustment is computed as follows:

$600 x 30% x (1 - .35) = <u>$117</u>

The investor's equity income and the carrying value of the investment account must both be reduced by $117. This adjustment corrects the investor's recognition of $90,000 (i.e., 30% x $300,000) of equity income, which included the $180 of pre-tax profit ($117 after-tax) not generated from transactions with independent parties.

Chapter 7 Accounting For Mergers and Acquisitions

INTRODUCTION

This chapter presents the accounting and analytical issues relating to mergers and acquisitions and consolidated financial statements. The accounting and reporting standards governing business combinations are set forth in FASB Statements Nos. 141(R), 142 and 160[1]. After a brief introduction discussing the legal forms of business combinations and an overview of consolidated financial statements, the accounting issues concerning the acquisition method of accounting and measuring and reporting goodwill will be presented.

LEGAL FORMS OF BUSINESS COMBINATIONS

A business combination can be implemented by using several different legal forms. The number of companies that survive the business combination can be used as a means of distinguishing the legal forms. Here are the legal forms of business combinations:

- a merger
- a consolidation
- an acquisition

Note that the boards of directors of the companies usually negotiate the terms of the combination, which is then approved by the stockholders of each of the combining companies. Although dependent on the state, usually two-thirds of each shareholder group must approve the business combination.

Under a statutory merger, one enterprise acquires all of the net assets of one or more other entities through an exchange of stock, payment of cash or other property or the issuance of debt instruments. The acquired entity ceases to exist as a separate legal entity, but could be maintained as a division of the acquirer. Specifically, under a legal merger, the parent is the sole owner of the subsidiary's stock, and votes to legally dissolve the subsidiary. The parent then records the assets and liabilities of the subsidiary on its own books (i.e., a net asset purchase). Here A + B = A.

In the case of a statutory consolidation, a new enterprise is formed to acquire two or more other enterprises through the exchange of voting stock. The acquired enterprises then cease to exist as separate legal entities. The new enterprise holds the stock of the previously separate companies and votes to dissolve the shares of both entities. The shareholders of the former enterprises now only hold the voting stock of the newly formed legal entity. Here A + B = C.

Finally, under a statutory (stock) acquisition, one enterprise pays cash or issues stock or debt for all or part of the voting stock of another enterprise. Both enterprises remain intact as separate legal entities. Maintaining the separate legal entities has some advantages. For example, if the parent decides to dispose of the subsidiary, it may be easier to sell the subsidiary's stock than its individual assets. In addition, if the subsidiary is a separate legal entity, it can still transact business in its own name (e.g., borrow additional capital). Here A + B = AB.

---

1. FASB ASC 805, ASC 350, ASC 810 [Predecessor literature: "Business Combinations," *Statement of Financial Accounting Standards No. 141* (R) (Norwalk, Conn.: FASB, 2007)]; [Predecessor literature: "Goodwill and Other Intangible Assets," *Statement of Financial Accounting Standards No. 142* (Norwalk, Conn.: FASB, 2001)]; [Predecessor literature: "Noncontrolling Interest in Consolidated Financial Statements," *Statement of Financial Accounting Standards No. 160* (Norwalk, Conn.: FASB, 2007)].

This is the only case where a legal parent-subsidiary relationship exists.

Unless noted otherwise, the discussion will assume a statutory (stock) acquisition and the need for an accounting consolidation. An accounting consolidation is the process of combining the financial statements of a parent company and one or more legally separate and distinct subsidiaries. The final combined statements will be the same under any legal form of combination.

CONSOLIDATED FINANCIAL STATEMENTS

The purpose of consolidated financial statements is to reflect the economic activities of an entity under common control, regardless of the separate legal existence of the individual subsidiaries. The consolidated financial statements are designed to present the "economic substance over the legal form of the separate businesses."

The basic principles of consolidation accounting relating to the (i) balance sheet and (ii) income statement are briefly discussed below.

The Consolidated Balance Sheet

In the preparation of a consolidated balance sheet, the accountant combines all asset, liability and stockholders' equity accounts but eliminates all transactions that are not objective or not "arms-length" such as:

1. The elimination of all intercompany receivables and payables.
2. The elimination of intercompany profit in inventory purchased by (upstream) or from (downstream) the parent at a marked-up transfer price.
3. The elimination of the parent's investment account against the stockholders' equity of the subsidiary. If less than 100% ownership, the difference between the total subsidiary stockholders' equity and the parent's claim to the subsidiary's net assets represents the noncontrolling interest (previously known as the minority interest).

The noncontrolling interest represents the outside shareholders' interest in the net assets of the consolidated subsidiary. It should be noted that even if the parent company owns less than 100% of the voting stock of the subsidiary, 100% of the assets and liabilities are included in the consolidated balance sheet at full fair value. This full fair value is attributable to both the controlling and the noncontrolling interest. The noncontrolling interest is also measured at fair value and is included in the stockholders' equity section of the consolidated balance sheet.

The attribution of full fair value to both the controlling and the noncontrolling interest is consistent with the entity theory of the firm. Under the entity theory, the firm is viewed as a single entity with values attributable to the controlling and the noncontrolling interest. That is, under the entity concept the consolidated financial statements are considered to be applicable to an economic entity that is owned by a controlling and a noncontrolling interest. When considered a single economic entity, the noncontrolling interest is revalued to reflect its full fair value and is presented with the other capital accounts in the stockholders' equity section of the consolidated balance sheet. The only exception to using full fair value in the measurement of the noncontrolling interest is in a reverse acquisition. Reverse acquisitions will be discussed in detail in a separate section of this chapter.

In subsequent accounting periods the noncontrolling interest is increased by its share of the subsidiary's net income and is reduced by its share of subsidiary net losses and dividends. In addition, any intercompany profit on intercompany sales to the parent is deducted from the noncontrolling interest's share of net income.

After all eliminations are made, the consolidated balance sheet should only reflect events and transactions between the consolidated entity and the "outside world" (i.e., third parties or firms outside the consolidated group).

The Consolidated Income Statement

In the preparation of a consolidated income statement, the accountant combines the revenues and expenses of the parent and its subsidiary companies, but eliminates all transactions not involving the outside world or third parties such as:

1. The elimination of all intercompany sales.
2. The elimination of all intercompany purchases.
3. The elimination of interest expense and interest income on intercompany loans.
4. The elimination of intercompany dividends.
5. The deduction (addition) of the "Net Income or (Loss) Attributable to the Noncontrolling Interest" on the consolidated income statement to reduce (increase) consolidated net income attributable to the controlling interest.

After all eliminations are made, the consolidated income statement should only reflect events and transactions between the consolidated entity and the "outside world" (i.e., third parties or firms outside the consolidated group).

Illustration: Net Income Attributable to the Noncontrolling Interest

To illustrate the presentation of net income attributable to the noncontrolling interest on the income statement, assume that Bennett Company holds an 80% interest in the BGO Group. During 20X9, the Bennett Company reported net income of $1,500,000 and the BGO Group reported net income of $200,000. This will result in $40,000 (i.e., 20% x $200,000) of the subsidiary's net income being attributed to the noncontrolling interest. The Bennett Company currently has 1,000,000 common shares outstanding. The calculation of consolidated net income is presented below. There are no preferred shares and no potentially dilutive securities outstanding.

Description	*Amount*
Net Income – Bennett Company	$1,500,000
Net Income – BGO Group	200,000
Net Income after tax	$1,700,000
Less: Net Income Attributable to the Noncontrolling Interest	(40,000)
Consolidated Net Income: Net Income Attributable to the Bennett Company	$1,660,000
Earnings per share Attributable to the Bennett Company Shareholders	$1.66

The financial statement effect of the net income attributable to the noncontrolling interest is presented in the financial modeling worksheet below. Note that the income attributable to the noncontrolling interest is a noncash charge against income and is an add back in the operating activities section of the cash flow statement.

FINANCIAL MODELING WORKSHEET

INCOME STATEMENT (FIRST)	
REVENUES:	
EXPENSES:	
Net Income Attributable to the Noncontrolling Interest	(40,000)
NET INCOME OR LOSS (a)	(40,000)

STATEMENT OF CASH FLOWS (THIRD)	
OPERATING ACTIVITIES:	
NET INCOME OR LOSS (a)	(40,000)
Add: Net Income Attributable to the Noncontrolling Interest	+40,000
Cash Flow from Operating Activities	- 0 -
INVESTING ACTIVITIES:	
FINANCING ACTIVITIES:	
INCREASE (DECREASE) IN CASH (b)	- 0 -
ADD: BEGINNING CASH BALANCE	
ENDING CASH BALANCE	

BALANCE SHEET (SECOND)			
ASSETS		LIABILITIES	
CURRENT ASSETS		CURRENT LIABILITIES	
CASH (b)	- 0 -		
		NONCURRENT LIABILITIES	
		Total Liabilities	
NONCURRENT ASSETS		STOCKHOLDERS' EQUITY	
		CAPITAL STOCK	
		APIC	
		RETAINED EARNINGS (a)	(40,000)
		Noncontrolling Interest	+40,000
TOTAL ASSETS	- 0 -	TOTAL LIABILITIES & STOCKHOLDERS' EQUITY	- 0 -

Debt on the Consolidated Balance Sheet

Consolidated debt may not legally represent a claim against the total assets of the consolidated group. Components of total debt are claims against the assets of the individual subsidiary incurring the obligation(s). Therefore, a creditor or financial analyst cannot adequately assess the risk involved with a particular loan agreement unless the individual subsidiary financial statements are analyzed. However, if the parent company specifically guarantees the obligations of the subsidiary, there is additional security for the creditor. In addition, even if the debt is not specifically guaranteed by the parent company and although not legally obligated to do so, the parent company is likely to cover a subsidiary's debt to maintain its own credit rating and financial reputation. In many cases a "comfort letter" is issued in which the acquiring company assures creditors that the newly acquired subsidiary will not be operated or managed in such a way as to impair its ability to repay any outstanding debt.

The difficulty in assessing the debt paying ability of a subsidiary in consolidated financial statements is prominent in a holding company structure.

The only function of a holding company is the hold stock in other, operating companies. The classic problem is that the holding company makes a relatively small equity investment to control a significantly large asset base. This results in a highly leveraged consolidated group where a small shift in profit margins can significantly impact the ability of the group to repay debt. A sample holding company structure is illustrated in the following spreadsheet.

Description	*Holding Company 1*	*Holding Company 2*	*Operating Company*	*Adjustments and Eliminations*	*Consolidated*
Assets	0.0	0.0	100.0		100.0
Investments	25.0	50.0	0.0	***a.*** (25.0) ***b.*** (50.0)	0.0
Total Assets	25.0	50.0	100.0	0.0	100.0
Liabilities	12.5	25.0	50.0		87.5
Shareholders' Equity	12.5	25.0	50.0	***a.*** (25.0) ***b.*** (50.0)	12.5
Total Liabilities & Sharehold-ers' Equity	25.0	50.0	100.0	0.0	100.0
Debt/Equity Ratio	1.0	1.0	1.0		7.0

Holding Company No. 1's only asset is its 100% investment in Holding Company No. 2. Holding Company No. 1s debt only covered by this investment. In addition, the only publicly traded equity is that of Holding Company No. 1. Holding Company No. 2's 100% investment in the Operating Company is its only asset and this asset is the only resource available to cover its debt. Only the Operating Company holds operating or income generating assets. The obligations of each company are not backed by the total assets of the consolidated group, unless specifically guaranteed by the company with the ability to pay. In fact, only $50.0 of the total $87.5 on consolidated debt is covered by operating assets. The other $37.5 in consolidated debt is only backed by investments in the other companies in the consolidated group. This means that a decline in the profitability of the operating company that reduces the value of the investment can impair the ability of the two holding companies to repay their debt.

It is also important to consider the other potential off-balance sheet obligations assumed by the acquirer (e.g., operating lease commitments).

ACCOUNTING FOR BUSINESS COMBINATIONS

There is presently only one GAAP method of accounting for business combinations. This method is the acquisition method (or the full fair value basis). Acquisition accounting must be used for all acquisitions and previous methods (i.e., the purchase and the pooling of interests methods) are no longer acceptable.

The Acquisition Method (The Full Fair Market Value Basis): Introduction

The use of the acquisition method implies that there is a dominant company in the transaction and this dominant party acquires, buys out or purchases the other company.

As is the case in any asset "acquisition," the transaction must be accounted for at the full fair value of the subsidiary on the date of the acquisition. The net assets of the subsidiary, including goodwill and the noncontrolling interest are all recognized and measured at full fair value.

The use of the acquisition method results in several analytical problems. These problems are based on the fact that the flow statements only reflect changes for the period from the date of acquisition to year end. The reason for not consolidating for the full year is that the fair values are only established as of the date of acquisition and this is the point where the new basis of accountability is established.

In the year of acquisition, a consolidated balance sheet is prepared as of the end of the year but the consolidated income statement can only be prepared from the date of acquisition. As noted above, the date of acquisition is the only date where the fair market values of the subsidiary's net assets are determined. Footnotes to the financial statements will provide income information on a pro forma basis whenever significant. The pro forma income information reflects the net income or net loss for the entire year, "as if" the entities were consolidated from the beginning of the fiscal year.

A consolidated statement of cash flows can be prepared for the entire year. However, the acquisition method results in several unique problems. The amount paid for the subsidiary's net assets is included in the consolidated investing activities. The total cash outflow in investing activities includes amounts paid for inventories, receivables, payables, accrued liabilities, etc., acquired on the date of the business combination. Without the acquisition, these changes would have been included in operating activities of the subsidiary. However, in the year of acquisition, the changes in the balance sheet for these operating cycle (noncash working capital) accounts will not equal the changes reported in the operating activities section of the statement of cash flows.

Any changes in noncash (operating) working capital accounts, caused by pre-acquisition events of the subsidiary, are included in the acquisition value and are ignored in the operating activities section of the cash flow statement. This means that balance sheet changes will not articulate with the changes in the noncash (operating) working capital items on the statement of cash flows.

An acquisition is one of three events causing changes in noncash working capital accounts on the balance sheet to differ from the change reported in the operating activities section of the cash flow statement. The other cases where there is lack of articulation between balance sheet changes and the change in operating working capital accounts on the cash flow statement are caused by divestitures and foreign currency translation adjustments. The effect of changes in foreign currency exchange rates is a separate category of cash flows on the statement.

This lack of articulation has a significant impact on operating working capital reported on the statement of cash flows. In addition, operating cycle ratios, such as day's payable, are distorted. This makes it difficult to determine liquidity and working capital needs (i.e., liquidity and debt capacity analysis will be distorted).

The effect of acquisitions and divestitures on any operating (noncash) working capital account, assuming no effect of exchange rate changes on cash is computed as follows:

Effect of Acquisitions and Divestitures = **Balance Sheet Change** – **Cash Flow Statement Change**

EXHIBIT 7.1 BRIGATTI, LTD CONSOLIDATED BALANCE SHEET

	June 1, 2012	June 1, 2011
	(millions)	
ASSETS		
Current assets:		
Cash and cash equivalents	$ 342.84	$ 420.6
Accounts receivable, net	581.04	546.84
Inventories	582.6	516.12
Deferred tax assets	38.88	89.76
Prepaid expenses and other	108.84	123.24
Total current assets	1,654.20	1,696.56
Property and equipment, net	658.56	585.48
Deferred tax assets	—	43.2
Goodwill	839.64	670.68
Intangible assets, net	310.2	56.4
Other assets	243.84	219.72
Total assets	$3,706.44	$3,272.04

EXHIBIT 7.2 BRIGATTI, LTD CONSOLIDATED STATEMENT OF CASH FLOWS

	Fiscal Years Ended		
	June 1, 2012		June 1, 2011
		(millions)	
Cash flows from operating activities:			
Net income	$ 369.6	$ 228.48	$ 203.04
Adjustments to reconcile net income to net cash provided by operating activities:			
Depreciation and amortization expense	152.4	122.52	102.72
Deferred income tax expense (benefit)	42.6	12.12	(6.12)
Minority interest expense	16.2	9.6	1.68
Equity in the income of equity-method investees	(5.16)	(7.68)	(6.6)
Non-cash stock compensation expense	31.92	15.48	4.92
Non-cash impairments of retail assets	12.96	1.8	—
Non-cash Jones-Related Litigation charge	—	120	—
Non-cash provision for bad debt expense	1.44	7.2	3.12
Loss on disposal of property and equipment	6.84	9.24	8.88
Non-cash foreign currency losses (gains)	6.36	(13.92)	(5.28)
Non-cash restructuring charges	5.4	—	23.52
Changes in operating assets and liabilities:			
Accounts receivable	(23.04)	(19.32)	(67.92)
Inventories	4.56	(28.2)	16.92
Accounts payable and accrued liabilities	46.92	(53.4)	56.52
Settlement of Jones – Related Litigation	(120)	—	—
Other balance sheet changes	(10.08)	54.48	(79.08)

Net cash provided by operating activities	538.92	458.4	256.32
Cash flows from investing activities:			
Acquisitions, net of cash acquired	(456.72)	(291.96)	(20.52)
Consolidation of RL Media cash	—	—	10.68
Capital expenditures	(190.32)	(208.92)	(151.56)
Net cash used in investing activities	(647.04)	(500.88)	(161.4)

Using Brigatti's 2012 Consolidated Financial Balance Sheet and Statement of Cash Flows as presented in Exhibits 7.1 and 7.2 we can determine the effect of acquisitions for the year, again assuming no effect of exchange rate changes on cash.

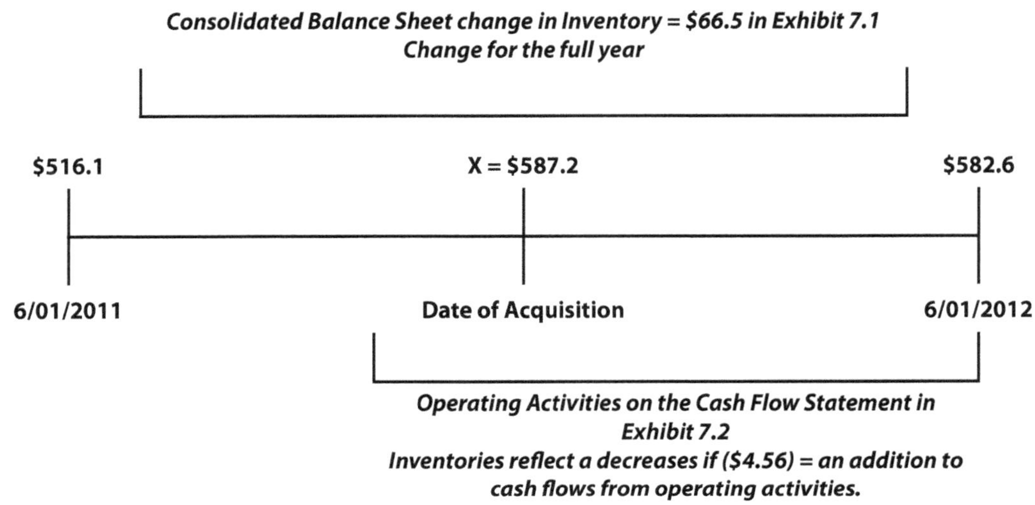

Effect of Acquisitions and Divestitures	=	Balance Sheet Change	-	Cash Flow Statement Change
+ $71.06	=	$66.5	-	(4.56)

Therefore, the effect of the acquisition was to increase inventory by $59.2 and results in an acquisition date inventory balance of $587.2 (i.e., $516.1 + 71.06).

The acquisition method is sometimes viewed as having additional disadvantages. For example, since the subsidiary's net assets are recognized and measured at full fair market value, charges for depreciation, depletion and amortization would increase and thereby reduce reported income. In addition, if the assets with increased carrying values (i.e., a "stepped-up basis") are sold, the gain on sale would be reduced or the loss on sale and the cost of goods sold for inventory would be increased. This is the "earnings drag" effect associated with acquisition accounting.

The existence of an earnings drag effect assumes that the net assets are written up to fair market value (FMV). If there were required write-downs to FMV, it could be considered an advantage of the acquisition method. Nonetheless, given historical cost-based accounting it is more common to experience the need for asset write ups.

Another disadvantage of the acquisition method is that the pre-acquisition retained earnings of the subsidiary cannot be brought across into the consolidated balance sheet because the companies were not under common control until the date of the acquisition. Only the subsidiary retained earnings generated after the date of the acquisition can be combined with the parent's retained earnings. As a result, only the parent company's equity is included in the consolidated financial statements on the date of acquisition.

The last disadvantage of acquisition accounting is that it usually results in goodwill being recorded on the consolidated balance sheet. The recognition of goodwill causes two analytical problems. Goodwill is no longer subject to amortization for financial reporting purposes. However, goodwill must be tested annually for impairment. An impairment write off will produces an additional earnings drag effect from use of the acquisition method.

Goodwill amortization may be tax deductible over a 15-year period. However, goodwill amortization is only tax deductible, (as a Section 197 intangible asset), in a net asset acquisition for cash. Goodwill amortization is not tax deductible in any cash for stock acquisition without a Section 338 (h) (10) election. As a result, goodwill could result in an earnings reduction from an impairment write off without the tax benefit of goodwill amortization.

Finally, the asset goodwill raises significant valuation questions in financial and credit analysis. The future economic benefit from goodwill is highly uncertain.

The general conclusion is that the acquisition method tends to be an income reducing accounting method.

PROFESSIONAL PRONOUNCEMENTS REGARDING BUSINESS COMBINATIONS: FASB STATEMENTS NOS. 141 (R), 142 AND 160

The FASB Statement No. 141(R) is the current guidance on accounting for business combinations. The standard is to be applied prospectively to all business combinations. This statement will be effective in fiscal 2009 for calendar year end companies. Early application and retrospective accounting are both prohibited.

FASB Statement No. 141(R) applies to all transactions meeting the definition of a business combination, as defined in (b) below. It does not apply to:

a. The formation of a joint venture.

b. The acquisition of an asset or a group of assets that does not constitute a business. Statement 141 (R) defines a business as an integrated set of activities and assets that are capable of being managed to provide a return to investors or economic benefit to owners, members or participants. The term capable increases the range of entities included within the scope of the standards. For example, the term capable will include entities not currently contracting with customers, such as development stage enterprises.

c. A combination between entities under common control (e.g., a parent transfers the net assets of a wholly owned subsidiary into the parent company and liquidates the subsidiary).

d. A combination between not-for-profit organizations or the acquisition of a for-profit business by a not-for-profit organization.

The Acquisition Method. All business combinations must be accounted for by applying the acquisition method. Application of the acquisition method requires four steps:

- Identification of the acquirer (This can result in a reverse acquisition where the legal subsidiary becomes the accounting parent or acquirer for purposes of accounting for the business combination).
- Determining the acquisition date.
- Recognizing and measuring the identifiable net assets acquired and any noncontrolling interest.
- Recognizing and measuring goodwill or a gain on a bargain purchase.

These four steps are discussed in the following sections.

STEP 1: Identification of the Acquirer

The acquirer is defined as the entity that gains control of the acquiree. The standards increase the means by which the acquirer gains control of the acquiree. FASB Statement No. 160 provides guidance regarding identification of the acquirer. This statement is similar to previous guidance in that the usual condition for control is defined as a majority voting interest. As a general rule, we must have ownership by one entity, either directly or indirectly of more than 50 percent of the outstanding voting shares of another entity, unless the other entity is in bankruptcy, in legal reorganization or under government imposed restrictions. In these last three cases, the acquirer cannot control the acquiree.

If the conditions discussed in the previous paragraph are not sufficient, FASB Statement 141 (R) provides other factors leading to control and defining the acquirer in a business combination affected by exchanging voting shares. For example, the other factors leading to control and identifying the acquirer include: the relative voting rights in the combined entity after the business combination; the existence of a large minority voting interest in the combined entity if no other owner or organized group of owners has a significant voting interest; the composition of the senior management of the combined entity; the terms of the exchange of equity interests.

The acquirer is typically the combining entity whose shareholders retain or receives the largest portion of the voting rights in the combined entity. In this case, consideration must be given to special voting arrangements, options, warrants or convertible securities. In addition, the acquirer can be identified as the combining entity whose single owner or organized group of owners holds the largest voting interest in the combined entity. The combining entity whose former management dominates the management of the combined entity is generally identified as the acquirer. Finally, the acquirer is typically the combining entity that pays a premium over the precombination value of the equity interests of the other combining entity or entities.

The FASB utilizes a broader or an expanded definition of what qualifies as a business combination. For example, an acquirer can use the acquisition method if that entity obtains control of the acquiree without the transfer of consideration (e.g., if the holder of voting shares gains a controlling interests when the participation rights of a majority interest expire). Control can also be obtained by contract without holding any voting interests in the other entity. In addition, the acquirer can be identified by being designated as the primary beneficiary of a variable interest entity that qualifies as a business under FIN 46R. Finally, a business combination can be implemented by combining two or more mutual entities (e.g., credit unions) or by acquiring development stage enterprises that meet the definition of a business under the current FASB standards.

STEP 2: Determination of the Acquisition Date and its impact on the Acquisition Price

The acquisition date is the date the acquirer obtains control of the acquiree which is typically the closing date. An exception is when the acquirer obtains control on a date earlier than the closing date by the terms of a written agreement. The acquisition date becomes a critical point under the acquisition method because it is the only point where the acquisition value is determined and measurement takes place. Part of the acquisition price is the fair value of the consideration transferred for the acquiree. For example, if equity is used to acquire the target company, the fair value of the acquirer's equity will be measured at the acquisition date and not at the announcement date.

STEP 3: Recognizing and measuring the identifiable net assets acquired and any noncontrolling interest

On the date of acquisition, identifiable tangible and intangible assets, goodwill or the gain on a bargain purchase, liabilities assumed and the noncontrolling interests in the acquiree must be measured at full fair value with limited exceptions.

Note that "full fair value" means that in all cases, (i.e., whether a 100% or partial acquisition is implemented), all net assets, including goodwill are recognized and measured as if there is a 100% acquisition of the target company. In addition, there is no allocation of the consideration transferred to the net assets acquired.

When the initial accounting (recognition and measurement process) is not complete by the end of the reporting period in which the business combination occurs, the acquirer can report provisional amounts for any items for which accounting information is incomplete. The maximum length of the measurement period is one year from the acquisition date. The measurement period ends whenever the acquirer obtains the necessary data to complete the financial information reported or determines that the additional data are not available. Any adjustments made during the measurement period are applied retrospectively and can result in restating prior period information, including adjustments to goodwill. Any adjustments made after the measurement period are recorded in earnings.

As a result, the acquisition date value of the business acquired is equal to the sum of:

- The fair value of the consideration transferred. Note that if securities are issued as part of the consideration transferred, they must be measured at fair value as of the acquisition date, regardless of factors that may influence the stock price including competitive bids by several potential acquirers and the impact of other events that occur between the announcement date and the acquisition date.
- The fair value of the noncontrolling interest in the acquiree.
- The fair value of the acquisition date equity interest previously held by the acquirer in a step acquisition. Here, the remeasurement of the existing equity held will result in a gain or loss recognized in the earnings of the acquirer.

There are several special measurement issues and modifications to the full fair value method. The key issues regarding tangible net assets are presented in Exhibit 7.3

EXHIBIT 7.3: DETERMINATION OF FAIR VALUES OF THE TANGIBLE NET ASSETS ACQUIRED

Net Asset Acquired	***Valuation Approach Per SFAS 141 (R)***
Marketable securities	Fair values, which, for trading and available for sale securities, are already reflected in the acquired company's balance sheet
Receivables	Present values of amounts to be received determined by using current interest rates, less allowances for uncollectible accounts
Inventories: Finished goods and merchandise inventories	Estimated selling prices less the sum of the costs of disposal and a normal profit
Inventories: Work in process inventories	Estimated selling prices less the sum of the costs of completion, costs of disposal, and a normal profit
Inventories: Raw material inventories	Current replacement cost
Plant and equipment: If expected to be used in operations	Current replacement costs for similar capacity unless the expected future use of the assets indicates a lower value to the acquirer
Plant and equipment: If expected to be sold	Fair value less cost to sell
Identifiable other assets (such as land, natural resources, and nonmarketable securities):	Appraised (fair) value
Liabilities (such as notes and accounts payable, long-term debt, pensions, warranties, claims payable)	Present value of amounts to be paid determined at appropriate current interest rates

The FASB provides an extensive list of identifiable intangible assets to be recognized and measured in a business combination at the date of acquisition. Exhibit 7.4 lists examples of the types of identifiable intangible assets that can be recognized and measured in a business combination.

EXHIBIT 7.4: CLASSIFICATION SCHEME FOR IDENTIFIABLE INTANGIBLE ASSETS

Identifiable Intangible Asset Acquired	*Items Included in the Classification*
Permits	1. Broadcast rights, defined as being a license to transmit over certain bandwidths in the radio frequency spectrum, granted by the operation of communication laws 2. Certification marks, or right to be able to assert that a product or service meets certain standards of quality or origin, such as "ISO 9000 Certified" 3. Collective marks, or rights to signify membership in an association 4. Construction permits, which are rights to build a specified structure at a specified location 5. Franchise rights, or permits to engage in a trade-named business, to sell a trademarked good, or to sell a service-marked service in a particular geographic area 6. Internet domain names 7. Operating rights, permits to operate in a certain manner, such as that granted to a carrier to transport specified commodities, and 8. Use rights, which are permits to use specified land, property, or air space in a particular manner, such as the right to cut timber, expel emissions, or land airplanes
Intellectual property	1. Copyrights, or the rights to reproduce, distribute, etc. an original work of literature, music, art, photography, or film 2. Newspaper mastheads, the rights to use the information that is displayed on the top of the first pages of newspapers 3. Patents, which are rights to make, use, or sell an invention for a specified period 4. Service marks, rights to use the name or symbol that distinguishes a service 5. Trade dress, defined as access to the overall appearance and image (unique color, shape, or package design) of a product; trademarks, which are rights to use the word, logo, or symbol that distinguishes a product; trade names, or the right to use the name or symbol that distinguishes a business; trade secrets, which consist of information, such as a formula, process, or recipe, that is kept confidential; and unpatented technology, or access to the knowledge about the manner of accomplishing a task
Technology tools	Computer software, including programs, procedures, and documentation associated with computer hardware, as well as databases, which are collections of a particular type of information, such as scientific data or credit information

Procurement rights	1. Construction contracts, which are rights to acquire the subject of the contract in exchange for taking over the remaining obligations (including any payments) 2. Employment contracts, or rights to take the seller's place as the employer under the contract and thus obtain the employee's services in exchange for fulfilling the employer's remaining duties, such as payment of salaries and benefits, under the contract 3. Lease agreements, which are rights to step into the shoes of lessees and thus obtain the rights to use assets that are the subject of leases, in exchange for making the remaining lease payments 4. License agreements, rights to access or use properties that are the subjects of licenses in exchange for making any remaining license payments and adhering to other responsibilities as licensee 5. Royalty agreements, which are rights to take the place of payors and thus assume the payors' remaining rights and duties under the agreements 6. Service or supply contracts, or rights to become the customer of particular contracts and thus purchase the specified products or services for the prices specified in those contracts
Competitor arrangements	1. Noncompete agreements, which are rights to assurances that companies or individuals will refrain from conducting similar businesses for specified periods; and 2. Standstill agreements, which convey rights to assurances that companies or individuals will refrain from engaging in certain activities for specified periods
Customer arrangements	1. Customer lists, defined as information about companies' customers, including names, contact information, and order histories that a third party, such as a competitor or a telemarketing firm would want to use in its own business 2. Customer relationships, or relationships between entities and their customers for which a. The entities have information about the customers and have regular contacts with the customers, and b. The customers have the ability to make direct contact with the entity 3. Contracts and related customer relationships which arise through contracts and are of value to buyers which can "step into the shoes" of the sellers and assume their remaining rights and duties under the contracts, and which have the promise that the customers will place future orders with the entity 4. Noncontractual customer relationships, arising through means such as regular contacts by sales or service representatives, the value of which are derived from the prospect of the customers placing future orders with the entities 5. Order or production backlogs, providing buyers rights to step into the shoes of sellers on unfilled sales orders for services and for goods in amounts that exceed the quantity of finished goods and work-in-process on hand for filling the orders

These identifiable intangible assets are separable from goodwill, either by using a contractual (legal) criterion or a separability criterion. To illustrate, covenants not to compete are contractual intangible assets while customer lists are separable intangible assets. A detailed discussion of accounting for intangible assets is presented in the next section.

ACCOUNTING FOR INTANGIBLE ASSETS UNDER SFAS NO. 142

Under FASB Statement No. 142, there are three classes of intangibles: (1) limited-life or finite life intangibles; (2) indefinite-life intangibles other than goodwill and (3) goodwill.

Limited Life Intangibles

Limited-life intangibles include assets such as leaseholds, copyrights, franchises, patents, etc. These intangible assets are capitalized only when purchased and must be expensed if internally created.

Limited-life intangibles are subject to amortization. Amortization represents systematic charges to expense over the estimated useful life of the intangible. Estimated residual values may be used, but this is not a common practice. Estimated useful lives are determined by consideration of legal, regulatory, contractual and competitive factors.

The standards do not strictly require either a specific method of amortization or a limit on useful life. However, the method of amortization should attempt to match the revenues generated from the use of the intangible. If a revenue stream cannot be reasonably estimated, the straight-line method should be used. There is a recommended 20 year maximum amortization period, but it can be avoided if there is evidence of cash flow generating ability beyond the 20 year period.

The implementation of maximum life of twenty years may be avoided if the asset generates clearly identifiable cash flows that are expected to continue for more than twenty years, and either (1) the asset is exchangeable or (2) control over the future economic benefits of the asset is obtained through contractual or other legal rights that extend for more than twenty years. Clearly identifiable cash flows are cash flows that may be associated with the specific intangible asset or with a group of assets that includes the intangible asset. Extended control over the economic benefits of an intangible asset can be achieved by renewal of legal or contractual rights. An example of such an asset would be a renewable broadcast license, expiring in two years, but which may be renewed indefinitely without any significant additional investment.

An identifiable intangible will be written down that asset's value is determined to be impaired. The future generating ability of the limited-life intangibles must be continually evaluated for impairment by applying the FASB Statement No. 144 requirements for non-current assets. For finite life intangible assets this involves using both the recoverability test and the fair value test. As in any test for asset impairment, there must be reasonable evidence of a loss of revenue generating ability. For example, new technology reduces the value of a capitalized patent. In cases were this evidence exists, the recoverability and fair value tests are employed.

In the recoverability test if the sum of the undiscounted cash flows over the remaining life of the asset is less than the carrying value, a possible impairment of value is indicated. If the sum of the undiscounted future cash flows exceeds the asset's carrying value, there is no impairment indicated. The fair value test follows and is only required in cases where impairment is indicated. If there is need for the fair value test, a write off is taken if the fair market value of the asset is less than its carrying value. Fair market value can be determined by quoted market prices, market comparables and discounted cash flow valuation. The fair value hierarchy provided by FASB No. 157 would be utilized for this purpose.

Indefinite-life Intangibles

The second category of intangible assets includes indefinite-life intangibles other than goodwill. An intangible is considered to have indefinite-life if there are no identifiable legal, regulatory, contractual or competitive factors that will limit the revenue generating ability of the asset. For example, customer lists, renewable licenses (e.g., broadcasting), renewable permits, trademarks and trade names (if registered, there are an indefinite number of renewals for 10 year periods). As is the case for all intangibles indefinite-life intangibles are capitalized only when purchased and are expensed when internally generated.

Indefinite-life intangibles are not subject to amortization. These intangibles have indefinite-life and not infinite life. As a result, amortization can begin as soon as a finite life is determined. Indefinite-life intangibles must also be tested for impairment at least annually. Again, there must be reasonable evidence of a loss of revenue generating ability. For example, satellite radio and MP3 technology can reduce the carrying value of renewable broadcast licenses for land based radio stations. In cases were this evidence exists, an impairment test is employed. However, because there is an indefinite-life the recoverability test does not apply. There is no recoverability test because the indefinite-life intangible would never fail the recoverability test with indefinite future cash flows.

Therefore, in cases where impairment is indicated, a write off is taken if the fair market value of the asset is less than its carrying value. Fair market value can be determined by quoted market prices, market comparables and discounted cash flow valuation. The fair value hierarchy provided by FASB No 157 would be utilized for this purpose.

Goodwill

Under the FASB Statement Nos. 141 (R) and 142, accountants are required to be more diligent in attempting to identify all intangibles. This is a critical step because any undiscovered intangible will be applied to goodwill. Since goodwill is not subject to amortization, the FASB was concerned that if the valuation is not carefully conducted, more of the acquisition value will be attributed to goodwill and without amortization expense the earnings drag effect can be minimized.

Other recognition and measurement issues on the date of acquisition include accounting for contingencies, transactions costs and contingent consideration.

Contingencies

FASB Statement 141(R) classifies contingencies as either contractual contingencies or noncontractutal contingencies.

Contractual contingencies

Contractual contingencies are also recognized at fair value at the date of acquisition (e.g., guaranty of debt). This means that the FASB Statement No. 5 criteria of probable and subject to reasonable estimation do not apply to the recognition and measurement of contractual contingencies acquired in the business combination. This includes both contingent assets and contingent liabilities. As a result, any assets and liabilities arising from contractual contingencies are measured at fair value, regardless of whether it is probable that the contingency will occur in the future.

Noncontractual contingencies

Noncontractual contingencies must meet a "more likely than not" condition for recognition and measurement at fair value at the acquisition date (e.g., pending litigation). If the noncontractutal contingency does not meet the "more likely than not" condition, the FASB Statement No. 5 criteria of probable and subject to reasonable estimation must be applied.

Note that the subsequent period changes in the recognized value of either type of contingency must be recognized in the earnings of the period of the change. A conservative approach is used in this regard. That is, the subsequent period adjustments will result in charges against earnings if the actual liability is higher or the actual asset is lower than the estimated amounts used on the date of acquisition.

Transaction costs

Transaction costs are not part of the acquisition value but are expensed as incurred. Transactions costs include professional fees (for accountants, appraisers, engineers, investment banks and lawyers), finder's fees, and incremental in-house or out-of-pocket costs specifically related to the acquisition. Recurring internal costs of maintaining an acquisitions department must be expensed as incurred (i.e., general and administrative expenses). All acquisition costs incurred by the target company should be expensed as incurred. The target's costs consist of management and staff time devoted to the merger.

DEBT AND STOCK ISSUE COSTS

Equity and debt issue costs are accounted for using the appropriate GAAP for these transactions. Debt and stock issue costs are accounted for in the same way as for any new security issuance. Debt and stock issue costs include printing, registration and underwriting fees.

Debt issue costs are capitalized as a deferred charge on the asset side of the balance sheet and are amortized over the life of the debt issue. Stock issue costs are usually recorded as reduction of the additional paid in capital on the issue. An alternative for stock issue costs is to record the amount as an intangible asset, "organization costs". This intangible can be amortized if considered a finite life intangible asset. The intangible asset treatment for stock issue costs is consistent with the asset classification of debt issue costs as a deferred charge.

An issue arises when the same investment bank is used by the acquiring company to provide advisory and valuation services, as well as underwriting securities used to implement the business combination. The SEC discusses the allocation of fees paid to an investment banker. Staff Accounting Bulletin (SAB) Topic 2A.6 indicates that the investment banker must allocate its fee between the costs of the acquisition (e.g., finder's fees) and debt and stock issue costs.

Contingent consideration

Contingent consideration is also measured at fair value at the acquisition date and is included in the consideration transferred to implement the business combination. This is true regardless of the potential difficulty in measuring the fair value of the contingent consideration. The uncertainty of the final amount of the contingent consideration is built into the fair value estimates used at the date of acquisition. Contingent consideration is still classified as either equity or a liability. The equity or liability classification is based on current FASB guidance. For example, FASB Statement No. 150 requires an issuer to classify as a liability any financial instrument issued in the form of shares that is mandatory redeemable and embodies an unconditional obligation requiring the issuer to redeem it by transferring its assets at a specified or determinable date (or dates) or upon an event that is certain to occur.

When classified as a liability the contingent consideration is measured at fair value and any remeasurement at settlement is recorded in income, unless the contingent arrangement involves a hedging instrument which will be accounted for in other comprehensive income. Contingent consideration classified as equity cannot be remeasured after the acquisition date and the settlement will be accounted for within equity.

STEP 4: Recognizing and measuring goodwill or a gain on a bargain purchase

One of the most significant issues addressed by the FASB standards involves the computation of goodwill and the treatment of a bargain purchase. The methodology employs the "entity theory" and the "full goodwill" approach. Under the entity theory, the combined entity is as a single economic unit comprised of a controlling and a noncontrolling interest. Full goodwill is measured as if the entire entity is acquired and the goodwill is attributed to both the controlling and the noncontrolling interests. The use of the entity theory and the full goodwill method has a major impact on the measurement of the net assets acquired and the valuation of the noncontrolling interest and goodwill.

Computing Goodwill or the Gain on a Bargain Purchase

According to FASB Statement No. 141(R), goodwill is measured as the excess of (a) over (b):

(a) The aggregate of:
1. The fair value of the consideration transferred.
2. The fair value of the noncontrolling interest in the acquiree.
3. The fair value of the acquisition date equity interest previously held by the acquirer in a step acquisition. Here, the remeasurement of the existing equity held will result in a gain or loss recognized in the earnings of the acquirer.

(b) The net of the acquisition date amounts of the identifiable assets acquired and liabilities assumed measured at fair value.

Again, under the full goodwill method, goodwill, (a – b), is computed as if there is always a 100% acquisition and is attributed to both the controlling and the noncontrolling interest. According to the entity theory and the full goodwill method, goodwill is measured at full fair value and is allocated between the two components of the single entity: the controlling and the noncontrolling interest.

Under FASB Statement No. 142, goodwill is not subject to amortization but must be tested for impairment. During the implementation of impairment tests, including the determination of the implied value of goodwill, the value of the reporting unit must be based on the acquisition method as required by FASB Statement No. 141(R).

A bargain purchase (also known as negative goodwill) results when (b) exceeds (a) and is recorded as a gain on the income statement on the date of acquisition.

In the case of a bargain purchase, the acquirer should reconsider the values used in the measurement and recognition process. If no adjustments are deemed necessary or if there is an excess after any adjustments, the acquirer recognizes the excess as a gain on the date of acquisition. Note that is a review of the values used and not a required reduction of the fair values assigned to long-lived assets as employed under prior standards.

Other Key Provisions of FASB Statement No. 141(R)

FASB Statement No. 141(R) includes other key provisions including the accounting for in-process research and development, treatment of anticipated restructuring charges, non-controlling interests in a reverse acquisitions and the allocation of income to the controlling and the noncontrolling interests.

(i) Accounting for In-Process Research and Development (R&D)

All In-Process R&D acquired in the business combination is to be recognized as an identifiable intangible asset and measured at fair value at the acquisition date. These R&D assets are considered to be indefinite-life intangibles and are not subject to amortization until the project is either considered complete or is deemed to be without future value to the combined entity. Of course, indefinite-life intangibles are subject to impairment testing. All future R&D costs, such as costs to complete the projects, must be expensed as incurred as required under FASB Statement No. 2.

(ii) Restructuring Charges

Any anticipated costs of restructuring that do not represent an actual obligation on the date of the acquisition are not be included in the measurement of a business combination (i.e., not part of the acquisition value). These costs will be recognized as incurred in periods subsequent to the acquisition. Only actual obligations for restructuring are recognized on the date of acquisition.

Noncontrolling interests in a reverse acquisition

In a reverse acquisition, the legal acquirer (legal parent) is identified as the accounting acquiree for financial reporting purposes. A reverse acquisition can occur if the shareholders of the legal subsidiary hold the majority of the voting shares of the legal parent company. The valuation of a noncontrolling interest in a reverse acquisition is based on the noncontrolling interest percentage of the book value of the legal subsidiary and not measured at fair value. With the exception of the reverse acquisition, the noncontrolling interest must be valued at full fair value at the acquisition date.

Definition of Consolidated Income and Earnings per Share

Consolidated income is defined as the income attributable to the parent plus the income attributable to the noncontrolling interest. However, earnings per share must only be reported on the income attributable to the shareholders of the controlling interest.

Accounting for the Noncontrolling Interest

Measurement and Reporting the Noncontrolling Interest

Under FASB Statement No. 160, the noncontrolling interest in a subsidiary (formerly known as the minority interest) shall be reported as part of consolidated equity and measured at full fair value. The effective date of FASB Statement No. 160 is the first annual reporting period beginning on or after December 15, 2008 (this is fiscal 2009 for calendar year entities). The presentation standards can be applied retroactively while other portions of the standard must be applied prospectively. Early adoption is prohibited.

By measuring the noncontrolling interest at full fair value, all assets and liabilities (including goodwill) are recognized, as if there is a 100% acquisition. Note that FASB Statement No. 160 does not apply to not-for-profit entities.

Fair value of the noncontrolling interest is determined by the market value of the noncontrolling interests' shares. If the shares are not publicly traded, other valuation methods shall be employed. FASB Statement No. 157 guidance is applied if the shares are not publicly traded. As noted earlier, the only exception to the fair value measurement of the noncontrolling interest is in a reverse acquisition. Here the noncontrolling interest is measured at its share of book value of the legal subsidiary.

Since consolidated income or loss is allocated between the controlling and the noncontrolling interests, the noncontrolling interest must continue to be attributed its share of consolidated losses even if that loss absorption results in a deficit (negative) balance for the noncontrolling interest.

Note that in a step acquisition (where the acquirer implements the business combination in stages), each previously acquired investment layer must be remeasured to fair value at the date of acquisition (i.e., the date control is obtained). The gain or loss on revaluation is recognized in income at the date of acquisition. The gain or loss computation will include any previously unrecognized gain or loss included in comprehensive income in prior periods.

Changes in the Acquirer's Ownership Interests (without loss of control)

Given that the noncontrolling interest is classified as a separate component of shareholders' equity, any changes in the acquirer's level of ownership will result in a capital transaction rather than a step acquisition. In a step acquisition control is obtained at a discrete point in time. A change in the level of ownership is considered a capital transaction as long as the acquirer had control over the acquiree both prior to and after the transaction. A change in the acquirer's ownership interest can occur if the subsidiary issues additional shares of voting shares or engages in treasury stock transactions or if the parent purchases additional shares of the subsidiary or sells some of its interest in the subsidiary. When there is a change in the acquirer's ownership interests, there are no changes in the measurement (i.e., carrying values) of the assets and liabilities (including goodwill). The adjustments are made to revalue the carrying amount of the noncontrolling interest on the balance sheet and any difference (i.e., "gain" or "loss") between the change in the noncontrolling interest and the fair value of the consideration paid or received in the transaction is recorded in the parent company's additional paid in capital.

Loss of Control and Deconsolidation

For any transaction that results in loss of control by the parent company, the parent will deconsolidate the subsidiary. As part of the deconsolidate process, the parent company must derecognize the subsidiary's assets, liabilities and equity. The realized gain or loss on the ownership interest sold is recognized in income. In addition, any equity interest retained by the parent company must be remeasured at fair value. The gain or loss on the remeasurement of the equity interest retained is also recognized in earnings.

Anti-manipulation Guidance

Since changes in control (e.g., deconsolidate) result in gains or losses reported in income, the FASB included guidance to avoid the possible earnings manipulation from implementing changes through a series of transactions. If any one of the following four criteria is met, a series of multiple transactions must be accounting for as a single event:

a. The separate transactions are entered into simultaneously or in contemplation of each other.
b. The separate arrangements form a single economic event designed to achieve an overall commercial effect.
c. The implementation of one transaction depends on the occurrence of one or more other transactions.
d. A single transaction in the group of events is not economically feasible unless combined with other transactions or arrangements.

The manipulation prevented by this guidance is based on the timing of the multiple arrangements. For example, in 20X8 an agreement is signed but is dependent on an event in 20X9 that completes the step acquisition, all gains or losses on revaluation of prior ownership interests will be recognized in 20X9 and not 20X8.

Disclosures in the Financial Statements

Relevant portions of the financial statements must be shown separately for the controlling and the noncontrolling interest. This means that not only will there be separate components of shareholders' equity and the allocation of consolidated income between the two components, but comprehensive income, discontinued operations and extraordinary items will be displayed or disclosed separately for the controlling and noncontrolling interests. There are also expanded disclosures that require a reconciliation of the beginning and ending balances of the equity attributable to the parent and noncontrolling interest and a schedule reflecting the impact of changes in the parent's ownership level on the amount of equity attributable to the parent.

V. ILLUSTRATIONS OF THE ACQUISITION METHOD AND OTHER PROVISIONS OF FASB STATEMENTS NO. 141(R) AND 160

The next section of the chapter will provide illustrations of the concepts discussed thus far.

100% Acquisition

Assume that the Buy Company acquires 100% of the Sell Company for $300 million in cash. The Buy Company does not hold any equity interest in the Sell Company prior to the date of acquisition. Information related to the acquisition is presented below (in millions).

Description	*Fair Value*	*Historical Cost*	*Write Up*
Sell Company Noncash Assets	$350	$290	$60
Sell Company Liabilities	$140	$110	$30
Noncontrolling Interest	N/A	N/A	N/A
Controlling Interest	$300	N/A	N/A
Equity interest previously held by the acquirer	N/A	N/A	N/A

Goodwill Computation:

Description	*Amount*
Fair value of consideration transferred	$ 300
Fair value of the noncontrolling interest	- 0 -
Fair value of the acquisition equity interest held by the acquirer	- 0 -
Total	$ 300
Fair value of the Sell Company net assets acquired ($350 – 140)	(210)
Goodwill (100% attributed to the acquirer)	$ 90

Consolidating Worksheet for the Statement of Financial Position on the Date of Acquisition (Numbers assumed except for the data previously provided):

Description	*Buy Co.*	*Sell Co.*	*Adjustments and Eliminations*	*Buy Co. & Subsidiary*
Cash	$400	$ - 0 -	-$300	$100
Noncash Assets	325	290	+60	675
Goodwill	- 0 -	- 0 -	+90	90
Total Assets	$725	$290	-$150	$865
Liabilities	$220	$110	$+30	$360
Stockholders' Equity	505	180	-180	505
Total Liabilities and Stockholders' Equity	$725	$290	-$150	$865

In the consolidating worksheet above, the business combination is reflected by the reduction of cash of $300, the write up of plant assets by $60 and liabilities by $30 and recognition of $90 of goodwill.

Since this is a 100% acquisition, the $180 book value of the subsidiary's net assets is eliminated in the stockholders' equity section of the balance sheet. Specifically, all of the subsidiary's common stock, additional paid in capital and retained earnings are removed from the acquisition date consolidated balance sheet. As a result, only the parent company's equity is reflected on the date of acquisition balance sheet. The subsidiary's stockholders' equity is eliminated from the acquisition date balance sheet for two reasons.

This equity was generated from a prior management group and the acquisition method represents a new basis of accountability. In addition, none of the subsidiary's shares are held by any investors outside the consolidated group. In subsequent periods, the growth in subsidiary retained earnings (but only from the date of acquisition), will be reflected in the consolidated financial statements. Here, the additional earnings were generated when the subsidiary was under the control of the current parent company. The future earnings of the consolidated entity will be reduced by the additional depreciation charges on the plant asset write up and the potential goodwill impairment.

Step Acquisition

Assume that the Buy Company holds a 10% interest in the Sell Company and accounted for this investment as part of its available for sale portfolio. The current carrying value of the investment is $40. Accumulated other comprehensive income includes $10 of previously unrecognized net gains on write ups to market value. At the end of the current year, the Buy Company acquires the remaining 90% of the Sell Company for $300 million in cash and gains control at this point. The current fair value of the 10% investment in Sell Company is $33 on the date of acquisition. Information related to the acquisition is presented below (in millions).

Description	***Fair Value***	***Historical Cost or Carrying Value***	***Write Up (Down)***
Sell Company Noncash Assets	$350	$290	$60
Sell Company Liabilities	$140	$110	$30
Noncontrolling Interest	N/A	N/A	N/A
Controlling Interest	$300	N/A	N/A
Equity interest previously held by the acquirer	$33	$40	($ 7)

Goodwill Computation:

Description	***Amount***
Fair value of consideration transferred	$ 300
Fair value of the noncontrolling interest	- 0 -
Fair value of the acquisition equity interest held by the acquirer	+ 33
Total	$ 333
Fair value of the Sell Company net assets acquired ($350 – 140)	(210)
Goodwill (100% attributed to the acquirer)	$ 123

Consolidating Worksheet for the Statement of Financial Position on the Date of Acquisition (Numbers assumed except for the data previously provided):

Description	*Buy Co.*	*Sell Co.*	*Adjustments and Eliminations*	*Buy Co. & Subsidiary*
Cash	$400	$ - 0 -	(b) -$300	$100
Noncash Assets	325	290	(b) +60 (a) - 7 (b) -33	635
Goodwill	- 0 -	- 0 -	(b) +123	123
Total Assets	$725	$290	-$157	$858
Liabilities	$220	$110	(b) + $30	$360
Stockholders' Equity Buy Company Sell Company	- - 505	 180	 RE (a)+ 3 AOCI (a) -10 (b) -180	 - 498
Total Liabilities and Stockholders' Equity	$725	$290	-$135	$858

As noted in entry (a) in the consolidating worksheet above, the previous investment in the subsidiary's is first remeasured to full fair value of $33, resulting in a write down and realized loss of $7. There is also a $10 reclassification out of accumulated other comprehensive income into a realized gain account and closed to retained earnings. This recognizes previously unrealized gains on the portfolio.

The business combination is reflected in entry (b) by the reduction of cash of $300, the write up of plant assets by $60 and liabilities by $30 and recognition of $123 of goodwill. The investment account, currently valued at $33 is removed as it represents a reciprocal account to the equity of the subsidiary. Therefore, the noncash asset change is $27 which is the asset write up of $60 and the elimination of the $33 investment against the shareholders equity of the subsidiary.

Since this is a 100% acquisition, the $180 book value of the subsidiary's net assets is eliminated in the stockholders' equity section of the balance sheet. Specifically, all of the subsidiary's common stock, additional paid in capital and retained earnings are removed from the consolidated balance sheet. As a result, only the parent company's equity is reflected on the date of acquisition balance sheet. Again, the subsidiary's stockholders' equity is eliminated from the acquisition date balance sheet for two reasons.

This equity was generated from a prior management group and the acquisition method represents a new basis of accountability. In addition, none of the subsidiary's shares are held by any investors outside the consolidated group. In subsequent periods, the growth in subsidiary retained earnings (but only from the date of acquisition), will be reflected in the consolidated financial statements. Here, the additional earnings were generated when the subsidiary was under the control of the current parent company. The future earnings of the consolidated entity will be reduced by the additional depreciation charges on the plant asset write up and the potential goodwill impairment.

Partial Acquisition-No Control Premium Paid by the Acquirer

Assume that the Buy Company acquires 80% of the Sell Company for $300 million in cash. The Buy Company does not hold any equity interest in the Sell Company prior to the date of acquisition. The 20% equity interest not acquired by the Buy Company is publicly traded and has a market value of $75 and a book value of $36 (20% x $180 Sell Company net assets).

Information related to the acquisition is presented below (in millions).

Description	*Fair Value*	*Historical Cost*	*Write Up*
Sell Company Noncash Assets	$350	$290	$60
Sell Company Liabilities	$140	$110	$30
Noncontrolling Interest – 20%	$75	36	N/A
Controlling Interest – 80%	$300	N/A	N/A
Equity interest previously held by the acquirer	N/A	N/A	N/A
Economic (Implied) Value of the Sell Company: ($75 / .20) =	$375	N/A	N/A
Control Premium: Price paid in excess of economic (implied) value: $300 – (80% x $375) = $300 – 300	- 0 -	N/A	N/A

Since the full fair value approach is used, we must compute an implied economic value of the subsidiary. This value represents the value for a 100% acquisition of the subsidiary. The computation divides the fair value of the noncontrolling interest shares by the percent of the noncontrolling interest. This gives an economic value that is not affected by the control premium paid. There is no control premium in this case because the parent pays exactly 80% of the economic value of the subsidiary.

The goodwill computation and the attribution of the goodwill to the controlling and the noncontrolling interests are presented below. The valuation of the noncontrolling interest is straightforward. It is simply the full fair value of the shares held by the noncontrolling interest.

Goodwill Computation:

Description	*Amount*
Fair value of consideration transferred	$ 300
Fair value of the noncontrolling interest	75
Fair value of the acquisition equity interest held by the acquirer	- 0 -
Total	$ 375
Fair value of the Sell Company net assets acquired ($350 – 140)	(210)
Goodwill (to be attributed or allocated to the controlling and the noncontrolling interest- see next table)	$ 165

Allocation of Goodwill:

Description	*Amount*
Total Goodwill	$ 165
Less: Control premium paid	(- 0 -)
Economic Value of Goodwill	$ 165
Goodwill attributed to the Controlling Interest: ($165 x 80%)	$132
Goodwill attributed to the Noncontrolling Interest ($165 x 20%)	33
Total Goodwill	$165
Alternatively: For the Controlling Interest	
Fair Value of the consideration transferred	$ 300
Fair Value of the net assets acquired (80% x $210)	168
Goodwill attributed to the Controlling Interest	$132
Goodwill attributed to the Noncontrolling Interest ($165 – 132)	$ 33

Note that there are two ways to compute the goodwill attributable to both groups. However, the alternative approach treats goodwill more like a residual value.

Consolidating Worksheet for the Statement of Financial Position on the Date of Acquisition (Numbers assumed except for the data previously provided):

Description	*Buy Co.*	*Sell Co.*	*Adjustments and Eliminations*	*Buy Co. & Subsidiary*
Cash	$400	$ - 0 -	-$300	$100
Noncash Assets	325	290	+ 60	675
Goodwill	- 0 -	- 0 -	+165	165
Total Assets	$725	$290	- $ 75	$940
Liabilities	$220	$110	+$ 30	$360
Stockholders' Equity:				
Buy Company	$ 505			$ 505
Sell Company		$ 180	-$180	- 0 -
Noncontrolling Interest	- 0 -	- 0 -	+ 75	75
Total Shareholders' Equity	$505	$180	- $105	$580
Total Liabilities and Stockholders' Equity	$725	$290	- $ 75	$940

In the consolidating worksheet above, the business combination is reflected by the reduction of cash of $300, the write up of plant assets by $60 and liabilities by $30, recognition of $165 of goodwill and creating the $75 noncontrolling interest

Since this is a 100% acquisition, the $180 book value of the subsidiary's net assets is eliminated in the stockholders' equity section of the balance sheet. Specifically, all of the subsidiary's common stock, additional paid in capital and retained earnings are removed from the consolidated balance sheet and replaced by the equity attributable to the controlling and the noncontrolling interests.

Partial Acquisition-Control Premium Paid by the Acquirer

Assume that the Buy Company acquires 80% of the Sell Company for $300 million in cash. The Buy Company does not hold any equity interest in the Sell Company prior to the date of acquisition. The 20% equity interest not acquired by the Buy Company is publicly traded and has a market value of $65 and a book value of $36 (20% x $180 Sell Company net assets). We now assume that the Buy Company paid a $40 control premium to implement the transaction. Information related to the acquisition is presented below (in millions).

Description	*Fair Value*	*Historical Cost*	*Write Up*
Sell Company Noncash Assets	$350	$290	$60
Sell Company Liabilities	$140	$110	$30
Noncontrolling Interest – 20%	$65	36	N/A
Controlling Interest – 80%	$300	N/A	N/A
Equity interest previously held by the acquirer	N/A	N/A	N/A
Economic (Implied) Value of the Sell Company: ($65 / .20) =	$325	N/A	N/A
Control Premium: Price paid in excess of economic (implied) value: $300 – (80% x $325) = $300 – 260	$40	N/A	N/A

Since the full fair value approach is used, we must compute an implied economic value of the subsidiary. This value represents the value for a 100% acquisition of the subsidiary. The computation divides the fair value of the noncontrolling interest shares by the percent of the noncontrolling interest. This gives an economic value that is not affected by the control premium paid. There is a control premium in this case because the parent pays $40 more than 80% of the economic value of the subsidiary.

The goodwill computation and the attribution of the goodwill to the controlling and the noncontrolling interests are presented below. The valuation of the noncontrolling interest is straightforward. It is simply the full fair value of the shares held by the noncontrolling interest.

Goodwill Computation:

Description	*Amount*
Fair value of consideration transferred	$ 300
Fair value of the noncontrolling interest	65
Fair value of the acquisition equity interest held by the acquirer	-0-
Total (Economic Value + Control Premium = $325 + 40)	$ 365
Fair value of the Sell Company net assets acquired ($350 – 140)	(210)
Goodwill (to be attributed or allocated to the controlling and the noncontrolling interest- see next table)	$ 155

Allocation of Goodwill:

Description	*Amount*
Total Goodwill	$ 155
Less: Control premium paid	(40)
Economic Value of Goodwill	$ 115
Controlling Interest Share of the economic value of goodwill: ($115 x 80%)	$ 92
Control Premium-100% attributed to the Controlling Interest	+ 40
Goodwill attributed to the Controlling Interest	$132
Goodwill attributed to the Noncontrolling Interest ($115 x 20%)	23
Total Goodwill	$155
Alternatively: For the Controlling Interest	
Fair Value of the consideration transferred	$ 300
Fair Value of the net assets acquired (80% x $210)	168
Goodwill attributed to the Controlling Interest	$132
Goodwill attributed to the Noncontrolling Interest ($155 – 132)	$ 23

Note that there are two ways to compute the goodwill attributable to both groups. However, the alternative approach treats goodwill more like a residual value.

Consolidating Worksheet for the Statement of Financial Position on the Date of Acquisition (Numbers assumed except for the data previously provided):

Description	*Buy Co.*	*Sell Co.*	*Adjustments and Eliminations*	*Buy Co. & Subsidiary*
Cash	$400	$ -0-	-$300	$100
Noncash Assets	325	290	+ 60	675
Goodwill	-0-	-0-	+155	155
Total Assets	$725	$290	-$ 85	$930
Liabilities	$220	$110	+$ 30	$360
Stockholders' Equity:				
Buy Company	$ 505			$ 505
Sell Company		$ 180	-$180	-0-
Noncontrolling Interest	-0-	-0-	+ 65	65
Total Shareholders' Equity	$505	$180	-$115	$570
Total Liabilities and Stockholders' Equity	$725	$290	-$ 85	$930

In the consolidating worksheet above, the business combination is reflected by the reduction of cash of $300, the write up of plant assets by $60 and liabilities by $30, recognition of $155 of goodwill and creating the $65 noncontrolling interest

Since this is a 100% acquisition, the $180 book value of the subsidiary's net assets is eliminated in the stockholders' equity section of the balance sheet. Specifically, all of the subsidiary's common stock, additional paid in capital and retained earnings are removed from the consolidated balance sheet and replaced by the equity attributable to the controlling and the noncontrolling interests.

100% Acquisition with a Bargain Purchase

Assume that the Buy Company acquires 100% of the Sell Company for $200 million in cash. The Buy Company does not hold any equity interest in the Sell Company prior to the date of acquisition. Information related to the acquisition is presented below (in millions).

Description	*Fair Value*	*Historical Cost*	*Write Up*
Sell Company Noncash Assets	$350	$290	$60
Sell Company Liabilities	$140	$110	$30
Noncontrolling Interest	N/A	N/A	N/A
Controlling Interest	$200	N/A	N/A
Equity interest previously held by the acquirer	N/A	N/A	N/A

Bargain Purchase (Negative Goodwill) Computation:

Description	*Amount*
Fair value of consideration transferred	$ 200
Fair value of the noncontrolling interest	- 0 -
Fair value of the acquisition equity interest held by the acquirer	- 0 -
Total	$ 200
Fair value of the Sell Company net assets acquired ($350 – 140)	(210)
Gain on the Bargain Purchase	($ 10)

Assuming that the Buy Company reconsidered the fair values used to measure the net assets acquired and determined that no adjustments are necessary. As a result, the gain on the bargain purchase will be $10 and recognized in earnings on the date of acquisition.

Consolidating Worksheet for the Statement of Financial Position on the Date of Acquisition (Numbers assumed except for the data previously provided):

Description	*Buy Co.*	*Sell Co.*	*Adjustments and Eliminations*	*Buy Co. & Subsidiary*
Cash	$400	$ - 0 -	-$200	$200
Noncash Assets	325	290	+60	675
Total Assets	$725	$290	-$140	$875
Liabilities	$220	$110	$+30	$360
Stockholders' Equity:				
Buy Company	505		+ 10	515
Sell Company		180	-180	- 0 -
Total Liabilities and Stockholders' Equity	$725	$290	-$140	$875

In the consolidating worksheet above, the business combination is reflected by the reduction of cash of $300, the write up of plant assets by $60 and liabilities by $30 and recognition of $10 gain on the bargain purchase. This gain is recognized in the earnings of the acquirer on the income statement and closed to its retained earnings account in the stockholders' equity section of the balance sheet.

Since this is a 100% acquisition, the $180 book value of the subsidiary's net assets is eliminated in the stockholders' equity section of the balance sheet. Specifically, all of the subsidiary's common stock, additional paid in capital and retained earnings are removed from the consolidated balance sheet. As a result, only the parent company's equity is reflected on the date of acquisition balance sheet. The subsidiary's stockholders' equity is eliminated from the acquisition date balance sheet for two reasons.

This equity was generated from a prior management group and the acquisition method represents a new basis of accountability. In addition, none of the subsidiary's shares are held by any investors outside the consolidated group. In subsequent periods, the growth in subsidiary retained earnings (but only from the date of acquisition), will be reflected in the consolidated financial statements. Here, the additional earnings were generated when the subsidiary was under the control of the current parent company. The future earnings of the consolidated entity will be reduced by the additional depreciation charges on the plant asset write up and the potential goodwill impairment.

REVERSE ACQUISITION (100% ACQUISITION)

In a reverse acquisition, the legal acquirer (legal parent) is identified as the accounting acquiree for financial reporting purposes. To illustrate, assume that on May 1, 20X9, the Buy Company issues 40,000 shares of its $1 par value common stock in exchange for all of the 10,000 shares of the Sell Company (i.e., a 4 to 1 exchange ratio). The fair value of the Buy Company stock is $20 per share and Sell Company shares trade for $80 per share. Therefore, the shares issued by the Buy Company have a total market value of $800,000 (i.e., 40,000 x $20) on the date of the acquisition.

As a result of the transaction, the Sell Company shareholders will hold 40,000 shares of the Buy Company's 70,000 outstanding shares, while the original Buy Company shareholders only hold 30,000 shares. It is assumed that the Buy Company's noncurrent assets are undervalued by $40,000 and the noncurrent assets of the Sell Company are undervalued by $22,000. The balance sheets of two unrelated companies on May 1, 20X9, the date of acquisition, are presented below.

Description	Buy Co.	Sell Co.
Cash	$ 10,000	$ 2,000
Current Assets	120,000	80,000
Noncurrent Assets	170,000	18,000
Total Assets	$300,000	$100,000
Liabilities	$ 70,000	$ 20,000
Stockholders' Equity		
Buy Company Common Stock - $1 par value	$ 30,000	
Sell Company Common Stock - $1 par value		$ 10,000
Retained Earnings	200,000	70,000
Total Stockholders' Equity	$230,000	$80,000
Total Liabilities and Stockholders' Equity	$300,000	$100,000

Assuming that no additional information is available regarding the composition of the combined entity's board of directors or senior management, the exchange of voting equity shares will result in the former shareholders of the Sell Company gaining control over the combined entity. This is shown in the following computation.

Buy Company Shares Issued and Outstanding	***Number of Shares***	***Percent Ownership***
Held by Buy Company Shareholders	30,000	3/7 = 42.86%
Held by Sell Company Shareholders	40,000	4/7 = 57.14%
Total	70,000	7/7 = 100.00%

After the exchange of voting shares, 57.14% (4/7) of the combined entity is owned by the Sell Company shareholders and this group controls the combined entity. Therefore, this transaction qualifies as a reverse acquisition and the Sell Company is the accounting acquirer (although it is the legal subsidiary). The Buy Company is the accounting acquiree (although it is the legal parent).

Determination of the Implied or Effective Consideration Transferred

Due to the fact that the Sell Company does not issue consideration to implement the business combination, an implied or effective consideration transferred must be determined.

The implied or effective consideration is determined by assuming that the Sell Company had to issue enough shares to acquire the Buy Company while at the same time maintain its 57.14% control or 4/7 share in the combined entity. From the Sell Company's perspective, 10,000 shares of its voting stock are outstanding before the transaction. Therefore, the number of shares to be issued to the Buy Company shareholders in order to have the Sell Company shareholders control 4/7 of the combined entity is determined below.

10,000 / (X + 10,000) = 4/7
10,000 = (X + 10,000) x 4/7
10,000 = 4/7 X + 5,714
4,286 = 4/7 X
X = 7,500 shares

The 17,500 shares could have also been obtained by dividing the percentage of control into the number of shares for the sell company (i.e. 17,500 = 10,000 ÷ 57.14%)

The Sell Company would have to issue 7,500 shares in exchange for the 30,000 shares of the Buy Company in order to control the same percentage of the 17,500 voting shares outstanding after the combination:

10,000 / 17,500 = <u>4/7 = 57.14%</u>

Given the fair value of the Sell Company's voting shares of $80 per share, the effective or implied fair value of the consideration transferred is equal to $600,000 ($80 x 7,500 shares). The $600,000 value is sufficient to acquire the 30,000 Buy Company shares ($600,000 / $20 = 30,000 shares). Alternatively,

7,500 shares of Sell Company = 30,000 shares of the Buy Company
(7,500 shares x $80) = (30,000 shares x $20) = $600,000

Note that where both companies are publicly traded, we could obtain the same result by determining a ratio of market price per share as illustrated below:

30,000 shares x ($20 / $80) = 7,500 shares

Goodwill Computation:

Description	*Amount*
Fair value of consideration transferred by the ***Sell Company*** ("as if" shares were issued by the Sell Company: 7,500 x $80)=	$ 600,000
Fair value of the noncontrolling interest	- 0 -
Fair value of the acquisition equity interest held by the acquirer	- 0 -
Total	$ 600,000
Fair value of the ***Buy Company*** net assets acquired:	
Current Assets ($10,000 cash +120,000 other current assets)	$ 130,000
Noncurrent Assets ($170,000 + 40,000 write up to FMV)	210,000
Less: Liabilities assumed	(70,000)
Fair value of the net assets acquired	($270,000)
Goodwill	$ 330,000

Note that the acquisition value is measured as the value of the implied consideration transferred by the Sell Company (the legal subsidiary) on an "as if" basis. Goodwill is then computed by assuming that the net assets of the Buy Company (the legal parent) are acquired at full fair value.

Consolidated Financial Statements in a Reverse Acquisition with 100% Ownership

The consolidated financial statements must be prepared in the name of the legal parent, the Buy Company (the accounting acquiree). In addition, on the consolidated balance sheet, the shareholders equity section will indicate the number of shares issued and outstanding for the legal parent, the Buy Company (i.e., 70,000 shares of $1 par value common stock). However, the number of outstanding shares for the legal parent, the Buy Company, is valued using the amounts applicable to the accounting acquiree, the Sell Company, including all contributed capital and retained earnings (i.e., the legal subsidiary's equity values are used to measure the legal parent company's book value per outstanding share). The consolidated balance sheet on the date of acquisition is presented below.

Consolidated Balance Sheet on the Date of Acquisition: 5-1-20X9

Description	Buy Company Acquiree (Legal Parent)	Sell Company Acquirer (Legal Subsidiary)	Adjustments and Eliminations	C Co (In the name of the Legal Parent)
Cash	$ 10,000	$ 2,000		$ 12,000
Current Assets	120,000	80,000		200,000
Noncurrent Assets	170,000	18,000	+$ 40,000	228,000
Goodwill	- 0 -	- 0 -	+ 330,000	330,000
Total Assets	$300,000	$100,000	+$370,000	$770,000
Liabilities	$ 70,000	$ 20,000	- 0 -	$ 90,000
Stockholders' Equity:				
Common Stock-$1 par (70,000 shares outstanding)	$ 30,000	$ 10,000	-30,000 +$600,000	$610,000
Retained earnings	200,000	70,000	-200,000	70,000
Total Stockholders' Equity	$230,000	$ 80,000	+$370,000	$680,000
Total Liabilities and Stockholders' Equity	$300,000	$100,000	+$370,000	$770,000

In the consolidating worksheet above, the business combination is reflected by the issuance of 40,000 Buy Company common shares using the $600,000 implied value of the consideration transferred by the Sell Company, the write up of the net assets by $40,000, the recognition of $330,000 of goodwill and the elimination of the carrying value of the Buy Company's common stock and retained earnings (i.e., $30,000 and $200,000 respectively).

Note that even though the only outstanding shares are the common shares of the Buy Company, the values assigned to those shares are based on the Sell Company values. Earnings per share must also be computed using the outstanding common shares of the Buy Company. The earnings per share computation is presented below.

CHANGES IN THE PARENT COMPANY'S LEVEL OF CONTROL (CHANGES IN A PARENT'S OWNERSHIP INTEREST IN A SUBSIDIARY)

Case 1: The Parent Company Sells a portion of its investment

Assume that the subsidiary company does not report any accumulated other comprehensive income. The Buy Company (the parent) currently owns 80% of the 1,000 outstanding voting shares of the Sell Company (the subsidiary). The value of the shares (i.e., the carrying value or book value of the investment) on the books of the Buy Company is $300 with the noncontrolling interest valued at $75. During the year, the Buy Company sells 80 shares to an unrelated entity for $40 in cash. The sale represents 8% of the outstanding shares of Sell Company. After the sale the Buy Company holds a 72% interest in the Sell Company and the noncontrolling interest is at 28%. Note that the total carrying value of the Sell Company equity does not change because the transaction simply moves a portion of the Sell Company equity attributed to the controlling interest to the noncontrolling interest.

This event is considered a capital transaction because the Buy Company controls the

Sell Company both before and after the sale of shares and any "gain" or "loss" on disposal is recognized as an adjustment to the parent company's additional paid in capital and is not recognized in earnings. The consolidated worksheet prior to the sale of the 8% interest is presented below.

Description	**Buy Co.**	**Sell Co.**	**Eliminations**	**Buy Co. & Subsidiary**
Cash and Investments	$100	$ -0-		$100
Investment in Sell Company	300	-0-	-$300	-0-
Noncash Assets	325	350		675
Goodwill	-0-	165	------	165
Total Assets	$725	$515	-$300	$940
Liabilities	$220	$140		$360
Stockholders' Equity				
Buy Company:	$505			$505
Sell Company:				
Controlling Interest	---	$300	-$300	
Noncontrolling Interest	---	75	--	75
Total Stockholders' Equity	$505	$375	-$300	$580
Total Liabilities and Stockholders' Equity	$725	$515	-$300	$940

With no changes in ownership or other transactions, the only consolidating adjustment at this point is to eliminate the parent's investment account against the stockholders' equity of the subsidiary (i.e., eliminate the reciprocal accounts).

However, with the sale of 8% of the investment results there is a 10% loss of Sell Company equity for the Buy Company and a transfer of $30 or the carrying value of the Sell Company equity from the controlling to the noncontrolling interest:

8% / 80% = 10% x $300 =	$30
Selling Price	$40
Carrying Value sold is transferred to the noncontrolling interest	(30)
Excess "Gain": Credit to Buy Company Additional Paid in Capital or increase in the APIC of the Buy Company	$10

The consolidating worksheet after the disposal of 8% of the investment is presented below. Note that:

- Due to the capital transactions treatment, there is no change in the carrying value of any of the consolidated net assets (except for the cash received on the sale).
- The effect on the Sell Company is a simple transfer of equity from the controlling to the noncontrolling interest.

Description	Buy Co.	Sell Co.	Entry	Buy Co. & Subsidiary
Cash	$100	$ - 0 -	(a) +$40	$140
Investment in Sell Company	300		(a) - 30 (c) -270	- 0 -
Noncash Assets	325	350		675
Goodwill	- 0 -	165		165
Total Assets	$725	$515	- $260	$980
Liabilities	$220	$140		$360
Stockholders' Equity				
Buy Company:	$505		(a) +$10	$515
Sell Company:				
Controlling Interest	---	$300	(b) -$30 (c) -270	- 0 -
Noncontrolling Interest	---	75	(b) +30	105
Total Stockholders' Equity	$505	$375	- $260	$620
Total Liabilities and Stockholders' Equity	$725	$515	- $260	$980

Entry (a) reflects that sale of the investment as a capital transaction with the "gain" recorded as an increase in the additional paid in capital of the parent company and a reduction of the controlling interest's share in the Sell Company. In entry (b) there is a reduction of the controlling interests' share of the Sell Company as $30 of the equity value is relinquished to the noncontrolling interest. Entry (c) removes the reciprocal accounts from the consolidated entity: the controlling interests share in the Sell Company and the balance of the investment account.

Case 2: The Subsidiary issues additional shares to an independent party

Assume that the subsidiary company does not report any accumulated other comprehensive income. The Buy Company (the parent) presently owns 80% of the 1,000 outstanding voting shares of the Sell Company (the subsidiary). The value of the shares (i.e., the carrying value or book value of the investment) on the books of the Buy Company is $300 and the noncontrolling interest is valued at $75.

During the year, the Sell Company issues an additional 250 voting shares to an unrelated entity for $55 in cash. Because the newly issued shares were previously unissued this transaction increases the number of outstanding shares. In addition, the noncontrolling interest now increases by 16% to 36% (i.e., 450 shares / 1,250 shares), with Buy Company relinquishing a proportionate interest of 16%, reducing its controlling share to 64% (i.e., 800 shares / 1,250 shares). The percentage decrease in the Buy Company's holding is 20% (16% / 80%).

Note that because the companies are measured at full fair value, the total carrying value of the Sell Company equity does not change. The transaction simply moves a portion of the Sell Company equity attributed to the controlling interest to the noncontrolling interest.

This event is considered a capital transaction because the Buy Company controls the Sell Company both before and after the issuance of additional voting shares and any "gain" or "loss" is recognized as an adjustment to the parent company's additional paid in capital and is not recognized in earnings.

The new shares issued by the subsidiary results in a 20% loss of Sell Company equity for the Buy Company and a transfer of $60 of the carrying value of the Sell Company equity from the controlling to the noncontrolling interest:

16% / 80% = 20% x $300 =	$60
Share Issue Price	$55
Carrying Value transferred to the noncontrolling interest	(60)
Deficiency "Loss": Debit to Buy Company Additional Paid in Capital or decrease in the APIC of the Buy Company	($5)

The consolidating worksheet after the issuance of 16% additional equity is presented below. Note that:

- Due to the capital transactions treatment, there is no change in the carrying value of any of the consolidated net assets (except for the cash received on the new share issue).
- The effect on the Sell Company is a simple transfer of equity from the controlling to the noncontrolling interest.

Description	Buy Co.	Sell Co.	Entry	Buy Co. & Subsidiary
Cash	$100	$ -0-	(a) +$55	$155
Investment in Sell Company	300		(b) -60 (c) -240	-0-
Noncash Assets	325	350		675
Goodwill	-0-	165		165
Total Assets	$725	$515	-$245	$995
Liabilities	$220	$140		$360
Stockholders' Equity				
Buy Company:	$505		(a) -5	$500
Sell Company:				
Controlling Interest	---	$300	(b) -60 (c) -240	-0-
Noncontrolling Interest	---	75	(a) +60	135
Total Stockholders' Equity	$505	$375	-$245	$635
Total Liabilities and Stockholders' Equity	$725	$515	-$245	$995

Entry (a) reflects that sale of the investment as a capital transaction with the "loss" recorded as a decrease in the additional paid in capital of the parent company and an increase in the value of the noncontrolling interest. In entry (b) there is the elimination of the parent's investment account against the controlling interest's share of the equity of the subsidiary. In addition, this entry also reflects a reduction of the controlling interests' share of the Sell Company as $60 of the equity value is relinquished to the noncontrolling interest. Entry (c) removes the reciprocal accounts from the consolidated entity: the controlling interests share in the Sell Company and the balance of the investment account.

Case 3: The Parent Company acquires additional shares of the subsidiary in the open market

Assume that the subsidiary company reports no accumulated other comprehensive income. The Buy Company (the parent) presently owns 80% of the 1,000 outstanding voting shares of the Sell Company (the subsidiary). The value of the shares (i.e., the carrying value or book value of the investment) on the books of the Buy Company is $300 and the noncontrolling interest is valued at $75.

During the year, the Buy Company pays $60 in cash to purchase an additional 120 shares of the Sell Company from the noncontrolling shareholders. The purchase represents 12% of outstanding voting common shares. This transaction reduces the noncontrolling interest by 60% (i.e., 12% / 20%) and increases the Buy Company's interest proportionately to a level of 92%.

Note that the total carrying value of the Sell Company equity does not change because the transaction simply moves a portion of the Sell Company equity attributed to the noncontrolling interest to the controlling interest. This event is considered a capital transaction because the Buy Company controls the Sell Company both before and after the acquisition of additional shares and any "gain" or "loss" is recognized as an adjustment to the parent company's additional paid in capital and is not recognized in earnings.

The purchase of the additional 12% of the outstanding share results in a 60% loss for the noncontrolling interest and a transfer of $45 of equity to the Buy Company.

12% / 20% = 60% x $75 =	$45
Purchase Price	$60
Carrying Value transferred to the controlling interest	(45)
Deficiency "Loss": Debit to Buy Company Additional Paid in Capital or decrease in the APIC of the Buy Company	($15)

The consolidating worksheet after the acquisition of 12% additional equity is presented below. Note that:

- Due to the capital transactions treatment, there is no change in the carrying value of any of the consolidated net assets (except for the cash paid for the shares purchase).
- The effect on the Sell Company is a simple transfer of equity from the noncontrolling to the controlling interest.

Description	Buy Co.	Sell Co.	Entry	Buy Co. & Subsidiary
Cash	$100	$ -0-	(a) -60	$ 40
Investment in Sell Company	300		(a) +45 (c) -345	-0-
Noncash Assets	325	350		675
Goodwill	-0-	165		165
Total Assets	$725	$515	-$360	$880
Liabilities	$220	$140		$360
Stockholders' Equity				
Buy Company:	$505		(a) -$15	$490
Sell Company:				
Controlling Interest	---	$300	(b)+$45 (c) -345	-0-
Noncontrolling Interest	---	75	(b) -45	30
Total Stockholders' Equity	$505	$375	-$360	$520
Total Liabilities and Stockholders' Equity	$725	$515	-$360	$880

Entry (a) reflects the purchase of an additional investment in the Sell Company as a capital transaction with the "loss" recorded as a decrease in the additional paid in capital of the parent company. There is a loss due to the fact that the parent company paid $60 for the additional shares but only gains $45 increased interest in the subsidiary. In entry (b) there is an increase in the controlling interests' share of the Sell Company as $45 of the equity value is relinquished by the noncontrolling interest. Entry (c) reflects the elimination of the parent's investment account against its controlling interest share of the net assets or shareholders' equity of the subsidiary.

Case 4: The Parent Company acquires additional shares of the subsidiary in the open market and the subsidiary has accumulated other comprehensive income

Assume that the subsidiary company reports $80 in accumulated other comprehensive income. The Buy Company (the parent) presently owns 80% of the 1,000 outstanding voting shares of the Sell Company (the subsidiary). The value of the shares (i.e., the carrying value or book value of the investment) on the books of the Buy Company is $300 and the noncontrolling interest is valued at $75.

During the year, the Buy Company pays $60 in cash to purchase an additional 120 voting common shares of the Sell Company from the noncontrolling shareholders. This purchase represents 12% of outstanding voting common shares. This transaction reduces the noncontrolling interest by 60% (i.e., 12% / 20%) and increases the Buy Company's interest proportionately to a level of 92%.

Note that the total carrying value of the Sell Company equity does not change because the transaction simply moves a portion of the Sell Company equity attributed to the noncontrolling interest to the controlling interest. This event is considered a capital transaction because the Buy Company controls the Sell Company both before and after the acquisition of additional shares and any "gain" or "loss" is recognized as an adjustment to the parent company's additional paid in capital and is not recognized in earnings.

The key difference in this case is that the subsidiary has accumulated other comprehensive income. The Sell Company's Stockholders' Equity section appears as follows:

Stockholders' Equity	Amount
Common Stock – no par	$ 95
Retained Earnings	200
Accumulated Other Comprehensive Income	80
Total Sell Company Stockholders' Equity	$375

The purchase of the additional 12% outstanding voting shares results in a 60% loss for the noncontrolling interest and a transfer of $45 of equity to the Buy Company.

12% / 20% = 60% x $75 =	$45
Purchase Price	$60
Carrying Value transferred to the controlling interest	(45)
Deficiency "Loss": Debit to Buy Company Additional Paid in Capital or decrease in the APIC of the Buy Company	($15)

In addition, there is a transfer of the noncontrolling interest's share of accumulated other comprehensive income to the controlling interest and this "gain" comes out of the additional paid in capital of the controlling interest (the Buy Company). Therefore, 60% x $80 = $48 of accumulated other comprehensive income is transferred into the Buy Company's accumulated other comprehensive income with a reduction of its additional paid in capital. This is simply a reclassification of existing balances in the stockholders' equity accounts.

The consolidating worksheet after the acquisition of an additional 12% of the outstanding shares is presented below. Note that:

- Due to the capital transactions treatment, there is no change in the carrying value of any of the consolidated net assets (except for the cash paid for the shares purchased).
- The effect on the Sell Company is a simple transfer of equity from the noncontrolling to the controlling interest.

Description	Buy Co.	Sell Co.	Entry	Buy Co. & Subsidiary
Cash and Investments	$100	$ - 0 -	(a) - 60	$ 40
Investment in Sell Company	300		(a) +45 (c) -345	- 0 -
Noncash Assets	325	350		675
Goodwill	- 0 -	165		165
Total Assets	$725	$515	-$360	$880
Liabilities	$220	$140		$360
Stockholders' Equity				
Buy Company: **Stockholders' Equity** **AOCI**	$505		(a) -$15 (d) – 48 (d) + 48	$442 48
				$490
Sell Company:				
Controlling Interest	---	$300	(b)+$45 (c) -345	- 0 -
Noncontrolling Interest	---	75	(b) -45	30
Total Stockholders' Equity	$505	$375	-$360	$520
Total Liabilities and Stockholders' Equity	$725	$515	-$360	$880

Entry (a) reflects the purchase of an additional investment in the Sell Company as a capital transaction with the "loss" recorded as a decrease in the additional paid in capital of the parent company. There is a loss due to the fact that the parent company paid $60 for the additional shares but only gains $45 increased interest in the subsidiary. In entry (b) there is an increase in the controlling interests' share of the Sell Company as $45 of the equity value is relinquished by the noncontrolling interest.

In entry (c) there is the elimination of the parent's investment account against the net assets or shareholders' equity of the subsidiary. Finally, entry (d) reflects the parent company's reclassification of $48 from additional paid in capital into accumulated other comprehensive income.

Earnings per Share

Earnings per share must be based on the weighted average shares outstanding for the legal parent, the Buy Company (the accounting acquiree). Assume that the Sell Company earnings for the year ended December 31, 20X8, (the year prior to the acquisition) amounted to $90,000, and the consolidated earnings for the year ended December 31, 20X9 (i.e., the first year-end following the acquisition) were $200,000. The earnings per share computation for the combined entity for the first year end following the transaction is presented below.

Description	Number of Shares
Number of shares deemed outstanding for the period 1-1-20X9 to 5-1-20X9 issued by the Buy Company in the reverse acquisition	40,000
Number of shares issued by the Buy Company on the date of acquisition 5-1-20X9.	30,000
Computation of the Weighted Average Number of Shares Outstanding:	
January 1, 20X9: 40,000 x 12/12 =	40,000
May 1, 20X9: 30,000 x 8/12 =	20,000
Weighted average number of common shares	60,000
Consolidated Earnings per Share: $200,000 / 60,000 =	$3.33 per share

In the presentation of comparative financial statements, the earnings per share of the Sell Company, the accounting acquirer must be restated based on the number of shares issued by the legal parent company, the Buy Company, in the reverse acquisition:

Restated Earnings per Share for 12-31-20X8 (the year prior to the business combination)

$$\frac{\text{Earnings of the Sell Company}}{\text{Common shares outstanding for the Buy Company in the Reverse Acquisition}} = \frac{\$90{,}000}{40{,}000} = \$2.25 \text{ per share}$$

Reverse Acquisition with a Noncontrolling Interest: An exception to measuring the Noncontrolling Interest at Fair Value

To illustrate a reverse acquisition with a noncontrolling interest, assume that on May 1, 20X9, the Buy Company issues 36,000 shares of its $1 par value common stock in exchange for 90% of the 10,000 shares of the Sell Company (i.e., 9,000 shares are exchanged). The exchange ratio is 4 to 1. The fair value of the Buy Company's common stock is $20 per share and Sell Company shares trade for $80 per share. Therefore, the shares issued by the Buy Company have a total market value of $720,000 (i.e., 36,000 x $20) on the date of the acquisition.

As a result of the transaction, the Sell Company shareholders hold 36,000 shares of the Buy Company's 66,000 outstanding shares, while the original Buy Company shareholders only hold 30,000 shares. It is assumed that the Buy Company's noncurrent assets are undervalued by $40,000 and noncurrent assets of the Sell Company are undervalued by $22,000. The balance sheets of two unrelated companies on May 1, 20X9, the date of acquisition, are presented below.

Description	*Buy Co.*	*Sell Co.*
Cash	$ 10,000	$ 2,000
Current Assets	120,000	80,000
Noncurrent Assets	170,000	18,000
Total Assets	$300,000	$100,000
Liabilities	$ 70,000	$ 20,000
Stockholders' Equity		
Buy Company Common Stock - $1 par value	$ 30,000	
Sell Company Common Stock - $1 par value		$ 10,000
Retained Earnings	200,000	70,000
Total Stockholders' Equity	$230,000	$80,000
Total Liabilities and Stockholders' Equity	$300,000	$100,000

Assuming there is no additional information regarding the composition of the combined entity's board of directors or senior management, the exchange of voting equity shares will result in the former shareholders of the Sell Company gaining control over the combined entity. That is:

Buy Company Shares Issued and Outstanding	***Number of Shares***	***Percent Ownership***
Held by Buy Company Shareholders	30,000	30/66 = 45.45%
Held by Sell Company Shareholders	36,000	36/66 = 54.55%
Total	66,000	66/66 = 100.00%

After the exchange of voting shares, 54.55% (36/66) of the combined entity is owned by the Sell Company shareholders and this group controls the combined entity. Therefore, this transaction qualifies as a reverse acquisition and the Sell Company is the accounting acquirer (although it is the legal subsidiary). The Buy Company is the accounting acquiree (although it is the legal parent).

Determination of the Implied or Effective Consideration Transferred

Due to the fact that the Sell Company does not issue consideration to implement the business combination, an implied or effective consideration transferred must be determined.

The implied or effective consideration is determined by assuming that the Sell Company had to issue enough shares to acquire the Buy Company while at the same time maintain its 54.55% control or 36/66 share in the combined entity. From the Sell Company's perspective, 9,000 of its 10,000 outstanding shares are exchanged in the transaction. Therefore, the number of shares to be issued to the Buy Company shareholders in order to have the Sell Company shareholders control 36/66 of the combined entity is determined below.

9,000 / (X + 9,000) = 36/66
9,000 = (X + 9,000) x 36/66
9,000 = 36/66 X + 4,909
4,091 = 36/66 X
X = 7,500 shares.

The Sell Company would have to issue 7,500 shares in exchange for all 30,000 shares of the Buy Company in order for the 90% participating Sell Company shareholders to control the same percentage of the 16,500 voting shares outstanding after the combination. Note that the Sell Company is assumed to acquire all 30,000 shares of the Buy Company because there is no noncontrolling interest in the Buy Company.

9,000 / 16,500 = 36/66 = 54.55%

The 16,000 shares could have also been obtained by dividing the percentage of control into the number of shares for the Sell Company (i.e. 16,500 = 9,000 ÷ 54.55%).

Given the fair value of the Sell Company's voting shares of $80 per share, the effective or implied fair value of the consideration transferred is equal to $600,000 ($80 x 7,500 shares). The $600,000 value is sufficient to acquire the 30,000 Buy Company shares ($600,000 / $20 = 30,000 shares). Alternatively,

7,500 shares of Sell Company = 30,000 shares of the Buy Company
(7,500 shares x $80) = (30,000 shares x $20) = $600,000

Note that where both companies are publicly traded, we could obtain the same result by determining a ratio of market price per share. For example,

30,000 shares x ($20 / $80) = 7,500 shares.

Goodwill Computation:

Description	***Amount***
Fair value of consideration transferred by the ***Sell Company*** ("as if" shares were issued by the Sell Company: 7,500 x $80)=	$ 600,000
Fair value of the noncontrolling interest (***Note:*** there is no noncontrolling interest in the Buy Company).	- 0 -
Fair value of the acquisition equity interest held by the acquirer	- 0 -
Total	$ 600,000
Fair value of the ***Buy Company*** net assets acquired:	
Current Assets ($10,000 +120,000)	$ 130,000
Noncurrent Assets ($170,000 + 40,000 write up to FMV)	210,000
Less: Liabilities assumed	(70,000)
Fair value of the net assets acquired	($270,000)
Goodwill	$ 330,000

Note that the acquisition value is measured as the value of the implied consideration transferred by the Sell Company (the legal subsidiary) on an "as if" basis. Goodwill is then computed by assuming that the net assets of the Buy Company (the legal parent) are acquired at full fair value.

Noncontrolling Interest in a Reverse Acquisition

A significant exception to the measurement and recognition guidelines of FASB Statements 141(R) and 160 is the valuation of the noncontrolling interest in the legal subsidiary for a reverse acquisition. In the case of a reverse acquisition, the noncontrolling interest is measured by multiplying the noncontrolling interest percentage against the carrying value of the legal subsidiary's net assets. This is a book value approach rather than the full fair value methodology employed in other computations. However, the use of the book value approach will not change the full goodwill valuation (i.e., goodwill is the same value as in the 100% acquisition case).

Noncontrolling Interest: Sell Company = 1,000 shares / 10,000 shares = 10%

The valuation of the noncontrolling interest is presented below:

Net Assets of the Sell Company	**$80,000**
Noncontrolling Interest Percentage	**10%**
Noncontrolling Interest	**$ 8,000**

Consolidated Financial Statements in a Reverse Acquisition with a Noncontrolling Interest

The consolidated financial statements must be prepared in the name of the legal parent, the Buy Company (the accounting acquiree). In addition, on the consolidated balance sheet, the shareholders equity section will indicate the number of shares issued and outstanding for the legal parent, the Buy Company (i.e., 66,000 shares of $1 par value common stock). However, the number of outstanding shares of the legal parent, the Buy Company, is valued using the amounts applicable to the accounting acquiree, the Sell Company, including all contributed capital and retained earnings (i.e., the legal subsidiary's equity values are used to measure the legal parent company's book value per outstanding share). The consolidated balance sheet on the date of acquisition is presented below.

Consolidated Balance Sheet on the Date of Acquisition: 5-1-20X9

Description	Buy Company Acquiree (Legal Parent)	Sell Company Acquirer (Legal Subsidiary)	Adjustments and Eliminations	C Co (In the name of the Legal Parent)
Cash	$ 10,000	$ 2,000		$ 12,000
Current Assets	120,000	80,000		200,000
Noncurrent Assets	170,000	18,000	+$ 40,000	228,000
Goodwill	- 0 -	- 0 -	+ 330,000	330,000
Total Assets	$300,000	$100,000	+$370,000	$770,000
Liabilities	$ 70,000	$ 20,000	- 0 -	$ 90,000
Stockholders' Equity:				
Common Stock-$1 par (66,000 shares outstanding)	$ 30,000	$ 10,000	-30,000 +$600,000 -1,000	$ - 0 - 609,000*
Retained earnings	200,000	70,000	-200,000 -7,000	63,000
Noncontrolling Interest	- 0 -	- 0 -	+8,000	8,000**
Total Stockholders' Equity	$230,000	$ 80,000	+$370,000	$680,000
Total Liabilities and Stockholders' Equity	$300,000	$100,000	+$370,000	$770,000

Notes:
** Common Stock Value = ($10,000 x 90% + $600,000 Implied Consideration Transferred) = $609,000*
*** Noncontrolling Interest Valuation = ($10,000 x 10% + $70,000 x 10%)= $8,000.*

In the consolidating worksheet above, the business combination is reflected by the issuance of 40,000 Buy Company common shares using the $600,000 implied value of the consideration transferred by the Sell Company, the write up of the net assets by $40,000, the recognition of $330,000 of goodwill and the elimination of the carrying value of the Buy Company's common stock and retained earnings (i.e., $30,000 and $200,000 respectively).

Note that even though the only outstanding shares are the common shares of the Buy Company, the values assigned to those shares are based on the Sell Company values. The noncontrolling interest is reflected by moving 10% of the book (carrying) value of the Sell Company's common stock and retained earnings into the noncontrolling interest account. So, in a reverse acquisition, the noncontrolling interest is not measured at full fair value but rather, it is carried at its percentage share of the stockholders' equity of the subsidiary.

CHANGES IN THE PARENT COMPANY'S LEVEL OF CONTROL (CHANGES IN A PARENT'S OWNERSHIP INTEREST IN A SUBSIDIARY)

Disclosure Required when there is a Change in the Parent's Ownership Interest

Whenever there is a change in the parent company's ownership interest, a disclosure must be provided in the notes to the consolidated financial statements indicating the net income attributable to the parent company and the changes in the parent's equity due to transfers to or from the noncontrolling interest.

To illustrate, assume that the net income for the current year for the Buy Company is $1,200 and the Sell Company reports $500 in net income. Assume also the due to the acquisition of an additional 12% of the outstanding shares of the subsidiary, the Buy Company company's controlling share of the Sell Company increases from 80% to 92%. In addition, its total additional paid in capital (APIC) is decreased by $63 as a result of the additional shares acquired (i.e., $15 from the share purchase and $48 from the reclassification into the parent's accumulated other comprehensive income. The following disclosure is required in the notes to the consolidated financial statements.

Buy Company Notes to the Consolidated Financial Statements Net Income attributable to the Buy Company and Transfers to and from the Noncontrolling Interests For the Year Ended December 31, 20X9	
Net Income attributable to the Buy Company: ($1,200 + 500 x 92%)	$ 1,660
Transfers (to) and from the Noncontrolling Interest: Decrease in Buy Company's Additional Paid in Capital from the purchase of an additional 12% interest in the Sell Company ($15 + 48)	(63)
Change from Net Income attributable to the Buy Company and transfers (to) and from the Noncontrolling Interest	$ 1,597

CHANGES IN A PARENT'S OWNERSHIP INTEREST IN A SUBSIDIARY: LOSS OF CONTROLLING INTEREST IN A SUBSIDIARY COMPANY AND DECONSOLIDATE

If an equity transaction results in a loss of control by the parent company, a deconsolidate of the subsidiary must be implemented. A gain or loss on deconsolidate is recognized in earnings, except for nonreciprocal transfers to shareholders (e.g., spin offs).

The gain or loss on deconsolidate is computed as the difference between (a) and (b):

(a) The aggregate of:
   1. The fair value of any consideration received.
   2. The fair value of any retained interest in the former subsidiary. (Here, the adjustment to bring the carrying value of the retained portion of the investment to fair value on date of deconsolidate results in a gain or loss recognized in earnings).
   3. The carrying value of any noncontrolling interest in the former subsidiary, including any accumulated other comprehensive income attributed to the noncontrolling interest.

(b) The carrying amount of the former subsidiary's assets and liabilities.

Illustration of Deconsolidate of a Subsidiary

The following consolidated balance sheet is provided on the date that the parent company (the Buy Company) sells all of its 80% interest in the Sell Company for $500 in cash. Assume that there is no accumulated other comprehensive income.

Buy Company ***Consolidated Balance Sheet*** ***At December 31 20X9***	
Cash	$100
Noncash Assets	675
Goodwill	155
Total Assets	$930
Liabilities	$360
Stockholders' Equity:	
Sell Company	$ - 0 -
Buy Company	505
Noncontrolling Interest	65
Total Shareholders' Equity	$570
Total Liabilities and Stockholders' Equity	$930

The carrying value of the subsidiary's net assets is presented below:

Noncash Assets	**$350**
Goodwill	**155**
Less: Liabilities	**(140)**
Net Assets	**$365**

Computation of the Gain or Loss on Deconsolidate:

Fair value of the consideration received	**$500**
Fair value of the retained interest in the former subsidiary	**- 0 -**
Carrying value of the noncontrolling interest	**65**
Total	**$565**
Carrying value of the subsidiary's net assets	**(365)**
Gain on deconsolidate	**$200**

The worksheet for the sale of the subsidiary and the deconsolidate is presented below. Note that the gain on the deconsolidate would be recognized in earnings and closed to retained earnings in the stockholders' equity section of the balance sheet. This is reflected as $200 increase in the stockholders' equity of the Buy Company. The other portions of the elimination entry reflect the increase in cash from the disposal the elimination of the values of the net assets assigned to the subsidiary company.

Buy Company ***Deconsolidate of the Sell Company***			
Account	***Consolidated***	***Elimination***	***Deconsolidated Buy Company Only***
Cash	$100	+$ 500	$ 600
Noncash Assets	675	-350	325
Goodwill	155	-155	- 0 -
Total Assets	$930	-$ 5	$ 925
Liabilities	$360	$-140	$ 220
Stockholders' Equity:			
Sell Company	$ - 0 -		$ - 0 -
Buy Company	505	+$ 200	705
Noncontrolling Interest	65	-65	- 0 -
Total Shareholders' Equity	$570	+ $135	$ 705
Total Liabilities and Stockholders' Equity	$930	-$ 5	$ 925

DISCLOSURES OF THE NONCONTROLLING INTEREST IN THE CONSOLIDATED FINANCIAL STATEMENTS

To illustrate the disclosure requirements of FASB Statements Nos. 141(R) and 160, assume that you are given the balance sheet for the Buy Company and Consolidated Subsidiary. This balance sheet is presented below.

Buy Company and Consolidated Subsidiary ***Consolidated Balance Sheets*** ***(in millions)***		
At December 31	***20X9***	***20X8***
Assets		
Cash	$ 550	$ 300
Noncash Current Assets	1,080	750
Noncurrent Assets	1,950	1,050
Total Assets	$3,580	$2,100
Liabilities		
Current Liabilities	$ 400	$ 400
Equity		
Stockholders' Equity: Buy Company		
Common Stock – no par (700 shares issued and outstanding)	$ 400	$ 400
Retained Earnings	1,945	1,000
Accumulated Other Comprehensive Income	590	200
Total Shareholders' Equity: Buy Company	$2,935	$1,600
Noncontrolling Interest	***$ 245***	***$ 100***
Total Shareholders' Equity	$3,180	$1,700
Total Liabilities and Stockholders' Equity	$3,580	$2,100

Assume that during 20X9, there was a $400 unrealized holding gain net of tax, on the financial instruments reported within the noncash current assets of the subsidiary. Of this amount, $390 is attributable to the Buy Company (97.5% assumed controlling interest) and $10 is attributed to the noncontrolling interest (2.5% assumed share). The subsidiary reported $5,400 net income after tax for the year ended December 31, 20X9. As a result, $5,265 (i.e., $5,400 x 97.5%) of the subsidiary's net income is attributed to the parent company and the $135 balance is attributed to the noncontrolling interest (i.e., $5,400 – 5,265). The consolidated income statement is presented below.

Buy Company and Consolidated Subsidiary Consolidated Statement of Earnings For the Year Ended December 31, 20X9	
Revenues	$4,000
Operating Expenses	(2,200)
Income Before Tax	$1,800
Provision for income tax	(720)
Net income	$1,080
Less: Net income attributable to the noncontrolling interest	(135)
Net income attributable to the Buy Company	$ 945
Basic Earnings per Share: Attributable to the Buy Company Common Shareholders	
$945 / 700 shares	$1.35
Amounts Attributable to the Buy Company Common Shareholders	
Income from continuing operations-net of tax	$ 945
Discontinued operations-net of tax	- 0 -
Net income	$ 945

Footnote: Noncontrolling Interest

Beginning Balance at January 1, 20X9	**$100**
Net income attributable to the noncontrolling interest	**$135**
Other comprehensive income attributable to the noncontrolling interest	**10**
Total Comprehensive Income attributed to the noncontrolling interest	**$145**
Ending Balance at December 31, 20X9	**$245**

Buy Company and Consolidated Subsidiary *Consolidated Statement of Comprehensive Income* *For the Year Ended December 31, 20X9*	
Net income	$1,080
Other comprehensive income net of tax: Unrealized holding gain	400
Comprehensive Income-net of tax	$1,480
Less: Comprehensive income attributable to the noncontrolling interest	(145)
Comprehensive Income attributable to the Buy Company	$1,335

Buy Company and Consolidated Subsidiary
Consolidated Statement of Changes in Shareholders' Equity
For the year ended December 31, 20X9

	Common Stock	*Retained Earnings*	*Accumulated Other Comprehensive Income*	*Noncontrolling Interest*	*Total*
Balance, January 1, 20X9	$400	$1,000	$200	$100	$1,700
Comprehensive Income					
Net Income		$ 945		$ 135	$ 1,080
Other Comprehensive Income: Unrealized Gain on Financial Instruments	---	---	390	10	400
Total Comprehensive Income	---	$ 945	$390	$145	$1,480
Balance, December 31, 20X9	$400	$1,945	$ 590	$ 245	$3,180

ACCOUNTING FOR INCOME TAXES WITH BUSINESS COMBINATIONS

Business combinations can be either taxable or nontaxable in nature.

In a taxable business combination, (e.g., a cash net asset purchase or a Section 338 election in a cash for stock acquisition), the total consideration transferred and the measured and recognized assets and liabilities for both tax and financial reporting purposes are reported at full fair value. However, in some cases these amounts can be different.

In a taxable business combination a temporary difference and deferred tax liability can be created by goodwill recognition and subsequent amortization in a net asset purchase if amortized 15 years for tax purposes and written off for financial reporting purposes, based on impairment tests. The deferred tax liability is not created on the date of acquisition but only when tax amortization begins. The deferred tax liability reverses when the goodwill is impaired for books or the acquiree is sold or ceases operations. Aside from the deferred tax liability generated by the tax amortization of goodwill, significant book tax differences are usually not expected on a taxable deal.

In a nontaxable business combination, (e.g., stock for stock exchange) the target company's tax bases for the various assets and liabilities are carried over, while for financial reporting, the assets acquired and liabilities assumed are recognized and remeasured at full fair value. Thus, in most cases, there will be significant differences between the tax and financial reporting bases in a nontaxable business combination.

So, both taxable and nontaxable business combinations can involve the application of deferred income tax accounting.

There are several key issues relating to accounting for income taxes when a business combination is implemented. These issues include the treatment of non-tax deductible goodwill and changes in valuation allowances for deferred tax assets.

First, the recognition of a deferred tax liability is prohibited when goodwill is either not recognized or not amortizable for tax purposes. For example, a deferred tax liability cannot be recognized for the excess reported (book) goodwill over tax goodwill because that portion of book goodwill has no tax implications.

With respect to valuation allowances for deferred tax assets, changes in the beginning of the year valuation allowances due to changes in circumstances affecting judgment regarding the realizability of the related deferred tax asset in future years should ordinarily be recognized in income from continuing operations. There are exceptions to the earnings effect of a change in valuation allowance: (1) changes in the valuation allowance made during the measurement period resulting from new information that existed at the acquisition date must be recognized as an adjustment to goodwill (reducing goodwill); (2) if goodwill is reduced to zero as a result of the adjustment process indicated in (1) above, any additional decreases in the valuation allowance shall be recognized as a gain on a bargain purchase (i.e., negative goodwill); and (3) there are other tax adjustments that can be credited or charged to contributed capital. For example, tax effects on items in comprehensive income.

The next section of this chapter provides illustrations of nontaxable and taxable business combination.

Illustration Case 1: Nontaxable Business Combination

Data for the Illustration: Assume that Nomiss, plc. acquires LODI Company in 20X9. The following data related to the transaction are presented below:

- The income tax rate is 35%.
- The acquisition of LODI Company was implemented by a transfer of consideration with a fair value of $1,000,000 in a nontaxable, stock for stock exchange.
- The fair values of assets acquired total $1,500,000.
- The carryover tax bases of assets acquired total $1,200,000 (target company's carryover basis).
- The fair and carryover tax bases of the liabilities assumed in the purchase are $500,000.
- The difference between the tax and fair values of the assets acquired, $300,000, (i.e., $1,500,000 – 1,200,000), consists of:
  - Taxable temporary differences of $400,000 and at 35% giving rise to a deferred tax liability of $140,000. For example, there is an excess book basis over the tax basis of depreciable assets acquired giving rise to future taxable amounts of $400,000 due to the lower future tax deductions relative to book.
  - There are also deductible temporary differences of $100,000, and at 35% giving rise to a deferred tax asset of $35,000. For example, there is an excess tax basis over the book basis of amortizable finite life intangible assets acquired, due to a portion of the intangible asset capitalized for tax purposes but already expensed on the financial statements resulting in future tax deductible amounts.

- There is no doubt as to the realizability of the deductible temporary differences in this case. Therefore, a valuation allowance against the deferred tax asset is not needed.

The amounts recorded to account for the nontaxable business combination transaction are as follows:

Consideration transferred (Fair value of the parent company shares issued)	$1,000,000
Fair value of the recognized net assets other than goodwill:	
Assets, other than goodwill and deferred tax assets	$1,500,000
Deferred tax assets (DTA-no valuation allowance)	35,000
Liabilities, other than deferred tax liabilities	(500,000)
Deferred tax liabilities (DTL)	(140,000)
Fair value of the identifiable net assets acquired	$895,000
Goodwill	$ 105,000

Since there is no goodwill for tax purposes, the entire amount of goodwill is excess book goodwill and no deferred tax liability is recognized.

Note: If the DTA and DTL at the date of acquisition were not recognized, there would be no goodwill for book purposes (i.e., Fair value of the consideration transferred = $1,000,000; Fair Value of net assets acquired = $1,000,000 = ($1,500,000 – 500,000).

Modification of the Nomiss plc. Illustration

In this case, assume that based on all available evidence (both positive and negative) at the acquisition date, Nomiss management believes that it is "more likely than not" that only $80,000 of future income will be available for realization of the benefits from the deferred tax asset. This assessment includes the reversal of future taxable amounts from the excess book basis of depreciable assets. The following analysis of the deferred tax asset made on the date of acquisition is presented below:

Description	***Pretax***	***Taxed at 35%***
Temporary deductible amounts (for the DTA)	$100,000	$ 35,000
Future income	(80,000)	(28,000)
Valuation allowance needed	$ 20,000	$ 7,000
Net DTA at the date of acquisition		$28,000

Based on the change of assumption regarding the need for a valuation allowance against the DTA, the amounts recorded to account for the business combination transaction are as follows:

Consideration transferred (Fair value of the parent company shares issued)	$1,000,000
Fair value of the recognized net assets other than goodwill:	
Assets, other than goodwill and deferred tax assets	$1,500,000
Deferred tax assets (DTA-net of valuation allowance)	28,000
Liabilities, other than deferred tax liabilities	(500,000)
Deferred tax liabilities (DTL)	(140,000)
Fair value of the identifiable net assets acquired	$888,000
Goodwill	$ 112,000

Since there is no goodwill for tax purposes, the entire amount of goodwill is excess book goodwill and no deferred tax liability is recognized.

Note: The valuation of goodwill is increased by $7,000 or the amount of the valuation allowance (i.e., $105,000 original goodwill + $7,000 valuation allowance = $112,000).

Assume that, one year after the acquisition, management now believes (based on all available evidence, both positive and negative), that it is "more likely than not" that all of the DTA benefits will be realized. That is, the valuation allowance is no longer necessary. According to the FASB standards, the elimination of the valuation allowance is to be recognized in earnings as a reduction of deferred income tax expense.

In this case valuation allowance will be reduced by $7,000 with a corresponding reduction of the (deferred) income tax expense. The balance of the DTA is increased to $35,000. The adjustment made in 2010 is reflected in the financial modeling worksheet below. The reduction of the valuation allowance increases the net realizable value of the deferred tax asset.

FINANCIAL MODELING WORKSHEET VALUATION ALLOWANCE ADJUSTMENT AFTER THE MEASUREMENT PERIOD

INCOME STATEMENT (FIRST)	
REVENUES:	
EXPENSES:	
Income Tax Expense (Negative Tax Expense – increases net income)	*+7,000*
NET INCOME OR LOSS (a)	*+7,000*

STATEMENT OF CASH FLOWS (THIRD)	
OPERATING ACTIVITIES:	
NET INCOME OR LOSS (a)	*+7,000*
Deduct: Valuation Allowance Adjustment	*(7,000)*
INVESTING ACTIVITIES:	
FINANCING ACTIVITIES:	
INCREASE (DECREASE) IN CASH (b)	*- 0 -*
ADD: BEGINNING CASH BALANCE	
ENDING CASH BALANCE	

BALANCE SHEET (SECOND)			
ASSETS		*LIABILITIES*	
CURRENT ASSETS		*CURRENT LIABILITIES*	
CASH (b)	*- 0 -*		
		NONCURRENT LIABILITIES	
		STOCKHOLDERS' EQUITY	
NONCURRENT ASSETS			
Deferred Tax Asset		*CAPITAL STOCK*	
(Valuation allowance)	*+ 7,000*	*APIC*	
Net Realizable Value		*RETAINED*	
		EARNINGS (a)	*+7,000*
		TOTAL LIABILITIES & STOCKHOLDERS' EQUITY	
TOTAL ASSETS	*+7,000*		*+7,000*

If this adjustment was made during the measurement period, the following entry would be made in the financial statements:

FINANCIAL MODELING WORKSHEET VALUATION ALLOWANCE ADJUSTMENT DURING THE MEASUREMENT PERIOD

INCOME STATEMENT (FIRST)	
REVENUES:	
EXPENSES:	
NET INCOME OR LOSS (a)	*- 0 -*

STATEMENT OF CASH FLOWS (THIRD)	
OPERATING ACTIVITIES:	
NET INCOME OR LOSS (a)	*- 0 -*
INVESTING ACTIVITIES:	
FINANCING ACTIVITIES:	
INCREASE (DECREASE) IN CASH (b)	*- 0 -*
ADD: BEGINNING CASH BALANCE	
ENDING CASH BALANCE	

BALANCE SHEET (SECOND)			
ASSETS		*LIABILITIES*	
CURRENT ASSETS		*CURRENT LIABILITIES*	
CASH (b)	*- 0 -*		
		NONCURRENT LIABILITIES	
		STOCKHOLDERS'	
NONCURRENT ASSETS		*EQUITY*	
Deferred Tax Asset		*CAPITAL STOCK*	
(Valuation allowance)	*+ 7,000*	*APIC*	
Net Realizable Value		*RETAINED*	
		EARNINGS (a)	*- 0 -*
Goodwill	*- 7,000*		
		TOTAL	
		LIABILITIES &	
		STOCKHOLDERS'	
TOTAL ASSETS	*- 0 -*	*EQUITY*	*- 0 -*

So, in this case goodwill and the valuation allowance will both be reduced by $7,000. The balance of the DTA is increased to $35,000 and goodwill is reduced to $105,000 (the same value as in the no valuation allowance case).

This second case reflects that general rule that measurement period adjustments are not included in earnings. The measurement period ends as soon as the acquirer obtains all necessary information to complete the financial information reported or determines that such information is not available. The maximum length of the measurement period is one year from the acquisition date.

Finally, if goodwill is reduced to zero as part of the adjustment process during the measurement period, any remaining adjustments to reduce the valuation allowance would be credited to the gain on a bargain purchase.

The accounting illustrated above applies to all deferred tax assets, even those created by net operating loss carry forwards. It should be noted that if a deferred tax asset is to be reduced in the future (either by an increase in the valuation allowance or a direct reduction of the deferred tax asset) it is treated as any asset impairment or write down and reflected in the earnings of the period in which the reduction is recognized. Again, all adjustments made beyond the measurement date must be reported in income.

Illustration Case 2: Taxable Business Combination

As noted earlier, there may not be many significant temporary book tax differences resulting from a taxable business combination as one would expect the fair value measurement and recognition to be similar for both book at tax purposes. Deferred tax assets and deferred tax liabilities, if any, would be measured and recognized in a typical fashion. However, one key issue results from the accounting for tax deductible goodwill.

When goodwill is tax deductible, the book and tax goodwill are separated into two components:

1. The lower of either book or tax goodwill (this creates a temporary book tax difference resulting in either a deferred tax asset or deferred tax liability, depending on the timing of the book impairment and the tax amortization).
2. The remainder: either the excess book goodwill over tax goodwill or the excess tax goodwill over book goodwill.

As noted earlier, when there is excess book goodwill over tax goodwill the recognition of a deferred tax liability is prohibited. When there is excess tax goodwill, complex set of computations are required. Excess tax goodwill results in an adjustment to book goodwill, reducing book goodwill by the amount of the deferred tax asset created by the future tax deductions.

Case 2A: Illustration of Tax Deductible Goodwill with Excess Book Goodwill

Assume that at the date of acquisition, book goodwill is $1,100 and tax goodwill is valued at $800. Following the guidelines of FASB Statement No. 141(R), the two components of goodwill are:

1. The lower of book goodwill or tax goodwill: Tax goodwill = $800. In this case, a deferred tax liability is created as soon as the tax amortization of goodwill begins for tax purposes. A deferred tax liability is not recognized on the date of acquisition. The deferred tax liability reverses when book goodwill is impaired or the reporting unit (e.g., the subsidiary or division acquired) is either sold or ceases operations. A deferred tax asset results if book impairment is recognized before tax amortization at initially larger amounts.
2. The remainder is the $300 excess book goodwill ($1,100 – 800). No deferred taxes are recognized on the excess book goodwill either at the acquisition date or in future periods.

Case 2B: Illustration of Tax Deductible Goodwill with Excess Tax Deductible Goodwill

Assume that at the acquisition date, book goodwill is $800 (before adjusting for the tax benefits of tax deductible goodwill), and tax goodwill is valued at $1,100. The applicable tax rate is 40%. Following the guidelines of FASB Statement No. 141(R), the two components of goodwill are:

1. The lower of book goodwill or tax goodwill: Book goodwill = $800 (before the adjustment for the tax benefits of tax deductible goodwill). The final amount of book goodwill will be determined by the computation presented below. Book goodwill is to be reduced by the deferred tax asset created by excess tax deductible goodwill.
2. The remainder is excess tax goodwill = $300 ($1,100 – 300). This will create a deferred tax asset on the date of acquisition and that will effectively reduce the amount of book goodwill. The amount of the deferred tax asset is determined by the following equation based on the preliminary temporary difference (PTD) amount:

$$DTA = [\,t / (1 - t)\,] \times PTD$$

This methodology must be employed to determine the amount of the deferred tax asset and the final amount of book goodwill. The equation for the DTA and the resulting amounts assigned to the DTA and book goodwill are presented in the next section.

Computations to determine the Deferred Tax Asset and the Adjusted (Final Amount of) Book Goodwill

This section provides the derivation of the DTA equation and the final values of goodwill and the DTA.

1. ***Variable definitions:***

t = tax rate
PTD = Preliminary Temporary Difference
FTD = Final Temporary Difference
Where:
FTD = PTD + DTA

DTA = Deferred Tax Asset
Where:
DTA = t x FTD

To determine the adjusted DTA, the following derivation is made:

$$FTD = PTD + DTA$$
$$FTD = PTD + (t \times FTD)$$
$$FTD - (t \times FTD) = PTD$$
$$FTD\,(1 - t) = PTD$$
$$FTD = PTD / (1 - t)$$

So, if the DTA = t x FTD, then by substitution for FTD the DTA defined in terms of the PTD is equal to:

$$DTA = t \times PTD / (1 - t)$$
$$\mathbf{DTA = [\,t / (1 - t)\,] \times PTD}$$

In this case:
t = .40

PTD	=	Tax Goodwill – Book Goodwill
$300	=	$1,100 - 800

DTA	= [t / (1 – t)] x PTD
DTA	= [.40 / (1 - .40)] x $300
DTA	= <u>$200</u>

So, the DTA is $200 which reduces book goodwill by the same amount.

After the acquisition date adjustment, book goodwill is now equal to $600 (i.e., $800 – 200) and the final temporary difference (FTD) is equal to $500:

FTD	=	PTD	+	DTA
$500	=	$300	+	200

Also:

FTD	=	Tax Goodwill	-	Book Goodwill
$500	=	$1,100	-	$600

So, given a 40% tax rate, the DTA is equal to $200 (i.e., $500 x 40%).

There will be a deferred tax liability created as soon as tax deductible amortization begins on the $600 (which is now the first component of goodwill). There is no deferred tax liability recognized on the date of acquisition. Again, the reversal of this deferred tax liability occurs when book goodwill is impaired or the reporting unit (e.g., the subsidiary or division acquired) is either sold or ceases operations.

In this example, the following financial modeling worksheet would reflect the entry that would be required on the financial statements to record the deferred tax asset and reduce the amount of book or reported goodwill by $200.

FINANCIAL MODELING WORKSHEET

INCOME STATEMENT (FIRST)	
REVENUES:	
EXPENSES:	
NET INCOME OR LOSS (a)	- 0 -

STATEMENT OF CASH FLOWS (THIRD)	
OPERATING ACTIVITIES:	
NET INCOME OR LOSS (a)	- 0 -
INVESTING ACTIVITIES:	
FINANCING ACTIVITIES:	
INCREASE (DECREASE) IN CASH (b)	- 0 -
ADD: BEGINNING CASH BALANCE	
ENDING CASH BALANCE	

BALANCE SHEET (SECOND)			
ASSETS		LIABILITIES	
CURRENT ASSETS		CURRENT LIABILITIES	
CASH (b)	- 0 -		
		NONCURRENT LIABILITIES	
		STOCKHOLDERS'	
NONCURRENT ASSETS		EQUITY	
Deferred Tax Asset	+ 200	CAPITAL STOCK	
		APIC	
Goodwill	-200	RETAINED	
		EARNINGS (a)	- 0 -
		TOTAL	
		LIABILITIES &	
		STOCKHOLDERS'	
TOTAL ASSETS	- 0 -	EQUITY	- 0 -

ACCRETION / DILUTION ANALYSIS IN PRO FORMA MERGERS

Accretion / Dilution Analysis is an analysis of the change in the acquirer's earnings per share (EPS) as a result of a merger or acquisition. The purpose of Accretion / Dilution Analysis is to estimate the change in stock price. The estimated change in stock price will help the analyst determine if existing shareholders will favor or oppose the proposed transaction. The following discussion will assume that the computation accretion or dilution is taken from the acquiring company's perspective. The same analysis can be conducted from the target company's perspective.

The basic procedure used in Accretion / Dilution Analysis involves three steps:

- Determine the standalone estimated or proforma net income and EPS for the target and the acquirer.
- Calculate financial statement adjustments, which include:
  - Additional interest expense on a debt financed deal.
  - Opportunity loss on a cash deal (i.e., lost interest income on investments or cost of not paying off existing debt with the cash used in the business combination).
  - Reduction of interest expense on debt refinancing.
  - Operating Synergies and cost savings, if any.
  - Amortization of intangibles with limited lives and additional depreciation, etc. due to asset write-ups.
  - Additional shares issued as part of the consideration given in the transaction and on assumed exercise of all outstanding options, convertibles, etc. (i.e. share count adjustments).
- Calculate the projected or pro forma EPS and compare to the standalone EPS of the acquirer.

Illustration of Accretion / Dilution Analysis

The following stand alone projected or proforma income information was obtained for the Buy Company and the Sell Company one year after the acquisition.

ACQUIRER AND TARGET STANDALONE PROJECTED OR PROFORMA INCOME STATEMENTS ONE YEAR AFTER THE ACQUISITION		
ACCOUNT	***BUY COMPANY***	***SELL COMPANY***
Sales	$ 100,000	$ 70,000
Less: Cost of goods sold	40,000	30,000
Gross profit	$ 60,000	$ 40,000
Less: Operating expenses	6,000	7,000
Operating income	$ 54,000	$ 33,000
Less: Interest expense	8,000	3,000
Less: Amortization of limited life intangible assets acquired	- 0 -	- 0 -
Less: Additional depreciation	- 0 -	- 0 -
Earnings before tax	$ 46,000	$ 30,000
Tax provision at 40%	18,400	12,000
Net income	$ 27,600	$18,000
Common shares outstanding	30,000 shs	10,000 shs
EPS	$.92 per share	$1.80 per share
Accretion / (Dilution) %	N / A	N / A

Assume that limited life intangibles of $20,000 were acquired on the transaction date. The limited life intangibles are amortized over a 10-year period and the $40,000 plant asset write-ups are also depreciated over a 10-year period. Based on these assumptions, the following consolidated income statements can be prepared. Note that both the intangible amortization and additional depreciation are computed on a straight-line basis without scrap value.

$$\textbf{Amortization Expense} = \frac{\$20{,}000}{10 \text{ years}} = \$2{,}000 \text{ per year}$$

$$\textbf{Additional Depreciation Expense} = \frac{\$40{,}000}{10 \text{ years}} = \$4{,}000 \text{ per year}$$

It is assumed that these are the only two adjustments needed in the analysis. The following illustrations use the same data from Cases A and B discussed earlier.

CASE A: Pro forma Income Statement – Acquisition Method used in a Cash Transaction

ACCOUNT	*BUY COMPANY*	*SELL COMPANY*	*ADJUSTMENTS*	*CONSOLIDATED NET INCOME*
Sales	$ 100,000	$ 70,000		$ 170,000
Less: Cost of goods sold	40,000	30,000		70,000
Gross profit	$ 60,000	$ 40,000		$ 100,000
Less: Operating expenses	6,000	7,000		13,000
Operating income	$ 54,000	$ 33,000		$ 87,000
Less: Interest expense	8,000	3,000		11,000
Less: Intangible amortization	- 0 -	- 0 -	2,000	2,000
Less: Additional depreciation	- 0 -	- 0 -	4,000	4,000
Earnings before tax	$ 46,000	$ 30,000		$ 70,000
Tax provision at 40%	18,400	12,000		28,000
Net income	$ 27,600	$18,000		$ 42,000
Common shares outstanding	30,000 shs	10,000 shs	-10,000 shs	30,000 shs
EPS	$.92 / share	$1.80 / share		$1.40 / share
Accretion / (Dilution) %	N / A	N / A		**(a) 52.2%**

(a) *([$1.40 - .92] / $.92) = 52.2%*
(b) ***NOTE:*** *A cash deal can be dilutive if there are target company losses and / or excessive charges for interest, depreciation, amortization, or if there are option or convertible contracts to be settled as part of the merger, etc.*

In this cash for stock deal, the number of shares outstanding do not change from the parent company's perspective. This results from the fact that we assumed that there were no option or convertible contracts that had to be settled as part of the merger deal. In this case, the deal is accretive by 52.2%, but as noted in the table, cash for stock deals can be dilutive where there are losses, excessive additional charges (earnings drag) or if there are option or convertible contracts to be settled.

CASE B: Pro forma Income Statement - Acquisition Method used in a Stock for Stock Transaction

It is assumed that the Buy Company controls the management and the board of directors of the combined entity. Therefore, the Buy Company is considered the accounting acquirer as well as the legal parent in this case, even though the former Sell Company shareholders hold a greater number of the Buy Company's voting shares (i.e., this deal does not qualify as a reverse acquisition).

ACCOUNT	BUY COMPANY	SELL COMPANY	ADJUSTMENTS	CONSOLIDATED NET INCOME
Sales	$ 100,000	$ 70,000		$ 170,000
Less: Cost of goods sold	40,000	30,000		70,000
Gross profit	$ 60,000	$ 40,000		$ 100,000
Less: Operating expenses	6,000	7,000		13,000
Operating income	$ 54,000	$ 33,000		$ 87,000
Less: Interest expense	8,000	3,000		11,000
Less: Intangible amortization	- 0 -	- 0 -	2,000	2,000
Less: Additional depreciation	- 0 -	- 0 -	4,000	4,000
Earnings before tax	$ 46,000	$ 30,000		$ 70,000
Tax provision at 40%	18,400	12,000		28,000
Net income	$ 27,600	$18,000		$ 42,000
Common shares outstanding	30,000 shs	10,000 shs	-10,000 shs +40,000 shs +30,000 shs	70,000 shs
EPS	$.92 / share	$1.80 / share		$.60 / share
Accretion / (Dilution) %	N / A	N / A		**(a) (34.8%)**

(a) *[$.60 - .92] / $.92) = (34.8%)*

(b) ***NOTE:*** *A stock deal can be accretive with higher target income, lower interest, depreciation and amortization charges or a more favorable exchange ratio. For example, if only 4,000 Buy Company shares are issued for all 10,000 Sell Company shares, the combined EPS is $1.24 ($42,000 / 34,000 shares). In this case, accretion is 34.8% or ([$.1.24 - .92] / $.92) = 34.8%.*

With the stock for stock deal, the number of outstanding shares generally increases from the parent company's outstanding shares. In Case B this share increase occurs primarily due to the exchange ratio assumed and makes the deal dilutive. As noted in the table, a higher target income, lower earnings drag adjustments, and a more favorable exchange ratio could make the stock for stock deal accretive.

PUSH DOWN ACCOUNTING

The concept of push down accounting is related to the acquisition method. Push down accounting is required by the SEC whenever the separate financial statements of a subsidiary are presented after there has been a "significant change in ownership." For example, separate statements are issued if the subsidiary has publicly traded securities. To date, the SEC has defined "significant" as a 95% to 100% change in ownership. However, a change of 90% to 95% will trigger push down accounting practice. The SEC regulations specifically indicate that push down accounting must be used whenever there is a 95% to 100% change in ownership. Push down accounting can be used on a voluntary basis if there is a 80% to

95% change in ownership. Finally, push down accounting cannot be used if there is a 50% to 80% change in ownership.

In all cases, the parent company must maintain control. Therefore, the noncontrolling interest, publicly traded debt and publicly traded preferred shares cannot be significant. As noted in the percentage guidelines, the noncontrolling interest cannot exceed 20%.

Under push down theory, whenever there is a significant change in the ownership of the voting common stock of a company, the economic effect of that change should be reflected on the financial statements of that company.

Essentially, push down accounting requires that the full fair values of the net assets of the subsidiary acquired in the purchase, including goodwill, be reflected (i.e., "pushed down") on the financial statements of the subsidiary. It should be noted that if push down accounting is not used in a legal stock acquisition, then, the only place where this revaluation process occurs is in the consolidated financial statements (i.e., the consolidating spreadsheet).

When push down accounting is used, the balance sheet for the subsidiary reflects the full fair value of its net assets (including goodwill). The income statement reflects profit or loss determined by utilizing depreciation, depletion, amortization, etc., and a cost of goods sold based on the revalued net assets.

To illustrate, assume that the Scarlet Company acquires the Knight Company. The Knight Company reported the following balance sheet on the date of acquisition.

Description	***KNIGHT AT HISTORICAL COST***
Cash	$ 10,000
Accounts receivable-net	5,000
Inventory	18,000
Equipment	80,000
Accumulated Depreciation	(15,000)
Goodwill	- 0 -
Franchises	4,000
Total assets	$102,000
Accounts payable	$ 2,000
Total liabilities	$ 2,000
Capital stock	$ 35,000
Additional paid-in capital	10,000
Retained earnings	55,000
Total liabilities and stockholders' equity	$102,000

Assume also that on the date of acquisition, the fair values of the subsidiary's net assets are measured and the following write ups are required to the subsidiary's net assets:

Inventory	**$ 1,900**
Equipment	**$ 9,500**
Goodwill	**$32,650**
Franchises	**$ 950**

If the principles of push down accounting were applied to the financial statements of the Knight Company, its balance sheet would appear as follows on the date of acquisition:

Description	***KNIGHT AT HISTORICAL COST***	***ADJUSTMENTS***	***KNIGHT PUSH DOWN BASIS***
Cash	$ 10,000		**$ 10,000**
Accounts receivable-net	5,000		**5,000**
Inventory	18,000	**(a) +1,900**	**19,900**
Equipment	80,000	**(a) +9,500**	**89,500**
Accumulated Depreciation	(15,000)		**(15,000)**
Goodwill	- 0 -	**(a) +32,650**	**32,650**
Franchises	4,000	**(a) +950**	**4,950**
Total assets	$102,000	**+ $ 45,000**	**$ 147,000**
Accounts payable	$ 2,000		**$ 2,000**
Total liabilities	$ 2,000		**$ 2,000**
Capital stock	$ 35,000		**$ 35,000**
Additional paid-in capital ***Push Down Capital (NOTE 1)***	10,000 - 0 -	**(a) + 45,000**	**10,000 45,000**
Retained earnings	55,000		**55,000**
Total liabilities and stockholders' equity	$102,000	**+$ 45,000**	**$ 147,000**

Notes to the Financial Statements:
NOTE 1: The total APIC is comprised of the original balance of $10,000 plus the net asset write up gains of $45,000 (i.e., gain on the $12,350 write-up of the company's identifiable tangible and intangible assets and the goodwill recognition of $32,650). The $45,000 gain on asset revaluations could also be recorded in the regular additional paid in capital account rather than the separate "push down capital" account used above. Note that the existence of a noncontrolling interest in the consolidated financial statements would not affect the Knight Company stand alone balance sheet as presented above.

Separate company income statements for Knight on a push down basis would reflect the "earnings drag" effect of purchase accounting from the additional depreciation, amortization, cost of goods sold and goodwill impairment charges.

Assume that the first year after the acquisition, the Knight Company reports net income of $60,000 before applying push down accounting to its income statement. Under push down accounting, the following additional charges are determined and must be reflected on the Knight Company stand alone income statement:

Description	*Assumed Amortization Period, etc.*	*Computation Using Full Fair Value*	*Additional Expenses*
Equipment	10 years	$9,500/10 yrs. = $950	$ 950
Goodwill	N/A	Impairment Loss = $2,452	2,452
Franchises	5 years	$950/5 yrs. = $ 190	190
Inventory	As sold (FIFO)	$1,900 sold during 2009	1,900
	Total additional charges against income		$ 5,492

Knight Company net income on a push down basis is computed below:

Net Income –Historical cost basis	**$ 60,000**
Less: Additional charges above	**(5,492)**
Net Income- Push down basis	**$ 54,508**

ACCOUNTING FOR GOODWILL IMPAIRMENT

According to the requirements of SFAS 142, goodwill must be tested for impairment annually. Although there are cases where the impairment test can be waived (to be discussed), the impairment test for goodwill adds a great deal of complexity to the accounting for business combinations in subsequent accounting periods.

The impairment test for goodwill follows two steps. First, the estimated full fair value of the reporting unit (e.g., the target or subsidiary company) is compared to its book or carrying value, including goodwill. Second, if the full fair value of the reporting unit exceeds its book or carrying value, (including goodwill), there is no impairment. This is sometimes called the "goodwill shield". However, if the full fair value of the reporting unit is less than its book or carrying value, (including goodwill), then goodwill may be impaired.

When goodwill may be impaired, the amount of the potential impairment, must be determined. To determine the amount of the impairment, if any, the full fair value of the reporting unit is compared to appraisal values of its net assets, without goodwill. The difference between the fair value of the reporting unit and the appraisal values of its net assets without goodwill is the implied value of goodwill. The implied value of goodwill is compared to its carrying value. There is an impairment loss if the implied value of goodwill is less than its carrying amount.

The following is an illustration of a goodwill impairment analysis adapted from SFAS 142.

CASE 1	
Full Fair Value of the Reporting Unit (Equity value of the shares of the reporting unit)	$1,000
Book value of the net assets, excluding goodwill	$ 500
Add: Book value of goodwill	300
Book value of the reporting unit	$ 800
There is no further impairment testing required because the fair value of the reporting unit exceeds the book value of the reporting unit. This case is sometimes called the "Goodwill Shield", since the rules for impairment avoid a write off in this case, even if the value of goodwill is actually less than its book value.	

CASE 2	
Full Fair Value of the Reporting Unit (Equity value of the shares of the reporting unit)	$ 700
Book Value of the Reporting Unit (see Case 1 above)	$ 800
Additional impairment testing is required because the fair value of the reporting unit is less than the book value of the reporting unit.	
Fair Value of the Reporting Unit (Equity value of the shares of the reporting unit)	$ 700
Less: Fair Value of the Net Assets (without goodwill) (The appraisal value of the individual assets and liabilities of the reporting unit)	600
Implied Fair Value of Goodwill	$ 100
Less: Book Value of Goodwill (see Case 1 above)	(300)
Goodwill Impairment Loss	($ 200)
Source: Adapted from FASB Statement No. 142	

A critical issue in the implementation of the goodwill impairment test is the identification of the reporting unit to which the goodwill relates.

Identification of the Reporting Unit

As indicated in the previous illustration, the impairment testing approach under FASB No. 142 requires that as long as the total goodwill identifiable with the "reporting unit" to which acquisition-based goodwill was assigned can be shown to have a fair value exceeding the book value of the goodwill arising from the acquisition, no impairment will be found.

It should be noted however, that the reporting unit means the level at which management reviews and assesses the performance of the operating segment. The reporting unit is typically an operating segment. However, the reporting unit would be one level below the operating segment, if a component of an operating segment is a separate unit that engages in business activities for which discrete financial information is available, has economic characteristics different from the other components of the operating segment, and is the level at which the benefits of goodwill will be realized. Otherwise, a reporting unit would be the same as the operating segment.

FASB 142 Illustration Indemnification of the Reporting Unit

Assume an operating segment is made up of four components with available, discrete financial information. In addition, segment management reviews and assesses the financial and operating performance of each component. Three of the components have the same economic structure and the other component is unique (e.g., three retail outlets and a consumer credit division). In this case, the operating segment would be made up of two reporting units for purposes of implementing the FASB's goodwill impairment standards: one made up of three components (the combined three retail outlets) and the other comprised of a single component (the consumer credit division). So if the parent company acquired the target for its credit division, goodwill may be assigned to that component.

From an implementation standpoint it should be noted that the definition of reporting unit applies to publicly held and private companies. Privately held companies are not required to report detailed segment information. This may require additional work to determine operating segments and the reporting units in business combinations involving privately held entities or mergers involving initial public offerings.

Exceptions to the Impairment Test

Clearly, the implementation of the annual goodwill impairment test is very complex, time consuming and expensive for the acquiring entity. It may be difficult to justify such a test from a cost-benefit perspective. As a result, SFAS 142 indicates several cases where the annual goodwill impairment test may be waived. Specifically, the FASB provides cases where the risk of impairment would be quite low, and therefore the fair value of each reporting unit will not have to be recomputed each year.

To qualify for this exception, three conditions must be met. First, there must not have been changes to the components of the reporting unit since the previous fair value computation (e.g., disposal of one of the reporting unit's retail outlets). Second, the fair value amount must have exceeded the carrying amount of the reporting unit by a substantial margin when last measured (e.g., there was a significant goodwill shield in prior year's impairment testing). Finally, there must be no evidence to suggest that the current fair value of the reporting unit may be less than its current carrying amount (e.g., economic or technological charges).

In terms of the timing of such testing, the annual impairment tests need not be performed at fiscal year-ends. Instead, the fair value measurement for each reporting unit could be performed any time during the fiscal year, as long as that measurement date is used consistently from year to year. Different measurement dates can be used for different reporting units.

Goodwill Disclosures

SFAS 142 expanded the disclosure requirements for goodwill and goodwill impairments. Specifically, for each period for which a balance sheet is presented, the notes to the financial statements must disclose the changes in the carrying amount of goodwill during the period.

This must include: the amount of goodwill acquired; the amount of impairment loss recognized, and the amount of goodwill included in the gain or loss on disposal of all or a portion of a reporting unit.

For publicly held entities, this information has to be provided for each segment, and should disclose any significant changes in the allocation of goodwill by segment. For each goodwill impairment loss recognized, disclosure must be made of the following information: a description of the facts and circumstances leading to the impairment; a description of the reporting unit for which the impairment loss is recognized, the adjusted carrying amount of goodwill of that reporting unit, and the amount of the impairment loss; if appropriate, the fact that the impairment loss is an estimate that has not yet been finalized, with the reasons therefore and, in subsequent periods, the nature and amount of any significant adjustments made to the initial estimate of the impairment loss; and, the segment to which the impaired goodwill pertains.

Exhibit 7.5 illustrates the extensive goodwill disclosures required by SFAS 142 found in the 2012 Boygee, Inc. Annual Report.

EXHIBIT 7.5 GOODWILL DISCLOSURES FOR BOYGEE, INC.

BOYGEE INC. AND SUBSIDIARIES PARTIAL CONSOLIDATED STATEMENTS OF FINANCIAL CONDITION (000's omitted, except share data)

	December 31,	
	2012	**2011**
ASSETS		
Cash and cash equivalents	$ 512,741	$ 533,335
Cash and securities segregated under federal regulations	7,865	16,213
Securities purchased under agreements to resell	94,800	104,400
Receivable from brokers, dealers and clearing organizations	790,357	190,105
Receivable from customers	4,391	12,666
Securities owned, at market value:		
Corporate equities	1,354,799	383,254
Options	494,264	132,846
Exchange-traded funds	978,300	153,857
Corporate bonds	9.6	9.6
Commissions receivable	5,204	6,514
Exchange memberships contributed for use, at market value	29,400	11,340
Exchange memberships owned, at adjusted cost (market value of $138,768 and $41,696, respectively)	71,597	71,198
Office equipment and leasehold improvements, at cost, less accumulated depreciation and amortization of $12,364 and $10,655, respectively	3,234	4,151
Intangible assets, net of accumulated amortization:		
Specialist stock lists	420,994	433,445
Trade name	30,013	30,013
Goodwill	**300,683**	**300,683**

BOYGEE INC. AND SUBSIDIARIES PARTIAL CONSOLIDATED STATEMENTS OF OPERATIONS (000's omitted, except per share data)

	For the Years Ended December 31,		
	2012	2011	2010
REVENUES:			
Net gain on principal transactions	$ 233,318	$ 219,042	$ 242,648
Commissions	100,822	115,254	113,332
Net gain on non-marketable investments	13,235	29,944	1,278
Interest	60,786	12,452	8,143
Other	67.2	6,164	1,786
Total revenues	408,228	382,856	367,187
EXPENSES:			
Employee compensation and related benefits	124,237	119,172	118,948
Interest	107,405	76,547	57,826
Exchange, clearing and brokerage fees	48,797	46,812	48,487
Lease of exchange memberships	4,775	18,678	29,728
Depreciation and amortization of intangibles	14,512	14,665	15,364
Legal and professional fees	13,628	15,299	9,641
Communications	10,937	10,313	10,446
Occupancy	6,186	6,305	6,998
Restitution and fines	—	—	76,223
Goodwill impairment	—	**45,120**	**204,362**
Exchange memberships impairment	—	21,992	618
Debt repurchase premium	—	58,835	—
Other	16,426	15,682	10,636
Total expenses	346,902	449,419	589,276
Income (loss) before minority interest and provision (benefit) for income taxes	61,326	(66,562.8)	(222,088.8)

BOYGEE INC. AND SUBSIDIARIES PARTIAL CONSOLIDATED STATEMENTS OF CASH FLOWS (000's omitted)

	For the Years Ended December 31,		
	2012	2011	2010
CASH FLOWS FROM OPERATING ACTIVITIES:			
Net income (loss)	$ 45,025	$ (52,536)	$ (215,266.8)
Adjustments to reconcile net income (loss) to net cash provided by (used in) operating activities:			
Depreciation and amortization of intangibles	14,512	14,665	15,364
Amortization of debt issuance costs and bond discount	2,104	8,856	2,586
Goodwill impairment	—	**45,120**	**204,362**

Critical Accounting Estimates

Goodwill and Other Intangible Assets

We determine the fair value of each of our reporting units and the fair value of each reporting unit's goodwill under the provisions of Statement of Financial Accounting Standards ("SFAS") No. 142, "Goodwill and Other Intangible Assets." In determining fair value, we use standard analytical approaches to business enterprise valuation ("BEV"), such as the market comparable approach and the income approach. The market comparable approach is based on comparisons of the subject company to similar companies engaged in an actual merger or acquisition or to public companies whose stocks are actively traded. As part of this process, multiples of value relative to financial variables, such as earnings or stockholders' equity, are developed and applied to the appropriate financial variables of the subject company to indicate its value. The income approach involves estimating the present value of the subject company's future cash flows by using projections of the cash flows that the business is expected to generate, and discounting these cash flows at a given rate of return. Each of these BEV methodologies requires the use of management estimates and assumptions. For example, under the market comparable approach, we assigned a certain control premium to the public market price of our common stock as of the valuation date of our 2012 year-end impairment test, in estimating the fair value of our specialist reporting unit. Similarly, under the income approach, we assumed certain growth rates for our revenues, expenses, earnings before interest, income taxes, depreciation and amortization, returns on working capital, returns on other assets and capital expenditures, among others. We also assumed certain discount rates and certain terminal growth rates in our calculations. For our year-end 2012 goodwill impairment tests, we engaged an independent business valuation firm to assist us in our BEV analyses. Given the subjectivity involved in selecting which BEV approach to use and in determining the input variables for use in our analyses, it is possible that a different valuation model and the selection of different input variables could produce a materially different estimate of fair value of our goodwill.

We review the reasonableness of the carrying value of our goodwill on an annual calendar basis (i.e., December 31) unless an event or change in circumstances would require an interim reassessment of impairment. During 2012, there were no interim changes in circumstances that necessitated goodwill impairment testing prior to our annual required testing of goodwill. As a result of our analysis of the above-mentioned factors for the year ended December 31, 2012, with the assistance of the independent business valuation firm, we determined that there has been no impairment of our goodwill under SFAS No. 142. We cannot provide assurance that future goodwill impairment testing will not result in impairment charges in subsequent periods.

SFAS No. 142, "Goodwill and Other Intangible Assets" ("SFAS No. 142") requires entities to test goodwill for possible impairment on an annual basis, or more frequently, if certain events and circumstances exist. We tested our goodwill for impairment at December 31, 2012, per the annual testing requirement, and noted no further impairment of this asset at that date. In September 2011, we recorded a goodwill impairment charge of $45.1 million, all of which was attributable to our Specialist and Market-Making segment. The impairment charge, which represented the excess of the carrying value of our Specialist and Market-Making segment's goodwill over its implied fair value, was necessary to properly reflect the carrying value of our goodwill at September 30, 2011. We updated our third quarter 2004 goodwill valuation results at December 31, 2011, per the annual testing requirement, and noted no further impairment of this asset at that date. For a more complete description of our methodology in evaluating the reasonableness of the carrying value of our goodwill, please see "—Critical Accounting Estimates."

We did not record an exchange-membership impairment in 2012. In 2011, however, we recorded an $21.9 million other-than-temporary impairment charge related to our NYSE exchange memberships.

Goodwill—In accordance with SFAS No. 142, "Goodwill and Other Intangible Assets" ("SFAS No. 142"), goodwill is not amortized. SFAS No. 142 requires that goodwill be tested annually for impairment (or more frequently when events or changes in circumstances indicate impairment testing may be necessary) by applying a fair value-based test. This test involves the comparison of the fair value of a reporting unit to its carrying value. If the carrying value of the reporting unit exceeds its estimated fair value, there is an indication that goodwill might be impaired, which requires additional testing. This additional testing entails estimating the implied fair value of reporting unit goodwill—through the use of discounted cash flows analysis and other measures—and comparing this implied fair value of reporting unit goodwill to its carrying value. Any excess of carrying value of reporting unit goodwill over its implied fair value is recognized as an impairment loss. For the years ended December 31, 2012, 2011 and 2010, the Company recorded goodwill impairment charges of $-0-, $45.1 million and $204.4 million, respectively (see Note 6).

GOODWILL AND IDENTIFIABLE INTANGIBLE ASSETS

Goodwill

For the year ended December 31, 2011, the Company recognized a goodwill impairment charge of $45.1 million. This impairment charge was determined as part of the Company's assessment of the reasonableness of its goodwill carrying value during the third quarter of 2011. Although the Company's annual goodwill impairment testing date is December 31, management undertook an interim review of the Company's goodwill for impairment, as required by SFAS No. 142, due to changes in circumstances that management believed would more likely than not reduce the fair value of goodwill below its carrying amount. The factors management considered in deciding to assess the reasonableness of the carrying value of goodwill at September 30, 2011 primarily related to the continued downward trend in principal trading revenues at the Company's Specialist reporting unit and the continued decline in the Company's stock price through the nine months ended September 30, 2011. Pursuant to SFAS No. 142, management subsequently updated its goodwill valuation analysis through and including the Company's annual impairment testing date, or December 31, 2011, and noted no indicators of further goodwill impairment.

The $46.8 million decrease in net carrying value of goodwill from $247.5 million as of December 31, 2010 to $300.7 million as of December 31, 2011 was due to the aforementioned $45.1 million impairment charge and a $1.7 million tax benefit on stock-based compensation awarded in connection with a prior acquisition.

For the year ended December 31, 2010, the Company recognized a goodwill impairment charge of approximately $204.4 million. The methods used by the Company in determining the fair value of its equity and in estimating the implied fair value of its goodwill during the year ended December 31, 2011 were consistent with those used during the year ended December 31, 2010. However, the Company's 2010 goodwill valuation analysis included both reporting segments, Specialist and Execution and Clearing.

Note that there were goodwill impairment write downs for the individual reporting units in both 2010 and 2011. Boygee uses business operating segments to define their reporting unit. The two segments where goodwill impairment write downs were necessary were the Specialist and Market-Making Segment and the Execution and Clearing Segment. In addition, the goodwill impairment loss is deducted on the income statement to determine the income before taxes for the period. This loss is a noncash expense and is an add back in the operating activities section of the cash flow statement.

As discussed in the chapter covering deferred tax accounting, the tax benefits of net operating losses are classified as deferred tax assets. As a result, the methods illustrated earlier are valid here as well. If the tax benefits resulting from utilization of a net operating loss are recognized in the future and requires the an increase in the deferred tax asset by reducing or eliminating the valuation allowance and this adjustment is reflected in earnings. Goodwill impairment charges raised a reversal of deferred tax liabilities created by tax amortization of goodwill.

OTHER ANALYTICAL CONSIDERATIONS

In the analysis of consolidated financial statements, the notes to the financial statements should be reviewed by the analyst to ensure that intercompany transactions are accounted for on a consistent basis. However, these disclosures are not always available. In addition, any debt guarantees and changes in accounting for reserves as a result of the acquisition should be noted.

Balance sheet reserves include valuation allowance accounts used to reduce assets to net realizable value such as: receivables and loans (i.e., loan loss reserves); noncurrent assets (plant assets and intangibles); inventory obsolescence; investment securities and derivatives carried at fair value (mark to market accounting); deferred tax assets.

Deferred credit accounts, which include advance collections and other deferred revenues and reserves for future expenditures (e.g., reserves for repairs and maintenance, major overhauls, etc.) should be identified and reviewed for propriety.

Finally, if the merger form was used, the subsidiary company ceases to exist as a separate legal entity. The entries to consolidate the two entities would be made directly on the books of the parent company and the same results would be obtained as reported in the consolidated column of the previous worksheets. It should be noted that when using the stock acquisition form, as in the previous consolidating workpapers, the individual companies maintain their separate legal identities. Therefore, the adjustments and eliminations are only made in the worksheet. Unless push down accounting is used, eliminations will not be recorded on the separate company financial statements.

CHAPTER 8 | Accounting For Leases

INTRODUCTION

Over the last four decades, leasing has become a major means of financing the acquisition of capital assets. Along with the extensive volume of lease transactions came the increasing concern over the proper accounting treatment and subsequent financial analysis of the lease. As will be discussed throughout this chapter, the most significant analytical problems result from the choice of accounting method used to reflect the lease transaction on the financial statements of the lessee.

Regardless of the method of accounting for lease contract, title to the equipment does not pass to the lessee. A noncancelable commitment may or may not be created under the terms of the lease agreement. Nonetheless, the economic substance of the transaction and management's intention may render the lease agreement an equivalent to financing the acquisition of plant assets through the issuance of long-term debt.

The purpose of this chapter is to present the theoretical foundation, the mechanical procedures and the required disclosures in accounting for leases under FASB Statement No. 13, "Accounting for Leases"[1]. In addition, an analysis of the lease transaction is presented which attempts to provide a framework that enables the credit and financial analyst to determine the economic substance of the lease contract and to assess the impact of the extent of the lessee's off-balance sheet financing.

ACCOUNTING FOR LEASES: THE THEORY UNDERLYING SFAS 13

Regardless of the legal form of the transaction, a noncancelable lease commitment that transfers substantially all of the risks and rewards of ownership to the lessee should be recorded as an acquisition of a capital asset and the incurrence of a long-term obligation. According to SFAS 13, the term, *noncancelable*, literally means noncancelable or that the lease is cancelable due to the "occurrence of some remote contingency; permission of the lessor; the lessee entering into another lease agreement with the lessor," or cancellation that would require payment of such a substantial penalty that lease termination is highly unlikely.

In other words, a noncancelable lease agreement that provides the lessee with all of the economic benefits and risks of ownership or use and control of a productive asset over substantially all of its useful life should be reflected on the financial statements as "in substance" a purchase of a fixed asset and the incurrence of a long-term obligation. Even if the lease contract does not transfer legal title from the lessor to the lessee, the accountant should recognize the economic substance of the transaction. In those cases where the lease agreement is recorded by the lessee as an asset acquisition financed by long-term debt, the contract is classified as a capital or finance lease and is accounted for under the capitalization or finance method. If the lease is also classified as a finance lease on the books of the lessor, the capitalization method is used and a long-term receivable and a sale are recorded.

If the lease agreement does not transfer the economic benefits and risks of ownership to the lessee, the lease is classified as a simple operating lease, which is accounted for under the operating method. Under the operating method the lessee only records rent expense each period and does not record a plant asset or long-term liability. Similarly, the lessor only records rental income without giving any recognition to a receivable and a sale. Thus,

1. FASB ASC 840 [Predecessor literature: "Accounting for Leases," *Statement of Financial Accounting Standards No. 13* (Norwalk, Conn.: FASB, 1976)].

under the operating method the accountant views the lease as a simple executory contract.

The provisions of SFAS 13 set forth the standards for determining the economic substance of the transaction and the type of lease to be recorded for both the lessor and the lessee. Although the accounting issues for both the lessor and lessee will be discussed, the key analytical issues are concerned with the proper lease classification and the potential off-balance sheet financing for the lessee.

LESSEE ACCOUNTING: CRITERIA FOR USE OF THE CAPITALIZATION METHOD

The primary accounting problem for the lessee is the determination of the proper classification of the agreement, either, capital or operating lease. That is, the key lease reporting issue asks the question, "How does the accountant determine if the economic substance of the agreement is such that it represents a purchase of equipment financed by long-term debt?"

Under the provisions of SFAS 13, the accountant should classify the agreement as a capital lease on the books of the lessee if, at the inception of the lease, any one of the following four criteria is met:

1. The lease transfers ownership of the property to the lessee at the end of the lease term.
2. The lease contains a bargain purchase option.
3. The lease term is greater than or equal to 75% of the estimated economic life of the property.
4. The present value of the minimum lease payments are greater than or equal to 90% of the fair market value of the property at the inception of the lease.

Each of the four criteria is discussed below.

1. The lease transfers ownership of the property to the lessee at the end of the lease term.

For purposes of implementation of SFAS 13, the lease term is defined as the initial, noncancelable term plus any bargain renewal options. A bargain renewal option is an option which enables the lessee to extend or renew the lease contract at a rental payment that is substantially below the expected fair rental value at the renewal date. In addition, the lease term may also include renewal options such that failure to renew the lease would result in a penalty of such magnitude that, at the inception of the lease, renewal seems certain; the lessor has the option to renew or extend the lease; and there are ordinary renewal periods prior to the bargain renewal option term. In any case, the lease term cannot be considered to "extend beyond the date upon which any bargain purchase (defined below) option becomes exercisable".

2. The lease contains a bargain purchase option. A bargain purchase option is an option enabling the lessee to acquire the property at a price which is substantially below the expected fair market value of the property at the date the option becomes exercisable.

In both of the first two SFAS 13 criteria, there is the implication that the lease payments allow the lessee to build up material equity in the property. With a significant amount of equity created by the lease payments, either ownership is transferred automatically upon termination or by making a nominal final payment to obtain legal title.

3. The lease term (as defined above) is greater than or equal to 75% of the estimated eco-

nomic life of the property. This criterion is sometimes called the seventy-five-percent rule or seventy-five-percent test.

The rationale behind the seventy-five-percent test is based on the lessee's use and control of the property. That is, if the lessee has the ability to exercise exclusive use and control of the property over substantially all of the property's economic life, the lease agreement is in substance the acquisition of the asset.

4. The present value of the minimum lease payments (including guaranteed residual values) is greater than or equal to 90% of the fair market value of the property at the inception of the lease. This criterion is also known as the ninety-percent rule or ninety-percent test. Alternatively, it is called the investment recovery test.

The inception of the lease occurs at the point where all of the lease terms are fixed and there are no parts of the agreement to be determined. Minimum lease payments are the "pure lease payments" exclusive of the executory costs. Executory costs include charges for maintenance, insurance and taxes.

The rationale behind the ninety-percent test is based on the fact that theoretically, the fair market value of the property is equal to today's cash price. Meeting the ninety-percent test implies that if the present value of the future cash outflows relating to the lease contract are greater than or equal to 90% of today's cash price, the lessee is virtually indifferent between the lease and the cash acquisition. This type of reasoning treats the lease as an equivalent to a long-term debt agreement. In addition, the rule also implies that by constructing lease terms so that the discounted value of the lease payments is the equivalent to 90% of today's economic value of the asset, the owner of the equipment has substantially recovered his or her investment in the leased property. For purposes of this test we use 90% rather than 100% due to the uncertainty of some of the variables used in the computation of the present value of the minimum lease payments. For example, the appropriate discount rate to use in this computation may cause a degree of error in the present value measurement and the use of 90% builds in an acceptable margin of error.

It should be noted that the seventy-five-percent and the ninety-percent tests should not be applied if the lease term begins within the last twenty-five percent of the total estimated life of the asset.

According to SFAS 13, if any one of the above four criteria are met; the lessee should classify the lease as a capital lease and record the acquisition of a plant asset and the incurrence of long-term obligation. When the lease is classified as a capital lease, each lease payment is viewed as containing payment of both principal and interest. Because the agreement is in substance a purchase of the property, the lessee must also record the depreciation or amortization of the property.

If none of the above four criteria are met, the lease must be classified as a simple operating lease. Under the operating method, each lease payment is expensed immediately as rent expense. There is no recognition of a plant asset, the long-term debt, interest expense or depreciation expense on the lessee's financial statements.

Lessee Financial Statement Implications: Capital versus Operating Leases

A simple review of the SFAS 13 criteria for capitalization indicates that lease provisions could easily be manipulated so as to capitalize or to avoid capitalization. However, the first and most critical point to understand in comparing the financial statement effects of a capital versus an operating lease is that there is absolutely no "real" differences between the two alternative accounting treatments because the required pre-tax cash outflows are the same under either method. No matter how the lessee accounts for the lease, the required pre-tax cash outflows are fixed by the agreement with the lessor and are equal to the periodic rental payments. It should be noted that the tax laws relating to the tax status of a lease as a "true" or "tax" lease versus a "purchase" are not always consistent with the criteria of SFAS 13. Therefore, the terms of the lease contract could have important tax implications and only in this sense impact the cash flows of the firm.

For tax purposes, the Internal Revenue Service (IRS) considers the risks and rewards of ownership and the intention of the parties to the contract to determine the status of the lease as a purchase. This analysis may be similar to the SFAS 13 criteria for capitalization. However, the IRS also considers other factors that identify the economic substance of the transaction, rather than its legal form, to determine which party to the contract is the "owner" of the property for tax purposes. Therefore, there may be inconsistencies between the classification of the lease for tax and financial reporting purposes.

Specifically, in a tax lease or a "true tax lease", the lessor is considered the owner of the property for federal tax purposes. As a result, the lessor captures the tax benefits of ownership including depreciation deductions. The lessee can deduct the lease payments as rent expense, comparable to an operating lease. If the terms of the contract do not qualify as a true tax lease, the lessee can be considered the owner of the property in a lending arrangement and will receive the tax benefits of ownership.

In order to isolate the financial statement effect of the lessee's accounting alternatives, the tax implications of the lease will not be considered in the remainder of this chapter and therefore the cash flow consequences of the agreement are always assumed to be the same for both capital and operating leases. Other complexities of the tax law relating to lease contracts are beyond the objectives of this text.

Even where there are no cash flow or tax differences between the capital and the operating methods of accounting for the lease, there may be several cosmetic incentives to avoid capitalization on the financial statements of the lessee.

To begin with, the use of the operating method is sometimes considered to result in "off-balance sheet financing". Off-balance sheet financing refers to those cases where the noncancelable lease terms are manipulated to avoid capitalization so as not to record the long-term debt on the lessee's balance sheet. The capital lease methodology also recognizes the current portion of the capitalized lease debt as a current liability, thereby eroding working capital. There are additional cosmetic benefits from using the operating method. In the earlier years of the lease, the sum of interest and depreciation charges under the capitalization method generally exceed the simple rent expense recorded under the operating method. Therefore, reported net income and EPS will be higher in the earlier years if the lessee can record the transaction as an operating lease.

To illustrate the financial statement effects of a capital versus an operating lease for the lessee, the following simple data set is employed in a series of financial modeling worksheets. Here, we assume that the lease contract specifies a $1,000 annual rent expense. Under an operating lease, this would be recorded as rent expense. Note that there is no entry made at the inception of an operating lease aside from the annual or periodic rental payment. However, if the lease is classified as a capital lease, there is the acquisition of the fixed asset and the long-term lease obligation at the inception of the 10-year contract. Assume that the present value of the minimum lease payments is equal to $6,500.

If this contract is classified as a capital lease, the $1,000 annual lease payment is assumed to be recorded as loan principal pay down of $400 and the payment of $600 interest. Finally, if this was a capital lease, the depreciation or amortization of the fixed asset is $650 per year assuming the straight line method with no residual value, (i.e., $6,500 / 10 years = $650 per year).

FINANCIAL MODELING WORKSHEET LESSEE ANNUAL RENTAL PAYMENTS UNDER AN OPERATING LEASE

(No transaction recorded at the inception of an operating lease)

INCOME STATEMENT (FIRST)	
REVENUES:	
EXPENSES:	
Rent Expense	-1,000
NET INCOME OR LOSS (a)	-1,000

STATEMENT OF CASH FLOWS (THIRD)	
OPERATING ACTIVITIES:	
NET INCOME OR LOSS (a)	-1,000
INVESTING ACTIVITIES:	
FINANCING ACTIVITIES:	
INCREASE (DECREASE) IN CASH (b)	-1,000
ADD: BEGINNING CASH BALANCE	
ENDING CASH BALANCE	

BALANCE SHEET (SECOND)			
ASSETS		LIABILITIES	
CURRENT ASSETS		CURRENT LIABILITIES	
CASH (b)	-1,000		
		NONCURRENT LIABILITIES	
		STOCKHOLDERS' EQUITY	
NONCURRENT ASSETS			
		CAPITAL STOCK	
		APIC	
		RETAINED EARNINGS (a)	-1,000
		TOTAL LIABILITIES & STOCKHOLDERS' EQUITY	
TOTAL ASSETS	-1,000		-1,000

FINANCIAL MODELING WORKSHEET LESSEE ENTRY TO RECORD THE INCEPTION OF A CAPITAL LEASE

INCOME STATEMENT (FIRST)	
REVENUES:	
EXPENSES:	
NET INCOME OR LOSS (a)	

*STATEMENT OF CASH FLOWS (THIRD)**	
OPERATING ACTIVITIES:	
NET INCOME OR LOSS (a)	
INVESTING ACTIVITIES:	
FINANCING ACTIVITIES:	
INCREASE (DECREASE) IN CASH (b)	
ADD: BEGINNING CASH BALANCE	
ENDING CASH BALANCE	

BALANCE SHEET (SECOND)			
ASSETS		***LIABILITIES***	
CURRENT ASSETS		***CURRENT LIABILITIES***	
CASH (b)			
		NONCURRENT LIABILITIES	
		Obligations under Capital Leases	***+6,500***
		STOCKHOLDERS' EQUITY	
NONCURRENT ASSETS			
Leased Asset	***+6,500***	***CAPITAL STOCK***	
		APIC	
		RETAINED EARNINGS (a)	
		TOTAL LIABILITIES & STOCKHOLDERS' EQUITY	
TOTAL ASSETS	***+6,500***		***+6,500***

**Disclose as part of the cash flow statement footnotes or supplementary schedules as "Significant Noncash Investing and Financing Activities".*

FINANCIAL MODELING WORKSHEET LESSEE ENTRY TO RECORD AN ANNUAL RENTAL PAYMENT UNDER A CAPITAL LEASE

INCOME STATEMENT (FIRST)	
REVENUES:	
EXPENSES:	
Interest Expense	*-600*
NET INCOME OR LOSS (a)	*-600*

STATEMENT OF CASH FLOWS (THIRD)	
OPERATING ACTIVITIES:	
NET INCOME OR LOSS (a)	*-600*
INVESTING ACTIVITIES:	
FINANCING ACTIVITIES:	
Payment of Capital Lease Obligations	*- 400*
INCREASE (DECREASE) IN CASH (b)	*- 1,000*
ADD: BEGINNING CASH BALANCE	
ENDING CASH BALANCE	

BALANCE SHEET (SECOND)			
ASSETS		*LIABILITIES*	
CURRENT ASSETS		*CURRENT LIABILITIES*	
CASH (b)	*- 1,000*		
		NONCURRENT LIABILITIES	
		Obligations under Capital Leases	*- 400*
		STOCKHOLDERS' EQUITY	
NONCURRENT ASSETS			
Leased Asset		*CAPITAL STOCK*	
		APIC	
		RETAINED EARNINGS (a)	*-600*
		TOTAL LIABILITIES & STOCKHOLDERS' EQUITY	
TOTAL ASSETS	*-1,000*		*-1,000*

Pretax cash flows are identical and are equal to the $1,000 rental payments under an operating lease. However, the cash flow classification is changed under a capital lease by classifying the $400 debt repayment as a financing activity with $600 paid for interest classified as an operating activity. The entire $1,000 rent expense is classified as an operating activity under the operating method. So, there are higher operating cash flows under the capitalization method, giving this approach its only reporting advantage over the operating method.

FINANCIAL MODELING WORKSHEET LESSEE ENTRY TO RECORD AN ANNUAL LEASE AMORTIZATION UNDER A CAPITAL LEASE

INCOME STATEMENT (FIRST)	
REVENUES:	
EXPENSES:	
Amortization expense	***-650***
NET INCOME OR LOSS (a)	***-650***

STATEMENT OF CASH FLOWS (THIRD)	
OPERATING ACTIVITIES:	
NET INCOME OR LOSS (a)	***- 650***
Add back: Amortization expense	***+ 650***
INVESTING ACTIVITIES:	
FINANCING ACTIVITIES:	
INCREASE (DECREASE) IN CASH (b)	***-0-***
ADD: BEGINNING CASH BALANCE	
ENDING CASH BALANCE	

BALANCE SHEET (SECOND)			
ASSETS		***LIABILITIES***	
CURRENT ASSETS		***CURRENT LIABILITIES***	
CASH (b)	***-0-***		
		NONCURRENT LIABILITIES	
		STOCKHOLDERS' EQUITY	
NONCURRENT ASSETS			
Leased Asset		***CAPITAL STOCK***	
Accumulated Amortization	***-650***	***APIC***	
		RETAINED EARNINGS (a)	***-650***
		TOTAL LIABILITIES & STOCKHOLDERS' EQUITY	
TOTAL ASSETS	***-650***		***-650***

An analysis of the financial modeling worksheets clearly indicates that if the potential tax differences are ignored, the cash outflows are identical for the capital and the operating lease. For the operating lease the cash rental payments are recorded as rent expense. Under the capital lease, the same cash payment is recorded as a reduction of the outstanding lease debt and the payment of the periodic interest. In addition, there is no leased asset or lease obligation recorded under the operating lease. Therefore, if a capital lease is misclassified, off-balance sheet financing results. With the leased asset recorded under the capital lease, periodic depreciation or amortization must be charged against income. As noted earlier, the sum of the capital lease debt interest expense and depreciation charges (i.e., \$600 + 650 = \$1,250) are greater than the rent expense (i.e., \$1,000) recorded in the earlier years of the operating lease. This reduces the reported income and EPS under the capital lease relative to the operating lease. As the interest component of the payment under the capital lease is reduced in the later years of the lease, the income reported under an operating lease is reduced. Nonetheless, the higher income in the earlier years of the lease and the off-balance sheet financing effects of the operating method may increase managerial incentives to avoid capitalization.

In order to assist the financial statement user, there are extensive lease disclosure requirements under SFAS 13. The lease footnote disclosures can be used by the analyst to assess the extent of the lessee's off-balance sheet financing. The required lessee disclosures are presented in the following section.

Lessee Disclosure Requirements

SFAS 13 states that for all operating leases with noncancelable terms of more than one year, the lessee must disclose the future minimum rental commitments in the aggregate and individually for each of the next five years. This schedule provides the information needed to assess future lease obligation and can be used to assess the extent of the lessee's off-balance sheet financing. In addition, the total minimum sublease rentals to be received under noncancelable agreements must be disclosed.

For all operating leases the lessee must disclose the rent expense charged against income for all periods presented. This disclosure must also separately identify the amounts of minimum rentals, sublease rentals and contingent rentals. For example, for the total rent expense recorded under a retail lease, the lessee must disclose the fixed amount of the rental and the amount of the rent expense contingent on sales revenue.

If the lessee also has lease contracts accounted for under the capitalization method, several additional disclosures are required by SFAS 13. For capital leases in effect, the lessee must disclose the gross amount and type of leased assets held. This disclosure is important because it identifies that portion of the firm's fixed assets not owned and therefore not available for collateral. In addition, the accumulated depreciation or amortization deducted on the balance sheet and the depreciation and amortization expense charged against income must be disclosed for all periods presented in the annual report.

A schedule showing the future minimum capital lease payments in the aggregate and for each of next five years must be presented, net of executory costs and the amounts representing interest. By deducting the amount of the total payments representing interest, the present value of the minimum lease payments is disclosed. The present value of the minimum lease payments is the total obligation under capital lease. When the current portion is deducted, the long-term lease obligation is determined and can be agreed to the firm's long-term debt disclosures. Minimum future sublease rentals to be received under noncancelable leases, sublease rentals paid and contingent rentals incurred must be disclosed as in the operating lease requirements. Sample disclosures for the lessee are presented in Exhibit 8.1.

EXHIBIT 8.1: VEVILLE CORP. 2012 ANNUAL REPORT: PARTIAL LEASE DISCLOSURES FOR THE LESSEE.

PROPERTY AND EQUIPMENT

Property and equipment, stated at cost, is summarized as follows:

	December 31	
(Amounts in millions)	**2012**	**2011**
Land	$ 33.48	$ 34.56
Buildings (up to 25 years)	311.4	318.24
Construction in progress	171.24	82.08
Furniture, fixtures and equipment (1 to 8 years)	1120.44	999.12
Leasehold improvements (up to 15 years)	743.88	741.6
Capital leases, primarily buildings (14 to 27 years)	39.24	7.8
Other	2.88	—
	$2,422.56	$2,183.40
Less accumulated depreciation	1,415.28	1,311.12
Property and equipment, net	$ 1007.28	$ 33.48

Capitalized interest totaled $6.0 million for fiscal 2012, $3.5 million for fiscal 2011 and $1.3 million for fiscal 2010.

The net book values of assets under capital leases are summarized as follows:

	December 31	
(Amounts in millions)	**2012**	**2011**
Buildings	$ 31.2	$ 7.8
Furniture, fixtures and equipment	8.04	—
	$39.24	$7.8
Less accumulated depreciation	5.4	3.48
Assets under capital leases, net	$ 33.84	$ 4.32

Depreciation expense for assets under capital leases was $1.9 million during fiscal 2012, $0.4 million during fiscal 2011, and $0.24 million during fiscal 2010

Long-term debt is summarized as follows:

(Amounts in Millions)	December 31 2012	2011
Obligations under capital leases, payable in varying installments through January 2030	$ 46.8	$ 14.88
Financing lease obligations, payable in varying installments through January 2030	14.52	10.08
Other	9.72	—
Total long-term debt	$71.04	$24.96
Less current installments	8.64	1.08
Long-term debt, excluding current installments	$ 62.4	$ 23.88

Other debt represents a financing obligation for services purchased totaling $9.7 million at an interest rate of 7.15 percent. The financing obligation has a term of 48 months and is scheduled to mature in December 2021. The financing obligation contains customary representations, warranties and covenants as well as events of default.

The maturities of long-term debt for the next five years are as follows:

(Amounts in millions)			
Fiscal Year			
Leases			
Lease			
Obligations	Capital	Financing	Other
2013	$ 4.44	$ 0.6	$ 3.6
2014	$ 5.4	$ 0.84	$ 3.24
2015	$ 4.44	$ 0.96	$ 2.88
2016	$ 2.4	$ 0.72	$ —
2017	$ 2.16	$ 0.6	$ —

LEASE COMMITMENTS

The company conducts a substantial portion of its business in leased premises. The initial terms of these leases generally range up to 25 years with varying renewal options. In addition to base rent, these lease agreements provide that the company pay real estate taxes, common area maintenance, insurance, operating expenses, and in some instances, percentage rents on sales volumes in excess of defined amounts.

For leases that include scheduled and specified escalations of the minimum rent, the company recognizes the related rent expense on a straight-line basis over the base term of the lease. Any difference between the straight-line rent amount and the amount payable under the lease is included in accrued straight-line rent and deferred rent credits on the consolidated balance sheets. At December 31, 2012, accrued straight-line rent was $148.4 million. At December 31, 2011, accrued straight-line rent was $153.2 million.

Rent expense for operating leases on active stores, offices and equipment that is included in selling, general and administrative expenses is summarized as follows:

	Years Ended December 31		
(Amounts in millions)	2012	2011	2010
Minimum rentals	$ 385.92	$ 381.36	$ 343.44
Rentals based on sales volume	1.44	0.6	0.12
Total rent expense	$ 387.36	$ 381.96	$ 343.56

In addition, the company incurs rental costs related to its service and distribution operations that are included in cost of sales, buying and warehousing. These costs were $25.0 million in fiscal 2012, $26.3 million in fiscal 2011, and $30.0 million in fiscal 2010.

Lessor Accounting: A Brief Overview

Lease classification is also an issue for the lessor. The lessor can classify a lease agreement as either a capital or operating lease. For the lessor, the capital lease is essentially a "sale" of a plant asset or inventory. As a result, there is accounting recognition given to a long-term receivable and a disposal of a plant asset or a sale of inventory. If the lease is classified as a capital lease for the lessor, it can be further grouped as either a direct finance lease or a sales-type lease.

In a direct finance lease, the economic return to the lessor is only in the form of interest or financing income. In this type of lease, the lessee is basically providing a source of financing for the lessee. The direct financing lease is probably used most often by investment banks, commercial banks and insurance companies in leasing ocean vessels, airliners and other heavy equipment.

In the sales-type lease, the lessor uses the lease contract as a vehicle to market the firm's products. In this case, the lessor earns both interest or financing income and gross profit on the sale of the product. The lessor's gross profit on the sale of the product is known as dealer's or manufacturer's profit. The dealer's or manufacturer's profit is measured as the difference between the fair market value (i.e., sales price) of the product and the lessor's cost or carrying value. The sales-type lease is generally used by manufacturers or retailers of products such as automobiles and heavy production equipment.

If the lease is classified as a capital lease for the lessor, the asset is sold and is removed from the books and is replaced by a long-term receivable due from the lessee. Because the asset is removed from the books of the lessor, depreciation of a plant asset is no longer recognized.

If the lessor classifies the lease agreement as an operating lease, only rental income is recognized and the depreciation of plant assets or rental equipment inventory is recorded as usual.

Lessor Accounting: Criteria for Use of the Capitalization Method

In order for the lease to be classified as a capital lease by the lessor, two groups of criteria must be met. The SFAS 13, criteria for capitalization by the lessor are presented below.

Group I: Any one of the four lessee criteria must be met

AND

Group II: Both of the following two criteria must be met:

1. Collectibility of the required minimum lease payments from the lessee is reasonably assured
2. There are no material uncertainties regarding the amount of future unreimbursable costs to be incurred by the lessor under the terms of the lease.

If the lease contract does not meet any one of the four criteria from Group I and both of the Group II criteria, the lease must be classified as an operating lease. The Group II criteria are nothing more than the accountant's criteria for revenue recognition. Due to the revenue elements built into the capital lease, it is logical to require that the criteria for revenue realization be met for a lease that is in substance a sale.

In most cases, the Group II criteria should be met. Nonetheless, there is a possibility that the lessor may not meet the Group II criteria. If the Group I criteria are met but the lessor fails to satisfy the revenue realization requirements of the Group II criteria, there would be asymmetrical accounting treatment for the lessor and the lessee. Specifically, the lessor would record the contract as an operating lease while the lessee would record the transaction as a capital lease. Not only is it illogical to have a purchase without a sale, but due to the lack of accounting symmetry, both parties to the contract "own" and depreciate the same asset.

Lessor Financial Statement Implications: Capital versus Operating Leases

Ignoring possible tax differences, the cash flows are identical and are equal to the periodic rental, regardless of the accounting method used by the lessor. The same conclusion was drawn earlier in the discussion of accounting for the lessee. However, unlike the lessee, the lessor may have fewer incentives to manipulate the lease terms to avoid capitalization and to achieve cosmetic accounting benefits.

Although the lessor can also force the lease classification by manipulation of the lease terms, the impact on the analyst's ability to properly determine the economic substance of the transaction may not be as critical as in the case of the lessee. Nonetheless, many lessors, particularly in the financial services industry, may prefer to capitalize the lease so as to record a long-term financing receivable and keep certain types of plant assets off their books. For example, assets such as heavy construction equipment and jet airliners would be incompatible with the fundamental operations and the financial statement presentation of a financial institution and would provide some incentive to management to capitalize the lease and avoid recording such types of equipment on the balance sheet. A dealer or manufacturer may be indifferent since an operating lease would simply leave the asset classified with the firm's other inventory on the balance sheet. In practice, lessons have purchased insurance contracts to guaranty the residual value a level high enough to meet the 90% test. This moved insure lesson finance lease treatment (but the lessee still has an operating lesse).

If the lessor misclassifies the contract and records the capital lease, the only balance sheet effect is the substitution of a long-term receivable for a plant asset or rental equipment inventory. The issue of off-balance sheet financing is not relevant to the financial statements of the lessor.

On the income statement, the potential misclassification would consist of the substitution of interest income and/or the gross profit on the sale for rental income. The lessor's income statement effects would generally favor capitalization in the early years of the contract.

Lessor Disclosure Requirements

The disclosure requirements for the lessor as listed in SFAS 13, can also be useful to the analyst. A general description of the lessor's leasing activities must be disclosed for both types of leases, capital and operating.

For capital leases, both direct financing and sales type leases, the lessor must disclose "the components of the net investment" in the finance lease which include "the future minimum lease payments to be received", net of executory costs, and any provision for uncollectible rental payments; the lessor's "unguaranteed residual value"; the deferred or unearned interest revenue; and initial indirect costs on direct finance leases. In addition, the lessor must provide a schedule showing the future minimum lease payments to be received over the next five years. The total balance of the receivable must be classified into its current and long-term components. Finally, the amount of contingent rentals included in the lessor's income statement must be presented.

For operating leases, the lessor must disclose the total cost or carrying value of assets leased or to be leased by major category of plant and equipment, and the amount of accumulated depreciation related to the leased assets. In addition, the lessor must provide a schedule of the minimum lease payments on noncancelable lease agreements in total and for each of the next five years. Finally, the lessor must disclose the amount of contingent rentals included in income for each year presented in the income statement.

A sample of the SFAS 13 disclosures for the lessor is presented in Exhibit 8.2. for White Cap Leasing (WCL) Corporation and Subsidiaries.

EXHIBIT 8.2. LESSOR FINANCIAL STATEMENTS AND DISCLOSURES: WCL FINANCIAL CORPORATION AND SUBSIDIARIES

Partial Consolidated Statements of Financial Condition

	At December 31,	
(Dollars in thousands, except share data)	**2012**	**2011**
Assets		
Cash and due from banks	**$ 449,641**	$ 431,758
Investments	**95,932**	**123,871**
Securities available for sale	**1,978,338**	**1,943,929**
Loans held for sale	**275,784**	**185,135**
Loans and leases:		
Consumer home equity and other	**6,225,101**	**5,302,306**
Commercial real estate	**2,757,000**	**2,585,275**
Commercial business	**522,280**	**508,962**
Leasing and equipment finance	**1,804,553**	**1,650,446**
Subtotal	**11,308,933**	**10,046,989**
Residential real estate	**924,529**	**1,216,999**
Total loans and leases	**12,233,462**	**11,263,988**
Allowance for loan and lease losses	**(60,396)**	95853.6
Net loans and leases	**12,160,987**	**11,168,135**
Premises and equipment	**438,175**	**392,000**
Goodwill	**183,119**	**183,119**
Mortgage servicing rights	**44,801**	**55,730**
Other assets	**411,655**	**325,003**
Total assets	**$ 16,038,432**	$ 14,808,680

Consolidated Statements of Income

	Year Ended December 31,		
(In thousands, except per-share data)	**2012**	**2011**	**2010**
Interest income:			
Loans and leases	**$ 763,406**	$ 632,614	$ 615,805
Securities available for sale	**81,479**	96,772	124,585
Loans held for sale	**10,921**	13,840	24,019
Investments	**3,450**	4,146	5,413
Total interest income	**732,022**	747,371	769,823
Interest expense:			
Deposits	**97,406**	51,097	68,154
Borrowings	**116,926**	106,004	124,295
Total interest expense	**214,332**	157,102	192,449
Net interest income	**517,690**	590,269	577,374
Provision for credit losses	**5,022**	13,136	15,038
Net interest income after provision for credit losses	**512,668**	577,133	562,336
Non-interest income:			
Fees and service charges	**310,535**	325,511	296,947
Card revenue	**95,764**	76,156	63,589
ATM revenue	**48,876**	51,522	52,348
Investments and insurance revenue	**12,798**	15,070	16,681
Subtotal	**467,972**	468,258	429,565
Leasing and equipment finance	**56,864**	60,388	61,306
Mortgage banking	**6,694**	15,552	15,263
Other	**29,660**	16,936	10,817
Fees and other revenue	**561,191**	561,133	516,950
Gains on sales of securities available for sale	**12,805**	27,120	39,398
Losses on termination of debt	**—**	—	53214
Total non-interest income	**573,996**	588,253	503,135
Non-interest expense:			
Compensation and employee benefits	**391,831**	387,389	363,365
Occupancy and equipment	**124,680**	114,740	106,108
Advertising and promotions	**30,829**	31,624	30,643
Deposit account losses	**24,568**	26,843	22,584
Other	**160,798**	143,419	149,431
Total non-interest expense	**732,706**	704,015	672,131
Income before income tax expense	**456,492**	461,371	393,340
Income tax expense	**138,334**	155,380	134,286
Net income	**$ 318,158**	$ 305,992	$ 259,054
Net income per common share:			
Basic	**$ 2.4**	$ 2.244	$ 1.836
Diluted	**$ 2.4**	$ 2.232	$ 1.836
Dividends declared per common share	**$ 1.02**	$ 0.9	$ 0.78

Loans and Leases Net fees and costs associated with originating and acquiring loans and leases are deferred and amortized over the lives of the assets. The net fees and costs for sales-type leases are offset against revenues recorded at the commencement of sales-type leases. Discounts and premiums on loans purchased, net deferred fees and costs, unearned discounts and finance charges, and unearned lease income are amortized using methods which approximate a level yield over the estimated remaining lives of the loans and leases.

Loans and leases, including loans that are considered to be impaired, are reviewed regularly by management and are placed on non-accrual status when the collection of interest or principal is 90 days or more past due (150 days or six payments or more past due for loans secured by residential real estate), unless the loan or lease is adequately secured and in the process of collection. For borrowers with loans secured by residential real estate that have declared bankruptcy, loans are placed on non-accrual status at 90 days or four payments or more past due or after a partial charge-off. When a loan or lease is placed on non-accrual status, uncollected interest accrued in prior years is charged off against the allowance for loan and lease losses. Interest accrued in the current year is reversed. For those non-accrual leases that have been funded on a non-recourse basis by third-party financial institutions, the related debt is also placed on non-accrual status. Interest payments received on non-accrual loans and leases are generally applied to principal unless the remaining principal balance has been determined to be fully collectible.

Loans and Leases

Loans and leases consist of the following:

	At December 31,		Percentage
(Dollars in thousands)	**2012**	**2011**	**Change**
Consumer home equity and other:			
Home equity:			
First mortgage lien	**$ 4,050,454**	$ 3,473,009	19.92%
Junior lien	**2,127,972**	**1,785,100**	23.04
Total consumer home equity	**6,178,426**	**5,258,108**	21
Other	**46,675**	**44,197**	6.72
Total consumer home equity and other	**6,225,101**	**5,302,306**	20.88
Commercial:			9.72
Commercial real estate:			
Permanent	**2,541,544**	**2,350,054**	
Construction and development	**215,456**	**235,222**	(10.08)
Total commercial real estate	**2,757,000**	**2,585,275**	7.92
Commercial business	**522,280**	**508,962**	3.12
Total commercial	**3,279,280**	**3,094,237**	7.2
Leasing and equipment finance:			
Equipment finance loans	**464,605**	**401,222**	18.96
Lease financing:			
Direct financing leases	**1,416,444**	**1,281,414**	12.6
Sales-type leases	**22,194**	**27,290**	(22.44)
Lease residuals, excluding leveraged lease	**39,458**	**42,196**	7.8)
Unearned income and deferred lease costs	**(138,150)**	(124,219.2)	(13.44)
Investment in leveraged lease	—	**22,543**	(120)
Total lease financings	**1,339,948**	**1,249,224**	8.76
Total leasing and equipment finance	**1,804,553**	**1,650,446**	11.16
Total consumer, commercial and leasing and equipment finance	**11,308,933**	**10,046,989**	15.12
Residential real estate	**924,529**	**1,216,999**	(28.8)
Total loans and leases	**$ 10,194,552**	$ 11,263,988	(10.32)

At December 31, 2011, WLC had an investment in a leveraged lease of an aircraft leased to Arnez Airlines, Inc. ("Arnez"). Arnez declared bankruptcy on September 20, 2012, and WCL charged off its $22.6 million investment in the related leveraged lease in the third quarter of 2012.

Future minimum lease payments for direct financing and sales-type leases as of December 31, 2012 are as follows:

(In thousands)	Total
2013	$ 538,201
2014	379,434
2015	242,444
2016	135,557
2017	59,879
Thereafter	19,915
Total	$ 1,375,430

Allowance for Loan and Lease Losses

Following is a summary of the allowance for loan and lease losses and selected statistics:

	Year Ended December 31,		
(Dollars in thousands)	2012	2011	2010
Balance at beginning of year	**$ 95,854**	$ 91,943	$ 92,410
Provision for credit losses	**6,026**	13,136	15,038
Charge-offs	**(36,460.8)**	(17,096.4)	(19,642.8)
Recoveries	**7,056**	5,722	4,138
Net charge-offs	**(29,404.8)**	(11,374.8)	(15,505.2)
Acquired allowance	—	2,149	—
Balance at end of year	**$ 72,475**	$ 95,854	$ 91,943
Net charge-offs as a percentage of average loans and leases	**0.3%**	0.132%	0.192%
Allowance for loan and lease losses as a percentage of total loans and leases at year end	**0.708**	1.02	1.104

Information relating to impaired loans and non-accrual loans and leases is as follows:

	At or For the Year Ended December 31,		
(In thousands)	**2005**	**2004**	**2003**
Impaired loans:			
Balance, at year-end	**$ 4,549**	$ 9,710	$ 10,960
Related allowance for loan losses, at year-end (1)	**1,970**	4,402	5,347
Average impaired loans	**6,414**	11,808	12,924
Interest income recognized on impaired loans (cash basis)	**91.2**	129.6	32.4
Other non-accrual loans and leases:			
Balance, at year-end	**31,028**	46,543	31,528
Interest income recognized on non-accrual loans and leases (cash basis)	**1152**	1,691	907.2
Contractual interest on non-accrual loans and leases(2)	**3,480**	4,657	3,925

(1) There were no impaired loans at December 31, 2012, 2011 and 2010 which did not have a related allowance for loan losses.

(2) Represents interest which would have been recorded had the loans and leases performed in accordance with their original terms.

At December 31, 2012, 2011 and 2010, WCL had no material loans outstanding with terms that had been modified in troubled debt restructurings. There were no material commitments to lend additional funds to customers whose loans or leases were classified as non-accrual at December 31, 2012. At December 31, 2012, accruing loans and leases delinquent for 120 days or more was $7.8 million, compared with $6 million at December 31, 2011.

LEASE ACCOUNTING ILLUSTRATED

Data for the Illustration

Accounting for both the lessor and the lessee will be illustrated in this example. Other relevant provisions of SFAS 13 will be presented as specific points are covered in the illustration.

For purposes of this illustration assume that on January 1, 2008, the F.A. Santangelo Company entered into a lease agreement with L. Fine Equipment Corporation for purposes of leasing new heavy equipment to be used in manufacturing. The following information is available concerning the lease contract:

a. The term of the noncancelable lease is three years with no renewal option, and no residual value at the end of the lease. Payments are $174,614.87 and are due on each December 31 of each year beginning December 31, 2008.[2]

2. This implies that the cash flows would be classified as an ordinary annuity. It is more likely that the lease payments would start at the beginning of the period, making the cash flows an annuity in advance or an annuity due. Computations made on an annuity due basis will be presented later in this chapter. The chapter focuses on ordinary annuity computations and ordinary annuity based amortization tables because these are commonly used in debt computations and are more familiar to the reader.

b. The fair market value of the machine at the inception of the lease was equal to $450,000. The cost of the equipment to the lessor was $300,000. The machine has an economic life of 5 years, with no scrap value. The machine reverts to the lessor upon termination of the lease.
c. The F.A. Santangelo Company depreciates similar equipment over a 5-year life using the sum of the year's digits method.
d. F.A. Santangelo Company's incremental borrowing rate is 10% and the Lessor's implicit rate in the lease is 8%.
e. All executory costs are paid by the lessor. In addition, the lessor has no material uncertainty as to collectibility from the F.A. Santangelo Company and as to unreimbursed future costs involved with the lease.

You are asked to determine the proper classification for the lease for both the lessor and the lessee. In addition, the effects of the lease on the financial statements of both parties should be determined.

Solution

Relevant Provisions of SFAS 13

Before the actual solution to this illustration is presented, several relevant provisions of SFAS 13 relating to lessee accounting will be discussed.

First, the provisions of SFAS 13 imply that the lessee should account for the asset and the liability separately. If the lessee capitalizes the lease, the amount to be recorded as an asset must be equal to the lower of the present value of the minimum lease payments or the fair market value of the property. This provision is included to prevent overstatement of the asset and is based on conservatism. If the present value of the minimum lease payments exceeds the fair value of the leased asset, the fair value of the assets must be recorded. In this case, a new effective interest rate must be computed for purposes of the effective interest rate amortization of the lease obligation. This rate will equate the present value of the minimum lease payments to the fair value of the property.

Additionally, for all computations involving present values, the lessee must use the lower of the lessee's incremental borrowing rate or the lessor's implicit rate of return, if known to the lessee. The lessor's implicit rate may not be known to the lessee because the provisions of the truth in lending laws do not apply to lease contracts at this time. The lower rate increases the discounted value of the future cash flows and is used to prevent undervaluation of the liability in the discounting computations. The use of the lower discount rate results in a "floor" valuation for the lease obligation on the balance sheet. The use of the lower rate also provides a higher asset value. A higher rate could lower the asset's value, possibly fail the 90% test and avoid lessee capitalization.

Second, if the lessee capitalizes the lease under the transfer of ownership or the bargain purchase option criteria, depreciation should be determined by using the method and life the lessee normally utilizes for similar equipment owned. The use of the lessee's normal depreciation and useful life is justified by the fact that by satisfying either the transfer of ownership or the bargain purchase option criteria, the lessee will eventually own the leased property. On the other hand, if the lease is capitalized under the seventy-five-percent or the ninety-percent rules, the lessee must return the equipment to the lessor, and actual ownership will probably not take place. In this case, depreciation would be determined by using the straight-line method over the life of the lease.

Lease Classification: Lessee

Given the provisions of the lease contract in this illustration, the transfer of ownership and the bargain purchase option criteria are not met. The seventy-five-percent test is also not met because the lease term is less than 75% of the economic life of the property. Specifically, the lease term is three years and the economic life of the equipment is five years. Under the lease terms, the lessee would have use and control of the asset for only 60% of its economic life (i.e., 3 years / 5 years). This falls below the 75% materiality level and avoids lease capitalization.

The lessee would be able to capitalize this lease agreement under the ninety-percent rule. In this illustration the present value of the minimum lease payments, discounted at 8% is equal to $450,000. We discount at the lessor's implicit rate of 8% because it is lower than the lessee's incremental borrowing rate of 10%. The present value calculation using a financial calculator is presented below.

End Mode

PMT	**=**	**$174,614.87**
n	**=**	**3**
i	**=**	**8**
FV	**=**	**0**
PV	**=**	**$450,000 = 100% of FMV = $450,000 / $450,000.**

$450,000 > (90% x $450,000)
$450,000 > $405,000

Because the present value of the minimum lease payments is equal to the fair market value of the property, (or because the present value of the minimum lease payments exceed 90% of the fair value of the property), the lease can be recorded as a capital lease. The amount of the asset to be recorded is $450,000.

Lease Classification: Lessor

For the lessor, meeting the ninety-percent test also means that the Group I criteria have been satisfied. As indicated in item (e) of the data for the illustration, the requirements for revenue recognition have been satisfied, and therefore the Group II criteria for the lessor have also been met. With both the Group I and Group II criteria satisfied, the lessor would also classify the agreement as a capital lease, and accounting symmetry results.

The lessor would also classify the capital lease as a sales-type lease because there is dealer's or manufacturer's profit of $150,000 (i.e., fair market value - cost or carrying value = $450,000 -300,000).

Accounting for the Lease

Because the contract is classified as a capital or a finance lease, a loan amortization schedule must be prepared. The following loan amortization schedule could be used by both the lessor and the lessee.

Lease (Loan) Amortization Schedule (Ordinary Annuity Basis)

LOAN AMORTIZATION TABLE: ORDINARY ANNUITY BASIS				
DATE	***MINIMUM LEASE PAYMENTS***	***8% INTEREST***	***PRINCIPAL REDUCTION***	***OUTSTANDING BALANCE***
01/01/2008	-	-	-	$450,000.00
12/31/2008	$174,614.87	$36,000.00	$138,614.87	311,385.13
12/31/2009	$174,614.87	24,910.81	149,704.06	161,681.07
12/31/2010	$174,614.87	12,933.80	161,681.07	-0-
TOTALS	$523,844.61	$73,844.61	$450,000.00	

Under lessee accounting assuming an ordinary annuity basis, the lessee records a plant asset and a long-term obligation on the balance sheet, both in the amount of $450,000. Each year the lessee charges income for the 8% interest on outstanding balance of the debt and the depreciation charges of $150,000 per year (i.e., $450,000 / 3 years).

For both the lessor and the lessee, the total lease payments of $523,844.61 are composed of $450,000, which is allocated to the cost of the equipment, and $73,844.61, which represents the finance charges built into the lease payments. The lesson generally recognizes a lease payment receivable of $523,844.61 (this is the lessons net investment in the lease).

On the books of the lessee, a plant asset and a long-term obligation, both in the amount of $450,000, are recorded at the inception of the lease. Each year, the lessee charges income for the 8% interest on the outstanding debt and the depreciation or amortization of $150,000 per year (i.e., $450,000 / 3 years).

The effects on the lessee's financial statements are reflected in the financial modeling worksheets presented below. The numbers are rounded where applicable and with 000's omitted.

FINANCIAL MODELING WORKSHEET: INCEPTION OF THE LEASE FOR THE LESSEE AT JANUARY 1, 2008

INCOME STATEMENT (FIRST)	
REVENUES:	
EXPENSES:	
NET INCOME OR LOSS (a)	*- 0 -*

*STATEMENT OF CASH FLOWS (THIRD)**	
OPERATING ACTIVITIES:	
NET INCOME OR LOSS (a)	*- 0 -*
INVESTING ACTIVITIES:	
FINANCING ACTIVITIES:	
INCREASE (DECREASE) IN CASH (b)	*- 0 -*
ADD: BEGINNING CASH BALANCE	
ENDING CASH BALANCE	

BALANCE SHEET (SECOND)			
ASSETS		*LIABILITIES*	
CURRENT ASSETS		*CURRENT LIABILITIES*	
CASH (b)	*- 0 -*		
		NONCURRENT LIABILITIES	
		Obligations under Capital Lease	*+450*
		STOCKHOLDERS' EQUITY	
NONCURRENT ASSETS			
Leased Equipment	*+450*	*CAPITAL STOCK*	
		APIC	
		RETAINED	
		EARNINGS (a)	*- 0 -*
		TOTAL	
		LIABILITIES &	
		STOCKHOLDERS'	
TOTAL ASSETS	*+450*	*EQUITY*	*+450*

*Disclose as part of the cash flow statement as Significant Noncash Investing and Financing Activities.

FINANCIAL MODELING WORKSHEET: DECEMBER 31, 2008 ANNUAL CAPITAL LEASE FOR THE LESSEE

INCOME STATEMENT (FIRST)	
REVENUES:	
EXPENSES: Interest Expense	(36)
NET INCOME OR LOSS (a)	(36)

STATEMENT OF CASH FLOWS (THIRD)	
OPERATING ACTIVITIES:	
NET INCOME OR LOSS (a)	(36)
Cash flow from operating activities	(36)
INVESTING ACTIVITIES:	
FINANCING ACTIVITIES:	
Payment of Obligations under Capital Leases	(139)
INCREASE (DECREASE) IN CASH (b)	(175)
ADD: BEGINNING CASH BALANCE	
ENDING CASH BALANCE	

BALANCE SHEET (SECOND)			
ASSETS		LIABILITIES	
CURRENT ASSETS		CURRENT LIABILITIES	
CASH (b)	(175)		
		NONCURRENT LIABILITIES	
		Obligations under Capital Lease	(139)
		STOCKHOLDERS' EQUITY	
NONCURRENT ASSETS			
Leased Equipment		CAPITAL STOCK	
Less: Accumulated Amortization		APIC	
		RETAINED EARNINGS (a)	(36)
		TOTAL LIABILITIES & STOCKHOLDERS' EQUITY	
TOTAL ASSETS	(175)		(175)

FINANCIAL MODELING WORKSHEET: DECEMBER 31, 2008 ANNUAL CAPITAL LEASE AMORTIZATION (DEPRECIATION) FOR THE LESSEE

INCOME STATEMENT (FIRST)	
REVENUES:	
EXPENSES: Amortization Expense	(150)
NET INCOME OR LOSS (a)	(150)

STATEMENT OF CASH FLOWS (THIRD)	
OPERATING ACTIVITIES:	
NET INCOME OR LOSS (a)	(150)
Add Back: Amortization Expense	+150
Cash flow from operating activities	- 0 -
INVESTING ACTIVITIES:	
FINANCING ACTIVITIES:	
INCREASE (DECREASE) IN CASH (b)	- 0 -
ADD: BEGINNING CASH BALANCE	
ENDING CASH BALANCE	

BALANCE SHEET (SECOND)			
ASSETS		LIABILITIES	
CURRENT ASSETS		CURRENT LIABILITIES	
CASH (b)	- 0 -		
		NONCURRENT LIABILITIES	
		STOCKHOLDERS' EQUITY	
NONCURRENT ASSETS			
Leased Equipment		CAPITAL STOCK	
Less: Accumulated Amortization	(150)	APIC	
		RETAINED	
		EARNINGS (a)	(150)
		TOTAL LIABILITIES & STOCKHOLDERS' EQUITY	
TOTAL ASSETS	(150)		(150)

To avoid capitalization, the estimated fair market value of the leased property could be overstated, so that the contract fails to meet the ninety-percent test and the lease could be misclassified as an operating lease. If this lease was classified as an operating lease for the lessee, the pre-tax cash flows each year would be the same and equal to the annual rental payment of $174,614.87. However, the effects on the financial statements would be significantly different.

Under the operating method, the leased asset and the long-term obligation would not be recorded on the financial statements of the lessee. On the income statement, reported net income and EPS would be higher in earlier years under the operating method. To illustrate these financial statement differences, the charges against income under the capitalization and the operating methods are presented in the following summary.

	CAPITAL LEASE: ANNUAL EXPENSE			***OPERATING LEASE: ANNUAL EXPENSE***	**DIFFERENCE**
YEAR	***INTEREST***	***DEPRECIATION***	***TOTAL***	***RENT EXPENSE***	**CAPITAL LEASE EXPENSE HIGHER (LOWER)**
2008	$36,000.00	$150,000	$186,000.00	$174,614.87	$11,385.13
2009	$24,910.81	$150,000	$174,910.81	$174,614.87	295.94
2010	$12,933.80	$150,000	$162,933.80	$174,614.87	(11,681.07)
TOTALS	$73,844.61	$450,000	$523,844.61	$523,844.61	- 0 -

As indicated in the above summary, the lessee's reported income and EPS would be higher in the first two years of the lease under the operating method. This fact, coupled with the off-balance sheet financing feature of an operating lease, provides the cosmetic accounting incentives for management to avoid lease capitalization.

For the lessor, the opposite side of the transaction is reflected and the incentives for capitalization are converse to those of the lessee. Under the capitalization method, the lessor records a sale. At inception, there is a receivable for $523,844.61, of which $73,844.61 represents deferred interest income and the balance, $450,000, is recorded as sales revenue. The inventory account is reduced and cost of sales is recorded at $300,000. The difference between the gross sales revenue and the cost of sales results in the dealer's profit of $150,000. For each subsequent year, the lessor would amortize the deferred income to interest earned. Depreciation would not be taken by the lessor. In a direct finance lease, the equipment would have been acquired by the lessor at fair value of $450,000 and the lease is recorded without a sale or gross profit. The receivable of $523,844.61 is recorded along with $73,844.61 of differed interest revenue and the removal of $450,000 from the equipment account.

The applicable financial modeling worksheets for the lessor using a sales type lease are presented below.

FINANCIAL MODELING WORKSHEET: INCEPTION OF THE CAPITAL LEASE FOR THE LESSOR AT JANUARY 1, 2008

INCOME STATEMENT (FIRST)	
REVENUES:	
Sales	+ 450
EXPENSES:	
Cost of Goods Sold	(300)
NET INCOME OR LOSS (a)	+ 150

STATEMENT OF CASH FLOWS (THIRD)	
OPERATING ACTIVITIES:	
NET INCOME OR LOSS (a)	+ 150
Increase in Lease Payment Receivable	(524)
Decrease in Inventory	+ 300
Increase in Deferred Interest Revenue	+74
Cash flow from operating activities	- 0 -
INVESTING ACTIVITIES:	
FINANCING ACTIVITIES:	
INCREASE (DECREASE) IN CASH (b)	- 0 -
ADD: BEGINNING CASH BALANCE	
ENDING CASH BALANCE	

BALANCE SHEET (SECOND)			
ASSETS		LIABILITIES	
CURRENT ASSETS		CURRENT LIABILITIES	
CASH (b)	- 0 -		
Inventory	(300)		
		NONCURRENT LIABILITIES	
		Deferred Interest Income (C)	+ 74
		STOCKHOLDERS' EQUITY	
NONCURRENT ASSETS			
Lease Payment Receivable (C)	+ 524	CAPITAL STOCK	
		APIC	
		RETAINED	
		EARNINGS (a)	+ 150
		TOTAL	
		LIABILITIES &	
		STOCKHOLDERS'	
TOTAL ASSETS	+ 224	EQUITY	+ 224

(c) Classify as current if leasing is a normal part of the lessor's operations.

FINANCIAL MODELING WORKSHEET: DECEMBER 31, 2008 ANNUAL CAPITAL LEASE COLLECTION AND RECOGNITION OF INTEREST REVENUE BY THE LESSOR

INCOME STATEMENT (FIRST)	
REVENUES:	
Interest Revenue	+ 36
EXPENSES:	
NET INCOME OR LOSS (a)	+ 36

STATEMENT OF CASH FLOWS (THIRD)	
OPERATING ACTIVITIES:	
NET INCOME OR LOSS (a)	+ 36
Decrease in Lease Payment Receivable	+ 175
Decrease in Deferred Interest Revenue	(36)
Cash flow from operating activities	+175
INVESTING ACTIVITIES:	
FINANCING ACTIVITIES:	
INCREASE (DECREASE) IN CASH (b)	+175
ADD: BEGINNING CASH BALANCE	
ENDING CASH BALANCE	

BALANCE SHEET (SECOND)			
ASSETS		LIABILITIES	
CURRENT ASSETS		CURRENT LIABILITIES	
CASH (b)	+ 175		
		NONCURRENT LIABILITIES	
		Deferred Interest Revenue	(36)
		STOCKHOLDERS' EQUITY	
NONCURRENT ASSETS			
Lease Payment Receivable	(175)	CAPITAL STOCK	
		APIC	
		RETAINED EARNINGS (a)	+ 36
		TOTAL LIABILITIES & STOCKHOLDERS' EQUITY	
TOTAL ASSETS	- 0 -		- 0 -

FINANCIAL MODELING WORKSHEET: DECEMBER 31, 2008 ANNUAL PAYMENT OF EXECUTORY COSTS BY THE LESSOR UNDER THE CAPITAL LEASE

INCOME STATEMENT (FIRST)	
REVENUES:	
EXPENSES:	
Insurance Expense	*(6)*
Maintenance Expense	*(3)*
NET INCOME OR LOSS (a)	*(9)*

STATEMENT OF CASH FLOWS (THIRD)	
OPERATING ACTIVITIES:	
NET INCOME OR LOSS (a)	*(9)*
Cash flow from operating activities	*(9)*
INVESTING ACTIVITIES:	
FINANCING ACTIVITIES:	
INCREASE (DECREASE) IN CASH (b)	*(9)*
ADD: BEGINNING CASH BALANCE	
ENDING CASH BALANCE	

BALANCE SHEET (SECOND)			
ASSETS		*LIABILITIES*	
CURRENT ASSETS		*CURRENT LIABILITIES*	
CASH (b)	*(9)*		
		NONCURRENT LIABILITIES	
		STOCKHOLDERS' EQUITY	
NONCURRENT ASSETS			
		CAPITAL STOCK	
		APIC	
		RETAINED	
		EARNINGS (a)	*(9)*
		TOTAL	
		LIABILITIES &	
		STOCKHOLDERS'	
TOTAL ASSETS	*(9)*	*EQUITY*	*(9)*

If the lease was misclassified as an operating lease, only the rental income of $174,614.87 would be recognized each year and the asset would be depreciated by the lessor. Once again, only cosmetic accounting differences would result in the financial statements. The pre-tax cash inflows to the lessor would be identical under either accounting method. The following summary compares the financial statement effects of a capital versus an operating lease for the lessor.

Year	Capital Lease Annual Income			Operating Lease Annual Income			Difference
	Profit	Interest	Total	Rent Income	Depreciation Expense **(a)**	Net	Capital Lease Profit Higher (Lower)
2008	$150,000.00	$36,000.00	$186,000.00	$174,614.87	($100,000.00)	$ 74,614.87	$ 111,385.13
2009	- 0 -	24,910.81	24,910.81	174,614.87	(100,000.00)	74,614.87	(49,704.06)
2010	- 0 -	12,933.80	12,933.80	174,614.87	(100,000.00)	74,614.87	(61,681.07)
Totals	$150,000.00	$73,844.61	$223,844.61	$523,844.61	($300,000.00)	$223,844.61	- 0 -

(a) The cost of the asset is assumed to be depreciated over the lease term using the straight-line method. (i.e., $300,000/3 years = $100,000/year)

As noted earlier, the capitalization method is generally preferred a lessor in the financial services industry. Reported net income and EPS would be higher in the first year of the lease. In addition, the finance lease receivable would replace plant and equipment held for lease on the balance sheet. Lessors in the insurance and banking industries prefer to reflect the finance receivable rather than the heavy manufacturing equipment on their balance sheets due to the incompatibility of reporting certain types of plant assets with the financial service assets employed in their core operations. This issue is less significant for a dealer or manufacturer lesser.

Annuity Due Application

If the lease payments began at the beginning of the year, the lease payments would represent an annuity due (i.e., beginning mode). In this case, the present value of the minimum lease payments would be equal to $486,000 (i.e., $450,000 x 1.08). In addition, assume that the fair market value of the equipment is also equal to $486,000, but the cost of the asset is assumed to remain at $300,000. The lease amortization table would be modified as follows:

AMORTIZATION TABLE: ANNUITY DUE BASIS					
DATE	***BEGINNING BALANCE OF THE LEASE OBLIGATION***	***MINIMUM LEASE PAYMENTS***	***BALANCE OF THE LEASE OBLIGATION AFTER PAYMENT***	***8% INTEREST***	***ENDING BALANCE OF THE LEASE OBLIGATION***
1/1/2008	$486,000.00	$174,614.87	$311,385.13	$ 24,910.81	$336,295.94
1/1/2009	336,295.94	174,614.87	161,681.07	12,934.80	174,615.87
1/1/2010	174,615.87	174,614.87	- 0 -	- 0 -	- 0 -
TOTALS		$523,844.61		$ 37,845.61	

The accounting issues and the financial statement implications for the annuity due basis would not change. The amortization table is different because the first payment is deducted from the debt immediately at the beginning of the period. Interest is computed on the "net debt", that is, the debt balance at the beginning of the period after the deduction of the payment. The ending balance of the lease obligation is the beginning balance, less the first payment and plus the interest for the period.

Accounting for Residual Values

Guaranteed Residual Value

Residual Values can be Guaranteed or unguaranteed. When the lease includes a residual value, the lease payments are reduced because the lessor's cost is partially recovered by the residual value. When the residual value is not guaranteed, its present value is deducted from the lessor's sales revenue and the cost of goods sold. This is due to the fact that the criteria for revenue recognition have not been met (i.e., material uncertainty as to collection of the residual value).

To illustrate the effect of a residual value, we will modify the lease case presented earlier. The data for the illustration are presented as follows. Assume that F.A. Santangelo Company enters a 3 year lease of property with a cost of $300,000 and a fair value of $450,000. There is a $20,000 residual value indicated in the lease contract. The lessor's implicit rate is 8% and is lower than the lessee's incremental borrowing rate of 10%. The lease payments are determined below:

End Mode (assume an ordinary annuity)

n = 3
i = 8
FV = $20,000 (Residual Value)
PV = $450,000
PMT = $168,454.41

Note that the lease payments were $174,614.87 in the case presented earlier *without* the residual value. The amortization table for the residual value case is presented below.

AMORTIZATION TABLE: ORDINARY ANNUITY BASIS				
DATE	***MINIMUM LEASE PAYMENTS***	***8% INTEREST***	***PRINCIPAL REDUC-TION***	***OUTSTANDING BAL-ANCE***
1/1/05	-	-	-	$450,000.00
12/31/05	$168,454.41	$36,000.00	$132,454.41	317,545.59
12/31/06	168,454.41	25,403.65	143,050,76	174,494.83
12/31/07	168,454.41	13,959.59	154,494.83	20,000.00
TOTALS	$505,363.23	$75,363.24	$430,000.00	

When there is a residual value, the total payments are reduced and this results in a lower principal pay-down. With less of the principal paid each period, the total interest cost is increased. The residual value is the ending balance of the lease payment receivable and the capital lease debt, if the lease is capitalized.

The accounting at the inception of the lease, at each lease payment and at the end of the year amortization is the same as without the residual value. However, the lessee would use a residual value in the amortization of the capitalized leased asset and therefore, there would be a net book value of the leased asset of $20,000 at the end of the lease. The other key accounting differences also only occur at the end of the lease term.

The following financial modeling worksheets are presented for the lessor and lessee at the end of the lease with a guaranteed residual value.

FINANCIAL MODELING WORKSHEET LESSOR: GUARANTEED RESIDUAL VALUE RECEIVED

INCOME STATEMENT (FIRST)	
REVENUES:	
EXPENSES:	
NET INCOME OR LOSS (a)	

STATEMENT OF CASH FLOWS (THIRD)*	
OPERATING ACTIVITIES:	
NET INCOME OR LOSS (a)	
INVESTING ACTIVITIES:	
FINANCING ACTIVITIES:	
INCREASE (DECREASE) IN CASH (b)	
ADD: BEGINNING CASH BALANCE	
ENDING CASH BALANCE	

BALANCE SHEET (SECOND)			
ASSETS		LIABILITIES	
CURRENT ASSETS		CURRENT LIABILITIES	
CASH (b)			
		NONCURRENT LIABILITIES	
		STOCKHOLDERS' EQUITY	
NONCURRENT ASSETS			
Equipment (or Inventory) at FMV	+20,000	CAPITAL STOCK	
Lease Payment Receivable	- 20,000	APIC	
		RETAINED	
		EARNINGS (a)	
		TOTAL	
		LIABILITIES &	
		STOCKHOLDERS'	
TOTAL ASSETS	- 0 -	EQUITY	- 0 -

*Disclose as part of the cash flow statement as Significant Noncash Investing and Financing Activities.

If the fair value of the property is less than the guaranteed residual value (i.e., the fair value), the lessor will collect the deficiency in cash from the lessee.

FINANCIAL MODELING WORKSHEET LESSOR: GUARANTEED RESIDUAL VALUE DEFICIENCY OF $5,000 RECEIVED

INCOME STATEMENT (FIRST)	
REVENUES:	
EXPENSES:	
NET INCOME OR LOSS (a)	

*STATEMENT OF CASH FLOWS (THIRD)**	
OPERATING ACTIVITIES:	
NET INCOME OR LOSS (a)	
Reduction of Lease Payment Receivable	***+5,000***
INVESTING ACTIVITIES:	
FINANCING ACTIVITIES:	
INCREASE (DECREASE) IN CASH (b)	***+5,000***
ADD: BEGINNING CASH BALANCE	
ENDING CASH BALANCE	

BALANCE SHEET (SECOND)			
ASSETS		***LIABILITIES***	
CURRENT ASSETS		***CURRENT LIABILITIES***	
CASH (b)	***+ 5,000***		
		NONCURRENT LIABILITIES	
		STOCKHOLDERS' EQUITY	
NONCURRENT ASSETS			
Equipment (or Inventory) at FMV	***+15,000***	***CAPITAL STOCK***	
Lease Payment Receivable	***- 20,000***	***APIC***	
		RETAINED EARNINGS (a)	
		TOTAL LIABILITIES & STOCKHOLDERS' EQUITY	
TOTAL ASSETS	***- 0 -***		***- 0 -***

FINANCIAL MODELING WORKSHEET LESSOR: GUARANTEED RESIDUAL VALUE DEFICIENCY OF $5,000 NOT RECEIVED

INCOME STATEMENT (FIRST)	
REVENUES:	
EXPENSES:	
Loss on Lease Residual Value	*-5,000*
NET INCOME OR LOSS (a)	*-5,000*

STATEMENT OF CASH FLOWS (THIRD)	
OPERATING ACTIVITIES:	
NET INCOME OR LOSS (a)	*- 5,000*
Loss on Lease Residual Value	*+5,000*
INVESTING ACTIVITIES:	
FINANCING ACTIVITIES:	
INCREASE (DECREASE) IN CASH (b)	*- 0 -*
ADD: BEGINNING CASH BALANCE	
ENDING CASH BALANCE	

BALANCE SHEET (SECOND)			
ASSETS		*LIABILITIES*	
CURRENT ASSETS		*CURRENT LIABILITIES*	
CASH (b)	*- 0 -*		
		NONCURRENT LIABILITIES	
		STOCKHOLDERS' EQUITY	
NONCURRENT ASSETS			
Equipment (or Inventory) at FMV	*+15,000*	*CAPITAL STOCK*	
Lease Payment Receivable	*- 20,000*	*APIC*	
		RETAINED EARNINGS (a)	*- 5,000*
TOTAL ASSETS	*- 5,000*	*TOTAL LIABILITIES & STOCKHOLDERS' EQUITY*	*- 5,000*

FINANCIAL MODELING WORKSHEET LESSEE: GUARANTEED RESIDUAL VALUE REQUIREMENT MET

INCOME STATEMENT (FIRST)	
REVENUES:	
EXPENSES:	
NET INCOME OR LOSS (a)	

STATEMENT OF CASH FLOWS (THIRD)*	
OPERATING ACTIVITIES:	
NET INCOME OR LOSS (a)	
INVESTING ACTIVITIES:	
FINANCING ACTIVITIES:	
INCREASE (DECREASE) IN CASH (b)	
ADD: BEGINNING CASH BALANCE	
ENDING CASH BALANCE	

BALANCE SHEET (SECOND)			
ASSETS		LIABILITIES	
CURRENT ASSETS		CURRENT LIABILITIES	
CASH (b)			
		NONCURRENT LIABILITIES	
		Lease Payment Receivable	- 20,000
		STOCKHOLDERS' EQUITY	
NONCURRENT ASSETS			
Leased Asset	- 20,000	CAPITAL STOCK	
		APIC	
		RETAINED	
		EARNINGS (a)	
		TOTAL LIABILITIES & STOCKHOLDERS' EQUITY	
TOTAL ASSETS	- 20,000		- 20,000

*Disclose as part of the cash flow statement as Significant Noncash Investing and Financing Activities.

FINANCIAL MODELING WORKSHEET LESSEE: GUARANTEED RESIDUAL VALUE DEFICIENCY OF $5,000 PAID

INCOME STATEMENT (FIRST)	
REVENUES:	
EXPENSES:	
Lease charge for deficiency in residual value	***-5,000***
NET INCOME OR LOSS (a)	***-5,000***

*STATEMENT OF CASH FLOWS (THIRD)**	
OPERATING ACTIVITIES:	
NET INCOME OR LOSS (a)	***-5,000***
INVESTING ACTIVITIES:	
FINANCING ACTIVITIES:	
INCREASE (DECREASE) IN CASH (b)	***+5,000***
ADD: BEGINNING CASH BALANCE	
ENDING CASH BALANCE	

BALANCE SHEET (SECOND)			
ASSETS		***LIABILITIES***	
CURRENT ASSETS		***CURRENT LIABILITIES***	
CASH (b)	***-5,000***		
		NONCURRENT LIABILITIES	
		Lease Obligation	***-20,000***
		STOCKHOLDERS' EQUITY	
NONCURRENT ASSETS			
Leased Asset	***-20,000***	***CAPITAL STOCK***	
		APIC	
		RETAINED EARNINGS (a)	***-5,000***
		TOTAL LIABILITIES & STOCKHOLDERS' EQUITY	
TOTAL ASSETS	***-25,000***		***-25,000***

*Disclose the reversal of the leased asset and lease obligation as part of the cash flow statement as Significant Noncash Investing and Financing Activities.

FINANCIAL MODELING WORKSHEET LESSEE: GUARANTEED RESIDUAL VALUE DEFICIENCY OF $5,000 NOT PAID

INCOME STATEMENT (FIRST)	
REVENUES:	
EXPENSES:	
NET INCOME OR LOSS (a)	-0-

*STATEMENT OF CASH FLOWS (THIRD)**	
OPERATING ACTIVITIES:	
NET INCOME OR LOSS (a)	-0-
INVESTING ACTIVITIES:	
FINANCING ACTIVITIES:	
INCREASE (DECREASE) IN CASH (b)	-0-
ADD: BEGINNING CASH BALANCE	
ENDING CASH BALANCE	

BALANCE SHEET (SECOND)			
ASSETS		*LIABILITIES*	
CURRENT ASSETS		*CURRENT LIABILITIES*	
CASH (b)	-0-		
		NONCURRENT LIABILITIES	
		Lease Obligation	-20,000
		STOCKHOLDERS' EQUITY	
NONCURRENT ASSETS			
Leased Asset	-20,000	*CAPITAL STOCK*	
		APIC	
		RETAINED EARNINGS (a)	
		TOTAL LIABILITIES & STOCKHOLDERS' EQUITY	
TOTAL ASSETS	-20,000		-20,000

*Disclose the reversal of the leased asset and lease obligation as part of the cash flow statement as Significant Noncash Investing and Financing Activities.

Unguaranteed Residual Value

When the residual value is not guaranteed, the earning process is not complete due to the uncertainty as to realization of the residual value. In this case all accounting entries and financial statement effects are the same with the exception of the date of inception of the lease and return of the equipment.

Continuing the previous illustration, at the inception of the lease, the present value of the $20,000 unguaranteed residual of $15,876.64, is deducted from the sales value and cost of goods sold (i.e., $20,000 x .794 the discount factor at 8% for 3 years). In this case, the lessor's sales would be reported at $434,123.36 and cost of goods sold is reduced to $284,123.37. All other accounting is the same for the lessor. There are no changes reflected on the books of the lessee.

THE CAPITALIZATION OF OPERATING LEASES FOR THE LESSEE: A DISCOUNTED CASH FLOW APPROACH

Although the previous discussion may point out some motivation for lessees to manipulate lease terms to achieve cosmetic accounting benefits on their financial statements, the key issue in credit and financial analysis is the proper determination of the economic substance of the lease transactions reported by the lessee. In this next section of the chapter, an analytical approach is presented that enables the analyst to capitalize operating leases for the lessee. This approach can assist the analyst in determining the extent of the lessee's off-balance sheet financing needed for effective credit and investment decisions.

The key reasons for the avoidance of lease capitalization by lessees has been noted several times throughout this chapter. By avoiding capitalization, the lessee can keep a significant amount of debt off the firm's balance sheets. Without the current portion of lease debt reported on the balance sheet, working capital is improved. In addition, in the earlier years of a capital lease, the lessee would report lower profit due to the excess interest and depreciation charges over the simple rent expense resulting from the operating lease.

The lessee can accomplish off-balance sheet financing by manipulation of lease terms to avoid capitalization. However, this managerial behavior results in serious problems for credit and financial analysts in the assessment of the lessee's debt paying ability and in the evaluation of other financial ratios.

To determine the extent of the lessee's off-balance sheet financing, most users of financial information have utilized the information provided in the footnotes to the lessee's financial statements. As noted earlier, the lessee's footnote disclosure indicates the minimum lease payments required over the next five years and over the remaining lease term in aggregate, for all noncancelable operating leases of terms of one year or more. In order to determine the effect of operating leases on the financial statements, credit and financial analysts should incorporate operating leases into the financial statements through analytical or constructive lease capitalization methods.

A frequently used method of incorporating operating leases into a lessee's balance sheet is the rating agency method (i.e., the method used by bond rating agencies). That is, various rules of thumb have been developed by rating agencies (e.g., Moody's and Standard and Poor's) to capitalize operating leases. These rules of thumb were originally designed for real estate leases, the most common type of lease arrangement at that time. At that point, multipliers as high as 10 times rent expense were used to proxy the capitalized lease debt. This was designed to capture the longer terms of the real estate debt. Therefore, using a multiplier of 10 was viewed as a representative present value factor for leases with extended terms. As will be illustrated later, the rating agency approach is conservative because it assumes that all operating leases have been misclassified. In addition, the rating agency approach is not consistent with the theoretically correct debt valuation using discounted cash flow computations.

The rules of thumb were adopted from "real estate capitalization rates". For long term real estate leases, terms can extend over 40 years. In this case, the number of periods in a discounted cash flow application would be so large that the cash flow term would approach perpetuity. As $n \rightarrow \infty$, the annuity discount factor, $\{[1 - 1 / (1+i)^n] / i\}$, approaches $1 / i$ where i is the capitalization rate. If discount rates at that time were 12.5%, then the capitalized lease value is computed as follows:

Capitalized Value **= Rent Expense x 1 / i =**
= Rent Expense x 1/ .125 =
= Rent Expense x 1/ (1/8) =
= Rent Expense x 8

Today, the lease obligation is estimated from the lease footnote information by using capitalization factors ranging from 6 to 8 times rent expense. The interest expense can be computed as 1/3 rent expense and depreciation may be estimated as 2/3 rent expense. The lower multipliers used in current practice reflect the use of shorter term leases (in addition to the traditional, longer term real estate lease).

The rating agency approach is a very tentative measure of the lease obligation and interest expense and may result in inaccurate predictions of the financial position of the lessee.

The following section of this chapter presents an alternative approach to the determination of the extent of the lessee's off-balance sheet financing. This approach is more consistent with the SFAS 13 requirements for lease capitalization by using a discounted cash flow (DCF) methodology. In addition, this method makes better use of the lessee's footnote disclosure which was designed to provide the user with enough data to determine the financial statement impact of operating leases that perhaps should have been capitalized. As with the rating agency rules of thumb, the DCF approach is conservative in that it assumes that all operating leases were misclassified. That is, all operating leases with noncancelable terms of one year or more were classified as operating leases as a result of managerial manipulation of lease terms to avoid capitalization. The DCF approach has recently been employed in practice by some rating agencies as an alternative to the basic rules of thumb.

An Alternative Approach to Capitalizing Operating Leases[3]

The illustration of lease accounting presented in this chapter indicated that according to the provisions of SFAS 13, the capitalized lease asset and obligation should be recorded at the lower of the fair market value of the asset or the present value of the future minimum lease payments. Although not discounted, the lessee's footnote information provides the future minimum lease payments required under operating leases with noncancelable terms of one year or more. This stream of payments becomes the input for the discounted cash flow (DCF) model. The future cash flows are only one of the three key variables needed to capitalize the operating leases for the lessee.

The Required Variables. To use any DCF model, three variables are required:

1. The stream of cash flows
2. The time period over which these cash flows will be received or paid
3. The discount rate of interest

In the case of the operating lease footnote information, the cash flows and the time period are readily available; however, the discount rate to use may be difficult to determine. An approach for estimating the discount rate to use is presented in the following section.

Using the Implicit Average Interest Rate

One alternative discount rate may be to use the firm's average interest rate on actual debt obligations, which can be obtained easily from the long-term debt footnote disclosure. If the lessee also reports capital lease obligations, a better alternative may be to use the implicit average rate of interest incurred on the firm's capitalized leases. This rate can be calculated from the lessee footnote disclosure for capital leases. In this footnote, the lessee is required

3. This section is adapted with permission from Alexander J. Sannella, "The Capitalization of Operating Leases: The Discounted Cash Flow Approach," *The Journal of Commercial Bank Lending (October, 1989) 49-55. Copyright, 1989, by Robert Morris Associates.*

to disclose the future minimum lease payments on noncancelable capital leases. The interest rate implicit in the lease footnote can be determined from a financial calculator.

Once the average discount rate on the firm's capital leases has been determined, the minimum lease payments on the lessee's operating leases can be discounted to compute the lease obligation, the interest expense and the extent of the lessee's off-balance sheet financing.

In the next section, an illustration of the discounted cash flow approach is provided. The results of this illustration are compared to the rating agency approach. It should be noted that the discounted cash flow approach only emphasizes the measurement of the effective operating lease debt. As a result, capitalized operating leases will understate fixed assets. While the DCF method provides the best method of measuring the effective operating lease debt, asset turnover and fixed asset turnover ratios will tend to be overstated by using this approach. Nonetheless, an analyst could use the discounted value as an estimate of both the leased asset and the long term obligation.

An Illustration of the DCF Approach to Capitalization of Operating Leases

In this section, the DCF approach is applied to the lease footnote information found in the 2012 financial statements of Token Corporation and Subsidiary Companies. Exhibit 8.3 below provides the Token 2012 lease footnote information.

EXHIBIT 8.3: TOKEN CORPORATION AND SUBSIDIARY COMPANIES: LEASE FOOTNOTE DISCLOSURES

Lease Obligations

Token leases aircraft, airport passenger terminal space, aircraft hangars and related maintenance facilities, cargo terminals, other airport facilities, other commercial real estate, office and computer equipment and vehicles.

At December 31, 2012, scheduled future minimum lease payments under capital leases (substantially all of which are for aircraft) and operating leases having initial or remaining noncancelable lease terms of more than one year were as follows:

(In millions)	Operating Leases		Capital
	Aircraft	Non-aircraft	Leases
Payable during -			
2013	938.4	586.8	212.4
2014	942	550.8	295.2
2015	913.2	534	376.8
2016	870	522	250.8
2017	835.2	506.4	519.6
After 2017	3,229.2	4,118.4	764.4
Total minimum lease payments	$7,728	$6,818	2419.2
Imputed interest (at rates of 1.5% to 10.0%)			(315.6)
Present value of minimum lease payments			2103.6
Current portion			(24)
Long-term obligations under capital leases			$2,080

As of December 31, 2012, we leased 310 mainline aircraft, 100 of which were under capital leases. These leases have initial terms of 15 to 36 years, and expiration dates ranging from 2013 through 2031. Under the terms of all leases, we have the right to purchase the aircraft at the end of the lease term, in some cases at fair market value and in others at fair market value or a percentage of cost.

Amounts charged to rent expense, net of minor amounts of sublease rentals, were $1.2 billion in 2012, $1.3 billion in 2011 and $1.4 billion in 2010.

CALCULATING THE AVERAGE DISCOUNT RATE

The first step in using the DCF approach is to calculate the average discount rate implicit in the firm's capitalized leases. This rate can be computed by using a cash flow routine on a financial calculator (i.e., the interval rate of return). The use of the cash flow routine on a financial calculator indicates that the implicit or average rate of interest is approximately 3.5%.

Given the implicit rate of interest, the DCF model can be applied to the footnote data disclosed. The only remaining problem is the distribution of the minimum future lease payments over the "After 2017" period. Without any other information, a viable solution is to assume that the aggregate cash flows for this period can be expressed as a terminal value or residual amount. The validity of the 305% implicit discount rate is tested in the following computation.

(1)	(2) Capital Leases	(3) Discount Factors at 3.5%	(4) DCF Valuation
In millions: Payable during -			
2013	$ 212	.966	$205
2014	295	.933	276
2015	377	.901	340
2016	251	.871	218
2017	520	.842	438
After 2017	764	.813	622
Total minimum lease payments	$ 2,419		
Imputed interest (at rates of 1.5% to 10.0%)	(316)		
Present value of minimum lease payments	**$2,103**		**$2,099**
Current portion	(24)		
Long-term obligations under capital leases	$2,079		

In column four of the above table, the individual cash outflows under the capital leases in column two are discounted to prove the accuracy of the implicit discount rate calculation. By multiplying the present value factors in column three by the reported minimum future lease payments in column two, the resulting discounted cash flows in column four amount to $2,099. When compared to the reported lease obligation of $2,103, the error is not significant.

The weighted average cost of debt capital is another alternative approach to estimate the implicit discount rate. As noted in the computation below, the average cost of debt capital is 7%. This is determined from the Long Term Debt Note as presented in Exhibit 8.3. The computation of the weighted average cost of debt capital for Token Corporation is presented in the table below.

(In millions) 2005	Debt Balance	Average Interest Rate	Average Interest Cost
Secured notes, 3.72% to 9.52%, averaging 6.67%, due through 2014	$6,907	.0667	$461
Debentures, 9.00% to 11.21%, averaging 9.89%, due through 2021	775	.0989	77
Municipal bonds, 5.63% to 6.38%, averaging 5.90%, due through 2035	521	.0590	31
Preferred securities of trust, 13.25%, due 2026	116	.1325	15
	$ 8,320		$584
Weighted average cost of debt = $584 / $8,320 =			**7%**

If we discount the capital lease flows at 7%, the present value is equal to $1,592 and is well below the present value computed above. Therefore using the implicit rate of 3.5% is the preferred alternative. The DCF approach to the capitalization of operating leases using 3.5% is discussed the next section.

Applicability to Future Lease Payments

The capitalization of Token's operating lease payments is presented in the following table.

(In millions)	Operating Leases		Total Operating Lease Payments	3.5% Discount Factors	DCF Valuation of Operating Lease Payments
	Aircraft	Non-aircraft			
Payable during -					
2013	$ 938.4	$ 568.8	$1,525.2	.966	$1,473.3
2014	942	550.8	1,492.8	.933	1,392.8
2015	913.2	534	1,447.2	.901	1,303.9
2016	870	522	1,392	.871	1,212.4
2017	835.2	506.4	1,341.6	.842	1,129.6
After 2017	3,229.2	4,118.4	7,342.6	.813	5,973.6
Total minimum lease payments	$ 7,728	$ 6,818	$14,546		$12,486
Imputed interest (at rates of 1.5% to 10.0%)			(2,060)		
Present value of minimum lease payments			$ 12,486		
Current portion **(a)**			(1,088)		
Long-term obligations under capitalized operating leases			$11,398		

(a) Current Portion = 2012 Total Payment – Interest Expense
Current Portion = 2012 Total Payment - 3.5% x Lease Debt)
Current Portion = $1,525 - (3.5% x $12,486)
Current Portion = $1,525 - 437
Current Portion = $1,088

With the discount rate equal to the average cost of lease debit of 3.5%, the same approach can be applied to the reported nominal minimum future lease payments reported under the firm's operating leases. As noted in the table above, the discounted cash flow approach would result in a capital lease obligation for the operating leases of $12,486 at December 31, 2012.

The bottom section of the above table presents parallel footnote information disclosed for the capital leases, presented by Token Corporation, and the capitalized lease information, as derived under the DCF approach. In this section, the current portion of the long-term lease obligation for the operating leases was determined to be $1,088 and the 2013 interest charge was estimate at $437.

The analyst can now utilize the data obtained by the constructive capitalization of the operating leases. Debt equity ratios and working capital computations can be recomputed by including the long term capitalized lease obligations and the current portion respectively. Interest coverage ratios can be modified by including the lease interest expense.

Applying the Rating Agency Approach

If the rating agency approach was applied to the Token Corporation footnote information presented in Exhibit 8.3, the capitalized lease obligation at December 31, 2012 would have been estimated at 8 times rent or $12,200 (8 X $1,525) and the interest expense for 2013would have been estimated at $508 ($1,525 / 3).

It should be noted that in practice, the analyst using the rating agency approach may also capitalize using the 2012 rent expense. However, because the DCF method uses future cash flows, the 2013 rent expense was used in the rating agency computations.

In this case, the results using the rating agency approach is not significantly different from the DCF methodology. In other cases, there can be significant differences between the two approaches. The DCF methodology estimates the capitalized operating lease debt at $12,486 and the corresponding interest expense is $437. Nonetheless, the DCF approach is considered preferable from an economic perspective. This is relevant given that the rating agency approach was designed for real estate leases, which only a portion of the total lease market. In addition, the DCF approach provides an estimate of lease debt and interest elements that are closer to the theoretically correct values that are more consistent with the computations prescribed by SFAS 13.

A Shortcut DCF Approach

The DCF model presented in the previous section of this chapter is superior to the rating agency approach in that it is consistent with the SFAS 13 computations for capital leases and makes better use of the information available in the lessee's footnote disclosure. One criticism, however, may be the complexity of the computations presented above as compared to the rating agency method.

If the lessee also reports capital lease transactions, a "shortcut" DCF model could be used as an alternative with minimal differences in the results obtained. As noted in computations above, regardless of the stream of lease payments, capital, or operating leases, the present value (PV) factors are the same. The constant PV factors can be factored out by calculating the average PV factor for the entire stream of capital lease cash outflows. The average PV factor can be obtained by the following ratio for the capital leases.

$$\textbf{Average PV Factor} = \frac{\textbf{PV of Minimum Lease Payments}}{\textbf{Total Minimum Future Lease Payments}}$$

Using the footnote information for Token Corporation in Exhibit 8.3, the Average PV Factor is $2,103 / $2,419 = .8694. The present value of the future minimum lease payments (i.e., the capitalized lease obligation) for the operating leases can be obtained by simply multiplying the average PV factor derived above by the total minimum future lease payments for the firm's operating leases.

As noted in the previous tables, in the case of Token Corporation the total minimum lease payments are equal to $14,546. The capitalized lease debt can be estimated at $12,646 or $14,546 X .8694 = $12,646.

Comparing this amount with the lease obligation of $12,486 computed in the tables above employing the full DCF methodology, the difference is $1,600 ($12,646 - 12,486). The difference would not have a material effect on the revised financial ratios using the capitalized operating lease debt. Therefore, the shortcut DCF model provides similar results as compared to the more complex approach but avoids the need for detailed computations. However, to the short-cut approach requires that the lessee also reports capital leases.

Conclusions: The DCF Approach

This section presented a DCF approach to the capitalization of operating leases on the financial statements of the lessee. The DCF model is viewed as a superior alternative to the rating agency rules of thumb for computing the extent of the lessee's off-balance sheet financing (i.e., the lease obligation) and the interest component of the lease payment. The DCF model is more consistent with the computation of the lease obligation for capital leases under SFAS 13, and makes better use of the footnote information required by this pronouncement and is therefore closer to the theoretically correct valuation of the lease debt.

A criticism of the DCF model may be the complexity of its computations as compared to the rating agency approach. To avoid this criticism, a shortcut approach was presented which provided similar results but with minimal computational effort.

It is believed that both DCF models are an improvement over the rating agency approach for credit-granting purposes and financial statement analysis in general. However, the DCF methodology focuses on the measurement of the effective operating lease debt, and as a result, it tends to understate fixed assets. Therefore, asset turnover and fixed asset turnover ratios will tend to be overstated. This fact simply seems to support the reality that operating leases continue to be problematic for creditors and financial analysts who seek a less complex way of measuring and understanding financial performance.

Chapter 9 | Computing Earnings Per Share

INTRODUCTION

Earnings per share (EPS) is a measure of operating performance used widely in credit and investment analysis. The EPS disclosure is probably the single most important financial statistic used in assessing the effectiveness of the management team in utilizing the economic resources entrusted to it by the common shareholders.

EPS is also used in the mechanistic valuation of common equity securities through the use of the price-earnings (P/E) multiple, and in the evaluation of the firm's ability to make dividend distributions to its common shareholders.

Due to the importance and extensive use of the EPS figure, the accountant provides the analyst with all required EPS information. The presentation of EPS on the face of the income statement is probably the only key financial ratio provided directly in the body of the financial statement. In all other cases, the analyst is required to use the information provided in the financial statements to compute financial ratios and other key statistics. Nevertheless, the EPS disclosure is subject to the same limitations of accrual basis accounting as all other financial information provided by the accountant in the annual report.

FASB Statement No. 128, "Earnings per Share"[1], establishes the standards for computing and disclosing earnings per share (EPS) for all companies with publicly held common stock or potential common stock (i.e., securities such as options, warrants, convertible securities or contingent share agreements). The statement simplifies the computation of EPS and makes the EPS computation and disclosures consistent with international accounting standards. Specifically, FASB No. 128 is nearly identical to International Accounting Standard (IAS) No. 33.

FASB No. 128 also requires a reconciliation of the numerator and denominator used in the EPS computation to the numbers reported in the financial statements. FASB Statement No. 129, "Disclosure of Information about Capital Structure"[2], simply consolidates prior standards regarding the disclosure of information about a firm's capital structure (e.g., liquidation preferences on preferred stock and redeemable preferred stock).

The importance of the EPS disclosure cannot be emphasized enough. EPS figures are continually reported in the financial press and are used by potential investors and the market in general to estimate the value of the company. In addition, clients are concerned with the impact on EPS from new capitalization, initial public offerings (IPOs), and from merger and acquisition activity (M&A).

Although the mandatory EPS information is provided on the face of the income statement, the analyst should still be familiar with the complexities of the EPS computation for purposes of making projections of EPS, conducting accretion / dilution analysis and for preparing proforma financial statements. For instance, an analyst may wish to determine the effect on reported EPS from additional debt financing versus equity financing. Similarly, the analyst may need a proforma calculation of EPS in order to assess the impact of a proposed merger on the reported EPS of the combined entity.

---

1. FASB ASC 260 [Predecessor literature: "Earnings per Share," *Statement of Financial Accounting Standards No. 128* (Norwalk, Conn.: FASB, 1997)].

2. FASB ASC 505 [Predecessor literature: "Disclosures of Information about Capital Structure," *Statement of Financial Accounting Standards No. 129* (Norwalk, Conn.: FASB, 1997)].

The purpose of this chapter is to present the reporting requirements SFAS 128 and to demonstrate the details of the EPS computation. In addition, several analytical issues related to the EPS disclosure will be discussed.

BASIC CONCEPTS IN COMPUTING EPS

Basic Or Unadjusted (Undiluted) EPS

Preferred Dividend Requirements.

In its simplest form, the basic or the unadjusted EPS is computed as follows:

$$\textbf{BEPS} = \frac{\textbf{Net Income - Preferred Dividend Requirements}}{\textbf{Weighted Average Number of Common Shares Outstanding}}$$

The basic EPS figure is generally considered inadequate because it may be overstated if there are potentially dilutive securities outstanding such as stock options or convertible securities. As will be discussed throughout this chapter, the basic EPS ratio will be modified and adjusted by the accountant to reflect the possible future impact of potentially dilutive securities outstanding. Thus, the accountant assumes a conservative position with respect to EPS in that the lower or diluted EPS figure, based on hypothetical events, is preferred to the actual, but potentially overstated, basic EPS amount.

The conservative position of the accountant is found in the rules that prohibit increasing EPS. Specifically, antidilution or accretion is not permitted. That is, any assumption regarding the hypothetical conversion or exercise of a potentially dilutive security that increases EPS cannot be included in the computation.

Weighted Average Number of Common Shares

Preferred dividend requirements represent the claims of senior equity securities. The claims of senior equity securities include current dividends declared on preferred stock or the current year's increase in dividends in arrears for undeclared dividends on cumulative preferred stock. This is only the increase in dividends in arrears for the current year and not the total balance of dividends in arrears. Only the increase in preferred dividends in arrears is used because all past dividends in arrears were already incorporated into prior years' EPS computations. Due to the exclusion of preferred shareholder claims, the numerator of the ratio is called "net income available to common." If there is a loss from continuing operations, loss per share is to be increased by the amount of preferred dividend requirements.

In computing the weighted average number of common shares, only "outstanding" shares are included. As discussed in the section of this text covering shareholders' equity, outstanding shares represent issued shares less treasury stock. The weighted average can be computed by weighting on a monthly, quarterly or daily basis. Although more complex, the daily weighting provides the more accurate computation. When share activity is not extensive, monthly and quarterly weighting provides sufficient accuracy and will be assumed throughout this chapter.

When computing the monthly weighted average, the weights used in the computation are the number of months from the date of the transaction to the date of the EPS computation. The following example provides an illustration of a basic weighted average computation.

Illustrations: Computation of the Weighted Average Number of Shares for the EPS Computation.

CASE I: WEIGHTED AVERAGE NUMBER OF SHARES: NO STOCK DIVIDENDS OR SPLITS

To illustrate the basic computation of the weighted average number of common shares outstanding without stock dividends and stock splits, assume that the Herman Corporation begins the current year with 10,000 common shares outstanding. Additional shares of 5,000 and 6,000 were issued on May 1 and October 1 respectively. In addition, the firm purchased 1,000 shares of treasury stock on July 1. The firm's year-end is December 31. Given this information the weighted number of common shares outstanding for the year is computed as follows:

DATE	***NUMBER OF SHARES***	***PERCENT OF YEAR (%)***	***SHARES x %***
1/1	BAL: 10,000	12/12	10,000
5/1	ISSUE: 5,000	8/12	3,333
7/1	T/STK: -1,000	6/12	-500
10/1	ISSUE: 6,000	3/12	1,500
12/31		***Weighted Average***	14,333

Quarterly Computations: (Discrete View)*

Quarter and Date of Transaction	***Number of Shares***	***Weight (Based on months)***	***Weighted Average Number of Shares***
First Quarter			
1/1	10,000	3/3	10,000
Weighted Average First Quarter			10,000

Quarter and Date of Transaction	***Number of Shares***	***Weight (Based on months)***	***Weighted Average Number of Shares***
Second Quarter			
4/1 **Beg. Bal.**	10,000	3/3	10,000
5/1	5,000	2/3	3,333
Weighted Average Second Quarter			13,333

Quarter and Date of Transaction	***Number of Shares***	***Weight (Based on months)***	***Weighted Average Number of Shares***
Third Quarter			
7/1 **Beg. Bal.**	10,000	3/3	10,000
7/1 **Beg. Bal.**	5,000	3/3	5,000
7/1	(1,000)	3/3	(1,000)
Weighted Average Third Quarter			14,000

Quarter and Date of Transaction	***Number of Shares***	***Weight (Based on months)***	***Weighted Average Number of Shares***
Fourth Quarter			
10/1 ***Beg. Bal.***	10,000	3/3	10,000
10/1 ***Beg. Bal.***	5,000	3/3	5,000
10/1 ***Beg. Bal.***	(1,000)	3/3	(1,000)
10/1	6,000	3/3	6,000
Weighted Average Fourth Quarter			20,000

Full Year:

Quarter	***Quarterly Weighted Average Number of Shares***	***Weight (Based on Quarter)***	***Weighted Average Number of Shares***
1	10,000	¼	2,500
2	13,333	¼	3,333
3	14,000	¼	3,500
4	20,000	¼	5,000
	57,333		
Weighted Average Full Year			14,333

****Under the discrete view of the quarter each quarter is cumulated as an independent, stand alone accounting period.***

Alternatively: 57,333 / 4 = 14,333 shares

CASE II: WEIGHTED AVERAGE NUMBER OF SHARES: WITH STOCK DIVIDENDS OR SPLITS

A fundamental concept in the EPS computation is the "if converted" assumption. Under the "if converted" assumption, accountants assume that hypothetical and actual conversions of potentially dilutive securities (e.g., stock options), and, actual stock dividends and stock splits occur at the beginning of the year (if the dilutive security is outstanding at the beginning of the year), or at the issue date of the potentially dilutive security, (if that security is issued during the year). This is a conservative assumption. The concept is considered conservative because, if we assume that all events increasing the number of common shares outstanding occur at the beginning of the year, they would receive a full 12-month (or quarter or 360 day) weight. Therefore, this assumption makes the security more dilutive and results in an even greater reduction of EPS.

In summary, the "if converted" assumption simply states that shares should be included in the EPS computation at the earliest possible point during the year. This determination can be made either at the beginning of the year or at the date when the potentially dilutive security was issued.

In the next illustration, there will be an application of the "if converted" assumption to stock dividends and stock splits in basic EPS. If there are actual stock dividends and stock splits during the year, an adjustment is needed in the weighted average computation to give "retroactive application" of the additional shares "as if" the event took place at the beginning of the year, (if the stock is outstanding at the beginning of the year), or the issue date of the stock, (if the stock is issued during the year). The retroactive application also applies to reverse splits.

In this case, the "if converted" assumption is applied to basic EPS to avoid management manipulation of EPS by the timing of stock dividends and stock splits. Other reasons for the retroactive application of stock dividends and stock splits are discussed in the next paragraph.

Unlike new issues and treasury share purchases, stock dividends and stock splits do not change cash or net assets. That is, stock dividends and stock splits do not change the economic resources available to generate income. As a result, including the additional shares on a retroactive basis does not mismatch the numerator and denominator of the EPS fraction. In addition, retroactive restatement results in the shares before and after the stock dividend or stock split stated on the same basis. The retroactive treatment also applies to stock dividends and stock splits (and reverse splits) implemented during the post-balance sheet period.

It should be noted that treasury stock transactions should be included in the weighted average computation only at the exact date of the acquisition. Again, the rationale behind the special treatment for splits and dividends is that these transactions do not involve corporate resources and therefore without "if converted" could be declared only at year end to avoid any dilution of the current year's EPS. The acquisition of treasury shares, although causing an increase in EPS, could involve substantial cash outflows. As a result, there could be a significant cost to achieve a cosmetic increase in EPS. In addition, it would be in management's best interests to acquire treasury shares earlier in the accounting period so as to maximize the increase in EPS with the fewest number of shares reacquired.

In applying the if-converted assumption to actual stock dividends and stock splits occurring during the period, an adjustment is needed in the weighted average computation in order to give retroactive application to the additional shares as if the event took place at the beginning of the period.

The above illustration is now modified to include a stock dividend. Assume that the Herman Corporation begins the year with 10,000 common shares outstanding. An additional 5,000 shares and 1,000 shares are issued on May 1 and November 1, respectively. In addition, a 10% stock dividend is declared and distributed on July 1. The firm's year-end is still assumed to be December 31. Given the revised assumptions, the weighted average number of common shares outstanding for the year is computed as follows:

DATE	***NUMBER OF SHARES***	***PERCENT OF YEAR (%)***	***SHARES x %***
1/1	BAL. 10,000	12/12	10,000
5/1	ISSUE: 5,000	8/12	3,333
	SUBTOTAL BEFORE DIVIDEND		13,333
7/1	***RETROACTIVE APPLICATION OF THE STOCK DIVIDEND (110%)***		x 1.10
	SUBTOTAL AFTER 10% DIVIDEND		14,666
11/1	ISSUE: +1,000	2/12	+167
12/31		***Weighted Average***	14,833

Quarterly Computations (Discrete View)

Quarter and Date of Transaction	***Number of Shares***	***Weight (Based on months)***	***Weighted Average Number of Shares***
First Quarter			
1/1	10,000	3/3	10,000
Weighted Average First Quarter			10,000

Quarter and Date of Transaction	***Number of Shares***	***Weight (Based on months)***	***Weighted Average Number of Shares***
Second Quarter			
4/1 ***Beg. Bal.***	10,000	3/3	10,000
5/1	5,000	2/3	3,333
Weighted Average Second Quarter			13,333

Quarter and Date of Transaction	***Number of Shares***	***Weight (Based on months)***	***Weighted Average Number of Shares***
Third Quarter			
7/1 ***Beg. Bal.***	10,000	3/3	10,000
7/1 ***Beg. Bal.***	5,000	3/3	5,000
7/1	***10% Stock Div.*** 1,500	3/3	1,500
Weighted Average Third Quarter			16,500

Quarter and Date of Transaction	***Number of Shares***	***Weight (Based on months)***	***Weighted Average Number of Shares***
Fourth Quarter			
10/1 ***Beg. Bal.***	10,000	3/3	10,000
10/1 ***Beg. Bal.***	5,000	3/3	5,000
10/1 ***Beg. Bal.***	***10% Stock Div.*** 1,500	3/3	1,500
11/1	1,000	2/3	667
Weighted Average Fourth Quarter			17,167

Full Year:

Quarter	Quarterly Weighted Average Number of Shares Previously Reported	Quarterly Weighted Average Number of Shares as Adjusted for 10% Stock Dividend	Weight (Based on Quarter)	Weighted Average Number of Shares
1	10,000	11,000	¼	2,750
2	13,333	14,666	¼	3,666
3	-	16,500	¼	4,125
4	-	17,167	¼	4,292
		59,333		
Weighted Average Full Year				14,833

Alternatively: 59,333 / 4 = 14,833 shares

The Effect of Mergers and Acquisitions on EPS

The computation of net income available to common and the weighted average number of common shares becomes more complex with the introduction of merger and acquisition activity.

Because the combination must now be accounted for under the acquisition method, net income is combined and the number of shares issued in the purchase are included in the EPS calculation only as of the date of acquisition. As noted in the chapter covering business combinations, proforma income and EPS information can be disclosed in a footnote, as if the combination took place as of the beginning of the year. However, there are no retroactive adjustments in an acquisition due to the theory underlying the transaction: there is an acquisition or takeover of one entity by another. All items of financial position and the results of operations are stated at the fair value as of the date of acquisition, and only proforma income information can be provided prior to that date. There is a new basis of accountability as of the date of the acquisition.

Simple and Complex Capital Structures

The need for and the extent of the adjustments to the basic EPS ratio will depend on whether the firm is considered to have a simple capital structure or a complex capital structure. The types of capital structure are defined by the accounting standards and are described in the sections that follow.

Simple Capital Structure

A firm is considered to have a simple capital structure if it only issues common and preferred stock, with no potentially dilutive securities. In the case of a simple capital structure, only a basic or unadjusted EPS disclosure is required. This is known as the single presentation.

Complex Capital Structure

A firm is considered to have a complex capital structure if it issues common and preferred stock, potentially dilutive securities and continent share arrangements. Potentially dilutive securities include options (i.e., employee stock options or call options including unissued stock subscriptions but not traded puts and calls); warrants (i.e., longer term options) and convertible securities (i.e., convertible preferred stock and convertible bonds). Contingent share arrangements include "earn out" provision of merger deals where additional shares are issued if a specified level of earnings are reached after a certain period of time following the business combination.

In the case of complex capital structure, the so-called dual presentation is required, unless the results are antidilutive. The dual presentation consists of basic EPS (BEPS) and diluted EPS (DEPS).

The Dual Presentation

As indicated in the previous section, if the firm is considered to have a complex capital structure a dual presentation is required unless the results are antidilotive. The dual presentation consists of basic EPS and diluted EPS.

Basic EPS (BEPS)

The objective of basic EPS is to measure the performance of an entity over the reporting period. As noted earlier, BEPS is computed by dividing income available to common shareholders by the weighted average number of common shares outstanding.

An exception to the above statement relates to contingent shares or contingently issuable shares. Contingent shares are shares that will be issued when certain conditions have been satisfied (e.g., passage of time, reaching a certain earnings level or an "earn out", opening a certain number of retail outlets, etc.). Contingently issuable shares are considered outstanding for BEPS as of the date that all necessary conditions have been satisfied. Contingent shares related to a "earn out" will not be included in BEPS because the final level of earnings is not known with certainty until year end, at which point the weight on the shares will be zero.

The "if converted" assumption is not used for contingent share agreements in BEPS. The shares are considered issued only as of the date all conditions are fully satisfied.

Diluted EPS (DEPS)

The objective of Diluted EPS is consistent with that of Basic EPS; to measure the performance of the firm over the reporting period after giving effect to all dilutive potential common shares that were outstanding during the period.

The computation of DEPS increases the denominator of the fraction to include the number of additional common shares that would have been outstanding if the dilutive potential common shares had been issued. The numerator of the EPS fraction is also adjusted for any interest or preferred dividends avoided on the assumed conversion of convertible securities. Interest on convertible debt is added back to net income after tax. There is no tax effect on preferred dividends because dividends are not expenses for financial reporting and are not usually deductible for tax purposes.

Additional details of the DEPS computation and disclosures will be discussed in the following sections of this chapter.

The "If Converted" Assumption Revisited

The requirement of a dual presentation for a firm with a complex capital structure expands the scope of the if-converted assumption. For diluted EPS, the if-converted assumption requires that:

(1) In general, all actual and hypothetical conversions or exercise of options take place at the beginning of the year if the dilutive security was outstanding for a full year. Conversion or exercise is assumed on the date of issuance, if the dilutive security was issued during the year. Specifically:

(i) If a dilutive security was issued during the year but not converted or exercised during the year, it is included in the weighted average computation "as if converted" only for the portion of the year outstanding. This is true unless its effect is antidilutive.

(ii) If a dilutive security is outstanding from the beginning of the year and is converted or exercised during the period, the "if converted" method is applied from the beginning of the period to the date of actual exercise or conversion. This is true unless its effect is antidilutive.

(iii) If a dilutive security is both issued and converted during the period, it is assumed to be converted only from the time of issuance to the date of actual exercise or conversion. This is true unless its effect is antidilutive.

It should be noted that for actual conversions during the year, actual conversions are given "if converted" treatment to be consistent with the treatment for hypothetical conversions. The additional shares issued on actual exercise or conversion are always included in the weighted average computation for BEPS from the date of actual exercise or conversion to year-end, even if antidilutive. The accounting question for DEPS is whether to give retroactive treatment for the additional shares from the beginning of the year or the date the potentially dilutive security was issued to the date of actual exercise or conversion. If the result of retroactive application of an actual conversion is antidilutive, it cannot be assumed.

(2) Interest on convertible debt, net of tax, and preferred dividends are avoided, (and added back to income available to common), for the periods of time indicated in (1) above on the securities assumed to be converted. The effective tax rate is used for the interest add back on converted debt securities.

Note that for any assumed conversion and exercise during the year, if there is more than one conversion rate or exercise price available on a dilutive security, the accountant would use the most advantageous rate or price from the standpoint of the security holder (i.e., resulting in the greatest number of common shares issued) for diluted EPS.

The implementation of the incremental effects of moving from basic EPS to diluted EPS is illustrated in the following table. The table provides the effects on the numerator and denominator of the EPS fraction as we move from basic to diluted EPS.

	DILUTED EPS		
BASIC EPS	***Convertible Preferred Stock***	***Convertible Debt***	***Options and Warrants***
Net Income – Preferred Dividend Requirements	+ Preferred Dividend Requirements	+ (1- t) x Effective Interest x Weight	+ 0 Assuming Qualified Stock Options
Weighed Average Number of Common Shares Outstanding	+ Number of shares assumed issued on conversion of convertible preferred shares x Weight	+ Number of shares assumed issued on conversion of convertible preferred shares x Weight	+ Number of incremental shares x Weight Incremental shares are equal to the number of shares issued on assumed exercise of "in the money" options less the assumed number of treasury shares purchased with the option proceeds.

Some of the requirements of the if-converted assumption as well as the other provisions of SFAS 128 are illustrated below

EPS Illustration: The "if converted" Assumption

The General Standards Corporation began 2008 with 400,000 common shares outstanding. On October 1, 2008, the company issued an additional 100,000 shares. The company also has $10,000,000 of 8% convertible bonds, convertible into 225,000 shares of common stock. None of the bonds were converted in 2008. The bonds were issued several years ago at par on a date when the market rate of interest on similar debt was also 8%. Therefore, the bonds were issued at their par value because the effective yield of the bonds at the time of issuance was equal to the coupon rate of 8%. The firm also has $1,150,000 par value, 5% nonconvertible, noncumulative preferred stock outstanding. The preferred shares were outstanding for a full year and the dividends were declared for 2008.

If the company's net income after tax was $3,500,000 and the company's effective tax rate was equal to 40%, determine basic and diluted EPS and provide all disclosures required under FASB No. 128.

Solution

The first step in the solution is to determine the basic or unadjusted EPS. This, in turn, requires the computation of the weighted average number of common shares outstanding.

Weighted Average Number of Shares = 400,000 + (3/12 x 100,000) = <u>425,000</u> Shares

Next, the preferred dividend requirements are computed and are equal to $57,500 ($1,150,000 X 5%). The resulting basic EPS is equal to $8.10 as computed below.

$$\text{Basic EPS} = \frac{(\$3{,}500{,}000 - 57{,}500)}{425{,}000 \text{ shares}}$$

$$= \frac{\$3{,}442{,}500}{425{,}000 \text{ shares}} = \$8.10 \text{ / share.}$$

The dual presentation is required if diluted EPS is less than basic EPS (i.e., the results are dilutive). With the existence of potentially dilutive securities in this case, a dual presentation may be required.

In this example, the only potentially dilutive security is the convertible debt. If its effects on EPS are dilutive, the convertible debt must be included in the determination of both diluted EPS. If we assume conversion, the debt would convert into 225,000 additional common shares. With the debt assumed to be converted as of the beginning of the year, the after tax interest savings is equal to $480,000 (i.e., [1 - 40%] X $800,000). The weights on both the additional common shares issued and the after tax interest savings on the assumed conversion are equal to 100% or 12 full months as the debt was outstanding for the full year.

The computation of diluted EPS is presented below.

$$\text{Diluted EPS} = \frac{\$3{,}500{,}000 - 57{,}500 + ([1-40\%] \text{ X } \$800{,}000)}{(425{,}000 \text{ shares} + 225{,}000) \text{ shares}}$$

$$= \frac{\$3{,}922{,}500}{650{,}000 \text{ shares}} = \$6.04 \text{ / share.}$$

Effect of Unusual Items

To illustrate the impact of unusual income statement items on the EPS computation, assume that the $3,500,000 net income reported in the previous illustration consists of the following: Note that the numerator is on adjusted for EPS from continuing operations.

Income from Continuing Operations	**$3,000,000**
Gain on Discontinued operations-net of tax	**500,000**
Net Income	**$3,500,000**

Under this assumption, the disclosure of basic EPS would consist of the following components:

$$\text{Basic EPS from Continuing Operations} = \frac{(\$3{,}000{,}000 - 57{,}500)}{425{,}000 \text{ shares}}$$

$$= \frac{\$2{,}942{,}500}{425{,}000 \text{ shares}} = \$6.92 \text{ / share.}$$

$$\text{Basic EPS On Discontinued Operations} = \frac{\$500{,}000}{425{,}000 \text{ shares}} = \$1.18 \text{ / share}$$

Basic EPS On Net Income = $6.92 + 1.18 = $8.10 / share

Under this assumption, the disclosure of diluted EPS would consist of the following components:

$$\text{Diluted EPS from Continuing Operations} = \frac{\$3{,}000{,}000 - 57{,}500 + ([1\text{-}40\%] \times \$800{,}000)}{(425{,}000 \text{ shares} + 225{,}000) \text{ shares}}$$

$$= \frac{\$3{,}422{,}500}{650{,}000 \text{ shares}} = \$5.27 / \text{share.}$$

$$\text{Diluted EPS On Discontinued Operations} = \frac{\$500{,}000}{650{,}000 \text{ shares}} = \$.77 / \text{share}$$

Diluted EPS On Net Income = $5.27 + .77 = $6.04 / share

Earnings per Share Disclosures

The following information will be disclosed on the face of the income statement directly below net income for the year. Note that the per share amounts for unusual items (discontinued operations) are not required to be shown on the face of the income statement but this is usually done on a voluntary basis.

	For the year ended 2002
Earnings per common share	
Income from continuing operations	$6.92
Gain on discounted operations	1.18
Net income	$8.10
Earnings per common share: assuming dilution	
Income from continuing operations	$5.27
Gain on discounted operations	.77
Net income	$6.04

Footnote Disclosure: The following is a reconciliation of the numerators and denominators of the basic and diluted EPS computations for "income from continuing operations." Note that FASB Statement No. 123, "Accounting for Stock-Based Compensation," requires additional disclosures specifically related to stock-based compensation arrangements.

Description	Income (Numerator)	Shares (Denominator)	Per-Share Amount
	For the Year Ended 2002		
Income from continuing operations	$3,000,000		
Less: Preferred dividend requirements	(57,500)		
Basic EPS			
Income available to common	$2,942,500	425,000	$6.92
Effect of Dilutive Securities			
8% Convertible Debt	480,000	225,000	
Diluted EPS			
Income available to common including the effect of assumed conversions	$3,422,500	650,000	$5.27

Note that this disclosure would include a detailed description of any dilutive securities excluded from the EPS computations because their effect was antidilutive.

THE TREASURY STOCK METHOD FOR THE USE OF THE HYPOTHETICAL PROCEEDS ON THE ASSUMED EXERCISE OF OPTIONS AND WARRANTS

When dealing with the assumed exercise of options (e.g., call options) and warrants, the accountant faces the additional problem of deciding what the corporation does with the proceeds from the exercise of these securities. The treasury stock method is used to account for the hypothetical proceeds received from the assumed conversion of options and warrants. Under the provisions of SFAS 128, the treasury stock method is used to account for the hypothetical proceeds received on the assumed conversion of options and warrants.

Under the treasury stock method, the accountant assumes that the hypothetical proceeds from the exercise are used to purchase treasury stock. Of course the security must be "in the money" to assume exercise. That is, the exercise price must be less than the market price. Not only is this a realistic condition (because an investor would not exercise if it was less expensive to purchase securities in the market), but also it results in "incremental shares". Incremental shares are required for dilution to take place. The proceeds received are based on an exercise price that is less than the market price. With the higher market price, the firm can buy back fewer shares than it issues, resulting in incremental shares.

The next question is to determine the market price to use for the assumed repurchase of treasury stock. If the accountant can assume the exercise of outstanding options and warrants, then he or she must use the average market price for the period (e.g., year, quarter) in all subsequent computations. According to FASB No. 128, the average market price should represent a "meaningful average." In theory, every market transaction for the period should be included in the computation. However, this may not be practical or cost effective, so, a simple average of weekly or monthly prices is usually more than adequate for purposes of this computation. In addition, if there is little fluctuation in share prices during the year, then the closing price is also considered a "meaningful average".

Note again that the exercise of options and warrants can be assumed only if the average market price is greater than the exercise price (i.e., the security is in the money) for the period of the EPS computation.

Using the average market price for the period under consideration, the number of incremental shares should be determined as follows:

$$\text{Incremental shares} = \text{Shares assumed issued} - \text{Treasury shares assumed acquired under the option}$$

$$\text{Treasury shares assumed acquired} = \text{Hypothetical Proceeds / Average Market Price}$$

Where:

$$\text{Hypothetical Proceeds} = \text{Shares assumed issued under the option} \times \text{Exercise Price}$$

Alternatively we have:

$$\text{Incremental Shares} = \frac{\text{Average Market Price - Exercise Price}}{\text{Average Market Price}} \times \text{Shares assumed issued}$$

In general, there is no "in the money" test in the accounting standards for convertible securities. That is, there is no condition requiring that the market value of the common shares issued on conversion exceed the implied strike price on convertible debt. This could result from the fact that most convertible securities are callable at the option of the issuing corporation. The call option can be used to force conversion when the call price is less than value of the equity securities received on conversion.

There are exceptions to this general accounting procedure. To begin with, convertible debt can be issued with a cash settlement option. These securities are known as "treasury stock convertibles" or "Instrument C" convertible debt. Treasury stock convertibles give the issuing corporation the option to settle the conversion provision in cash. This feature creates a put option and the need for an "in the money" test. In this case we use the reverse treasury stock method. The reverse treasury stock method will be discussed in a subsequent section of this chapter.

Another exception occurs in the case of convertible securities issued with a beneficial conversion option. This class of convertible debit was discussed in a previous chapter of this text. To conduct an "in the money" test for this class convertible debt, an implied strike price must be estimated. To illustrate, assume that a corporation issues convertible debt with a par value of $1,000 and each bond is convertible into 250 shares of common stock. In this case there is an implied strike price of $4 per share (i.e., $1,000 par value / 250 shares). If the market price of the company's shares exceeds $4 per share the convertible bonds are in the money and conversion can be assumed for the EPS computation.

The following example illustrates the use of the treasury stock method in the EPS computation.

EPS Illustration: The Treasury Stock Method

Assume that the Woody Corporation earned an after-tax net income of $5,000,000 for fiscal 2008. The firm's tax rate was equal to 40%. The weighted average number of shares was equal to 3,000,000 shares, which was also equal to the number of outstanding shares at year end.

The average for the year market price for Woody's common stock was $40 per share while the year-end closing price was $57 per share. Woody had outstanding options outstanding to acquire 1,000,000 shares of common stock at an exercise price of $30/share. The exercise price was below the market price of the stock for the entire year, so that the options were in the money for the period of the EPS computation.

Woody also had 100,000 shares of $100 par value, 10% nonconvertible, noncumulative preferred stock outstanding as of the beginning of the year. The dividend rate is $2 per share and dividends were declared by the Board of Directors. Based on this information, you are asked to compute both basic and diluted EPS and provide the disclosures required under SFAS 128.

Solution

The first step in any EPS computation is the determination of the unadjusted or basic EPS for the period.

The preferred dividend requirements for the EPS computation are $200,000 (i.e.,.100,000 x $2 = $200,000). Basic EPS is presented below:

$$\text{Basic EPS} = \frac{\$5{,}000{,}000 - 200{,}000}{3{,}000{,}000 \text{ shares}} = \$1.60 \text{ / share}$$

The only potentially dilutive securities in Woody's capital structure are the options. The preferred shares are not convertible and are not potentially dilutive. Given that the options are potentially dilutive, the treasury stock method must be employed to determine if there are incremental shares that are needed for dilution to take place.

The hypothetical proceeds from the exercise of options are equal to $30,000,000 (i.e., 1,000,000 X $30). Using the average market price of $40 per share, the proceeds are sufficient to purchase 750,000 treasury shares ($30,000,000/$40). Therefore, there are 250,000 incremental shares (i.e., 1,000,000 - 750,000).

Alternatively,

$$\text{Incremental Shares} = \frac{\text{Average Market Price} - \text{Exercise Price}}{\text{Average Market Price}} \times \text{Shares Assumed Issued}$$

$$\text{Incremental Shares} = \frac{\$40 - 30}{\$40} \times 1{,}000{,}000 = 250{,}000 \text{ shares}$$

Diluted EPS is Computed below.

$$\text{Diluted EPS} = \frac{\$5{,}000{,}000 - 200{,}000}{(3{,}000{,}000 + 250{,}000)\text{ shares}} = \$1.48 / \text{Share}$$

Earnings per Share Disclosures

The following information will be disclosed on the face of the income statement directly below net income for the year. Note that the per share amounts for unusual items (e.g. discontinued operations) are not required to be shown on the face of the income statement, but is usually done on a voluntary basis.

	For the year ended 20XX
Earnings per common share	
Net income	$1.60
Earnings per common share: assuming dilution	
Net income	$1.48

The following is a reconciliation of the numerators and denominators of the basic and diluted EPS computations for "income from continuing operations." Note that FASB Statement No. 123, "Accounting for Stock-Based Compensation," requires additional disclosures specifically related to stock-based compensation arrangements.

	For the Year Ended 20XX		
Description	***Income (Numerator)***	***Shares (Denominator)***	***Per-Share Amount***
Income from continuing operations	$5,000,000		
Less: Preferred dividend requirements	(200,000)		
Basic EPS			
Income available to common	$4,800,000	3,000,000	$1.60
Effect of Dilutive Securities			
Options and warrants	- 0 -	250,000	
Diluted EPS			
Income available to common including the effect of assumed exercise of the options	$4,800,000	3,250,000	$1.48

This disclosure would include a detailed description of any dilutive securities excluded from the EPS computations because their effect was antidilutive.

OTHER ISSUES IN THE EPS COMPUTATION

Contingent Share Arrangements with Diluted Earnings per Share

Shares that are contingently issuable upon the satisfaction of certain conditions are considered outstanding and included in the computation of diluted EPS as follows:

- If all necessary conditions have been satisfied by the end of the period, the shares will be included in the computation as of the beginning of the period or as of the date of the contingent agreement, if later.
- If all necessary conditions have not been satisfied by the end of the period, the number of contingently issuable shares included in the diluted EPS computation would be based on the number of shares issuable if the end of the reporting period was the end of the contingency period. For example, if a contingent share agreement is based on earnings for the period ended 6/30/2009 and that earnings level was reached at 12/31/2008, the contingent shares will be included in the diluted EPS figure for the year ended 2008. This treatment is based on the assumption that the current amount of earnings will remain unchanged until the end of the agreement.

As mentioned earlier, the additional shares should also be included in the denominator of basic EPS only as of the date when all conditions of a contingent share arrangement have been satisfied. The primary exception relates to a contingency based on earnings (e.g., an "earn out"). Because the amount of earnings may change in a future period when the contingency date is reached, basic EPS cannot include the contingently issuable shares based on earnings since all necessary conditions have not been satisfied. Even in those cases where the contingent level of earnings is met at the end of a contingency period that coincides with the end of the reporting period, the additional shares contingent on earnings would *not be included* in basic EPS. This results from the fact that the contingent level of earnings is only known (the contingency is satisfied) at the end of the reporting period where the weight on the shares would be zero.

Antidilution

The computation of diluted EPS cannot assume a conversion, exercise or contingent issuance of securities that would increase EPS (i.e., have an antidilutive on EPS). Of course, shares issued on actual conversion, exercise or satisfaction of certain conditions for which the effect was antidilutive would be included in the computation of the weighted average number of common shares outstanding but only from the date of actual conversion, exercise or satisfaction of certain conditions. That is, the "if converted" method would not be assumed when its effect is antidilutive.

In testing for dilution (or antidilution), each issue of potential common shares should be considered in sequence from the most dilutive to the least dilutive. That is, the potential common shares with the lowest "earnings per incremental share" should be included in the diluted EPS computation before those with higher earnings per incremental share. This is known as antidilution sequencing. An illustration of antidilution sequencing is presented below.

Illustration: Antidilution Sequencing

Assume that Classic Company provides the following information for the year ended December 31, 2008.

Classic reported net income available to common of $3,000,000 for the year. This amount is net of a deduction of $96,000 for preferred dividends (see the information below). The company is subject to a 40% tax rate. Classic reported 600,000 shares of common stock outstanding for the entire year. The average market price of the Company's common stock was $25 per share for the year.

The company also had the potentially dilutive securities outstanding for the full year. These securities included options to acquire 30,000 shares of common stock at an exercise price of $20 per share. Several years ago, the Company issued 24,000 shares of $4 convertible preferred stock. Each preferred share is convertible into 1 share of common stock. The board of directors declared the preferred dividends for the year. Finally, Classic issued $3,000,000 face value, 5% convertible bonds at par on January 1, 2008. Each $1,000 par value bond is convertible into 250 shares of common stock. Based on this information, you are asked to compute basic and diluted EPS and provide the disclosures required by SFAS 128.

Solution

Since there are several potentially dilutive securities in the company's capital structure, Classic must employ antidilution sequencing. The first step is to prepare the incremental per share effect of each of the potentially dilutive securities and rank each from lowest to the highest amount.

The options required the use of the treasury stock method. The computations for the treasury stock method are presented below.

$$\text{Incremental Shares} = \frac{\text{Average Market Price} - \text{Exercise Price}}{\text{Average Market Price}} \times \text{Shares Assumed Issued}$$

$$\text{Incremental Shares} = \frac{\$25 - 20}{\$25} \times 30{,}000 = \underline{6{,}000} \text{ shares}$$

or

Hypothetical option proceeds = $20 x 30,000 = $600,000

Treasury shares = $600,000 / $25 = 24,000 shares

Incremental shares = 30,000 - 24,000 = <u>6,000</u> shares

Computations relating to the convertible preferred stock and the convertible bonds are presented below.

Preferred dividends = $4 x 24,000 = <u>$96,000</u>

Debt interest after tax = $3,000,000 x 5% = $150,000 x (1 - .4) = $90,000

Shares issued on assumed debt conversion:

$3,000,000 / $1,000 = 3,000 bonds x 250 shares per bond = 750,000 shares.

The incremental per share effects and the ranking from lowest to highest is determined in the following table:

Determination of Earnings per Incremental Share				
Potentially Dilutive Security	***Increase in Income***	***Increase in the Number of Common Shares***	***Earnings per Incremental Share***	***Rank for Order of Entry into the Diluted EPS Computation***
Options	- 0 -	6,000	$ - 0 -	1st
Convertible preferred stock	$96,000	24,000	$4.00	3rd
5% convertible bonds	$90,000	750,000	$ .12	2nd

The potentially dilutive securities should be brought into the diluted EPS computation individually in sequence rather than in the aggregate. The sequence flows from the most dilutive to the least dilutive. In this case the order is: options, convertible bonds and convertible preferred stock.

Computation of Diluted Earnings per Share using Antidilution Sequencing				
Description	***Income Available to Common***	***Common Shares***	***Per Share***	
Basic EPS	$3,000,000	600,000	$5.00	
1st: Options	- 0 -	6,000		
	$3,000,000	606,000	$4.95	***Dilutive***
2nd: 5% convertible bonds	90,000	750,000		
	$3,090,000	1,356,000	$2.28	***Dilutive***
3rd: Convertible preferred stock	96,000	24,000		
	$3,186,000	1,380,000	$2.31	***Antidilutive***

Because diluted EPS increases from $2.28 to $2.31 when the convertible preferred shares are included in the computation, these shares are antidilutive and must be excluded from the computation of diluted EPS. As a result, diluted EPS is reported as $2.28.

Sample EPS disclosures are shown in Exhibit 9.1.

EXHIBIT 9.1: BROWN CORPORATION AND SUBSIDIARIES EARNINGS PER SHARE DISCLOSURES

Consolidated Statements of Earnings
Brown Corporation and Subsidiaries

	Years ended December 31,		
($ in millions, except per share amounts)	2012	2011	2010
Net sales	$ 6,901.44	$ 6,528.24	$ 5,972.40
Costs and expenses			
Cost of sales (excluding depreciation and amortization)	5,786.88	5,320.20	4,896.24
Depreciation and amortization	256.2	258.12	246.6
Acquisition costs (gains)	25.44	(18.24)	(4.44)
Selling, general and administrative	277.92	321.48	281.04
	6,346.44	5,881.56	5,419.44
Earnings before interest and taxes	555	646.68	552.96
Interest expense			
Interest expense before debt refinancing costs	116.52	124.44	151.08
Debt refinancing costs	23.16	–	18.24
Total interest expense	139.68	124.44	169.32
Earnings before taxes	415.32	522.24	383.64
Tax provision	(11.16)	(167.04)	(120.12)
Noncontrolling	(0.96)	(1.2)	(1.2)
Equity in results of affiliates	18.6	0.72	13.56
Net earnings	**$ 313.8**	**$ 354.72**	**$ 275.88**
Earnings per share (Note 20):			
Basic	$ 2.916	$ 3.204	$ 2.472
Diluted	$ 2.856	$ 3.12	$ 2.412
Weighted average shares outstanding (000s) (Note 20):			
Basic	129,310	133,015	134,052
Diluted	131,678	136,548	137,130
Cash dividends declared and paid, per share	$ 0.48	$ 0.42	$ 0.288

Notes to Consolidated Financial Statements
Brown Corporation and Subsidiaries

20. Earnings Per Share

The following table provides additional information on the computation of earnings per share amounts. Share and per share information have been retroactively restated for the two-for-one stock splits.

($ in millions, except per share amounts)	Years ended December 31, 2012	2011	2010
Diluted Earnings per Share:			
Net earnings	$ 313.8	$ 354.72	$ 275.88
Weighted average common shares (000s)	129,310	133,015	134,052
Dilutive effect of stock options and restricted shares	2,369	3,533	3,078
Weighted average shares applicable to diluted earnings per share	131,678	136,548	137,130
Diluted earnings per share	$ 2.856	$ 3.12	$ 2.412

Certain options have been excluded from the computation of the diluted earnings per share calculation since they were anti-dilutive (i.e., the exercise price exceeded the average closing market price of common stock for the year). A total of 851,100 options at an exercise price of $47.69 and 767,280 options at an exercise price of $33.79 were excluded for the years ended December 31, 2012 and 2010, respectively. There were no anti-dilutive options for the year ended December 31, 2011.

NET LOSS PER SHARE

When additional shares are included in the denominator of the diluted EPS ratio for continuing operations it will always result in antidilutive per share amounts when there is a loss from continuing operations (after increasing the loss for any preferred dividends). Therefore, no potential common shares should be included in the computation of any diluted EPS amounts when a loss from continuing operations exists, even if the firm reports a net income for the period. A loss from continuing operations can be more than offset by an extraordinary gain resulting in a net income for the period.

To illustrate, assume you are given the following information about the PJS Company:

- Outstanding shares = 20,000 shares.
- Shares "issuable" on options = 10,000 "incremental" shares
- Two cases are presented below:

	Case A	***Case B***
Income (Loss) from continuing operations	**$500,000**	**($600,000)**
Extraordinary item (net of tax)	**(600,000)**	**500,000**
Net Income (Loss)	**($100,000)**	**($100,000)**
Basic EPS (20,000 shares): • ***Continuing Operations*** • ***Extraordinary Items*** • ***Net Income***	**$25** **(30)** **($ 5)**	**($30)** **25** **($ 5)**
Diluted EPS (30,000 shares): • ***Continuing Operations*** • ***Extraordinary Items*** • ***Net Income***	**$17** **(20)** **($ 3)**	***Antidilutive***

Note for Case A: The results are considered dilutive as long as EPS on income from continuing operations is reduced when the options are considered, even if EPS on net income is higher for DEPS than BEPS (i.e., ($3) > ($5)).

Exhibit 9.2 illustrates disclosures when a net loss per share is reported.

EXHIBIT 9.2 SAMPLE DISCLOSURES FOR NET LOSS PER SHARE ARE PRESENTED BELOW

Roe Incorporated

Consolidated Statements of Operations	*(Dollars in millions, except per share)*		
	2012	2011	2010
Net sales	$ 2,215	$ 2,046	$ 2131.2
Cost of sales	1,400	1,248	1359.6
Selling, general and administrative expenses	432	417.6	477.6
Research and development	46.8	50.4	63.6
Goodwill and intangible asset amortization (Note 5)	9.6	10.8	28.8
Other operating expense (income), net (Note 21)	20.4	55.2	(19.2)
Profit from operations	306	264	220.8
Interest and debt expense (Note 25)	157.2	118.8	244.8
Preferred security distributions of subsidiary trusts		69.6	69.6
Other expense, net (Note 18)	34.8	138	9.6
Income (loss) before income taxes and equity income (loss)	114	(62.4)	(103.2)
Provision (benefit) for income taxes (Note 10)	25.2	(3.6)	16.8
Income (loss) before equity income (loss)	88.8	(58.8)	(120)
Equity income (loss) of affiliated companies, net of tax	-	2.4	(10.8)
Net income (loss) from continuing operations before discontinued Operations and extraordinary items	88.8	(56.4)	(130.8)
Net income (loss) on discontinued operations, net of tax (Note 30)	4.8	(235.2)	67.2
Net income (loss) before extraordinary items			
in accounting principle	93.6	(291.6)	(63.6)
Extraordinary items, net of tax	(39.6)	(441.6)	
Net income (loss)	$ 54	$ (733.2)	$ (63.6)
Earnings (loss) per share (Note 18)			
Basic earnings (loss) per share			
Continuing operations	$ 0.828	$ (0.528)	$ (1.248)

Discontinued operations	$ 0.048	$ (2.22)	$ 0.636
Cumulative effect of changes in accounting principle	$ (0.372)	$ (4.164)	$
Net income (loss)	$ 0.504	$ (6.912)	$ (0.612)
Weighted average number of shares (millions)	129.36	127.2	125.76
Diluted earnings (loss) per share			
Continuing operations	$ 0.828	$ (0.528)	$ (1.248)
Discontinued operations	$ 0.048	$ (2.22)	$ 0.636
Cumulative effect of changes in accounting principle	$ (0.372)	$ (4.164)	$
Net income (loss)	$ 0.504	$ (6.912)	$ (0.612)
Weighted average number of shares (millions)	129.48	127.2	125.76

The accompanying accounting policies and notes are an integral part of the consolidated financial statements.

18. Earnings (Loss) per Share

The following table shows the amounts used in computing earnings (loss) per share and the effect on income (loss) and the weighted-average number of shares of dilutive common stock:

(Dollars in millions, except per share)

	2012		2011		2010	
	Earnings (loss)	Income (loss) per share	Loss	Loss per share	(Loss) income	(Loss) earnings per share
Basic:						
Continuing operations	$ 88.8	$ 0.828	$ (56.4)	$ (0.528)	$ (130.8)	$ (1.248)
Discontinued operations	14.8	0.048	(235.2)	(2.22)	67.2	0.636
Extraordinary items	(39.6)	(0.372)	(441.6)	(4.1647)	-	-
Net income (loss)	$ 54	$ 0.504	$ (733.2)	$ (6.912)	$ (63.6)	$ (0.612)
Weighted average number of basic shares (millions)	129.36 (b)		127.2 (b)		125.76 (b)	
Diluted:						
Continuing operations	$ 88.8	$ 0.828	$ (56.4)	$ (0.528)	$ (1.308)	$ (1.248)
Discontinued operations	4.8	0.048	(235.2)	(2.22)	67.2	0.636
Extraordinary items	(39.6)	(0.372)	(441.6)	(4.164)	-	-
Net income (loss)	$ 54	$ 0.504	$ (733.2)	$ (6.912)	$ (63.6)	$ (0.612)
Weighted average number of diluted shares (millions)	129.48 (a,b)	127.2 (a,b)	125.76	(a,b)	104.8 (a,b)	

(a) For the years ended December 31, 2012, 2011 and 2010, the Company had approximately 0.24 million convertible subordinated debentures. However, the common stock shares into which these debentures are convertible have not been included in the dilutive share calculations for the years 2011 and 2010 because the impact of their inclusion would be anti-dilutive.

(b) The Company has restated its basic and diluted weighted-average number of shares pursuant to the method prescribed by SOP 93-6 which requires the exclusion of unallocated employee stock ownership plan shares from the calculation of shares outstanding (see Note 1).

Hansen Company Consolidated Statements of Operations
Years Ended December 31

(In millions except per share amounts)	**2012**	2011	2010
Net sales	**$ 20,112**	$ 19,220	$ 18,980
Cost of sales	**16,030**	16,397	15,136
Administrative and selling expenses	**1,438**	1,357	1,340
Research and development expenses	**539**	547	608
Total operating expenses	**18,007**	18,301	17,084
Operating income	**2,105**	919	1,896
Interest expense	**596**	835	913
Interest income	**(32)**	(43)	(30)
Other expense (income), net	**252**	(22)	14
Non-operating expense, net	**816**	770	898
Income from continuing operations before taxes	**1,289**	149	998
Federal and foreign income taxes	**383**	127	426
Income from continuing operations	**906**	22	572
Loss from discontinued operations, net of tax	**(1,064)**	(908)	(407)
Income (loss) before extraordinary items	**(158)**	(887)	(166)
Extraordinary gain (loss) from debt repurchases, net of tax	**(612)**	(19)	—
Net income (loss)	**$ (768)**	$ (906)	$ 166
Earnings per share from continuing operations			
Basic	**$ 2.23** $	$ 0.06	$ 1.69
Diluted	**2.22**	0.06	1.68
Earnings (loss) per share			
Basic	**$ (1.91)**	$ (2.54)	**$** 0.49
Diluted	**(1.88)**	(2.51)	0.48

Notes to Consolidated Financial Statements:

Basic earnings per share (EPS) is computed by dividing net income by the weighted- average shares outstanding during the period. Diluted EPS reflects the potential dilution that could occur if securities or other contracts to issue common stock were exercised or converted into common stock or resulted in the issuance of common stock that then shared in the earnings of the entity.

The weighted-average shares outstanding for basic and diluted EPS were as follows:

(In thousands)	**2012**	2011	2010
Average common shares outstanding for basic EPS	**481,733**	428,060	406,088
Dilutive effect of stock options, restricted stock, and equity security units	**7,904**	5,527	3,253
Shares for diluted EPS	**489,637**	433,587	409,341

Stock options to purchase 28.4 million, 24.6 million, and 26.8 million shares of common stock outstanding at December 31, 2012, 2011, and 2010, respectively, did not affect the computation of diluted EPS. The exercise prices for these options were greater than the average market price of the Company's common stock during the respective years.

Stock options to purchase 21.5 million, 18.6 million, and 12.1 million shares of common stock outstanding at December 31, 2012, 2011, and 2010, respectively, had exercise prices that were less than the average market price of the Company's common stock during the respective periods and are included in the dilutive effect of stock options, restricted stock, and equity security units in the table above.

The Reverse Treasury Stock Method for Written Put Options

Contracts that require the firm repurchase its own shares (e.g. written put options or forward purchase contracts), will be reflected in the computation of diluted EPS if the effect is dilutive. The reverse treasury stock method is also used for treasury stock convertibles (i.e., Instrument C convertible securities). These contracts are "in the money" if the exercise price is greater than the market price of the shares for the period. In this case, the firm agrees to purchase the shares at the exercise price. The holder of such an option would only exercise if the exercise (selling) price is higher than the market price.

For contracts that are in the money, the dilutive effects are determined by the reverse treasury stock method:

- Issuance of sufficient common shares will be assumed at the beginning of the period (at the average market price during the period) to raise sufficient proceeds to satisfy the contract.
- The proceeds from the issuance of the shares will be used to buy back the shares as specified by the contract.
- The incremental shares (the difference between the shares issued and the shares received from satisfying the repurchase contract) will be included in the denominator of diluted EPS.

To illustrate, assume that Sipping Ltd. grants 1,000 put options with an exercise price of $30. The average market price for the period was $25 per share. Because the exercise price of the put option exceeds the average market price for the period, the put options are "in the money."

In computing diluted EPS at the end of the period, Sipping would assume that it issued 1,200 shares at $25 per share (i.e., [1,000 x $30] / $25 = $30,000 / $25 = 1,200 shares). This generates the $30,000 needed to satisfy the conditions of the put option contract. The difference between the 1,200 shares issued and the 1,000 shares reacquired under the terms of the put option contract results in 200 incremental shares and would be added to the denominator of diluted EPS.

THE TWO-CLASS METHOD[3]

Under FASB Statement No. 128, the two-class method applies to all entities with more than one class of nonconvertible securities. Application of the two-class method has been clarified by the emerging issues task force. Some companies that issue securities that are entitled to participate in dividends with common stocks will report lower earnings per share under a new consensus by the Emerging Issues Task Force than under previous requirements. The consensus clarifies what is meant by a "participating security," provides guidance on applying the two-class method for computing EPS, and requires affected companies to retroactively restate EPS amounts presented.

The two-class method is an earnings allocation formula for computing EPS. It determines EPS for each class of common stock and participating securities according to dividends declared or accumulated and participation rights in undistributed earnings. Statement 128 requires companies with participating securities or more than one class of common stock to use this method to compute EPS.

A Participating Security

Companies found it difficult to apply the description of a participating security in Statement 128, so the EITF developed this formal definition of the term: "A security that may participate in undistributed earnings with common stock, whether that participation is conditioned upon the occurrence of a specified event or not, regardless of the form of participation."

Under this definition, securities or other contracts that entitle their holders to obtain common stock (such as options, warrants, forwards, convertible debt, and convertible preferred stock) are participating securities if they can participate in undistributed earnings with common shareholders. According to the consensus, awards accounted for under stock-compensation literature, such as options and non-vested stock, are not considered participating securities for EPS purposes before they are fully vested, even if such instruments entitle their holders to receive dividends along with holders of common stock prior to vesting.

Provisions of convertible securities that reduce the conversion price or increase the conversion ratio when dividends to common shareholders are declared are not participation features for EPS computations. In contrast, a provision in a forward contract to issue an entity's equity shares that reduces the contract price per share when dividends are declared is a participation right for EPS calculations, assuming it noncontingently transfers value to the holder of the forward contract if dividends are declared. All of the forward contract's relevant terms must be considered in determining whether value is noncontingently transferred to the holder of the forward contract.

---

3. The following is adapted from KPMG's ***Defining Issues***, April 2004, No. 04-8., "Participating Securities" for EPS Calculations."

Allocating Earnings and Losses

Net earnings must be reduced by the amount of dividends declared in the current period for each class of stock and by the contractual amount of dividends or other participation payments that are paid or accumulated for the current period. Undistributed earnings for a period should be allocated to a participating security based on the contractual participation rights of the security to share in those current earnings assuming all earnings for the period are distributed.

This is not a fair value analysis. It is an allocation process based on the terms of the securities. An entity would allocate losses to a participating security in periods of net loss if the participating security's contractual terms provide not only the right to participate in the issuer's earnings, but also an obligation to share in the issuing entity's losses on a basis that is objectively determinable.

For purposes of applying this guidance, a participating security holder has an obligation to share in the losses of the issuing entity if the holder is obligated to fund the issuing entity's losses (i.e., the holder is obligated to write a check) without any corresponding increase in the holder's investment interest) or if losses incurred by the issuing entity reduce the participating security's principal or mandatory redemption amount. A holder is not obligated to share in the losses of the issuing entity solely because the losses reduce the holder's liquidation preference or reduce the issuing entity's ability to pay dividends to the participating security holder in the future.

The two-class method is now required for participating convertible securities when computing basic EPS. This changes earlier GAAP guidance, which permitted companies to make an accounting policy election to use the if-converted method, rather than the two-class method, in the basic EPS computation as long as the if-converted method was not less dilutive than the two-class method. The consensus supersedes the earlier guidance.

Presentation and Disclosure

Presentation of basic and diluted EPS for securities other than common stock is not required, but it is permitted. What is required is the adjustment to the earnings that are used to compute EPS for the common stock. The consensus does not affect Statement 128's other required disclosures, including basic and diluted EPS for each class of common stock (e.g., presentation of EPS information for tracking stocks continues to be required).

ILLUSTRATION: BASIC EPS WITH PARTICIPATING CONVERTIBLE PREFERRED STOCK

Assume that AW Company has 10,000 shares of common stock and 5,000 shares of preferred stock outstanding during 20X4, and has net income of $115,000. Each share of preferred stock is convertible into two shares of common stock. The preferred stock is entitled to a non-cumulative annual dividend of $5 per share. After the common stock has been paid a dividend of $2 per share, the preferred stock then participates in any additional dividends on a 40:60 per share ratio with the common.

This results in the following allocation percentages:

Common: 10,000 shares x .60	=	6,000 weighted shares
Preferred: 5,000 shares x .40	=	2,000 weighted shares

Giving common 6/8 or 75% of the undistributed earnings and preferred 2/8 or 25% of the undistributed earnings.

For 20X4, assume that a total of $53,000 of dividends have been distributed and the common shareholders have been paid $26,000 (or $2.60 per share), and the preferred shareholders have been paid $27,000 (or $5.40 per share).

Description	***Preferred***	***Common***	***Total***
Regular preferred dividend: (5,000 shares x $5)	$25,000		$25,000
Common dividend: (10,000 x $2)		$20,000	20,000
Total before participation			$45,000
Preferred participation: ($53,000 – 45,000 = $8,000 X 25%)	2,000		2,000
Common participation: ($53,000 – 45,000 = $8,000 X 75%)		6,000	6,000
Total Dividend Distribution	$27,000	$26,000	$53,000
Outstanding shares	5,000	10,000	
Income allocated to Basic EPS	$5.40	$2.60	

Basic earnings per share under the two-class method for 20X4 would be computed as follows:

Net income		**$115,000**
Less dividends paid:		
Common	**$26,000**	
Preferred	**27,000**	**53,000**
Undistributed 20X1 earnings		**$ 62,000**

Allocation of undistributed earnings:

To preferred:

25% x $62,000 = $15,500

$15,500 ÷ 5,000 shares = $3.10 per share

To common:

75% x $62,000 = $46,500

$46,500 ÷ 10,000 shares = $4.65 per share

The basic earnings per share amounts are presented below:

Description	Preferred	Common
Distributed earnings (as above)	$5.40	$2.60
Undistributed earnings	3.10	4.65
Totals: BEPS	$8.50	$7.25

Basic EPS without application of the Two-Class method is presented below: (based on preferred dividends declared):

$$\text{Basic EPS} = \frac{(\$115{,}000 - 27{,}000)}{10{,}000 \text{ shares}}$$

$$= \frac{\$88{,}000}{10{,}000 \text{ shares}} = \$8.80 \text{ / share.}$$

Note that there is an 18% (i.e., ($8.80 – 7.25) / $8.80 = 18%) decrease in basic EPS from the application of the two-class method.

V. FASB STATEMENT NO. 129, "DISCLOSURE OF INFORMATION ABOUT CAPITAL STRUCTURE"

FASB Statement No. 129 requires detailed disclosures of information about a firm's capital structure. The Statement consolidates the various disclosure requirements found in several other pronouncements. The provisions of FASB Statement No. 129 are applicable to both public and nonpublic entities.

The Statement's required disclosures must include the following information:

- Dividend and liquidation preferences
- Participation rights
- Call prices and dates
- Conversion or exercise prices or rates and pertinent dates
- Sinking fund requirements
- Unusual voting rights
- Significant terms of contracts to issue additional shares
- The aggregate or per share amounts at which preferred stock may be called or is subject to redemption through sinking fund operations or otherwise
- The aggregate or per share amounts of arrearages in cumulative preferred dividends

The Statement also requires the following disclosures with respect to the liquidation preferences of preferred stock and redeemable preferred stock.

Liquidation preference of preferred stock

When the firm issues preferred shares with preference in involuntary liquidation considerably in excess of par or stated value, the liquidation preference should be disclosed in the equity section of the balance sheet, either parenthetically or in the footnotes to the financial statements.

Redeemable stock

When an entity issues redeemable stock, it should disclose the amount of redemption requirements, separately by issue or combined, for all issues of capital stock that are redeemable at fixed or determinable prices on fixed or determinable dates in each of the five years following the latest balance sheet presented.

CHAPTER 10 Revenue and Expense Recognition Issues

INTRODUCTION: CONCEPTS RELATED TO THE INCOME STATEMENT

Revenue and expense recognition have become critical issues in financial reporting. The acceleration or deferral of revenues and expenses can be used by management as a tool to smooth income and achieve other objectives of a firm's financial reporting strategy. The manipulation of revenue and expense recognition has been cited in many recent financial reporting failures and has prompted standard setters to reconsider the propriety of income reporting and disclosure.

This chapter discusses key concepts and issues related to revenue and expense recognition and will focus on the analytical problems that result from employing various earnings management techniques. The conceptual foundation underlying revenue and expense recognition forms the basis of accrual account and measurement issues on the income statement.

The concepts identified with the income statement are concerned with revenue and expense recognition and provide the foundation for the accrual basis of accounting.

The two primary concepts related to the income statement are the revenue realization concept and the matching principle.

Revenue Realization Concept

According to the FASB in Statement of Financial Accounting Concepts No. 5, "Recognition and Measurement in Financial Statements of Business Enterprises"[1], revenue is recognized when a transaction occurs and (1) the revenue is realized or realizable and (2) the revenue is earned.

Revenue from a transaction must meet both criteria in order to be recognized. Revenue is generally considered realized when cash is received for the sale of a product or performance of a service. Revenue generally becomes realizable when a promise to pay is received in exchange for the sale of a product or performance of a service. The promise to pay could be verbal (account receivable) or written (note receivable).

Revenue is generally earned when a legally enforceable exchange takes place (e.g., consideration has been tendered and the buyer takes possession of the product or benefits from the performance of a service).

An alternative and perhaps more practical view of revenue recognition states that revenue is recognized when: (1) an exchange has taken place and (2) the earning process is essentially complete. The earning process is complete when there are no material uncertainties as to future costs to be incurred and collectibility.

Both definitions of revenue recognition are supported by the SEC in Staff Accounting Bulletins 101 and 104 [2]:

Revenue generally is realized or realizable and earned when all of the following criteria are met:

---

1. Predecessor literature "Recognition and Measurement in Financial Statements of Business Enterprises," *Statement of Financial Accounting Concepts No. 5* (Stamford, Conn.: FASB, December 1984).

2. FASB ASC 605, ASC 605 [Predecessor literature: "Revenue Recognition in Financial Statements," *Staff Accounting Bulletin No. 101* (Washington, D.C.: SEC, Decemeber 2003)].

1. There is persuasive evidence that an arrangement exists
2. Delivery has occurred or services have been rendered
3. The seller's price to the buyer is fixed or determinable, and
4. Collectibility is reasonably assured.

The theory and the accounting rules governing revenue recognition seem to imply that implementation of these standards should be straightforward with little room for discretion. However, there have been several revenue recognition concept implementation problems in practice. For example, software manufacturers deferred and amortized a portion of revenues earned from the sales of its packaged software products using the theory that, due to the material uncertainties involved with the future costs of supporting the new products, the earnings process was not substantially complete at the point of sale. In addition, the revenue could not be recognized for the customer support because the product support was not delivered and there was no exchange.

Although deferral of revenue recognition for the undelivered product support is justified by current accounting standards, some software manufacturers may have taken an overly aggressive position in delaying revenue recognition for its promise to deliver customer service on its products. If one can argue that the earnings process was not complete, then revenue should not be recognized in the year of the sale (and in the year of cash receipts) In this case, cash flow preceded revenue recognition. This is sometimes called "cookie jar" or "rainy day" reserves.

The Matching Principle

Expense recognition is governed by the matching principle. Under the matching principle, expenses (costs) are to be recognized only in the period in which the related revenues (benefits) are received. This principle will justify "capitalization" of the cost of a productive asset (e.g., delivery van). Capitalization is also called the deferral or prepayment of cost or recording cost as an asset. The accountant will expense (depreciate or amortize) this capitalized cost only in the future when revenues are earned (e.g., deliveries are made).

As is the case with revenue recognition reporting issues, the expense/capitalization alternative is a key issue in the analysis of financial statements and continues to create implementation problems for the expense recognition. Specifically, the matching principle could be used in practice to justify the improper deferral (capitalization) of a cost as an asset in the current year and only expensed and matched against revenues in the future. This practice would overstate assets and book value over the asset's life. Income will be overstated in the current period and would be understated in all subsequent periods through the amortization or depreciation process, unless the cost deferral can be implemented each year.

For example, internet provides capitalized part of the cost of mailing free "starter" disks as "deferred advertising" on the asset side of the balance sheet. The argument in this case was that these starter disks would generate additional subscriptions and the proportion of these advertising dollars that increased sales can be estimated. The portion of the total cost of mailing expected to increased revenue was deferred and amortized over the average subscription period. The SEC criticized this practice and these entities were forced to take a one-time charge to write off the balance of its deferred advertising. AOL no longer follows this practice.

The Cash Basis Versus the Accrual Basis of Accounting

Only the accrual basis of accounting is acceptable under GAAP.

Under the cash basis, revenues are recognized only when cash is received and expenses are recognized only when cash is paid. This approach to revenue and expense recognition is not acceptable because it only measures cash receipts and disbursements and does not measure economic activity. In addition, net income can be manipulated by the "timing" of cash flows.

Under the accrual basis, revenues are recognized when earned according to the revenue realization concept and expenses are recognized when incurred according to the matching principle, regardless of when cash is received or paid. The accrual basis gives rise to "accruals" (the economic event is recognized before the cash event) and "deferrals" (the economic event is recognized after the cash event). It should be noted that the statement of cash flows is not a violation of the accrual basis of accounting. Rather, it should be viewed as presenting the cash flows that result from the economic activity properly reported under the accrual basis of accounting.

CURRENT REVENUE AND EXPENSE RECOGNITION ISSUES

The previous discussion clearly indicates that revenue and expense recognition continues to be a difficult issue for standard setters to resolve in practice. The primary problems in revenue and expense recognition focus on the issue of whether or not reported earnings reflect the underlying cash flows of the firm. There are several key issues in revenue recognition. These issues include; gross versus net presentation of revenue on the income statement; barter transactions and other nonmonetary exchanges; channel stuffing, trade loading, winter or seasonal dating of accounts receivable; sales with the right to return; software revenue recognition; contract accounting and installment sales. Each of these issues will be discussed in the following sections of this chapter.

Gross versus Net Presentation of Revenues

The issue in this case is whether a company should recognize revenue as the gross amount billed to the customer or whether the company should recognize revenue based on the net proceeds. The net proceeds represent the amount collected from the customer, less the amount returned to the supplier for the product or service provided.

The key issue here is whether the seller has earned a "commission" from the supplier of the goods or services provided. Although we have standards governing this issue (to be discussed below), this is still an important issue because revenue recognition is a major concern for financial statement users as firm valuation can be based on revenue multiples in lieu of multiples of earnings. This is particularly true if the entity being valued has not generated earnings for the period under consideration.

To resolve the issue of gross versus net presentation of revenue, the EITF reached a consensus on Issue No. 99-19[3]. This standard was based on SEC Staff Accounting Bulletin No. 101, "Revenue Recognition in Financial Statements." In SAB 101, the SEC indicated that if a company acts as an agent or broker, without assuming the risks and rewards of ownership of the product, revenues should be reported net, not gross.

3. FASB ASC 605 [Predecessor literature: *EITF Issue No. 99-19*, "Reporting Revenue Gross as a Principal versus Net as an Agent," *Emerging Issues Task Force Abstracts* (July 20, 2000)].

In making the determination of whether to recognize revenue on a net or gross basis, the SEC indicates that there are several factors to consider. These include:

1. Whether the entity acts as a principal or an agent in the transactions.
2. Whether the entity takes title to the property (here, title means "possession", involving general inventory risks).
3. Whether the entity has the normal risks and rewards of ownership.
4. Whether the entity acts as an agent or broker (including performing services, in substance, as an agent or broker) with compensation on a commission or fee basis.

The gross versus net presentation issue came to forefront of financial accounting and reporting with the explosion of the Dot Com companies during mid to late 1990s. The classic illustration in this regard relates to Priceline.com's revenue recognition policies. Specifically, Priceline recognized both revenue from sales and the costs of sales while functioning as an agent. As most readers are aware, Priceline search for low airline fares, rental car rates and hotel charges, buy tickets, and then resells them to customers.

At that time, Priceline argued that it absorbed the risk of ownership because it actually acquires the tickets and includes them in an inventory account. However, the ticket purchase only occurs if there is a guaranteed customer. Therefore, in this case, Priceline does not actually take "possession"from an economic perspective because there is no inventory risk in the normal course of business. Prior to the implementation of SAB 101, Priceline's sales resulted in a material overstatement due to the company's use of a net revenue recognition methodology.

The following illustration provides a comparison of the gross and net methods for recognizing revenue from agent type sales transactions.

Illustration:

Costline.com receives an order for a $1,000 airline ticket earning a commission as agent of $400 (i.e., cost of $600). Recording this transaction on both a gross and net basis is presented below.

Description	Gross	Net
Sales	$1,000	$ 400
Cost of goods sold	(600)	- 0 -
Gross profit	$ 400	$ 400
Operating expenses	(1,300)	(1,300)
Net Loss	($ 900)	($ 900)

The issue illustrated in this case is the fact that although the gross profit and net loss reported will be the same under either method, sales are significantly overstated by employing the gross method. In this case if a financial analyst prepares a valuation model for Costline.com, the analyst would use a multiple of revenues as one means to value the company. With the reported net loss, a multiple of earnings would not be utilized. Costline's management has an incentive to overstate revenues to enhance the analyst's valuation of the firm.

Additional analytical problems emerge when a firm acts as both an agent and a typical retailer or wholesaler. In this case, sales would be recorded on both and net and gross basis.

This could also occur when a firm changes from gross to net revenue reporting. In either case, gross profit margins and trends become distorted by reporting sales on a net basis or by changing from a gross to a net sales basis.

For example, assume a firm has $1,000 of regular retail sales and $500 of agent sales. Both types of sales have a 40% cost component. If the entity records the agent sales on gross basis, they would add $500 to their $1,000 regular retail sales and include the 40% cost of sales or $200 to the $400 cost of sales for the regular retail sales. The additional gross profit on the agent sale equals $300 ($500 revenue less the $200 cost of goods sold).

On a net basis, the company would simply add the $300 commission on the agent sales to the $1,000 regular retail sales. The cost of sales would only relate the retail sales and would not vary from the $400 amount.

Description	Regular Retail Sales	Rental + Agent Sales: Gross Basis	Rental + Agent Sales: Net Basis
Sales	$1,000	$ 1,500	$ 1,300
Cost of goods sold	(400)	(600)	(400)
Gross profit	$ 600	$ 900	$ 900
Gross profit margin	60%	60%	69%

In the case of both regular retail and agent type sales, the use of the net basis actually improves the gross profit margin (i.e., gross profit divided by sales). The gross profit margin using the gross sales basis is 60% while the gross profit margin using net agent reporting is 69%. An analyst should determine the methods used in order to compare firms on the save bases.

Another related problem involves the proper classification of shipping charged to customers. If shipping charges are included in revenue and operating expenses, it overstates gross profit margins. So, if shipping charged to customers is included in revenues (e.g. identified separately from revenues from product sales), shipping costs should be classified as part of the firm's cost of goods sold.

A sample disclosure for Acquarius Concerts for 1999 (prior to SAB 101's effective date) presented in Exhibit 10.1 illustrates the use of gross revenue recognition for agent or commission basis transactions.

EXHIBIT 10.1: ACQUARIUS CONCERTS INCORPORATED 1999 ANNUAL REPORT

Acquarius Concerts incorporated statements of operations
(In thousands, except per share data)

	Year Ended December 31, 1999	1998
Revenues	$578,892	$42,284
Cost of revenues:		
Product costs	507,667	40,195
Service costs	1,828	3,635
Total costs of revenues	509,495	43,830
Gross profit (loss)	69,397	(1,546)
Operating expenses:		
Depreciational Expense	1,198,598	69,575
Sales and marketing	95,492	29,266
General and administrative	33,131	21,605
Systems and business development	16,828	13,358
Total operating expenses	1,344,049	133,804
Operating loss	(1,274,652)	(135,349)
Interest income	9,001	657.6
Other expense	(457.2)	
Total other income (expense)	8,544	657.6
Net loss	(1,266,108)	(134,692)
Accretion on preferred stock	(10,025)	(2,620)
Net loss applicable to common stockholders	($1,276,133)	($137,311)
Net loss applicable to common stockholders per basic and diluted common share	($9.48)	($1.69)
Weighted average number of basic and diluted common shares outstanding	161,546	97,477

See notes to financial statements.
NOTES TO FINANCIAL STATEMENTS

2. SUMMARY OF SIGNIFICANT ACCOUNTING POLICIES

Revenues and Cost of Revenues — The Company recognizes and records revenues in a variety of ways depending on the product or service sold. With respect to concert ticket sales, the Company recognizes as revenue the amount received from the customer, net of taxes, and records as the cost of revenue the amount that the Company pays the respective concert promoter.

Barter Transactions and Other Nonmonetary Exchanges

Another area of concern for financial analysts is the recognition of income or loss on exchanges of nonmonetary assets. Barter transactions are generally considered nonmonetary exchanges, and are accounted for using the rules found in FASB Statement No. 153, "Exchanges of Nonmonetary Assets-an amendment to APB Opinion No. 29"[4].

A nonmonetary transaction is generally measured at the fair value of the consideration given or consideration received, which ever is more clearly evident. Fair value is determined using the SFAS 157 methodology. However, revenue (i.e. gain or loss) should only be recognized if the transactions have "commercial substance." An exchange transaction has commercial substance if the future cash flows change as a result of the transaction. In other words, if the economic positions of the parties to the transaction change, the exchange is said to have commercial substance. Future cash flows and the economic positions of the parties to the transaction can change if the exchange involves either similar assets (one truck is exchanged for another) or dissimilar assets (land is exchanged for a building). Specifically, for asset swaps the general rule for valuation of the new asset received is that it should be recorded at the fair market value of the consideration given up (i.e., this is your cost or what you give up in the transaction).

According to SFAS 153, fair value is the basis for recording exchanges of nonmonetary assets only if the transaction has "commercial substance." Recording at fair value generally results in a gain or loss on the exchange. It should be noted that the FASB did not modify the procedures for recognizing income on an exchange where cash is received. If cash ("boot") is received, then there is a partial sale to the extent of cash received. That is, income can be recognized in proportion to the cash received on an exchange lacking commercial substance. This percentage is equal to the ratio of cash received to the total value received (i.e., the fair value of the asset received plus the cash received). If the percentage of cash received is 25% or greater, the cash received is considered material and the transaction is classified as a monetary transaction with the total gain recognized. All material losses are recognized in all exchanges (with or without commercial substance). These cases are recognized to avoid overrating the asset.

If there is an exchange with commercial substance, the transaction is recorded at fair value and all gains and losses are recognized. The gain or loss is determined as the difference between the carrying value and the fair value of the asset given up in the exchange. If that fair value is not clearly evident, the fair value of the consideration received should be used. If the exchange lacks commercial substance, the transaction is recorded at book value (historical cost) and no gains or losses are recognized.

For example, assume that the Drifter Too Company exchanges a piece of equipment with Bleak Enterprises, LLC. The equipment was on Drifter Too's books at a net carrying value of $100,000 and had a fair value of $120,000. The fair value of the asset received is $150,000. Assume also that the transaction has commercial substance and can be recorded at fair value (with a gain or loss recognized).In this case, Drifter Too records the new asset at the fair value of the consideration given, $120,000 and recognizes a gain of $20,000 on the exchange. The financial modeling worksheet for this transaction is presented below.

---

4. FASB ASC 845 [Predecessor literature: "Exchanges on Non-Monetary Assets-an amendment of *APB Opinion No. 29*," *Statement of Financial Accounting Standards No. 153* (Norwalk, Conn.: FASB, 2004)].

FINANCIAL MODELING WORKSHEET EXCHANGE OF PLANT ASSETS WITH COMMERCIAL SUBSTANCE

INCOME STATEMENT (FIRST)	
REVENUES:	
Gain on Plant Asset Exchange	*+20,000*
EXPENSES:	
NET INCOME OR LOSS (a)	*+20,000*

STATEMENT OF CASH FLOWS (THIRD)	
OPERATING ACTIVITIES:	
NET INCOME OR LOSS (a)	*+20,000*
Less: Gain on Plant Asset Exchange	*(20,000)*
INVESTING ACTIVITIES:	
FINANCING ACTIVITIES:	
INCREASE (DECREASE) IN CASH (b)	*-0-*
ADD: BEGINNING CASH BALANCE	
ENDING CASH BALANCE	

BALANCE SHEET (SECOND)			
ASSETS		*LIABILITIES*	
CURRENT ASSETS		*CURRENT LIABILITIES*	
CASH (b)	*-0-*		
		NONCURRENT LIABILITIES	
		STOCKHOLDERS' EQUITY	
NONCURRENT ASSETS			
Old Asset at Carrying Value	*(100,000)*	*CAPITAL STOCK*	
New Asset at Fair Value	*+120,000*	*APIC*	
		RETAINED EARNINGS (a)	*+20,000*
		TOTAL LIABILITIES & STOCKHOLDERS'	
TOTAL ASSETS	*+20,000*	*EQUITY*	*+20,000*

Assume now that the transaction lacks commercial substance and can only be recorded at book or carrying value of the old asset. There is no gain or loss recorded on this transaction. In this case, Drifter Too records the new asset at the carrying value of the consideration given, $100,000 and effectively defers the gain of $20,000 on the exchange. Alternatively, the new asset is recorded at the fair value of the consideration given less the deferred gain (i.e., $100,000 = $120,000 – 20,000). Note that if there was a deferred loss, the loss would be added to the fair value of the old asset unless the loss was material. Again, all material losses are recognized. In both cases, the deferred gain (loss) is recognized over the life of the new asset through lower (higher) depreciation charges. The financial modeling worksheet for this transaction is presented below.

FINANCIAL MODELING WORKSHEET EXCHANGE OF PLANT ASSETS LACKING COMMERCIAL SUBSTANCE

INCOME STATEMENT (FIRST)	
REVENUES:	
EXPENSES:	
NET INCOME OR LOSS (a)	- 0 -

STATEMENT OF CASH FLOWS (THIRD)	
OPERATING ACTIVITIES:	
NET INCOME OR LOSS (a)	- 0 -
INVESTING ACTIVITIES:	
FINANCING ACTIVITIES:	
INCREASE (DECREASE) IN CASH (b)	- 0 -
ADD: BEGINNING CASH BALANCE	
ENDING CASH BALANCE	

BALANCE SHEET (SECOND)			
ASSETS		LIABILITIES	
CURRENT ASSETS		CURRENT LIABILITIES	
CASH (b)	- 0 -		
		NONCURRENT LIABILITIES	
		STOCKHOLDERS' EQUITY	
NONCURRENT ASSETS			
Old Asset at Carrying Value	(100,000)	CAPITAL STOCK	
New Asset at Fair Value – Deferred Gain	+100,000	APIC	
		RETAINED	
		EARNINGS (a)	- 0 -
		TOTAL	
		LIABILITIES &	
		STOCKHOLDERS'	
TOTAL ASSETS	- 0 -	EQUITY	- 0 -

Barter transactions can be considered a component of nonmonetary asset exchanges. Barter transactions are used frequently in many types of companies. Some examples include advertising swaps engaged in by "dot-com" enterprises, and the excess capacity swaps of fiber optic communications concerns. The reporting issue for barter transaction was that at times they involved immediate recognition of revenues and deferred recognition of costs, (e.g., recognize revenue in the year of the agreement and recognize cost in the year the advertisement runs or the capacity is used). However, these events were equal exchanges not providing economic profits to either party. Revenues are artificially increased in that it is recognized without any future cash realization. In addition, these examples do not represent completion of the normal earnings process (e.g., fiber optic networks were created to sell communications services to end users, not to swap capacity with other similar operations). The transaction may not have commercial substance, (See Exhibit 10.2).

Barter Advertising Transactions

Advertising barter transactions have increased in recent years, particularly between internet companies. Similar to the gross versus net presentation of revenue, the swapping of equal value internet advertising would increase revenue and expenses by the same amount and would result in no effect on net income. Nonetheless, as illustrated in the gross revenue approach for agent sales, equity valuation could be enhanced by the increase in revenue recognized on the advertising swap.

The FASB addressed the issue of advertising barter transactions in EITF Issue No. 99-17, "Accounting for Advertising Barter Transactions"[5]. In EITF 99-17, the FASB indicates that the primary problem is that the revenues recognized in the barter transactions will not result in cash flow realization and as noted earlier there no effect on net income. The practice may lead to overstated revenues and artificially inflated market capitalization. The issue addressed by the EITF is determine if an internet barter transaction qualifies as a nonmonetary exchange of rights to the benefits of web site advertising that would properly result in recording revenues and expenses on the income statement.

In this regard, the EITF reached a consensus decision that revenue and expense should be recognized in a barter transaction only if the fair value of the advertising exchanged is determinable based on a company's historical practice of cash sales of similar types of advertising with buyers unrelated to the counterparty in the barter transaction. The EITF went on to say that the historical practice of cash sales must have occurred no more than six months prior to the barter transaction. Previous cash sales are to be used to benchmark the fair value of the barter transaction and as a result, barter revenues and expenses can be recognized only up to the amount of previous cash transactions. In addition, the bartered advertisement must be essentially the same as the advertisement sold for cash (e.g., same type of advertisement, same length, same web site, etc).

In those cases where the fair value of advertising "sold" cannot be established under the above EITF 99-17 guidelines, the transaction must be recorded at the book or carrying amount of the advertising "sold." The book value of the advertising given up in the exchange should be equal to due to the fact that advertising is not to be deferred or capitalized and as a result, it will have a zero carrying value.

Finally, the FASB requirements indicate that companies engaging in advertising barter transactions must disclose the barter amounts in the footnotes to the financial statements as a percentage of total revenue. A sample disclosure of advertising barter transactions for Berry, Inc. in its 2012 annual report is presented in Exhibit 10.2.

EXHIBIT 10.2. BERRY, INC. 2012 ANNUAL REPORT FOOTNOTE DISCLOSURE FOR ADVERTISING BARTER TRANSACTIONS

Barter Transaction: In 2012, the Company entered into one barter transaction to exchange services for advertising. The transaction was recorded at the estimated fair value of the services expected to be received. Revenue of $450,000 from this transaction was recognized in 2012, when the service was provided and will be expensed during 2013, when the advertising is provided to Berry.

5. FASB ASC 605 [Predecessor literature: *EITF Issue No. 99-17,* "Accounting for Advertising Barter Transactions," *Emerging Issues Task Force Abstracts* (January 20, 2000)].

Capacity Trades

The SEC has ruled on capacity trades and the concluded that such nonmonetary exchanges should not be considered revenues. The ruling is again supported by the notion that capacity trades are exchanges of noncash assets and the exchange does not have commercial substance. Accordingly, the transaction is recorded at book value without income or loss recognition, assuming no cash is tendered as part of the agreement.

Trade Loading and Channel Stuffing

Trade loading and channel stuffing are ways to enhance revenues without necessarily violating the GAAP conditions for revenue recognition, but raise questions regarding ethical and transparent reporting practices.

Trade loading has been practiced by the tobacco industry. For example, the tobacco companies offer incentives to their wholesale distributors to accept a significantly greater amount of inventory than they could possibly resell in that year. This practice accelerates sales in one year, at the expense of sales in the next, unless this practice can be repeated each year. That is, current sales are accelerated with the knowledge that the wholesale distributors of the tobacco product will not be able to accept as much inventory next year. As a result, next year's sales will be reduced. The practice simply shifts sales up to the current period.

The computer software industry engages in a similar practice called channel stuffing. Software distributors can offer their distributors significant discounts and recorded sales as soon as the software was shipped. Again, this overloads or "stuffs" the distribution channels and causes an increase in current sales and the expense of sales in the future (unless channel stuffing can be repeated in subsequent accounting periods).

Another technique to accelerate sales is called winter or seasonal dating of accounts receivable. This technique is used often by manufacturers of building products. Construction is limited to certain months during cold weather periods of the year. If sales of building products were based on seasonal demand, revenues would spike during warmer months and decline during cold periods. To avoid extreme volatility in sales volume, manufacturers will produce and ship on a regular basis to construction companies, but during winter months, allow these companies to repay in the spring (i.e., possibly 90 days after the sale).

A key analytical problem involved with seasonal dating of accountings receivable is that although it inflates revenues, this will have an adverse impact on days sales outstanding. In addition, cash collection is dependent on the success of the construction company a full season from the date of sale. A possible modeling technique to analyze seasonal dating of accounts receivable is to compute a ratio of cash collected from customers to sales. This may be useful in identifying these types of practices. Cash collected from customers can be estimated by taking reported sales and deducting the increases in accounts receivable or adding the decrease in accounts receivable. Analysis of the trend in days sales outstanding can also be useful in this regard.

Sales with the Right to Return

When a company sells with the right to return, the key factor for revenue recognition is the ability to make reasonable estimation of returns. It is clear that when a customer is given the right to return purchases, the amount of revenue recognized is contingent on the amount of units returned to the seller. The contingency element added to the sales transaction creates uncertainty as to the amount of revenue to be recognized on the sale.

FASB Statement No. 48, "Revenue Recognition When the Right to Return Exists"[6], requires that the sale cannot be recorded on the date the exchange takes place, unless a reasonable estimate of returns can be made. SFAS 48 also includes several factors that may impair a firm's ability to estimate returns. For example, the length of the return period, a lack of historical experience (as with a new product), the susceptibility of the product to external factors such as obsolescence, and the absence of a large volume of transactions.

SFAS 48 specifies six conditions or criteria that must be met in order for a sale with the right to return to be recorded as revenue. Specifically in situations where the seller gives the customer the right to return the product, the FASB indicates that these exchanges are not to be recognized as revenue unless all of the following six criteria are met:

a. The seller's price to the buyer is substantially fixed or determinable at the date of sale.
b. The buyer has paid the seller, or the buyer is obligated to pay and the obligation is not contingent on resale of the product.
c. The buyer's obligation to the seller would not be changed in the event of theft or physical destruction or damage of the product.
d. The buyer has economic substance apart from that provided by the seller.
e. The seller does not have significant future performance obligations to directly bring about the resale of the product by the buyer.
f. The amount of future returns can be reasonably estimated.

If all six conditions are met, a sale is recorded. However, if any one of these conditions is not met, the transaction should be recorded as a consignment sale. Here, when the products are shipped, the merchandise inventory is taken off the books and replaced by an account called "inventory on consignment" (a simple reclassification without any effect on total inventory). This entry is reversed whenever inventory is returned. If the inventory is sold, the cash receipt and the sales are recorded and the cost of goods sold is charged. The inventory on consignment is removed from the books, reducing inventory levels only at that point.

As is typical in rule based accounting, even with a clear set of conditions there are potential analytical problems that may arise from the implementation of SFAS 48. Specifically, the ability to estimate future returns is the key factor for revenue recognition. This estimate is subject to judgement and if optimistic, sales growth can be overestimated, with subsequent future cash flows not realized.

Alternatively, some firms may record the transaction as a sale and provide a full allowance for sales returns against the revenue. In this case, the net sales amount is still zero. Depending on the financial statement presentation, the gross sales amount can be overstated if this approach is used (i.e., the allowance is placed below the sales line).

The last and least acceptable alternative is to record a receivable and a liability for repurchase. The liability actually represents deferred revenue that is to be recognized when the inventory is sold by the purchaser (i.e., accounts receivable and deferred revenues will be overstated).

In addition to the six SFAS 48 criteria, SEC SAB 101 lists other factors that may impair a firm's ability to make a reliable estimate of returns. Companies that place significant reliance on distributors to market their products, such as pharmaceutical and computer software firms, may face additional risks that will impair the firms ability to estimate the level of

6. FASB ASC 605 [Predecessor literature: "Revenue Recognition When Right of Return Exists," *Statement of Financial Accounting Standards No. 48* (Norwalk, Conn.: FASB, 1981)].

returns. An analyst should carefully consider the following factors in assessing the quality of the revenues reported by firms in industries where giving customers the right to return is a common practice. The SAB 101 factors include:

- Significant increases in distributor inventory, (channel stuffing)
- An inability to determine inventory levels in the distribution channel and the current level of sales to end users
- The anticipated introduction of new products that may render current products in the distribution channel obsolete
- The significance of a particular distributor to a company's sales or a particular reporting segment
- The newness of a product
- The introduction of competitors' products with superior technology or greater expected market acceptance

All of the above factors indicate an increased probably of merchandise returns. Where possible returns can be reasonably estimated, the next step is to validate that an adequate allowance for sales returns is provided. In addition, if the SFAS 48 and SAB 101 risk factors prevent the company from making a reasonable estimate of returns, the accountant must confirm that related shipments are not recorded as sales until the right of return expires. In this case, cash may be received well in advance of revenue recognition creating deferred revenue.

Software Revenue Recognition

The basic principles underlying software revenue recognition are found in the EITF No. 00-21, "Accounting for Revenue Arrangements with Multiple Deliverables"[7] and AICPA's Statement of Position (SOP) No. 97-2, "Software Revenue Recognition"[8] and Statement of Position (SOP) No. 98-9, "Modification of SOP 97-2, With Respect to Certain Transactions"[9].

To understand software revenue recognition, transactions must be separated into two categories; long term contracts and multiple deliverable arrangements.

Long term contracts include contractual arrangements involving significant delivery, subsequent production, modification or customization of software. Here a long term contract is used where an extended period of time is needed to have the software fully functional. These types of arrangements are to be accounted for using contract or percentage of completion accounting. Contract accounting will be discussed in a later section of this chapter.

Multiple deliverable arrangements or MDAs represent a second major type of software contractual arrangements with single or multiple deliverables (elements). Here there are separate elements that become usable or fully functional as delivered.

Under SOP 97-2, all four of the following criteria must be met in order to recognize revenue on single or multiple element software contracts (i.e., multiple deliverables):

---

7. FASB ASC 605 [Predecessor literature: *EITF Issue No. 00-21*, "Revenue Arrangements with Multiple Deliverables," *Emerging Issues Task Force Abstracts* (May 15, 2003)].

8. FASB ASC 985 [Predecessor literature: "Software Revenue Recognition," *Statement of Position 97-2* (New York: AICPA, 1997)].

9. FASB ASC 985 [Predecessor literature: "Modification of SOP 97-2, Software Revenue Recognition," *Statement of Position 98-9* (New York: AICPA, 1998)].

1. There is persuasive evidence that an arrangement exists
2. Delivery has occurred or services have been rendered
3. The seller's price to the buyer is fixed or determinable, and
4. Collectibility is reasonably assured.

These four requirements replicate the SAB No. 101 conditions for revenue recognition.

If it is determined that revenue should be recognized, there are two methods of revenue recognition for multiple deliverables (MDAs); the relative fair market value method and the Residual Method. Both methods are discussed in detail in the following sections.

The Relative Fair Market Value Method

If all MDA elements have objective, reliable estimates of fair market value, then the relative fair market value method can be employed. The fair value is best estimated by using "vendor specific objective evidence" or VSOE. VSOE will be discussed below.

When implementing the relative fair value method, if a delivered element has an objective, "stand alone" value to the customer and there is an objective fair value for all contract elements, then the delivered element can be separated and the total contract price can be allocated to the elements on a relative fair market value basis. In all cases, the delivered element must be fully functional, or one can say that the item must be fully functional to be considered "delivered."

Illustration

A software designer signs a contract to bundle three products into a single contract. The contract price including installation is $1,000. The three products have stand alone fair values as follows: P1 = $400; P2 = $300 and P3 = $500. If P2 was delivered and installed, revenue would be recognized for $250. If the total contract price was collected, $750 would remain unearned or deferred. That is:

Description	Stand Alone Fair Value	Relative Fair Value	Contract Price	Revenue Recognized
P1: Undelivered	$ 400	.3333	$1,000	$ 333
P2: Delivered	***300***	***.2500***	***$1,000***	***250***
P3: Undelivered	500	.4167	$1,000	417
Total	$1,200	1.0000	$1,000	$1,000

Assume the total contract price was collected, $250 is earned and $750 would remain unearned or deferred [($1,000 – 250) = $750.]

Fair value is best estimated by using vendor specific objective evidence (VSOE). VSOE of fair value is defined as the price charged by the software vendor for the same element sold separately. However, if a component is not sold separately, the most probable price established by management is considered the fair value of the element as long as the price is not expected to change before the component is sold separately. The determination of fair value based on VSOE was not charged by the fair value measurement requirements of FASB 157.

The financial modeling worksheet for the relative fair value approach is presented below.

FINANCIAL MODELING WORKSHEET SOFTWARE REVENUE RECOGNITION: RELATIVE FAIR VALUE METHOD

INCOME STATEMENT (FIRST)	
REVENUES:	
Sales	***+250***
EXPENSES:	
NET INCOME OR LOSS (a)	***+250***

STATEMENT OF CASH FLOWS (THIRD)	
OPERATING ACTIVITIES:	
NET INCOME OR LOSS (a)	***+250***
Increase in unearned revenues	***+750***
INVESTING ACTIVITIES:	
FINANCING ACTIVITIES:	
INCREASE (DECREASE) IN CASH (b)	***+1,000***
ADD: BEGINNING CASH BALANCE	
ENDING CASH BALANCE	

BALANCE SHEET (SECOND)			
ASSETS		***LIABILITIES***	
CURRENT ASSETS		***CURRENT LIABILITIES***	
CASH (b)	***+1,000***	***Unearned revenue***	***+750***
		NONCURRENT LIABILITIES	
		STOCKHOLDERS' EQUITY	
NONCURRENT ASSETS			
		CAPITAL STOCK	
		APIC	
		RETAINED	
		EARNINGS (a)	***+250***
		TOTAL	
		LIABILITIES &	
		STOCKHOLDERS'	
TOTAL ASSETS	***+1,000***	***EQUITY***	***+1,000***

The Residual Method. The residual method is applicable where not all MDA elements have a fair value and revenue is to be recognized on a delivered element. Without having a fair value for all MDA elements, the relative fair value approach cannot be applied. Under these circumstances, SOP No. 98-9 amended SOP No. 97-2 to permit the use of the residual approach of software revenue recognition when the criteria for revenue recognition are met (i.e., the SAB 101 conditions) and the VSOE of fair value of all undelivered elements is available, but the VSOE of fair value of one or more delivered elements is not available. If the VSOE of the delivered elements are available, the relative fair value approach could be employed.

In this case the fair value assigned to the undelivered elements is deferred until earned, and the excess contract price or the residual, is allocated to the delivered elements and is recognized as revenue in the current period.

That is:

Revenue recognized on the Delivery of Elements (Residual)	=	Total Contract Price	–	FMV of Undelivered Elements (Deferred) based on VSOE

It should be noted that if the VSOE of fair value for the delivered elements is known but the VSOE of fair value for the undelivered elements is unknown, the entire contract price is deferred and no revenue can be recognized in the current period. So, you must have VSOE of fair value for undelivered elements in order to recognize revenue under the residual approach. In addition, the deferred revenue allocated to undelivered elements cannot later be adjusted, unless it becomes probable that the amount allocated to an undelivered element of the arrangement will result in a loss. Due to conservatism, the loss must be recognized immediately recognized.

Illustration

A software designer created proprietary software for a large financial services company. Along with the software, the designer will include four years of free service.

Assuming all four criteria for revenue recognition are met, you are provided with the following information related to the contract:

1. Total contract price = $20,000.
2. Four-year "free" service contract (undelivered) = $8,000 (based on VSOE when a four-year service contract is sold separately).
3. VSOE of fair value for the delivered software is not available.

Using the Residual Method we have:

Revenue recognized on the Delivery of Elements (Residual)	=	Total Contract Price	–	FMV of Undelivered Elements (Deferred) based on VSOE
$12,000	=	$20,000	–	$8,000

The $8,000 deferred revenue on the service contract will be amortized over the period of the contract (i.e., four years in this case) and recognized in income at $2,000 per year. Again, if the VSOE of fair value for the service contract (i.e., the undelivered element) was not available, even if the fair value of the delivered element is known, all of the revenue is deferred and amortized over the period of the service contract, or until a reliable VSOE of fair value exists.

The financial modeling worksheet for the residual method is presented below. Note that the $8,000 unearned revenue is classified as a current liability for simplicity. This account would typically be classified as current and noncurrent depending on the expected timing of delivering the customer service.

FINANCIAL MODELING WORKSHEET SOFTWARE REVENUE RECOGNITION: RESIDUAL METHOD

INCOME STATEMENT (FIRST)	
REVENUES:	
Sales	+12,000
EXPENSES:	
NET INCOME OR LOSS (a)	+12,000

STATEMENT OF CASH FLOWS (THIRD)	
OPERATING ACTIVITIES:	
NET INCOME OR LOSS (a)	+12,000
Increase in unearned revenues	+8,000
INVESTING ACTIVITIES:	
FINANCING ACTIVITIES:	
INCREASE (DECREASE) IN CASH (b)	+20,000
ADD: BEGINNING CASH BALANCE	
ENDING CASH BALANCE	

BALANCE SHEET (SECOND)			
ASSETS		LIABILITIES	
CURRENT ASSETS		CURRENT LIABILITIES	
CASH (b)	+20,000	Unearned revenue	+8,000
		NONCURRENT LIABILITIES	
		STOCKHOLDERS' EQUITY	
NONCURRENT ASSETS			
		CAPITAL STOCK	
		APIC	
		RETAINED	
		EARNINGS (a)	+12,000
		TOTAL LIABILITIES & STOCKHOLDERS' EQUITY	
TOTAL ASSETS	+20,000		+20,000

Sample disclosures of software revenue recognition for PAS Systems are presented in Exhibit 10.3. PAS System's balance sheet indicates both short and long term unearned revenue accounts. This classification is based on the expected timing of revenue recognition. The cash flow statement indicated both the advance collection for unearned, undelivered elements as well as the portion of unearned revenue recognized during this period. Finally, PAS System's footnotes outline the company's revenue recognition policies and provide details regarding its multiple deliverable arrangements.[10]

10. The FASB recently issued a new standard contained in ASC 606-25-65-1 that becomes effective in 2011 but early adoption is permitted. Under the new guidance, the term "selling price" will replace the term "fair value" to emphasize the fact that these values are based on the entity's assumptions and do not reflect the assumptions of a market participant. In addition, the new standard will allow third party evidence if VSOE is not available and an estimated selling price if neither is available. The fact that a selling price will always be available, the new standard eliminates the use of the residual method.

EXHIBIT 10.3: PAS SYSTEMS ANNUAL REPORT: 2012 FINANCIAL STATEMENTS AND FOOTNOTE DISCLOSURES

BALANCE SHEETS

(In millions)

December 31	2012	2011
Assets		
Current assets:		
Cash and equivalents	$8,056.8	$5,821
Short-term investments (including securities pledged as collateral of $3,065 and $-)	32,936.4	39,480
Total cash and short-term investments	40,993.2	45,301
Accounts receivable, net of allowance for doubtful accounts of $142 and $171	11,179.2	8,616
Inventories, net	1,773.6	589.2
Deferred income taxes	2,328	2,041
Other	2,538	1,937
Total current assets	$58,812	$58,484
Property and equipment, net	3,652.8	2,815
Equity and other investments	11,078.4	13,205
Goodwill	4,639.2	3,971
Intangible assets, net	646.8	598.8
Deferred income taxes	3,133.2	4,345
Other long-term assets	1554	1,559
Total assets	$83,516	$84,978
Liabilities and stockholders' equity		
Current liabilities:		
Accounts payable	$3,491	$2,503
Accrued compensation	2,326	1,994
Income taxes	1,868	2,424
Short-term unearned revenue	10,966	9,002
Securities lending payable	3,740	—
Other	4,540	3,607
Total current liabilities	$26,930	$16,877
Long-term unearned revenue	2,117	1,665
Other long-term liabilities	6,344	4,158
Commitments and contingencies		
Stockholders' equity:		
Common stock and paid-in capital – shares authorized 24,000; outstanding 10,062 and 10,710	70,806	72,496

(In millions)

December 31	**2012**	**2011**
Retained earnings (deficit), including accumulated other comprehensive income of $1,229 and $1,426	(22681.2)	(37,458)
Total stockholders' equity	48,125	57,738
Total liabilities and stockholders' equity	$83,516	$84,978

See accompanying notes.

PARTIAL CASH FLOWS STATEMENTS

(In millions)

Year Ended December 31	**2012**	**2011**	**2010**
Operations			
Net income	$ 15,119	$ 14,705	$ 9,802
Depreciation, amortization, and other noncash items	1083.6	1026	1,423
Stock-based compensation	2,058	2,938	6,881
Net recognized gains on investments	324	(632.4)	(1,555)
Stock option income tax benefits	(106.8)	801.6	1,320
Excess tax benefits from stock-based payment arrangements	19,744	–	–
Deferred income taxes	–	(214.8)	(1,775)
Unearned revenue	–	16,597	14,132
Recognition of unearned revenue	(17,675)	(15,503)	(15,032)
Accounts receivable	(2,485)	(1,492)	(824.4)
Other current assets	(1,686)	(294)	573.6
Other long-term assets	(58.8)	25.2	40.8
Other current liabilities	(174)	475.2	1,835
Other long-term liabilities	1,528	1,494	730.8
Net cash from operations	$17,285	$19,926	$17,551

See accompanying notes.

NOTE 1 ACCOUNTING POLICIES

REVENUE RECOGNITION

Revenue is recognized when persuasive evidence of an arrangement exists, delivery has occurred, the fee is fixed or determinable, and collectibility is probable. We enter into certain arrangements where we are obligated to deliver multiple products and/or services (multiple elements). In these arrangements, we generally allocate the total revenue among the elements based on the sales price of each element when sold separately (vendor-specific objective evidence).

Revenue for retail packaged products, products licensed to original equipment manufacturers, and perpetual licenses for current products under our volume licensing programs generally is recognized as products are shipped, with a portion of the revenue recorded as unearned due to undelivered elements including, in some cases, free post-delivery telephone support and the right to receive unspecified upgrades/enhancements on a when-and-if-available basis. The amount of revenue allocated to undelivered elements is based on the vendor-specific objective evidence of fair value for those elements using the residual method. Under the residual method, the total fair value of the undelivered elements, as indicated by vendor-specific objective evidence, is recorded as unearned, and the difference between the total arrangement fee and the amount recorded as unearned for the undelivered elements is recognized as revenue related to delivered elements. Unearned revenue due to undelivered elements is recognized ratably on a straight-line basis over the related product's life cycle.

NOTE 2 UNEARNED REVENUE

Unearned revenue is comprised of the following items:

Volume licensing programs – Represents customer billings for multi-year licensing arrangements, paid either up front or annually at the beginning of each billing coverage period, which are accounted for as subscriptions with revenue recognized ratably over the billing coverage period.

Undelivered elements – Represents free post-delivery telephone support and the right to receive unspecified upgrades/enhancements on a when-and-if-available basis. The amount recorded as unearned is based on the sales price of those elements when sold separately and is recognized ratably on a straight-line basis over the related product's life cycle. The percentage of revenue recorded as unearned due to undelivered elements ranges from approximately 18% to 35% of the sales price for PAS V, approximately 10% to 22% of the sales price for PAS VI Professional, and approximately 1% to 12% of the sales price for desktop applications, depending on the terms and conditions of the license and prices of the elements. Product life cycles are currently estimated at three and one-half years for PAS operating systems and two years for desktop applications.

Other – Represents payments for post-delivery support and consulting services to be performed in the future, online advertising for which the advertisement has yet to be displayed, maintenance and enhancement billings, and other billings that are accounted for as subscriptions, and other agreements where PAS is committed to the delivery of future enhancements, products, or services, including the TV platform.

The components of unearned revenue were as follows:

(In millions)

December 31	2012	2011
Volume licensing programs	$9,193.2	$7,200.0
Undelivered elements	2,479.0	2,543.0
Other	1,410.0	1,258.0
Unearned revenue	$13,082.0	$11,000.0

Unearned revenue by segment was as follows:

(In millions)

December 31	2006	2005
Client	$3,420.0	$3,224.0
Server and Tools	4,550.0	3,658.0
Information Worker	4,331.0	3,377.0
Other segments	781.2	741.6
Unearned revenue	$13,082.0	$10,976.0

Contract Accounting (Revenue recognized before Delivery)

As discussed in Chapter 1, revenue is typically recognized at the point of sale. The point of sale is where there is an exchange (i.e., delivery takes place) and completion of the earnings cycle. The earnings cycle is essentially completed when there are no material uncertainties as to collection and future costs to be incurred. In addition, legal title usually passes from the seller to the buyer at the point of sale.

Accounting for long term contracts creates an exception to the general rule of recognizing revenue at the point of sale or at delivery. This is due to the fact that with a long term contract, the product or service provided is actually delivered in installments, even if legal title does not pass from the seller to the buyer until the end of the contract term.

Contract accounting is applicable to long-term construction projects, long-term software design projects, (other than MDAs), and research and development contracts. The primary accounting issue is the estimation of revenues, costs and the degree of completion (i.e., the extent of delivery) for the extended term of the contract.

There are two methods of accounting for long term contracts. These are the percentage-of completion method and the completed-contract method. As will be discussed, the percentage of completion method permits recognition of revenue and costs over the life of the long-term contract, while the completed contract method only permits revenue and cost recognition at the end of the contract when title passes from the seller to the buyer.

AICPA Statement of Position (SOP) 81-1," Accounting for Performance of Construction-Type and Certain Production Type Contract"[11] lists the criteria that must be met in order to use the percentage of completion basis.

The first and most important criterion is that the firm has the ability to make reasonably reliable estimates of the extent of progress toward completion, contract revenues, and contract costs. Next, there must be enforceable rights on both sides of the contract. Finally, the specific performance on both sides of the contract must be anticipated. That is the buyer must be financially capable to liquidate its obligations and the seller or contractor must be able to deliver the finished product.

The percentage of completion method can be used only if all of these conditions are met. If all of the conditions of the percentage of completion method are not met, then the completed contract method must be used. Again, under the completed contract method all revenue and costs should be recognized in the period that the contact is completed.

The completed-contract method should be used only when an entity has primarily short-term contracts, the conditions for using the percentage-of-completion method cannot be met, or there are inherent hazards in the contract beyond normal, recurring business risks. Of course, immaterial and short-term contracts can be accounted for under the completed contract method.

The AICPA clearly indicates that the percentage-of-completion method and the completed-contract method are not alternatives and all of the above conditions must be met in order to use the percentage of completion method.

11. FASB ASC 605 [Predecessor literature: "Accounting for Performance of Construction-Type and Certain Production-Type Contracts," *Statement of Position 81-1* (New York: AICPA, 1981)].

Percentage-of-Completion Method

Under the percentage-of-completion method, revenue on long-term contracts is recognized as work is delivered. Costs incurred under the contract plus gross profit earned to date are recorded in a "construction or work in process" account (i.e., an inventory account designated as CIP or WIP respectively). The amount of revenue recognized in each accounting period is based on a percentage of the total revenue to be recognized on the contract.

The key condition for the use of the percentage of completion method is the ability to make reliable estimates of revenue, costs and degree of completion. There are two ways to determine the degree of completion: input and output measures. Input measures include the number of hours expended or costs incurred. Output measures can be based on physical progress, such as the number of miles of road completed or the use of engineering estimates to determine the degree or completion

The most practical input measure is the "cost to cost" approach. Under the cost to cost approach, the percentage used to estimate the degree completed is measured as the total actual costs incurred on the contract to date divided by the estimated total costs. Estimated total costs are equal to the total actual costs incurred to date plus the estimated costs to complete.

From the financial reporting perspective, there are several advantages of the percentage of completion method as compared to the completed contract method. These financial reporting benefits include:

1. Provides a better measure of economic activity.
2. Better matches costs and revenues.
3. Better measures assets ("the right to bill") and liabilities ("obligation to perform") under the terms of the long-term contract.

Failing to provide these reporting and disclosure benefits represents the disadvantages of the completed contract method.

Illustration

Assume that Lorenzo Construction Corporation has been engaged to build a factory for the Pooley Products Group, LLC. The details of the contract indicate that the expected completion date is three years and total contract price is $72,000,000.

The following table provides a summary of costs incurred, estimates of the degree completed, revenue and costs recognized and the amount of billings and collection per year. Assume that all contract costs are paid in cash in the year incurred.

Description	*2008*	*2009*	*2010*
Actual costs incurred per year	$21,600,000	$3,480,000	$34,920,000
Cumulative actual costs incurred to date	$21,600,000	$25,080,000	$60,000,000
Estimated costs to complete	32,400,000	40,920,000	-0-
Estimated cumulative total costs	$54,000,000	$66,000,000	$60,000,000
Estimated gross profit	$18,000,000	$6,000,000	$12,000,000

Estimated degree completed: Costs to date / Estimated total cost	$21,600 / $54,000 = 40%	$25,080 / $66,000 = 38%	$60,000 / $60,000 = 100%
Revenue recognized this year = (% x $72,000,000) - cumulative prior year revenue recognized	$28,800,000 – 0 = $28,800,000	$27,360,000 – 28,800,000 = ($1,440,000)	$72,000,000 – 27,360,000 = $44,640,000
Gross profit recognized this year = (% x estimated gross profit) - cumulative prior year gross profit recognized)	$7,200,000 – 0 = $7,200,000	$2,280,000 – 7,200,000 = ($4,920,000)	$12,000,000 – 2,280,000 = $9,720,000
Progress billings on CIP each year	$24,000,000	$24,000,000	$24,000,000
Cash collected each year	$18,000,000	$24,000,000	$30,000,000

Construction in Progress Account Activity	
Description	***Amount***
2008: Actual cost incurred	$21,600,000
2008: Gross profit recognized	7,200,000
2008 Balance	$28,800,000
2009: Actual cost incurred	3,480,000
2009: Gross profit recognized	(4,920,000)
2009 Balance	$27,360,000
2010: Actual cost incurred	34,920,000
2010: Gross profit recognized	9,720,000
2010 Balance	$72,000,000

The CIP account is an inventory account representing the right to bill. A contra inventory account called "billing on CIP" is used to offset CIP since it represents advance selling (and possible collections) and the obligation to perform. The net balance of these two accounts creates either an asset or liability position for the entity.

Note that decreases in the CIP account can occur with contract completions and reversal of profit due to cost overruns or revisions of the percentage completed. This second case implies that prior year's profit could have been overstated.

The balance sheet account balances are presented in the following table (000s omitted).

Description	***2008***	***2009***	***2010***
CIP (Right to Bill)	**$28,800**	**$ 27,360**	**$72,000**
Less: Billings on CIP (Obligation to perform)	**(24,000)**	**(48,000)**	**(72,000)**
Net Asset (Liability)	**$ 4,800**	**($20,640)**	**- 0 -**

The resulting net asset represents "unbilled receivables" or the right to bill. The net liability represents an "overbilling" (advance billings) and the obligation to perform. A significant change in the net asset or net liability position could indicate a change in the estimation techniques used in determining the degree completed.

A significant analytical problem can arise because reported contract profitability can be over-or-understated by manipulating the percentage completed or estimates of contract costs. This means that there is a high degree of uncertainty regarding the quality of earnings reported under the percentage of completion basis. An analysis of changes in the net asset or net liability position of the contractor may indicate unusual changes in the estimation of the degree completed. Again, increases in the estimated degree of completion increases the CIP account and the net asset position. Another analytical problem is that the timing of revenue recognition and the timing of cash flows are not articulated.

If cash is collected in advance (and the contractor is in a net liability position), there is a possibility that the cash may no longer be available to complete the contract. This could impair the contractor's ability to deliver on the contract. Conversely, if there is a significant net asset position (i.e., an increasing trend in unbilled receivables), it could mean that the buyer has little capital at risk and can walk away from the contract.

Although there are disclosures for contracts accounted for under the percentage of completion basis, the information provided may not be adequate to assess the potential earnings management afforded by the discretion in the use of estimates. The financial statements reflect the profit recognized and either the net asset or net liability position of the contractor. The financial modeling worksheet for 2008 (the first year of the contract) is presented below.

FINANCIAL MODELING WORKSHEET FOR 2008 (000S OMITTED)

INCOME STATEMENT (FIRST)	
REVENUES: Contract Revenues	+28,800
EXPENSES: Contract Expenses	(21,600)
NET INCOME OR LOSS (a)	+7,200

STATEMENT OF CASH FLOWS (THIRD)	
OPERATING ACTIVITIES:	
NET INCOME OR LOSS (a)	+7,200
Increase in CIP-Net Asset Position	(4,800)
Increase in A/R	(6,000)
Cash flow from Operating Activities	(3,600)
INVESTING ACTIVITIES:	
FINANCING ACTIVITIES:	
INCREASE (DECREASE) IN CASH (b)	(3,600)
ADD: BEGINNING CASH BALANCE	
ENDING CASH BALANCE	

BALANCE SHEET (SECOND)			
ASSETS		LIABILITIES	
CURRENT ASSETS		CURRENT LIABILITIES	
CASH (b)	(3,600)		
CIP	+28,800		
Billings on CIP	(24,000)		
Net CIP	+4,800	NONCURRENT LIABILITIES	
Accounts Receivable	+6,000		
		STOCKHOLDERS' EQUITY	
NONCURRENT ASSETS			
		CAPITAL STOCK	
		APIC	
		RETAINED EARNINGS (a)	+7,200
		TOTAL LIABILITIES & STOCKHOLDERS' EQUITY	
TOTAL ASSETS	+7,200		+7,200

When the current estimates of total contract revenue and contract cost indicate that a loss is expected, the entire expected contract loss must be recognized in the period in which it becomes evident under both the percentage-of-completion and the completed-contract-methods.

In addition to normal financial statement disclosures, contractors should disclose:

a. The method of recognizing revenue
b. The basis used to classify assets and liabilities as current
c. The basis for recording inventory
d. The effects of any revisions of estimates
e. The amount of backlog on incomplete contracts
f. The details about receivables

Contract losses must be accrued on all fixed contracts. This would not be an issue for cost-plus contracts. Here, the contractor has a built in cost recovery and estimated losses are not likely to occur under normal circumstances.

Financial disclosures for contract accounting are presented for Cascade Communications, Inc. in Exhibit 10.4. Cascade provides an excellent illustration of the required disclosures for the percentage of completion method. CIP and excess billing are shown separately on both the balance sheet and statement of cash flow. In addition, the income statement provides separate disclosure in the footnotes.

EXHIBIT 10.4: CONTRACT DISCLOSURES FOR CASCADE COMMUNICATIONS 2012 ANNUAL REPORT

CONSOLIDATED BALANCE SHEETS

(in millions, except share data)

	December 31, 2012	December 31, 2011
ASSETS		
Current assets:		
Cash and cash equivalents	$ 472.68	$ 784.08
Contracts in process	3,485.28	2,374.80
Deferred income taxes	276.72	152.52
Other current assets	137.52	58.56
Total current assets	4,372.20	3,369.96
Property, plant and equipment, net	789.12	668.4
Goodwill	8,279.76	4,865.76
Identifiable intangible assets	495.36	222.96
Deferred debt issue costs	91.92	43.2
Other assets	262.56	166.68
Total assets	$ 14,290.92	$ 9,336.96
LIABILITIES AND SHAREHOLDERS' EQUITY		
Current liabilities:		
Accounts payable, trade	$ 571.32	$ 337.8
Accrued employment costs	561.24	365.04
Accrued expenses	206.4	83.64
Billings in excess of costs and estimated profits	256.8	165.96
Customer advances	116.64	128.76
Income taxes	83.04	101.28
Other current liabilities	429.72	228.48
Total current liabilities	2,225.16	1,410.96
Pension and postretirement benefits	522.72	490.92
Deferred income taxes	142.92	9.6
Other liabilities	353.64	144.96
Long-term debt	5,560.20	2,627.76
Total liabilities	8,804.64	4,684.20
Commitments and contingencies (see Note 10)		
Minority interests	97.44	93
Shareholders' equity:		

	2012	2011
Class A common stock; $1 par value; in 2012 and in 2011 Class B common stock; $1.50 par value, authorized, issued and outstanding)	3,648.96	3,336.60
Retained earnings	1,854.00	1,315.08
Unearned compensation	(21.48)	(4.68)
Accumulated other comprehensive loss	(92.64)	(87.24)
Total shareholders' equity	5,388.84	4,559.76
Total liabilities and shareholders' equity	$ 14,290.92	$ 9,336.96

See notes to consolidated financial statements.

PARTIAL CONSOLIDATED STATEMENTS OF OPERATIONS (in millions, except per share data)

	Year Ended December 31,		
	2012	**2011**	**2010**
Sales:			
Contracts, primarily U.S. Government	$ 10,259.04	$ 7,386.72	$ 5,282.04
Commercial, primarily products	1074.6	889.68	791.88
Total sales	11,333.64	8,276.40	6,073.92
Costs and expenses:			
Contracts, primarily U.S. Government	9,159.96	6,572.16	4,636.56
Commercial, primarily products:			
Cost of sales	698.64	550.8	500.4
Selling, general and administrative expenses	200.16	169.68	168.72
Research and development expenses	78.84	85.44	71.04
Total costs and expenses	10,137.60	7,378.08	5,376.72
Operating income	1196.04	898.32	697.2
Other expense (income), net	6.6)	8.76)	0.24)
Interest expense	245.04	174.36	159.24
Minority interests in net income of consolidated subsidiaries	11.64	10.68	4.2
Loss on retirement of debt		6	13.44
Income before income taxes	945.96	716.04	520.56
Provision for income taxes	335.76	257.76	187.44
Net income	$ 610.2	$ 458.28	$ 333.12
Class A earnings per common share:			
Basic	$ 5.136	$ 4.248	$ 3.468
Diluted	$ 5.04	$ 3.996	$ 3.144
Class B weighted average common shares outstanding:			
Basic	142.56	129.36	115.2
Diluted	145.44	140.88	136.68

See notes to consolidated financial statements.

CONSOLIDATED STATEMENTS OF CASH FLOWS (in millions)

	Year Ended December 31,		
	2012	2011	2010
Operating activities:			
Net income	$ 610.2	$ 458.28	$ 333.12
Loss on retirement of debt	-	6	13.44
Depreciation	135.96	109.92	92.76
Amortization of intangibles and other assets	47.4	32.88	21.72
Deferred income tax provision	166.32	148.08	113.64
Minority interests in net income of consolidated subsidiaries	11.64	10.68	4.2
Contributions to employee savings plans	76.44	64.56	47.4
Amortization of deferred debt issue costs (included in interest expense)	6.24	8.64	9.6
Other non-cash items	9.96	(1.44)	0.48
Subtotal	1064.16	837.6	636.36
Changes in operating assets and liabilities, excluding acquired amounts:			
Contracts in process	(249.96)	(294.48)	(144.48)
Other current assets	(4.2)	(18.36)	(2.04)
Other assets	(40.08)	(39.6)	(19.08)
Accounts payable, trade	112.08	74.64	(23.4)
Accrued employment costs	64.32	65.76	24.72
Accrued expenses	26.64	(4.08)	6.84
Billings in excess of costs and estimated profits	20.04	16.92	21.96
Customer advances	(11.4)	40.44	(5.76)
Income taxes	79.8	64.68	52.92
Other current liabilities	(15.24)	(24.6)	(43.44)
Pension and postretirement benefits	(33)	11.4	6.12
Other liabilities	6.24	8.64	22.8
All other operating activities	(3.24)	5.88	13.8
Subtotal	(48)	(92.76)	(89.04)
Net cash from operating activities	1016.16	744.84	547.32

NOTES TO CONSOLIDATED FINANCIAL STATEMENTS

2. Summary of Significant Accounting Policies

Revenue Recognition: The majority of the Company's direct and indirect sales to the U.S. Government and certain of the Company's sales to allied foreign governments and commercial customers are within the scope of SOP 81-1, ARB 43 and ARB 45 and sales and profits on them are recognized using percentage-of-completion (POC) methods of accounting. Sales and profits on fixed-price production contracts under which units are produced and delivered in a continuous or sequential process are recorded as units are delivered based on their contractual selling prices (the "units-of-delivery" method). Sales and profits on each fixed-price production contract under which units are not produced and delivered in a continuous or sequential process, or under which a relatively few number of units are produced, are recorded based on the ratio of actual cumulative costs incurred to the total estimated costs at completion multiplied by the total estimated contract revenue, less cumulative sales recognized in prior periods (the "cost-to-cost" method).

Under the POC methods of accounting, a single estimated total profit margin is used to recognize profit for each contract over its entire period of performance, which can exceed one year. Losses on contracts are recognized in the period in which they are determined. The impact of revisions of contract estimates, which may result from contract modifications, performance or other reasons, are recognized on a cumulative catch-up basis in the period in which the revisions are made.

Sales and profits on cost-reimbursable type contracts that are within the scope of ARB 43, in addition to SOP 81-1, are recognized as allowable costs . The costs are incurred on the contract at an amount equal to the allowable costs plus the estimated profit. The estimated profit on a cost-reimbursable contract is generally fixed or variable based on the contractual fee arrangement. Incentive and award fees on these contracts are recorded as sales when the conditions under which they are earned are reasonably assured of being met and can be reasonably estimated.

Sales and profits on time and material type contracts are recognized on the basis of direct labor hours expended multiplied by the contractual fixed rate per hour plus the actual costs of materials and other direct non-labor costs.

Contracts in Process: Contracts in process include receivables and inventories for contracts that are within the scope of SOP 81-1, ARB 43 and ARB 45, as well as receivables and inventories related to other contractual arrangements. Billed Receivables represent the uncollected portion of amounts recorded as sales and billed to customers for all revenue arrangements, net of allowances for uncollectible accounts. Unbilled Contract Receivables represent accumulated incurred costs and earned profits or losses on contracts in process that have been recorded as sales, primarily using the cost-to-cost method, which have not yet been billed to customers. Inventoried Contract Costs represent incurred costs on contracts in process that have not yet been recognized as costs and expenses because the related sales, which are primarily recorded using the units-of-delivery method, have not been recognized. Contract costs include direct costs and indirect costs, including overhead costs.

4. Contracts in Process

The components of contracts in process are presented in the table below. The unbilled contract receivables, inventoried contract costs and unliquidated progress payments are principally related to contracts with the U.S. Government and prime contractors or subcontractors of the U.S. Government.

	December 31, 2012	December 31, 2011
	(in millions)	
Billed receivables, net of allowances of $19.6 million and $16.5 million	$ 1,285.44	$ 938.28
Unbilled contract receivables, gross	1,696.92	972.84
Less: unliquidated progress payments	-282.72	-215.16)
Unbilled contract receivables, net	1,414.20	757.68
Inventoried contract costs, gross	635.76	519.24
Less: unliquidated progress payments	-77.4	-61.08)
Inventoried contract costs, net	558.36	458.16
Inventories at lower of cost or market	227.28	220.68
Total contracts in process	$ 3,485.28	$ 2,374.80

Unbilled Contract Receivables. Unbilled contract receivables represent accumulated incurred costs and earned profits on contracts (revenue arrangements), which have been recorded as sales, but have not yet been billed to customers. Unbilled contract receivables arise from the cost-to-cost method of revenue recognition that is used to record sales on certain fixed-price contracts.

Unbilled contract receivables from fixed-price type contracts are converted to billed receivables when amounts are invoiced to customers according to contractual billing terms, which generally occur when deliveries or other performance milestones are completed. Unbilled contract receivables also arise from cost-reimbursable type contracts and time-and-material type contracts, for revenue amounts that have not been billed by the end of the accounting period due to the timing of preparation of invoices for customers. The Company believes that approximately 95% of the unbilled contract receivables at December 31, 2012 will be billed and collected within one year.

Installment Sales: (Cash Basis- Revenue Recognized After Delivery)

When revenue is recognized after the exchange takes place, accountants are employing a cash basis. The cash basis is used in these situations because there are material uncertainties as to future collectibility. In this case, the earnings process is not complete and revenue cannot be recognized at point of delivery. Gross profit is deferred until cash is collected. There are two methods used to for the deferral of revenue recognition until cash is collected. The two methods are the installment method and the cost recovery method. Only installment sales are discussed in this chapter.

APB Opinion No. 10, "Omnibus Opinion-1966"[12], indicated that the installment method of recognizing revenue is generally not acceptable, and can be use in limited circumstances. The installment method can be used where the terms of sale provide for collection over an extended period of time. In addition to the long term nature of the receivable, there is no reasonable basis for estimating the degree of collectibility (i.e., due to the high degree of uncertainty as to collection).

Under the installment method, revenue and cost of sales are deferred until cash is collected and gross profit is realized is proportionate to the amount of cash collected. Specifically, the gross profit (sales less cost of goods sold) on the installment sale is deferred until cash receipt takes place. This means that sales and the cost of sale are record in the usual way during the accounting period. Installment accounts receivable are a separate category of receivables and are always classified as current if installment sales are a part of normal operations, regardless of the length of the collection period under contract. Otherwise, the receivables are classified as current or noncurrent based on expected collection date.

At the end of the accounting period, the portion of gross profit not matched with cash receipts is deferred. The deferred gross profit account is a liability account and can be current or noncurrent, classified in the same way as the installment sale receivable.

The amount of gross profit associated with cash received is recognized as income. It is important to note that the gross profit rate for each accounting period must be identified and matched with the cash received from the receivables for that year in the revenue recognition process.

The installment method is used in certain equipment manufacturing (e.g., farm equipment), furniture manufacturing and real estate transactions. According to FASB Statement No. 66, "Accounting for Sales on Real Estate"[13], the installment sales method of accounting must be used for a real estate sale that meets all of the following criteria:

12. FASB ASC 605 [Predecessor literature: "Omnibus Opinion-1966," *Opinions of the Accounting Principles Board No. 10* (New York: AICPA 1966)].

13. FASB ASC 360 [Predecessor literature: "Accounting for Sales of Real-Estate," *Statement of Financial Accounting Standards No. 66* (Norwalk, Conn.: FASB, 1982)].

- The period of cancellation of the sale with refund of the down payment and any subsequent payments has expired;
- Cumulative cash payments equal or exceed 10% of the sales value; and
- The seller is financially capable of providing all promised contract representations (i.e., land improvements, off-site facilities).

Illustration

Assume you are provided with the following information from McManus Ltd.

	2008	2009	2010
Installment sales	$904,000	$ 992,000	$1,044,000
Cost of installment sales	494,940	528,240	587,250
Gross profit	$409,060	$ 463,760	$ 456,750
Rate of Gross Profit:			
Gross Profit / Installment Sales	45%	47%	44%
Cash Receipts from:			
2008 Sales	$340,000	$ 384,000	$ 180,000
2009 Sales		492,000	348,000
2010 Sales			588,000
Total cash collected in 2009		$876,000	
Increase in 2009 Accounts Receivable: ($992,000 – 876,000)		$116,000	

Only the 2009 financial results will be provided. The financial statement effects for 2008 and 2010 are the same, but the only the 2009 financial modeling worksheets are presented below.

The gross profit recognized in 2009 is equal to the sum of the cash received in 2009 multiplied by the gross profit rate for year of receivable collected. Specifically, there is $384,000 cash collected in 2009 from 2008 installment sales. The 2008 gross profit rate is 45% so the gross profit recognized in 2009 on collections on 2008 sales is $172,800 (i.e., $384,000 X .45). The balance of the cash collected in 2009, $492,000, is from 2009 and therefore gross profit is recognized at 47% (the 2009 gross profit rate). The gross profit recognized on 2009 sales is $231,240, (i.e. $492,000 X .47). The total gross profit recognized in 2009 is $404,040 and the $59,720 balance of the $463,760 total gross profit is 2009 is deferred until cash is collected.

When interest is involved in installment sales, it should be accounted for separately as interest income in the period received. Uncollectible installment accounts receivable are typically accounted for as regular accounts receivable. However, repossessions can provide additional security on bad debts related to installment sales receivable.

FINANCIAL MODELING WORKSHEET FOR 2009

INCOME STATEMENT (FIRST)	
REVENUES: Installment Sales	*+992,000*
EXPENSES: Cost of Goods Sold	*(528,240)*
GROSS PROFIT	*463,760*
NET DEFERRED GROSS PROFIT	*(59,720)*
NET INCOME OR LOSS (a)	*404,040*

STATEMENT OF CASH FLOWS (THIRD)	
OPERATING ACTIVITIES:	
NET INCOME OR LOSS (a)	*+404,040*
Increase in A/R	*(116,000)*
Decrease in Inventory	*+528,240*
Increase in Deferred Gross Profit	*+59,720*
Cash Flow from Operating Activities	*+876,000*
INVESTING ACTIVITIES:	
FINANCING ACTIVITIES:	
INCREASE (DECREASE) IN CASH (b)	*+876,000*
ADD: BEGINNING CASH BALANCE	
ENDING CASH BALANCE	

BALANCE SHEET (SECOND)			
ASSETS		*LIABILITIES*	
CURRENT ASSETS		*CURRENT LIABILITIES*	
CASH (b)	*+876,000*	*Deferred Gross Profit*	*+59,720*
Installment A/R	*+116,000*		
Inventory	*(528,240)*		
		NONCURRENT LIABILITIES	
		STOCKHOLDERS' EQUITY	
NONCURRENT ASSETS			
		CAPITAL STOCK	
		APIC	
		RETAINED EARNINGS (a)	*+404,040*
		TOTAL LIABILITIES & STOCKHOLDERS' EQUITY	
TOTAL ASSETS	*+463,760*		*+463,760*

Repossessions

When it is determined that an installment receivable is not collectible, that account should be written off and the deferred gross profit related to the uncollectible installment sale receivable must also be removed from the financial statements. The repossessed assets are recorded in a repossessed merchandise inventory account and fair value. The difference between the net asset value related to the installment contract (i.e., net asset value = installment sale receivable – deferred gross profit) and the fair value of the repossessed merchandise is recorded as a gain or loss on repossessions.

Illustration

Assume that Aton Corporation reports the 2010 balance of installment sales receivable of $200,000 for one of its major customers. The deferred gross profit related to the installment sale receivable is $80,000.

At the end of 2010, Anton determines that the account is uncollectible and decides to repossess the merchandise. Merchandise related to the above balances is repossessed with a fair market value of $100,000. Since the net asset value related to the installment sale contract is $120,000 (i.e., Installment sale receivable = $200,000, - deferred gross profit = $80,000) is greater the fair value of the repossessed inventory of $100,000, there is a $20,000 loss on repossession recognized in income from continuing operations.

The financial modeling worksheet related to the repossession is presented below.

FINANCIAL MODELING WORKSHEET 2009 REPOSSESSION OF INVENTORY

INCOME STATEMENT (FIRST)	
REVENUES:	
EXPENSES:	
Loss on Repossession	(20,000)
NET INCOME OR LOSS (a)	(20,000)

BALANCE SHEET (SECOND)			
ASSETS		LIABILITIES	
CURRENT ASSETS		CURRENT LIABILITIES	
CASH (b)	- 0 -	Deferred Gross Profit	(80,000)
Installment Sales Receivable	(200,000)		
Repossessed Inventory	+100,000		
		NONCURRENT LIABILITIES	
		STOCKHOLDERS' EQUITY	
NONCURRENT ASSETS			
		CAPITAL STOCK	
		APIC	
		RETAINED EARNINGS (a)	(20,000)
TOTAL ASSETS	(100,000)	TOTAL LIABILITIES & STOCKHOLDERS' EQUITY	(100,000)

STATEMENT OF CASH FLOWS (THIRD)	
OPERATING ACTIVITIES:	
NET INCOME OR LOSS (a)	(20,000)
Decrease in Installment Sales Receivable	+200,000
Increase in Reposessed Inventory	(100,000)
Decrease in Deferred Gross Profit	(80,000)
INVESTING ACTIVITIES:	
FINANCING ACTIVITIES:	
INCREASE (DECREASE) IN CASH (b)	- 0 -
ADD: BEGINNING CASH BALANCE	
ENDING CASH BALANCE	

Sample disclosures for the installment sales method are presented in Exhibit 10.5 for KAST, Inc. Note that installment sales receivable are reported on the balance sheet as both current and noncurrent assets. The same is true for deferred revenues reported in the liability section. These accounts are key adjustments in the statement of cash flows. The company's footnotes explain it's revenue recognition policies and the use of the in statement method.

EXHIBIT 10.5: KAST, INC. AND SUBSIDIARIES: 2006 ANNUAL REPORT DISCLOSURES FOR INSTALLMENT SALES

CONSOLIDATED BALANCE SHEETS

	March 31,	
	2012	2011
		(restated)
	(dollars in millions)	
ASSETS		
CURRENT ASSETS		
Cash and cash equivalents	$ 2,197	$ 3,395
Marketable securities	40.8	355.2
Trade and installment accounts receivable, net	606	931.2
Federal and state income taxes receivable		66
Deferred income taxes	273.6	127.2
Other current assets	60	122.4
TOTAL CURRENT ASSETS	3,178	4,997
INSTALLMENT ACCOUNTS RECEIVABLE, due after one year, net	538.8	714
PROPERTY AND EQUIPMENT		
Land and buildings	585.6	712.8
Equipment, furniture, and improvements	1,279	1100.4
	1,865	1,813
Accumulated depreciation and amortization	-1104	-1066.8
TOTAL PROPERTY AND EQUIPMENT, net	760.8	746.4
PURCHASED SOFTWARE PRODUCTS, net of accumulated amortization of $4,299 and $3,899, respectively	553.2	871.2
GOODWILL, net of accumulated amortization of $1,409 and $1,416, respectively	6,370	5,453
DEFERRED INCOME TAXES	180	250.8
OTHER NONCURRENT ASSETS	945.6	643.2
TOTAL ASSETS	$ 12,526	$ 13,675

LIABILITIES AND STOCKHOLDERS' EQUITY		
CURRENT LIABILITIES		
Current portion of long-term debt and loans payable	$ 1.2	$ 991.2
Government investigation settlement	2.4	183.6
Accounts payable	493.2	212.4
Salaries, wages, and commissions	350.4	309.6
Accrued expenses and other current liabilities	447.6	444
Deferred subscription revenue (collected) — current	1,820	1,688
Deferred maintenance revenue	300	324
Taxes payable, other than income taxes payable	154.8	142.8
Federal, state, and foreign income taxes payable	444	427.2
Deferred income taxes	38.4	114
TOTAL CURRENT LIABILITIES	4,052	4,837
LONG-TERM DEBT, net of current portion	2,172	2,172
DEFERRED INCOME TAXES	55.2	224.4
DEFERRED SUBSCRIPTION REVENUE (COLLECTED) — NONCURRENT	537.6	327.6
OTHER NONCURRENT LIABILITIES	92.4	63.6
TOTAL LIABILITIES	6,910	7,625
STOCKHOLDERS' EQUITY		
Preferred stock, no par value, 30,000,000 shares authorized, no shares issued		
Common stock, $0.10 par value	75.6	75.6
Additional paid-in capital	5,394	5,333
Retained earnings	2,100	2,021
Accumulated other comprehensive loss	-160.8	-91.2
Unearned compensation	-7.2	-13.2
Treasury stock, at cost, of 60,000,000 and 45,000,000 shares, respectively	-1785.6	-1274.4
TOTAL STOCKHOLDERS' EQUITY	5,616	6,050
TOTAL LIABILITIES AND STOCKHOLDERS' EQUITY	$ 12,526	$ 13,675

KAST INC. PARTIAL CONSOLIDATED STATEMENTS OF CASH FLOWS

	Year Ended March 31,		
	2012	2011	2010
		(restated) (in millions)	(restated)
OPERATING ACTIVITIES:			
Net income (loss)	$ 190.8	$ 28.8	$ (33.6)
Income from discontinued operations, net of tax	3.6	—	73.2
Adjustment to gain on disposal of discontinued operations, net of tax	—	(2.4)	—
Income (loss) from continuing operations	187.2	31.2	(106.8)
Adjustments to reconcile income (loss) from continuing operations to net cash provided by continuing operating activities:			
Depreciation and amortization	699.6	692.4	716.4
Provision for deferred income taxes	(408)	(230.4)	(361.2)
Non-cash compensation expense related to stock and pension plans	118.8	139.2	178.8
Gain on asset divestitures	(8.4	—	(22.8)
Non-cash charge for in-process research and development	21.6	—	—
Foreign currency transaction (gain) loss — before taxes	(10.8)	9.6	49.2
Shareholder litigation settlement	—	19.2	189.6
Impairment charges for capitalized software	—	—	4.8
Changes in other operating assets and liabilities:			
Decrease in trade and installment receivables, net — current	328.8	454.8	285.6
Decrease in noncurrent installment accounts receivable, net	170.4	200.4	542.4
Increase in deferred subscription revenue (collected) — current	178.8	196.8	264
Increase (decrease) in deferred subscription revenue (collected) — noncurrent	214.8	(9.6)	110.4
Decrease in deferred maintenance revenue	(24)	(32.4)	(66)
Increase in taxes payable, net	90	196.8	42
Restitution fund, net	(180)	171.6	12
Restructuring and other, net	67.2	3.6	—
Increase (decrease) in accounts payable, accrued expenses and other	127.2	(169.2)	70
Changes in other operating assets and liabilities, excluding effects of acquisitions and divestitures	82.8	158.4	(387.6)
NET CASH PROVIDED BY CONTINUING OPERATING ACTIVITIES	1,656	1,832	1,535

Note 1 — Significant Accounting Policies

Basis of Revenue Recognition: The Company recognizes revenue pursuant to the requirements of Statement of Position (SOP) 97-2, "Software Revenue Recognition," issued by the American Institute of Certified Public Accountants, as amended by SOP 98-9 "Modification of SOP 97-2, Software Revenue Recognition, With Respect to Certain Transactions." In accordance with SOP 97-2, the Company begins to recognize revenue from licensing and supporting its software products when all of the following criteria are met: (1) the Company has evidence of an arrangement with a customer; (2) the Company delivers the products; (3) license agreement terms are deemed fixed or determinable and free of contingencies or uncertainties that may alter the agreement such that it may not be complete and final; and (4) collection is probable.

Note 9 — Trade and Installment Accounts Receivable

The Company uses installment license agreements as a standard business practice and has a history of successfully collecting substantially all amounts due under the original payment terms without making concessions on payments, software products, maintenance, or professional services. Net trade and installment accounts receivable represent financial assets derived from the committed amounts due from the Company's customers that have been earned by the Company. These accounts receivable balances are reflected net of unamortized discounts based on imputed interest for the time value of money for license agreements under our prior business model, unearned revenue attributable to maintenance, unearned professional services contracted for in the license agreement, and allowances for doubtful accounts. These balances do not include unbilled contractual commitments executed under the Company's current business model. Such committed amounts are summarized in Management's Discussion and Analysis of Financial Condition and Results of Operations. Trade and installment accounts receivable are comprised of the following components:

	December 31 2012	December 31, 2011
		(restated)
	(in millions)	
Current:		
Accounts receivable	$ 993.6	$ 952.8
Other receivables	92.4	46.8
Unbilled amounts due within the next 12 months — prior business model	304.8	469.2
Less: Allowance for doubtful accounts	(30)	(42)
Less: Unearned revenue — current	(754.8)	(495.6)
Net trade and installment accounts receivable — current	$ 606	$ 931.2
Noncurrent:		
Unbilled amounts due beyond the next 12 months — prior business model	$ 613.2	$ 910.8
Less: Allowance for doubtful accounts	(24)	(63.6)
Less: Unearned revenue — noncurrent	(50.4)	(133.2)
Net installment accounts receivable — noncurrent	$ 538.8	$ 714

The components of unearned revenue consist of the following:

	December 31, 2006	December 31 2005 (restated)
	(in millions)	
Current:		
Unamortized discounts	$ 52.8	$ 74.4
Unearned maintenance	4.8	27.6
Deferred subscription revenue (billed, uncollected)	640.8	376.8
Unearned professional services	56.4	16.8
Total unearned revenue — current	$ 754.8	$ 495.6
Noncurrent:		
Unamortized discounts	$ 40.8	$ 94.8
Unearned maintenance	9.6	38.4
Total unearned revenue — noncurrent	$ 50.4	$ 133.2

CHAPTER 11 | Special Income Statement Items and Other Issues in Full Disclosure

INTRODUCTION

The income statement is the primary source of information regarding the firm's ability to generate future cash flows needed to repay debt and to make earnings distributions to stockholders. For decades, accountants have debated the appropriateness of including unusual or nonrecurring items on the income statement. The current reporting standards are essentially based on a modified form of the all-inclusive concept of income. Under the modified all-inclusive concept, all items of profit and loss, except those events properly classified as prior period adjustments and components of other comprehensive income, should be reported on the income statement.

The original all-inclusive concept of income has been modified over the last 35 years. With the completion of the work of the AICPA's Study Group on the Objectives of Financial Statements in 1973[1], there has been a greater emphasis on reporting an accrual basis net income that is more closely related to the underlying cash flows of the firm. As a result of the work of the Study Group, the FASB requires that financial statements prepared in accordance with GAAP include a statement of cash flows. The cash flow statement will be discussed in detail in the last chapter of this text. In addition to the required cash flow statement, the accounting profession has now begun to exclude from reported income those items not reasonably expected to be converted into cash in the short run. These items are reported on the balance sheet as accumulated other comprehensive income as a component of total stockholders' equity. Some of these items discussed in previous chapters of this text include cumulative gain or loss on foreign currency translation adjustments, pension adjustments needed to reflect the funded status of the pension plan on the balance sheet and the cumulative unrealized gain or loss on adjustments to fair value the available for sale portfolio of investment securities and derivative financial instruments.

Aside from prior period adjustments and the other comprehensive income adjustments to stockholders' equity on the balance sheet, all other items of profit and loss must be reported on the income statement. This means that the income statement includes events and transactions that are normal and recurring as well as those that would be considered unusual, infrequent or both by a financial statement user.

In order to assist the credit and financial analyst in assessing the quality of accounting earnings and the degree of accounting risk associated with the reported income figure, the accounting profession identifies what it considers to be unusual and nonrecurring items.

The present income statement format divides the income statement into two major sections: (1) income (loss) from continuing operations, and (2) income or loss from unusual, nonrecurring or otherwise special events and transactions. These special items are identified by a separate "net of tax" treatment on the income statement. The following sample income statement will illustrate the current reporting format.

---

1. *Objectives of Financial Statements* (New York: American Institute of Certified Public Accountants, October, 1973).

Sample Corporation ***Income Statement*** ***For the Year Ended 12/31/XX***
Sales
Less: Cost of Goods Sold
Gross Profit (Margin)
Less: Operating Expenses
Add or deduct: Unusual **or** infrequent items
Income before Tax
Less: Income Tax Expense **(T)**
Income From Continuing Operations
ACCOUNTANT'S DIVIDING LINE
Gain (Loss) from Discontinued Operations -- Net of Tax **(T)**
Extraordinary Gain or Loss -- Net of Tax **(T)**
Net Income **(E)**
(T) *Along with reporting Prior Period Adjustments - Net of Tax as an adjustment to opening retained earnings on the balance sheet, the matching of the tax expense to the item that gives rise to the tax on the financial statements, within the same accounting period, is known as "Intraperiod Tax Allocation."* ***(E)*** *Earnings per share are usually reported below net income for each income statement category. That is, the disclosure includes EPS from income from continuing operations, EPS from discontinued operations, EPS on extraordinary items, and EPS from net income.*

As noted earlier, the purpose for using this income statement reporting format and EPS disclosures is to provide sufficient information to make a proper assessment of the quality of accounting earnings, in the aggregate and for each income statement category. For example, income generated from normal, continuing operating activities is considered to be of higher "quality" than an extraordinary gain because normal operating activities are frequent and recurring events that can be used to project the future cash flows of the firm. Extraordinary items and any of the unusual or special events noted in the sample income statement are nonrecurring and will not generate cash flows on a regular basis. As a result, the unusual items cannot be relied upon as a source of dividend distributions or principal and interest payments on corporate debt.

In the following sections of this chapter, the special income statement items will be discussed in detail. In addition, other events such as loss contingencies, related party transactions, segment disclosures and interim financial reporting will be presented. These issues impact full disclosure and the transparency of financial information.

SPECIAL INCOME STATEMENT ITEMS

Accounting for Extraordinary Items

According to APB Opinion No. 30, "Reporting the Results of Operations"[2], extraordinary items are defined as those material items with a character significantly different from the normal activities of the business and would not be expected to recur on a regular basis.

In order to operationalize the concept of an extraordinary item, Opinion 30, sets forth two specific criteria that must be met in order for an event to be classified as an extraordinary item. To be classified as an extraordinary item, the material event or transaction must be both:

1. Unusual in nature, and
2. Infrequent in occurrence, within the environment in which the firm operates.

It is interesting to note that in a literal application of the second criterion, a major loss of inventory due to a flood, in an area where there is frequent flooding, is not considered an extraordinary item because of the environment in which the firm operates.

Satisfying both of the Opinion 30 criteria may be difficult in practice, and this in fact was one of the objectives of Opinion 30. Prior to Opinion 30, the criteria for classification of an event as extraordinary were somewhat vague and left much of the classification choice to the discretion of management. If management believed that financial statement users discounted extraordinary items, an unusual transaction resulting in significant gains could be classified as part of normal operating income while material losses could be classified as extraordinary. This practice is sometimes known as "classificatory smoothing of income with extraordinary items".[3] The two Opinion 30 criteria severely limit this type of smoothing behavior.

Although the Opinion 30 criteria would be difficult to meet in practice, they would usually be satisfied in the case of any of the following three events:

1. A major casualty (e.g., fire, flood, earthquake, etc.);
2. Expropriation of assets by government;
3. Prohibition under a newly enacted law or regulation.

Unless each of these events is expected in the environment in which the firm operates.

At times it may be difficult to distinguish between the continuing operations of a business and extraordinary items. For example, the write-off of obsolete inventory is an expected part of most business operations, although it may not be frequent in occurrence. As a result, it would not qualify as an extraordinary item. However, if the government (e.g., the Food and Drug Administration) prohibited the sale of a certain inventory item, and the entire inventory of this item was written down to a zero value, this loss would then qualify as an extraordinary item.

In addition to meeting the specific criteria of Opinion 30, certain events not meeting the criteria may still be classified as extraordinary if required by a specific FASB professional pronouncement.

---

2. FASB ASC 225 [Predecessor literature: "Reporting the Results of Operations," *Opinions of the Accounting Principles Board No. 30* (New York: AICPA 1973)].

3. Joshua Ronen and Smirch Sedan, *Smoothing Income Numbers* (Reading, MA: Addison-Wesley Publishing Company, 1981).

It should be noted that the materiality of extraordinary items must be judged individually and not in the aggregate. Extraordinary items should be presented on the income statement after the gain or loss from discontinued operations but before net income.

A sample disclosure of an extraordinary item by Hummer Utility Company, Inc. in its 2012 annual report is presented in Exhibit 11.1. The details explaining the extraordinary loss are presented on one footnote.

EXHIBIT 11.1: EXTRAORDINARY ITEM DISCLOSURES AND PARTIAL INCOME STATEMENT FOR HUMMER UTILITY COMPANY, INC.

HUMMER UTILITY COMPANY, INC. AND SUBSIDIARY COMPANIES CONSOLIDATED STATEMENTS OF OPERATIONS For the Years Ended December 31, 2012, 2011 and 2010 (in millions, except per-share amounts)

	2012	2011	2010
REVENUES			
Utility Operations	$ 13,432	$ 12,797	$ 13,236
Gas Operations	555.6	3,682	3,720
Other	546	615.6	843.6
TOTAL	14,533	17,094	17,800
EXPENSES			
Fuel and Other Consumables Used for Electric Generation	4,310	3,671	3,776
Purchased Energy for Resale	824.4	804	848.4
Purchased Gas for Resale	307.2	3,368	3,420
Maintenance and Other Operation	4,379	4,440	4,531
Asset Impairments and Other Related Charges	46.8	-	780
Gain/Loss on Disposition of Assets, Net	(144)	(4.8)	(57.6)
Depreciation and Amortization	1,582	1,560	1,568
Taxes Other Than Income Taxes	915.6	876	841.2
TOTAL	12,221	14,714	15,708
OPERATING INCOME	2,312	2,380	2,092
Investment Income	126	39.6	30
Carrying Costs	66	362.4	-
Allowance For Equity Funds Used During Construction	25.2	18	16.8
Investment Value Losses	(8.4)	(18)	(84)
Gain on Disposition of Equity Investments, Net	67.2	183.6	-
INTEREST AND OTHER CHARGES			
Interest Expense	836.4	937.2	976.8
Preferred Stock Dividend Requirements of Subsidiaries	8.4	7.2	10.8
Minority Interest in Finance Subsidiary	-	-	20.4
TOTAL	844.8	944.4	1008
INCOME BEFORE INCOME TAX EXPENSE, MINORITY INTEREST		0	0
EXPENSE AND EQUITY EARNINGS	1,744	2,021	1046.4
Income Tax Expense	516	686.4	429.6
Minority Interest Expense	4.8	3.6	2.4
Equity Earnings of Unconsolidated Subsidiaries	12	21.6	12

INCOME BEFORE DISCONTINUED OPERATIONS, EXTRAORDINARY **LOSS AND CUMULATIVE EFFECT OF ACCOUNTING CHANGES**	1,235	0 1,352	0 (626.4)
DISCONTINUED OPERATIONS, Net of Tax	32.4	99.6	726
EXTRAORDINARY LOSS, Net of Tax	(270)	(145.2)	-
CUMULATIVE EFFECT OF ACCOUNTING CHANGES, Net of Tax			
Accounting for Risk Management Contracts			(58.8)
Asset Retirement Obligations	(20.4)		290.4
NET INCOME	$ 976.8	$ 1,307	$ 132
WEIGHTED AVERAGE NUMBER OF BASIC SHARES OUTSTANDING	468	475.2	462
BASIC EARNINGS (LOSS) PER SHARE			
Income Before Discontinued Operations, Extraordinary Loss and Cumulative Effect of Accounting Changes	$ 3.168	$ 3.42	$ 1.62
Discontinued Operations, Net of Tax	0.084	0.252	(1.884)
Extraordinary Loss, Net of Tax	(0.696)	0.372	
Cumulative Effect of Accounting Changes, Net of Tax	(0.048)		0.612
TOTAL BASIC EARNINGS PER SHARE	$ 2.508	$ 3.3	$ 0.348
WEIGHTED AVERAGE NUMBER OF DILUTED SHARES OUTSTANDING	469.2	475.2	462
DILUTED EARNINGS (LOSS) PER SHARE			
Income Before Discontinued Operations, Extraordinary Loss and Cumulative Effect of Accounting Changes	$ 3.156	$ 3.42	$ 1.62
Discontinued Operations, Net of Tax	0.084	0.252	(1.884)
Extraordinary Loss, Net of Tax	(0.696)	(0.372)	
Cumulative Effect of Accounting Changes, Net of Tax	(0.048)	-	0.612
TOTAL DILUTED EARNINGS PER SHARE	$ 2.496	$ 3.3	$ 0.348
CASH DIVIDENDS PAID PER SHARE	$ 1.704	$ 1.68	$ 1.98

See Notes to Consolidated Financial Statements.

NOTE 10:
EXTRAORDINARY ITEMS

Results for 2012 reflect net adjustments made by Hummer to its net true-up regulatory asset for the PUCT's final order in its True-up Proceeding issued in February 2013. Based on the final order, net true-up regulatory asset was reduced by $461 million. Of the $461 million, $414 million ($270 million, net of tax) was recorded as an extraordinary item in accordance with SFAS 101 "Regulated Enterprises - Accounting for the Discontinuation of Application of FASB Statement No. 71" (SFAS 101) and is reflected in our Consolidated Statements of Operations as Extraordinary Loss, Net of Tax.

In the fourth quarter of 2011, as part of its True-up Proceeding, Hummer made net adjustments totaling $222 million ($145 million, net of tax) to its stranded generation plant cost regulatory asset related to its transition to retail competition. These net adjustments were recorded as an extraordinary item of $145 million net of tax in accordance with SFAS 101 and are reflected in our Consolidated Statements of Operations as Extraordinary Loss, Net of Tax.

The losses in Exhibit 11.1 are classified as extraordinary because the write down of the regulatory assets was due to government regulations and the classification is also required by SFAS 101[4]. It should be mentioned that since there are few standards requiring extraordinary item treatment and given the difficulty in meeting the FASB criteria, one should expect a minimal number of companies reporting extraordinary items. This means that there are a significant number of unusual or infrequent events that are now reported routinely as components of income from continuing operations. The analytical issues surrounding the unusual or infrequent items are discussed in the next section.

EVENTS AND TRANSACTIONS THAT ARE UNUSUAL IN NATURE OR INFREQUENT IN OCCURRENCE BUT NOT BOTH

In practice, there are a significant number of transactions that are either unusual in nature or infrequent in occurrence, but not both.

Disposals of plant and equipment are not considered part of the normal operations of a service business. However, these events could be recurring. For example, a computer systems design firm could turnover its fleet of automobiles every three years. On the other hand, events such as the write-off of obsolete inventory or the write-off of a receivable from a major customer may not occur frequently, but must be considered a normal part of doing business. In both examples, the events are special either due to their unusual nature or infrequent occurrence. Nevertheless, these events do not meet both of the Opinion 30 criteria for classification as an extraordinary item, and would not be reported as such, unless the disposal of the fleet of automobiles, the write-off of the obsolete inventory and the receivable write-off were caused by a major casualty, expropriation by government or a prohibition under a newly enacted law or regulation.

If the event is not classified as an extraordinary item, the question for the accountant is how to properly report these events on the current income statement and the question for the analyst is to determine if the accountant's classification is satisfactory for a proper determination of the operating strength of the firm.

Reporting Issues

With respect to the accountant's classification question, Opinion 30 provides guidance as to the treatment of events that are either unusual or infrequent, but not both. If the gain or loss results from a transaction that is unusual in nature or infrequent in occurrence, but not both, its income statement disclosure depends on the materiality of the item.

1. If the gain or loss is not material in amount, the gain or loss is combined with other items of revenue and expense within the "income from continuing operations" section of the income statement and is not disclosed separately.
2. If the gain or loss is material in amount, the gain or loss is disclosed as a separate line item in the "income from continuing operations" section of the income statement. That is, the significant unusual or infrequent item would be presented above the "accountant's dividing line" on the current income statement. Examples include the gain or loss from disposal of property, plant and equipment, restructuring charges, inventory obsolescence reserves, environmental liability accruals, write offs for asset impairments, unless caused by a major casualty, expropriation, or a prohibition under a newly enacted law or regulation.

4. FASB ASC 980 [Predecessor literature: "Regulated Enterprises-Accounting for the Discontinuation of Application of *FASB Statement No. 71*," *Statement of Financial Accounting Standards No. 101* (Norwalk, Conn.: FASB, 1988)].

The disclosure required in item (2) above is similar to an extraordinary item in that it results in separate presentation on the income statement. However, several differences in presentation are required in order to distinguish these events from extraordinary items. To begin with, the unusual or infrequent gain or loss cannot be shown net of tax. In addition, there cannot be a separate EPS presentation for the unusual or infrequent gain or loss.

Sample disclosures of nonrecurring write-offs for items that are unusual in nature or infrequent in occurrence but not both reported in the 2012 annual report of Medina, Inc. are presented in Exhibit 11.2. These items include restructuring charges, asset impairments and litigation settlements. Footnote four provides an explanation of these items.

Analytical Issues

The issue for the credit and the financial analyst is to determine the proper treatment of the unusual or infrequent items in assessment of the future cash flows of the firm. It is clear from the Medina disclosures in Exhibit 11.2 that in substance, there is little difference between the nonrecurring write-offs and the extraordinary loss presented in Exhibit 11.1. For the Hummer Utility Company.

In this case, the credit and financial analyst should probably classify the restructuring charges and asset impairment write off, etc., as "extraordinary" items when assessing the quality of accounting earnings or conducting a trend or comparative analysis over several years.

Careful examination of Exhibits 11.1 and 11.2 points out another problem for the analyst. In both cases the term "operating income" includes unusual or infrequent items such as gain and loss on the disposal of plant assets, asset impairment charges, restructuring charges and litigation settlements. This requires an additional step to determine if any of these line items are "recurring" and whether the item should be included in an analyst's measure of EBIT and EBITDA in either the historical or estimation periods of a financial projection.

EXHIBIT 11.2: SAMPLE DISCLOSURES FOR UNUSUAL OR INFREQUENT ITEMS (BUT NOT BOTH) FOR MEDINA, INC.

Consolidated Statements of Operations

(in millions, except amounts per share)

	Years ended December 31,		
	2012	2011	2010
Product revenue	$ 2,548.80	$ 2,525.28	$ 2,291.40
Service revenue	383.76	364.68	339.6
Total revenue	2,932.56	2,889.96	2,631.00
Cost of sales	1,579.80	1,526.40	1,373.76
Gross profit	1,352.76	1,363.56	1,257.24
Operating costs and expenses			
Selling, general and administrative	782.76	727.2	666.36
Research and development	250.68	240	233.16
Restructure charge (credit)	43.68	(0.84)	22.2
Asset impairments	28.8	—	—
Litigation settlements	—	—	(59.88)
Total operating costs and expenses	1105.92	966.36	861.84
Operating income	246.84	397.2	395.4
Non-operating (income) expense			
Interest income	(21.72)	(15.84)	(11.88)
Interest expense	52.56	43.44	48.24
Other, net	17.28	35.76	31.68
Total non-operating expense	48.12	63.36	68.04
Earnings before income taxes	198.72	333.84	327.36
Income taxes	18	80.76	78.72
Net income	$ 180.72	$ 253.08	$ 248.64
Basic earnings per share	$ 2.904	$ 4.104	$ 4.056
Diluted earnings per share	$ 2.784	$ 3.852	$ 3.852
Weighted average number of shares outstanding (in thousands) Basic	74,748	73,972	73,454
Diluted	77,833	78,928	77,392

Restructuring Activities and Asset Impairments

Restructuring Activities—In June 2012, the Company announced a strategic reorganization of its business. The objective of the restructure is to better enable the Company to leverage its personnel, technologies and products. As a result of these activities the Company expects to eliminate approximately 1,500 positions worldwide. A charge of $41.8 million was recorded in 2012 for severance and related benefits for affected employees. Additional charges may also be incurred in 2013 as other aspects of the reorganization are implemented.

Asset Impairments—As a result of the restructuring activities, the Company exited certain non-strategic products and products under development. Additionally, the Company exited certain non-strategic product lines and certain non-core product lines.

As it was determined that the Company no longer had significant sales and cash flow expectations for the assets related to the above projects and product lines, as well as other less significant products, the Company recorded a $28.8 million charge to write-off patents, licenses and other related assets. The patent amounts were written down to their estimated fair values as determined by their discounted cash flows. Additionally, charges of $2.8 million were recorded in cost of goods sold for inventory write-offs related to products that are no longer being offered by the Company, and $1.9 million in selling, general and administrative expenses for other costs related to the restructuring.

The previous discussion indicates that the provisions of Opinion 30 may have substituted one analytical problem for another. Prior to Opinion 30, the analyst was faced with the problem of determining if management was attempting to smooth income through the improper classification of items as extraordinary or ordinary income. With Opinion 30, the classification of events as extraordinary is relatively limited. However, the classification of a gain or loss as an unusual or infrequent item, together with the related disclosures, may result in the additional problem of carefully analyzing this information and possibly reclassifying them as extraordinary in the analysts' trend analysis or cash flow projections.

Although the provisions of Opinion 30 have resulted in a significant improvement in classification and reporting of extraordinary items, proper analysis of unusual or infrequent events remains a continuing problem for the credit and financial analyst.

Analytical Restatement

As noted earlier, in both Exhibits 11.1 and 11.2, the gain or loss from unusual or infrequent items is reported as a component of operating income. However, the analyst usually reclassifies such items as extraordinary, if material and if not expected to recur over the projection period. In this case, the item would not be considered in an analyst's EBIT or EBITDA projections. This analytical restatement is performed because the items are considered nonrecurring or unusual, regardless of the accountant's classification as operating income. An example of the analytical restatement is presented below for Medina, Inc. as presented in Exhibit 11.2 for 2012.

In the following analytical restatement, it is assumed that the analyst has determined that the restructuring charges and the asset impairment write off should be considered nonrecurring. As a result, these charges are removed from the analyst's measure of EBIT and are reclassified as "extraordinary" for modeling purposes. It is likely that an analyst would use a normalized tax rate in building a financial projection (e.g., 40%). The illustration below assumes that the effective tax rate is used. The effective tax rate is 9.1% and determined from the actual income statement by dividing tax expense by earnings before tax (i.e., $15.0 / $165.6). The use of the effective tax rate results in the same bottom line for both the reported net income and the analytically restated net income. This bottom line equality is sometimes desired by an analyst. The resulting EBIT of $266.1 is properly determined for analytical purposes.

Actual		*Analytical Restatement*	
Total revenue	$2,932.6	Total revenue	$2,,932.6
Cost of goods sold	1,579.8	Cost of goods sold	1,579.8
Gross profit	$1,352.8	Gross profit	$1,352.8
Operating costs and expenses:		Operating costs and expenses:	
Selling, general and administrative	$782.8	Selling, general and administrative	$782.8
Research and development	250.7	Research and development	250.7
Restructuring charge	43.7	Total	$ 1,033.5
Asset impairments	28.8	Operating Income (EBIT)	$ 319.3
Total	$ 1,105.9	Non-operating (income) & expense:	
Operating income	$ 246.8	Interest income	($21.7)
Non-operating (income) & expense:		Interest expense	52.6
Interest income	($21.7)	Other net	17.3
Interest expense	52.6	Total	$ 48.2
Other net	17.3	Income before "Extraordinary" items	$ 271.1
Total	$ 48.2	Income taxes @ a 9.1% effective rate	24.7
Earnings before tax	$ 198.7	Income after tax before "Extraordinary" items	$ 246.4
		Restructuring charge (net of tax)	39.6
		Asset impairments (net of tax)	26.1
Income taxes @ a 9.1% effective rate	18.0		
Net income	$ 180.7	Net income	$ 180.7

There is another analytical issue to consider. Because management has a great deal of discretion as to when it faces up to these types of charges, the write-off, etc., many of the charges may actually represent an adjustment of prior years' income overstatements or an attempt to smooth future years' income (i.e., taking a big bath this year). As a result, the nonrecurring charges cannot be ignored as they may impact assessment of earnings growth trends. An analyst must also distinguish between those nonrecurring items with cash flow implications and those without any real effects. As noted earlier, a decision must be made as to the recurring nature of items that may generally be unusual or infrequent, but occur each year of the analysis' estimation (i.e., historical) period.

ACCOUNTING FOR DISCONTINUED OPERATIONS

Accounting for discontinued operations is presently governed by the rules set forth by FASB Statement No. 144 "Accounting for the Impairment or Disposal of Long-Lived Assets"[5]. Under SFAS 144 the reporting requirements for discontinued operations now apply to a "component of an entity" and are not restricted to a defined business segment. According to SFAS 144, a component of an entity is "clearly distinguishable" from the rest of the entity because it has its own operations and cash flows. SFAS 144 indicates that the component must be separate: physically, operationally and for financial reporting purposes, from the other components of the business. Also, management regularly assesses the component's income and cash flows.

As noted above the discontinued operations include a disposal of a component of a business, a business segment or a major product line. The component can also be held for sale. The FASB requires the disclosure of a separate income statement category "Discontinued Operations" showing the total gain or loss from the discontinued operation, net of tax.

5. FASB ASC 360 [Predecessor literature: "Accounting for the Impairment or Disposal of Long-Lived Assets," *Statement of Financial Accounting Standards No. 144* (Norwalk, Conn.: FASB 2001)].

Income Statement Disclosures

The gain or loss, (net of tax), from the discontinued operation consists of two elements. The two elements can be disclosed separately on the face of the income statement or in a single line item with the details of the two portions provided in a footnote. The two elements of the gain or loss on discontinued operations are the profit or loss from the discontinued component's operations and the gain or loss on actual disposal.

1. The profit or loss from operations of the discontinued component. This is shown net of tax. This component is nothing more than an "income statement" for the discontinued operation from the beginning of the year to the end of the year (if the disposal does not take place during the year), or the disposal date, (if the component is sold during the year). Segregating these revenues and expenses from continuing operations assists the financial statement user in projecting the future cash flows of the firm. Recurring cash flows cannot be expected in the future from the discontinued operation.
2. The gain or loss from the disposal of the component. This element includes the gain or loss on the sale of the investment in the discontinued subsidiary, division, etc. The sale of the investment consists of either a sale of ownership shares or individual net assets. Future losses (and gains) may not be anticipated or estimated and only recognized when incurred. If however the component is held for sale, an impairment loss can be recognized as the difference between the fair value and the carrying value of the business component.

Qualifications

FASB Statement No. 144 requires that discontinued operation disclosures are required for any business component that has either been disposed of or is currently held for sale if both of the following conditions are met:

- The operations and cash flows of the component have been or will be removed from the ongoing operations of the entity as a result of the disposal transaction, and
- The entity will have no significant continuing involvement in the operations of the component after the disposal transaction.

For example, if General Electric Company sells its interest in NBC Broadcasting, it should qualify for discontinued operations treatment, but if Sears discontinues its sporting goods departments it may not qualify. However, since SFAS 144 no longer requires that the discontinued operation be a segment, it provides a much broader coverage of what qualifies for discontinued operations treatment. For example, if Yum Brands decides to close all its KFC restaurants in New York City, it could qualify as a discontinued operation if it meets the SFAS 144 criteria.

Income Statement Disclosures

In the period in which a component of an entity is either classified as held-for-sale or has been disposed of, the results of operations of that component and any gain or loss recognized on disposal is reported as a separate component of income, before extraordinary items (if any). The income statements of any prior periods being presented should be restated to also reflect the results of operations of the component as discontinued operations. All amounts should be reported less applicable income taxes (benefits), as shown in Exhibit 11.3.

This example shows the loss on disposal on the face of the income statement. Alternatively, the amount can be shown in the notes to the financial statements, as long as the disclosure identifies the caption in the income statement in which the loss in included. A sample footnote is also provided in Exhibit 11.3.

Assets and Liabilities of a Discontinued Operation

Assets and liabilities of a disposal group classified as held-for-sale are presented separately in their respective sections of the balance sheet. Offsetting of these amounts is not permitted. The balance sheet presentation for assets and liabilities of a discontinued component are also presented in Exhibit 11.3. Note any assets held for sale are carried at the lower of carrying value or fair value and are not depreciated.

EXHIBIT 11.3: DISCONTINUED OPERATIONS DISCLOSURES FOR WALKER INDUSTRIES

Walker Industries 2012 Annual Report

Partial Consolidated Statements of Earnings ($ in millions, except per share amounts)

For the Fiscal Years Ended	December 31, 2012	December 31, 2011	December 31, 2010
Revenue	$ 29,456	$ 25,135	$ 21,253
Cost of goods sold	22,020	18,852	16,729
Gross profit	7,436	6,283	4,524
Selling, general and administrative expenses	5,872	5,071	3,434
Operating income	1,565	1,212	1,089.6
Net interest (expense) income	(9.6)	4.8	21.6
Earnings from continuing operations before income tax expense	1,555	1,217	1,111.2
Income tax expense	595.2	470.4	427.2
Earnings from continuing operations	***960***	***746.4***	***684***
Loss from discontinued operations (Note 8), net of $20.4 and $142.8 tax	***(34.8)***	***(529.2)***	—
Loss on disposal of discontinued operations (Note 8), net tax	***(79.2)***	—	—

Partial Consolidated Balance Sheets ($ in millions, except per share amounts)

Assets	**December 31, 2012**	**December 31, 2011**
Current Assets		
Cash and cash equivalents	$ 3,120	$ 2,297
Receivables	411.6	374.4
Merchandise inventories	3,128	2,492
Other current assets	208.8	237.6
Current assets of discontinued operations	—	***476.4***
Total current assets	6,869	5,878
Property and Equipment		
Land and buildings	580.8	249.6
Leasehold improvements	1033.2	862.8
Fixtures and equipment	2,581	2,530
Property under master and capital lease	93.6	64.8
	4,289	3,707
Less accumulated depreciation and amortization	1,596	1,232
Net property and equipment	2,693	2,474
Goodwill, Net	572.4	514.8
Intangible Assets	37	39.6
Other Assets	170	138
Noncurrent Assets of Discontinued Operations	—	***188.4***
Total Assets	$ 8,652	$ 9,233

Liabilities and Shareholders' Equity	**December 31, 2012**	**December 31, 2011**
Current Liabilities		
Accounts payable	$ 3,042	$ 2,634
Unredeemed gift card liabilities	360	266.4
Accrued compensation and related expenses	322.8	208.8
Accrued liabilities	778.8	645.6
Accrued income taxes	456	448.8
Current portion of long-term debt	441.6	1.2
Current liabilities of discontinued operations	—	***384***
Total current liabilities	5,401	4,589
Long-Term Liabilities	296.4	344.4
Long-Term Debt	578.4	993.6
Noncurrent Liabilities of Discontinued Operations	—	***30***

Footnotes:

8. Discontinued Operations

In July 2011 we committed to a plan to sell HEBB products. The loss from discontinued operations for fiscal 2012 includes a loss on the disposal of discontinued operations (which was primarily non-cash) of $79.2, net of tax. In accordance with FASB No. 144, financial results of our discontinued operations are reported separately as discontinued operations for all periods presented.

During fiscal 2011, we recorded an after-tax, non-cash impairment charge of $369.6 for the full write-off of goodwill related to our acquisition of HEBB Products. In addition, we recorded an after-tax, non-cash charge of $9.6 for the change in our method of accounting for HEBB vendor allowances. The charges are classified as cumulative effects of changes in accounting principles in discontinued operations (see Note 1, Summary of Significant Accounting Policies, above).

Also during fiscal 2011, in accordance with FASB No. 144, we recorded an impairment charge of $199.2 before tax in "(Loss) earnings before income taxes" related to a reassessment of the carrying value of HEBB's long-lived assets. We determined fair values utilizing widely accepted valuation techniques, including discounted cash flows. We based fair values on the then-current expectations for the business in light of the then-existing retail environment and the uncertainty associated with future trends in prerecorded music products.

The financial results of HEBB, included in discontinued operations, were as follows:

For the Fiscal Years Ended	**Dec. 31, 2012**	**Dec. 31, 2011**	**Dec. 31, 2010**
Revenue	$ 424.8	$ 2,072	$ 2,263
(Loss) earnings before income taxes	(55.2)	(292.8)	12
Loss before the disposal and the cumulative effect of accounting changes, net of $17, $119 and $10 tax, respectively	(34.8)	(150)	—
Loss on disposal of discontinued operations, net of $0 tax	(79.2)	—	—
Cumulative effect of change in accounting principles, net of $5 tax	—	(379.2)	—
Loss from discontinued operations, net of tax	(114)	(529.2)	—

There were no assets or liabilities of HEBB included in our balance sheet at December 31, 2012. The current and noncurrent assets and liabilities of HEBB as of December 31, 2011, were as follows:

	December 2011
Cash and cash equivalents	$ 2.4
Receivables	3.6
Merchandise inventories	379.2
Other current assets	91.2
Current assets of discontinued operations	**$ 476.4**
Net property and equipment	$ 82.8
Other assets	105.6

Noncurrent assets of discontinued operations	**$**	**188.4**
Accounts payable	$	249.6
Accrued compensation and related expenses		16.8
Accrued liabilities		117.6
Current liabilities of discontinued operations	**$**	**384**
Long-term liabilities	$	24
Long-term debt		6
Noncurrent liabilities of discontinued operations	**$**	**30**

Analytical Issues

Although there are adequate disclosures under SFAS 144, there are several issues to consider in the analysis of discontinued operations. To begin with, the analyst must be aware of the restatement of prior periods' financial statements in the year of the measurement date. There will be several line items on the income statement and balance sheet that will be reduced by the removal of the revenues, expenses, assets and liabilities of the discontinued component. The segregation of these line items could result in a significant distortion and a lack of comparability in a time series of financial ratios. In this case, the analyst may consider using the footnote disclosures to compute financial ratios both "with and without" the discontinued operation. In this way, the analyst can analytically restate the financial statements and compute ratios, etc., as if the component was not discontinued, and restore comparability with prior years. This approach can be useful in determining the extent of the bias created by the accounting for discontinued operations, but the restated ratios should not be used in projections. Only the numbers generated by the continuing components of the business will create future cash flows and enhance firm value. In this case, the analyst must carefully examine the footnote information provided in order to determine the significance of the key income statement line items, the net assets of the discontinued operation and the possible distortion of financial ratios and other statistics based on total assets, plant assets and liabilities. These details are included in the footnote disclosure in Exhibit 11.3

For purposes of projections and modeling it is only useful to employ the data "as reported" with the results of operations and financial condition of the discontinued component eliminated. In this case, using three years of historical income information and two years of balance sheet data for obtaining trends and relationships to be used in the estimation period of the model may be the most practical solution to the estimation problem when there are discontinued components. By excluding the discontinued component, financial statistics would more properly reflect the expected, recurring operating strength of the firm and would provide better information for projecting the firm's future cash flows.

Another problem for the analyst is to determine if all discontinued operations are properly identified in the financial statements. The vague criteria of SFAS 144 may result in a discontinued component not qualifying for discontinued operations treatment on the income statement. For example, if the accountants and the management of the firm determine that a component to be disposed of is not "clearly distinguishable" from the other operations of the firm, this component would not be reported as a discontinued operation. This event could be reported as a restructuring rather than a discontinued operation. Without discontinued operations treatment, all of the revenue, expenses, assets and liabilities of the discontinued component may still be combined within the continuing operations of the firm. In this case, the analyst must examine the footnotes to the financial statements for information regarding the disposal of the component and make the appropriate adjustments to the income, assets and liabilities of the continuing operations. Again, by excluding the discontinued component, financial statistics would more properly reflect the expected, recurring operating strength of the firm and would provide better information for projecting the firm's future cash flows.

Although reported "below the line" and excluded from projections of sustainable income and cash flows, management's strategy for exiting the line of business must be considered by an analyst. This includes the implications for future business policies and modifications to the firm's lines of business.

ACCOUNTING CHANGES

Accounting Changes (APB Opinion No. 20-revised by FASB Statement No. 154)[6]

All accounting changes violate the consistency principle of accounting. However, accounting changes are permitted as long as adequate disclosure is available to assist financial statement users in restoring comparability with prior years' financial information presented.

The major types accounting changes are:

1. Change in accounting estimate.
2. Change in accounting principle or method.
3. Change in the reporting entity.
4. Correction of an error made in previously issued financial statements classified as a prior period adjustment.

We will focus on changes in accounting estimate and changes in accounting principle in this chapter.

There are two approaches to reporting accounting changes. These are the retroactive or retrospective type change and the prospective type change. The following sections of this chapter will review the advantages and disadvantages of the two approaches. It should be noted that the income statement cumulative effect type change is no longer acceptable under GAAP.

The retrospective or the retroactive type accounting change

In a Retroactive-Effect Type Change, all prior years' financial statements presented in the annual report are restated "as if" the newly adopted principle had always been used. In addition, opening retained earnings in the first balance sheet presented is adjusted for the cumulative effect of applying the new principle in all prior years.

This type of change is preferred from an analyst's perspective, because the retroactive application of the new standard will restore comparability with prior years. In addition, a large cumulative effect on the income statement in the year of the change is avoided. A cumulative effect adjustment can be very material in amount and distort net income and earnings per share. The large cumulative effect adjustment can be a distraction in the analysis

6. FASB ASC 250 [Predecessor literature: "Accounting Changes and Error Corrections- a replacement of *APB Opinion No. 20 and FASB Statement No. 3*," *Statement of Financial Accounting Standards No. 154* (Norwalk, Conn.: FASB, 2005)].

of financial statements and is no longer permitted.

A prospective or future adjustment

In the case of a prospective type accounting change, the change is made in the current year (i.e., the year of the change) and all future years. Prior periods are not adjusted and there is also no cumulative effect on the income statement. Opening retained earnings are not adjusted in the first balance sheet presented

A prospective adjustment does not restate prior years' information and eliminates the large cumulative effect adjustment on the face of the income statement in the year of the change.

FASB Statement No. 154 eliminates the use of the cumulative effect type of change and requires retrospective adjustments for all changes in accounting principle, except where it is impractical to do so (to be discussed). In addition, SFAS 154 also requires prospective adjustments for all changes in accounting estimate.

Application of retroactive accounting treatment is impractical if any one of the following three conditions exist:

1. The effects of the retroactive application are not determinable.
2. Retroactive application requires assumptions about management's intent in a prior period.
3. Retroactive application requires significant estimates for a prior period, and the availability of the necessary information to determine these estimates cannot be objectively verified.

If any one of these three conditions exists, retroactive application cannot be implemented and the change in accounting principle is applied prospectively. An example of an "impractical change in accounting principle" is a change to the LIFO method. Determination base layers of inventory at prior year's prices would be impractical from a cost-benefit perspective.

Change in Accounting Estimate

As noted above, a change in accounting estimate must be applied prospectively. A change in accounting estimate involves revisions of estimates used in accounting for areas such as the bad debts expense, depreciation, depletion and amortization and accounting for pensions. Estimates are a natural part of the accounting process. Changes in estimate are expected, particularly with experience and as new information become available. Therefore, changes in estimates are not viewed as unusual events. Any adjustments made are "prospective in nature". That is, the new estimate is implemented in the year of the change and in all future years. No retroactive adjustments are made to previously issued financial statements.

For example, assume a firm acquires a plant asset for $1,000. It is depreciated on the straight-line basis over a 10-year period and with no scrap value. Annual depreciation is $100 per year, (i.e., $1,000/10 years). After six years, when the asset's net book value is $400, (i.e., $1,000 - ($100 x 6 yrs)), the company believes the asset will be productive for another 8 years. Therefore, the revised depreciation is $50 / per year, (i.e., $400/8 years). The revised depreciation is used from the year of the change to the date of disposal or another accounting change. All prior years are not restated. If the effect of this change on net income is material, it must be disclosed in the footnotes to the financial statements.

At times it is difficult to differentiate between a change in accounting estimate and change in accounting principle. This is true in the case of a change in depreciation method. The FASB classifies a change in depreciation method as a "change in accounting estimate that is affected by a change in accounting principle". A change in depreciation method is based on many changes in estimate regarding the future economic benefits to be derived from the use of the asset, etc. So, a change in depreciation method is accounted for as a change in accounting estimate.

Change in Accounting Principle

A change in accounting principle must be accounted for on a retroactive basis, unless it is impractical to do so. The change in principle can be voluntary or mandatory (e.g., a new FASB standard is issued).

A change in accounting principle involves changing from one GAAP method to another. For example, a switch from the average cost method to the FIFO method of accounting for inventory for financial reporting purposes qualifies as a change in accounting principle.

The change in GAAP accounting method results in a violation of the consistency principle of accounting. When consistency is violated, the financial statements are no longer comparable from period to period. Nevertheless, consistency does not prohibit changes in accounting principle. The change is acceptable as long as there is adequate accounting for the change and disclosure of its effects in the financial statements.

As noted earlier, in a retroactive-effect type change, all prior years' financial statements presented in the annual report are restated "as if" the newly adopted principle had always been used. In addition, opening retained earnings for the first balance sheet presented is adjusted for the cumulative effect of applying the new principle in all prior years.

Accounting for a Change in Principle

As discussed earlier, when a company changes from one GAAP method of accounting to another, the consistency principle of accounting is violated. Consecutive years' financial statements are no longer comparable when consistency is violated. The accounting profession permits changes in principle and violations of consistency as long as there is adequate disclosure. Disclosure is adequate when it restores comparability and is transparent.

For any change in accounting principle, the following footnote disclosures must be provided. In the year of the change, (and for all subsequent years in which the year of the change is included in the annual report), a footnote to the financial statements should include the following information:

1. The nature of the change, (e.g., "...effective January 1, 2008, the company changed its method of accounting for inventory from the FIFO method to the Average Cost method").
2. Management's justification for the change, (e.g., "...management believes that the new method of accounting for inventory valuation will better match costs and revenues or better reflect the company's operations").
3. The effect of the change on net income after tax (i.e., "...net income after tax would have been $1,000,000, ($1.23 per share) greater if the FIFO method (i.e., the old method) was still used").

The last footnote requirement assists the user in restoring comparability with prior years. That is, the footnote information can be used to restate the current year's income to what it would have been under the old method. However, this restatement is only useful in determining the extent of the bias resulting from the retroactive accounting change. Of course, only the financial information computed using the new method would be useful making future years financial projections.

Illustration: Retroactive Application of an Accounting Change. Assume that at the beginning of 2008, the firm elects to switch from the FIFO method to average cost method of accounting for inventory cost for financial reporting purposes. The firm still uses FIFO for tax purposes and is subject to a 40% tax rate Cost of goods sold under both methods is presented in the table below.

YEAR	***Cost of Goods Sold FIFO - Old***	***Cost of Goods Sold Average Cost Method- New***
2004	$7,000	$8,000
2005	5,000	6,000
2006	6,000	7,000
2007	4,000	5,000
2008	2,000	3,000

Given this data, you are asked to compute the effects of the change, prepare the financial modeling worksheet reflecting implementation of the change and summarize the required financial statement disclosures. The calculation of the effects of the change from the FIFO to average cost method is presented in the following table.

	PRIOR YEARS			***FIRST BALANCE SHEET PRESENTED***	***YEAR OF THE CHANGE***
METHOD	***2004***	***2005***	***2006***	***2007***	***2008***
FIFO – OLD	$7,000	$5,000	$6,000	$4,000	$2,000
AVERAGE COST-NEW	8,000	6,000	7,000	5,000	3,000
	($1,000)	($1,000)	($1,000)	($1,000)	($1,000)

TOTAL PRE-TAX CUMULATIVE EFFECT = ($4,000)

Summary Cumulative Effect:
Before Tax: ($4,000)
After Tax : ($2,400)

PRE-TAX CUMULATIVE EFFECT FOR THE FIRST BALANCE SHEET PRESENTED = ($3,000)

Summary Cumulative Effect:
Before Tax: ($3,000)
After Tax : ($1,800)

INFORMATION FOR FOOTNOTE DISCLOSURE:
"NET INCOME AFTER TAX WOULD HAVE BEEN $600 (I.E., $1,000 X [1 - 40%]) GREATER IF FIFO WAS STILL USED BY THE FIRM."

FINANCIAL STATEMENT PRESENTATION STATEMENTS OF INCOME			
	2008	**2007***	**2006***
REVENUES (assumed)	$20,000	$32,000	$31,000
COST OF GOOD SOLD (ALL YEARS ON AVERAGE COST)	(3,000)	(5,000)	(7,000)
OPERATING EXPENSES (assumed)	(4,000)	(8,000)	(5,000)
DEPRECIATION EXPENSE (assumed)	(3,000)	(3,000)	(4,000)
NET INCOME BEFORE TAX.	$ 10,000	$ 16,000	$ 15,000
INCOME TAX EXPENSE @ 40%	(4,000)	(6,400)	(6,000)
NET INCOME	$ 6,000	$ 9,600	$ 9,000
**** = 2007 AND 2006 Restated to reflect the new method of accounting.***			

Partial Balance Sheet	***2008***	***2007***
Assets		
CURRENT ASSETS:		
Inventory ***(Prior years' change only)*** ***(Effect from applying to 2007)***		(3,000) (1,000)
Deferred Tax Asset ***(Prior years' change only: $3,000 X 40%)*** ***(Effect from applying to 2007: $1,000 X 40%)***		+1,200 + 400
Net Balance Sheet Effect in 2004		($2,400)
Stockholders' Equity		
Beginning Retained Earnings (as previously reported – assumed)		
Less: Cumulative effect from a change to the Average Method of Accounting for Inventory –Net of tax		(1,800)
Beginning Retained Earnings (as adjusted)		
Net Income (Effect from applying new method in 2007		(600)
		($2,400)

For purposes of this illustration, the balance sheet effects for the first year presented have been separated into the current year's effect (i.e., 2007), and the effects for all prior years. For example, inventory is reduced $4,000 through 2007. However, $1,000 of this reduction applies to 2007 and the remaining $3,000 is due to adjustments for all prior years. The same presentation applies to the deferred tax asset and the retained earnings adjustments. A deferred tax asset is created because the firm still uses FIFO for tax, computes taxable income using a lower cost of goods sold and pays more tax today, relative to book using average cost.

FINANCIAL MODELING WORKSHEET FOR THE BEGINNING OF THE YEAR OF THE CHANGE, 2008

INCOME STATEMENT (FIRST)	
REVENUES:	
EXPENSES:	
NET INCOME OR LOSS (a)	

STATEMENT OF CASH FLOWS (THIRD)	
OPERATING ACTIVITIES:	
NET INCOME OR LOSS (a)	
INVESTING ACTIVITIES:	
FINANCING ACTIVITIES:	
INCREASE (DECREASE) IN CASH (b)	
ADD: BEGINNING CASH BALANCE	
ENDING CASH BALANCE	

BALANCE SHEET (SECOND)			
ASSETS		***LIABILITIES***	
CURRENT ASSETS		***CURRENT LIABILITIES***	
CASH (b)			
Inventory	***(4,000)***		
		NONCURRENT LIABILITIES	
		STOCKHOLDERS'	
NONCURRENT ASSETS		***EQUITY***	
Deferred Tax Asset	***1,600***	***CAPITAL STOCK***	
		APIC	
		RETAINED	
		EARNINGS (a)	***(2,400)***
		TOTAL	
		LIABILITIES &	
		STOCKHOLDERS'	
TOTAL ASSETS	***(2,400)***	***EQUITY***	***(2,400)***

The effects of the change will be reflected in the first balance sheet presented (i.e., 2007). Sample disclosures for a retroactive accounting change are presented in Exhibit 11.4 below.

EXHIBIT 11.4: RETROACTIVE ACCOUNTING CHANGE DISCLOSURES FOR THE HOLLY GROUP 2012 ANNUAL REPORT

Footnote Disclosures:

19. Accounting Changes

As of January 1, 2012, the Company changed the method of determining the cost of certain U.S. inventories which previously utilized the LIFO method to the FIFO method. The change was made as the FIFO method more accurately reflects the replacement cost of inventory. The Company has operated in a low inflationary environment, and frequently a deflationary environment, for a number of years, thus reducing any potential advantages of the LIFO method in matching current revenues with current costs. Additionally, the change enhances the comparability of the Company's financial statements with its peers' as FIFO is the predominant method utilized in its industry. As a result, all inventories are now valued at the lower of cost, determined on a FIFO basis, or market. All previously reported results have been restated to reflect the retroactive application of the accounting change as required by APB Opinion No. 20, "Accounting Changes."

Item 6. Selected Financial Data

	2012	2011	2010	2009	2008
Per common share					
Net income					
Basic	**$ 3.072**	$ 1.788	$ 1.836	$ 1.716	$ 1.236
Diluted	**2.976**	1.728	1.788	1.68	1.212
Dividends paid	**1.008**	0.96	0.96	0.96	0.96
Stockholders' equity (at year-end)	**19.752**	18.108	17.28	13.668	13.452
Stock price (at year-end)	**39.6**	31.812	38.772	24.42	28.788
For the year *(in thousands)*					
Net sales	**$1,322,609**	$ 1,193,651	$ 1,068,982	$ 940,843	$ 922,585
Operating income	**104,034**	69,098	62,201	53,126	48,205
As a percent of sales	**7.9%**	5.8%	5.8%	5.6%	5.2%
Income before income taxes and cumulative effect of a change in accounting principle	**$ 94,153**	$ 51,632	$ 45,842	$ 39,052	$ 27,973
Income taxes	**21,064**	10,321	6,347	6,889	5,137
Net income	**72,620**	41,311	39,496	32,162	22,836
As a percent of average stockholders' equity	**16.2%**	10.1%	11.8%	12.3%	9.1%
Depreciation and amortization	**$ 41,830**	$ 41,012	$ 41,485	$ 40,351	$ 44,454
Capital expenditures	**31,316**	34,211	22,076	23,240	29,828
Average common shares outstanding - basic	**28,319**	27,727	25,770	22,500	22,207
Year-end financial position *(in thousands)*					
Working capital	**$ 144,970**	$ 151,996	$ 159,542	$ 144,102	$ 104,442
Current ratio	**1.5 to 1**	1.6 to 1	1.7 to 1	1.9 to 1	1.5 to 1
Property, plant and equipment	**$ 188,467**	$ 199,541	$ 184,906	$ 191,328	$ 183,532
Total assets	**1,199,890**	1,124,354	1,006,121	792,295	775,844
Long-term debt and notes payable	**343,230**	321,654	289,220	265,154	277,729
Stockholders' equity	**474,246**	199,541	395,224	259,124	248,282
Debt as a percent of total capitalization	**42%**	43.3%	42.3%	50.6%	52.8%
Year-end statistics					
Employees	**7,446**	6,047	7,231	6,206	6,180

ACCOUNTING FOR CONTINGENCIES

Introduction

FASB Statement No. 5, "Accounting for Contingencies"[7], defines a contingency as an existing condition, situation or set of circumstances involving uncertainty as to possible gain (i.e., a gain contingency or a contingent asset) or loss (i.e., a loss contingency or a contingent liability), to a firm that will ultimately be resolved when one or more future events occur or fail to occur.

As indicated by the FASB's definition of a contingency, there are two types of contingencies: a gain contingency and a loss contingency. The actual accounting for the contingency will depend on its type. In general, there are three possible accounting alternatives for a contingency. These are:

1. Recognize (accrue) the contingent event in the current financial statements and disclose in the footnotes;
2. Disclose the event only in the footnotes to the financial statements;
3. Make no disclosure.

As will be discussed in the following sections, the accounting alternative actually used will not only depend on the type of contingency, but will also depend on the probability of future occurrence and the ability to estimate the amount of the contingent event.

Accounting for Gain Contingencies

A gain contingency is an uncertain right or claim, which may become a valid property right in the future. Due to conservatism, contingent assets are never recorded or accrued in the accounts and the financial statements, and are disclosed in the footnotes only when there is almost complete certainty of realization in the future. Examples of gain contingencies that may be disclosed in the footnotes to the financial statements include favorable settlements of tax disputes with the IRS or favorable settlements of litigation.

Accounting for Loss Contingencies

A loss contingency or a contingent liability is a potential obligation whose realization is dependent upon the occurrence of some future event or the failure of the event to occur. In the case of a loss contingency, all three accounting alternatives are used. The particular alternative used is dependent on the probability of occurrence and the ability to provide a reasonable estimation of the future loss.

Recognition of the Loss Contingency in the Financial Statements

An estimated loss is accrued and charged against income, and a liability is recorded or an asset is reduced if both of the following SFAS 5, criteria are met:

1. Prior to the issuance of the financial statements there is evidence that it is "probable" that a liability has been incurred or an asset has been reduced as of the date of the financial statements;

7. FASB ASC 450 [Predecessor literature: "Accounting for Contingencies," *Statement of Financial Accounting Standards No. 5* (Norwalk, Conn.: FASB, 1975)].

2. The amount of the loss is subject to "reasonable estimation".

Common examples of loss contingencies that are accrued and reported on the financial statements are the bad debt expense, environmental remediation costs and product warranty accruals.

According to FASB Interpretation No. 14, "Reasonable Estimation of the Amount of a Loss", the term subject to "reasonable estimation" can include a range of possible amounts. When one amount in the range appears to be the best estimate at the time the financial statements are prepared, that amount is accrued. If no amount in the range appears to be the better estimate, the accountant would accrue the low end of the range and disclose the high end of the range in the footnotes to the financial statements.

Footnote Disclosure of Loss Contingencies

If the amount of the loss is not subject to reasonable estimation, but the loss is material and "reasonably possible", the loss contingency should be disclosed in the footnotes to the financial statements. The footnote disclosure should include a description of the nature of the contingency and an estimate of the possible loss, an estimated range of the loss or a statement that an estimate of the loss cannot be made. This type of disclosure is quite common for pending litigation with uncertain outcomes and guarantees of the debt of others. A sample litigation footnote is presented in Exhibit 11.5.

EXHIBIT 11.5: LORENZO AND COMPANY LITIGATION DISCLOSURES

Contingencies

On June 30, 2012, Stillwell Partners filed suit against the Company in the U.S. District Court for the Southern District of New York asserting that the Company's plumbing products infringe certain Stillwell patents. On September 19, 2012, Stillwell filed an additional claim against the company.

The Company believes that it has meritorious defenses to each of the above-mentioned suits pending against the Company and is engaged in a vigorous defense of each of these matters.

The Company is also involved both as a plaintiff and a defendant in other legal proceedings and claims that arise in the ordinary course of business.

In the opinion of management, any such future charges, individually or in the aggregate, could have a material adverse effect on the Company's consolidated results of operations and consolidated net cash flows in the period or periods in which they are recorded or paid.

Loss Contingencies without Disclosure

If the probability of the occurrence of the loss contingency is "remote", the event may not be disclosed in the financial statements. However, due to conservatism, most accountants would make some disclosure of the event, even if the footnote includes a statement that legal counsel and the management of the firm do not expect the loss to be realized or that the ultimate realization of the loss contingency would not materially affect the financial statements.

Exhibit 11.6 presents an illustration of contingency footnotes where the firm does not expect a material adverse impact on the financial statements, but still makes a disclosure due to conservatism. This disclosure also includes an example of recording a contingent liability for probable claims.

EXHIBIT 11.6: COMMITMENTS AND CONTINGENCIES FOOTNOTE FOR MORRISON INTERNATIONAL

Note 11– Commitments and Contingencies

At December 31, 2012, we were involved in several legal actions. The outcome of these legal actions cannot be predicted with certainty. However, management, based upon advice from legal counsel, believes such actions are either without merit or will not have a material adverse effect on our financial position or results of operations. In fiscal 2011, we recorded a $7.2 million liability for probable unasserted claims. There was no change in the status of these claims at June 30, 2006. As such, this amount continues to be accrued at December 31, 2012.

At December 31, 2012, our Board of Directors had authorized the repurchase of a total of up to 24 million shares of common stock. Through December 31, 2012, we had acquired and placed in treasury 18,000,000 shares of our common stock at a total cost of $612.9 million. We expect future share repurchases to be funded primarily with cash generated by operations.

Analytical Issues

By setting strict conditions under which a loss contingency can be recognized in the accounts and the financial statements, SFAS 5 reduced (but did not completely eliminate) the flexibility available to management with respect to the creation of "reserves". These reserves were traditionally used by management as income-smoothing devices. For example, if management expected a sharp decrease in earnings next year, it could create a reserve for repairs and maintenance in the current year. The current addition to the reserve would be charged against this year's income as an operating expense while the cumulative balance of the allowance (reserve) for repairs and maintenance or a liability for future repairs and maintenance would be reported on the balance sheet. By reducing this year's income, next year automatically looks better. In addition, when there is an actual cash outflow for repairs and maintenance next year or in the future, it would be changed against the allowance (reserve) or it would reduce the liability. The actual repairs and maintenance and the cash paid would have no effect on the income reported in subsequent accounting periods. The SFAS 5 restrictions on the use of reserves have been supported by subsequent authoritative pronouncements.

Although SFAS 5 significantly reduced the use of reserves in the financial statements, the analyst must still examine the financial statements for the creation of reserves as income-smoothing devices. Liberal interpretation of the loss recognition criteria of SFAS 5 (i.e., the loss is "probable" and subject to "reasonable estimation") may result in the creation of many loss reserves. Common examples include reserves for obsolete inventory and other deferred costs.

The analytical problem with income smoothing is that it artificially shifts accrual-based accounting income between periods. This could be done to reduce the variation in the trend of accounting earnings. In addition, smoothing devices and unusual write-offs are used in "big bath" accounting. When a company is incurring large losses, write-offs of items such as obsolete inventory and previously deferred costs increase the loss even further. By increasing the loss, future recovery seems more significant than would otherwise be the case. In addition, these write-offs may be a way to "clean house" because many of the items in inventory and deferred costs may have been known to be of little value, but management was reluctant to write these items off during years of marginal profitability.

The use of reserves and other unusual changes against income may also represent a signal by management that next year will result in below normal operating performance. Regardless of the reason for the creation of the reserve or the write-off, the analyst should be aware of these items and their effect on the quality of accounting income.

In the year the reserves are created or the write-off is taken, income will be understated. In the year when the events provided for by the reserve or the charge-off result in cash outflows, accounting income will be overstated. The analyst should make "qualitative adjustments" to the accrual basis income reported in these accounting periods. In addition, analysis of the cash flow statement will provide information regarding the cash consequences of the items accounted for by the reserve method.

Finally, if the loss contingency involves a material amount, the independent registered public accounting firm may modify its audit opinion as to a material uncertainty. This modification would involve an explanatory paragraph discussing the contingency and referring to the contingent liability footnote disclosure in the financial statements. As with the accrual of the loss, the extent of modification of the auditor's opinion depends on the probability of occurrence of the contingency.

OTHER ISSUES IN FULL DISCLOSURE

Related Party Transactions

A related party has the ability to significantly influence the policies of the company. The transactions between the related party and the company may not be objectively determined (i.e., not "arms-length"). For example, a transaction between two closely held companies, owned by the same family, would probably not be objectively determined. Therefore, the accountant must disclose the economic substance of the transaction, regardless of its legal form. According to FASB Statement No. 57, "Related Party Disclosures"[8], a related party footnote disclosure would include the nature of the relationship (e.g. dependency) and the nature and the amounts of the transactions involving the company and the related party.

The analyst should consider the related party footnote disclosure in the assessment of the future operating strength of the firm. If a significant part of the company's revenues are generated from transactions with related parties, the firm may be less profitable than reflected by the accounting income numbers when eliminating sales to related parties.

When related parties exist, the analyst should obtain the financial statements of the related party. An examination of the long-term debt and other footnotes to the financial statements of the related party could reveal guarantees of the related party's debt made by the company. This could have a significant effect on the lending decision made by the credit analyst.

Sample related party transaction disclosures are presented in Exhibit 11.7.

8. FASB ASC 850 [Predecessor literature: "Related Party Disclosures," *Statement of Financial Accounting Standards No. 57* (Norwalk, Conn.: FASB, 1982)].

EXHIBIT 11.7: SAMPLE RELATED PARTY DISCLOSURE

Note 14 RELATED PARTY TRANSACTIONS

We have regular transactions in the normal course of business with Redding, INC., and Chandor Company. At December 31, 2012, we owned 40% of Redding and 24.6% of Chandor. In 2012, we recorded $37.2 million in sales related to Redding and $12.4 million related to Chandor. We also had expenses related to services provided by Redding and Chandor of $3.5 million and $7.7 million, respectively.

We have ongoing purchase commitments with JP and Heatsafe, our two partnership investments. These future commitments are for the purchase of a minimum of $51 million and $16.6 million of newsprint in 2013 with JP and Heatsafe, respectively, at current market prices. We also have a sales commitment with AJ to supply them with 50% of their newsprint requirements, which in 2013 will be approximately $33.9 million. We have the resources necessary to fulfill these commitments in 2013.

Segment Reporting

According to SFAS 131[9], an operating segment is defined as a component of an enterprise engaged in business activity for which it may earn revenues and incur expenses, about which separate financial information is available that is evaluated regularly by the chief operating decision makers in deciding how to allocate resources and in assessing performance.

As evident by the SFAS 131 definition, management can continue to exercise judgment in determination of their company's operating segments. However, the FASB's objective is to ensure that the segment information provided in external financial reports conforms to the segment information used internally by the company's management. The first key management decision in implementing SFAS 131 is to determine which operating segments are reportable segments. SFAS 131 provides guidelines to help identify a reportable segment.

Reportable Segments

A segment is considered to be a reportable segment if it is considered significant or material. The materiality level is 10% and is applied to three financial statement statistics for a company's operating segment. The financial statement statistics employed are revenues, operating profit and assets. The SFAS 131 materiality tests are listed below.

- ***Revenues test.*** A segment is considered a reportable segment if its revenue (unaffiliated and intersegment) is at least 10% of the combined revenue (unaffiliated and intersegment) of all operating segments.
- ***Operating profit and loss test.*** A segment is classified as a reportable segment if its operating profit (loss) is computed as revenues minus operating expenses. Both revenues and operating expenses consist of unaffiliated and intersegment components. The absolute amount of that segment's operating profit or loss is at least 10% of the greater, in absolute amount, of:
    1. Combined operating profits of all operating segments reporting a profit.
    2. Combined operating losses of all operating segments reporting a loss.

9. FASB ASC 280 ["Reporting Disaggregated Information about a Business Enterprise," *Statement of Financial Accounting Standards No. 131* (Norwalk, Conn.: FASB, 1997)].

- ***Assets test.*** A segment is included as a reportable segment if its assets are at least 10% of the combined assets of all operating segments. Segment assets are those assets used exclusively by the segment and any allocated portion of assets shared by two or more segments. Assets held for general corporate purposes are not assigned to segments.

The 10% tests will take into account comparability of presentation over several accounting periods. If a segment fails to meet the tests in the current year, but was included as a reportable segment in prior years and will probably meet the 10% tests in the future, it is considered reportable in the current year to maintain comparability. Similarly, if a segment was never reportable in prior years, but meets the 10% tests in the current year, that segment may be not be included for comparability purposes.

A 75% test must also be used to ensure that the reportable segments represent a significant amount of the company's revenues. Specifically, the combined unaffiliated revenue of all reportable segments must be at least 75% of the combined unaffiliated revenue of all operating segments. If the 75% test is not met, additional segments must be included as reportable segments until 75% of total revenue is reached.

Prior to conducting the 10% tests and deciding on a reportable segment, the company can combine operating components with similar characteristics. In deciding on "similarity", the operating components must have all of the following factors in common;

1. The nature of the products and services
2. The nature of the production processes
3. The type of customer for their products and services
4. The methods used to distribute their products or provide their services
5. The nature of the regulatory environment

At this point, it is possible that the combined segment could meet the 10% test. It should be noted that the firm could elect to disclose information about other segments that are not considered reportable for purposes of implementing SFAS 131.

Finally, to avoid including an "overload" of segment information and enhance the usefulness of the line of business disclosures, the FASB recommends that no more than 10 segments should be presented.

Segment Disclosures

SFAS 131 requires several disclosures regarding the enterprise's reportable segments. The disclosures should contain financial information about each reportable segment. Here financial information includes five key financial statement elements: revenues; operating profit (loss); segment assets; depreciation, depletion and amortization expense and capital expenditures.

In the general information section of the disclosure, an explanation of how management identified the enterprise's reportable segments should be included with information indicating if operating segments have been aggregated. General information also includes a description of the types of products and services generated from each reportable segment.

Information about reported segment profit and loss, segment assets and the basis of measurement is also disclosed. The revenues and expenses included in segment profit and loss and the determination of segment assets is included in the footnote.

An important element of the segment disclosure is the reconciliation of segment information to the consolidated financial statements. In addition, the amount of sales dollars generated from external parties for each product and service should be provided, if practical. Segment information regarding domestic and foreign operations is also provided.

Major customers

If an enterprise earns 10% or more of its revenue on sales to a single external customer, that fact and the amount of revenue from each such customer must be disclosed by segment.

Sample operating segment disclosures for Debow Company and Consolidated Affiliates are presented in Exhibit 11.8.

EXHIBIT 11.8: DEBOW COMPANY AND CONSOLIDATED AFFILIATES 2011 ANNUAL REPORT: SEGMENT DISCLOSURES

From the Management's Discussion and Analysis Section

Segment Operations

Operating segments comprise our six businesses focused on the broad markets they serve:

- Industrial
- Consumer
- Supplier
- Direct Sales
- Commercial
- Government

Segment profit is determined based on internal performance measures used by the Chief Executive Officer to assess the performance of each business in a given period. In connection with that assessment, the Chief Executive Officer may exclude matters such as charges for restructuring; rationalization and other similar expenses; in-process research and development and certain other acquisition-related charges and balances; technology development costs; certain gains and losses from dispositions; and litigation settlements or other charges, responsibility for which preceded the current management team.

Segment profit always excludes the effects of principal pension plans and results reported as discontinued operations and accounting changes. Segment profit excludes or includes interest and other financial charges and income taxes according to how a particular segment's management is measured–excluded in determining segment profit, which we refer to as "operating profit".

Summary of Operating Segments

	Debow Company and consolidated affiliates				
(In millions)	**2012**	2011	2010	2009	2008
REVENUES					
Industrial	**$ 50,164**	$ 44,848	$ 43,883	$ 48,143	$ 43,703
Consumer	**39,157**	36,866	29,986	31,385	31,321
Supplier	**18,184**	16,147	12,238	10,746	10,091
Direct Sales	**17,627**	15,463	8,245	8,579	6,923
Commercial	**24,775**	23,429	20,312	18,826	17,532
Government	**23,299**	18,881	15,414	12,319	11,410
Total segment revenues	**173,206**	155,634	130,078	129,997	120,979
Corporate items and eliminations	**6,437**	5,743	5,386	6,630	8,090
CONSOLIDATED REVENUES	**$ 179,642**	$ 161,377	$ 135,463	$ 136,627	$ 129,070

SEGMENT PROFIT					
Industrial	**$ 9,323**	$ 8,156	$ 8,834	$ 11,014	$ 9,443
Consumer	**3,071**	2,200	1,662	2,204	3,170
Supplier	**3,198**	2,743	2,041	1,855	1,798
Direct Sales	**3,710**	3,070	2,398	1,990	1,690
Commercial	**5,148**	4,284	3,488	2,604	2,141
Government	**3,660**	3,024	2,593	2,159	1,922
Total segment profit	**28,110**	23,477	21,017	21,826	20,164
Corporate items and eliminations	**-1161.6**	-392.4	60	2,419	1,386
Debow interest and other financial charges	**-1718.4**	-1174.8	-941	-569	-980.4
Debow provision for income taxes	**-3300**	-2367.6	-2857	-4604.4	-5031.6
Earnings from continuing operations before accounting changes	**21,930**	19,542	16,519	18,958	15,538
Earnings (loss) from discontinued operations, net of taxes	**-2306.4**	640.8	2,468	-739.2	1,356
Earnings before accounting changes	**19,624**	20,183	18,988	18,218	16,894
Cumulative effect of accounting changes	-	-	-587	-1218	-344.4
CONSOLIDATED NET EARNINGS	**$ 19,624**	$ 20,183	$ 18,283	$ 17,000	$ 16,549

Revenues of our businesses include income from sales of goods and services to customers and other income.

Sales from one component to another generally are priced at equivalent commercial selling prices.

Revenues originating from operations based in the United States were $107,864 million, $98,578 million and $83,998 million in 2012, 2011 and 2010, respectively. Revenues originating from operations based outside the United States were $71,778 million, $62,800 million and $51,466 million in 2012, 2011 and 2010, respectively.

	Assets			**Property, plant and equipment additions**			**Depreciation and amortization**		
	At December 31			For the years ended 31-Dec			For the years ended 31-Dec		
(In millions)	2012	2011	2010	2012	2011	**2010**	2012	2011	2010
Industrial	$ **107,466**	99,358	$ 91,422	$ **5,026**	4,726	$ 4,248	$ **2,923**	2,594	$ 2,492
Consumer	49,867	50,448	48,431	5,240	4,933	2,646	3,950	3,950	2,746
Supplier	**29,593**	29,845	12,979	**552**	1,908	346.8	**740.4**	678	333.6
Direct Sales	**37,435**	41,047	13,943	**330**	1,427	145.2	**406.8**	327.6	140.4
Commercial	**228,655**	221,266	206,965	**6,511**	5,488	6,169	**3,178**	3,326	2,933
Government	**190,595**	181,506	127,836	**226.8**	260.4	229.2	**471.6**	400.8	331.2
Corporate items and eliminations	**164,399**	277,139	275,818	**238.8**	232.8	302.4	**249.6**	294	447.6
Total	**$ 808,010**	900,608	$ 777,394	$ **18,125**	18,974	**$** 14,087	$ **11,920**	11,572	$ 9,424

	Interest and other financial charges			Provision for income taxes		
(In millions)	2005	2004	2003	2005	2004	**2003**
Industrial	$ **2,047**	$ 1,723$	1,483	$ **(242.4)**	$ 74.4	$ 291.6
Consumer	**643.2**	631.2	721.2	**76.8**	(148.8)	(198)
Direct Sales	**7,072**	5,664	5,556	**1165.2**	1,373	591.6
Commercial	**6,532**	4,277	3,235	**634.8**	538.8	549.6
Corporate items and eliminations(b)	**1,931**	1,692	1,556	**2,990**	2,346	3,379
Total	$ **18,224**	$ 13,987$	12,552	$ **4,625**	$ 4,183	$ 4,614

Property, plant and equipment associated with operations based in the United States were $31,368 million, $30,263 million and $24,709 million at year-end 2012, 2011 and 2010, respectively. Property, plant and equipment associated with operations based outside the United States were $49,666 million, $45,461 million and $32,560 million at year-end 2012, 2011 and 2010, respectively.

Major Analytical Issues in the Application of Segment Reporting Requirements

There are three major analytical issues in the application of SFAS 131. These involve the definition of an industry segment, the allocation of common or joint costs, and transfer pricing

Definition of an Industry Segment

The FASB did not prescribe the procedures to be used in defining an industry segment. A firm could use SIC codes, geographic limits, legal entities, components or divisions. As a result, there is no standard definition of an industry segment reported under SFAS 131. Thus, the Industrial Division of Debow could be operating in a completely different industry from the industrial division of a competing company. Due to the lack of guidance from the FASB, an analyst cannot easily compare the segments of different firms, even if the firms are operating in the same industry.

The Allocation of Common or Joint Costs and Transfer Pricing

The FASB requires the disclosure of segment operating profit after the allocation of common costs. The common or joint costs are costs incurred at the corporate level for the benefit of more than one line of business. Common costs include corporate administration, centralized information technology operations, corporate advertising and executive compensation.

The SFAS 131 requirement that operating profit be determined after the allocation of common costs raises problems for financial statement analysis. One issue results from the fact that there are no guidelines provided regarding the composition of the common cost pools and as to the methods of allocation. As a result of this flexibility, some firms allocate all common costs to industry segments, while others leave some or all of the common costs unallocated and charge these costs to the "corporate segment". For example, corporate interest and pension costs are typically not allocated to the firm's business segments. These costs are also found in Debow's segment disclosures in Exhibit 11.8.

There is also no uniformity as to the definition of a common cost. Some firms may consider centralized information technology services as a common cost and thereby subject to allocation. Other firms may consider centralized information technology services as a pure corporate function and would not allocate costs of operating the information technology operations to the industry segments. In addition, regardless of the composition of the common cost pool, the method of allocation selected could "shift" profit between segments, and could be used as a means of concealing the relative profitability of the individual segments from competitors.

Another problem results from the fact that there is no uniformity as to the disclosures of the composition of the common cost pool and the methods of allocation used. In general, this information is not disclosed in the segment footnote.

Joint or common assets can also be allocated if a reasonable basis for that allocation exits. Disclosure of direct segment assets and the joint or indirect assets allocated to the segment should be disclosed. Similar to the allocation of common costs, the basis for allocation of joint assets is somewhat subjective and raises questions as to the quality of segment information.

Due to these and other problems, segment information is generally considered "soft" in the sense that it is significantly influenced by managerial discretion and involves a great deal of subjectivity in its preparation and disclosure. As long as the total of the segment operating profit is equal to the consolidated total on the income statement, management can manipulate the individual segment profitability. Exhibit 11.8 shows that Debow's 2012 consolidated net earnings of $19,624 are reconciled by segment in the disclosure.

Although segment information is of low quality and results in a high level of accounting risk, it is the only line of business information available in the annual report and could be used as the starting point for a more detailed analysis of the firm. Finally, the FASB requires companies to use the same transfer pricing system in their segment disclosures as they use for internal or management control purposes.

Interim Reporting

The professional standards governing interim or quarterly reporting are found in APB Opinion No. 28, "Interim Financial Reporting"[10]. In general, the provisions of Opinion 28 require that the same accounting principles be used in the quarterly report as are used in the annual financial statements. However, there are several significant exceptions to this general rule.

Interim reporting standards only require the inclusion of an income statement. However, the inclusion of a balance sheet and the statement of cash flows are recommended. In addition, the interim financial statements differ from the annual report with respect to accounting for inventory in several key areas. First, the gross profit method of estimating inventory value can be used during interim periods. Second, interim period liquidations of LIFO layers are not recognized in the interim financial statements, if replacement of the layers is expected by year end. Third, interim financial statements are not audited and are clearly labeled as such. Finally, write-offs of obsolete inventory can be deferred.

Other issues to be considered in the analysis of quarterly financial information result from the different views of interim reporting. The two concepts of interim reporting are discussed in the following sections.

---

10. FASB ASC 270 [Predecessor literature: "Interim Financial Reporting," Opinions of the Accounting Principles Board No. 28 (New York: AICPA 1973)].

The Discrete versus the Integral View of Reporting

The Discrete View

Under the discrete approach, each interim reporting period is treated as a separate accounting period. As a result, accruals and deferrals are accounted for as if the interim period was a complete, self-contained accounting period. For example, if a company prepays a six-month insurance policy on January 2nd, it would be fully expired by year end, December 31st. However, if the firm follows the discrete view of the quarter, the firm would defer the expense at acquisition and capitalize it as a prepaid asset. The deferred asset cost would be amortized to expense on a monthly basis. Therefore, at the end of the first quarter, three months or one-half of the deferred asset is expired and would be charged to expense. The other half would be reported on the balance sheet as a deferred asset.

Although the discrete view is not favored by the APB in Opinion 28, it is still employed by many firms for certain financial statement items, such as large advertising expenditures extending beyond the quarter in which the payment was made.

The Integral View

Under the integral approach, the interim reporting period is viewed as an integral part of the annual reporting period. Therefore, items such as accruals and deferrals are accounted for by considering what would occur for the entire year. In the prepaid insurance example, the entire prepayment on January 2nd would be charged to expense immediately because there would be no asset value remaining (i.e., it would be fully expired) by December 31st. The integral view is favored by the accounting profession in Opinion 28. Although considered the preferred approach, the application of the integral view has resulted in several implementation problems in practice. Some of these problems include the following.

1. Practice has varied widely (i.e., discrete or integral treatment) in accounting for material advertising expenditures extending beyond the quarter of cash disbursement.
2. A great deal of subjectivity must be employed in recording expenses on an interim basis that require information for the entire accounting period. For example, charges against income for the bad debt provision, write-off of obsolete inventory and accrued pension expense require information for the full accounting period if reliable accruals are to be recorded.
3. In determining the income tax provision for each interim period, the amount of income for that period would not provide an appropriate level of income for determining the tax rate to use from the graduated tax rate schedule. As a result, FASB Interpretation No. 18, "Accounting for Income Taxes in Interim Periods"[11], requires that the estimated annual effective tax rate must be applied to the year-to-date income at the end of each interim period.
4. Extraordinary items and the gain or loss from discontinued operations should be recognized in the quarter in which it actually occurs. Retroactive accounting changes are treated in the same way as on the annual report. That is, if there is an accounting change during the year, prior quarters are restated to reflect the effect of the retroactive change in accounting principle.

---

11. FASB Interpretation No. 18, ASC 740 [Predecessor literature: "Accounting for Income Taxes in Interim Periods (APB Op. No. 28)" (Norwalk, Conn.: FASB 1977)].

5. The EPS for each quarter must be determined as if the interim period was a discrete annual period. Therefore, each quarter "stands alone" as a discrete accounting period and all of the SFAS 128 requirements are applied as if the quarter is a complete accounting period. For example, the average stock price used in implementing the treasury stock method is the average price for the period. The period using the discrete approach is the quarter. As a result, options could be in the money for the quarter and not for year end, and vice versa.

The implementation problems noted above will result in quarterly information that is less reliable than the information contained in the annual report. In essence, the accountant is trading off relevance for reliability. Quarterly data are more timely, and therefore more relevant to the financial statement user. However, the more timely the data, the greater the use of estimates and subjective judgments, making the interim information less reliable. If the analyst is aware of the limitations of interim financial information, quarterly reports can still be used, but used with caution.

Sample 10K and 10Q quarterly financial data for 2012 for Oliver, Inc. are presented in Exhibit 11.9.

EXHIBIT 11.9: OLIVER, INC. 2012 QUARTERLY FINANCIAL DATA DISCLOSURES

Quarterly Financial Data (Unaudited)

Quarterly financial data does not always reveal the trend of Oliver's business operations due to nonrecurring items and seasonal weather patterns, which affect earnings, and related components of net revenues and operating income.

(in millions, except per share data)	First Quarter	Second Quarter	Third Quarter	Fourth Quarter
2012				
Gross revenues	$3,219.96	$1,627.68	$1,397.64	$ 3,233.64
Operating Income	525.24	143.28	111.84	363
Income from Continuing Operations	250.44	9.48	(6.96)	87.36
Income (Loss) from Discontinued Operations — net of taxes	(2.88)	37.32	(1.2)	(0.54)
Change in Accounting — net of taxes		—	—	(0.36)
Net Income (Loss)	247.56	46.8	(8.16)	81.6
Basic Earnings Per Share of Common Stock				
Continuing Operations	0.924	0.036	(0.024)	0.324
Discontinued Operations	(0.012)	0.144	(0.012)	(0.024)
Basic Earnings (Loss) Per Share	$ 0.912	$ 0.18	$ (0.036)	$ 0.3
Diluted Earnings Per Share of Common Stock				
Continuing Operations	0.924	0.036	#0.024	0.324
Discontinued Operations	(0.012)	0.132	(0.012)	(0.024)
Diluted Earnings (Loss) Per Share	$ 0.912	$ 0.168	$ (0.036)	$ 0.3

From the Third Quarter 10Q Filing
Item 1: FINANCIAL STATEMENTS
Oliver Inc. Partial Statements of Consolidated Income (unaudited)

	Three Months Ended September 30,		Nine Months Ended September 30,	
(in millions, except per share amounts)	**2012**	2011	**2012**	2011
Net Revenues				
Gas Distribution	**$ 456.12**	$ 395.04	**$ 3,438.24**	$ 3,124.80
Gas Transportation and Storage	**214.92**	223.68	**865.2**	885.84
Electric	**458.04**	366	**1135.08**	1009.32
Other	**267.48**	189.12	**802.08**	613.32
Gross Revenues	**1,396.56**	1173.84	**6,240.60**	5,633.28
Cost of Sales	**667.32**	466.92	**3,510.12**	2,998.80
Total Net Revenues	**729.24**	706.92	**2,730.48**	2,634.48
Operating Expenses				
Operation and maintenance	**391.8**	338.76	**1178.4**	1066.08
Depreciation and amortization	**163.32**	150.72	**489.12**	453.6
Impairment and loss (gain) on sale of assets	—	-0.012	**24.48**	1.08
Other taxes	**62.28**	63.84	**258.12**	238.92
Total Operating Expenses	**617.4**	553.2	**1,950.12**	1,759.68
Operating Income	**111.84**	153.72	**780.36**	874.8

Oliver Inc.: Partial Consolidated Balance Sheet

(in millions)	**September 30, 2012** (unaudited)	December 31, 2011
ASSETS		
Property, Plant and Equipment		
Utility Plant	**$ 19,800.60**	$ 19,432.92
Accumulated depreciation and amortization	**(8994.96)**	(8697.24)
Net utility plant	**10,805.64**	10,735.68
Other property, at cost, less accumulated depreciation	**505.32**	513
Net Property, Plant and Equipment	**11,310.96**	11,248.68
Investments and Other Assets		
Assets of discontinued operations and assets held for sale	**41.64**	46.32
Unconsolidated affiliates	**84.48**	77.04
Other investments	**138.24**	135.6
Total Investments and Other Assets	**264.36**	258.96
Current Assets		
Cash and cash equivalents	**1119**	35.4
Restricted cash	**2.16**	67.56
Accounts receivable (less reserve of $57.2 and $55.6, respectively)	**526.32**	1066.92
Gas inventory	**799.8**	543.48
Underrecovered gas and fuel costs	**276**	352.56
Materials and supplies, at average cost	**85.32**	84.72
Electric production fuel, at average cost	**33.12**	35.04
Price risk management assets	**445.2**	73.32
Exchange gas receivable	**249.84**	203.52
Regulatory assets	**215.28**	163.44
Prepayments and other	**103.68**	115.32
Total Current Assets	**3,855.72**	2,741.28
Other Assets		
Price risk management assets	**257.52**	177.96
Regulatory assets	**661.32**	682.08
Goodwill	**4,412.76**	4,424.64
Intangible assets	**598.2**	624.36
Deferred charges and other	**217.68**	227.4
Total Other Assets	**6,147.48**	6,136.44
Total Assets	**$ 21,578.52**	$ 20,385.36

The accompanying Notes to Consolidated Financial Statements are an integral part of these statements.

Oliver Inc.: Statements of Consolidated Cash Flows (unaudited)

Nine Months Ended September 30, (in millions)	**2012**	2011
Operating Activities		
Net income	**$ 286.2**	$ 332.28
Adjustments to reconcile net income to net cash from continuing operations:		
Depreciation and amortization	**489.12**	453.6
Net changes in price risk management activities	**(102.84)**	3.84
Deferred income taxes and investment tax credits	**(68.16)**	(7.08)
Deferred revenue	**13.92**	(26.04)
Amortization of unearned compensation	**7.92**	8.28
Loss (Gain) on sale of assets	**(1.68)**	1.08
Loss on impairment of assets	**26.16**	
Income from unconsolidated affiliates	**(4.2)**	(1.32)
Loss (gain) from sale of discontinued operations	**(57.36)**	1.92
Loss (income) from discontinued operations	**24.12**	(5.4)
Amortization of discount/premium on debt	**20.44**	16.68
Other adjustments	**(1.56)**	(2.28)
Changes in assets and liabilities:		
Accounts receivable	**508.56**	474.72
Inventories	**(255.12)**	(148.44)
Accounts payable	**(116.64)**	(235.68)
Customer deposits	**3.24**	2.04
Taxes accrued	**(9.24)**	(59.28)
Interest accrued	**75.48**	70.2
(Under) Overrecovered gas and fuel costs	**77.64**	18.6
Exchange gas receivable/payable	**(26.4)**	9.36
Other accruals	**(1.44)**	(45.84)
Prepayment and other current assets	**19.56**	49.32
Regulatory assets/liabilities	**(21)**	48.84
Postretirement and post employment benefits	**49.92**	18.96
Deferred credits	**(6.84)**	(13.68)
Deferred charges and other noncurrent assets	**15.84**	(21.6)
Other noncurrent liabilities	**14.28**	29.16
Net Cash Flows from Continuing Operations	**929.16**	972.24
Net Cash Flows used for Discontinued Operations	**-20.88**	-0.12)
Net Cash Flows from Operating Activities	**908.28**	972.12
Investing Activities		
Capital expenditures	**(488.28)**	(458.76)
Proceeds from disposition of assets	**8.88**	7.08
Other investing activities	**142.92**	(3.48)
Net Cash Flows used for Investing Activities	**(336.48)**	(455.16)

Financing Activities		
Issuance of long-term debt	**1,200.00**	—
Retirement of long-term debt	**(139.08)**	(282.96)
Change in short-term debt	**(369.12)**	(8.52)
Issuance of common stock	**47.16**	13.32
Acquisition of treasury stock	**(2.04)**	(4.44)
Dividends paid — common shares	**(225.12)**	(219)
Net Cash Flows from (used for) Financing Activities	**511.8**	(501.6)
Increase in cash and cash equivalents	**1083.6**	15.36
Cash and cash equivalents at beginning of year	**35.4**	32.52
Cash and cash equivalents at end of period	**$ 1119**	$ 47.88
Supplemental Disclosures of Cash Flow Information		
Cash paid for interest	**289.08**	278.16
Interest capitalized	**1.56**	2.28
Cash paid for income taxes	**116.88**	164.16

The accompanying Notes to Consolidated Financial Statements are an integral part of these statements.

NiSource Inc.: Statements of Consolidated Comprehensive Income (unaudited)

	Three Months Ended September 30,		Nine Months Ended September 30,	
(in millions, net of taxes)	**2012**	2011	**2012**	2011
Net Income (Loss)	**$ (8.16)**	$ 34.56	**$ 286.2**	$ 332.28
Other comprehensive income, net of taxes				
Foreign currency translation adjustment	—	—	—	0.84
Net unrealized gains on cash flow hedges	**113.28**	21.72	**132.72**	32.04
Net gain (loss) on available for sale securities	**(0.24)**	0.36	**0.36**	0.84
Minimum pension liability adjustment	**(27.24)**	5.52	**(27.24)**	5.52
Total other comprehensive income, net of taxes	**85.8**	27.6	**105.84**	39.24
Total Comprehensive Income	**$ 77.64**	$ 62.16	**$ 326.7**	$ 371.52

The accompanying Notes to Consolidated Financial Statements are an integral part of these statements.

Chapter 12 The Statement of Cash Flows: Preparation and Analysis

INTRODUCTION

The analytical problems resulting from the flexibility afforded to management within the framework of accrual basis accounting have been discussed at length in the previous chapters of this text. Nevertheless, GAAP generally prohibits the use of the cash basis of accounting for preparation of the income statement and the statement of financial position. The cash basis has been criticized because of its failure to adequately measure economic activity. In addition, the cash basis allows even greater manipulation of the results of operations through management's ability to control the timing of cash receipts and cash disbursements.

Notwithstanding the persuasive arguments against the cash basis of accounting, credit and financial analysts find cash flow information an invaluable resource in determining an entity's ability to repay principal and interest on outstanding debt and to provide a dividend return to stockholders. For years it seemed paradoxical that information regarding a firm's cash flows was excluded from the reported financial statements and the related footnotes. Without this information, much of which was dependent on internal data, the credit and financial analyst was forced to rely on crude measures of cash flow. This paradox was resolved with the issuance of FASB Statement No. 95, "Statement of Cash Flows."[1]

SFAS 95 requires the inclusion of a Cash Flow Statement (CFS) as one of the three basic financial statements to be provided in order to issue financial information in accordance with GAAP.

CASH FLOW REPORTING STANDARDS

The Need for Cash Flow Reporting

SFAS 95 was issued by the accounting profession as a direct response to the recommendations of the financial community. In the early 1980s it became apparent that credit and financial analysts were increasingly dissatisfied with the funds flow information provided by the financial reporting model. The diversity of reporting practices for the funds flow statement made it difficult for the analyst to determine the cash flow for the individual firm both in the current year and over time, and made it virtually impossible to compare the cash flows between firms within the same industry.

Credit and financial analysts have expressed several reasons for their preference for accurate cash flow information. As implied throughout the previous chapters, accrual basis net income may not be related to the net cash flows generated from operations. This point is clear when one considers the extensive use of deferrals and capitalization of costs. In addition, working capital may not adequately reflect the liquidity of the firm. The high debt levels of many firms, particularly with LBO activity and the ever present possibility of corporate bankruptcies, have made cash flow analysis an even more critical component in the evaluation of credit and investment alternatives.

---

1. FASB ASC 230 [Predecessor literature: "Statement of Cash Flows," *Statement of Financial Accounting Standards No. 95* (Norwalk, Conn.: FASB, 1987)].

The Objectives of Cash Flow Reporting

Under SFAS 95, the CFS is a basic financial statement that summarizes the cash inflows and outflows for a firm over a period of time. It is a flow statement that is used to explain the change in cash and cash equivalents (to be discussed). The statement can also be useful in explaining and reconciling many other significant changes in the financial position of the firm when the CFS is used with the other financial statements and related footnote disclosures.

The cash flow statement is also important in completing the financial reporting cycle and enhancing the articulation among the financial statements. The financial reporting cycle is illustrated in the following diagram.

To illustrate:

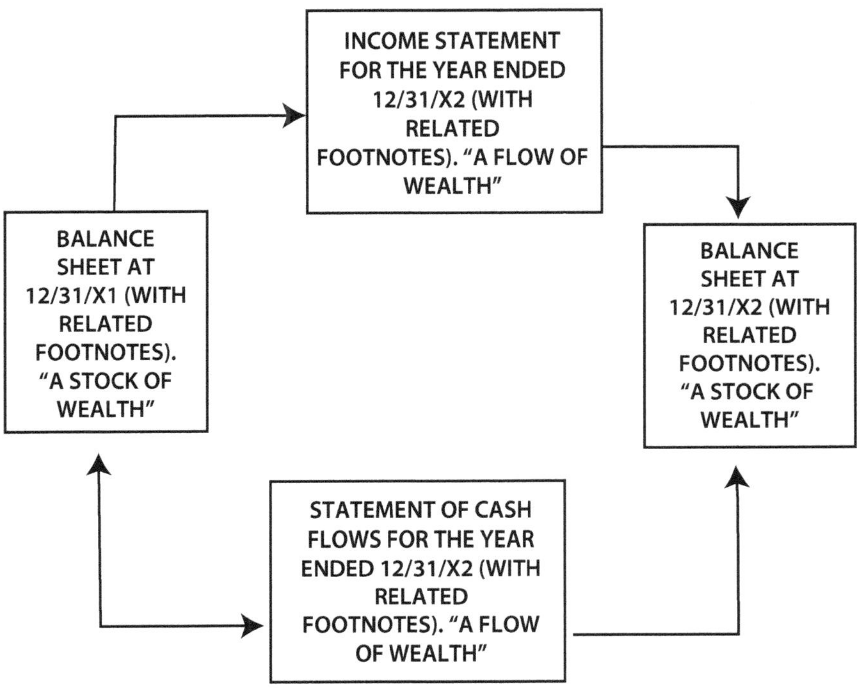

The balance sheet is the only permanent element of the financial reporting cycle. Each year the balance sheet changes by income and cash flows. Income flows impact the balance sheet through the closing of net income into retained earnings. The statement of cash flows is useful in explaining other balance sheet changes, but only if the transactions affecting the balance sheet are cash changes. Nonetheless, significant noncash events are disclosed in the footnotes to the financial statements. Therefore, the financial reporting cycle is closed by the two flow statements and the related footnotes to the financial statements. The flow statements are temporary accounts and will start next year with no balance and the beginning balance sheet indicates the cycle again for the next reporting period including the prior year's closing balance. This also maximizes the articulation among the financial statements and helps meet the FASB's objectives for cash flow reporting.

Objectives of the Cash Flow Statement

Specifically, SFAS 95 established two primary objectives for cash flow reporting. The primary purpose of the CFS is to provide information about the cash receipts and cash payments of the firm over a period of time.

The first objective of cash flow reporting relates to the current operating cash flows of the firm which are associated with net income for the period and the certain noncash or operating working capital items on the statement of financial position. Operating or noncash working capital items typically relate to cash flows from changes in current accounts such as accounts receivable, inventory, accounts payable and taxes payable.[2]

A secondary purpose of the CFS is to provide information about a firm's financing and investing activities. These activities relate to debt and equity financing and investments in plant and equipment, as well as other current and noncurrent assets.

Both of the SFAS 95 objectives imply that the CFS should provide information needed by the analyst to assess the ability of the firm to generate positive future cash flows from operations, in order to pay dividends, meet debt service requirements, and assess the firm's future needs for external financing and therefore its financial flexibility. Because of the inherent deficiencies of accrual basis accounting, the CFS can also assist the analyst in assessing the quality of reported net income and the level of accounting risk associated with the accrual basis financial statements. In addition, because of the extensive use of deferrals, accrual basis net income has become further removed from the underlying cash flows of the firm. Therefore, a CFS may be viewed as a means of assessing the "quality" of the firm's accounting earnings.

Definitions and Issues Related to the Cash Flow Statement

Under SFAS 95, the caption "cash and cash equivalents" replaces the concept of the fund. This caption is a much broader concept than cash, and now the CFS is designed to explain the change in the firm's cash and cash equivalents.

According to SFAS 95, the term "cash equivalents" includes "short-term, highly liquid investments" with original maturities of three months or less from the date of purchase which were acquired by the firm by using cash in excess of its immediate cash requirements. It is in the sense of using excess cash that these types of investments are cash substitutes and will be converted back into cash if needed in the operating cycle. In addition, SFAS 95 includes cash equivalents within the cash concept because the acquisition and disposal of investments of this nature are considered part of the firm's overall cash management activities and therefore should not be considered within the operating, investing and financing activities of the entity.

The term "original maturities of three months or less" used in SFAS 95, requires that there must be three months to maturity at the time the investment is acquired by the firm. For example, a three-year treasury instrument purchased with two months to maturity qualifies as a cash equivalent, while a three-year treasury instrument acquired three years ago does not become a cash equivalent when it reaches three months to maturity. Therefore, the determination of a cash equivalent is made only at acquisition and is not modified in subsequent accounting periods. Clearly, it is management's intention at the date of acquisition and not the time to maturity that determines a security's status as a cash equivalent.

2. Operating working capital could include cash if cash is an integral part of operations (e.g., retail industry).

SFAS 95 also requires that cash and cash equivalents on the CFS agree with the same financial statement items on the balance sheet. Only investments such as treasury bills, commercial paper and money market funds usually qualify as cash equivalents. Short-term marketable securities such as investments in common stock and corporate debt will generally not qualify as cash equivalents and should be shown as a separate line item in the current asset section of the balance sheet.

Finally, SFAS 95 requires that the firm disclose its policy regarding the definition and composition of its cash equivalents. The firm should disclose the specific criterion used to classify an investment as a cash equivalent (i.e., investments with original maturities with three months or less) along with the types of securities included within this category.

Classification of Cash Flows by Activity or Function

A functional or activity format must be used under SFAS 95. The FASB identifies three classifications of cash flow activity which are designed to meet the stated objectives of cash flow reporting. A CFS should classify cash receipts and disbursements into three major categories. These are operating activities, investing activities and financing activities. The discussion that follows assumes an industrial rather than financial service or regulated entry unless noted otherwise.

Operating Activities

In SFAS 95, cash flows from operating activities are defined as the cash effects of economic events that enter into the determination of net income or loss for the period, regardless of source. A firm's income statement and noncash or operating working capital items related to operations from the statement of financial position form the basis for net cash flows from operating activities. SFAS 95 indicates that cash flows from operations include the following activities.

Cash Inflows:

- From the sale of goods and services
- From interest and dividend income

Cash Outflows:

- To suppliers for inventory, utilities and other services
- To employees for services
- To government agencies for taxes
- To creditors for interest paid, net of amounts capitalized

It should be noted that by requiring a CFS and the determination of cash flow from operating activities, the FASB is not advocating a cash basis of accounting. As noted earlier, the accrual basis must still be used to properly measure the results of operations from economic activities. Cash flow from operations is designed to report the net cash generated from the year's economic activity, as measured under the accrual basis.

The definition of operating activities used in the CFS is not consistent with the usual concept of operating income (or EBITDA) as used in finance. Using a pure definition of operations, income from operations excludes other income and other expense items such as interest income, interest expense and dividends received. On the other hand, net cash flow from operating activities as defined by SFAS 95 includes taxes paid, interest income and interest expense and dividends received, while excluding all items of revenue and expense without cash consequences. In addition, SFAS 95 does not classify operating cash flows by source such as miscellaneous income and expense. As a result, operating cash flows from the CFS cannot always be related to a specific line item on the income statement. These points will be discussed further in the analysis of the CFS.

Investing Activities

The net cash flows from investing activities generally relate to the cash receipts and disbursements from the acquisition and disposal of noncurrent assets such as plant and equipment and long-term investments, and from the acquisition and disposal of short-term investments not qualifying as cash equivalents. Specifically, SFAS 95 indicates that cash flows from investing activities should include:

Cash Inflows:

- From the sale of property, plant and equipment
- From the sale of debt or equity investments, both short and long term
- From the collection of principal on loans to others

Cash Outflows:

- For the acquisition of property, plant and equipment, including
- Interest capitalized on construction in progress
- For the acquisition of investments in debt or equity securities, both short and long term
- For making loans to others

Note again that interest received and interest paid are classified as operating activities and not as part of the investing cycle.

Financing Activities

The final classification of cash flows for a firm without foreign operations involves cash receipts and payments related to debt and equity financing, including dividend distributions to owners. According to SFAS 95 financing activities include the following cash flows.

Cash Inflows:

- From the issuance of debt securities, both short and long term
- From the issuance of common or preferred stock

Cash Outflows:

- To redeem or retire debt securities, both short and long term
- To purchase treasury stock or retire capital stock
- To make dividend distributions to stockholders

The SFAS 95 cash flow classifications are critical to credit and financial analysis because it is the source of the cash flow and not the amount that is useful in assessing the ability of the firm to repay principal and interest and to make future dividend distributions. Specifically, cash generated from operating activities is of higher "quality" than cash generated from borrowing or from the disposal of productive assets. Thus, the rationale behind these classifications is similar to the justification for the income statement captions "income from continuing operations" and "extraordinary items." As noted earlier, the SFAS 95 does not require cash flows to be identified with the income statement captions, so that a line item cash flows from extraordinary items, discontinued operations, etc., may not reported on the CFS.

Gross versus Net Presentation for Investing and Financing Activities and the Application of SFAS 95 to Financial Institutions

Individual items within the investing and financing activities section of the CFS must be shown on a gross cash flow basis. This generally results in a direct cash flow computation for investing and financing activities. For example, acquisitions and disposals of plant assets must be disclosed separately and cannot be netted out as either a net cash inflow or outflow. Although the FASB did not specifically exempt financial institutions from the requirements of SFAS 95, certain exceptions were permitted in to accommodate financial institutions. For example, net presentation is allowed for balance sheet items with "quick turnover and short maturities" such as short-term investments, loans receivable and demand deposits, "provided that the original maturities of these items are three months or less." A net presentation is also permitted in those cases where the financial institution is substantially holding or disbursing cash on behalf of its customers (e.g., commercial letters of credit) and for all credit card receivables. The exception was made for credit card receivables because a customer generally has the option to pay off the credit card balance within 30 days. As a result, the FASB considered these receivables to have original maturities of less than three months.

The gross presentation was originally required for all longer term assets and liabilities such as investment securities, commercial loans, real estate loans, installment loans and certificates of deposit. However, the financial community generally believed that the gross presentation for transactions of financial institutions provided information of little value that was quite costly to generate and disseminate through the CFS. Therefore, SFAS 95 was amended to permit banks, savings institutions and credit unions to report in the CFS net cash receipts, any payments for deposits made and withdrawn, time deposits made and withdrawn, and loans made and collected.

Cash Flow Classifications Involving Multiple Activities

In those cases where the cash flow classification is not clear, the FASB indicated that the cash flow classification should be based on the dominant source of the cash flow. For example, an auto manufacturer that temporarily uses vehicles for key employees, but ultimately sells the automobiles, would classify the production as an operating activity and not as an investment in plant and equipment.

Significant Events Not Affecting Cash Flows

A firm will generally engage in many significant transactions that do not have immediate cash flow consequences. For example, events such as the acquisition of plant and equipment financed by a bond issue, debt converted into common stock or the declaration of dividend scan have a significant impact on the financial position of the firm but do not have an effect on cash flow. According to SFAS 95, all non-cash flow events should not be included within the CFS. However, if significant, non-cash flow events must be disclosed in a footnote or a separate schedule. These events may be disclosed in a footnote or separate schedule using the caption, "significant noncash investing and financing activities."

PREPARATION OF THE CASH FLOW STATEMENT: THEORETICAL MODEL AND REPORTING FORMATS

Theoretical Model for the Cash Flow Statement

As noted earlier, the cash flow statement is also useful in explaining balance sheet changes, so it is logical to build a cash flow statement from balance sheet changes. The cash flow statement is really nothing more that a statement of changes in financial position on a cash basis. Building the cash flow statement directly from balance sheet changes is reflected in the following theoretical model.

ASSETS	=	**LIABILITIES**	+	**STOCKHOLDERS' EQUITY**
(Uses of Funds)	=	**(Sources of Funds)**		
(Noncash asset changes are inversely related to cash flows)		**(Liability and Equity changes are directly related to cash flows)**		
CASH + OCA + NCA	=	**CL + NCL**	+	**CS + RE**

Where:

OCA	=	**Other Current Assets (other than cash and short term investments)**
CL	=	**Current Liabilities (assumes no short term debt)**
NCA	=	**Noncurrent Assets**
NCL	=	**Noncurrent Liabilities**
CS	=	**Capital Stock**
RE	=	**Retained Earnings**

Subtracting other current assets and noncurrent assets from both sides of the equation we have:

CASH = +CL - OCA + NCL - NCA + CS + RE

The change in these line items results in the model for the statement of cash flows.

ΔCASH	=	+ΔCL- ΔOCA	+ΔNCL	-ΔNCA	+ΔCS	+ ΔRE
		Operating	Financing	Investing	Financing	

+ ΔRE → Net Income (Loss) (Operating Activities) | Dividends (Financing Activities)

The theoretical model can be used to analyze any transaction and its effect on the statement of cash flows. For example, the acquisition of a plant asset is a noncurrent asset (NCA) and has a negative cash flow effect. It is classified on the statement as an investing activity.

The statement can be rearranged to reflect the noncash or operating working capital format.

ΔCASH = - [ΔOCA - ΔCL] -ΔNCA +ΔNCL +ΔCS + ΔRE

ΔCASH = - INVESTMENT IN NONCASH WORKING CAPITAL - ΔNCA +ΔNCL +ΔCS + ΔRE

Reporting Formats for the Cash Flow Statement

There are two acceptable formats for the preparation of the CFS. These are the Indirect Method (the Reconciliation Format) and the Direct Method (the Income Statement Format). Although both methods are acceptable under SFAS 95, the direct method is preferred by the FASB, but to date is the least popular in practice.

The only difference between these two approaches is the method used to determine cash flows from operating activities. The determination of net cash flow from investing and financing activities always follows a direct format approach and will be identical under either reporting format.

In the determination of cash flow from operating activities, changes in working capital items such as increase (decrease) in accounts receivable, inventories, and accounts payable can be shown on a net basis. In addition, net cash flows from operating activities must be the same under either reporting format.

The Indirect Method: The Reconciliation Format

Under the indirect method, aggregate accrual basis net income from the income statement is converted to cash generated from operating activities by applying a series of adjustments or reconciling items to the net income figure. A statement of cash flows for Association Inc. and Subsidiaries is presented in Exhibit 12.1. Note that cash flow from operating activities can begin with either net income or net loss.

The first line of the CFS is net income from the income statement, and the bottom line is cash and cash equivalents reported on the balance sheet. The three statements provided in Exhibit 12.1 can be tied together by tracing the line items mentioned above (i.e. articulation).

EXHIBIT 12.1: ASSOCIATION INC. AND SUBSIDIARIES 2012 CONSOLIDATED FINANCIAL STATEMENTS

CONSOLIDATED STATEMENTS OF CASH FLOWS
For the Years Ended December 31, 2012, 2011 and 2010
(In millions)

	For the Years Ended December 31,		
	2012	**2011**	**2010**
CASH FLOWS FROM OPERATING ACTIVITIES:			
Net income (loss)	$ 180.84	$ (161.28)	$ 103.68
Adjustments to reconcile net income (loss) to net cash provided by operating activities:			
Equity in earnings of unconsolidated affiliates	(17.04)	(10.92)	(8.28)
Minority interest	0.36	1.2	2.04
Non-cash restructuring expenses	1.08	—	—
Non-cash impairment of long-lived assets and goodwill	—	249.6	—
Unrealized gain on futures contracts	(27.96)	—	—
Stock based compensation expense	34.56	14.28	7.32
Depreciation and amortization	44.88	51.12	55.32
Deferred income taxes	14.28	3.84	(0.24)
Other (gains), losses and expenses, net	(3.48)	16.44	15.84
Changes in assets and liabilities, net of effects of divestitures:			
Accounts and notes receivable	(64.32)	(68.76)	(145.2)
Inventories	0.12	(33.96)	(0.96)
Other current assets	(19.44)	(9.6)	(2.64)
Accounts payable	77.28	(18.48)	1.8
Accrued expenses	48.36	2.88	23.52
Income taxes payable and receivable	27.72	(7.68)	28.56
Long-term warranty, deferred income and other liabilities	(20.28)	(3.12)	16.8
Net cash (used in) provided by operating activities from discontinued operations	(2.52)	43.32	(0.48)
Net cash provided by operating activities	274.44	68.88	68.04

CASH FLOWS FROM INVESTING ACTIVITIES:			
Proceeds from the disposal of property, plant and equipment	0.84	1.8	12.24
Purchases of property, plant and equipment	(75.96)	(48.36)	(47.64)
Dividends from affiliates	—	3.36	—
Additional investment in affiliates	—	(4.4)	(0.72)
Proceeds from disposal of investments (continuing operations)	47.16	—	10.68
Net cash provided by (used in) investing activities from discontinued operations	3	26.16	(-1.44)
Net cash used in investing activities	(24.96)	(21.48)	(26.88)
CASH FLOWS FROM FINANCING ACTIVITIES:			
Short-term (repayments) borrowings, net	(5.04)	2.4	(8.16)
Long-term debt (repayments) borrowings, net	(43.56)	(67.56)	(18.48)
Revolver long-term (repayments) borrowings, net	(6)	2.46	3.6
Sales of common stock	30.96	24.48	15
Payments of deferred financing costs	(2.04)	(0.36)	(3.24)
Repurchases of common stock	(18.96)	(0.12)	(-0.48)
Excess tax benefits related to share based payments	6.12	—	—
Cash dividends paid	(29.76)	(27.36)	(26.52)
Net cash used in financing activities	(68.28)	(66.12)	(38.28)
INCREASE (DECREASE) IN CASH AND CASH EQUIVALENTS	181.2	(18.72)	17.136
EFFECT OF EXCHANGE RATES ON CASH AND CASH EQUIVALENTS	1.92	0.48	(0.84)
CASH AND CASH EQUIVALENTS, beginning of year	73.08	91.32	17.136
CASH AND CASH EQUIVALENTS, end of year	$ 256.2	$ 73.08	$ 17.136
Supplementary disclosures of cash flow information:			
Cash paid during the year for:			
Interest	$ 19.56	$ 35.64	$ 36.12
Income taxes (net of refunds)	$ 79.32	$ 20.88	$ 10.92

ASSOCIATION INC. AND SUBSIDIARIES
PARTIAL CONSOLIDATED BALANCE SHEETS
As of December 31, 2012 and 2011
(In millions, except share data)

	As of December 31,	
	2012	**2011**
ASSETS		
CURRENT ASSETS:		
Cash and cash equivalents	$ 256.2	$ 73.08
Accounts and notes receivable, net	610.08	567
Inventories	290.88	296.64
Deferred income taxes	24.36	15.72
Other assets	75.12	55.08
Assets held for sale	—	6.12
Total current assets	1,256.64	1013.64
PROPERTY, PLANT AND EQUIPMENT, net	306.84	280.8
GOODWILL	268.68	270.48
DEFERRED INCOME TAXES	86.28	99.36
OTHER ASSETS	166.68	158.04
TOTAL ASSETS	$ 2,085.12	$ 1,822.32

ASSOCIÀTION INC. AND SUBSIDIARIES
PARTIAL CONSOLIDATED STATEMENTS OF OPERATIONS
For the Years Ended December 31, 2012, 2011 and 2010
(In millions, except per share data)

	For the Years Ended December 31,		
	2012	**2011**	**2010**
NET SALES	$ 4,039.4	$ 3,579.2	$ 3,347.9
COST OF GOODS SOLD	2,709.8	2,382.2	2,215.9
Gross Profit	1,329.6	1,197.0	1,132.0
OPERATING EXPENSES:			
Selling, general and administrative expense	1,082.9	991.3	940.3
(Gains), losses and other expenses, net	(62.2)	—	2.3
Restructuring charge	2.9	—	—
Goodwill impairment	1.9	249.6	—
Operational income (loss) from continuing operations	304.1	(43.9)	189.4
INTEREST EXPENSE, net	18.5	32.6	34.1
OTHER EXPENSE (INCOME)	3.6	(1.0)	(2.9)
Income (loss) from continuing operations before income taxes	282.0	(75.6)	158.2
PROVISION FOR INCOME TAXES	99.5	36.6	54.1
Income (loss) from continuing operations	182.5	(112.2)	104.0
DISCONTINUED OPERATIONS:			
Loss from operations of discontinued operations	2.4	46.7	0.1
Income tax (benefit) expense	(0.6)	(11.2)	0.24
Loss on disposal of discontinued operations	0.1	17.9	—
Income tax benefit	(0.2)	(4.3)	—
Loss from discontinued operations	1.7	49.1	0.36
Net income (loss)	$ 180.84	$ (161.28)	$ 103.68

Common adjustments or reconciling items used in the indirect format are presented below. Notice that there are two groups of adjustments used in operating activities. The first makes add backs and deductions for noncash expenses and revenues respectively. The second group includes adjustments for change in operating working capital accounts.

NET INCOME (ACCRUAL BASIS).

ADJUSTMENTS TO RECONCILE NET INCOME TO NET CASH PROVIDED BY OPERATIONS

ADDITIONS:

- Depreciation, Depletion and Amortization Expense and Bad Debt Expense
- Compensation Expense paid in Stock Options
- Amortization of Bond Discounts and other Deferred Charges
- Increase in Deferred Income Tax Liability or decrease in the Deferred Tax Asset
- Losses recognized for investments accounted for under the Equity Method
- Loss on sale of long-term assets and investments
- Unrealized losses on investment trading securities and certain derivatives.
- Dividend distributions in excess of Equity Income
- Minority interest share of income
- Increase in Long Term Pension Obligations
- Noncash charges for Discontinued Operations and Extraordinary Items

Operating (Noncash) Working Capital Accounts:

- Decreases in current assets other than investments (trade receivables, inventory, prepaid expenses)
- Increases in current liabilities other than short term debt and dividends payable (accounts payable, accrued liabilities)

DEDUCTIONS:

- Amortization of Bond Premiums and other Deferred Credits
- Decrease in the Deferred Tax Liability or increase in the Deferred Tax Asset
- Undistributed Income under the Equity Method
- Gain on sale of long-term assets and investments
- Unrealized gains on investment trading securities and certain derivatives
- Minority interest share of a net loss
- Decrease in Long Term Pension Obligations
- Noncash gains from Discontinued Operations and Extraordinary Items

Operating (Noncash) Working Capital Accounts:

- Increases in current assets other than investments(trade receivables, inventory, prepaid expenses)
- Decreases in current liabilities other than short term debt and dividends payable (accounts payable, accrued expenses)

NET CASH FLOWS PROVIDED BY OPERATIONS (CASH BASIS NET INCOME)

The Direct Method: The Income Statement Format

Under the direct method of determining net cash generated from operating activities, the accrual basis income statement is disaggregated and each line item is adjusted to convert that particular line item from the accrual basis to the cash basis. In substance, a cash basis income statement is prepared. It should be noted that the same adjustments (i.e., reconciling items) are applied to the individual line items of the income statement under the direct method as were applied against aggregate net income under the indirect method.

At a minimum, according to SFAS 95, the following line items must be included in the operating cash flow section using the direct format.

- Cash collected from customers, lessees, licensees, etc.
- Interest and dividends received
- Other operating cash receipts, if any
- Cash paid to employees and other suppliers of goods and services
- Interest paid, net of amounts capitalized
- Income taxes paid
- Other operating cash disbursements, if any.

Determination of Operating Cash Flow Line Items Under the Direct Method

Under the direct method (income statement format), the accrual basis income statement is disaggregated and each line item is converted to the cash basis. The following tables should be used in determining cash inflows and cash outflows for the minimum line items required under the direct method. Note that in all cases the use of ( ) indicates that there is negative cash flow or a use of cash.

1. Cash Collected From Customers:
Sales -Accrual Basis
(Less: Increase in Accounts Receivable, net)
OR
Add: + Decrease in Accounts Receivable, net
Cash Collected From Customers

The computation of cash paid for merchandise purchased requires two steps. First, accrual basis purchases must be determined from an analysis of cost of goods sold and changes in inventory balances. Second, the cash paid for the acquisition of merchandise is determined by an analysis of the change in accounts payable. The computations used in the two-step approach are illustrated in 2a and 2b below.

2. Cash Paid for Merchandise Purchased (Requires Two Steps):
(a) Determination of Accrual Basis Purchases:
(Cost of Goods Sold -Accrual Basis)
(Add: Increase in Inventory)
OR
Deduct: + Decrease in Inventory
(Purchases on the Accrual Basis)
(b) Determination of Cash Paid for Merchandise Purchased:
(Purchases on the Accrual Basis from (a) above)
(Add: Decrease in Accounts Payable)
OR
Deduct: + Increase in Accounts Payable
(Cash Paid for Merchandise Purchased)

3. Cash Paid to Employees for Wages:

(Wage Expense - Accrual Basis)

(Add: Decrease in Wages Payable)

OR

Deduct: + Increase in Wages Payable

(Cash Paid to Employees for Wages)

The general formula for determining cash paid to employees for salaries and wages can be used for computing cash paid for most other operating expenses. Cash paid for prepaid or deferred expenses, interest expense and income taxes are illustrated below. This example highlights insurance expense but cash paid for prepaid or deferred expenses first would employ the same formula for determining the cash outflow.

4. Cash Paid for Insurance and Other Prepaid (Deferred) Expenses:

(Insurance Expense Accrual Basis)

(Add: Increase in Prepaid Insurance)

OR

Deduct: + Decrease in Prepaid Insurance

(Cash Paid for Insurance)

(Cash paid to suppliers for merchandise is usually combined with cash paid to employees and cash paid for operating expenses such as insurance).

The line item entitled "cash paid to employees and suppliers of goods and services" on the CFS usually consists of cash paid for merchandise plus cash paid to employees for wages. It is not uncommon to combine cash paid for other operating expenses such as insurance in this line item. Otherwise, a separate line item entitled "cash paid for other operating expenses" could be utilized. In many cases, the income statement line item entitled "selling, general and administrative expenses" (SG&A) is the starting point for cash paid for operating expenses. In addition to the adjustments for changes in payables, prepaid expenses, and other assets, adjustments to SG&A would include the elimination of noncash expenses. Noncash expenses include depreciation, depletion, amortization and the bad debts expense.

5. Cash Paid for Interest: (Required Disclosure under the Indirect Method)

(Interest Expense -Accrual Basis)

(Add: Decrease in Interest Payable)

OR

Deduct: + Increase in Interest Payable

(Cash Paid for Interest)

6. Cash Paid for Income Taxes: (Required Disclosure under the Indirect Method)

(Income Tax Expense - Accrual Basis)

(Add: Decrease in Income Taxes Payable)

OR

Deduct: + Increase in Income Taxes Payable

AND

(Add: Decrease in a Deferred Tax Liability or increase in a Deferred Tax Asset)

OR

Deduct: + Increase in a Deferred Tax Liability or decrease in a Deferred Tax Asset

(Cash Paid for Income Taxes)

A sample direct method format cash flow statement is presented for Rivers Group in Exhibit 12.2.

EXHIBIT 12.2: DIRECT CASH FLOW FORMAT: RIVERS GROUP:

Consolidated Cash Flow Statement
Rivers Group 1 January–31 December

in millions	**Note**	**2012**	**2011**
Proceeds from sale of goods and services		83823.6	73328.4
Payments to suppliers of goods and services and of other operating expenses		(42553.2)	(36766.8)
Payments to employees, pensions, social security tax and tax deductions		(11562)	(11136)
Proceeds from interest income		416.4	387.6
Proceeds from other financial income		194.4	708
Payments of interest expenses		(1875.6)	1633.2
Payments of other financial expenses		(58.8)	(80.4)
Other proceeds and payments related to operating activities		4.8	(26.4)
Payment of income taxes and public duties		(1581.6)	(1992)
Net cash flow from operating activities (1)		**26808**	**22789.2**
Proceeds from sale of property, plant and equipment and intangible assets		646.8	314.4
Purchase of property, plant and equipment and intangible assets		(17055.6)	(13935.6)
Cash receipts from sale of subsidiaries and associated companies, net of cash sold		888	1018.8
Cash payments on purchase of subsidiaries and associated companies, net of cash purchased		(9753.6)	(7537.2)
Proceeds from sale of other investments		1846.8	4752
Payments for other investments		(570)	(250.8)
Net cash flow from investment activities		**(23997.6)**	**(15637.2)**

Proceeds from non-current liabilities	6861.6	2983.2
Proceeds from current liabilities	7268.4	66
Payments on non-current liabilities	(5668.8)	(7252.8)
Payments on current liabilities	(3451.2)	(969.6)
Proceeds from issuance of shares, inclusive from minority interests	88.8	56.4
Shares buy back	(2720.4)	(2424)
Payment of equity and dividends to minorities in subsidiaries	(262.8)	(248.4)
Payment of dividends	(3114)	(2116.8)
Net cash flow from financing activities	**(998.4)**	**(9906)**
Effect on cash and cash equivalents of changes in foreign exchange rates	258	(321.6)
Net change in cash and cash equivalents	**2070**	**(3075.6)**
Cash and cash equivalents as of 1 January	6097.2	9172.8
Cash and cash equivalents as of 31 December	**8167.2**	**6097.2**
(1) Reconciliation		
Profit after taxes	10960.8	8895.6
Profit after taxes from discontinued operations	4.8	-
Taxes	4143.6	2953.2
Profit before taxes	**15109.2**	**11848.8**
Income taxes paid	(1642.8)	(1819.2)
Net (gain) loss including write-downs and change in fair value of financial items	(1114.8)	(3793.2)
Depreciation, amortization and write-downs	14557.2	17001.6
Associated companies	(1479.6)	(1183.2)
Changes in inventories	(44.4)	(94.8)
Changes in accounts receivable and prepayments from customers	1990.8	114
Changes in accounts payable and prepaid expenses	488.4	284.4
Difference between expensed and paid pensions	253.2	320.4
Currency (gains) losses not relating to operating activities	(21.6)	68.4
Change in other accruals	(1287.6)	42
Net cash flow from operating activities	**26808**	**22789.2**

Comparison of the Reporting Formats

The computations presented above indicate that statement preparation under the direct method are more complex, more time consuming and therefore more costly than under the indirect approach. Nevertheless, the direct method is preferred by the FASB. The FASB justified its position by stating that a CFS based on cash receipts and disbursements is easier to understand. In addition, cash flow projections are more accurate if based on the disaggregated line items than if the total cash flow from operations is used.

A major disadvantage of the direct method is that the line items included within the operating cash flows section cannot be traced and agreed to any other financial statement line item. On the other hand, the individual reconciling items used in the indirect approach can generally be agreed to the information included in other financial statements. This results in stronger articulation among the financial statements. As a result of these and other criticisms of the direct method, the indirect method is used most often in practice.

Before presenting a detailed illustration, the following brief example permits an overview comparison of the direct and indirect methods.

Assume you are provided with the following partial income and balance sheet information for the current year.

Income Statement	***Amount***
Sales	$ 3,000
Depreciation Expense	(600)
Selling General and Administrative Expenses	(400)
Tax Expense	(200)
Net Income	$1,800
From the Balance Sheet:	
Increase in Accounts Receivable	$200
Increase in Accounts Payable	$100
Decrease in Tax Payable	$100

Based on this information, cash flow from operating activities can be determined.

Cash Flow Statement: Indirect Method: Reconciliation Format:	
Operating Activities:	
Net income	$1,800
Add back: Depreciation	+ 600
Increase in Accounts Receivable	(200)
Increase in Accounts Payable	+ 100
Decrease in Tax Payable	(100)
Cash flow from operating activities	$2,200

Note that for the direct method below, the same adjustments are made as used in the indirect method. However, the direct method applies the adjustments to each income statement line item, converting each line item from the accrual to the cash basis. The indirect method applies the adjustments against aggregate net income. The indirect method applies the adjustments vertically and the direct method applies the adjustments horizontally. This is illustrated in the following line item computations for the direct method.

Direct Method: Income Statement Format: Computations			
Description	**Amount**	**+/− Adjustments =**	**Cash Flow**
Sales	$3,000	Increase in A/R (200)	$2,800
Depreciation Expense	(600)	Depreciation Expense +600	- 0 -
SG&A Expense	(400)	Increase in A/P +100	(300)
Tax Expense	(200)	Decrease in Tax Payable (100)	(300)
Net Income	$1,800		
Cash flow from operating activities			$2,200

Using the computations above, the direct method operating activities can be determined.

Cash Flow Statement: Direct Method or Income Statement Format:	
Operating Activities:	
Cash Collected from Customers	$2,800
Cash Paid to Suppliers	(300)
Cash Paid for Taxes	(300)
Cash flow from operating activities	$2,200

SFAS 95 Disclosure Requirements

As noted earlier, an underlying requirement of SFAS 95 is that the same net cash flow from operating activities is presented, regardless of the reporting format used. Consistent with this requirement, SFAS 95 also stipulates that there must be sufficient disclosures to enable the user to convert from one reporting format to the other. For example, if the firm uses the direct method, the firm must disclose the reconciliation of accrual basis net income and cash flows from operations as required under the indirect approach in a separate schedule or footnote. This direct method disclosure is exactly the same as the operating activities section determined under the indirect method.

If the firm reports the CFS under the indirect method, income taxes paid and interest paid (net of amounts capitalized) must be disclosed in a footnote or a separate schedule. This can also be used to convert operating cash flows to an approximate cash EBITDA. For both the direct and the indirect method, the firm must disclose its policy regarding its definition and composition of cash equivalents.

Foreign Currency Cash Flows Under SFAS 95

For firms with foreign operations or foreign transactions, there are two additional reporting requirements under SFAS 95. First, the firms must present the reporting currency (e.g., the U.S. dollar) equivalent of the foreign currency cash flows using the exchange rate in effect at the time related "cash flows" took place or at the average rate for the year, regardless of the functional currency. This requirement involves three steps: (a) obtain a statement of cash flows in the foreign currency from all foreign operations; (b) translate into the reporting currency (e.g., the U.S. dollar) using the rate in effect when the transactions took place or at the average rate for the year; and (c) consolidate (b) with the U.S. CFS.

Under the second requirement, the effect of exchange rate changes on foreign currency cash balances is to be presented as a separate classification of cash flow activities. That is, a CFS prepared for a firm with foreign operations would appear as follows.

Net Cash Provided by:
Operating Activities
Investing Activities
Financing Activities
Effect of Exchange Rate Changes on Cash

Change in Cash and Cash Equivalents

The effect of exchange rate changes on foreign cash balances is not a cash receipt or cash disbursement, but is needed as part of the reconciliation of the net change in cash and cash equivalents for the year. Because it is not an operating, financing or investing activity, the separate caption is created. Finally, any foreign currency transaction gains (losses) are reported as decreases (increases) in the reconciliation of accrual basis net income and net cash flow in the operating activities section of the CFS prepared under the indirect method.

PREPARATION OF THE CASH FLOW STATEMENT: AN ILLUSTRATION

The following tables present the statements of income and retained earnings for the year ended December 31, 2009 and the comparative balance sheets for the Gibson Corporation at December 31, 2009 and 2008.

Gibson Corporation ***Statements of Income and Retained Earnings*** ***For the Year Ended December 31, 2009***		
Sales		$500
Less: Cost of Goods Sold		
Inventory 1-1-X4	$120	
Purchases	560	
Cost of Goods Available for Sale	$680	
Inventory 12-31-X4	(300)	
Cost of Goods Sold		(380)
Gross Profit		$120
Less: Operating Expenses:		
Selling, General & Administrative Expenses	$30	
Depreciation Expense	22	
Income Tax Expense	21	
Interest Expense	10	(83)
Net Income		$ 37
Retained Earnings 1-1-X4		40
Less: Dividends		(12)
Retained Earnings 12-31-X4		$ 65

Gibson Corporation Balance Sheets, December 31, 2009 and 2008		
	2009	2008
ASSETS:		
Cash and Cash Equivalents	$ 60	$ 85
Accounts Receivable - net	95	70
Inventory	300	120
Prepaid Expenses	140	90
Plant Assets	194	255
Accumulated Depreciation	(99)	(100)
Total Assets	$690	$520
EQUITIES:		
Accounts Payable	$ 53	$ 50
Accrued Taxes Payable	50	30
Long Term Debt	222	100
Capital Stock	300	300
Retained Earnings	65	40
Total Equities	$690	$520

In addition, an examination of the footnotes to the financial statements and management's discussion and analysis revealed that during 2009, Gibson paid $105,000 in cash for new equipment and financed an additional $22,000 in plant acquisitions by borrowing the full amount on a long-term note from the manufacturer. The company also disposed of a piece of equipment for $165,000 in cash, which was also equal to its net book value. Finally, Gibson borrowed an additional $100,000 from the Country National Bank.

Given this information, cash flow statements can be prepared under either the direct or indirect reporting formats. The first step in constructing a CFS under either method is to isolate the changes in balance sheet items between 2008 and 2009 and classify these changes by activity or cycle: operating, investing or financing. The analysis of changes in balance sheet items is presented below. Note that the change in cash is not included in any classification because this change is the bottom line "answer" for the cash flow statement.

ANALYSIS OF CHANGES IN BALANCE SHEET ITEMS				
	Activity	2009	2008	CHANGE
ASSETS:				
Cash and Cash Equivalents	Answer	$ 60	$ 85	($ 25)
Accounts Receivable - net	Operating	95	70	25
Inventory	Operating	300	120	180
Prepaid Expenses	Operating	140	90	50
Plant Assets	Investing	194	255	(61)
Accumulated Depreciation	(a)	(99)	(100)	(1)
Total Assets		$690	$520	
EQUITIES:				
Accounts Payable	Operating	$ 53	$ 50	$ 3
Accrued Taxes Payable	Operating	50	30	20
Long Term Debt	Financing	222	100	122
Capital Stock	Financing	300	300	-0-
Retained Earnings	(b)	65	40	25
Total Equities		$690	$520	

(a) Accumulated deprecation is changed by depreciation expense (operating) and disposals of plant assets (investing)

(b) The retained earnings account changes by net income (operating) and dividends (financing if dividends are paid).

Using the information provided above, the individual line items for the cash flow from operations under the direct method can be determined. These line items are presented below ($000's omitted).

1. Cash Collected From Customers During the Year.

Sales	$500
Less: Increase in Accounts Receivable - net	(25)
Cash Collected From Customers	$475

This illustration points out one of the problems in constructing a CFS from published annual reports. Specifically, much of the actual CFS is based on internally generated information which is not disclosed in the annual report. In this case, the bad debts expense is not disclosed. As a result, it cannot be used to determine cash collected from customers and it cannot be deducted from operating expenses as an adjustment for noncash expenses. Overall, the cash flow from operations will not be affected by the misstatement. However, the individual line items will not be correct. Therefore, if the analyst converts from the indirect to the direct format the resulting operating cash flows will generally be correct, but the individual line items may only be approximate.

2. Cash Paid to Suppliers.

Cost of Goods Sold	($380)
Add: Increase in Inventory	(180)
Purchases (Accrual Basis)	($560)
Less: Increase in Accounts Payable	3
Cash Paid to Suppliers	($557)

3. Cash Paid for Operating Expenses.

General Expenses	($ 30)
Add: Increase in Prepaid Expenses	(50)
Cash Paid for Operating Expenses	($ 80)

4. Cash Paid for Income Taxes (Required disclosure for the indirect method).

Income Tax Expense	($ 21)
Less: Increase in Income Taxes Payable	20
Cash Paid for Income Taxes	($ 1)

5. Cash Paid for Interest (Required disclosure for the indirect method).

Interest Expense	($10)
Add: Increase in Interest Payable ***or***	+ 0
Less: Decrease in Interest Payable	(0)
Cash Paid for Interest	($10)

Because the balance sheet does not reflect any liabilities for interest or dividends, it can be assumed that interest paid in cash is $10,000 and cash dividends paid equal $12,000.

After the above line items are computed, it is recommended that the analyst reconcile all other changes in balance sheet line items. This step is needed to provide a logic check for all prior computations. It is also important to reconcile all changes in account balances. These computations are used to ensure that all balance sheet changes are fully explained. The other reconciliations are provided below. For example, the cost of plant assets sold can be determined as follows:

Plant Assets:

Beginning Balance	$255
Add: Capital Expenditures	127
Subtract: Cost of Plant Assets Sold	***X = (188)***
Ending Balance	$194

Similarly, the accumulated depreciation removed on the disposal of the plant asset can be determined as follows:

Accumulated Depreciation:

Beginning Balance	$100
Add: Depreciation Expense	22
Subtract: Accumulated Depreciation Removed on Sale	***X = (23)***
Ending Balance	$ 99

Therefore, the net book value of plant assets removed on the disposal is equal to $165 (i.e., cost – accumulated depreciation = $188 – 23), which is consistent with the additional information provided earlier: the asset was sold for its net book value of $165 with no gain or loss on the transaction.

Retained Earnings and Dividends Paid:

Beginning Balance	$40
Add: Net Income	37
Subtract: Dividends Declared	***X = (12)***
Ending Balance	$ 65
Dividends Declared	$12
Change in Cash Dividends Payable	- 0 -
Dividends paid	$12

Long Term Debt:

Beginning Balance	$100
Add: Borrowing for Capital Expenditures	22
Cash Borrowing	100
Subtract: Debt Retirement or repayment	0
Ending Balance	$222

Given the preliminary computations, the cash flow statements prepared under both the direct and indirect methods are provided with required disclosures.

The CFS for the Gibson Corporation prepared under the direct format is presented below The supplementary schedules and required disclosures for the direct method are also presented.

GIBSON CORPORATION STATEMENT OF CASH FLOWS (DIRECT METHOD) FOR THE YEAR ENDED DECEMBER 31, 2009		
CASH FLOW FROM OPERATING ACTIVITIES:		
Cash received from customers		$475
Cash paid to suppliers and employees	($557)	
Cash paid for other operating expenses	(80)	
Interest paid (net of amounts capitalized)	(10)	
Income taxes paid	(1)	(648)
Net cash provided (used) by operating activities		($173)
CASH FLOWS FROM INVESTING ACTIVITIES:		
Proceeds from the sale of facility	$ 165	
Capital Expenditures	(105)	
Net cash provided by investing activities		60
CASH FLOWS FROM FINANCING ACTIVITIES:		
Proceeds from issuance of Long Term Debt	$100	
Cash dividends paid	(12)	
Net cash provided from financing activities		88
NET DECREASE IN CASH AND CASH EQUIVALENTS		($ 25)
CASH AND CASH EQUIVALENTS, BEGINNING OF YEAR		85
CASH AND CASH EQUIVALENTS, END OF YEAR		$ 60

Required Disclosures and Supplementary Schedules Under the Direct Approach

1. Reconciliation of Net Income and Net Cash Provided by Operating Activities.

Income from continuing operations	$ 37
Adjustments to Reconcile Net Income to Net Cash Provided by Operating Activities:	
Depreciation expense	22
Changes in Current Assets and Liabilities	
Increase in accounts receivable	(25)
Increase in prepaid expenses	(50)
Increase in inventory	(180)
Increase in accrued taxes payable	20
Increase in accounts payable	3
NET CASH PROVIDED (USED) BY OPERATING ACTIVITIES	***($173)***

The above reconciliation is also provided in the operating cash flows section of the CFS prepared under the indirect method.

2. Disclosure of Significant Noncash Investing and Financing Activities.

Equipment with a value of $22 was purchased through the issuance of a long-term note in the amount of $22.

3. Accounting Policy for Definition of Cash Equivalents.

For purposes of the Statement of Cash Flows, the Company considers all highly liquid debt instruments purchased with a maturity of three months or less to be cash equivalents.

The CFS for the Gibson Corporation prepared under the indirect method is presented in following statement. The supplementary schedules and required disclosures for the indirect format are presented below.

GIBSON CORPORATION STATEMENT OF CASH FLOWS (INDIRECT METHOD) FOR THE YEAR ENDED DECEMBER 31, 2009		
CASH FLOW FROM OPERATING ACTIVITIES:		
Income from continuing operations	$ 37	
Adjustments to Reconcile Net Income to Net Cash Provided by Operating Activities:		
Depreciation expense	22	
Changes in Current Assets and Liabilities		
Increase in accounts receivable	(25)	
Increase in prepaid expenses	(50)	
Increase in inventory	(180)	
Increase in accrued taxes payable	20	
Increase in accounts payable	3	
NET CASH PROVIDED (USED) BY OPERATING ACTIVITIES		($173)
CASH FLOWS FROM INVESTING ACTIVITIES:		
Proceeds from the sale of facility	$ 165	
Capital Expenditures	(105)	
Net cash provided by investing activities		60
CASH FLOWS FROM FINANCING ACTIVITIES:		
Proceeds from issuance of Long Term Debt	$100	
Cash dividends paid	(12)	
Net cash provided from financing activities		88
NET DECREASE IN CASH AND CASH EQUIVALENTS		($ 25)
CASH AND CASH EQUIVALENTS, BEGINNING OF YEAR		85
CASH AND CASH EQUIVALENTS, END OF YEAR		$ 60

Required Disclosures and Supplementary Schedules Under the Indirect Approach

1. Supplemental Disclosure of Cash Flow Information

Cash Paid During The Year For:

Income taxes paid	$ 1
Interest paid (net of amounts capitalized)	$ 10

2. Supplemental Schedule of Noncash Investing and Financing Activities: Same As Under The Direct Method

3. Disclosure of Accounting Policy Regarding the Definition of Cash Equivalents: Same As Under The Direct Method

AN ANALYSIS OF THE CASH FLOW STATEMENT

As indicated in the previous sections of this chapter, the CFS is a key analytical tool for both the credit and financial analyst. There were several reasons noted why the CFS is critical to any successful analysis. However, the analyst must be aware of the problems involved in the analysis of the CFS. The following sections present the analytical advantages and disadvantages of the CFS as required under SFAS 95.

Usefulness of the Cash Flow Statement

There are many analytical advantages of using the CFS required by SFAS 95. First, the CFS summarizes all cash flow information regarding operating, financing and investing activities. Although this information could probably be obtained from other financial statements and footnote disclosures, the CFS proves to be more useful in that it provides this information in a single, concise statement that avoids the difficulties involved in reconstructing cash flow information from multiple sources. In addition, by providing a CFS that clearly specifies the sources and uses of cash by activity, the analyst can better identify the cash effects of the key transactions of the firm and can understand the underlying economic substance of events reported under the accrual basis. By forcing the definition and classification of cash flows, SFAS 95 enables the analyst to avoid other crude and inaccurate measures of cash flow such as net income plus depreciation.

Second, although the indirect method is used most often in practice, the disclosures required by SFAS 95 enable the analyst to convert from the indirect method to the direct method. If the analyst prefers the direct format, in total or for particular line items, the conversion can be made from the indirect format information and disclosures. For example, an analysis of the ratio of cash collected from customers divided by sales may provide a better measure of revenue overstatement than traditional turnover ratio analysis.

The direct method is preferred by the FASB and is also preferred by many credit and financial analysts. As noted earlier, when forecasting future cash flows, the use of a disaggregated time series will result in more accurate projections than if aggregated data are used. In addition, credit and investment risk are closely related to fluctuations in the individual components of cash flow from operating activities. If the indirect format is used, only fluctuations in the total operating cash flow are available. Therefore, the conversion to the direct method may result in cash flow statistics that are more accurate in credit and investment analyses.

Third, due to the problems with accrual basis net income, cash flows from operations may be a more reliable measure of operating performance in credit and investment analysis. For example, increases in sales and net income may not enhance the firm's ability to meet scheduled debt payments and to make dividend distributions if sales and net income are not converted into cash. It is for this reason that many financial analysts compute a measure of the quality of accrual basis net income. The quality of earnings is measured by the ratio of operating cash flows to net income. In addition, many bond rating agencies and investment banks evaluate debt coverage by both a times-interest-earned ratio and a ratio of cash flow to long term debt or total debt.

Finally, by using the activities or cycles provided in the CFS, an analyst can assess the growth stage of the client's business life cycle. The four typical growth stages are a rapid growth stage, a sustained growth stage, a mature stage and a declining stage.

During the rapid growth stage, an analyst can expect negative cash flows from operations as the client needs to build up inventory levels for future expansion and experiences increases in accounts receivable as high year end sales are still uncollected. Large investments are made in this stage and with the negative operating cash flow, these capital investments must be financed through the debt and equity markets. As a result, high negative investing and high positive financing cash flows are expected during the rapid growth stage of a client's life cycle.

When the client reaches the sustained growth stage, operating cash flows become positive and can be use to help finance the continued investment in capital projects needed to expand or replace existing productive capacity. Some external financing is still required as operating cash flows are still not sufficient to cover all investing activities. Therefore, during the sustained growth stage, there are still high negative investing cash flows and positive financing cash flows are expected but not as material as during the rapid growth stage of a client's life cycle.

In the mature stage of a business life cycle, operating cash flows increase further and are used to finance moderate capital projects. However, as these investment opportunities begin to dry up during the mature stage, excess operating cash flows can be used to pay off debt and with lack of investment projects, the firm begins to buy back treasury shares. In this stage, an analyst can expect high operating cash flows with lower negative investing and financing activities.

During the declining stage of the clients business life cycle, operating cash flows are still positive, but are declining. In addition, there are few investment opportunities available. Therefore, the operating cash flows are primarily used to repay debt and purchase treasury stock.

Some Analytical Problems

In addition to the benefits of using the CFS, there are several analytical problems that the analyst must consider in the assessment of the credit and investment risk of the firm.

To begin with, and most important, the analyst must not place undue reliance on the firm's operating cash flows. Accrual basis net income measures economic activity; operating cash flows do not. Operating cash flows can only be generated from the economic activities of the firm. Therefore, operating cash flows must be analyzed in conjunction with the examination and analysis of the other financial statements and the related footnote disclosures.

Second, the analyst must be aware of the inconsistencies in terminology and presentation between the CFS and other information contained in the annual report. As noted earlier, net cash flows from operations includes taxes paid dividend and interest income, and interest expense but excludes all items of profit and loss without any cash effects. The term operating income as used in financial analysis excludes other income such as dividends and interest and omits interest expense. Thus, the term "operations" has quite different meanings for the financial analyst and accountant in the financial statements. In addition, SFAS 95 does not require the identification of cash flows from unusual sources such as discontinued operations and extraordinary items. Again, it is difficult to relate cash flow items to the line items of the income statement under the indirect method.

Similarly, because the CFS only reflects the cash consequences of transactions, the statement will not always articulate well with changes in line items on the statement of financial position. For example, if there are dividends payable, dividends paid on the CFS will not agree with the total dividend declaration on the statement of retained earnings. In the same way, a full understanding of other key changes in the statement of financial position may require additional information such as noncash acquisitions of plant and equipment or bond conversions.

Fourth, in converting from the indirect to the direct method, many inaccuracies can result due to the lack of disclosure of internal information. For example, the change in accounts payable is generally used to adjust the cost of sales in deriving cash paid to suppliers.

However, the balance in accounts payable may actually relate to the acquisition of goods and services other than inventory.

A major criticism of the CFS is found in lack of articulation with balance sheet changes in a year of a divestiture or a business combination accounted for under the acquisition method. When a business combination is accounted for under the acquisition method, the cash paid for the net assets acquired is included as a cash outflow in investing activities. The total in investing activities includes inventories, receivables, payables, accrued liabilities, etc., acquired on the date of the business combination. Without the acquisition, these changes would have been included in operating activities of the subsidiary. However, in the year of acquisition, the changes in the balance sheet for these operating cycle (noncash working capital) accounts will not equal the changes reported in the operating activities section of the statement of cash flows.

Acquisitions and divestitures are one of two events causing changes in noncash working capital accounts on the balance sheet to differ from the change reported in the operating activities section of the cash flow statement. The other case results from foreign currency translation adjustments. The effect of changes in foreign currency exchange rates is a separate category of cash flows on the statement.

The effect of acquisitions and divestitures, assuming no effect of exchange rate changes on cash is computed as follows:

Effect of Acquisitions Divestitures = **Balance Sheet Change** − **Cash Flow Statement Change.**

Using the data from Donovan's 2012 annual report as presented in Exhibit 12.3 (in millions) and assuming that there are no effects of foreign currency exchange rates on cash, we can determine the effect of acquisitions on the lack of articulation between the balance sheet changes and the changes in the cash flow statement. This exhibit also provides an illustration of disclosure of noncash events and other supplemental cash flow information.

EXHIBIT 12.3: DONOVAN CONSOLIDATED STATEMENTS OF CASH FLOWS AND CONSOLIDATED BALANCE SHEETS

PARTIAL CONSOLIDATED STATEMENTS OF CASH FLOWS

(Dollars in Millions) (Note 1)	2012	2011	2010
CASH FLOWS FROM OPERATING ACTIVITIES			
Net earnings	$12,493	10,211	8,636
Adjustments to reconcile net earnings to cash flows:			
Depreciation and amortization of property and intangibles	2,512	2,549	2,243
Purchased in-process research and development	434.4	21.6	1101.6
Deferred tax provision	(55.2)	(597.6)	(864)
Accounts receivable allowances	(37.2)	3.6	7.2
Changes in assets and liabilities, net of effects from acquisitions:			
Increase in accounts receivable	(681.6)	(133.2)	(829.2)
(Increase)/decrease in inventories	(475.2)	13.2	46.8
(Decrease)/increase in accounts payable and accrued liabilities	(1093.2)	728.4	2,630
Decrease/(increase) in other current and non-current assets	744	(474)	(895.2)
Increase in other current and non-current liabilities	411.6	1035.6	637.2

NET CASH FLOWS FROM OPERATING ACTIVITIES	14,252	13,357	12,714
CASH FLOWS FROM INVESTING ACTIVITIES			
Additions to property, plant and equipment	(3,158)	(2,610)	(2,714)
Proceeds from the disposal of assets	184.8	284.4	402
Acquisitions, net of cash acquired (Note 17)	(1184.4)	(696)	(3,374)
Purchases of investments	(6,792)	(13,940)	(9,108)
Sales of investments	11,024	14,473	9,674
Other (primarily intangibles)	(409.2)	(327.6)	(310.8)
NET CASH USED BY INVESTING ACTIVITIES	(334.8)	(2,816)	(5,431)
SUPPLEMENTAL CASH FLOW DATA			
Cash paid during the year for:			
Interest	$61	266.4	247.2
Income taxes	4,115	4,656	3,775
SUPPLEMENTAL SCHEDULE OF NONCASH INVESTING AND FINANCING ACTIVITIES			
Treasury stock issued for employee compensation and stock option plans, net of cash proceeds	$982	962.4	1086
Conversion of debt	442.8	126	2.4
ACQUISITIONS			
Fair value of assets acquired	$1,354	714	3,762
Fair value of liabilities assumed	(169.2)	(18)	(387.6)
Net cash paid for acquisitions	$1,184	696	3,374

PARTIAL CONSOLIDATED BALANCE SHEETS

December 31, (Dollars in Millions Except Share and Per Share Data)	2012	2011
ASSETS		
CURRENT ASSETS		
Cash and cash equivalents	$19,266	11,044
Marketable securities	99.6	4,417
Accounts receivable trade, Net	8,412	8,197
Inventories	4,751	4,493
Deferred taxes on income	2,214	2,084
Prepaid expenses and other receivables	2,930	2,549
TOTAL CURRENT ASSETS	37,673	32,784

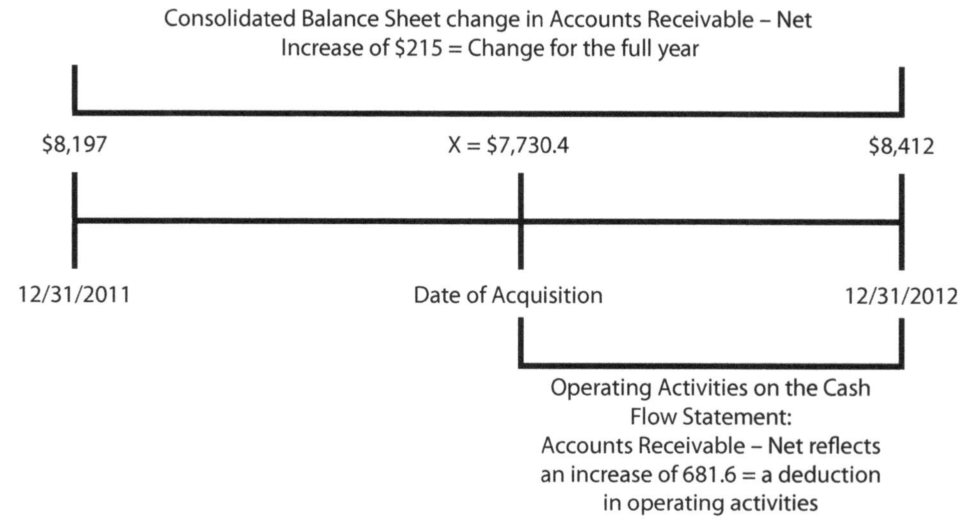

Effect of Acquisitions		Balance Sheet		Cash Flow Statement
Divestitures	=	**Change**	-	**Change**
($466.6)	=	**$215**	-	**681.6**

So the effect of the acquisition was to decrease accounts receivable – net by $466.6 and results in an acquisition date accounts receivable balance of $7,730.4 (i.e. $8,197 – 466.6).

Another analytical problem is found in the effect of exchange rate changes on cash. The statement of cash flows is prepared using an annual average exchange rate to normalize the choice of functional currency (i.e., temporal versus current rate method). An average rate is also used for the flow statements. Under either the temporal or the current rate method, balance sheet accounts such as accounts receivable would be translated on the balance sheet using the current rate at the balance sheet date. The difference between using the average rate on the statement of cash flows and the current rate on the balance sheet is reported as the “Effect of Exchange Rate Changes on Cash,” which is a separate caption on the cash flow statement. This is required by FASB Statement No. 95 but may not always be followed in practice.

To illustrate, assume the increase in the accounts receivable of foreign subsidiary is 100 local currency units (LC). The current exchange rate is $1.06 = 1LC and the average rate is $1.02 = 1LC. The change in accounts receivable is included in the consolidated balance sheet using the current rate. Therefore the balance sheet change in accounts receivable is $106 (i.e., $1.06 x 100 LC). In the operating activities section of the cash flow statement, the average rate is used. Therefore, the increase in accounts receivable is deducted at $102 (i.e., $1.02 x 100 LC). The difference is reported as the effect of exchange rate changes on cash. That is, $4 (100LC x [$1.06 – 1.02]) is deducted in this separate category of the statement of cash flow. Together, $106 is deducted from total cash flows (i.e., $102 in operating activities and $4 in the separate caption), which is equal to the change in the balance sheet account $106).

A final problem arises in the analysis of the CFS because the bad debts expense is generally not disclosed in the footnotes to the statement of financial position. Without this information the analyst cannot accurately convert sales to cash collected from customers. The cash paid for operating expenses will also be misstated because of the inability of the analyst to exclude the noncash bad debts expense. It should be noted that although the individual line items will be only approximations, the net cash flow from operating activities should be correct.

If possible, it is best to identify the bad debt expense and add this back to net income as the noncash component of the decrease in accounts receivable-net. This will allow the analyst to isolate the decrease in accounts receivable resulting from cash collections from customers.

To illustrate, assume the company begins with accounts receivable-net of $25,000 and ends the year with a balance of $22,000. The bad debt expense for the year is $2,000 and no accounts were written off. Accounts receivable — net decreased by $3,000, but $2,000 of the increase is due to the increase in the allowance for uncollectible accounts. Therefore, only $1,000 is the net change in accounts receivable due to cash collections during the year. The company reported a net income of $18,000 for the year. If the bad debt expense is not isolated, the operating activities section of the cash flow statement appears as follows (assuming the indirect method only for the information provided):

Operating Activities:	
Net income	$18,000
Add: Decrease in accounts receivable-net	3,000
Operating cash flow	$21,000

If the bad debt expense is known by the analyst, the cash flow statement can be reported as follows:

Operating Activities:	
Net income	$18,000
Add: Bad debt expense	2,000
Add: Decrease in accounts receivable	1,000
Operating cash flow	$21,000

In computing cash collected from customers, it is more appropriate to use a disclosure in accounts receivable of $1,000 than $3,000 when adding it back to sales.

Additional data should be used when analyzing the CFS. If an analyst prefers to convert from the indirect to the direct format, care must be taken not to ignore the possible signals contained in the individual reconciling items used in the indirect method. For instance, a decrease in prepaid expenses such as rent, insurance or supplies results in an adjustment that increases cash flow. However, a decrease in the acquisition of items such as operating supplies could signal an expected slowdown in future operations. Therefore, knowledge of the relationships between the CFS and the other financial information provided as well as familiarity with the operations of the firm and the industry are critical for making sound investment and credit decisions.

An analysis of financing and investing activities also requires additional sources of information. Although these activities indicate the sources of financing, both internal and external, and how earnings are reinvested, the analyst needs to consider the signals regarding expansion or contraction of future operations. Disclosure of the type of capital expenditure is not required by SFAS 95. Therefore, additional information is needed to identify the exact areas of acquisition and disposal of plant assets and if there are noncash acquisitions and disposals. The segment footnote may be useful for this purpose.

If expansion is financed by debt or additional equity, the analyst must consider the availability of future cash flows. The long-term debt and stockholders' equity footnotes must be examined in order to determine the extent of future debt service, preferred dividends in arrears and scheduled mandatory redemptions of debt and redeemable preferred stock. Given these commitments, the bottom line net cash flow may not be "free" for use in future operations.

The above discussion indicates that the analyst must never lose sight of the fact that a proper analysis of cash flow can only be made within the overall analysis of the firm. The overall analysis requires additional information from the annual report and other sources such as economic and industry publications.

Index

Applied Financial Accounting: Implication for Analysts

W

www.ingramcontent.com/pod-product-compliance
Ingram Content Group UK Ltd.
Pitfield, Milton Keynes, MK11 3LW, UK
UKHW051029041026
15470UKWH00015B/1790

9 781601 820037